ROUTLEDGE HANDBO
POSTCOLONIAL POLITICS

Edited by Olivia U. Rutazibwa and Robbie Shilliam

LONDON AND NEW YORK

First published 2018
by Routledge
2 Park Square, Milton Park, Abingdon, Oxon OX14 4RN

and by Routledge
52 Vanderbilt Avenue, New York, NY 10017

First issued in paperback 2020

Routledge is an imprint of the Taylor & Francis Group, an informa business

British Library Cataloguing in Publication Data
A catalogue record for this book is available from the British Library

Library of Congress Cataloging in Publication Data
A catalog record for this book has been requested

ISBN 13: 978-0-367-58081-0 (pbk)
ISBN 13: 978-1-138-94459-6 (hbk)

Typeset in Bembo
by Apex CoVantage, LLC

ROUTLEDGE HANDBOOK OF POSTCOLONIAL POLITICS

Engagements with the postcolonial world by International Relations scholars have grown significantly in recent years. The *Routledge Handbook of Postcolonial Politics* provides a solid reference point for understanding and analyzing global politics from a perspective sensitive to the multiple legacies of colonial and imperial rule.

The *Handbook* introduces and develops cutting-edge analytical frameworks that draw on Black, decolonial, feminist, indigenous, Marxist and postcolonial thought as well as a multitude of intellectual traditions from across the globe. Alongside empirical issue areas that remain crucial to assessing the impact of European and Western colonialism on global politics, the book introduces new issue areas that have arisen due to the mutating structures of colonial and imperial rule.

This vital resource is split into five thematic sections, each featuring a brief, orienting introduction:

- Points of departure
- Popular postcolonial imaginaries
- Struggles over the postcolonial state
- Struggles over land
- Alternative global imaginaries

Providing both a consolidated understanding of the field as it is, and setting an expansive and dynamic research agenda for the future, this handbook is essential reading for students and scholars of International Relations alike.

Olivia U. Rutazibwa is Senior Lecturer in International Development and European Studies, University of Portsmouth, UK.

Robbie Shilliam is Professor of International Relations at Queen Mary University of London, UK.

CONTENTS

ILLUSTRATIONS

Figure

Tables

CONTRIBUTORS

Hisham Aidi currently teaches Political Science and African Studies at Columbia University's School of International and Public Affairs, USA. He is the author of *Redeploying the State* (2008) and co-editor, with Manning Marable, of *Black Routes to Islam* (2009). Since 2007, he has been a contributing editor of *Souls: A Critical Journal of Black Culture, Politics and Society*. Aidi is author most recently of *Rebel Music: Race, Empire and the New Muslim Youth Culture* (2014), winner of the American Book Award for 2015.

A. Haroon Akram-Lodhi is Professor of Economics and International Development Studies in the Department of International Development Studies at Trent University, Canada. He is also the Editor-in-Chief of the *Canadian Journal of Development Studies* and an Associate Editor of *Feminist Economics*. A Fellow of Food First, the Institute for Food and Development Policy, Haroon Akram-Lodhi also holds adjunct appointments at several universities in the United States, Mexico and Canada.

Mary Tuti Baker comes from the island of O'ahu. Her mother's mother is from Hawaii Island, her mother's father from Kauai and her father's family is from the gulf coast of Texas. She is a Kanaka 'Ōiwi (Native Hawaiian) scholar grounded in her kinship relationship to Hawai'i and committed to futures for the islands that are anchored in place-based Kanaka 'Ōiwi values. She is currently a PhD candidate at the University of Hawai'i at Mānoa, USA, writing on indigenous ideologies and post-colonial futures.

Gurminder K. Bhambra is Professor of Sociology at the University of Warwick, UK, and Guest Professor of Sociology and History at the Centre for Concurrences in Colonial and Postcolonial Studies at Linnaeus University, Sweden. She is author of *Connected Sociologies* (2014) and *Rethinking Modernity: Postcolonialism and the Sociological Imagination* (2007), which won the 2008 Philip Abrams Memorial Prize for best first book in sociology. She has co-edited four collections, *Silencing Human Rights* (2009), *1968 in Retrospect* (2009), *African Athena* (2011) and *European Cosmopolitanisms* (2016). She also set up the Global Social Theory (globalsocialtheory.org) website to support students and academics interested in social theory in a global perspective.

Pinar Bilgin is Professor of International Relations at Bilkent University, Turkey. She is the author of *Regional Security in the Middle East: A Critical Perspective* (2005), *The International in Security, Security in the International* (2016), and co-editor of *The Routledge Handbook of International Political Sociology* (2017) and *Asia in International Relations: Unthinking Imperial Power Relations* (2017). Her articles have appeared in *Review of International Studies, Political Geography, European Journal of Political Research, Third World Quarterly, Security Dialogue, Foreign Policy Analysis, International Theory, International Relations* and *Geopolitics*. She is an Associate Member of Turkish Academy of Sciences, and co-editor of Palgrave book series, 'Critical Security Studies in the Global South'. Her research agenda focuses on critical approaches to security studies.

Ijahnya Christian has served both government and civil society in the fields of social development, cultural preservation and environmental management in the Caribbean. She has drafted position papers for Anguilla's engagement with the UN Special Committee on Decolonisation and contributed to the island's report at the UN Fourth World Conference on Women in Beijing. She has also participated in Commonwealth People's Forum in Durban and Abuja, and in the African Union's technical meetings on the African Diaspora. As a founding member of the Caribbean Rastafari Organisation, she was the first Rastafari representative on the executive of the Caribbean Pan-African Network. In 2010 she repatriated to Ethiopia after declining the award of Order of the British Empire. She is an advisor to the Empress of Zion international organisation of Rastafari women, and to Positive Action Charity, which operates Yawenta Children's Center for children affected by HIV and AIDS in Shashemene. Her dream is to visit every African country, and her metaphor for living is that of a lion aspiring to be an ant.

Deep K. Datta-Ray is an Associate Professor at O.P. Jindal Global University, India, and earlier was a business consultant for ten years with firms in London, New York, Singapore and Mumbai. Prior to his DPhil in International Relations from the University of Sussex, UK, and MA in War Studies from King's College London, he received a BA(Hons) in Chinese History from SOAS University of London. He was raised in various European cities, Singapore, Honolulu and Calcutta, and his academic interests lie at the intersection of everyday violence and the ethics of its negotiation by individuals, institutions and states, in particular, in India, the United States and China.

Aparna Devare is an Assistant Professor in the Department of Political Science, University of Hyderabad, India. Her book is titled *History and the Making of a Modern Hindu Self* (2011) and she has published articles in *Postcolonial Studies, Contexto Internacional, International Political Sociology* and *International Journal of Political Theory*, along with several chapters in edited books. She has published on themes such as religion and politics, the politics of history writing, Indian political thinkers and their negotiation with modernity, violence and colonialism. Her broad research purpose is to look at the intersection of non-western political thought, concepts and practices, and international relations defined as intercultural relations.

Dilar Dirik is an activist of the Kurdish women's movement and writes on freedom struggles in Kurdistan for an international audience. She is working on her PhD in the Department of Sociology at the University of Cambridge, UK.

Emilio Distretti is Assistant Professor of Urban Studies and Spatial Practices at Al-Quds Bard College for Arts and Sciences in Abu Dis in the Occupied Palestinian Territory, as well as

Research Fellow at the Kenyon Institute – Council for British Research in the Levant in East Jerusalem. He holds a PhD in Aesthetics and Politics of Representation from the School of Art and Design, UK. His research interests are multidisciplinary with a strong emphasis on global politics and international relations in their intersections with new materialism, postcolonial theory, critical geography and theories of space.

Joy Lehuanani Enomoto is currently pursuing a dual masters in Library and Information Science, and Pacific Island Studies. She is a mixed-media artist living in Honolulu, Hawai'i. She is of Native Hawaiian, African-American, Japanese, Caddo Indian and Punjabi descent. Her work engages ancestral memory, social justice and other issues currently affecting Pacific peoples. Her work has been featured in *Finding Meaning: Kaona and Contemporary Hawaiian Literature*, *Amerasia Journal*, *Bamboo Ridge: Journal of Hawai'i Literature and Arts* and *Hawai'i Review*.

Peo Hansen is Professor of Political Science at the Institute for Research on Migration, Ethnicity and Society, Linköping University, Sweden. He is a former senior fellow at the Remarque Institute at New York University, and his research areas include European integration, EU migration policy, postwar European geopolitics and the history of colonialism and decolonisation. His most recent book is *Eurafrica: The Untold History of European Integration and Colonialism* (co-authored with Stefan Jonsson, 2014). He is currently writing a book on Europe's migration crises.

Eiichi Hoshino is Professor in the Faculty of Law and Letters at the University of the Ryukyus Japan. He obtained an MA in International Studies from Graduate School of International Studies (GSIS), University of Denver, USA. His research interests include international relations and the political economy of aid. He is co-editor of *Self-determinable Development of Small Islands* (2016).

Rosalba Icaza is a decolonial feminist and International Studies scholar with 15 years of research and teaching experience on gender and development, international political economy and research methodologies. Her publications have advanced a critical re-thinking of the modern/colonial notion of region and regionalism, and a critical enquiry of the knowledges and cosmovisions that have been actively produced as backward or sub-altern by established knowledge practices. She has published across different disciplines including International Relations, Global Sociology, Gender, Feminism and Development Studies. Her latest article 'Decolonial feminism and global politics: Border thinking and vulnerability as a knowing otherwise' is part of the book *Critical Epistemology of Global Politics,* edited by Sebastien Weier and Marc Woons for E-International Relations. In 2016, Icaza acted as Senior Researcher of the University of Amsterdam Diversity Commission. She is Senior Lecturer of Governance and International Political Economy at the International Institute of Social Studies, Erasmus University of Rotterdam, the Netherlands.

Stefan Jonsson is Professor at the Institute for Research on Migration, Ethnicity and Society, Linköping University, Sweden. He holds a PhD from the Graduate Program in Literature at Duke University, USA, and was a postdoctoral fellow at the Getty Research Institute and Visiting Professor at the University of Michigan, USA, and Pontifical Catholic University, Brazil. His writings include *Subject Without Nation* (2000), *A Brief History of the Masses* (2008), *Crowds and Democracy* (2013), and most recently *Eurafrica: The Untold History of European Integration and Colonialism* (co-authored with Peo Hansen, 2014) and *Austere Histories in European Societies* (co-edited with Julia Willén, 2016). Jonsson is also a critic at Sweden's major newspaper *Dagens Nyheter.*

Christine M. Klapeer is currently a Lecturer in Gender and Development Studies at Bayreuth University, Germany; from 2011 to 2016 she held a postdoctoral position with an emphasis on 'transnational sexualities and development politics' at the University of Vienna, Department of Development Studies. She received her doctorate in Political Science from the University of Innsbruck and has been teaching 'critical' development studies, feminist political theory and postcolonial queer studies at various universities, including the Central European University Budapest. Her research interests include trans/national LGBTIQ movements and queer politics, intersectional and race critical perspectives on articulations and political economies of sexual rights and sexual citizenship, constructions and figurations of (dissident) sexualities and genders in development policies, and development discourse. Her third book, entitled *Queer G(r)ifts. Development Politics, LGBTIQ Rights and the Trajectories of Transnational Queer Solidarity*, is in preparation.

Rahel Kunz is a Senior Lecturer at the Institute of Political, Historical and International Studies, University of Lausanne, Switzerland. Her research interests are feminist international political economy, gender issues in migration and development, gender and security sector reform, and feminist poststructuralist and postcolonial thought. She has published in *International Political Sociology*, *Journal of European Integration*, *Migration Studies*, *Review of International Political Economy* and *Third World Quarterly*, and is the author of *The Political Economy of Global Remittances: Gender, Governmentality and Neoliberalism* (2011).

Denize LeDeatte 'Artist named Iesha' has a career history which straddles numerous industry sectors. She has studied at Croydon College of Art, City Lit and Putney School of Art. Denize also has a background in economic development, business, management, training and recruitment; as well as European funding contract management and project management of transnational multiple partner programmes across Europe. Past employers include: Wandsworth Borough Council, Tesco, British Airways – (Peach Personnel), United Nations – (Paragon Training), Oxfam – (Women's' Design Service). Additionally her Third Sector experience is diverse and spans a period of over 30 years. More recently, as Artist named Iesha, she has been developing a body of work (African Violet) within her practice; she is a Fellow of the RSA and both a British & European Women Inventor and Innovators Network awards recipient for creativity and social change. This combined with the backdrop of her management background propels her to her current space and direction of "Creative Brokerage" at Peach Mango Maverick©. Peach Mango Maverick© is both an artwork and an artists' practice which explores social challenges through arts.

L.H.M. Ling is Professor of International Affairs at The New School in New York, USA. She has authored *Postcolonial International Relations* (2002), *Transforming World Politics* (co-authored with A.M. Agathangelou, York University, 2009), *The Dao of World Politics* (2014) and *Imagining World Politics* (2014). Two books are forthcoming: *A Worldly World Order* and *Between India and China* (co-authored with Payal Banerjee, Smith College). Anthologies include *Asia in International Relations* (co-edited with Pinar Bilgin, 2017), *India China* (2016) and *Four Seas to One Family* (co-edited with Tan Chung, in Chinese and English, 2015). Ling's articles have appeared in academic journals such as *International Studies Quarterly*, *International Relations of the Asia-Pacific*, *Millennium*, *Postcolonial Studies*, *International Feminist Journal of Politics*, along with popular sites like the *Huffington Post*. She is co-editor with John M. Hobson (Sheffield University) of 'Global Dialogues', a book series at Rowman & Littlefield International.

Xin Liu is currently a Research Associate at the University of Sussex, UK. His research centres on 'globalising' mainstream international theories by introducing non-European experiences of modernity as correctives to the profane and rigid frameworks of Eurocentric international relations. Liu's research also aims at highlighting and mapping out the global interconnections of non-Western subjects in augmenting modern categories such as nationalism, political justice and citizenship. He is working on a couple of journal articles that explore the premodern origins of international systems in Asia-Pacific, together with a monograph that explains the modern Chinese revolution as an internationally generated phenomenon.

Alanna Lockward is a Berlin- and Santo Domingo-based Dominican author, curator and filmmaker. She is the Founding Director of Art Labour Archives, an exceptional platform that has spiralled consistently on theory, political activism and art since 1996. Her interests are Caribbean marronage discursive and mystical legacies in time-based practices, critical race theory, decolonial aesthetics/aesthesis, Black feminism and womanist ethics. Lockward is the author of *Apremio: apuntes sobre el pensamiento y la creación contemporánea desde el Caribe* (2006), a collection of essays; and the short novel *Marassà & The Nothingness* (2016) and *Un Haití Dominicano. Tatuajes fantasmas y narrativas bilaterales* (1994–2014), a compilation of her investigative work on the history and current challenges between both island-nations (2014). She is Adjunct Professor of Audiovisual Theory and Investigative Journalism at Pontificia Universidad Católica Madre y Maestra, Dominican Republic; has been a Guest Lecturer at the Humboldt Universität zu Berlin, the Decolonial Summer School Middelburg, the University of Warwick, Dutch Art Institute and Goldsmiths University of London; and has been a panellist at the University of Kwa-Zulu Natal, South Africa, and Duke, Columbia and Princeton Universities, USA. She is Academic Advisor of Transart Institute and is Associated Scholar of Young Scholars Network Black Diaspora and Germany. She has conceptualised and curated the ground-breaking transdisciplinary meeting BE.BOP. BLACK EUROPE BODY POLITICS (2012–2016). Lockward has received awards by the Allianz Cultural Foundation, the Danish Arts Council and the Nordic Council of Ministers. Her first documentary project on Black Liberation Theology and the transnational history of the African Methodist Episcopal Church (AME) received the production prize FONPROCINE 2013.

D. Keali'i MacKenzie is of mixed Kanaka Maoli, European and Chinese descent. He was born and raised in Springfield, Massachusetts in what are the traditional lands of the Nipmuc and Pocumtuck nations. He received a Master of Arts in Pacific Islands Studies and a Master of Library and Information Science, both from the University of Hawai'i at Mānoa, USA. His academic articles have appeared in *The Contemporary Pacific* and *The American Mosaic: The American Indian Experience*. He is a Poet-Facilitator for the Honolulu-based non-profit Pacific Tongues.

Nivi Manchanda is a Lecturer in International Politics at Queen Mary University of London, UK. Her research interests include race, gender and the legacies of colonialism in International Relations. She is currently working on a book manuscript entitled *Bulletpoints: The Imperial Politics of Knowledge Production about Afghanistan,* which is based on her award-winning PhD thesis. She is co-editor of *Race and Racism in International Relations: Confronting the Global Colour Line* (2015) and co-convenor of the Colonial, Postcolonial and Decolonial British International Studies Association working group.

Soumaya Mestiri is a philosopher who teaches at the Université de Tunis, Tunisia. She has previously written books on John Rawls and has translated the medieval Persian philosopher Al-Farabi, the philosopher and mathematician Al-Kindi, and the polemical, theologian and naturalist Al-Jahiz. Her recent work engages with the relationship between feminism, western society and Islamic society. She has recently published *Decolonising Feminism: A Transcultural Approach* (2016).

Andile Mngxitama is the President of Black First Land First a Black Consciousness and Pan Africanist movement in South Africa. He is a former Member of Parliament and co-editor of *BIKO LIVES! The Contested Legacies of Steve Biko*. Mngxitama is also the founding member of the Landless People's Movement and the founding editor of *New Frank Talk*, a journal on the Black condition.

Sabelo J. Ndlovu-Gatsheni is Professor and Director of Scholarship in the Change Management Unit in the Vice-Chancellor's Office at the University of South Africa in Pretoria. He is former Founding Head of the Archie Mafeje Research Institute for Applied Social Policy based at the same institution. His research is into African intellectual history, African political thought, African identity, African nationalism, Zimbabwean and South African history and politics, as well as decolonial theory/postcolonial theory. His major recent publications include *Decolonizing the University, Knowledge Systems and Disciplines in Africa* (2016), *The Decolonial Mandela: Peace, Justice and the Politics of Life* (2016); and *Joshua Mqabuko Nkomo of Zimbabwe: Politics, Power and Memory* (2017).

Swati Parashar is Associate Professor at the School of Global Studies, University of Gothenburg, Sweden. During 2016, she was a Visiting Fellow at the Centre for the Study of Developing Societies, Delhi. Her research engages with the intersections between feminism and postcolonialism, focused on conflict and development in South Asia. She is the author of *Women and Militant Wars: The Politics of Injury* (2014) and has edited the Special Issue of *Postcolonial Studies* (Volume 19, 2016: Issue 4) on 'Feminism Meets Postcolonialism: Rethinking Gender, State and Political Violence.'

Ajay Parasram is Assistant Professor in the departments of International Development Studies and History, Dalhousie University on unceded Mi'kmaq territory, Halifax, Canada. Parasram's research is concerned with the violence of universal thinking encoded and normalised in the practice of international relations broadly conceived.

Desirée Poets was born and raised in Rio de Janeiro after the multicultural turn in Latin America and has been undertaking her PhD in International Relations at the University of Aberystwyth, Wales, UK. As part of her PhD project, she has worked and built solidarities with urban indigenous groups and urban *quilombola* communities in the cities of Rio de Janeiro, São Paulo and Belo Horizonte. Poets has published in academic and non-academic channels about the struggles with which she has become involved, including the activist journalism platform 'Rio On Watch', as well as the *Bulletin of Latin American Research*.

Althea-Maria Rivas is an Assistant Professor at York University, Canada. Her research interests are race and global politics, gender, peace and security, migration, and feminist and postcolonial theory and pedagogy. She is also a Research Associate at the Harriet Tubman Institute for Research on Africa and its Diasporas at York University.

Olivia Umurerwa Rutazibwa is a Belgo-Rwandan Senior Lecturer in European and International Development Studies at the University of Portsmouth, UK. Her research centres around ways to decolonise thinking and practices of International Solidarity by recovering and reconnecting philosophies and enactments of dignity and self-determination in the postcolony: autonomous recovery in Somaliland, Agaciro in Rwanda and Black Power in the USA; a book on this is in preparation. She has published in *Postcolonial Studies*, *Ethical Perspectives*, *Journal of Intervention and Statebuilding*, and *Journal of Contemporary European Studies*. She is associate editor of *International Feminist Journal of Politics* and is the former Africa desk editor, journalist and columnist at the Brussels-based quarterly *MO* Magazine* for which she occasionally continues to write.

Giorgio Shani is Professor and Chair of Politics and International Relations and Director of the Rotary Peace Center at International Christian University, Japan. From 2016–17, he was Visiting Senior Fellow at the Centre of International Studies at the London School of Economics and Political Science. Educated at the University of London, he is author of *Sikh Nationalism and Identity in a Global Age* (2008) and *Religion, Identity and Human Security* (2014). He has published widely in internationally reviewed journals including *International Studies Review*, *The Cambridge Review of International Affairs* and *Postcolonial Studies*. He is a series editor of *Critical Perspectives on Religion in International Politics* (Rowman and Littlefield International) and currently serving as President of the Asia-Pacific region of the International Studies Association.

Robbie Shilliam is Professor of International Relations at Queen Mary University of London, UK. He is author of *The Black Pacific: Anticolonial Struggles and Oceanic Connections* (2015) and co-editor of *Meanings of Bandung: Postcolonial Orders and Decolonial Visions* (2016). He is co-editor of the book series *Kilombo: International Relations and Colonial Questions* (Rowman & Littlefield International).

Archana Thapa is an independent scholar, writer and theatre artist based in Kathmandu, Nepal. Her areas of research are feminist perspective in epistemology, gender studies, media and popular culture, art and artivism in Nepal, and theatre in Nepal. She practises an interdisciplinary approach to seek alternative knowledge(s), and her academic papers and articles are published in national and international journals and magazines. She compiled, edited and published two collections of Nepali women's personal narrations, *Telling A Tale* and *Swaastitwako Khoj* (*A Search for Self*), as well as her book of short stories, *Kathaputala (A Puppet)* (2017). Thapa founded Akshar Creations Nepal, a home-based publishing house, which publishes books on non-mainstream topics and traditions. She campaigns for women's writing and women's public participation. She also leads Aahwaan Group, an informal discussion group, to enhance the quality of inclusive public dialogue to explore uncharted territories of knowledge.

Lisa Tilley is currently a Leverhulme Fellow in the School of Politics and International Relations at Queen Mary University of London, UK. Her Leverhulme project, 'Race, Intimacy and Extraction on an Internal Frontier', investigates how race is produced and deployed in relation to cultures of intimacy and in the service of extraction along the frontiers of global capital. She has previously published work in relation to debates within political economy, political ontology, post/decolonial thought and decolonial methodology. She is also co-convenor of the Colonial, Postcolonial, Decolonial Working Group within the British International Studies Association, co-convenor of the Raced Markets collective research project, and Associate Editor of *Global Social Theory*.

ACKNOWLEDGEMENTS

The authors would like to thank the editors at Routledge for their help and support. We would also like to thank our advisory board for guidance and suggestions: Pal Ahluwalia, Gurminder K. Bhambra, Aparna Devare, Peo Hansen, Kim Hutchings, Stefan Jonsson, L.H.M. Ling, Kamran Matin, Sabelo Ndlovu-Gatsheni, Alf Nilsen, Amy Niang, Swati Parashar, Mustapha Pasha, Sanjay Seth, Giorgio Shani, Ritu Vij and Heloise Weber. Finally, we would like to thank all our contributors for their intellectual generosity in providing such a set of worthy contributions.

1
POSTCOLONIAL POLITICS
An introduction

Olivia U. Rutazibwa and Robbie Shilliam

Introduction

Engagements with the postcolonial critique by students of politics have grown significantly in recent years. Indeed, whilst it is still not generally acknowledged, it is nowadays at least not quite so controversial to think that the legacies of colonial rule and imperial administration continue to impact upon global politics. For example, development projects have been increasingly entangled with security concerns in post-conflict scenarios across the Global South leading some to liken present-day humanitarianism to the 'civilising missions' of nineteenth-century imperialism (Paris 2002). Alternatively, consider the deep challenges to national belonging in the Global North prompted by an increasingly multicultural citizenry, wherein a quotidian conviviality is currently being attacked by far-right movements and terrorist actors. To the extent that diverse populations in the North often hail from past colonies in the South, we could apprehend multiculturalism as an effect of the empire returning home (see Bhambra and Narayan 2017).

This *Handbook* gathers a multitude of theoretical and empirical inquiries so as to provide the reader with a broad survey of the ways in which global politics can be critically appraised as *postcolonial* politics. But the label 'postcolonial' is not without its own controversies. So, in the process of curating the *Handbook* we, as editors, have conceived of the postcolonial in a specific way. Rather than claiming allegiance to any one intellectual tradition, we utilise the 'postcolonial' as a heuristic device that sensitises the thinker to the multiple, contending and overlapping legacies of colonial rule and imperial administration that inform contemporary global politics. The provocation of 'post' lies, therefore, in a double re-engagement with global politics as both historically constituted through colonialism and presently delineated by struggles over colonial legacies even in an era where, formally speaking, colonialism has mostly ended. Addressing this provocation is what we take to be the task of 'postcolonial critique'. At a minimum, postcolonial critique stretches our imagining of what politics does and should entail. At a maximum, postcolonial critique impels us to pluralise, enrich and even rethink the methods, methodologies, concepts, actors and narratives we deploy in order to make sense of global politics. In short, postcolonial critique helps us to apprehend global politics as, fundamentally, postcolonial politics.

In putting together this *Handbook* we were guided by three aims. Firstly, we wanted the contributions to showcase a plurality of approaches to and applications of postcolonial critique. In this respect, and as we shall explain further in a following section, we did not wish to make this solely a handbook of 'postcolonial theory'. Rather, we have collected a diversity of approaches all of which, in various ways, make substantive engagements with global politics. Secondly, we wanted to puncture the circumscription of postcolonial critique within the politics of the old Commonwealth territories of the British empire and within the English language. This tendency, as we admit below, is difficult to avoid in the academic formation of postcolonial critique. Nonetheless, we have sought, as much as possible, to also engage with intellectuals, traditions and politics on the edges of or even outside of the Anglosphere. And thirdly, we also wanted to address a critique of knowledge production germane to postcolonial critique, namely, the 'silencing' and/or exclusion of voices. To this effect, we have solicited the work of 'practitioner' intellectuals alongside 'academic' ones, as well as those who work between the two spheres.

The *Handbook* provides an expansive set of inquires that equips the reader with the dispositions, concepts and empirics with which to confront and address imaginary and methodological Eurocentrism. In this context, imaginary Eurocentrism refers to an inability to conceive of reality outside of a gaze that assigns superiority and exceptionality to Europe – and by extension the Global North – and a belief that it developed in isolation (see e.g. Wallerstein 1997; Amin 1989). Methodological Eurocentrism points at a systematic reproduction of this bias in the chosen tools and approaches to study the 'global', favouring scholars, questions, theories and concepts derived from a (putatively) European – and 'Northern' – experience to make sense of the 'Rest', as well as a professed preference for a Cartesian division between nature and culture, for the rational, falsifiable and often linear, over other (sources of) knowledges as the basis of science (see e.g. Hall 1992; McLennan 2000).

In this respect, we also hope that the *Handbook* might enable the reader to move beyond the deconstructive impetus to only speak back to Eurocentrism and towards a creative (re) construction of alternatives. Certainly, alternative ways of thinking and acting are pressing to the extent that postcolonial politics can be considered as historically and presently exemplary of the systematic imposition of extreme inequality, exclusion and violence on a global scale. In this respect, we hope that the *Handbook* will enable and encourage the reader to carefully and critically consider from where and with whom our story of politics starts, what imaginaries are implicated in popular narratives of global politics, how these imaginaries are complicit in variously scaled struggles over resources and the modern state, and what alternative imaginaries might be embedded in political projects that have sought – and still seek – to put an end to colonial legacies.

In what remains of this introduction, we firstly induct the reader into the stakes at play in approaching global politics as, specifically, *postcolonial* politics. We then identify and weave together a variety of strands of intellectual inquiry to further induct the reader into the pursuit of 'postcolonial critique'. Finally, we lay out and justify the organisation of the *Handbook*.

Why postcolonial politics?

We start by providing some provocations with which to think differently about recent crises in global politics. Facing the fallout of the financial crash at the end of 2007, we witnessed a Europe incapable of stepping out of pre-existing policy 'solutions' such as the brutal austerity measures inflicted on Greece. We especially witnessed blame being attributed to the behaviours and characteristics of the victims – indolent, lazy, unproductive. This response was provided as if such negative characterisations of subject populations had not been roundly deployed during colonial rule as a way to justify external interventions into discrete economies and societies (see especially Alatas 2012). Neither did these responses consider the fact that austerity measures had been tried before in the Global South through the Northern-authored Structural Adjustment Policies of the 1980s and subsequent Poverty Reduction Strategy Papers dictated by the World Bank and International Monetary Fund Such long-term interventions have been judged widely unsuccessful in relieving public debt. (see e.g. Ostry, Loungani and Furceri 2016; Geo-Jaja and Mangum 2001)

The effect of these long-term economic interventions was made evident when in 2013 the Global North woke up to the Ebola crisis in West Africa. That it was not necessarily the disease itself that killed people *en masse*, but rather the place where one contracted it (for patients in Spain or the USA it was not necessarily fatal), was a fact rarely meditated upon in media commentary. Crucially, the West African states at the centre of the outbreak had experienced years of externally mandated economic discipline that hollowed out their public health systems to be replaced by a patchwork of resources provided by non-governmental organisations and Northern charities. Indeed, global health governance, as Sophie Harman (2017) argues, is 'geared towards mitigating risks to people living in developed countries'. And while lack of local access to medicines and healthcare in the Global South might be bemoaned, meanwhile the production of drugs is dependent upon patent laws, intellectual property rights and international trade regulations, most of which benefit pharmaceutical companies supported by governments of the Global North (see e.g. Turshen 2014: 351).

However, the recent refugee crisis in Europe has demonstrated just how hard it is to contain disease, war, poverty and instability within the global South (see especially Kaplan 2001). The pathologies of Northern-led global governance are perhaps at their most extreme when it comes to the movement of people. Take the Mediterranean, now one of the deadliest sea-crossings in the world, with peoples fleeing persecution and instability in Eritrea, Somalia, Sudan, Nigeria, Mali, etc. That European governments have been, at least to some extent, instrumental in fomenting the conditions for the movement of people presently seeking asylum in Europe is often lost in political debate.

The 2011 Libya war, prosecuted in the main by the USA, Canada, Britain, France and Italy to remove Gaddafi from power, has had the effect of increasing the mobility of terrorist groups in the Sahel as well as emboldening people-smuggling activities that channel asylum seekers through Libya to Lampedusa and other Italian islands in the Mediterranean (Brantner and Toaldo 2015; Kuperman 2015). The internationalisation of the Syrian war, along with the long-term fallout of the Afghanistan war – both conflicts in which North American and European polities have played significant roles – has drastically compounded the flow of peoples seeking refuge within 'fortress Europe'. These extremely complex geo-politics certainly cannot be reduced to an original colonial sin, wherein European powers, especially in the late nineteenth and early twentieth centuries variously governed over these territories and peoples. Yet these imperial histories still seem to be binding European polities and politics to their past mandates.

For instance, although asylum seekers – including children – have regularly died at sea in horrific circumstances, right-wing forces in Europe have continued to demonise those who survive the journey as bearers of violent and backward cultures as well as economic burdens. True, much has been made (rightly so) of the hospitality of some European publics and politicians towards asylum seekers. But we should remember that, on a global scale, Europe is a small player in the hosting of refugees. As has always been the case, the majority of displaced peoples in the Global South have relocated either elsewhere in their own countries or into neighbouring countries. Additionally, consider this striking story. In 1943, 6,000 Greeks, fleeing Nazism, crossed to Turkey and there, having made arrangements with the British government, were taken via the Sinai to Djibouti and also to Dire Dawa and Addis Ababa in Ethiopia. After the liberation of Greece, most returned home, but some remained. Today, people flee the other way across the Mediterranean to an impoverished and crumbling Greece, which is beset by an imposed austerity regime. In 1943, Ethiopia had barely recovered from the appalling and savage occupation of fascist Italy. Yet still, Ethiopia welcomed the Greeks. Hospitality – even when it is extended – is not solely a European invention.

We have given these provocations less as arguments-within-themselves and more as means to sensitise the reader to some key propositions of the study of global politics as *postcolonial* politics, which we will now outline.

Firstly, a great deal of global politics is predicated upon – and complicit in reproducing – inequality, exclusion and violence. Secondly, a great deal of the structures underpinning such politics are inherited, in various and often mediated ways from European and North American colonial rule and imperial administration. Thirdly, and conversely, whenever global attention is paid to issues that first and foremost pertain to and affect the Global South, common-sense analysis invariably posits an idealised Euro- or Western-centric benchmark to which the governments and peoples of the South are cast as aberrations to the 'norm' or 'not-there-yet'. However, fourthly, rather than the North being rendered geographically and temporally distinct to the South (i.e. 'things are simply different over there' and 'they are behind us'), global politics is more adequately apprehended in terms of an interconnected space constituted by actors who exist contemporaneous to each other (see, in general, Fabian 1983; and more specifically, Bhambra 2015).

Let us dwell for a moment on this last proposition. The study of politics has, like many areas of academic inquiry, responded positively to the claim that, post-Cold War, a new stage of modernity has been reached with the globalisation of heretofore national structures, processes, problems and belongings. The propositions outlined above would imply that, in fact, politics has been global for a long time, even in the so-called 'nation-state' era, due to the consolidation, continuation, rearrangement and contestation of the principles of colonial rule and imperial administration (see, for example, Krishna 2009; Hawley and Krishnaswamy 2008). This recognition speaks to why we should study global politics as *postcolonial* politics.

But this proposition requires some crucial clarifications. Firstly, the legacies of colonial rule and imperial administration are mutable. To put it another way, the *principles* of the rule have survived the end of the *rule* itself. Therefore, if we define colonial rule and imperial administration as 'colonialism' then we can define these afterlives as 'coloniality', i.e. the principles and rationalities of colonial and imperial rule that survive even in the absence of formal colonialism (see e.g. coloniality of power: Quijano 2000, 2007; of being: Wynter 2003; Maldonado-Torres 2007; of gender: Lugones 2008; global coloniality: Escobar 2004; Mignolo 2012) Indeed, many – perhaps most – postcolonial polities, and not only old-imperial centres, still govern through these principles. Take, for instance, the music of Fela Kuti, who bemoans the 'colonial mentality' of his 'native' elites in Nigeria. In short, one does not need to be a coloniser – nor a white male – to govern through colonial rationalities.

Secondly, there is a South in the North. Returning to our first remarks above, peoples from the old colonies have regularly migrated to the imperial centres in various capacities (as students, workers, servants, family members, businesspeople, diplomats and asylum seekers) and there they have created new communities or diasporas. Since at least the 1960s, these movements have given rise to debates over multiculturalism, tolerance and belonging, which inflect local and national politics with 'postcolonial' issues (see, for example, the Salman Rushdie affair mentioned below). To put it another way, if we take global politics to be postcolonial politics, then we cannot make categorical distinctions between local, national and global 'levels' of politics.

Thirdly, there is also a North in the South. Wealth and power have never only been accumulated by the elites of the Global North, and this is especially the case with the rise of China, India, Saudi Arabia, Brazil, Singapore, Nigeria, South Africa, etc., as centres in their own right, of resource extraction, industry, services and finance. Moreover, these economic practices are often undertaken by advancing the principles provided by colonialism. One can posit, then, that the elites of the South represent – at least to some extent – the interests of the Global North more so than the experiences of most of their own populations (see, for example, Bond 2013). But at the same time, Southern elites might struggle against their Northern counterparts. In short, there is as much 'politics' in the South as in the North, even if their cadencies might be somewhat distinct.

And fourthly, on this note, postcolonial politics is composed not only of the imposition of inequality, exclusion and violence drawn from the principles of colonialism. Just as much, postcolonial politics is composed of contestations against these impositions – from the 'grassroots' to the 'elites'. There is no postcolonial politics without contention over the continued existence of coloniality.

In pursuit of a more adequate understanding of these political dynamics, intellectuals have variously deployed a 'postcolonial critique'. And it is to this body of work that we now turn.

What is postcolonial critique?

So far, we have introduced the 'postcolonial' as a heuristic device that sensitises the thinker to the multiple, contending and overlapping legacies of colonialism. We now want to substantiate some of the intellectual projects that might conceivably resonate with this heuristic. Leela Gandhi (1998, viii) argues that postcolonial critique 'seems to lack an "originary moment" or a coherent methodology'. Gandhi's caution is well taken. Hence, rather than claim an originating moment or a singular tradition of postcolonial critique, we will instead weave together diverse strands of thought into a patchwork material for the reader to examine.

If not enjoying a singular originating moment, postcolonial critique was first named as a definitive approach in the late 1980s and in the fields of English and Commonwealth literature specifically (see Ashcroft and Griffiths 1988; Mishra and Hodge 1991). At its most general level, the project announced by postcolonial critique sought to destabilise the separation of the imperial centre from the colonial peripheries in narratives of nation-building and emergence of the modern subject/citizen. The 'post' in postcolonial functioned, therefore, not as an escape from history but as a marker of limits: to think beyond colonialism was to unavoidably grapple with the intellectual and practical legacies of empire.

But as soon as this project was named, so too was it questioned. Take, for instance, Ella Shohat's (1992) sympathetic criticism published in the aftermath of the 1990–1 Gulf War, the first major conflict pursued by the USA as the Cold War finished. Shohat questioned why the academy was far more comfortable discussing postcolonialism instead of neocolonialism, and suggested that the former term had a 'depoliticising' effect. Shohat's argument is important. However, we should also remember that the actual literature associated with postcolonial critique has often invoked viscerally political responses outside of academia. Most famous, in this regard, is the publication in 1988 of Salman Rushdie's *The Satanic Verses,* which led to a fatwa being issued by Ayatollah Ruhollah Khomeini, the first Supreme Leader to emerge from the Iranian Revolution, ordering the author's death. In many ways, the 'Rushdie affair' signposted future contentions over tolerance and multiculturalism in the imperial centres of the Global North (see Mazrui 1990; Asad 1990).

In response to Shohat, Arif Dirlik (1994) mounted a more hostile attack, arguing that postcolonial critique provided an 'incorporative function' for post-Cold War global capitalism by bringing 'Third World intellectuals' into the 'First World' academy on the terms of the latter's 'concerns and orientations' (see also Appiah 1991, 149; Ahmad 1994). Dirlik might have overstated the case; nonetheless, it is clear that, in literature at least, postcolonial critique has enjoyed an intimate relationship with British empire in so far as Englishness had by the late nineteenth century become a key modality of imperial belonging, and was taught, as such, to 'native elites' (see Gikandi 1997). Nonetheless, a counterpoint can be found in Ngũgĩ wa Thiong'o's (1986) influential argument (born out of his own travails with the postcolonial Kenyan state) that in order to decolonise the mind, one must produce literature in one's indigenous languages. It is important to note that Thiong'o first gave the series of lectures that formed his famous book *Decolonising the Mind* at the University of Auckland, Aotearoa New Zealand, in 1984. And at this point in time Māori activists had included the teaching of Te Reo, the indigenous language, as part of their demands for reparative justice against the crimes of British settler colonialism.

While postcolonial critique was named and consolidated largely in English and Commonwealth literature, the project that it expounded was homologous to a variety of other extant and contemporaneous work spread across the humanities and social sciences. Take, for instance, cultural criticism, and Edward Said's (2003) seminal argument that the Orient was a colonial construction rather than a place to be discovered. Add to this Homi Bhabha's (1984) claim that the colonial influence on non-European cultures has, as an act of mimicry, produced difference rather than sameness. Consider, also, Ashis Nandy's (1983) psychological critique of colonial elites, who seek to purify themselves of the 'native' within them. What might be said to draw together these strands of inquiry is a claim that, rather than governing over pre-existing formations, colonialism *creates* cultures and sentiments in the core and periphery. Colonialism is culturally transformative and on a global scale.

Next to cultural critique, we must acknowledge the seminal importance of historiographical engagements with colonialism. Dominating this field, the Marxist tradition has sought in multiple ways to account for the historical expansion of capitalism through imperial vectors (see, for example, Brewer 2002; Panitch and Leys 2003). We do not wish to place Marxism in categorical opposition to postcolonial critique, and rather support attempts to find resonances (as well as dissonances) between the two (internally heterogeneous) approaches to historical inquiry (Matin 2013; Rao 2016; see also Bhambra 2011). That being said, of more direct importance for our present inquiry into postcolonial critique is the emergence in the early 1980s of a collective of historians of India influenced by the work of famous Marxist historian of English culture, E.P. Thompson.

The Subaltern Studies collective came to prominence by questioning the elitist biases of narratives of Indian nation-building provided both by the imperially inflected Cambridge School and (Indian) Marxism. Instead, Ranajit Guha (1983, 1996) implored historians to listen to the 'small voices', especially those of the peasantry, even when the latter articulated a 'pre-political' register that spoke of gods rather than profane social forces. Subsequent works arising out of the collective challenged the 'modular' narrative of nation-building, which presumed a similar, sequential process for each polity (see Kaviraj 2005). Unlike in imperial Europe, colonial rule, argued Partha Chatterjee (1986), drastically attenuated the public sphere, leading to postcolonial publics being constituted from the ostensibly 'private' elements of religion, etc. More recently, historians emerging from the collective such as Dipesh Chakrabarty (2000, 2002) have sought to cultivate a 'subaltern historiography' that seeks to learn the limits of modernity from subaltern narratives.

But the Subaltern Studies project also came under fire, most famously by Gayatri Spivak (1988), who posed a set of questions: was it possible to recover the political consciousness of the subalterns in terms of a knowledge untainted by the exercise of colonial power? And to what extent was the notion of a 'resisting subject' itself a category born of European fantasies of their own mastery? In other words, could intellectual elites ever 'represent' the subaltern with fidelity? Spivak's addressing of these questions via the figure of the female subaltern consolidated, in the eyes of the Western academy, a feminist strand of postcolonial thought. However, we should remember that the necessarily multi-faceted – or 'intersectional' – critique of gender, sexuality, race and empire that feminist postcolonial critique requires had already arrived in the academy via multiple routes (see, for example, Moraga, Anzaldúa, and Bambara 1981; Mohanty 1984).

Spivak's mobilisation of the figure of the 'subaltern' also signalled the incorporation of postcolonial critique into poststructural critique. In effect, the elite/subaltern problematic became transposed into the self/other problematic (see especially Prakash 1994). And by this logic, the unknowable subaltern now marked the limit of the will to total knowledge of the modern self. One of the more influential projects arising from the aligning of poststructural and postcolonial critique has been to examine how colonialism was not only concerned with resource extraction but at the same time with the disciplining of the subaltern. Utilising Michel Foucault's latter-day work, scholars have explored 'colonial governmentality', the project to produce out of the subaltern a political subject amenable to being governed along modern rationalities (see for example Scott 1995; Chatterjee 2006).

Cognate projects have also appeared in critical legal studies. Consider, especially, the development of Third World Approaches to International Law (TWAIL). Intellectuals associated with this approach initially took their empirical touchstone to be the Bandung Conference of 1955, wherein Asian and African polities sought to provide a different rule-set of global governance to the antipathies of Cold War politics, one based instead on the principles of peaceful coexistence, self-determination and anti-racialism. Scholars such as Bhupinder Chimni (Anghie and Chimni 2003), Anthony Anghie (2005) and Makau Mutua (2001) have since identified the imperial determinants of international law which produced and perhaps still uphold the principle of colonial difference. Along racialised lines produced through imperial administration, this principle, argue TWAIL scholars, renders some polities as subjects of intervention and others as sovereign subjects, and some peoples as victims or savages and others as saviours of human rights.

These are some of the strands that, although not always marked as 'postcolonialism', certainly contribute to a more acute investigation of global politics as postcolonial politics. So far, however, we have worked our way through disciplinary alignments. But some strands also appear as more distinctly 'national' intellectual traditions.

Alongside Shohat, Dirlik and others, Stuart Hall (1995), Britain's premier public intellectual of the twentieth century, also provided a contribution to the debate on postcolonial critique. However, Hall's prior (collective) work through the 1970s and 80s had pre-empted many of the issues arising out of the predominantly North American debate. Hall is famous for exploring the way in which culture and ideology came to inflect in Britain's post-imperial morass through popular authoritarianism, Thatcherism, moral panics, racist law and order agendas (Hall et al. 1978; Hall 1979). Intellectuals who gestated their ideas within the spaces carved out by Hall were also, by the early 1990s, contributing to the wider academic debate on what we would now call postcolonial critique. Paul Gilroy (1993), for instance, moved from a concern over race, culture and nation in Britain to an immensely influential study of Black modernity in North America.

In this respect, we might also consider the ways in which the predominantly North American tradition of Black Studies has resonated with the postcolonial critique despite the relative paucity of intellectuals actively working across both fields. With the post-emancipation rise of the Historically Black Colleges and Universities (HBCUs) in the USA, Black intellectuals struggled to define and delineate the nature and scope of Black study. One iconic debate positioned Booker T. Washington against W.E.B. Du Bois – the former advocating a compromise position limiting Black study to technical arts, the latter arguing for racial equality and the Black pursuit of 'liberal education' alongside whites (Du Bois 1961; see also Jarratt 2009). Fast forward, now, to the civil rights and Black power era, and we find Black students engaged in months-long strike action in order to compel San Francisco State University to inaugurate Black Studies. Sociologist Nathan Hare (1969) was eventually hired to put together such a programme, which placed special emphasis on the organic involvement of Black communities in the teaching and delivery of a Black-centred liberal arts curriculum. Meanwhile, an elderly Trinidadian Marxist, C.L.R. James (1984), wrote with concern as to the potential bureaucratisation and ghettoisation of Black Studies in the USA academy. Black History, as James (1993) had argued decades before, should be apprehended as quintessentially American – and Global – history.

We confess that our recounting of these traditions is perhaps too partial to the Anglosphere – and certainly English speaking – world. In fact, the label 'postcolonial' does not travel so smoothly outside of this world. Yet this is not to deny the import of intellectual work cognate to the postcolonial critique emanating from, for example, the Francophone world (see, for example, Wilder 2015). It was, after all, the French minister, Jules Ferry who coined the term 'mission civilisatrice' (civilising mission), i.e. the duty of the 'superior races' to civilise the 'inferior races'. And it was a French demographer and anthropologist, Alfred Sauvy, who in 1952 coined the term Tiers Monde (Third World) to identify the 'non-aligned' countries of the Cold War. One year prior, French anthropologist Georges Balandier (1951) had published 'La situation coloniale: approche théorique', which sketched out a research programme remarkably similar to postcolonial critique in so far as it put forward the theoretical premise that colonising and colonised societies were irreducibly interconnected. As testimony to this interconnection, the Black Writers and Artists Congress convened in 1956 at the Sorbonne's Descartes Amphitheatre, attended by, amongst others, Léopold Sédar Senghor, Aimé Césaire, Jacques Rabemananjara, Jean Price-Mars, and Frantz Fanon.

We therefore need to draw attention to wider, regional complexes of critical thought on postcolonial politics that exceed the Anglosphere. For this purpose, let us first recognise that postcolonial critique has demonstrated a notable focus on nineteenth-century imperialism, the role of the imperial state and the epistemic imposition of European temporalities and narratives upon understandings of colonial and postcolonial culture. Moreover, key nodes of this body of work (e.g. Subaltern Studies) refer to a South Asian cartography. Alternatively, the Modernity/Coloniality/Decoloniality (MCD) project, largely enunciated in the Spanish and Portuguese languages, and whilst initially engaging with Subaltern Studies, has nonetheless turned attention to 1492, the colonisation of the Americas, the role of settler colonialism and plantation economies, the ontological question of who counts as 'human', and the possibility of 'delinking' from colonial knowledge structures via the marginalised yet still living knowledge traditions of enslaved and indigenous peoples (see, for example, Dussel 2008; Mignolo 2007; Quijano 2000; Vasquez 2011; Grosfoguel 2007; Domingues 2013).

Because the MCD project has grown in popularity in recent years, we want to make three points that might help the reader better situate it within the patchwork of postcolonial critique. Firstly, whilst the 'postcolonial' and 'decolonial' in many ways represent distinct – and for some no doubt conflicting – dispositions, nevertheless, their resonances have also been productively mobilised (Bhambra 2014). Secondly, as was the case with Subaltern Studies, so too has the MCD project increasingly engaged with issues of gender and sexuality, with some scholars directly mobilising the tradition of 'intersectional' analysis that is seminal to Black Feminist scholarship (Lugones 2010; Icaza and Vazquez 2016; see also Combahee River Collective 2000; Hill Collins and Bilge 2016). And thirdly, the many diverse traditions of indigenous knowledge, if seminally influential to the MCD project, have still retained their intellectual and political distinctiveness as they have entered the Western academy through the work of specific scholars. These bodies of critique draw upon centuries of resistance to post-apocalyptic settler colonialism in the lands now known as the Americas (for example Cusicanqui 1990, 2015; Simpson 2014; Coulthard 2014), in the islands of the Pacific (for example Trask 2005; Smith 1999; Teaiwa 2004; Hau'ofa 2010) and elsewhere.

Indeed, many of the strands of what we are here heuristically weaving into postcolonial critique have their filaments rooted in the extra-academic intellectual work undertaken in the anti-racist, anti-colonial, independence and liberation struggles of the late nineteenth and twentieth centuries. Take, for instance, the rich vein of critical discussions of nationalism, democracy and independence provided by Rabindranath Tagore, Babasaheb Ambedkar, Jawaharlal Nehru, José Martí and Jean-Price Mars. Take also the ethics and politics of resistance grappled with by Mahatma Gandhi, Sayyid Qutb, Mahmoud Darwish, and Samih al-Qasim. Consider the theorisations of (world) revolution provided by Manabendra Nath Roy, Chairman Mao, Zhou Enlai, Ali Shariati, Huey P. Newton, Elaine Brown, Amílcar Cabral and Walter Rodney. And then reflect on the visions of internationalism cultivated by Amy Ashwood Garvey, Amy Jacques Garvey, Marcus Garvey, Haile Selassie I, Chief George Manuel, Fidel Castro, Che Guevara, Muammar Gaddafi and Samora Machel. Finally, let us remember the critiques of racism and humanism developed by Suzanne Césaire, Aimé Césaire, Frantz Fanon, Steve Biko and Robert Sobukwe.

Of course, none of these works are unambiguous, nor are they un-contested, and together they betray a myriad of political positions and theoretical lines of argumentation. Be that as it may, these works remain fundamental to the fabric of postcolonial critique, woven through the political organisations and movements associated with, e.g. Asian-African solidarity, the Non-Aligned Movement, Tricontinentalism, Anti-Apartheid, the indigenous Fourth World, Pan-Africanism, Pan-Arabism and the Intifada. The intellectuals recounted above are also, mainly, male. And this gendered partiality in recording, publishing and disseminating anti-colonial thought must be addressed more directly. For intellectual work that critically addresses colonial and imperial rule has always been generated by women even if they have remained, in many cases, un-named contributors to collective knowledge traditions.

Given this very practical political history, it should not come as a surprise that the study of International Relations (IR) has always been part of the patchwork of postcolonial critique. One can think, for instance, of the engagement by the 'Howard School' with imperial administration in the first part of the twentieth century (Vitalis 2015), the World Order Models Project of the Cold War era (Falk 1978) or simply in terms of the contribution of iconic individuals such as Ali Mazrui (1964). But since the 1990s, postcolonial critique has become more and more influential to the field (see especially Darby 1997; Chan, Mandeville and Bleaker 2001; Chowdhry and Nair 2004; Shilliam 2011; Seth 2013; Tickner and Blaney 2013). Specifically, postcolonial critique has been mobilised to address international law, governance and diplomacy (Grovogui 1996; Bowden 2014; Phạm and Shilliam 2016), global articulations of race (Doty 1993; Persaud 1997; Krishna 2001; Hobson 2012; Anievas, Manchanda and Shilliam 2015), international political economy (Sylvester 1999; Blaney and Inayatullah 2010; Agathangelou and Ling 2009), war and intervention (Barkawi and Laffey 2006; Muppidi 2012; Sabaratnam 2016; Rutazibwa 2014) and sovereignty and subjecthood (Lightfoot 2016; Sajed 2012; Pasha 2012; Jabri 2013; Shani 2014).

These are some – but by no means all – of the diverse intellectual and political strands that we are weaving together to form the intellectual material of postcolonial critique. This material is avowedly a patchwork, comprising distinctive yet criss-crossing narratives, temporalities, agents, structures, movements, concepts, traditions and dispositions. And so, in closing this section, we want to repeat the point that we are using the 'postcolonial' as a heuristic device. Heuristically we wish to call attention to the crossings and entanglements of these intellectual strands; but in this endeavour, we have no wish to refute their distinctive provenances and dispositions as they critically inquire into global politics. The reader will make up their own mind as to what strands and connections interest them the most.

Organisation of the *Handbook*

We have introduced the subject matter of this *Handbook* by outlining the substance of global politics as *postcolonial* politics, as well as its intellectual investigation through postcolonial critique. We have also suggested that intellectual and political responses to the legacies of colonialism are often hard to entirely disentangle. Likewise, all the chapters in this *Handbook* demonstrate an application of postcolonial critique in its many variants, and an engagement with the strikingly diverse substance of global politics. We have curated these chapters into sections, each of which has its own introduction that details the general theme in relation to the contents of its chapters. In lieu of these more specific introductions we now briefly rehearse the rationale for each section.

We begin with a section entitled 'Points of Departure'. Eurocentrism proposes an imperial origin to the thought and practice of politics such that (post)colonial subjects never create their own worlds but only receive the ready-made world of the coloniser. Alternatively, the chapters in this section introduce the reader to diverse, relatable and contestable points of departure into the issues and prospects of postcolonial politics. Many of these departure points are situated amongst peoples who are presumed to have no history prior to colonialism; and even when the departure point is the imperial centre itself, this centre is narrated differently from the perspective of postcolonial critique. Hence, this section encourages the reader to become disposed towards a multitude of points of departure into global politics rather than accept the apparently unassailable and singular centre-point of Eurocentrism.

'Popular Postcolonial Imaginaries' then draws the reader to a critical engagement with some key elements of the contemporary political lexicon. Specifically, this section calls attention to how coloniality might inhere in the very concepts that we deploy to make sense of global politics. Put another way, the principles of colonialism have become embedded within conceptual vocabularies to the point where they form the 'common-sense' of political analysis. The chapters in this section use postcolonial critique to make un-common many of the Eurocentric assumptions that accompany discussions of, for example, terrorism, tribalism, diplomacy and development. This exercise confirms what we have suggested above, namely, that it is academically important and politically urgent to read global politics more adequately as *postcolonial* politics.

The postcolonial state is central to postcolonial politics. Rather than being the moment when colonialism finishes, independence from colonial and imperial rule in the form of the 'nation state' might better be identified as the moment when the (idealised) Eurocentric conception of politics and governance becomes universalised. The section 'Struggles over the Postcolonial State' helps the reader to scope out the essentially contested nature of the postcolonial state and its oftentimes schizophrenic nature: on the one hand, as an entity that is supposed to protect the independence and self-determination of previously colonised peoples; on the other hand, as an entity that impels elites to govern through principles and rationalities inherited from colonialism. Some of the chapters in this section also draw attention to the monumental influence that the state-form exerts on actors in contexts where European colonialism was only partially enacted or derivatively entertained.

At the centre of the colonial project is a claim on land and the resources that it holds. This claim was often justified in terms of cognitively reducing the inhabitants of land-to-be-colonised to savages who had no conception of property ownership or rights. And such claims were most often pursued by enclosing land by violent and even genocidal methods. The section 'Struggles over Land' addresses this fundamental issue of global politics. Of course, land is considered less fundamental to the political calculus in Northern societies, or at least, it is parsed more immediately through notions of property, community, nationalism and citizenship. Nonetheless, land remains central to the calculus of global politics understood as postcolonial politics, being parsed through concerns over food sovereignty, economic dispossession, environmental degradation and even spiritual belonging. The chapters in this section address these concerns, which can be mapped onto whole continents, seas of islands or, simply, a place called home.

The last section, 'Alternative Global Imaginaries', returns us to the multiple horizons encountered in the first section, 'Points of Departure'. But here, the focus is avowedly on mobilising past and present contestations over global politics to envisage alternative political projects. The chapters in this section engage the global imaginary to conceive of different ways of providing human security, of cultivating global solidarities, of inter-connections from the artistic to the diplomatic, of pursuing ethics of repair and healing, and even of teaching global politics differently. All the contributions challenge the reader to think despite, against, besides or beyond colonialism and coloniality, and to envisage scenarios wherein global politics might no longer be synonymous with *postcolonial* politics.

Bibliography

Agathangelou, Anna, and L.H.M. Ling. 2009. *Transforming World Politics: From Empire to Multiple Worlds*. London: Routledge.

Ahmad, A. 1994. *In Theory: Classes, Nations, Literatures*. London: Verso.

Alatas, Syed Hussein. 2012. *The Myth of the Lazy Native: A Study of the Image of the Malays, Filipinos and Javanese from the 16th to the 20th Century and Its Function in the Ideology of Colonial Capitalism*. Hoboken: Taylor and Francis.

Amin, Samir. 1989. *Eurocentrism*. New York: NYU Press

Anghie, Anthony. 2005. *Imperialism, Sovereignty, and the Making of International Law*. Cambridge: Cambridge University Press.

Anghie, Antony, and B. S. Chimni. 2003. 'Third World Approaches to International Law and Individual Responsibility in Internal Conflicts.' *Chinese Journal of International Law* 2: 77–104.

Anievas, Alexander, Nivi Manchanda, and Robbie Shilliam. 2015. *Race and Racism in International Relations: Confronting the Global Colour Line*. London: Routledge.

Appiah, Kwame Anthony. 1991. *In My Father's House: Africa in the Politics of Culture*. London: Methuen.

Asad, Talal. 1990. 'Multiculturalism and British Identity in the Wake of the Rushdie Affair.' *Politics & Society* 18 (4): 455–80.

Ashcroft, Bill, and Gareth Griffiths. 1988. *The Empire Writes Back: Theory and Practice in Post-Colonial Literatures*. London: Routledge.

Balandier, Georges. 1951. 'La Situation Coloniale: Approche Théorique.' *Cahiers Internationaux de Sociologie* 11: 44–79.

Barkawi, Tarak, and Mark Laffey. 2006. 'The Postcolonial Moment in Security Studies.' *Review of International Studies* 32 (2): 329–52.

Bhabha, Homi. 1984. 'Of Mimicry and Man: The Ambivalence of Colonial Discourse.' *October* 28 (April): 125–33.

Bhambra, Gurminder K. 2011. 'Talking among Themselves? Weberian and Marxist Historical Sociologies as Dialogues without "Others".' *Millennium: Journal of International Studies* 39 (3): 667–81. doi:10.1177/0305829811401119.

Bhambra, Gurminder K. 2014. *Connected Sociologies*. London: Bloomsbury Academic Press.

Bhambra, Gurminder K. 2015. 'The Refugee Crisis and Our Connected Histories of Colonialism and Empire.' *Sicherheits Politik-Blog*. http://www.sicherheitspolitik-blog.de/2015/10/01/the-refugee-crisis-and-our-connected-histories-of-colonialism-and-empire/.

Bhambra, Gurminder K., and John Narayan, eds. 2017. *European Cosmopolitanism: Colonial Histories and Postcolonial Societies*. London: Routledge.

Blaney, David L., and Naeem Inayatullah. 2010. *Savage Economics: Wealth, Poverty, and the Temporal Walls of Capitalism*. Basingstoke: Routledge.

Bond, Patrick. 2013. 'Sub-Imperialism as Lubricant of Neoliberalism: South African "Deputy Sheriff" Duty within BRICS.' *Third World Quarterly* 34 (2): 251–70.

Bowden, Brett. 2014. *The Empire of Civilization: The Evolution of an Imperial Idea*. Chicago: University of Chicago Press.

Brantner, Franziska, and Mattia Toaldo. 2015. 'Friede in Libyen Löst Flüchtlingsproblem.' *Frankfurter Rundschau*, May 15. www.fr.de/politik/meinung/gastbeitraege/libyen-fluechtlinge-friede-in-libyen-loest-fluechtlingsproblem-a-470390.

Brewer, Anthony. 2002. *Marxist Theories on Imperialism: A Critical Survey*. London: Routledge.

Chakrabarty, Dipesh. 2000. *Provincializing Europe: Postcolonial Thought and Historical Difference*. Princeton, N.J.: Princeton University Press.

———. 2002. *Habitations of Modernity: Essays in the Wake of Subaltern Studies*. Chicago: University of Chicago Press.

Chan, S., P. Mandeville, and P. Bleaker, eds. 2001. *The Zen of International Relations: IR Theory from East to West*. Basingstoke: Palgrave.

Chatterjee, Partha. 1986. *Nationalist Thought and the Colonial World: A Derivative Discourse?* Delhi: Oxford University Press.

———. 2006. *The Politics of the Governed*. New York, Chichester: Columbia University Press.

Chowdhry, G., and S. Nair, eds. 2004. *Power, Postcolonialism and International Relations*. London: Routledge.

Combahee River Collective. 2000. 'The Combahee River Collective Statement.' In *Home Girls: A Black Feminist Anthology*, edited by Barbara Smith, 264–74. New Brunswick: Rutgers University Press.

Coulthard, Glen. 2014. *Red Skin, White Masks: Rejecting the Colonial Politics of Recognition*. Minneapolis: University of Minnesota Press.

Cusicanqui, Silvia Rivera. 1990. 'Liberal Democracy and Ayllu Democracy in Bolivia: The Case of Northern Potosí.' *The Journal of Development Studies* 26 (4): 97–121.

———. 2015. *Sociología de la Imagen: Miradas Ch'ixi Desde la Historia Andina*. Buenos Aires: Tinta Limón.

Darby, P. 1997. *At the Edge of International Relations: Postcolonialism, Gender and Dependency*. London: Pinter.

Dirlik, Arif. 1994. 'The Postcolonial Aura: Third World Criticism in the Age of Global Capitalism.' *Critical Inquiry* 20 (2): 328–56.

Domingues, José Maurício. 2013. *Global Modernity, Development, and Contemporary Civilization: Towards a Renewal of Critical Theory*. London: Routledge.

Doty, Roxanne Lynn. 1993. 'The Bounds of 'Race' in International Relations.' *Millennium* 22 (3): 443–61.

Du Bois, William Edward Burghardt. 1961. *The Souls of Black Folk*. New York: Crest Books.

Dussel, Enrique D., ed. 2008. *Coloniality at Large: Latin America and the Postcolonial Debates*. Durham: Duke University Press.

Escobar, Arturo. 2004. 'Beyond the Third World: Imperial Globality, Global Coloniality and Anti-globalisation Social Movements.' *Third World Quarterly* 25(1): 207–230.

Fabian, Johannes. 1983. *Time and the Other: How Anthropology Makes Its Object*. New York: Columbia University Press.

Falk, Richard. 1978. 'The World Order Models Project and Its Critics: A Reply.' *International Organization* 32 (2): 531–45.

Gandhi, Leela. 1998. *Postcolonial Theory: A Critical Introduction*. Sydney: Allen & Unwin.

Geo-JaJa, M. A. and Mangum, G. 2001. 'Structural Adjustment as an Inadvertent Enemy of Human Development in Africa.' *Journal of Black Studies* 32 (1): 30–50.

Gikandi, Simon E. 1997. *Maps of Englishness: Writing Identity in the Culture of Colonialism*. New York: Columbia University Press.

Gilroy, Paul. 1993. *The Black Atlantic: Modernity and Double Consciousness*. Cambridge, MA: Harvard University Press.

Grosfoguel, R. 2007. 'The Epistemic Decolonial Turn: Beyond Political-Economy Paradigms.' *Cultural Studies* 21 (2–3): 211–23.

Grovogui, Siba N'Zatioula. 1996. *Sovereigns, Quasi Sovereigns, and Africans: Race and Self-Determination in International Law*. Minneapolis: University of Minnesota Press.

Guha, Ranajit. 1983. 'The Prose of Counterinsurgency.' *Subaltern Studies* II.

———. 1996. 'The Small Voice of History.' *Subaltern Studies IX*, 1–12.

Hall, Stuart. 1979. 'The Great Moving Right Show.' *Marxism Today*, January: 14–20.

———. 1992. 'The West and the Rest: Discourse and Power.' In *Formations of Modernity*, edited by Stuart Hall and Bram Gieben, 275–320. Oxford: Polity Press.

———. 1995. 'When Was 'the Post-Colonial'? Thinking at the Limit.' In *The Postcolonial Question: Common Skies, Divided Horizons*, edited by Iain Chambers and Lidia Curti, 242–60. London: Routledge.

Hall, Stuart, C. Critcher, T. Jefferson, J. Clarke, and B. Roberts. 1978. *Policing the Crisis: Mugging, the State, and Law and Order*. London: Macmillan.

Hare, Nathan. 1969. 'A Conceptual Proposal for a Department of Black Studies.' In *Shut It Down! A College in Crisis*, 159–67. Washington: U.S. Government Printing Office.

Harman, Sophie. 2017. 'How Can a Woman Survive Ebola and Then Die in Childbirth? The Shame of Global Health Governance.' *Huffington Post*, March 2. http://www.huffingtonpost.co.uk/sophie-harman/how-can-a-woman-survive-e_b_15084078.html.

Hau'ofa, Epeli. 2010. *We Are the Ocean: Selected Works*. Honolulu: University of Hawaii Press.

Hawley, John Charles, and Revathi Krishnaswamy. 2008. *The Postcolonial and the Global*. Minneapolis: University of Minnesota Press.

Hill Collins, Patricia, and Sirma Bilge. 2016. *Intersectionality*. Cambridge: Polity Press.

Hobson, John M. 2012. *The Eurocentric Conception of World Politics: Western International Theory, 1760–2010*. Cambridge: Cambridge University Press.

Icaza, Rosalba, and Rolando Vazquez. 2016. 'The Coloniality of Gender as a Radical Critique of Developmentalism.' In *The Palgrave Handbook on Gender and Development: Critical Engagements in Feminist Theory and Practice*, edited by Wendy Harcourt, 62–76. London: Palgrave Macmillan.

Jabri, Vivienne. 2013. *The Postcolonial Subject: Claiming Politics/ Governing Others in Late Modernity*. London: Routledge.

James, C. L. R. 1984. 'Black Studies and the Contemporary Student.' In *At the Rendezvous of Victory*, 186–201. London: Allison & Busby.

———. 1993. *American Civilization*. Cambridge, MA: Blackwell.

Jarratt, Susan C. 2009. 'Classics and Counterpublics in Nineteenth-Century Historically Black Colleges.' *College English* 72 (2): 134–59.

Kaplan, Robert D. 2001. *The Coming Anarchy: Shattering the Dreams of the Post-Cold War*. Vintage.

Kaviraj, Sudipta. 2005. 'On the Enchantment of the State.' *Archives Européennes de Sociologie* 46 (2): 263–96.

Krishna, Sankaran. 2001. 'Race, Amnesia, and the Education of International Relations.' *Alternatives* 26 (4): 401–24.

———. 2009. *Globalization and Postcolonialism: Hegemony and Resistance in the Twenty-First Century*. Lanham, MD: Rowman & Littlefield.

Kuperman, Alan J. 2015. 'Obama's Libya Debacle: How a Well-Meaning Intervention Ended in Failure.' *Foreign Affairs* 94: 66–77.

Lightfoot, Sheryl. 2016. *Global Indigenous Politics: A Subtle Revolution*. London: Routledge.

Lugones, Maria. 2008. 'The Coloniality of Gender.' *Worlds & Knowledges Otherwise, Spring*. 1–17.

———. 2010. 'Towards a Decolonial Feminism.' *Hypatia* 25 (4): 742–59.

Maldonado-Torres, Nelson. 2007. 'On the Coloniality of Being: Contributions to the Development of a Concept.' *Cultural Studies* 21(2–3): 240–70.

Matin, Kamran. 2013. 'Redeeming the Universal: Postcolonialism and the Inner Life of Eurocentrism.' *European Journal of International Relations* 19 (2): 353–77.

Mazrui, Ali. 1964. 'The United Nations and Some African Political Attitudes.' *International Organization* 18 (3): 499–520.

Mazrui, Ali A. 1990. 'The Satanic Verses or a Satanic Novel? Moral Dilemmas of the Rushdie Affair.' *Alternatives* 15 (1): 97–121.

McLennan, Gregory. 2000. 'Sociology's Eurocentrism and the "Rise of the West" Revisited'. *European Journal of Social Theory*. 3(3): 275–91.

Mignolo, Walter. 2007. 'Delinking: The Rhetoric of Modernity, the Logic of Coloniality and the Grammar of De-Coloniality.' *Cultural Studies* 21 (2): 449–514.

———. 2012. *Local Histories/Global Designs: Coloniality, Subaltern Knowledges, and Border Thinking*. Princeton University Press.

Mishra, Vijay, and Bob Hodge. 1991. 'What Is Post(-)colonialism?' *Textual Practice* 5 (3): 399–414.

Mohanty, Chandra Talpade. 1984. 'Under Western Eyes: Feminist Scholarship and Colonial Discourses.' *Boundary 2* 12/13 (April): 333–58.

Moraga, Cherríe, Gloria Anzaldúa, and Toni Cade Bambara. 1981. *This Bridge Called My Back: Writings by Radical Women of Color.* Watertown, MA: Persephone Press.

Muppidi, Himadeep. 2012. *The Colonial Signs of International Relations.* New York: Columbia University Press.

Mutua, Makau. 2001. 'Savages, Victims, and Saviors: The Metaphor of Human Rights.' *Harvard International Law Journal* 42: 201–45.

Nandy, Ashis. 1983. *The Intimate Enemy: Loss and Recovery of Self Under Colonialism.* Delhi: Oxford.

Ostry, J.D., Loungani, P. and Furceri, D. 2016. 'Neoliberalism: Oversold.' *Finance & Development* 53 (2): 38–41.

Panitch, Leo, and Colin Leys. 2003. *Socialist Register, 2004: The New Imperial Challenge.* London: Merlin.

Paris, Roland. 2002. 'International Peacebuilding and the "Mission Civilisatrice."' *Review of International Studies* 28: 637–56.

Pasha, Mustapha Kamal. 2012. 'Islam and the Postsecular.' *Review of International Studies* 38 (5): 1041–56.

Persaud, R. 1997. 'Frantz Fanon, Race and World Order.' In *Innovation and Transformation in International Studies*, edited by S. Gill and J.H. Mittelman, 170–84. Cambridge: Cambridge University Press.

Phạm, Quỳnh N, and Robbie Shilliam. 2016. *Meanings of Bandung: Postcolonial Orders and Decolonial Visions.* London: Rowman & Littlefield International.

Prakash, Gyan. 1994. 'Subaltern Studies as Postcolonial Criticism.' *The American Historical Review* 99 (5): 1475–90.

Quijano, Aníbal. 2000. 'Coloniality of Power and Eurocentrism in Latin America.' *International Sociology* 15 (2): 215–32.

———. 2007. 'Coloniality and Modernity/Rationality.' *Cultural Studies* 21(2–3): 168–78.

Rao, Rahul. 2016. 'Recovering Reparative Readings of Postcolonialism and Marxism.' *Critical Sociology* OnlineFirst.

Rutazibwa, Olivia Umurerwa. 2014. 'Studying Agaciro: Moving Beyond Wilsonian Interventionist Knowledge Production on Rwanda.' *Journal of Intervention and Statebuilding* 8 (4): 291–302.

Sabaratnam, Meera. 2016. *Decolonizing Intervention: International Statebuilding in Mozambique.* London: Rowman & Littlefield International.

Said, Edward W. 2003. *Orientalism.* London: Penguin.

Sajed, Alina. 2012. *Postcolonial Encounters in International Relations: The Politics of Transgression in the Maghreb.* London: Routledge.

Scott, David. 1995. 'Colonial Governmentality.' *Social Text*, no. 43: 191–220.

Seth, Sanjay. 2013. *Postcolonial Theory and International Relations: A Critical Introduction.* London: Routledge.

Shani, Giorgio. 2014. *Religion, Identity and Human Security.* London: Routledge.

Shilliam, Robbie. 2011. *International Relations and Non-Western Thought: Imperialism, Colonialism and Investigations of Global Modernity.* London: Routledge.

Shohat, Ella. 1992. 'Notes on the "Post-Colonial."' *Social Text*, no. 31/32: 99–113.

Simpson, Audra. 2014. *Mohawk Interruptus: Political Life Across the Borders of Settler States.* Durham: Duke University Press.

Smith, Linda Tuhiwai. 1999. *Decolonizing Methodologies: Research and Indigenous Peoples.* London: Zed Books.

Spivak, Gayatri Chakravorty. 1988. 'Can the Subaltern Speak?' In *Marxism and the Interpretation of Culture*, edited by C. Nelson and L. Grossberg, 271–313. Houndsmills: Macmillan.

Sylvester, Christine. 1999. 'Development Studies and Postcolonial Studies: Disparate Tales of the "Third World."' *Third World Quarterly* 20 (4): 703–21.

Teaiwa, Teresia. 2004. 'Black in the Blue Pacific.' *The Other Voices International Project* 3. http://othervoicespoetry.org/vol3/teaiwa/index.html.

Thiong'o, Ngũgĩ wa. 1986. *Decolonising the Mind: The Politics of Language in African Literature.* Nairobi: Heinemann.

Tickner, Arlene Beth, and David L Blaney. 2013. *Claiming the International.* London: Routledge.

Trask, Haunani-Kay. 2005. *From a Native Daughter: Colonialism and Sovereignty in Hawai'i.* Honolulu: University of Hawai'i Press.

Turshen, Meredith. 2014. 'A Global Partnership for Development and Other Unfulfilled Promises of the Millennium Project.' *Third World Quarterly* 35 (3): 345–57

Vasquez, Rolando. 2011. 'Translation as Erasure: Thoughts on Modernity's Epistemic Violence.' *Journal of Historical Sociology* 24 (1): 27–44.

Vitalis, Robert. 2015. *White World Order, Black Power Politics: The Birth of American International Relations.* Ithaca: Cornell University Press.

Wallerstein, Immanuel. 1997. 'Eurocentrism and Its Avatars: The Dilemmas of Social Science'. *Sociological Bulletin.* 46(1): 21–39.

Wilder, Gary. 2015. *Freedom Time: Negritude, Decolonization, and the Future of the World.* Durham: Duke University Press.

Wynter, Sylvia. 2003. 'Unsettling the Coloniality of Being/Power/Truth/Freedom: Towards the Human, after Man, Its Overrepresentation: An Argument.' *CR: The New Centennial Review.* 3(3): 257–337.

PART I

Points of departure

2
INTRODUCTION

The consolidation of prosperity, peace and freedom in the Global North has traditionally been credited to enlightenment and industrialisation wherein modernity congeals as a globally unprecedented system of thought and historic advent. In text book renditions, modernity is mostly presented as a phenomenon that arose in an isolated European context by design (bordering on manifest destiny) or by chance. Explicitly or implicitly, Eurocentrism holds that European modernity entails forms of political, economic and social governance that are practically and morally superior to, and desirable over, any other civilisational development in human history.

We start this Part with the claims made on behalf of European modernity because it is from this logic that prominent actors in the Global North have often engaged with the Global South, shaping, cajoling, bribing or bombing the peoples of the latter into the former's own (idealised and partial) image. International diplomacy, trade liberalisation, democratisation and aid policies, military/humanitarian interventions and even global governance and climate change are still very much issues that are on the whole conceived as the diffusion of modernity from the North to South. Moreover, this logic of normative and technical primacy remains undisturbed by more pessimistic narratives that identify – or even propose – a 'retreat' of the Global North in the face of contestation or rejection from the Global South. Hence, in the Eurocentric conception of the modern world, the projection of the other as inferior, dangerous, less capable or 'not there yet' is naturalised conceptually and narratively. And it is this naturalisation that makes global politics quintessentially postcolonial politics.

But what if we were to start the story some-where and some-when else? What happens when Europe – as a geographic and historical place of isolated, exceptional and superior development, as an idea, as the telos of humanity – ceases to be the centre of our imagination and study of global politics? For one, it would be untenable to study the industrial, political and other revolutions associated with modernity in the absence of the contributions of, resistances of and murderous violence suffered by colonised and enslaved peoples before and during the rise of these continuously commemorated developments in Europe. We hasten to add that we are signalling for these colonial histories and imperial entanglements to be considered not merely as derivative to, but as fundamentally constitutive features of, the logic of what most call 'modernity'.

The chapters in this Part tackle Eurocentrism by proposing different points of departure, thus showcasing the possibilities of thinking global politics *otherwise*. These departure points re-connect pasts – from the most 'local' to the global – which colonial and Eurocentric knowledge production have tended to fragment, obfuscate and present as distinct, separate or unworthy. Many of these departure points are located amongst peoples and places who are too often cast as not having meaningful history prior to colonialism. These different locations bring forth different issues for consideration, or require us to approach familiar issues in unfamiliar ways. Even when the point of departure is the imperial centre itself, this centre looks differently from the perspective of postcolonial critique.

Our first point of departure lies in a vision of indigenous futures. We consider this to be an extremely radical departure point given the assumption, underlining most narratives of global politics and practices of global development, that the 'indigenous' is a thing of the past and exists in the present only as a relic. And even sympathetic voices tend to narrate indigenous peoples as having been annihilated in colonial genocides. Mary Tuti Baker firmly foregrounds the indigenousness of Hawai'i, forcefully annexed to the USA in 1898. Drawing attention to the concepts of *aloha ʻāina* (love for the land) and *waiwai* (abundance), and through the works of two communities, Baker introduces the organising principle of *anarcha-indigenism*: a meeting place between a world view grounded in indigenous land-based practice and knowledge systems with anarchist principles of fluid leadership and horizontal power structures. Baker's illuminating account of the two chosen communities – one in rural Molokai and the other Ho'oulu Āina, a nature reserve in urban Honolulu – speaks to recurrent themes, tropes and concerns in postcolonial politics. It allows for a range of colonial assumptions and ways of knowing to be pierced: the urban rural divide and the systematic casting of the indigenous in the rural and the past; and the supremacy of the modern concept of progress and development. Baker's chapter instead offers alternative imaginaries of economies of abundance and indigenous futures.

In Chapter 4, Peo Hansen and Stefan Jonsson fundamentally reappraise the historical study of a key imperial centre. The European integration project is usually presented as an exclusively intra-European affair, cast as the quintessential example of peace-making by forging economic ties of mutual dependency. Breaking the isolationist bias of this European integration narrative, Hansen and Jonsson offer a fundamentally different reading of the purpose and constitutive actors of the European integration project. As in that period most European nations were still engaged in formal colonisation, it is indeed curious how the overseas territories are systematically cut out of most narratives of intra-European institutional development. The chapter instead, retrieves the forgotten plans for Eurafrica, and discusses how the project that culminated in the 1957 Treaty of Rome, was congenitally a colonial one: one that sought larger scale burden-sharing and institutional locking-in of the African continent at the service of the survival of Europe. The chapter's alternative account of the European integration project does not only illuminate our understanding of the past, but also raises some very important theoretical questions about contemporary globalisation processes and EU-Africa relations in particular.

Pinar Bilgin's chapter reflects on the question of whether 'security' – a key concept in the study of global politics – should be a point of departure for postcolonial critique. The chapter engages with this question by offering a conversation between three approaches to the question of security. After having detailed the standard realist account of security, Bilgin engages with cosmopolitan approaches that explicitly include the security of peoples understood as located someplace else. Here, humanity as a whole is supposedly the point of reference. Bilgin then addresses postcolonial critiques that reveal how cosmopolitanism flattens out the violent histories that have marked and shaped the global point of reference and continues to shape interactions between peoples in the present day. Postcolonial scholarship points towards the inescapability of the top-down imposition (e.g. North–South) of universalised understandings of cosmopolitan security. The question is then maybe less about whether security should be a point of departure for postcolonial engagements with the global, even though the security of peoples is somehow an important and recurrent concern in postcolonial thinking. Bilgin rather wishes to deploy postcolonial critique to think more adequately about security, especially in terms of the violence that pushes a particular notion of security on the postcolonial world as the universal norm to follow.

In the Chapter 6, Rosalba Icaza offers an alternative point of departure for feminist engagements with global social struggles for justice. Feminism, in all its different shapes and forms, has gained traction, and has over the years been successful in foregrounding gender as a point of departure in the struggles for justice. Nonetheless, what remains obscured is the coloniality embedded in the concept of gender and its subsequent deployments in different sites. Therefore the point of departure for Icaza's 'decolonial feminism' approach is not gender but coloniality. Through three vignettes of contemporary social struggles across Abya Yala (Americas), the chapter builds on co-learned and co-created insights and accounts of/with those resisting violent forms of power that destroy land, women's lives and hopes. This departure point allows for a detailed development of what decolonial feminism stands for and how it allows for thinking and doing global politics *otherwise*. For one, Icaza's approach has profound methodological implications, including the need for un-learning our privilege, in producing knowledge *about and for* the communities impacted by the destruction of their livelihoods and environment, and re-learning from communal forms of resistance.

The point of departure for Sabelo J. Ndlovu-Gatsheni's chapter is that of race as a structuring principle of global politics. Ndlovu-Gatsheni draws attention to the fact that the colonial processes of *dis-membering* – the ontological splitting up of humanity, in which the colonised and enslaved peoples are dehumanised at the service of the coloniser's 'will to power' – is still very much a defining feature of global politics today. But equally present are the decolonial countermoves of *re-membering* – in the words of Ngũgĩ wa Thiong'o: 'the quest for wholeness, a quest that has underlain African struggles since the Atlantic slave trade' – at the service of the 'will to live'. This ontological split, contends Ndlovu-Gatsheni, is racialised, and it is racism that created and sustains it. Blackism, therefore, is connected to the subaltern on the one side, and Whitism and the will to power, on the other. By deploying race as a point of departure in his analysis of contemporary global politics, Ndlovu-Gatsheni is able to foreground the fact that the aim of postcolonial politics should not merely be about including Blackism into Whitism, but that true liberation cannot but be conceived as something that goes beyond that, to a place where whiteness and blackness as a binary state of being no longer exist.

3

WAIWAI (ABUNDANCE) AND INDIGENOUS FUTURES

Mary Tuti Baker

Introduction

Our story of indigenous futures and economies of abundance focuses on two communities in Hawai'i. Both are part of a global network of native spaces whose diverse practices coalesce around the organizing principle of anarcha-indigenism, a world-view grounded in indigenous land-based practice and knowledge systems that articulate with anarchist principles of fluid leadership and horizontal power structures. Indigenism is a fabric of social relationships that builds upon a people's kinship with a particular place, embodied in reciprocal relations between humans and non-humans of that place.[1] This examination of anarcha-indigenism in practice problematizes dichotomies of coloniality, particularly the dichotomy between rural and urban spaces. I want to trouble the settler colonial assumption that indigenous communities only exist in rural spaces and pre-modern temporalities, and that the 'indigenous' is a remnant of the past rather than a preferred alternative future.[2]

I begin by introducing the places that are the focus of this chapter and my relationship to them. In both places Kānaka 'Ōiwi figure prominently. Kanaka 'Ōiwi refers to the people who trace their genealogy to the first people of this land. Other terms which I use interchangeably with this one include Native Hawaiian, Kanaka Maoli, and Kanaka.[3] Rural Moloka'i is predominantly Kanaka 'Ōiwi. Living on a remote island with one supermarket, Moloka'i residents develop a close relationship to that which feeds them – the 'āina (land). The second stop on our journey is Ho'oulu 'Āina, a 100-acre nature preserve run by a community health center in Honolulu's urban core. At Ho'oulu 'Āina, planting and restoring the natural habitat is a part of a community health regime. Both communities exist in a space that is actively modeling Kanaka 'Ōiwi 'āina-based social practices like aloha 'āina (love for the land) and waiwai (abundance); practices that demand that humans participate in communal, reciprocal relationships with each other and with the non-human world.

I am Kanaka 'Ōiwi. My mother's mother has genealogical roots on Hawai'i Island and my mother's father has genealogical roots on Kaua'i, at the other end of the archipelago. I grew up in a suburb of Honolulu, a graduate of the Kamehameha Schools, an institution endowed by the will of the last descendant of Hawai'i's first monarch, Kamehameha. The school's mission is to educate Native Hawaiians to become good and industrious men and women.[4] The school was my anchor to being Hawaiian, as were my Native Hawaiian grandparents. We ate Hawaiian food, sang Hawaiian songs, danced hula and we always referred to Hawaiian culture in the past tense. The goal of school and family was to socialize me into the capitalist political economy of the United States. During the politically and socially unsettling late twentieth century, a time of resurgence in Kanaka ʻŌiwi values and practices, I was forced to re-evaluate my position as a privileged Hawaiian.[5] I began a critical investigation of Hawaiʻi's colonial history and began the hard work of (re)learning what it means to be Hawaiian. My work on aloha ʻāina and waiwai in places like Molokaʻi and at Hoʻoulu ʻĀina has been a part of this learning process. Integrating the resurgent values and practices of my ancestors into daily life is a constant challenge in a society that is deeply invested in a capitalist economy and settler colonial power structures. These resurgent practices anticipate what I call indigenous futures in which they are not merely counter-hegemonic but the norm.

The belief that Western ingenuity will meet any challenge that arises in the natural or man-made world dominates neoliberal dreams of the future. This world, made better through technology, is anticipated in institutions like Singularity University or the aerospace corporation SpaceX. Singularity University's mission is to prepare scientist-entrepreneurs to utilize the 'exponentially growing technologies, such as biotechnology, artificial intelligence and neuroscience, to address humanity's grand challenges: education, energy, environment, food, health, poverty, security, space and water.'[6] SpaceX designs, manufactures and launches advanced rockets and spacecraft to revolutionize space technology, with the ultimate goal of enabling people to live on other planets. The CEO of SpaceX, Elon Musk, recently proclaimed that there were 'two fundamental paths' facing humanity today. 'One is that we stay on Earth forever and then there will be an inevitable extinction event. The alternative is to become a spacefaring civilization, and a multi-planetary species.'[7] Whether it is colonizing other planets or solving pressing problems on Earth using Western technology, these models depend on global capital for success, which means that global capital is setting the agenda and providing the solutions to a consuming public. Indigenous futures do not preclude science and human technology but these futures do demand that goals are pursued within an ethic of reciprocity and responsibility to human and non-human.

As the Zapatistas proclaim: "In the world of the powerful there is no space for anyone but themselves and their servants. In the world we want everyone fits."[8] Capitalism and colonialism, particularly settler colonialism, have historically left no room for other ways of being. During Western colonial expansion, Indigenous lifeways were threatened, obscured, and made irrelevant to survival. These lifeways were not eliminated but they certainly went underground. In the epithet above, the Zapatista Army of National Liberation responds to this colonial power structure with a dream of an alternative world where many worlds fit. This sentiment is echoed by Ziauddin Sardar who writes that the future is colonized by a singular vision of humanity in which globalizing forces of neoliberal capitalism – forces that equate with 'the values and canonical myths' of Western society – are in control. Just as colonialism has obscured the histories of colonized peoples, it also obscures our futures through hegemonic discourse of the foregone and predetermined. In order to survive these globalizing forces, Sardar writes, Indigenous Peoples must, 'start to think more concretely and imaginatively about the future' in order to open the future to non-Western possibilities 'and move from *the* future to a *plethora of futures*.'[9] I liken this visioning of a world where many worlds fit to active dreaming in the present, in anticipation of futures based in Indigenous values and economies of abundance.

It is a daunting task to challenge the notion that Western progress and development are the best, the right, the only trajectory for humanity. This belief in Western progress has fueled the colonial conquest of the last five hundred years; it has built empires based on resource exploitation and land dispossession; and it has attempted to eliminate the Indigenous populations that resisted this conquest. Neoliberal globalization is an intensification of this colonial expansion, but whereas early colonialism was controlled by the state, the present iteration of colonial domination seeks to globalize corporate control of human behavior. This new form of colonialism goes beyond exploiting resources by promoting 'a dominant set of cultural practices and values, one vision of how life is to be lived at the expense of all others.'[10]

Indigenous Peoples have been fighting colonial control of their lifeways for generations. They continue to fight on many fronts: from within the colonial legal system by demanding Native rights, and on the ground where they physically blockade destruction of their sacred lands.[11] In addition to these acts of resistance, Indigenous Peoples are engaged in resurgence. Resurgence involves acts of reinforcing the knowledge and values of ancestors in the practice of daily life in anticipation of futures where these values are the norm. These strategies of demand, block and resurgence are powered by indigenous cosmologies that settler colonial capitalist regimes, try as they might, have not been able to eliminate. I refer to cosmologies in the plural because the world of Indigenous futures is a world, as the Zapatistas declare, where many worlds fit. Unlike the homogenized, profaned future that corporate and state hegemonic powers offer as the only future possible, Indigenous futures actively dream a world of diverse peoples rooted to place and living in close relationship to the human and non-human world.

This chapter dares to articulate indigenous futures based on the values of aloha ʻāina and waiwai. The close relationship of Kānaka ʻŌiwi to the non-human world is reflected in the language itself. ʻĀina translates as land or earth. The word is derived from ʻai to eat and is glossed as that which feeds. Aloha ʻāina then is an abiding care for the land and all that feeds us. Wai is the word for fresh water and the doubling of 'wai' yields 'waiwai', the word for abundance and wealth. The land feeds us and fresh water creates abundance. In what follows, we first visit the island of Molokaʻi where Kanaka ʻŌiwi and settler allies alike are integrating aloha ʻāina and waiwai into community-based development. Subsequently, we visit Hoʻoulu ʻĀina, an urban nature preserve operated by a community health center that integrates aloha ʻāina and waiwai into a comprehensive health-care system. Finally, we consider the ways that these two places are practicing decolonial futures in the present.

Grounded normativity on Molokai

> Molokai is the last Hawaiian island. We who live here choose not to be strangers in our own land. The values of aloha ʻāina and mālama ʻāina (love and care for the land) guide our stewardship of Molokai's natural resources, which nourish our families both physically and spiritually. We live by the historic legacy of pule oʻo (powerful prayer) left to us by our kūpuna (elders/ancestors). We honor our island's Hawaiian cultural heritage, no matter what our ethnicity, and that culture is practiced in our everyday lives. Our true wealth is measured by the extent of our generosity.[12]

On Molokai, the most meaningful evidence of resurgence lies in the community's ability to determine its own economic development priorities. These priorities are based on a set of principles articulated in various community-based development documents and summarized in the community vision statement above. Embedded in this statement is the call to individuals to be stewards of the island's resources and to take on the responsibility of ensuring that the resources are protected and available for generations to come. Sustainability starts with the community living with the land and its natural resources, that is, with people who are intimate with rather than strangers to the place where they live.

On Moloka'i, Kanaka 'Ōiwi constitute the majority of the island's approximately 7,000 residents.[13] In addition to Kanaka 'Ōiwi, Molokai's population includes longtime residents (predominantly descendants of plantation workers) and recent arrivals (predominantly propertied white Americans). According to standards set by the neoliberal state, Molokai is a distressed community. Unemployment is high, and many residents live below the poverty line.[14] There are also few amenities on the island, and most residents who make a commitment to living on Molokai provide for themselves by hunting, fishing and gardening. Families and neighbors commonly share work and resources.[15] Molokai has a vibrant sustenance economy defined by relationships of sharing and reciprocity. Rather than use the more common term subsistence, I use sustenance, a concept developed by environmental activist Vandana Shiva. Subsistence is too often associated with the bare life of the subaltern, whereas sustenance emphasizes the active participation of people, not only in their own survival but in their thriving as well. 'In the sustenance economy,' Shiva writes, 'people work to directly provide the conditions necessary to maintain their lives.'[16] This sustenance economy operates alongside the ubiquitous market economy defined by profit-taking and resource exploitation. The richness of the sustenance lifestyle empowers the residents to resist being victimized by the capitalist model of modernity that operates with structures of deficit, and measures well-being in terms of monetary wealth.

The community standard for good development is expressed in the vision statement cited above, which Molokai residents have used extensively to leverage public and private funds for community-based development. The vision statement articulates community priorities for development that can be presented to the outside. The foremost consideration is that development projects follow the principle of aloha 'āina: to love and care for the land and its resources. Projects need to protect the island's cultural and natural resources at the same time as providing meaningful livelihood and affordable housing for the island's residents.

The vision statement has also been deployed with varying degrees of success to galvanize community resistance to exploitation of Molokai resources by transnational capital. Transnational corporate notions of economic progress are very different from community-based notions. For the most part, the handful of transnational corporations doing business on the island measures wealth in terms of capital accumulation rather than generosity. This leads to a complex, ongoing and ever-shifting power dynamic within and between community and corporations. In 2006, community protest stopped a luxury housing development at La'au Point, an environmentally sensitive shoreline area of the island. Members of the community have also resisted, with varying degrees of success, an industrial-scale wind farm and production of genetically modified seed corn on the island.[17]

Political organizing on Molokai draws on social relations and practices that have evolved over centuries of living on the island. These social relations are a part of an ethical framework of grounded normativity, a concept developed by Dene scholar Glen Coulthard.[18] Indigenous struggles that are anti-colonial and anti-capitalist, Coulthard explains, are 'deeply *informed* by what the land as mode of reciprocal *relationship* ... teaches us about living our lives in relation to one another and our surroundings in a respectful, nondominating and nonexploitative way.'[19] The 'Ōiwi value of aloha 'āina is an expression of grounded normativity. Aloha 'āina engenders community strategies for development on Molokai that anticipate nondominating and nonexploitative Indigenous futures.

Ho'oulu 'Āina

I would like to now turn to an articulation of grounded normativity in a very different place, an urban environment facing a different set of challenges that requires a different set of strategies. Ho'oulu 'Āina is an agricultural park on the island of O'ahu situated in the upland edge of the ahupua'a of Kalihi.[20] Before colonization, extended family units in this ahupua'a cultivated plots of land along the streams that ran from the lush upland forests through fertile estuaries and on into the ocean depths. Today, Kalihi is a working-class community in the urban core of Honolulu. Streams flowing from the forested uplands are confined to a man-made channel system by the time they reach the middle-class developments and the sprawling low-income public housing. In the lowlands, the banks of the sluggish canals are crowded with warehouses, industrial complexes and the occasional encampment of houseless people. The water's journey ends at Māmala Bay, where on its eastern edge, cargo is unloaded at the docks of Honolulu harbor, and on the western edge, hundreds of flights an hour arrive and depart at Honolulu International Airport.

Ho'oulu 'Āina is part of Kokua Kalihi Valley Comprehensive Family Services (KKV). In addition to providing medical, dental and behavioral health care, KKV also promotes 'health by sharing food and laughter, celebrating elders and children, dancing, planting, and remembering how to be a community.'[21] The majority of the patients at KKV are immigrants from the Philippines, Marshall Islands, Samoa and other Pacific island groups, as well as Native Hawaiians living in the valley. KKV introduces Ho'oulu 'Āina on its website with this:

> KKV sees the 'āina [land] as a vital member of the community, and so we are pleased to offer opportunities for community gardening, reforestation, environmental education and the preservation of land-based cultural knowledge at Ho'oulu 'Āina (the Kalihi Valley Nature Preserve). In this "welcoming place of refuge for people of all cultures," healing the land heals us as well.[22]

Ho'oulu 'Āina's beginnings go back to a decades-long struggle between residents and the State and private developers over the best use for the land. One resident involved in the struggle suggested to her doctor that KKV create a park on the land where the community could garden and enjoy outdoor activities.[23] The desire of residents in the valley to protect the health of the land and the desire of KKV to protect the health of the people converged, and Ho'oulu 'Āina came into being. The collective activities of the organization are effectively operationalizing transformative social relations involved with food production and healing arts. These social relations are an example of anarcha-indigenism. I offer as examples of the modeling of these principles my first experience volunteering at Ho'oulu 'Āina, and a lesson in waiwai economics.

Just past a wooden bridge over a free-flowing Kalihi Stream, shaded by green and lush forest, is the turn into the Ho'oulu 'Āina driveway. The only sign marking the driveway reads: 'This land is your grandmother and she loves you.' Driving into the gravel parking lot, I am immediately immersed in community. To the right is controlled chaos in and around a large open tent. A line of sorts snakes from a table at the entrance of the tent across the lawn. On the left, at the far edge of the lawn, is an ahu (stone altar). Offerings of a hand of banana and ti leaf woven into a shiny green lei have been placed on the rock structure. Beyond the ahu is a lush border of greenery and glimpses of a massive ulu tree, papaya trees, and rows of garden greens. Beyond that, Norfolk pines reach upward through a vertical spread of albizia and, towering above the forest canopy, the green peaks of the Ko'olau mountains touch the sky. The air is cool and the sun brilliant.

At the tent, the volunteer coordinator and her helpers distribute waiver forms to newcomers. 'Please sign the waiver. You have to do it once a year,' they implore the crowd. I sign the legal form filled with language of warranties and responsibilities, and then sign in for the day on a more welcoming sheet that asks:

'What's your name? Where are you from? How are you feeling?'

A double subjectivity is embedded in this protocol of signing-in. On the one hand, the waiver forms interpellate us as subjects of the state and its legal system. The daily sign-in sheet, on the other hand, reinforces the volunteer's relationship to homeland and personal well-being.

Like ripples through water, word spreads that it's time to begin. People gravitate to the lawn. The leader of the opening protocol calls out:

'Aloha! ... Aloha! Please join the circle.'

> As the crowd of around 100 people forms into a circle she continues:
>
> Welcome to Ho'oulu 'Āina. We begin every community workday with an aloha circle. In this circle we ask you to share three names. First your name, then the name of the place you call home, and finally the name of someone you're bringing with you today. It could be a kupuna who has passed on or someone you hold dear. The first introduction though is to the 'āina. We are in a 100-acre nature preserve that encompasses two 'ili 'āina or land divisions. We are standing in the 'ili of 'Ōuaua and makai of us is Māluawai.

After we introduce ourselves and speak the name of our home and someone dear to us, work crew leaders describe the projects for the day: harvesting herbs, weeding and harvesting in the vegetable garden, weeding in the Pasifika agro-forest, planting bananas in the upper garden, preparing lunch in the kitchen, and participating in the story crew. Roles in the organization, like circle leader, sign-in coordinator, and work crew leaders are responsibilities with permeable boundaries. At community workdays, volunteers who have been participating at the park for a long time lead work parties, orient newcomers, and participate in capacities similar to those of paid staff.

The leader then reminds everyone present to be mindful while working and to take care of each other. Individual accountability to the collective whole is a guiding principle of both anarchism and indigenism. She then closes the opening protocol with an oli (Hawaiian chant) that honors the 'āina of Kalihi.

Controlled chaos resumes as volunteers self-select into one of six work crews. Self-selection is a marker of anarchist social organization. Everyone there is asked to take personal responsibility for their participation in the workday. I join the story crew. The leader of this group is a staff member who is responsible for writing reports to foundations that support Ho'oulu 'Āina programs. She wants to build a database of stories from volunteers to share with funders. The three of us in the story crew are to visit each work site observing, listening, and asking participants to respond to the prompt 'this place is...' At the end of the workday the leader will compile our stories into a narrative she can use in grant reports.

For the next two hours, I move from the kitchen to the organic garden in 'Ōuaua, to the Pasifika agro-forest to the upper gardens of Māluạwai, observing and listening. In the kitchen as we prepared vegetables for lunch, I asked the choppers to finish the sentence 'Ho'oulu 'Āina is....' A woman carefully slicing carrots quietly responds, 'This place is hard to pronounce.' She seemed to shy away from her spontaneous outburst but was bolstered when others around the table agree. A staff member also chopping vegetables is surprised. She didn't realize this could be a problem. The ensuing discussion centered on how to help those not familiar with the

Hawaiian language to become more comfortable with the language. Here is an example of the anarchist principle of horizontal leadership. At the table a relative newcomer's experience of place is taken as seriously as someone who has worked at the park for years.

In the upper garden area of Māluawai, young people are busy digging holes for banana shoots. I ask what Ho'oulu 'Āina means to them. 'We love this place and this place loves us,' one of them shouts and returns to digging. This is a common sentiment. People who spend any time working at Ho'oulu 'Āina develop this kind of reciprocal relationship of aloha with place.

While in Māluawai, I engage in a lengthy conversation with a staff person who has lived and worked at Ho'oulu 'Āina for most of the ten years that the park has been in operation. He works primarily in the dense forest of trees and underbrush separating the Māluawai garden from the garden and gathering place in 'Ōuaua. 'Aren't all the invasive plants a challenge?' I ask him. He points to a tree at the edge of the jungle that surrounds the clearing. It is perhaps a foot and a half in diameter, growing tall and straight.

> That's an albizia. They are damaging forests all over Hawai'i. We can't let those trees take over our forests. But *that* tree – it does not make sense to cut down *that specific tree.* Someday it could make a good canoe.

Like many other introduced species, albizia (*Falcataria moluccana*), a native to lowlands in the Molucca Islands (Indonesia), was brought to Hawai'i as an ornamental as well as to reforest the land after imported ungulates caused massive de-forestation.[24] This is yet another example of colonial violence to the land brought about by the introduction of foreign species that destroy native eco-systems. The point being made by the staff person, though, was that although invasive species need to be removed in order to reach the long-term goal of returning water flow to this 'āina and revitalizing native eco-systems, each patch of land with its trees, and underbrush and microorganisms must be analyzed based on many possible models, not just a single model. All this information is processed collectively into continually evolving plans of action. 'Knowledge comes from working the 'āina,' he tells me. Having lived and worked at Ho'oulu 'Āina for ten years, he has come to understand that the 'āina is sacred. The land itself demands that we respect the mana (divine power) of all plants growing in the forest, including, he emphatically adds, invasive species. After a contemplative moment, he declares:

We are not planning for five years or even fifteen years. Our plan is for two hundred years.

I have returned to Ho'oulu 'Āina many times since this first day. At community workdays I join hundreds of others cultivating food at the various garden sites, clearing invasive species and restoring eco-systems in the forest. Working the land in a place like Ho'oulu 'Āina requires that those who show up collectively engage with networks of humans, plants, animals, weather, dirt, and rock in complex relationships of knowledge cultivation. This is the essence of grounded normativity.

According to Puni Jackson, the program director at the park, Ho'oulu 'Āina operates on the 'Ōiwi economic principle of waiwai, associating wealth with abundance, generosity, sharing and reciprocity. These principles are structured into community workdays. At the end of these workdays the fruits and vegetables that were harvested that day are put out on tables for participants to take home. Everyone is encouraged to take food for their own table and to share with family and friends. In addition to the giveaway, food grown in the garden is distributed to the elderly and others in Kalihi who have limited access to fresh vegetables and fruits. The produce is also used at Roots, the restaurant operated by KKV.

At one such community workday, I participated in a lesson in the economics of abundance. Volunteers are in line for lunch while others are taking vegetables from the table laid out with the day's harvest. I am eating lunch at the registration table with some of the Hoʻoulu ʻĀina staff. A young woman approaches with bags of fresh produce and hands me $20, a gesture I read as payment for the vegetables. I tell her that Hoʻoulu ʻĀina doesn't take money for the vegetables. The volunteer coordinator sitting next to me intercedes, pulling from her registration folder a small plastic bag with some money already in it. 'We'll be happy to take your donation though,' she says and graciously accepts the gift.

Hoʻoulu ʻĀina has consciously structured food sharing so that there is no direct correlation between the bulging bag of fresh organic vegetables that the volunteer had helped harvest and the $20 in her hand. The vegetables are hers because she showed up and participated. She freely gives the $20 in recognition that Hoʻoulu ʻĀina needs cash to operate. This is a very different social relation from purchasing food at a supermarket. It models an alternative future where money and barter exchange systems operate side by side.

Conclusion

As a young person growing up in suburban Honolulu, aloha ʻāina and waiwai were not prevalent concepts. At school I was taught that satisfaction was derived from being productive in the capitalist economic system, but I also inherited from my family a latent love for place and desire to live in an environment where generosity was the norm. In this chapter I examined the ways in which waiwai and aloha ʻāina are the embodiments of place-based knowledge and values, and I argued that they are resurgent today in the everyday practices of two very different populations – one rural and the other urban.

It is important that Hoʻoulu ʻĀina and the Molokai community be read together in order to problematize the dichotomies of coloniality. Rural Molokai is perceived as an authentic indigenous space – an idea that is reinforced by Molokai residents themselves who refer to their island as 'the most Hawaiian island.'[25] This subjectivity affirms the perception that the colonized indigenous subject is enclosed in the rural. Indigenous practice at Hoʻoulu ʻĀina demonstrates the viability of these practices outside of the confines of the rural. Both communities exist in a space that is actively modeling Kanaka ʻŌiwi ʻāina-based social practices such as waiwai and aloha ʻāina, practices which demand that humans participate in communal reciprocal relationships with one another and with the non-human world.

Both communities also operate within the hegemony of the capitalist economy. On Molokai practices which are born out of ancestral knowledge and lifeways are integrated into a community development strategy that also seeks to include state and private capital investment. Hoʻoulu ʻĀina actively pursues monetary support from institutional donors as well as individual participants. The ability of the Molokai community and Hoʻoulu ʻĀina to operate in both economic spheres disrupts the colonial hold on the future referred to above by Sardar. The colonial future is a continuation of current trajectories in which human-designed technology alone can solve the Earth's problems. To move out of a colonized future into a truly post-colonial future requires that these relationships be torn down so that new relationships can emerge. Molokai and Hoʻoulu ʻĀina are part of a network of communities that are modeling these new relationships.

The future is a dream that as a global society we are collectively dreaming. What values are we carrying forward in this dreaming? As the dream world unfolds into the present, communities – including the two profiled in this chapter – are actively dreaming post-colonial worlds, Indigenous futures: a world where many worlds fit.[26]

Bibliography

'Albizia Tree Removal Project.' *Harold L. Lyon Arboretum*, September 20, 2014. https://manoa.hawaii.edu/lyonarboretum/albizia-tree-removal-project-details/.

Alfred, Taiaiake. *Wasáse: Indigenous Pathways of Action and Freedom*. Peterborough, Ont: Broadview Press, 2005.

Baker, Mary 'Tuti'. 'Resisting Neoliberal Capitalism: Sustainable Self-Determination on Molokai, Hawai'i.' *International Journal of Critical Indigenous Studies* 4, no. 1 (2011): 12–20.

Beamer, B. Kamanamaikalani. *No Mākou Ka Mana: Liberating the Nation*. Honolulu Hawai'i: Kamehameha Publishing, 2014.

Cluett, Catherine. 'Molokai Group Unites Against Industrial Wind.' *Molokai Dispatch*, June 5, 2011, online edition, sec. 'Energy'. http://themolokaidispatch.com/molokai-group-unites-against-industrial-wind.

Coulthard, Glen. *Red Skin, White Masks: Rejecting the Colonial Politics of Recognition*. Minneapolis: University of Minnesota Press, 2014.

Day, Richard J. F. '"Anarcha-Indigenism", an edited excerpt of a conference paper presented by Richard J.F. Day.' *Void Mirror*, January 4, 2012. http://voidmirror.blogspot.com/2012/01/anarcha-indigenism-edited-excerpt-of.html.

———. *Gramsci Is Dead: Anarchist Currents in the Newest Social Movements*. London: Pluto Press, 2005.

Ferguson, Kathy. 'Becoming Anarchism, Feminism, Indigeneity.' *Affinities: A Journal of Radical Theory, Culture, and Action* 5, no. 1 (August 30, 2011). http://www.affinitiesjournal.org/index.php/affinities/article/view/19.

Fujikane, Candace, and Jonathan Y. Okamura, eds. *Asian Settler Colonialism: From Local Governance to the Habits of Everyday Life in Hawai'i*. Honolulu: University of Hawai'i Press, 2008.

Goodyear-Ka'ōpua, Noelani, Ikaika Hussey, and Erin Kahunawaika'ala Wright, eds. *A Nation Rising: Hawaiian Movements for Life, Land, and Sovereignty*. Durham: Duke University Press Books, 2014.

Hamilton, Chris. 'Molokai Ranch: A Year after Closure, Times Are Hard but Spirit Is Alive', Mauinews.com, 'News, Sports, Jobs, Visitor's Information', April 19, 2009. www.mauinews.com/page/content.detail/id/517428.html?nav=10.

Institute for Alternative Futures. 'Case Study: Kokua Kalihi Valley Comprehensive Family Services.' Institute for Alternative Futures, 2010. www.altfutures.org/pubs/leveragingSDH/IAF-KKV-CaseStudy.pdf.

'Ka Honua Momona, Intl.' Accessed April 22, 2013. www.kahonuamomona.org/.

Kame'eleihiwa, Lilikalā. *Native Land and Foreign Desires: Pehea Lā E Pono Ai?* Honolulu: Bishop Museum Press, 1992.

'Kamehameha Schools – Bernice Pauahi Bishop's Will and Codicils.' Accessed November 14, 2013. www.ksbe.edu/pauahi/will.php.

Klein, Naomi. *This Changes Everything: Capitalism vs. the Climate*. New York: Simon & Schuster Paperbacks, 2015.

Kokua Kalihi Valley website. 'Home.' Accessed September 29, 2016. http://kkv.net/.

Lasky, Jackie. 'Indigenism, Anarchism, Feminism: An Emerging Framework for Exploring Post-Imperial Futures.' *Affinities: A Journal of Radical Theory, Culture, and Action* 5, no. 1 (August 30, 2011). www.affinitiesjournal.org/index.php/affinities/article/view/72.

Matsuoka, Jon K., Davianna McGregor, and Luciano Minerbi, eds. *Governor's Moloka'i Subsistence Task Force Final Report*. Honolulu: The Task Force, 1994.

Maui County Data Book 2015. Accessed April 14, 2017. www.hisbdc.org/BusinessResearchLibrary/MauiCountyDataBook2015.aspx.

McGregor, Davianna. *Nā Kua'āina: Living Hawaiian Culture*. Honolulu: University of Hawai'i Press, 2007.

Moloka'i Community. 'Moloka'i: Future of a Hawaiian Island.' *Hulili: Multidisciplinary Research on Hawaiian Well-Being* 5 (2008): 13–63.

Moloka'i Enterprise Community. 'Moloka'i Rural Empowerment Zone Application Submitted to the United States Department of Agriculture,' October 9, 1998.

Molokai Hawaii Visitor Guide. *Molokai Hawaii Visitor Guide*. Accessed May 1, 2017. http://visitmolokai.com/wp/.

Phillips, Brandt, Reddick & Assoc. (Hawaii). *Lā'au Point: Draft Environmental Impact Statement, West Moloka'i, Moloka'i, Hawai'i*. Honolulu, Hawaii: PBR Hawaii, 2008.

Sardar, Ziauddin. 'The Problem of Futures Studies.' In *Rescuing All Our Futures: The Future of Futures Studies*, ed. Ziauddin Sardar, 9–18. Praeger, 1999.

Shiva, Vandana. *Earth Democracy: Justice, Sustainability, and Peace*. Cambridge, MA: South End Press, 2005. 'So, What Is SU?' *Singularity University*. Accessed September 29, 2016. http://singularityu.org/overview/.

Trask, Haunani-Kay. *From a Native Daughter: Colonialism and Sovereignty in Hawai'i*. Rev. ed. Honolulu: University of Hawai'i Press, 1999.

Wolfe, Patrick. 'Settler Colonialism and the Elimination of the Native.' *Journal of Genocide Research* 8, no. 4 (December 2006): 387–409.

Woolf, Nicky. 'SpaceX Founder Elon Musk Plans to Get Humans to Mars in Six Years.' *The Guardian*, September 28, 2016, sec. 'Technology'. www.theguardian.com/technology/2016/sep/27/elon-musk-spacex-mars-colony.

Yamashita, Matt. *Molokai – Return to Pono*, 2008. www.youtube.com/watch?v=KclJtYFawyw&feature=youtube_gdata_player.

Yamashita, Todd. 'Monsanto Could Be Its Own Worst Enemy.' *The Molokai Dispatch*. July 23, 2008. www.themolokaidispatch.com/monsanto-could-be-its-own-worst-enemy.

Young, Kanalu G. Terry. *Rethinking the Native Hawaiian Past*. Native Americans (Garland Publishing, Inc.). New York: Garland Pub, 1998.

Notes

1 Principles of anarcha-indigenism are developed in: Lasky, 'Indigenism, Anarchism, Feminism'; Ferguson, 'Becoming Anarchism, Feminism, Indigeneity'; Day, 'Void Mirror.' For another theorization of the intersection of indigenous political action and anarchism, see Alfred, *Wasa'se*.

2 For a discussion of settler colonialism and attempts at eliminating the native, see Wolfe, 'Settler Colonialism and the Elimination of the Native.'

3 For an explanation of the use of this term see Young, *Rethinking the Native Hawaiian Past*.

4 'Kamehameha Schools - Bernice Pauahi Bishop's Will and Codicils.'

5 For more on this resurgence and the movement for Kānaka 'Ōiwi self-determination, see Trask, *From a Native Daughter*, Kame'eleihiwa, *Native Land and Foreign Desires*; Beamer, *No Mākou Ka Mana: Liberating the Nation*; Fujikane and Okamura, *Asian Settler Colonialism*; Goodyear-Ka'Ōpua, Hussey, and Wright, *A Nation Rising*.

6 'So, What Is SU?'

7 Woolf, 'SpaceX founder Elon Musk plans to get humans to Mars in six years.'

8 Adapted from 'The Fourth Declaration of the Lacandon Jungle.' www.struggle.ws/mexico/ezln/jung4.html. Accessed 1/15/15.

9 Sardar, 'The Problem of Futures Studies,' 15. Emphasis is mine.

10 Ibid., 12.

11 For more on politics of demand and blockade, see Day, *Gramsci Is Dead*; Klein, *This Changes Everything*.

12 Various places where I found this vision statement include: McGregor, *Nā Kua'āina*, 194; Moloka'i Community, 'Moloka'i: Future of a Hawaiian Island'; Phillips, Brandt, Reddick & Assoc. (Hawaii), *Lā'au Point*; Moloka'i Enterprise Community, 'Moloka'i Rural Empowerment Zone Application Submitted to the United States Department of Agriculture'; 'Ka Honua Momona, Intl.'

13 Maui County Data Book 2015, 11.

14 Hamilton, 'Molokai Ranch: A Year after Closure, Times Are Hard but Spirit Is Alive,' Mauinews.com, 'News, Sports, Jobs, Visitor's Information', *The Maui News*.

15 Matsuoka, McGregor, and Minerbi, *Governor's Moloka'i Subsistence Task Force Final Report*.

16 Shiva, *Earth Democracy*, 17.

17 On Lā'au Point, see Baker, 'Resisting Neoliberal Capitalism: Sustainable Self-Determination on Moloka'i, Hawai'i.' On wind power, see Cluett, 'Molokai group unites against industrial wind.' Accessed 8/20/2011. On Monsanto, see Yamashita, 'Monsanto could be its own worst enemy.'

18 Coulthard, *Red Skin, White Masks*.

19 Ibid., 60.

20 Ahupua'a is a traditional Hawaiian land division that generally runs from the mountain forest to the ocean depths.

21 Kokua Kalihi Valley website, 'Home'.

22 'Ho'oulu 'Aina – Kokua Kalihi Valley.' Accessed November 11, 2013, www.kkv.net/index.php/hooulu-aina.

23 Institute for Alternative Futures, 'Case Study: Kokua Kalihi Valley Comprehensive Family Services,' 3.

24 'Albizia Tree Removal Project.'

25 'Molokai Hawaii Visitor Guide'; Yamashita, *Molokai – Return to Pono*.

26 Mahalo (thanks) to Puni Jackson and the staff at Ho'oulu 'Āina for their support of this project and to colleague Mo Wells for cogent comment on early versions of this chapter. I take responsibility for the ideas expressed in this text.

4
EUROPEAN INTEGRATION AS A COLONIAL PROJECT

Peo Hansen and Stefan Jonsson

Introduction

For a long time, studies of colonialism and imperialism focused primarily on once colonised societies where the traces and consequences of colonialism lay immediately open to anyone's experience. In recent decades, and in large part due to postcolonial scholarship, which has disclosed that colonising societies were just as much influenced by colonialism as the colonised ones, there has also emerged an impressive body of research that traces colonialism's influence on the national cultures and histories of a number of European states, and not just those that had explicit colonial ambitions. This research testifies to the fact that colonialism lingers on as a touchy and salient issue in national imaginaries and cultural identities, as well as in national high politics. Meanwhile, the urgency of a series of contemporary developments and projects should challenge research also to go beyond the methodological nationalism or, better, methodological colonial statism often inherent in such studies.

In this chapter we attend to 'the European project', or more specifically the project of European integration. Challenging received ideas in scholarship, we suggest a new point of departure for the analysis of the relation between Europe and Africa in the interwar and postwar eras. By demonstrating that the early European integration that culminated in the Treaty of Rome in 1957 in fact was a colonial enterprise that incorporated all the member states' colonies within its institutional framework, we also point to the crucial implications that this has had for postcolonial relations between what is today the European Union and the former colonies in Africa.

In reconceiving historical European integration as a colonial project, we also discuss the implications of this for contemporary conceptions of European integration. Provided that European integration in the postwar period to a large extent revolved around matters of trade, the EEC being a 'customs union', our intuition should tell us that such a project ought to have been deeply concerned with colonial affairs, particularly because the future of the French empire and its trading bloc seemed to hinge on France's ability to preserve and consolidate its colonial economy. It should be equally safe to assume that the general political and geopolitical situation of the latter part of the 1940s and the 1950s, so profoundly marked by colonial crises and colonial wars, should have left a strong imprint on the various initiatives to bolster postwar Western European cooperation. To imagine that these circumstances did not affect European integration would be as counterintuitive as to imagine European integration to have been unaffected by the Cold War. Yet, this is how things are portrayed in just about all of today's standard histories of European integration (see further, Hansen and Jonsson 2014a). The chapter seeks to clarify this puzzle and lacuna, focusing, *inter alia*, on the need to rethink the concepts and remodel the interpretive frames within which the history of European integration traditionally has been understood and explained.

The Great War and Europe's decline

The interconnection between the history of colonialism and the history of European integration is best exposed by a compelling geopolitical figure once known as *Eurafrica*. As we have shown elsewhere, early efforts to unify Europe – in the period from, say, 1920 to 1960 – systematically coincided with efforts to stabilise the colonial system in Africa (Hansen and Jonsson 2011; 2012; 2013; 2014a; 2014b).

It may be said that European integration was from its very outset, as it took shape after the First World War, a geopolitical project. This is also the way in which the earliest advocates of pan-European collaboration viewed the matter. Reflecting both the aggressive lust for imperial expansion and the nervous obsession with Europe's uncertain fate in a new global situation after 1918, geopolitical science in its original sense was a theory that envisioned the world order as a struggle between various polities (Heffernan 2009). It saw states as dynamic and transmutable, owning specific quantities of energy and vitality often measured in population and production figures, which were subsequently translated into territorial reach. The 'vital force' of a certain polity would thus also determine what 'space' or 'scale' it needed to adequately develop its capacities. In geopolitical theory, political boundaries were unfixed and turned into elastic demarcations, shrinking or expanding depending on the force of a particular state and on the counter-force exerted by its neighbours and enemies.

The outcome of the First World War, with the imperial expansion of European powers to some extent curbed by the emergence of new global powers to the east and the west, made European debate and politics ripe for geopolitical speculations and calculations as to the future of the comparatively small and fragmented European metropolitan states, which now had to look for new ways of ensuring the development and progress of their populations and economies. In this perspective, the integration of Europe's productive and strategic capacities was imperative. This is how political scientist Rudolf Kjellén, the inventor of the concept of geopolitics, described the dire situation of Europe in 1914:

> The European federation has not yet been seriously placed on the agenda, but it carries an old legacy; and what used to be a vague idea is now emerging as a necessity in the interest of Europe's self-preservation. Only through union [or amalgamation] can the present European states remain resistant to their rapidly growing adversaries, which already count their territories in two-figure millions and their populations in three-figure millions while they at the same time are self-sufficient in food production. We can already witness the shadows of the American, Russian and Yellow perils being cast over our continent. Thus, has Europe come under pressure that in due time will win out over the mighty facts and traditions that still split Europe into several sovereign small parts.
>
> (Kjellén 1914, 194)

In the interwar period, a fatigued and crisis-ridden Europe had to face the prospect of its diminishing global significance compared to the rising powers: the United States and the new Soviet Union. In this situation, Kjellén's geopolitical prognosis gained relevance, and European leaders and thinkers placed European integration high on the agenda. The Italian geopolitical theorist Paolo d'Agostini Orsini di Camerota asserted that Europe had become old and in desperate need of injections of fresh energy and blood (Orsini de Camerota 1934, 4).

European integration thus found its real support only after the spiritual shock, economic collapse and political destruction inflicted by the Great War. In this post-catastrophic atmosphere of anxiety and pessimism, where nationalist hubris was defeated and imperial Europe was perceived as being in decline, the grand geopolitical narrative of European integration took shape. 'Europe no longer rules in the world', wrote Spanish philosopher José Ortega y Gasset in 1929 (Ortega y Gasset 1929/1957, 129). As the demographer Lothrop Stoddard stated in his influential 1922 (and 1935) work, the First World War and the ensuing reorganisation of world politics amounted to a collapse of the political universe, which 'in one cataclysmic event' had lost the sun around which the planets moved in cosmic harmony. That sun was the 'European comity of nations', now being replaced by terrifying geopolitical processes that the title of Stoddard's book summed up as *The Rising Tide of Colour Against White World-Supremacy* (Stoddard 1922/2003, 198–221; 1935, 31–174). A number of European thinkers of the interwar period – from Oswald Spengler and Martin Heidegger to Edmund Husserl and Paul Valéry – expounded similar views. They were reflected in intellectual interventions, policy proposals and political initiatives that aimed to save the position of Europe and the white race by reigniting its dynamism and bolstering its growth through a more thorough integration of the resources under its control. If this did not happen, there would be disintegration and destruction (see e.g. Pasture 2015).

Paneuropa and the African roots of European integration

The most influential of these proposals for European integration was presented by Richard von Coudenhove-Kalergi in his 1923 pamphlet, *Paneuropa*. This booklet launched his Pan-European Union movement, which was to gather both sizeable and influential intellectual and political support from the best and the brightest of his generation, including Nobel laureates Albert Einstein, Gerhart Hauptmann, Selma Lagerlöf, Thomas Mann, Nathan Söderblom, as well as statesmen like Winston Churchill, Konrad Adenauer, Ignaz Seipel, Karl Renner, Joseph Caillaux and Aristide Briand. For the late Walter Lipgens, a leading scholar on the history of European integration, *Paneuropa* was by far the most important of the many proposals for European collaboration of the 1920s. Moreover, this pamphlet largely mirrored the world view of internationalists and liberal progressives of the era (Lipgens 1982, 38).

According to the Pan-European movement, a united Europe was paramount for political reasons, or simply to prevent a repetition of the First World War. This was the argument for peace. Or as Coudenhove-Kalergi proclaimed: 'The alternatives today are clear: Pan-Europe or war!' (Coudenhove-Kalergi 1927, 1). A united Europe was desirable also for cultural reasons, as history seemed to indicate that Europe made up some sort of civilisational unity. 'Pan-Europe should be the political expression of the European cultural community', Coudenhove-Kalergi explained. All the 'linguistic nations' of Europe would be gathered into 'one single racial nation', just as the pan-Hellenic movement in ancient times brought together the city-based polities of Greece 'into one great nation for all Hellenics'. Pan-Europe's self-proclaimed 'cultural aim' was thus 'the self-knowledge of the European race as an occidental nation' (Coudenhove-Kalergi 1928, 8).

Perhaps most importantly, the Pan-European movement put forward a third, economic argument for continental integration. The organisation's economic programme, authored by the economist Otto Deutsch, listed three imminent threats to the European economy: 'the danger of a collapse of all industries' without close access to raw materials; 'the danger of a complete impoverishment of the European population because of increasing unemployment, decreasing production, capital export and indebtedness'; and 'the danger that the European economy in general will become completely dependent on North American capital'.

As a remedy, Deutsch outlined an economic programme that would abolish trade barriers and economic imbalances such as those caused by the reparations forced on Germany by the Treaty of Versailles. The programme also proposed a planned economy as well as a thorough 'Taylorisation of the European industrial totality' (Deutsch 1927, 7). However, this would not suffice to catch up with the rapidly growing US and Soviet economies. These countries enjoyed the advantage of organising their economies on a continental scale, thus making them self-sufficient for most raw materials and providing greater markets for the sale of their products. Accordingly, the Pan-European economic zone suggested by Deutsch also presupposed, as 'an indispensable supplement', 'the communal exploitation of the Pan-European colonies from an economic viewpoint' (Deutsch 1927, 8).

Gradually, then, the economic perspective became a geopolitical one that touched on the sensitive issue as to whether Europe would ever again attain its global influence. In this context, the African continent was seen as a necessary condition for economic recovery and also as a sufficient reason for European unification. The Pan-European strategy designated Africa 'Europe's plantation', a reservoir of agricultural produce, subsoil mineral resources and hydro-electric power. Coudenhove-Kalergi certainly spoke for the majority of Europe's political and intellectual elite when he in 1929 pushed for a Pan-European colonial management of Africa and recounted what Africa offered: 'Africa could provide Europe with raw materials for its industry, nutrition for its population, land for its overpopulation, labour for its unemployed, and markets for its products' (Coudenhove-Kalergi 1929, 3).

Coudenhove-Kalergi's arguments for assimilating Africa converged into one big argument for the unification of Europe. The common or synergetic exploitation of Africa was so unquestionably attractive and beneficial that it constituted in itself a reason for European states to make common cause. A geopolitical calculation based on two symbiotic benefits emerged: the new geopolitical sphere of a united Europe would be sustainable and prosperous thanks to its incorporation of Africa, and correspondingly, the bonds between once-antagonistic European states would be strengthened by the shared goal of developing Africa. As Coudenhove-Kalergi proclaimed: 'The African problem thus brings us back to Europe. Africa cannot be made available if Europe does not unite' (Coudenhove-Kalergi 1929, 18). In short, Europe's unification would start off in Africa. The joint European colonisation of Africa was highlighted in Article 13 of the draft of a Pan-European pact of 1930 as one of the organisation's defining priorities: 'All European citizens shall enjoy equal economic rights in the tropical colonies of Africa' (Coudenhove-Kalergi 1930, 149).

Postwar developments and Treaty of Rome as a treaty on Eurafrica

Even as Eurafrica was transformed from a geopolitical representation with utopian overtones in the 1920s into a political reality in the 1950s, it always marked the site where interests in European integration overlapped with colonial ambitions. According to the Eurafrican idea, European integration would come about only through a coordinated exploitation of Africa, and Africa could be efficiently exploited only if European states combined their economic and political capacities. In 1957, these two propositions interlocked, contributing to the establishment of the European Economic Community (EEC), which in leading political circles and major news media was simultaneously perceived as the creation of Eurafrica.

The twelve years from the end of the First World War to the establishment of the EEC saw the birth of numerous initiatives and institutions aiming to bring about European integration. They all stressed the importance of Africa. As French historian Yves Montarsolo (2010, 91) remarks, 'each time a new "European" institution saw the day, Africa was always at the heart of all concerns.' Scholarly, political and journalistic accounts at the time thus provide ample testimony to the fact that European integration was inextricably bound up with a Eurafrican project. The architects of European integration clearly understood that the west European landmass lacked the natural resources necessary for Europe's rebuilding into a viable geopolitical and geo-economic power bloc able to compete with the emerging superpowers to the east and west, as well as to prevent Bandung's anti-colonial momentum from intervening in African affairs.

A few representative illustrations will here have to suffice to sketch out the contours of these postwar efforts at Eurafrican integration (see further, Hansen and Jonsson 2014). Immediately after the war's end, for instance, Britain's foreign secretary Ernest Bevin announced his 'Third World Power' project, which aimed to integrate particularly the African colonies and their vast natural resources into a Western European Union and sphere of influence able to challenge the hegemonic ambitions of the US and the Soviet Union. Founded on a close colonial cooperation between Britain and France, such a project, Bevin asserted in the autumn of 1948, 'could have US dependent on us, and eating out of our hand, in four or five years. Two great mountains of manganese are in Sierra Leone, etc. US is very barren of essential minerals and in Africa we have them all' (quoted in Kent 1989, 66; see also Kent 1992; Deighton 2006). In accordance with Coudenhove-Kalergi's formula, a Western European bloc, or a 'Third World Power' on a par with the US and the Soviet Union, was then to emerge chiefly as a result of a successful European joint venture in Africa. Or as Britain's Chancellor of Exchequer, Stafford Cripps, spelled it out before the African Governor's Conference in November 1947:

> The economies of Western Europe and Tropical Africa are so closely interlocked in mutual trade, in the supply of capital and in currency systems that their problems of overseas balance are essentially one. Tropical Africa is already contributing much, both in physical supplies of food and raw materials and in quite substantial net earnings of dollars from the sterling area pool. The further development of African resources is of the same crucial importance to the rehabilitation and strengthening of Western Europe as the restoration of European productive power is to the future progress and prosperity of Africa. Each needs and is needed by the other. In Africa indeed is to be found a great potential for new strength and vigour in the Western European economy and the stronger that economy becomes the better of course Africa will fare.
>
> (Quoted in Kent 1989, 58–9)

Under the headline 'Cripps says colonies hold key to survival', *The New York Times* (1947) underscored that Cripps' contention 'has been widely accepted by the country's top economists and business men'.

But it was the Council of Europe (CE), also established in 1949, that endeavoured to take the Eurafrican project to the next level. The CE grew out of the European Movement and its Congress of Europe in The Hague in 1948. Many of the Congress' participant groupings adhered to the Eurafrican tenet concerning the imperative necessity of developing African colonies for the collective benefit of a war-torn Western Europe striving to emerge as a 'third force' in world politics. For instance, in its 'Draft of a Federal Pact', one of the Congress' major players, the European Union of Federalists, proclaimed:

> Europe as an entity will be viable only if the links which unite it with countries and dependent territories [...] are taken into account. The era of national ownership of colonial territories is past. [...] From now onwards a common European policy of development for certain regions of Africa should be taken in hand (quoted in Hick 1991, 90).

Subsequently, Eurafrica would emerge as one of the Council of Europe's defining priorities (see Palayret 2005, 200–13; Heywood 1981). The unanimous adoption of the *Strasbourg Plan* by the CE's Consultative Assembly in 1952 reflects the Eurafrican momentum during the 1950s (Council of Europe 1952). Built in part on the previous colonial planning within the Organisation for European Economic Cooperation (OEEC 1951; today's OECD), the Plan set out to resolve Western Europe's chronic dollar deficit. As the main solution to this difficult problem, the Plan pointed to the joint utilisation of colonial Africa's vast and largely untapped natural resources; or as the chairman of the CE's Committee on Economic Questions and former French prime minister Paul Reynaud had it: 'We must also, if free Europe is to be made viable, jointly exploit the riches of the African continent, and try to find there those raw materials which we are getting from the dollar area, and for which we are unable to pay' (Council of Europe 1952, 135).

By this means Western Europe could begin its ascent to become 'a third economic group standing mid-way between the Communist and the dollar areas' (Council of Europe 1952, 15). However, since the large-scale investments required could not be borne by the colonial powers alone, the Plan was adamant that all the Council members (by now 14 countries) needed to contribute. As pointed out by the UK representative to the Council of Europe, Lord Layton, 'it is clear that we have to think of these overseas territories not as the possessions of any one country [...]; they have to be integrated with all the countries of Europe and all the overseas territories' (Council of Europe 1952, 140). This chimed with practically all of the representatives. For instance, Denmark's Hermod Lannung emphasised

> the overriding importance of greater co-operation and of a major joint European effort in Africa if we do not wish to see Africa lost to European influence, culture, trade, etc., and, in the long run, for that influence to be replaced by that of another continent.

Europe had just lost the 'battle of Asia', Lannung warned, and now its nations needed to unite in order to not also lose 'the battle of Africa'. 'Here we have before us a great concrete and practical task which calls for the utmost collaboration of us all' (Council of Europe 1952, 154).

While highly indicative of the zeitgeist, the plans drawn up within the Council of Europe generated little in terms of concrete results. Much of this though was sought to be compensated for by the Rome Treaty agreement in 1957. Just to cite a few of many pertinent illustrations of this, we can turn to West Germany's foreign minister, Heinrich von Brentano, and his communication to Adenauer on December 8 1956, as the treaty negotiations were reaching their final stage:

> In principle, the demand for inclusion of the overseas territories should be welcomed. Since many years and in numerous European organisations, as in the Council of Europe and the OEEC, plans have been worked out which have had as their aim the joint exploitation of the overseas territories by the European states. Until now the

> realisation of this has failed [...]. Within the frame of the Schuman Plan it also did not succeed to push through the inclusion of the overseas territories in the European Coal and Steel Community. However, in all these negotiations no doubts were ever expressed, from the perspective of the majority of the European states, and especially from the perspective of the Bundesrepublik, that the joint inclusion of the overseas territories is desirable. Precisely from the German side it has been repeatedly complained that the Schuman Plan did not provide for the inclusion of the overseas territories. The significance of this persistent demand of the European states and especially also of the Bundesrepublik has in no way been diminished by the most recent events in world politics. There can remain no doubt that a conflict is emerging over the overseas territories, especially the African territories, between on the one hand the communist states and on the other hand the western community of states. The outcome of this conflict will have a great, if not decisive importance as concerns the future constellation of power in the worldwide context. It follows from all this, that the demand for an inclusion of the overseas territories must not just be accepted, but welcomed (Brentano 1956).

This letter shows that although West Germany fought France in the negotiations on financial details, particularly concerning the exact contributions of the respective member states to the investment fund that would fund development projects in the associated territories, it enthusiastically embraced France's demand, and the inclusion of the colonies, as a geopolitical imperative of the highest order. Most commentators dealing with the Treaty negotiations have failed to distinguish that disagreement as to the details of the association of the mostly African colonies did not mean disagreement on the principles of colonial association as such (Hansen and Jonsson 2014a: Ch. 4).[1] Indeed, the Rome Treaty negotiations on Eurafrican colonial association are replete with precisely this consensus dictum, the only delegation occasionally voicing a principled dissent being the Dutch one.

This overarching consensus also comes to the fore with great clarity in the work by the intergovernmental Ad-Hoc Overseas Territories Group, chaired by Belgian diplomat Albert Hupperts and launched as part of the treaty negotiation on Belgium's foreign minister Paul-Henri Spaak's initiative in late November 1956. On 18 December 1956 the group circulated a draft of a preamble to its final report that was presented to the Heads of Delegation of the Intergovernmental Conference two days later. It is a highly interesting document because it contains all the general geopolitical, political and economic issues at stake in the Rome Treaty negotiations. Hupperts presents it as a first balance sheet of the advantages of the association of the overseas territories:

> Economically speaking, the European member states of the common market have an essential need for the cooperation and support that the overseas territories – particularly the African ones – are able to offer in order to establish long-term balance of the European economy. The sources of raw material, variegated and abundant, which the overseas territories dispose of are likely to ensure for the entirety of the European economy of the common market the indispensable foundation for an expanding economy and present the additional advantage of being situated in countries whose orientation may be influenced by the European countries themselves. In addition to the mineral riches of all kinds and the agricultural and exotic products of the overseas countries, it is fair to mention as a concrete incentive, the results of very recent prospections in the petroliferous area carried out in connection with the systematic inventorying of the immense African reserves of metals, phosphates, hydraulic energy, etc.

Further down in the preamble, comparison is made with the Marshall plan for Europe, and it is asserted that the association of the overseas territories should be undertaken in the same spirit. The preamble concludes:

> The proposed enterprise entails consequences of major importance for the future of Europe. […] In aiding Africa and supporting itself on her, the community of the six is able to furnish Europe with its equilibrium and a new youth. It is in this perspective that all other elements of information assembled in the present report should be understood.
>
> (Conférence intergouvernmentale, 1956)

Shortly thereafter, Robert Schuman weighed in on the treaty negotiations with a forceful plea for Eurafrican integration that partly echoed the ad-hoc group's report. 'Eurafrica', he asserted,

> does not just signify the creation of a system of assistance; but the constitution of an economic whole, of a true association, in the interior of which a reciprocity of advantages and a communal politics of development will be put to work.
>
> (Schuman 1957a)

In words alluding to the Suez crisis, Schuman went on to add Eurafrica's by now much rehearsed geopolitical rationale, arguing that since the Soviet quest for world hegemony had set its eyes on Africa, 'we should respond through the institution of a true community between the peoples of Europe and of Africa, the notion of which is at the basis of the Eurafrican idea' (Schuman 1957b, 21).

For France's socialist-led government, under Guy Mollet, such staunch support from the opposition was of course welcomed, especially since Paris was in the midst of an international propaganda drive to seek support for its Algerian policy *precisely* by linking it to the ongoing negotiation on Eurafrican integration. On January 9, 1957 the French government, through Mollet, issued a statement on France's position concerning the Algerian situation that directly addressed the UN General Assembly. Mollet ends his note on Algeria with reference to Eurafrica:

> France is negotiating at this time with her European partners for the organization of a vast common market, to which the Overseas Territories will be associated. All of Europe will be called upon to help in the development of Africa, and tomorrow Eurafrica may become one of the principal factors in world politics. Isolated nations can no longer keep pace with the world. What would Algeria amount to by itself? On the other hand, what future might it not have, as one of the foundations of the Eurafrican community now taking shape?
>
> (Mollet 1957)

By February 1957 an agreement emerged that inserted into the draft treaty a series of special trade rules and a special colonial investment fund that forcibly associated half of Africa, and also parts of the West Indies and Oceania, to the EEC. The agreement had been long in the making, with numerous technical issues that had to be ironed out in hard negotiations. But, by early 1957, consensus was in sight not only as to the general desirability of some kind of Eurafrican collaboration but also in terms of its concrete institutional organisation.

The agreement was struck on 20 February 1957 at the Heads of Government meeting in Paris, under the chairmanship of Mollet. The settlement, which was to be codified in the Rome Treaty's Part IV (Articles 131–6) entailed first of all a trade agreement according to which, in principle, all associated colonies would gain access to the common market on equal terms, just as all the six member states would gain access to trading and investment opportunities in the associated areas on equal terms. Second, the association entailed the creation of an investment fund that would finance social and economic development in the associated territories. Contributions to the fund, totalling USD 581.25 million for the initial five years would be divided between the member states but with West Germany and France shouldering the brunt, or USD 200 million each. Nine tenths of the fund would go to projects in the French territories. Third, it was stipulated that these measures would be implemented for a five-year term, after which it would be renewed, and it was also understood that the full realisation and implementation of this common market would take twelve to seventeen years.

The day after the Paris conference, *Le Monde* remarked that the agreement had a distinct French colouring, primarily because of the association of French Africa, the investment fund and the inclusion of Algeria (1957a).[2] Next day's editorial was wholly devoted to the association of the OCTs enabled by the EEC, *Le Monde* now unequivocally asserting that the 'Eurafrica' that has just been established by the Six 'is not incompatible with the maintenance of the French Union. On the contrary, it may provide a last chance for it to evolve in a better climate.' (1957b) Thus, it was not merely a European, but more correctly a Eurafrican, Common Market that had been adopted in Paris, and this was seen as an undertaking in which colonial overseas territories were projected to remain integrated for the long term.

As Paul-Henri Spaak in late February 1957 summarised, the intergovernmental negotiations in Paris that were about to be confirmed by the signing of the Rome Treaty (which took place on in Rome on March 25), he singled out the establishment of the EEC not just as 'the most important event in the history of Europe since the French Revolution'. He also emphasised the world-historical and geopolitical importance of the EEC. A 'great historical decision' had been made in Paris on February 20, namely to 'admit into the Common Market, on certain terms, the overseas territories'. By adding the African territories, the market would include more than 200 million inhabitants and Europe would have access to the raw materials necessary for its sustainability, Spaak told his audience. For this chieftain of European integration, the constitution of a community incorporating Europe and Africa was thus the boldest part of the Rome Treaty: 'Would it not be a success, if we could realise the dream of Eurafrica, which, after the reunion in Paris, seems able to become reality?' (Spaak 1957)

Spaak's speech disproves the claim that imperial ambitions had little to do with the emerging Common Market. In fact, imperial politics formed an integral part of the motives of most of the founders of the EEC (e.g. Spaak, Jean Monnet, Robert Schuman, Konrad Adenauer and Guy Mollet). They all wanted the EEC to correspond to the geopolitical constellation that went by the name of Eurafrica.

In the early days of the EEC, it was generally recognised that parts of Africa and the Common Market were bound together in one imperial polity. The foremost manifestation of this polity was the European Commission's Directorate General for the overseas territories, or the DG VIII, which in 1958 began its work under the (French) Commissioner Robert Lemaignen. Lemaignen structured the EEC's Eurafrican activities into four areas, based on the Commission's interpretation of the Treaty of Rome: research and programme activities; cultural and social questions; trade matters; and financing of development through the investment fund (Lemaignen 1964, 119). Initiatives in each area ensued from Lemaignen's policy statement that 'the European community was a common good for all its participants including all the African peoples.' In 1964 the Commissioner summarised the first five years at the DG VIII, affirming that 'a broad foundation had been laid for the Eurafrican economic symbiosis', adding that this was 'an essential element of the world of tomorrow' (Lemaignen 1964, 160).

The 'foundation' in question was the Yaoundé Convention, signed in 1963, between the EEC and eighteen newly independent former French and Belgian colonies, which prolonged the Rome Treaty's Eurafrican association regime into the postcolonial era. The European Commission and Robert Lemaignen – in charge of carrying out much preparatory work for the convention within its DG VIII – were thus successful in their pursuit to model Yaoundé on Rome's association regime. Despite formal independence, then, the eighteen African states had no real leverage to negotiate at Yaoundé. Rather, as Emily Jones puts it, 'the EEC presented its offer to the Francophone Associates as a *fait accompli* and they accepted it'; 'the outcome reflected the EEC's interests and the eighteen Francophone African countries exerted minimal influence'." (Jones 2014, 8)

To no little extent, then, Yaoundé took care to secure a continuity between the colonial Eurafrican association regime, as established by the Rome Treaty in 1957, and the subsequent association regime that was established between the EEC and the newly independent African states. Whether such a scenario was on the cards, and whether it was to be welcomed or shunned, was of course the subject of much debate prior to Yaoundé, not the least amongst African movements and leaders. As we shall come back to below, African leaders such as Kwame Nkrumah and Guinea's Ahmed Sekou Touré saw the EEC's Eurafrican association regime as detrimental to both national independence and Pan-African solidarity. By contrast, Tunisian president Habib Bourguiba believed that the EEC's association regime contained a 'true opportunity' for both continents. Yet, as long as France conducted a 'full-scale war' against the Algerian people, Eurafrica, along with the plans for developing the Sahara's oil and mineral resources, would come to nothing. Hence Bourguiba's ultimate prediction: 'Eurafrica will die in Algeria' (*Der Spiegel* 1957). Such views also manifested themselves institutionally within the Pan-African movement in West Africa and Central Africa.

If these voices represented both pessimistic and moderate African opinions on Eurafrica at the crucial moment of decolonisation, Félix Houphouët-Boigny – a member of Mollet's government as the first-ever West African delegated minister, and subsequently the first president of Ivory Coast – led the group of African supporters and ambassadors of EEC's Eurafrican vision. Here, African independence was approached as best conducted in close partnership with the former colonial powers. As it turned out, and as manifested in Yaoundé, the majority of African leaders saw little choice but to follow Houphouët-Boigny's example (Hansen and Jonsson 2014a).

This trajectory was analysed early on by Immanuel Wallerstein (2005/1961, 1967: 129–51), who assessed the Rome Treaty's impact on Africa's economic and political structures in the early 1960s. As he argued, the association of the African colonies to the EEC raised forbidding obstacles to attempts at creating African integration and unity. Most of the newly independent African states found it more practical to consolidate links with the EEC than to realise the ideas presented by the movements for African unity. The same conclusion was reached by the United Nations Economic Commission for Africa, which pointed at the 'danger that the Rome Treaty may tempt [the Associated States] to prefer the short-run advantage of tariff concessions [in EEC markets] to the long-run gains of industrial development'; and that 'association with EEC can easily tend to perpetuate economic dependency' (UN 1960: 14). Wallerstein describes the process of decolonisation in Africa as a political compromise between the colonial metropolitan governments and the nationalist leadership of Africa.

Explaining and conceptualising Eurafrica's historiographical disappearance

The documents that we have referred to in this chapter are fragments of a larger discourse that for lack of space we cannot reconstruct in any detail here (for an in-depth account, see Hansen and Jonsson 2014a). Why has *this* history of colonialism been consigned to oblivion? Why is it virtually unknown that most of the visions, movements and concrete institutional arrangements working towards European integration in the postwar period placed Africa's incorporation into the European enterprise as a central objective? One reason is that the history of the EU is usually bent to fit Eurocentric presuppositions or even, as we pointed out, has been elaborated into a self-legitimising myth. Another reason is that the histories of Europe and Africa are mostly conceived as endogenous continental narratives. A third one, also mentioned, is that the history of colonialism is typically told as a history of the colonial systems of the colonial/imperial states. If world history and global processes are cut up and edited by such devices, Eurafrica drops out of the picture, because it belongs to a geopolitical constellation that cannot be mapped by way of continental or national categories.

Let us analyse these circumstances in more detail. We mentioned that the history of colonialism is often treated as the sum-total of the colonial systems of various colonial/imperial states. Historians of colonialism seem still constrained by the national and linguistic barriers laid in place by the old colonial powers; and, at best, they compensate for this by engaging in traditional exercises of comparative history that never approach the intergovernmental and supranational levels and logics of European integration.

Having said this, we should of course also note the obvious fact that the growing field of postcolonial studies is indeed examining the impact of colonialism and decolonisation on historical as well as current notions of Europe and European identity; and, as such, it highlights that colonialism also needs to be approached as a shared (Western) European experience which in many ways transgresses particular national outlooks. Nevertheless, this research also suffers from an almost complete lack of engagement with the question of European integration (for an example, see Chakrabarty 2000). Considering that critical explorations of notions of 'Europe' are the hallmark of postcolonial studies, this neglect constitutes a puzzle, particularly in view of the fact that no project since European colonialism has carried itself more proudly *in the name of Europe* than the historical European integration and the current European Union. As such, postcolonial studies have failed to apply its sophisticated utilisation of discourse theory and analysis to the institutional settings (Connelly 2000) – such as the EU – where 'European' policy is actually being articulated and where the official historiography is being propagated.

Additionally, the disappearance of Eurafrica also has to do with the fact that the Eurafrican project does not fit a couple of dominant historiographical paradigms, in which the postwar relation between Europe and Africa is refracted through what has been called 'the Cold War lens' (Connelly 2000), or has been told as a narrative structured around a presumed historical rupture of decolonisation. Most accounts of EU history are informed by a strict adherence to a Cold War analytical framework as developed within, *inter alia*, International Relations theory.

In placing its empirical focus squarely on the Cold War's European scene, this framework is destined to neglect Africa and the North–South dimension as factors impacting and shaping the historical trajectory of European integration, and the import of colonialism is at best treated in a cursory fashion. Interestingly, scholarship on the Cold War's Third World scene is similarly afflicted by this failure to spot European integration's strong bearing on postwar colonialism and decolonisation. In his otherwise authoritative *The Global Cold War*, for instance, Westad (2005) makes no mention whatsoever of European integration. Even when speaking about postwar efforts made by colonial and former colonial powers to incorporate colonies and newly independent states into various larger colonial and/or international organisational frameworks (e.g. the British Commonwealth, the French Union and French Community), Westad's (2005: 97–8) account fails to mention the arguably most important such organisational framework, namely the EEC's association of colonial territories and, with the Yaoundé Convention, former colonies.

It is of course true that the path toward European integration was heavily conditioned by the Cold War, as were also the paths toward independence taken by anticolonial movements in

Africa and Asia. The very designation of the newly independent states as a 'third world' – supplementing the capitalist 'first world' and the socialist 'second world' – seems to have been perpetuated by the Cold War global order. However, in the 1950s this influence was overdetermined by a concerted European effort to secure supremacy over Africa and thus establish a 'third' geopolitical sphere, Eurafrica. This would grant Europe a measure of geopolitical leverage and secure its economic sustainability, and at the same time defend Europe's interests against challenges posed by anti-colonial insurrections and wars of liberation –Vietnam, Algeria, Cameroon, to mention a few. It would also serve to impede the nonaligned movement of former colonies, those that convened at the Bandung meeting, or transformed the United Nations General Assembly into a platform for debating global injustices, or mobilised a united Pan-African front against Europe's colonial powers.

Faced with these foreign-policy challenges it was rational for the six European states that founded the EEC in 1957 to develop and modernise their imperial policy, as it were. The European integration process provided an opportunity for doing that, just as the geopolitical changes affecting the imperial order in the postwar context provided an opportunity for European integration. Taken together, these processes generated an internationalisation of colonialism, what Nkrumah (1962, 12) denounced as 'collective colonialism', or what Europeans may have perceived as a 'reformed colonialism'. For it should be remembered that the EEC, in justifying the association of the overseas territories as a way of improving the social and economic development of the colonies, in many ways did not differ from an older imperialism which had justified itself in much the same way.

Yet, by bringing such a policy to an international and supranational level, the EEC's association of overseas countries and territories allowed Europe to posit its presence and interests in Africa as a new relationship of 'interdependence' – a buzz word in the 1950s – or mutual association, outwardly accommodating the demands of the anticolonial movements, but keeping the European role as patron and tutor intact.

For the African countries that in the same year of 1957 began liberating themselves, Eurafrica was an arrangement that allowed the political elites of what subsequently became (nominally) independent states to posit themselves as partners in a world of 'interdependent' states and regional formations, while at the same time loyally accommodating the economic demands and policies of their former colonial masters. This was to be conducted through arrangements – such as the Yaoundé Convention – from which both camps would reap huge benefits, at the cost of the majority of Africans for whom decolonisation did not seem to happen or turned out to be 'a non-event', as Achille Mbembe puts it (2010, 58).

Thus, if the misrecognition that prevents us from relating the EU to colonial history is dispelled, and if the history of Eurafrica is put back into the picture, we understand why decolonisation never constituted a significant rupture with the past – except in states where leaders and movements explicitly tried to break with the colonial rulers. EEC's 'offer' of association to the common market here turned out to be an efficient antidote to Pan-Africanism, and this may even be said to have been its true historical purpose: to adjust Europe's foreign policy, modes of economic extraction and means of production to a nominally independent Africa, while ensuring that the continent's resources remained within Europe's reach.

The success of this strategy is amply illustrated in Arnold Rivkin's (at the time, Development Advisor to the World Bank) enthusiastic account (from 1966) of the EEC's 'fruitful' Eurafrican association scheme. 'Guinea's attitude', Rivkin (1966: 40) writes disparagingly, has:

> been one of hostility to the association of other African states with the EEC. President Touré has viewed, not without reason, the existence of so attractive an alternative as

> the European Common Market as a serious obstacle to the achievement of his original Pan-African designs.

In Rivkin's view, then, Guinea and Ghana's stance on EEC association 'as a new neo-colonial application of the old "divide and rule" principle' cannot amount to anything but a mistaken obstinacy, totally at odds with these countries' own best interests.

As Nkrumah had it, the Treaty of Rome and the EEC marked 'the advent of neo-colonialism in Africa' (quoted in Martin 1982: 229), whereby association represented a newfangled arrangement for 'collective colonialism which will be stronger and more dangerous than the old evils we are striving to liquidate' (Nkrumah 1962, 12; see also Asante 1993: 740). More specifically, leaders such as Nkrumah and Touré saw the EEC's Eurafrican design not only as strategy to foil national independence in Africa per se; more importantly perhaps, they also saw it as a deliberate attempt to frustrate the formation of any types of independently organised African integration and regionalisation schemes – among numerous proposals we could mention the joint Ghana–Guinea proposals for an African Common Market (see Ki-Zerbo 2013, 257–380).

Having fulfilled this task, Eurafrica disappeared from the political agenda by the mid-1960s, as the EEC and various other international organisations and actors by then developed more efficient and less costly arrangements through which European interventions in African affairs could continue, but now entirely in the guise of development, aid and diplomatic counselling. At this point, we understand why it makes sense to forget the history of Eurafrica and repudiate the idea that the EU has something to do with the history of colonialism. For when facts are reassembled, it becomes clear that the foundation of the EEC as well as the establishment of independent Africa was as much a continuation of old policies as a rupture and a new start.

Perhaps, all this can be summed up by an observation made some years ago by philosopher V.Y. Mudimbe. Enunciations about Africa or interventions in Africa say less about Africa than about European subjects of knowledge being 'prisoners of epistemological frames that only unfold the consequences of their own postulates' (Mudimbe 1974, 93). In this sense, the history of Eurafrica, as it marks out the intersection of the history of European integration and the history of colonialism, indicates the necessity of perceiving Europe and Africa, particularly in International Relations theory and EU studies, from the perspective of a truly global history and theory.

By the same token, Eurafrica also becomes vital for our comprehension of the current EU–African relations. As few could have failed to notice, the past fifteen years or so have seen a renewed and rapidly increasing interest in Africa on the part of the European Union. As a topical example, we could point to the current high-level negotiations whereby the EU seeks to 'muster adequate leverage' vis-à-vis countries in North- and Sub-Saharan Africa to have them prevent migration and sign readmission agreements as preconditions for receiving aid and investments (European Commission 2015, 10–14). As reported, 'Angela Merkel is stepping up diplomatic efforts to stem migrant flows to Europe as part of what Berlin terms a "Marshall Plan for Africa".' (*Financial Times* 2017).

Many of these developments are outgrowths of the 'Strategic Partnership' that was agreed between the EU and Africa in 2007. As was stated in the partnership, or the so-called Lisbon Declaration: 'We have come together in awareness of the lessons and experiences of the past, but also in the certainty that our common future requires an audacious approach, one that allows us to face with confidence the demands of our globalizing world.'

'On a global scale', the Declaration went on, 'we have today an increased understanding of our vital interdependence and are determined to work together in the global arena on the key political challenges of our time, such as energy and climate change, migration or gender issues.' Furthermore, the Lisbon Summit also made sure to perpetuate the myth of EU–African relations as being of an exclusively *post*-colonial nature, hailing the summit as offering 'a unique opportunity jointly to address the common contemporary challenges for our continents, in the year that we celebrate the 50th anniversary of the European integration and the 50th anniversary of the beginning of the independence of Africa' (Lisbon Declaration – EU Africa Summit 2007). It was also made clear that the new 'partnership' between the EU and Africa should amount to more than a mere expansion of the long-standing EU–African association regime, as currently codified in the Cotonou Agreement (Yaoundé and Lomé's successor).

Hence, Africa is now approached as an indispensable 'partner' in the EU's pursuit of a number of key objectives: geopolitical and security concerns (e.g. scarce strategic raw materials, terrorism, 'illegal immigration', disease control, and food and energy security); economic concerns (e.g. raw materials and expanding outlets for investment in Africa's emerging markets); and demographic and labour market concerns (e.g. labour immigration from Africa).

Conclusion

As is well known, all established and emerging global powers are today involved in an increasingly fierce battle over Africa's riches. Researchers and global media even suggest that we are witnessing a 'new scramble for Africa'. To be sure, EU leaders are always fast to deny any such allegation. Distancing themselves from other major stakeholders – foremost China but also the USA, India, Russia, Brazil, the Gulf States, and Japan – they instead insist that the EU's African engagement is guided by 'interdependence' and committed to a mutually beneficial 'partnership of equals' that will promote development, economic growth, democratic governance, human rights, and peace and prosperity on the African continent.

The history of Eurafrica helps us understand this so-called new scramble for Africa, how it can happen and which stakes are involved. For in order to think theoretically about globality today, it is fundamental to know how the global was conceived in the past – that is, in historical times. Eurafrica was an intellectual endeavour and a political project that from the 1920s saw Europe's future survival – its continued existence in history as a power-shaping global history – as totally bound up with Europe's successful merger with Africa. That is, Europe could rise out of the two world wars only in the shape of Eurafrica. Today, even as the Eurafrican project is largely forgotten, the content of current EU policy-making towards its African 'partner' demonstrates that it has continued influence under the surface; and the only way to comprehend the deep structures of current EU–African relations is to bring this history to life.

Bibliography

Asante, S. K. B. (1993) 'Pan-Africanism and regional integration'. In Mazrui, A. A. (ed.) *General History of Africa VIII: Africa since 1935*. Oxford: Heinemann.

Brentano, H. (1956) Letter to Konrad Adenauer, 8 Dec. 1956. Politischen Archivs des Auswärtigen Amts, PA AA. B 10 Abteilung II, Politische Abteilung, Bd. 915 (Brüsseler Integrationskonferenz).

Chakrabarty, D. (2000) *Provincializing Europe*. Princeton: Princeton UP.

Conférence intergouvernmentale (1956): 'Projet de préambule, établi par le Président du groupe ad hoc territoires d'outre-mer'. MAE 818 f/56. HAEU (Historical Archives of the European Union), CM 3/ NEGO–252 (Conférence intergouvernmentale: Historique de l'article 131 du traité).

Connelly, M. (2000) 'Taking off the Cold War lens: visions of North-South conflict during the Algerian War for Independence'. *American Historical Review*, 105 (3): 739–69.

Coudenhove-Kalergi, R. N. (1923/1925) *Paneuropa*, 2nd ed., Vienna: Paneuropa-Verlag.
——(1927) 'Alarm', *Paneuropa* 3 (4): 1–5.
——(1928) 'Die europäische Nationalbewegung', *Paneuropa* 4 (1): 1–12.
——(1929) 'Afrika', *Paneuropa* 5 (2): 3–18.
——(1930) 'Entwurf für einen Paneuropäischen Pakt', *Paneuropa* 6 (5): 149–65.
Council of Europe (1952) *The Strasbourg Plan*. Strasbourg: Secretariat-General Council of Europe.
Deighton, A. (2006) 'Entente neo-coloniale? Ernest Bevin and the proposals for Anglo-French Third World power, 1945–1949'. *Diplomacy and Statecraft* 17: 835–52.
Der Spiegel (1957) 'Wenn ein Volk seinen Verstand verliert', 18 September.
Deutsch, O. (1927) 'Paneuropäisches Wirtschaftsprogram', *Paneuropa* 3 (1): 7–17.
Dimier, V. (2014) *The Invention of a European Development Aid Bureaucracy: Recycling Empire*, Houndmills: Palgrave Macmillan.
Dodds, K. and Atkinson, D. (eds) (2009), *Geopolitical Traditions: A Century of Geopolitical Thought*, London: Routledge.
Enders, U. and Henke, J. (eds) (2000) *Die Kabinettsprotokolle der Bundesregierung*. Vol. 10, 1957 (München: R. Oldenbourg Verlag).
European Commission (2015) 'EU Action Plan on return', COM (2015) 453 final, Brussels, 9. 9.
Financial Times (2017) 'Merkel advocates investment to stem migrant flows', 1 March, www.ft.com/content/b9251d82-fe5e-11e6-96f8-3700c5664d30.
Gilbert, M. (2008) 'Narrating the process: questioning the progressive story of European integration'. *Journal of Common Market Studies* 46 (3): 641–62.
Hansen, P. and Jonsson, S. (2011) 'Bringing Africa as a 'dowry to Europe': European integration and the Eurafrican Project'. *Interventions* 13 (3): 443–63.
——(2012) 'Imperial origins of European integration and the case of Eurafrica: a reply to Gary Marks' "Europe and Its Empires"'. *Journal of Common Market Studies* 50 (6): 1028–41.
——(2013) 'A statute to Nasser? Eurafrica, the colonial roots of European integration, and the 2012 Nobel Peace Prize'. *Mediterranean Quarterly* 24 (4): 5–18.
——(2014a) *Eurafrica: The Untold History of European Integration and Colonialism*. London: Bloomsbury Academic.
——(2014b) 'Another colonialism: Africa in the history of European integration'. *Journal of Historical Sociology* 27 (3), 442–61.
Heffernan, M. (2009), '*Fin de Siècle, Fin du Monde*: On the origins of European geopolitics', in Klaus Dodds and David Atkinson (eds), *Geopolitical Traditions: A Century of Geopolitical Thought*, London: Routledge, pp. 27–51.
Heywood, R. W. (1981) 'West European community and the Eurafrica concept in the 1950s'. *Journal of European Integration* 4 (2): 199–210.
Hick, A. (1991) 'The 'European Movement"'. In Lipgens, W. (ed.) *Documents on the History of European Integration*, vol. 4. Berlin: Walter de Gruyter.
Jones, E. (2014) 'When do "weak" states win? A history of African, Caribbean and Pacific countries manoeuvring in trade negotiations with Europe'. *GEG Working Paper* 2014/95 (December 2014), The Global Economic Governance Programme, University of Oxford.
Kent, J. (1989) 'Bevin's imperialism and the idea of Euro-Africa, 1945–49'. In Dockrill, M. and Young, J. W. (eds) *British Foreign Policy, 1945–56*. Houndmills: Macmillan.
——(1992) *The Internationalisation of Colonialism: Britain, France, and Black Africa, 1939–1956*. Oxford: Clarendon Press.
Ki-Zerbo, L. (2013) (ed.) *Le mouvement panafricaniste au vingtième siècle*, Dakar: Codesria; Paris: Organisation internationale de la francophonie.
Kjellén, R. (1914), *Samtidens stormakter*, vol. 1, Stockholm: Hugo Gebers Förlag. (Translated into German as *Die Großmächte der Gegenwart*, Leipzig: Teubner, 1914).
Le Monde (1957a) Editorial: 'Première étape vers l'Eurafrique', 21 February 1957.
——(1957b) Editorial: 'Bulletin de l'étranger: Un point de départ?', 22 February 1957.
Lemaignen, R. (1964) *L'Europe au berceau: Souvenirs d'un technocrate*. Paris: Plon.
Lipgens, W. (1982) *A History of European Integration, Volume 1 1945–1947*. Oxford: Clarendon Press.
Lisbon Declaration – EU Africa Summit (2007) Lisbon, 8–9 December, www.africa-eu-partnership.org/sites/default/files/documents/eas2007_lisbon_declaration_en.pdf.
Martin, G. (1982) 'Africa and the ideology of Eurafrica: neo-colonialism or pan-Africanism?'. *The Journal of Modern African Studies* 20 (2): 221–38.

Mbembe, A. (2010) *Sortir de la grande nuit: Essai sur l'Afrique décolonisée*. Paris: Éditions La Découverte.
Migani, G. (2008) *La France et l'Afrique sub-saharienne, 1957–1963: Histoire d'une décolonisation entre idéaux eurafricains et politique de puissance*, Brussels: Peter Lang.
Mollet, G. (1957) 'Text of the French government's statement on Algeria', 9 January, 1957. HAEU, Dep. Emile Noël, EN–2736 (EN.01–04.01–Discours de Guy Mollet 1956–58).
Montarsolo, Y. (2010) *L'Eurafrique – contrepoint de l'idée d'Europe: Le cas français de la fin de la deuxième guerre mondiale aux négociacions des Traités de Rome*.
Mudimbe, V. Y. (1974) *L'Autre face du Royaume: une introduction à la critique des langages en folie*. Lausanne: L'Age d'Homme.
Nkrumah, K. (1962) 'Address to the Nationalists' Conference, June 4, 1962'. Accra.
OEEC (Organisation for European Economic Cooperation) (1951) *Investments in Overseas Territories in Africa, South of the Sahara*. Paris: OEEC.
Orsini di Camerota, P. D. (1934) *Eurafrica: L'Africa per l'Europa, l'Europa per l'Africa*, Rome: Paolo Cremonese.
Ortega y Gasset, J. (1929/1957) *The Revolt of the Masses*, New York: Norton.
Palayret, J-M. (2005) 'Les mouvements proeuropéens et la question de l'Eurafrique, du Congrès de La Haye à la Convention de Yaoundé (1948–1963)'. In Bitsch, M-T. and Bossuat, G. (eds) *L'Europe unie et l'Afrique: de l'idée d'eurafrique à la convention de Lomé I*. Brussels: Bruylant.
Pasture, P. (2015) *Imagining European Unity since 1000 AD*, Houndmills: Palgrave Macmillan.
Rivkin, A. (1966) 'Africa and the European Common Market: a perspective'. *Monograph Series in World Affairs* 3 (4), Denver: University of Denver.
Schuman, R. (1957a) 'Unité européenne et Eurafrique: Politique révolutionnaire. Aperçu d'ensemble'. *Union française et Parlement*, January, 1–3.
——(1957b) *France-Forum*. 21 February.
Spaak, P-H. (1957) 'L'Alliance occidentale et le destin de l'Europe', *Mars et Mercure*, no. 3 (March 1957): 7–9.
Stoddard, L. (1922/2003) *The Rising Tide of Colour Against White World-Supremacy*, Honolulu: University Press of the Pacific.
——(1935) *The Clashing Tides of Colour*, New York: Charles Scribner's Sons.
The New York Times (1947) 'Cripps says colonies hold key to survival', 13 November.
Treaty establishing the European Economic Community (1957) (Rome, 25 March).
UN (1960) 'The impact of Western European integration on African trade and development', UN Economic and Social Council Document E/CN.14/72, 7 December.
Wallerstein, I. (2005/1961, 1967) *Africa: The Politics of Independence and Unity,* Lincoln: University of Nebraska Press (new ed.).
Westad, O. A. (2005) *The Global Cold War: Third World Interventions and the Making of Our Times*, Cambridge: Cambridge University Press.
Zeleza, P. T. (2005) 'Africa: the changing meanings of "African" culture and identity'. In Abiri, E. and Thörn, H. (eds), *Horizons: Perspectives on a Global Africa*. Göteborg: Museion, Göteborg University.

Notes

1 In the entire body of scholarship, Guia Migani (2008: 54) is the only one who explicitly and, against the received idea, correctly points out that 'the criticisms [of West Germany, Italy, the Netherlands and Luxembourg against the French-Belgian association proposal] all concerned the modalities of association; nobody explicitly contested the principle that the African territories would participate in the Common Market'.

5
SECURING THE POSTCOLONIAL

Pinar Bilgin

Introduction

This chapter considers the following question: Should 'security' be a point of departure when thinking about the postcolonial? In considering this question, I will focus on recent debates on cosmopolitanism and security. Cosmopolitan approaches to security have focused on concerns with the security of peoples beyond one's own borders plus the global environment (Linklater, 2005, Burke, 2013). Doing so while avoiding treating the postcolonial in a top-down manner (i.e. by presuming to know the best ways to address security in the global South) has turned out to be a challenge for students of world politics.

In what follows, I will distinguish between three perspectives. First there are those who limit the scope of security to their immediate community understood as the state. This is the *standard realist perspective* on security that is skeptical of cosmopolitan concerns and places the responsibility for insecurities experienced in the global South at the doorstep of the postcolonial. Second, there are the proponents of *cosmopolitan approaches to security* who treat humanity and the global environment as the referent of security, without distinguishing between 'us' and 'them'. Yet, cosmopolitan approaches have been received critically for remaining oblivious to the 'dark side' of cosmopolitanism (Mignolo, 2003; Rao, 2010) and the persistence of inequalities created during the age of colonialism and beyond (that is, the 'colonial present' (Gregory, 2004)). Third, there are the students of *postcolonial studies* who have indeed pointed to cosmopolitanism's 'dark side' but also called for a more expanded approach to cosmopolitanism (Grovogui, 2005; Grovogui, 2011; Jabri, 2012).

While 'security' may not necessarily invoke warm feelings in the mind of the postcolonial, securing peoples and the global environment has nevertheless continued to top postcolonial state agendas (Abraham, 2009, Tickner and Herz, 2012). Accordingly, my concern with 'securing the postcolonial' is less about asking whether 'security' should be a point of departure when thinking about the postcolonial world. Rather, I am concerned with giving the postcolonial center-stage when discussing the ways in which 'security' is given prominence when thinking about the global South. Accordingly, I emphasise that thinking critically about security involves considering the contributions and contestations of the postcolonial. The alternative is presuming existing conceptions of security and statehood that shape existing practices to be 'universal', without considering aforementioned limitations rooted in their 'particularity' (Bilgin, 2016a).

The point here is not to replace one particular with another, but to highlight the particularity that passes as universal and consider ways of broadening their basis (Grovogui, 2005).

Before proceeding, one clarification is in order. If it appears that I refer to 'the postcolonial' and 'the global South' interchangeably, this is not because I collapse one into the other. Rather, it is because I consider postcolonial statehood to cover not only those states that were directly or indirectly colonised, but also in terms of the trials and travails of new or non-members vis-à-vis the international society. Following Stuart Hall, I understand colonialism as '[referencing] something more than direct rule over certain areas of the world by the imperial powers'. Rather, it '[signifies] the whole process of expansion, exploration, conquest, colonisation and imperial hegemonisation which constituted the "outer face", the constitutive outside, of European and then Western capitalist modernity after 1492' (Hall, 1996: 249). As such, I understand postcolonial insecurities as endured by all those in the global South who were written out of that particular narrative.

The first section outlines the standard realist perspective on security pertaining the global South. The two sections that follow counterpose criticisms of the standard realist approach from cosmopolitan and postcolonial perspectives. The concluding section suggests that advancing our thinking about security in the global South requires engaging with the postcolonial critique of the 'dark side' cosmopolitanism while carefully distinguishing it from the communitarianism of (subaltern) realism.

Standard realist approach to security in the global South

During the Cold War, concerns regarding security in the global South were never very far from the agendas of great powers. For the two superpowers, securing the global South took the form of securing the allegiance of the newly independent states vis-à-vis one's Cold War adversary. While both superpowers considered themselves as countering colonialism and contributed to post-Second World War de-colonisation, they were not necessarily viewed as such by the postcolonial (see, for example, Muppidi, 1999; Niva, 1999). For the former colonial powers, in turn, concerns with securing access to primary resources, cheap labor and markets comprised the definition of security in the global South.

In the post-Cold War era, the realist agenda on securing the global South came to focus on concerns with checking the rise of aspiring great powers (such as China and India), and addressing so-called 'state failure' (as in Somalia and Haiti). As such, the standard realist approach to security in the global South is conditioned by a particular notion of statehood shaped by the memories of and theorising about the trajectory of statehood in Western Europe. While such memories and theorising have been shown to be erroneous by historical sociologists (Halperin, 1997; also see Milliken and Krause, 2002), they have nevertheless been allowed to shape the standard realist approach to security and inform policy practices vis-à-vis the global South (Bilgin and Morton, 2002; Bilgin and Morton, 2004).

Throughout the Cold War and beyond, the postcolonial has suffered disproportionately as the great powers have sought to render 'universal' what are essentially 'particular' approaches to security. Approaches such as humanitarian intervention, state-building or security sector reform are informed by 'particular' notions of 'statehood' and 'security', and are designed to consider and address the concerns of those who have taken active part in their conceptualisation. Yet, those who have sought to apply these approaches in myriad places often overlook their 'particularity'. The problem at hand is essentially a mismatch between the dynamics on the ground in the global South and local actors' understanding of those dynamics on the one hand, and, on the other hand, 'particular' assumptions regarding 'statehood' and 'security' shaping those approaches that are presented as having 'universal' applicability. What is labeled as the 'problem of local ownership' (that global South actors do not seem to embrace those practices introduced by state and non-state actors from the global North) is one instance of such mismatch (Nathan, 2007; Mac Ginty and Richmond, 2013). That said, while 'the problem of local ownership' has been diagnosed as one consequence of such a mismatch, views differ as to what is the best way of addressing its ramifications for security in the global South (compare Brigg and Bleiker, 2011; Bilgin, forthcoming).

Central to our purposes here is the standard realist narrative on how security in the global North has been maintained. At the risk of oversimplification, the standard narrative tells the story of how building 'strong' states in the global North has given way to the building of a security community comprising Western Europe (the European Community/Union) and the North Atlantic (NATO) (Buzan, 1991). Since states in the global South have remained 'weak', this narrative suggests, they have not been successful in addressing the violent consequences of the anarchical condition. Accordingly, the responsibility for insecurities experienced in the global South is placed on the doorstep of the postcolonial. For instance, the absence of 'strong' states and observance of so-called 'failed' states is explained with reference to those states' internal dynamics. While there often is some acknowledgement of colonialism, there is almost no recognition of the persistent dynamics behind such 'failure' or the erroneous notion of statehood as background to the framing of current dynamics as a 'failure' (Bilgin and Morton, 2002; Bilgin and Morton, 2004).

A particularly striking example of this approach is the debate on the so-called 'zone of peace' and 'zone of war', which is staged often without considering the historical or contemporary relationships between the two zones (Goldgeier and McFaul, 1992). At best, these relationships are recognised in their most historical form, by way of noting the ills of colonialism. Yet, it is often acknowledged that the 'colonial present' (Gregory, 2004) has shaped the experiences of the postcolonial in more ways than one. In some instances the 'colonial present' has taken the form of former colonial powers preserving historical relationships, albeit in new forms, as with Britain's entangled ties with the Arabian peninsula, including but not limited to oil imports and arms exports (Vitalis, 2002; Vitalis, 2007).

In some other instances, the 'colonial present' has taken the form of actors in the global North temporalising difference and spatialising time, treating the global South as lagging behind and therefore more suited for the use of violent practices that are no longer considered as suitable for use in the global North (Bilgin, 2016b). Examples include the conduct of the Global War on Terror (GWoT) in the global South, including the US-led coalition's invasion of Iraq in 2003 and the dropping of the so-called 'mother of all bombs' (i.e. the most powerful non-nuclear weapon produced thus far) in Afghanistan in pursuit of Al Qaeda amidst an escalated drone warfare campaign that followed the withdrawal of US troops from Afghanistan; and US and its GWoT allies' close collaboration, throughout the 2000s, with authoritarian states in the global South for the pursuit and interrogation of suspected terrorists (Joffé, 2008; Jabri, 2013).

The point is that the standard realist narrative on security in the global South has rested on 'particular' notions of statehood and security that limit the understanding of postcolonial insecurities. As a result, the narrative on the emergence of 'strong' states and the building of a security community in the global North is told without acknowledging the historical or contemporary relationships with the global South. Even as the historical ills of colonialism are acknowledged, the 'colonial present' is not considered in terms of persistent trends in North–South relations, or in terms of the resilience of factors that conceal how the emergence of a 'zone of peace' in the global North has been tied up with the persistence of a 'zone of war' in the global South (Barkawi and Laffey, 1999).

Cosmopolitan approaches to security

Cosmopolitan approaches to security have been built upon three main bodies of thinking: the contributions of English school theorists on the necessity of norms and (cautious) solidarism in the international arena (Wheeler, 2000); the Aberystwyth school's emancipatory approach to security theorising (Booth, 2007); and post-structuralist sensibilities regarding the (re)production of boundaries and insecurities through practices of security (Bigo, 2008). Contra popular portrayals, the critical difference between standard realist and cosmopolitan approaches is not their preferred instruments (military versus non-military) but the referent of security. Where standard realist approaches privilege one's own community ('us' versus 'them'), cosmopolitan approaches have preferred to cross state borders and treated humanity *and* the global environment as the referent of security (Linklater, 2005). Accordingly, contributors to this body of thinking conceptualised military intervention as an expression of solidarity beyond borders. While most such interventions have taken North-to-South direction, more recently some Southern actors have adopted the same body of cosmopolitan norms in South-to-South interaction as well (such as Brazil in Haiti) (Müller, 2016).

The latest strand in this body of theorising is Anthony Burke's (2013, 2015) 'security cosmopolitanism', which draws from all three aforementioned traditions. The cosmopolitan aspect of Burke's approach crystallises when arguing against the standard realist perspective that prefers to limit the scope of security to one's own community (i.e. the state). Stated in terms of his affinities with post-structuralist approaches to security theorising, Burke has underscored Vivien Jabri's (2007, 2013) emphasis on the limits of liberal cosmopolitanism as security governance. In offering this line of critique, Jabri has highlighted past and present injustices and violence committed in the name of cosmopolitan interventionism. Hence Jabri's (2007) call for pursuing 'cosmopolitan solidarity' and not 'cosmopolitan security'. In distinguishing between the two, Jabri highlighted the top-down character of present-day cosmopolitan interventionism and underscored the need for considering insecurities in the global South as voiced by the postcolonial, and offering help as needed without presuming that 'we' know what others' insecurities are and/or the best ways of addressing them. As such, Jabri called for checking against the global North's top-down military interventionism vis-à-vis the global South that has characterised both the standard realist approach and some of its cosmopolitan critics who, however inadvertently, run the risk of sliding into neo-imperialism.

While Jabri has done away with 'security' and called for 'cosmopolitan solidarity', Burke has retained both cosmopolitanism and security while theorising differently about both. In doing so, he has aligned his thinking with Ken Booth's (2007) emphasis on the politics of security and the need for an emancipatory approach to security that crosses borders (while remaining cautious about humanitarian intervention, see (Booth, 1994)). Yet at the same time, Burke has sought to push Booth's emancipatory approach to security further by underscoring post-structuralist sensibilities regarding 'security as a set of promises and dangers' (Burke, 2013; see also, Bigo, 2008; Abraham, 2009).

Before turning to the postcolonial critique of security, let me discuss, however briefly, a body of thought that has drawn upon the aforementioned critique of cosmopolitanism while pushing for a return to a communitarianism that is characteristic realism, namely, subaltern realism. Maintaining that states in the global South are 'late' arrivals to the international society, Mohammed Ayoob (1997, 1998) asked for them to be given the space and the time to grow up and become 'strong' states and not be targeted for cosmopolitan engagement. Cosmopolitan engagement by the global North with the global South, suggested Ayoob, would arrest their development, disallowing the kind of security community that was generated in the global North. Then, different from the postcolonial critics of security (see below), Ayoob suggested that insecurities experienced by peoples and other non-state actors as well as the global environment are exigencies of the process of building 'strong' states in the global South. Only through building 'strong' states, he suggested, could security in the global South be ensured.

Space does not permit dwelling upon the ways in which Ayoob's criticism failed to identify the particularity of standard realist approach to statehood and security, thereby failing to broaden their basis from the perspective of the subaltern (Bilgin, 2016a). What is significant for our purposes here is that Ayoob marshaled the critique against cosmopolitan approaches to security to insist on the need for a communitarian approach to security akin to standard realist approaches. This is not an entirely consistent position to take, for the same body of criticism also identifies the limitations of the statist approach to security as assumed by the postcolonial state (see, for example, Krishna, 1999; Biswas, 2001; Rao, 2004; Abraham, 2006) – the very group of states that Ayoob seeks to strengthen vis-à-vis their own peoples.

Furthermore, what Ayoob failed to note was that critiquing cosmopolitanism does not necessarily warrant disallowing all forms of cosmopolitan engagement beyond borders. As seen above, critical IR scholars' contributions to debates on rights resist those attempts to limit the scope of security to those within one's own borders on communitarian grounds. Rather, their critique is conditioned by the historical legacy of cosmopolitanism and those who have hesitated to broaden the scope of security beyond their immediate community even when acting in the name of cosmopolitanism. The point being that the proponents of subaltern realism, while drawing upon postcolonial critique of cosmopolitanism's 'dark side', have used such a critique as a stepping stone for arguing against cosmopolitan engagement *in toto*. In doing so, they favoured the postcolonial state, but not peoples (or the global environment), as the ultimate referent of security (Bilgin, 2016a).

Postcolonial critique

Viewed from the global South, a cosmopolitan approach to security may not necessarily come across as a solution not only because of what 'security' has entailed (as critiqued by Jabri, see above) but also because what 'cosmopolitanism' invokes in the minds of the postcolonial. For, different memories of experiences with cosmopolitanism prevail in the global South versus the global North. The global North favours a cosmopolitan stance for the ability to think and act beyond one's borders, and experiences moments of self-doubt only when criticised on grounds of neo-imperialism. The global South, in turn, carries different memories of past instances of North-to-South cosmopolitan engagement. Yet, the proponents of cosmopolitan approaches often overlook such differences between the North and the South. Even those who are concerned with the problem of so-called 'lack of local ownership' in the global South, explain away what they observe by invoking 'cultural' differences, thereby overlooking the 'colonial present' that has shaped North-to-South interventionism (Bilgin, 2016b).

For instance, where students of English School theorising observe a broadening of the consensus on norms, the postcolonial critics have cautioned against mistaking the postcolonial's entry into the international society for the universalisation of its constitutive norms. As Shogo Suzuki (2005) has argued with reference to the case of imperial Japan, the postcolonial viewed the international society as 'Janus-faced' precisely because of the incongruity between members' treatment of fellow members versus not-yet members such as Japan. Accordingly, the postcolonial's stance vis-à-vis such a 'Janus-faced' international society was characterised by ambivalence. The new entrants often observed but not totally embraced the constitutive norms of the international society. Their thinking was that the members of the international society themselves were not entirely consistent in enforcing those norms vis-à-vis non-members (Suzuki, 2009). Put differently, in the experience of not-yet members, what the founding members of the international society viewed as constitutive norms were not applied universally but only toward fellow members. And yet, cosmopolitan approaches to security have not always been forthcoming in offering such self-critique.

One such critique can be found in the writings of Beate Jahn (1998: 631) who has noted that thinkers such as Samuel von Pufendorf and Emmerich de Vattel, whose writings Linklater's studies were built upon, 'did not develop universal ideas but rather universal *yardsticks* which were supposed to provide them with a justification *not* to extend equal rights to others'. Accordingly, argues Jahn, Linklater's model excludes others at the moment of inclusion:

> For it is on the basis of the 'inclusion' into humanity defined as European rationality, European political organization, European capitalism or forms of communication and morality that alternative forms of rationality, political organization, modes of production or forms of communication and morality are excluded, not only from the higher echelons of humanity, but also from certain concrete legal and moral rights.
>
> (Jahn, 1998: 636–7)

Put differently, what the critics consider problematic about cosmopolitan approaches' adoption of universals is not only that 'particular' universals are imposed in seeking to improve the human condition in different parts of the world, but that they have been applied arbitrarily and that cosmopolitan scholars have had precious little to say about that (Grovogui, 2006).

The 'arbitrary' application of 'universals' has long constituted a challenge for the notion of 'universals'. Consider Siba Grovogui's critique of Linklater's cosmopolitan outlook. Recognising Linklater's attempt to 'extend rights' beyond state borders, Grovogui has also pointed to the problems involved. Where Linklater saw difficulties in terms of previous failures to think and act beyond borders, Grovogui has insisted that the problem lies elsewhere. The issue is not only one of overcoming past instances of 'exclusion' noted Grovogui, but also diagnosing the 'mechanisms of exclusion' and the ways in which such mechanisms have persisted. Grovogui wrote:

> Such criticisms do not conceive prior misapplication or suspension of international morality (likened metonymically to a liberal constitutional regime) as a mere problem of exclusion. They involve considerations of the very terms of the constitutional order – the implicated political imaginaries, juridical and moral systems, and their base-notions of communities and obligations – as mechanisms of exclusion.
>
> (Grovogui, 2006: 48–9)

While the cosmopolitan case is often made with reference to a choice between applying existing norms universally or having no universals at all, Grovogui argued differently. There is no reason, he wrote, to suppose that what are portrayed as 'universals' are indeed universal or that they are the only possible definition of rights that could be used to render a definition truly universal. To quote Grovogui again:

> Non-Western legal and moral systems do – and have – provided sufficient or equally compelling rationales for the idea of enforceable rights to protect humans, which may be extended to include a responsibility to protect victims and a duty to prosecute violators.

> Second, human-rights related obligations and duties can be defended without conceding the universality and conclusiveness of Western ideas and practices of human rights.
> (Grovogui, 2011: 45–6)

The postcolonial critics' point being that 'extending rights' beyond state borders as per the cosmopolitan agenda need to be coupled with taking stock of the context in which those rights were defined as 'rights' to the exclusion of other rights. Accordingly, taking a cosmopolitan approach to security seriously would likely involve taking the critique of cosmopolitanism seriously – not to give up on thinking and acting beyond borders as per (subaltern) realism (see above) but to

> broaden cosmopolitan perspectives...to come up with methods of translation that render intelligible beliefs, attitudes and values and, therefore, institutions, idioms and political languages that, although not organically linked, may converge in their teleology.
> (Grovogui, 2005: 112)

From a postcolonial perspective, then, the problem of the co-called 'lack of local ownership' would not be explained away by invoking 'cultural' differences but by highlighting an inability to recognise 'the value of parallel or non-Western moral thoughts and ethics and their justifications, intellectual programs and political agendas' (Grovogui, 2005: 112).

Conclusion

Critiquing the 'dark side' of cosmopolitanism does not warrant security communitarianism. The latter is preferred by standard realist and subaltern realist approaches to security. Postcolonial scholars' contributions to debates on cosmopolitanism resist those attempts to limit the scope of security to one's own community on 'culturalist' grounds. As such, they are more closely aligned with the cosmopolitan perspective on security than with the subaltern realist approach.

Students of subaltern realism indicated awareness of postcolonial insecurities insofar as they marshaled the postcolonial critics' interrogations of the 'dark side' of cosmopolitanism; yet they overlooked another side of such insecurities when they unreservedly pushed for statist approaches to security. Herein lies the significance of taking 'security' as a point of departure for the postcolonial. For, those critics who claim to speak on behalf of the postcolonial have insisted on the need for a statist approach to security in the global South. That students of subaltern realism do so while knowing fully well that state-focused security practices may or may not produce security for peoples in whose name security is sought is a point that cannot be overemphasised. Examples include those who live next to military bases and bear the brunt of the rise of militarism; men and women who are dis/empowered in different ways during wartime; or the most vulnerable in the society whose insecurities are overlooked while designing and implementing so-called 'smart sanctions' (Enloe, 1990; Sharoni, 1998; Drury and Peksen, 2014).

Another such danger is the persistence of neo-imperial interventionism, which has been justified on cosmopolitan grounds (thereby deviating from the previously self-regarding justifications for military intervention offered by the standard realist approaches), maintaining that 'empire is good for the periphery because it brings good governance to "rogue" or "failed" states, thereby ensuring greater respect for the human rights of their inhabitants' (Rao, 2004: 146). From this perspective, security is a 'public good supplied by the US empire' and neo-imperialist interventionism is justified for reasons of security in the global South.

However, as Rahul Rao (2004: 162–3) has noted, public goods are supposed to be 'non-excludable (it is impossible to prevent non-contributors from enjoying the good) and joint (a number of actors are able simultaneously to consume the same produced unit of the good without detracting from each other's enjoyment)'. Yet, cautioned Rao, security does not always fit this definition, as it has (historically or currently) been pursued through acts of neo-imperial interventionism. Furthermore, even when no intervention takes place, as with the experience of building a security community in North America and Western Europe, security still does not emerge as a public good. For, the experience of building security communities in one part of the world has had implications for in/security elsewhere (Barkawi and Laffey, 1999).

The broader point being that, while underscoring the need to address insecurities beyond one's borders, the proponents of cosmopolitan approaches to security have not yet fully considered the contributions and contestations of the postcolonial as regards the limits of thinking and practices shaped by global North's conceptions of 'statehood' and 'security'. In contrast, students of postcolonial studies have expressed their critique of cosmopolitanism not to make a case for communitarism but to call for broadening its bases beyond current thinking and practices. Indeed, postcolonial critique is conditioned by the historical legacy of cosmopolitanism and those who have hesitated to broaden the scope of security beyond their immediate community even when acting in the name of cosmopolitanism. Accordingly, advancing our thinking about security in the global South requires carefully distinguishing the communitarianism of (subaltern) realism from the cosmopolitanism of postcolonial approaches *and* identifying the grounds for learning and solidarity between security cosmopolitanism and the postcolonial critique.

Bibliography

Abraham, I. 2006. 'The ambivalence of nuclear histories'. *Osiris*, 6:21, 49–65.

—— 2009. 'Seguranca/security in Brazil and the United States'. In: Gluck, C. and Tsing, A. L. (eds.) *Words in Motion: Toward a Global Lexicon*. Duke University Press.

Ayoob, M. 1997. 'Defining security: a subaltern realist perspective'. *Critical Security Studies*, 121–46.

—— 1998. 'Subaltern realism: international relations theory meets the Third World'. In: Neuman, S. G. (ed.) *International Relations Theory and the Third World*. London: Macmillan.

Barkawi, T. and Laffey, M. 1999. 'The imperial peace: democracy, force and globalisation'. *European Journal of International Relations*, 5, 403–34.

Bigo, D. 2008. 'International political sociology'. In: Williams, P. D. D. (ed.) *Security Studies: An Introduction*. London: Routledge.

Bilgin, P. 2016a. *The International in Security, Security in the International*. London: Routledge.

—— 2016b. 'Temporalizing security: securing the citizen, insecuring the immigrant in the Mediterranean'. In: Agathangelou, A. M. and Killian, K. D. (eds.) *Time, Temporality and Violence in International Relations: (De) Fatalizing the Present, Forging Radical Alternatives*. London: Routledge.

Bilgin, P. forthcoming. 'Worlding conflict resolution and mediation expertise in the "Global South"'. In: Leander, A. and Waever, O. (eds.) *Exclusive Expertise*. London: Routledge.

Bilgin, P. and Morton, A. D. 2002. 'Historicising representations of "failed states": beyond the Cold-War annexation of the social sciences?' *Third World Quarterly*, 23, 55–80.

—— 2004. 'From "rogue" to "failed" states? The fallacy of short-termism'. *Politics*, 24, 169–80.

Biswas, Shampa. 2001. '"Nuclear apartheid" as political position: race as a postcolonial resource?' *Alternatives: Global, Local, Political*, 26:4, 485–522.

Booth, K. 1994. 'Military intervention: duty and prudence'. *Political Quarterly*, 65, 56–56.

—— 2007. *Theory of World Security*. Cambridge: Cambridge University Press.

Brigg, M. and Bleiker, R. (eds.) 2011. *Mediating Across Difference: Oceanic and Asian Approaches to Conflict Resolution*. University of Hawaii Press.

Burke, A. 2013. 'Security cosmopolitanism'. *Critical Studies on Security*, 1, 13–28.

—— 2015. 'Security cosmopolitanism: the next phase'. *Critical Studies on Security*, 3, 190–212.

Buzan, B. 1991. 'Is international security possible?' In: Booth, K. (ed.) *New Thinking about Strategy and International Security.* London: Harper Collins.

Drury, A. C. and Peksen, D. 2014. 'Women and economic statecraft: the negative impact international economic sanctions visit on women'. *European Journal of International Relations,* 20, 463–90.

Enloe, C. 1990. *Bananas, Beaches and Bases: Making Feminist Sense of International Politics.* Berkeley: University of California Press.

Goldgeier, J. M. and Mcfaul, M. M. 1992. 'A tale of two worlds: core and periphery in the post-Cold War era'. *International Organization,* 46, 467–91.

Gregory, D. 2004. *The Colonial Present.* Oxford: Wiley.

Grovogui, S. N. 2005. 'The new cosmopolitanisms: subtexts, pretexts and context of ethics'. *International Relations,* 19, 103–13.

—— 2006. *Beyond Eurocentrism and Anarchy: Memories of International Order and Institutions.* New York: Palgrave Macmillan.

—— 2011. 'To the orphaned, dispossessed, and illegitimate children: human rights beyond republican and liberal traditions'. *Indiana Journal of Global Legal Studies,* 18, 41–63.

Hall, S. 1996. 'When was "the post-colonial"? Thinking at the limit'. In: Chambers, I. and Curti, L. (eds.) *The Post-Colonial Question: Common Skies, Divided Horizons.* London: Routledge.

Halperin, S. 1997. *In the Mirror of the Third World: Capitalist Development in Modern Europe.* Ithaca, NY: Cornell University Press.

Jabri, V. 2007. 'Solidarity and spheres of culture: the cosmopolitan and the postcolonial'. *Review of International Studies,* 33.

—— 2012. 'Cosmopolitan politics, security, political subjectivity'. *European Journal of International Relations,* 18, 625–44.

—— 2013. *The Postcolonial Subject: Claiming Politics/Governing Others in Late Modernity.* London: Routledge.

Jahn, B. 1998. 'One step forward, two steps back: critical theory as the latest edition of liberal idealism'. *Millennium: Journal of International Studies,* 27, 613–41.

Joffé, G. 2008. 'The European Union, democracy and counter-terrorism in the Maghreb'. *Journal of Common Market Studies,* 46, 147–71.

Krishna, S. 1999. *Postcolonial Insecurities: India, Sri Lanka, and the Question of Nationhood.* Minneapolis: MN, University of Minnesota Press.

Linklater, A. 2005. 'Political community and human security'. In: Booth, K. (ed.) *Critical Security Studies and World Politics.* Lynne Rienner.

Mac Ginty, R. and Richmond, O. P. 2013. 'The local turn in peace building: a critical agenda for peace'. *Third World Quarterly,* 34, 763–83.

Mignolo, W. 2003. *The Darker Side of the Renaissance: Literacy, Territoriality, and Colonization.* Ann Arbor, MI: University of Michigan Press.

Milliken, J. and Krause, K. 2002. 'State failure, state collapse, and state reconstruction: concepts, lessons and strategies'. *Development & Change,* 33, 753.

Müller, M.-M. 2016. 'Entangled pacifications: peacekeeping, counterinsurgency and policing in Port-au-Prince and Rio de Janeiro'. In: Hönke, J. and Müller, M.-M. (eds.) *The Global Making of Policing: Postcolonial Perspectives.* London: Routledge.

Muppidi, H. 1999. 'Postcoloniality and the production of international insecurity: the persistent puzzle of US-Indian relations'. In: Weldes, J., Laffey, M., Gusterson, H. and Duvall, R. (eds.) *Cultures of Insecurity: States, Communities, and the Production of Danger.* Minneapolis: University of Minnesota Press.

Nathan, L. 2007. *No Ownership, No Commitment: A Guide to Local Ownership of Security Sector Reform.* Birmingham, UK: University of Birmingham.

Niva, S. 1999. 'Contested sovereignties and postcolonial insecurities in the Middle East'. In: Weldes, J., Laffey, M., Gusterson, H. and Duvall, R. (eds.) *Cultures of Insecurity: States, Communities, and the Production of Danger.* Minneapolis: University of Minnesota Press.

Rao, R. 2004. 'The empire writes back (to Michael Ignatieff)'. *Millennium-Journal of International Studies,* 33, 145–66.

—— 2010. *Third World Protest: Between Home and the World.* Oxford: Oxford University Press.

Sharoni, S. 1998. 'Gendering conflict and peace in Israel/Palestine and the North of Ireland'. *Millennium: Journal of International Studies,* 27, 1061–90.

Suzuki, S. 2005. 'Japan's socialisation into Janus-Faced European international society'. *European Journal of International Relations,* 11, 137–64.

—— 2009. *Civilization and Empire: China and Japan's Encounter with European International Society*, London, New York: Routledge.

Tickner, A. and Herz, M. 2012. 'No place for theory? Security studies in Latin America'. In: Tickner, A. and Blaney, D. (eds.) *Thinking International Relations Differently*. London: Routledge.

Vitalis, R. 2002. 'Black gold, white crude: an essay on American exceptionalism, hierarchy, and hegemony in the Gulf'. *Diplomatic History*, 26, 185–213.

—— 2007. *America's Kingdom: Mythmaking on the Saudi Oil Frontier*. Stanford: Stanford University Press.

Wheeler, N. J. 2000. *Saving Strangers: Humanitarian Intervention in International Society*. Oxford: Oxford University Press.

6

SOCIAL STRUGGLES AND THE COLONIALITY OF GENDER

Rosalba Icaza

Introduction

Today, as the last natural resources are located in first nation people's land, it seems that the ecological frontier coincides with an epistemic human frontier. For example, the resource war we are facing is one in which first nations are struggling to preserve their lands, their rivers and mountains, dignity, and their right to self-determination (Icaza and Vazquez 2017). What can we learn from these ongoing social struggles resisting violent forms of power destroying land, women's lives and hope? This question inspires the steps taken in this chapter.

We start by sharing three small vignettes which aim to transmit how different social struggles for land, women lives and hope, which are place-based[1] yet connected to global dynamics of violence and extermination, are taking place across Abya Yala[2] (Americas). This is followed by a brief introduction to decolonial thinking key concepts. In the third and final step, two questions are asked and some initial reflections provided: what is decolonial feminism and what might happen to the way we make sense of social struggles in global politics when gender is understood from its underside, coloniality?

The key objective of this chapter is to generate even more questions to the imagined potential readers: people interested in global politics, their actors and current processes, and in particular, people aiming to think and relate to global politics and each other *otherwise*.[3] To that effect, throughout the chapter some collective and individual reflections are shared. These have emerged from co-learning moments and encounters *with*[4] people who within and/or outside academia are generating *otherwise* forms of thinking, sensing and relating to land, life and women's struggles across the Americas (Barbosa, Icaza and Ocampo 2015).

Contrary to mainstream academic style that makes absent the person(s) who writes the text to such an extreme degree that her emotion-less and body-less knowledge appears to arise naturally from a distant/abstract space, this text starts with a positioning of the self that writes as a *yosotras (I-we)*[5]: '*I speak to "us" because from there I see the possibility of building worlds where life is born and grows without fear, with the possibility of recognizing our vulnerability and perseverance*' (CarteArte 2016). To write as an I-we, to write as *yosotras,* not only questions dominant forms of representing and writing about the world, people and their struggles, but also highlights the fact that the ideas in this chapter, like any other knowledge, emerge from co-learning moments and encounters (Leyva 2013; Icaza 2015a). I-we wrote in this specific form with the intention of generating a dialogue in the form of questions that generate even more questions: 'asking, we walk', said the Zapatistas.

This form of writing, knowing and sharing from a communal self is what decolonial thinker Rolando Vazquez calls a trans-decolonial move as one that:

> enact[s] relational forms of personification that are often not only in a fluidity of genders but also in a non-individualized position, in a fluidity between the communal and a plural self, and a non-anthropocentric position, in a fluidity between earth and the communal vulnerable self, a communal self.
>
> (Vazquez 2017a forthcoming)

Situating knowledge

Land

> *In our cosmovisions, we are beings coming from Earth, Water and Corn*
> *We Lenca people are the ancestral guardians of rivers*
> *protected by the spirits of girls who teach us that*
> *giving our lives in multiple ways to defend the rivers*
> *is to give life for the well-being of humanity and this planet.*
> *Wake up, Wake up humanity! There is no more time!*
> *Our conscience will be shaken by the fact that we are only contemplating*
> *our own destruction by capitalist, racist and patriarchal predation.*
> *The Rio Gualcarque has called us, as well as the other rivers*
> *that are being seriously threatened around the world*
> *We must go.*
> *The Mother Earth, militarized, enclosed, poisoned,*
> *where the elementary rights are systematically violated,*
> *requires us to act.*

These are the words of Lenca indigenous leader Berta Caceres' acceptance speech at the Goldman Environmental Award Ceremony of 2015.[6] Berta dedicated the award to '*all rebellions, to my mother and to the people of Agua Blanca and COPINH*'. COPINH is the Honduras-based *Consejo Civico of Organizations Populares e Indigenas*:

> an Indigenous Lenca organization made up of 200 Lenca communities in the western Honduran states of Intibuca, Lempira, La Paz, and Santa Barbara. COPINH was born in 1993 when the Indigenous and popular movements in the Honduran state of Intibuca came together to stop logging and advance popular struggles. Today, COPINH encompasses four states in western Honduras and struggles for the rights of the Lenca people, including environmental, cultural, economic, social, health, education, and Indigenous rights. COPINH defends the Lenca territory and our natural resources as part of our Lenca cosmovision of respect for Mother Earth.[7]

In recent years, Berta leaded COPINH's struggle against the world largest dam construction 'Agua Zarca Dam' in the Gualcarque River. Sadly, a few months after her speech at the Goldman Environmental Award Ceremony, Berta was assassinated, presumably by members of the private security forces of DESA, the local owner and developer of the project. In April 2016, as part of a group of students and colleagues at the Institute of Social Studies[8] and neighbors from The Hague, the city that hosts the International Criminal Court, we welcomed Berta's family and COPINH. Their visit was part of an international tour supported by different human rights organizations[9] to raise awareness not only of the growing local opposition to the Agua Zarca Dam but also to claim justice for Berta's assassination. As The Hague also hosts FMO, the Dutch development bank which is partially financing the construction of the hydroelectric plant at the Gualcarque River, these organizations organized a demonstration outside FMO's headquarters, accompanied by some ISS students and staff.

A few weeks after the demonstration, FMO suspended but did not cancel their financial involvement and established a fact-finding commission to Honduras that delivered their final report in October 2016.[10] COPINH and Berta's family continue to reject FMO conclusions: 'The [FMO] report selectively chooses to repeat DESA's narrative and allegations, often without verifying the facts, while excluding significant information that challenges this narrative and reflects the disastrous reality of the Agua Zarca Hydroelectric Project.'[11]

Some months ago, Berta's daughter and I came together once more. This time we were members of one of the few initiatives in Latin America and the Caribbean involved in collaborative research and coalition-building with social movements: the Transnational Network of Other Knowledges, hosted by the Latin American Council of Social Sciences (CLACSO).[12] To this day, Berta's daughter's message at ISS still resonates in me: *Berta didn't die, she multiplied.* This is the message that also inspired a tribute to Berta at the 2016 Goldman Environmental Prize Ceremony by poets Leslie Valencia, Terisa Siagatonu and Erika Vivianna Céspedes: '*Bertha, as indigenous women, we know that death is just the Earth's way of reminding us who we belong to*...'[13]

As this chapter was being written, and amidst the monothematic media obsession with Donald Trump's new set of US/Mexican policies on trade, immigration and security, the sad news that came from Mexico has already been sidelined: Tarahumara leader Isidro Baldenegro Lopez, 2005 Goldman Environmental awardee,[14] was assassinated. Like his own father some decades ago, Isidro was killed by clandestine loggers who over the years have tried to stop Tarauhmara people's struggles to defend the communal forest of *Coloradas de la Virgen*.

> In a world predominantly run under the modern logic that prioritizes the economy over anything else (including life), spirituality challenges its very logic since it's founded on a way of relating to the world that prioritizes life, the relationship to every being: rocks, plants, rivers, animals, people and spirits. Midwives who carry the knowledge learned in dreams taking care of life and growing the plants they need for this, people who run Temazcales from one lineage or another in their many perhaps hybrid forms, they are all guardians of the heart of the earth, resisting with their bodies and their practices the violence of discrimination, coloniality, neoliberalism, epistemicide, development and its institutions.[15]

We wonder if Isidro's struggle, like the struggles of many other 'Guardians of the heart of the Earth' in Mexico and around the world would be once more be condemned to oblivion or not? Maybe Isidro will not die but multiply too?

Women's lives

Traigo un infierno	*I am carrying the hell inside me*
(Makila 69)[16]	
Te gusta la mala vida	*You like evil life,*
me dicen los muertos	*death people tell me*
Te gusta la mala vida	*You like evil life,*

me dicen los muertos
Y a mi me da por reir
mientras les digo que si
Me voy a escapar otra vez al amor
Traigo un infierno muy dentro de mi
que va a estallar, que va a estallar
Hay una guerra en este pais
que ya estallo,
que ya estallo
Hay una guerra en este pais
en contra de ti
Hay una guerra en contra de mi
Hay una Guerra en este pais
que ya estallo,
que ya hasta yo,
que ya hasta tu puedes morir
(Obeja Negra featured by Makila 69)[17]
Ninguna Guerra en mi nombre
Genocidas primeros mandatarios
Ninguna Guerra en nuestro nombre
Desde la Frontera Norte
No se nos olvidan
las miles de voces
Acalladas de mujeres
Que no tuvieron la oportunidad
De retumbar en estas bocinas
y esta palabra
Asi que tremendo ruido por aquellas
Que no lograron hacerlo
Por que estamos locas
Y seguiremos locas
Y regresaremos
y nuestra venganza sera ser felices
Y sonreir, y caminar seguras
Libres, sin miedo, unidas, vivas!
Vivas nos queremos
Vivas, nos queremos

death people tell me
And I laugh
while I tell them Yes
I am going to escape once more to love
I am carrying the hell inside me
it is going to blow up, to blow up
There is a war in this country
that has already blown up
that has already blown up
There is a war in this country
against you
There is a war in this country against me
There is a war in this country
that has already blown up
that even me
that even you could die

Any war in my name
Genocidal country leaders
Any war in our names
From the Northern border
We do not forget
the thousands of women's voices
silenced
That did not have opportunity
to rumble in these horns
and these words
So, let's make a tremendous noise for them
who were not able to make it
Because we are crazy
We will be crazy
We will return
and our revenge will be to be happy
and smile, and walk safe
free, without fear, united… Alive!
Alive we want to be
Alive, we love each other

Above are the lyrics of two different songs. The first one '*Traigo un infierno*' was written by Mexican artist Nidia Barajas from *Makila 69*, an electro acoustic duet formed with her male partner and bass player, El Alas Blissett. The second one is an intervention by *Obeja Negra* (*Black Sheep*), a female Mexican rapper and member of *Batallones Femeninos*.[18] The three of them were born in the Mexico–US border cities of Tijuana or Ciudad Juarez, the latter, the so-called Mexican capital of femicides and drug-related murders, and were invited to perform at the Zapatista Arts Festival COMPARTE held in San Cristobal de las Casas, Chiapas, Mexico in the summer of 2016.[19]

After some brief conversations and informal exchanges with them, *Obeja Negra* shared the manifesto *CarteArte: Abajo y a la Izquierda en Morado.*[20] The document, a collaborative product of conversations among women in Mexico, delineates feminist political and epistemic principles for liberation within and in spite of '*machista*/misogynist leftist activism': '*I am learning that "we" is political and ethically built, not by sexual determination, nor by gender roles, but from the social class "we" are*' (CarteArte 2016).

CarteArte as a collective exercise also denounces the appropriation of women struggles by people like us, writing from a comfortable paid position in a European University and occupying positions of racial/socio-economic/gender/sexual privilege, while also calling for life and care of each other.

A few months ago, through social media we learned that *Obeja Negra* and Batallones Femeninos have been actively engaged in supporting the families of the disappeared students of Ayotzinapa.[21] This is how we also learned that in December 2016, *Obeja Negra* was illegally detained by local authorities in Oaxaca, Mexico. It was through social media that we supported the campaign for her release.[22] Is this how support from positions of privilege contributes to the enactment of a collective self? We keep ourselves asking this.

Hope

A few months ago, again through social media we were listening to the messages of the Water Defenders at Standing Rock opposing the Dakota Access Pipeline (DAPL). [23] Here is the testimony of Phyllis Young, former councilwoman for the Standing Rock Sioux Tribe and Central Oceti Sakowin camp organizer:

> It's about the whole world. It's about Mother Earth, having endured her suffering for this long, she needs our help. She needs our protection. She's a female, and Indigenous people are the keepers of Mother Earth. We're obligated to keep her water for her, and maintain the life as created, and for us. We have deep spiritual obligation to protect our place.[24]

Phyllis' words make us feel a sense of hope that is nested in caring for the Earth. This kind of hope not only stems from practices of organizing resistance modeled according to the future we aspire to, or what some call politics of hope (i.e. Dinnerstein 2014). It is also a kind of hope embedded in the certainty of past struggles that determines who we are but also the way ahead of us (Vazquez 2017b, forthcoming). Hope can be seen in the struggles for autonomy by Indigenous people and those of African descent in Latin America and the Caribbean, who are oriented towards a politics of dignity (Icaza and Vazquez 2017, forthcoming).

> The moment is critical: the pipeline is near completion and still must be stopped before it reaches the Missouri river...We have been met along our trip so far with amazing acts of solidarity and donations from store clerks and people along the way when we tell them we are going to Standing Rock. Thank all of you for your support, please donate and continue posting and talking about the historic and inspiring Standing Rock fight to stop the DAPL. Love and Solidarity!! Never Give Up.'[25]

The call was clear once more. We were called to support a 'we', and so we did.

Making sense of social struggles for land, women's lives and hope in global politics

When confronted with experiences of social struggles for land, women's lives and hope across the Global South/North divide, one of the common starting points in global politics in thinking *about* these struggles is capitalism as the dominant mode of production. By taking capitalism as a starting point, Lenca, Tarahumara and Sioux people's resistance to either a hydroelectric plant, illegal logging or a pipe line can be explained as one of many contemporary struggles against accumulation by land dispossession, while their cruel assassinations have been one of the many costs of the battle against global predatory capitalism. From such a point of departure, the attempt to understand what role the racialization of originary people in Abya Yala might play, alongside the complex effects experienced, negotiated and resisted by communities inhabiting sacred ancestral territories, can be seen as a distraction introduced by well-intentioned academics like us.

But then, what allows a few to generate analysis and knowledge on land dispossession and about 'others' struggles against it? Indigenous scholar Linda Tuhiwai Smith (2012) has explained the role that 'academic research' has historically played in the subjugation of indigenous peoples. Outsider experts not only speak for those subjugated by capital but also extract their knowledges for their own personal and professional benefit. The lack of attention to this academic extractivism as part of the problem, of what needs to be transformed, has been a constant. In contrast, attention to academic extractivism allows us to ask who and when, why and where knowledge is generated, opening the possibility of a knowing that sits in bodies and territories and their local histories, in contrast to a disembodied, abstract knowledge with universalist pretentions (Mignolo 2003, 2010).

Meanwhile, when taking gender as a key starting point in the understanding of struggles for land, women's lives and hope, the complex effects in power relations within communities of people affected by trends in land dispossession become central in intellectual and policy oriented enquiries. In particular, changing gender power relations within the communities and of the communities with state and capital actors (i.e. from local government to security forces) are key in thinking about these social struggles.

From this starting point, the struggles pursued by artists/activists such as Makila 69 and *Obeja Negra*, their lyrics and aesthetics could be seen as not only reflecting their commitment to social justice for women, but also as expressing non-heteronormative ideals about what it means to be a female and an artist resisting the violent destruction of women's bodies in Mexico. However, what troubles us is that by taking gender as a starting point, we generate the invisibility of other ways of understanding, sensing and relating to what now is named 'nature', 'culture', 'body', 'women'. This operation is inevitably marked by coloniality and this is to what we turn next.

On decolonial thinking

Decolonial thinking has been recently contributed to an effort to understand social struggles in global politics (Icaza 2015b, 2010; Icaza and Vazquez 2013). Coloniality refers to:

> long-standing patterns of power that emerge in the context of colonialism, which redefine culture, labor, intersubjective relations, aspirations of the self, common sense, and knowledge production in ways that accredit the superiority of the colonizer. Surviving long after colonialism has been overthrown, coloniality permeates consciousness and social relations in contemporary life.
>
> (Mendoza 2016; 114)

Hence, coloniality is not colonialism, but a complex set of logics (e.g. dehumanization of the colonized) that is common to all forms of colonialism: Spanish, Dutch, British, settler, and non-settler (Lugonés 2010a, 2010b; Mignolo 2003, 2013; Quijano 2000; Vazquez 2014). Decolonial thinkers consider both modern and historical outcomes of colonialism.

> The colony is both the condition of possibility and the proving ground of the Western nation-state, and rights-bearing citizenship tethered to men of property. In other words, the freedom of the European and the colonial settler depends on the unfreedom of the colonized.
>
> (Mendoza 2016: 113)

Coloniality of power, a term originally coined by Peruvian sociologist Anibal Quijano, puts forward the idea that racialization was key for colonization (Quijano 2000). Moreover, this notion explains that 'the basic and universal social classification of the population of the planet in terms of the idea of "race" is introduced for the first time' with the conquest of the Americas (Lugonés 2010a: 371). From this perspective 'Western modernity' constitutes a dominant project of civilization that claimed universality for itself at the moment of the violent encounter with 'the Other' and the subsequent concealment of this violence. This seminal encounter goes back to 1492 when *Abya Yala* was conquered by the Spanish empire and the genocide of millions of indigenous peoples, their knowledge and ways of being in the world took place (Mignolo 2003; Quijano 2000). Therefore, hegemonic histories of modernity locating its beginning in the eighteenth century as a product of the Renaissance or the Industrial Revolution are not accepted but challenged (Icaza 2017, forthcoming).

Coloniality (of power, capitalism, gender, being, knowledge) as the underside of modernity constitutes an epistemic location from which reality is conceived. This is a dominant *locus of enunciation* from where one thinks/senses/relates with human and non-human 'others' in hierarchical and often violent forms (Mignolo 2003; Vazquez 2014). The starting point of early decolonial writings was the affirmation that 'there is no modernity without coloniality'. As co-constitutive binomial, modernity/coloniality was defined as a structure of management that operates by controlling the economy, authority (government, politics), knowledge and subjectivities, gender and sexuality (Mignolo 2013; Quijano 2000).

More recently, modernity/coloniality as the binomial around which gravitates decolonial thinking has as a departure point the acknowledgment of the limits and exteriority of modernity (Vazquez 2014: 173). This is to mark a contrast with the thinking centered in the Western philosophical tradition, in which modernity in its different facets (i.e. unfinished, plural and hybrid, postmodern, global, postcolonial and so on) is assumed as the totality of our reality.

> For decolonial thinking modernity (with its modernities) cannot claim to cover all the historical reality. There is an outside, something beyond modernity... ways of living and inhabiting the world that come from other geo-genealogies, non-Western and non-modern.
>
> (Vazquez 2014: 173)

The above means that, for example, the ancestral relation of Lenca people with the Balcarque river, of Sioux people with the Missouri River, of Tarahumara people with the forest of Coloradas de la Virgen, is of course touched by modernity/coloniality and can be explained through its frameworks of understanding as pure superstition or as cultural discourse that claims a place in the politics of representation. However, this relationship also transcends and exceeds these frameworks.

Vazquez (2017b) reminds us of notions of the communal and the ancestral self in originary people's philosophies in Abya Yala as belonging to other geo-genealogies. Meanwhile, the work of Mexican ethno-historian feminist Sylvia Marcos (2006) on Mesoamerican civilizations' eroticism and spirituality reveals the existence of fluid dualities 500 years before non-binary sexualities were 'theorized' by feminists. But most importantly, Marcos' notion of fluid dualities in relation to sexuality reveals an exteriority to Western feminist anti-essentialist approaches to sexuality, and with it a starting point to think about ways of being erotic *otherwise*. In both cases, the work ofVazquez and Marcos informed by Mesoamerican philosophies showcases a point of departure other than Western philosophical traditions.

Therefore, to be conscious about modernity's underside (coloniality) grants a decolonial perspective to one's own perspective which becomes a thinking, sensing and doing that is situated in the exteriority of 'modernity' (e.g. Dussel 2001; Vazquez 2014: 173). This exteriority to modernity, nonetheless, 'should not be thought as a pure outside, untouched by the modern: it refers to an outside that is precisely constituted as difference by hegemonic discourse' (Escobar 2007: 186).

Modernity/coloniality has recently been explained as two different historical movements or forms of relationship with reality which highlight their different loci of enunciation: the historical movement of modernity from which hegemony and privilege has named reality, for example, the name given to 'civilized and uncivilized people', and more recently 'developed and under-developed countries' and their peoples as always lacking or in need of experts and professionals of development (Escobar 1995). Meanwhile, the historical movement of coloniality is a moment in which the negation of realities and worlds *otherwise* (i.e. the Gualquarque river and the Missouri river in a sacred relationship) that go beyond the dominant modern geo-genealogy of modernity takes place, for example, when knowledge systems outside or in the margins of human rationality are denied validity (i.e. a sacred relationship) (Vazquez 2014; Icaza 2015).

The decolonial option is a third movement in which trajectories in knowledges and cosmovisions that have been actively produced as backward or 'sub-altern' by hegemonic forms of understanding resistance to land dispossession and destruction of women's bodies become politically visible (Santos et al. 2007). This has been explored in relation to *sumak kawsay* (the good living) and global trade politics in South America (Walsh 2011) and in relation to customary law, the monocultural perception of 'human rights' and global social dissent (Icaza 2015; Suarez-Krabbe 2016). Decoloniality has also been defined by Mexican-American teachers in the US as a 'political, epistemological and spiritual project' that deliberately attempts to disengage from' coloniality (Cervantes and Saldana 2015: 86).

Meanwhile, decolonial thinkers interested in a shift towards a knowing that sits in bodies and territories and their local histories have considered border thinking and border subjectivities as decolonial ways of knowing, sensing and relating to the world (Mignolo 2010; Mignolo and Tlostanova 2006). Nigerian poet Ijeoma Umebinyuo[26] helps us to express what border subjectivity might feel for some of us:

So, here you are,
Too foreign for home
Too foreign for here
Never enough for both

Border thinking as an *embodied consciousness* allows a thinking from concrete incarnated experiences of colonial difference and the wounds left on us (Lugonés 1992; Icaza and Vazquez 2016). As such, it is a possibility for a critical re-thinking of the geo and body politics of knowledge, the modern/colonial foundations of political economy analysis, and of gender (Mignolo and Tlostanova 2006; Grosfoguel 2007; Lugonés 2010a, 2010b).

Decolonial feminism and the coloniality of gender

So, what is decolonial feminism? To date, feminisms have been successful in introducing the category 'gender' not as a biological fact but as a historically constructed set of social relations of power. Once this idea is taken as a point of departure, feminist analyses informed, for example, by Marxism stress the role of capitalist primitive accumulation as having a prominent role in shaping social relations and laying ground for the centrality of the material in gender (e.g. Federici 2014).

On the other side of the intellectual spectrum informed by Western philosophy, post-structuralist feminist approaches have over the years conducted research on the inter-subjective cultural meanings of gender to explain the construction of hierarchies of 'value' (Peterson 2003). In this way, their emphasis on discourses on sexual difference, understood as meaning systems, are seen as imposing heteronormativity (e.g. Griffin 2007). Meanwhile, post-colonial feminist approaches by exploring the colonial imperative to control bodies and sexualities provide us with analyses on how this complex operation works for the benefit of empires (Peterson 2003).

In all these feminist approaches, gender might be differently conceptualized and articulated, but nonetheless is a common point of departure. Gender might be socially constructed hence highly contextual, or fluid and performative, entangled with race and/or class, sexuality and so on, but always a point of departure. This is precisely a stark difference with Maria Lugones' decolonial feminism for whom gender is not the point of departure but coloniality.

Elsewhere, we have argued that the work of feminist philosopher, popular educator and decolonial thinker Maria Lugonés constitutes a powerful perspective for a critical re-thinking of social resistance to neoliberalism in global politics (Icaza 2010; Icaza and Vazquez 2016; Icaza 2017, forthcoming). Lugonés' decolonial feminism acknowledges 'gender' as a key analytical category, but is engaged with its coloniality. This means an interest/focus on the underside of gender. This involves, among many other aspects, to acknowledge the complex and violent effects that 'gender' as a mainstream category in many feminisms has in the co-production of ways of being and sense of one's relation to different worlds (human and non-human) as non-existent together with the subsequent concealment of such operation (Icaza and Vazquez 2016).

Meanwhile, Lugonés' central concept of coloniality of gender allows us to understand the historical movement towards the imposition of a global Eurocentered capitalist heterosexual order that today is still in place (Lugonés 2007). From this perspective, class and race, but also gender are understood as social categories that were imposed in the colonial encounter through different technologies of dehumanization (Lugonés 2007). In other words, sexual difference was imposed as a system of sociability for some, but not to all bodies (Lugones 2007, 2010a, 2010b). This means accepting the separation of humans from non-humans as being central to colonization: while gender granted a civilized status to those men and women who inhabit the domain of the human, those who lack gender are subject to gross exploitation or outright genocide (Lugonés 2010a, 2010b). This is why for Lugonés 'the Other has no gender [because] only the civilized are men or women. Indigenous people of the Americas and enslaved Africans were classified as not human species – as animals, uncontrollably sexual and wild' (Lugonés 2010: 743). The coloniality of gender is then an invitation to consider 'gender' geo-historically as a colonial construct, and not a universal condition that existed before colonization (Icaza and Vazquez 2016).

> The colonizers used gender to break the will of indigenous men and women, imposing new hierarchies that were institutionalized with colonialism. The bodies of women became the terrain on which indigenous men negotiated survival under new colonial

> conditions ... systemic sexual violence the dark side of modern/colonial gender system still present to this day.
>
> (Mendoza 2015: 116)

Therefore, for us as decolonial feminists, the point of departure then is not gender, but classification and dehumanization of some but not all bodies. 'If I am right about the coloniality of gender in the distinction between the human and the non-human, sex has to stand alone...sex was made to stand alone in the characterization of the colonized' (Lugonés 2010b: 744). Gender is then a characteristic of humanity imposed as a sexual order differently according to racial lines (Lugonés 2010b).

As a consequence of this, gender as a universalism becomes visible from its coloniality, from what erases or disregards, for example, the sense of communal selves of originary women in Mesoamerica being classified as 'backward', or 'reproducing heteronormativity', a 'culturalist discourse' or 'identity politics'. It is from this point of departure that we can start to see the limitations and violence of the category gender. 'Coloniality of gender is useful precisely because it situates gender in relation to the genocidal logic of the coloniality of power (classification of people on the basis of race)' (Mendoza 2016: 118). In other words, this means that gender contributes to a genocidal logic that currently is expressed in violent forms of dehumanization as the racialization of certain bodies; the non-normative bodies, and that also is expressed in femicides, trafficking and the killing of indigenous people (Lugonés 2010a, 2010b; Mendoza 2016).

Conclusion: feminist decolonial un-learnings and re-learnings

As a final step, we ask ourselves what might happen to the way 'we' think about social struggles for land, women's lives and hope, using the coloniality of gender as our point of departure? To take coloniality of gender as our point of departure implies not to seek to classify what these struggles are or are not, but to learn how they challenge the logics of coloniality. An example of these logics, which has been pervasive and deeply ingrained in modern/colonial academia, is our impulse to classify and name what our human and non-humans others are or do (Santos et al. 2007; Vazquez 2014). For example, in global politics analyses dealing with transborder forms of resistance, the dominant impulse has been to explain whether these are sufficiently counter-hegemonic or revolutionary, or not, and to what extent these contribute to the destabilizing of dominant discourses and representations (i.e. Icaza 2010; Icaza and Vazquez 2016).

Once our task is no longer to contribute to the logic of 'classification' of what a social struggle is or is not, we might ask ourselves how we make sense of social struggles of peoples and their communities without (re)colonizing such experiences. Such a questioning has inspired the embodied thought and praxis that this chapter aims to explore. However, the implications of such questioning are more far-reaching than this short text, and bring forward the task of decolonisation of gender and the effects of this on feminist and non-feminist practices of knowledge within and outside the academia. An endeavor of such magnitude calls for a collective effort in the decolonizing of our methodologies (Smith 2012) and ways of working, which means not doing research *on behalf of* or *about* these struggles but allowing these resistances to challenge the 'us' we are aiming to enact. And this is happening in contexts of horror and extreme forms of violence that lead us to question ourselves how to advocate for life, as a political act: one that vindicates lives, bodies, and voices in communal projects (Silva Londoño 2017).

As an epistemic proposal, the coloniality of gender call us to be attentive to our points of departure and to position ourselves on the side of what has been produced as inexistent – women of color, indigenous women, trans women – by logics of dehumanization and classification of white, Western, bourgeois, Eurocentered frameworks of knowledge, including some feminisms (Lugonés 2010a, 2010b). This attention might lead us to be brave enough to raise questions about life: whose life are we talking about? Whose bodies are being made dispensable and disregarded by the logic of coloniality? How do we take part in this?

Coloniality of gender as a point of departure allows us to learn from the 500-year-old resistance of originary people in Abya Yala when addressing the above questions from our different collective life projects. It is from this point of departure that we have been able to perceive what the Zapatists in Mexico or Nasa people in Colombia (Suarez-Krabbe 2016) called the *Death Project* as what has been consuming land, women's lives and hope. But most importantly, in listening about the Death Project we have realized that we are all implicated at different levels and to different extents in such a project: through our patterns of consumption and socio-economic privilege that are sustained by trends of exploitation of certain bodies and destitution of lands and through our modern/colonial subjectivities and sublime forms of self-control that are sustained in the disdain of some forms of knowing and sensing (Suarez-Krabbe 2016; Vazquez 2017b).

To confront this means for some of us to embark on processes of un-learning privileges (epistemic, racial, socio-economic, etc.) and of re-learning from communal forms of resistance (Esteva et al. 2013) to the Death Project of coloniality. If gender is a social construct, hence not natural but imposed as a way of organizing/controlling societies, then who imposed it over whom, what existed before and what still remains? These are the questions that might inspire more questions to come.

Bibliography

Anzaldúa, Gloria (1987) *Borderlands/La Frontera: The New Mestiza*. Aunt Lute Books.

Barbosa da Costa, L., R.A. Icaza Garza, and A.M. Ocampo Talero, (2015). 'Knowledge about, knowledge with: dilemmas of researching lives, nature and genders otherwise.' In W. Harcourt and I.L. Nelson (eds.), *Practising Feminist Political Ecologies* (260–85). London: Zed Books.

Brown, Leslie and Susan Strega (ed.) (2005), *Research and Resistance. Critical, Indigenous, and Anti-Oppressive Approaches*. Canadian Scholars' Press/Women's Press, Canada.

CarteArte (2016) 'CarteArte: Abajo y a la Izquierda en Morado'. Unpublished document.

Cervantes, Marco Antonio and Liliana Patricia Saldana (2015) 'Hip hop and nueva canción as decolonial pedagogies of epistemic justice', *Decolonization: Indigeneity, Education & Society* Vol. 4, No. 1, 2015, 84–108.

Dinnerstein, Ana (2014) *The Politics of Autonomy in Latin America: The Art of Organising Hope*. Palgrave MacMillan.

Dussel, Enrique (2001) 'Eurocentrismo y modernidad (Introducción a las lecturas de Frankfurt), en Mignolo (comp.) *Capitalismo y Geopolítica del Conocimiento. El Eurocentrismo y la Filosofía de la Liberación en el de Bate Intelectual Contemporáneo*. Bs. Aires, Signos: 57–70.

Escobar, Arturo (1995). *Encountering Development: The Making and Unmaking of the Third World*. Princeton: Princeton University Press.

—— (2004) 'Beyond the Third World: imperial globality, global coloniality and anti-globalisation social movements', *Third World Quarterly*, Vol. 25, No. 1, 'After the Third World?' 207–30.

—— (2007) 'World and knowledges otherwise: the Latin American modernity/coloniality research program', in *Cultural Studies*, 21: 2, 179–210.

Esteva, Gustavo, Jerome Baschet, Vilma Almendra and Emmanuel Rozental (2013). 'Reberlarse desde el nosotros. Porque desde el abismo es imposible vivir sin luchar'. Queretaro, Mexico: En Cortito que es largo. Publicacion Autogestiva y sin patrón.

Federici, S. (2014) 'Caliban and the witch: women, the body and primitive accumulation'. *Autonomedia*: USA.

Griffin, Penny (2007) 'Neoliberalism and the World Bank: economic discourse and the (re)production of gendered identity(ies)', *Policy Futures*, Vol. 5 (2).

Grosfoguel, Ramon (2007) 'The epistemic decolonial turn: beyond political economy paradigms'. *Cultural Studies*, Vol. 21, no. 2–3, 211–23.

Icaza, Rosalba (2010) 'Global Europe, guilty! Contesting EU neo-liberal governance to Latin America', in *Third World Quarterly*, 3 (12), 123–39.

—— (2015a) 'Testimony of a pilgrimage: (un)learning and re-learning with the South'. In M. Barahona and Z. Arashiro (eds.), *Women in Academia Crossing North–South Borders: Gender, Race and Displacement.* Lanham, Maryland: Lexington Books, 1–26.

—— (2015b) 'The permanent people's tribunals and indigenous people's struggles in Mexico: between coloniality and epistemic justice?' *Palgrave Communications*, 1 (online). Open Access: http://www.palgrave-journals.com/articles/palcomms201520.

—— (2017 forthcoming) 'Decolonial feminism and global politics: border thinking and vulnerability as a knowing otherwise'. In: Marc Woons and Sebastian Weier (eds.), *Developing a Critical Epistemology of Global Politics*, E-International Relations.

Icaza, Rosalba and Rolando Vazquez (2013) 'Social struggles as epistemic struggles'. *Development and Change*, Vol. 43, 6, 683–704.

—— (2016) 'The coloniality of gender as a radical critique of developmentalism'. In W. Harcourt (ed.), *The Palgrave Handbook on Gender and Development: Critical Engagements in Feminist Theory and Practice* (62–73). Basingstoke, UK: Palgrave Macmillan.

—— (2017 forthcoming) 'Notes on decolonizing development', in Josef Estermann, ed. *Entwicklungsbegriff auf dem Prüfstand – Wie wir die Zukunft im Norden und Süden gestalten möchten*, Comundo: Lucerne, Switzerland.

Leyva Solano, Xochitl (2013) 'Y/osotras ¿Mi/nuestras Luchas Epistémicas Creativas?' In Obra Colegiada del SVI. México, Seminario Virtual Internacional (SVI). Unpublished document.

Leyva, Xochitl et al. (2015) 'Practicas otras de conocimiento(s). Entre Crisis, entre Guerras'. San Cristobal de las Casas, Chiapas, Mexico: Cooperativa Editorial Retos.

Lugonés, Maria (1992) 'On borderlands/La Frontera: an interpretative analysis', in *Hypatia*, Vol. 7, 4, 31–7.

—— (2007) 'Heterosexualism and the colonial modern gender system', *Hypatia*, Vol. 22, 1, Winter. Accessible at: https://muse.jhu.edu/article/206329.

—— (2010a) 'The coloniality of gender'. In Walter Mignolo and Arturo Escobar (eds.), *Globalization and the Decolonial Option.* London: Routledge, 367–90.

—— (2010b) 'Towards a decolonial feminism'. *Hypatia*, vol. 4, 742–59.

Marcos, Sylvia (2006) *Taken from the Lips: Gender and Eros in Mesoamerican Religions.* Leiden: Brill.

Mendoza, Breny (2016) 'Coloniality of gender and power: from postcoloniality to decoloniality'. In *The Oxford Handbook of Feminist Theory*, Lisa isch and Mary Hawkesworth, (eds.), Oxford: Oxford University Press, 100–21.

Mignolo, Walter (2013) 'Dewesternization, rewesternization and decoloniality: the racial distribution of capital and knowledge', public lecture given at the Centre for the Humanities, University of Utrecht, May 13th, 2013.

—— (2010) Delinking: 'The rethoric of modernity, the logic of coloniality and the grammar of decoloniality', in Walter Mignolo and Arturo Escobar, (eds.), *Globalization and the De-Colonial Option.* London: Routledge, 303–68.

—— (2003) *Historias Locales/Diseños Globales: Colonialidad, Conocimientos Subalternos y Pensamiento Fronterizo.* Madrid: Ediciones Akal.

Mignolo, Walter and Madina V. Tlostanova (2006) 'Theorising from the borders: shifting to geo and body politics of Knowledge', in *European Journal of Social Theory*, Vol. 9, 2, 205–21.

Peterson, Spike V. (2003) *A Critical Rewriting of Global Political Economy: Integrating Reproductive, Productive, and Virtual Economies.* London: Routledge/RIPE Studies in Global Political Economy.

Quijano, Anibal (2000) 'Coloniality of power, ethnocentrism, and Latin America', *Nepantla*, Vol. 1, 3, 533–80.

Santos, Boaventura, J.A. Nunes and M.P. Meneses (2007) 'Opening up the canon of knowledge and recognition of difference', in B. de Sousa Santos (ed.), *Another Knowledge is Possible: Beyond Northern Epistemologies.* London: Verso.

Silva Londoño and Diana Alejandra (2017) 'Somos las vivas de Juárez: hip-hop femenino en Ciudad Juárez'. *Revista Mexicana de Sociologia*, Vol. 79, 1.

Smith, Linda Tuhiwai (2012) *Decolonizing Methodologies: Research and Indigenous People.* Second edition. London: Zed Books.

Suarez-Krabbe, Julia (2016) *Race, Rights and Rebels. Alternatives to Human Rights and Development from the Global South*. London: Rowman and Littlefield.

Trejo Mendez, Paulina (2006) 'The guardians of the heart of the earth'. Unpublished manuscript.

Vazquez, Rolando (2017a forthcoming) 'Precedence, trans★, and the decolonial.' *Angelaki: Journal of Theoretical Humanities,* special issue 'Tranimacies: Intimate Links between Animal and Trans★ Studies.' 22.2 (June).

—— (2017b forthcoming) 'Precedence, earth and the anthropocene: decolonizing design', in *Design Philosophy Papers*, Special Number on Design for/by the Global South, edited by Tony Fry.

—— (2014) 'Colonialidad y Relacionalidad', in Maria Eugenia Borsani y Pablo Quintero (comp.) *Los Desafíos Decoloniales de Nuestros Días: Pensar en Colectivo*. Neuquen, Argentina: EDUCO/Universidad Nacional de Comahuep, 173–96.

Walsh, Catherine (2011) 'The (de)coloniality of knowledge, life and nature: the North America-Andean Free Trade Agreement, indigenous movements and regional alternatives', in Johan Shefner and Patricia Fernandez Kelly (eds.), *Globalization and Beyond: New Examinations of Global Power and its Alternatives.* Pennsylvania State University Press, 228–49.

Notes

1 The notion of place-based struggles considers place as 'a site of live cultures, economies and environments rather than nodes in a global and all-embracing capitalist system' (Escobar 2004, 223).

2 Abya Yala is the name given by originary people to the territory now known as the Americas before the colonial encounter in 1492.

3 The term otherwise is used here as 'another way of thinking, *un paradigm otro*" (Escobar 2007: 179).

4 The shift from doing research *about* to research *with* is not only a textual one, but an epistemic/political/ethical one. It entails being aware of extractivist forms of knowledge for the sake of one's interest, career or privileges (e.g. Smith 2012; Brown and Strega 2005). It also entails the embrace of the principles of collaborative/activist/engaged research and reflects on the dilemmas posed by these principles when conducting research (see: Barbosa, Icaza and Ocampo 2015; Leyva et al. 2015).

5 Yosotras literal translation from Spanish means me–us. It was developed by Mexican anthropologist Xochitl Leyva to think-write-sense from a *yosotras* (me–us) to emphasize the co-creation of learning and writing practices within collective endeavours and organizations (Leyva 2013).

6 This is the author's translation from Spanish to English. Source: https://www.youtube.com/watch?v=AR1kwx8b0ms

7 COPINH: the name in English can be translated as Civic Council of Popular and Indigenous Organizations of Honduras. COPINH official website description in English can be found at: http://copinhenglish.blogspot.nl/p/who-we-are.html

8 www.iss.nl

9 For example, Impunity Watch (http://www.impunitywatch.org/html/index.php) and the School of Americas Watch (http://www.soaw.org/)

10 See: https://www.fmo.nl/agua-zarca

11 See executive summary of COPINH analysis at: https://www.copinh.org/media/documents/2016/09/copinh-fmo-report-response-english.pdf

12 See: https://www.clacso.org/grupos_trabajo/detalle_gt.php?ficha=995&s=5&idioma= http://www.encuentroredtoschiapas.jkopkutik.org/index.php/es/

13 See: https://www.youtube.com/watch?v=yMybBm6RT5g

14 See: https://www.theguardian.com/world/2017/jan/18/isidro-baldenegro-lopez-killed-goldman-environmental-prize-mexico-berta-caceres

15 Paulina 'Sat' Trejo Mendez shares her unpublished text 'Guardians of the Heart of the Earth'. Paulina is a PhD researcher at ISS and can be contacted at: trejomendez@iss.nl

16 '*Traigo un infierno'*, Nidia Barajas, Lyrics: el Alas Blissett, music. Makila 69, Ni Diosa ni Diablo, ElectroAcusTrip Hope. Creative Commons Attribution License (reuse allowed). Published on May 10, 2014 on YouTube. Video available at: www.youtube.com/watch?v=zXWKRGOLW6M. Accessed on July 21, 2017.

17 '*Si*', Maquila 69 featured Obeja Negra, Concert at Paliacate, July 30, 2016, San Cristobal de las Casas, Chiapas, Nidia Barajas, Lyrics: el Alas Blissett, music. Makila 69, Ni Diosa ni Diablo, ElectroAcusTrip

Hope. Creative Commons Attribution License (reuse allowed). Published on YouTube on Aug 2, 2016. Video available at: www.youtube.com/watch?v=SqJjooysSuM. Accessed on July 21, 2017.

18 Nidia, and Batallones Femeninos lyrics inspire anti-patriarchal, anti-capitalist, anti-racist principles and life projects. Batallones Femeninos and Makila 69 do not participate in commercial musical circuits nor in state-funded artistic initiatives and all their songs are free to download from the internet.

19 COMPARTE has two meanings in Spanish: it literally translates as Sharing but it also means COMPA, the short way to speak about a companiero/companiera (partner) and ART, implying that the festival involved art that is committed in different ways and extents to Zapatista struggles for social justice. See: http://enlacezapatista.ezln.org.mx/2016/07/08/the-comparte-festival-and-solidarity/

20 CarteArte has two meanings in Spanish: the act of sending letters, which implies a dialogue, and the activity of writing letters as an Art. Meanwhile, abajo y a la izquierda, is the Zapatista's way of referring to a position that is crucial in institutionalization and elitisms of 'official' leftist organizations and political parties in Mexico. A sincere thanks to Obeja Negra for sharing this document.

21 On September 26 2014, the town of Ayotzinapa in the State of Guerrero, Mexico made world news headlines when 42 male students at the Raúl Isidro Burgos Rural School, some of them minors and indigenous, were kidnapped and, according to Mexico's attorney general's office, killed and burned by members of the drug cartel *Guerreros Unidos.*

22 According to the Mexican National Network of Female Defendants of Human Rights (RNDDHM), Obeja Negra's detention was part of the state's strategy to criminalize activists and social dissent. http://im-defensoras.org/2016/12/carta-publica-rnddhm-denuncia-y-condena-la-detencion-ilegal-de-susana-molina/

23 See: www.standingrock.org

24 Source: http://www.ecowatch.com/indigenous-women-dakota-access-pipeline-2069613663.html?utm_source=CR-TW&utm_medium=Social&utm_campaign=ClimateReality

25 Personal email exchange with a Water Defendant. November 3, 2011.

26 All Ijeoma Umebinyuo are available at: http://theijeoma.tumblr.com/

7
RACISM AND 'BLACKISM' ON A WORLD SCALE

Sabelo J. Ndlovu-Gatsheni

Introduction

The 'postcolonial' is yet to be born. This is because colonialism if it was ever buried, it was buried alive. This means that those conditions that were the ground for colonialism's making continue to constitute a stronghold on the so-called 'postcolonial' world. Therefore, at the very centre of contemporary 'postcolonial' politics are two opposing imperatives; namely, the long-standing imperial colonial logic of 'dismemberment' of the colonised people underpinned by the 'will to power' and the decolonial politics of 're-membering' predicated on the 'will to live' as leitmotif of liberation philosophy. At the centre of this global state of politics is a resilient but invented ontological split, which gave birth to blackness on a world scale on the one side and whitism on a world scale on the other side. The long-term consequences of this invented ontological split has come back to haunt the contemporary modern world with virulence, challenging the logics of an imagined postraciality that was said to have emerged with the election of Barack Obama in 2008 as the first black president of the United States of America (Goldberg 2015).

Racist configuration of the world is the fuel and justification for the 'will to power.' Racism is anti-human. It is opposed to the existence of a genuine 'postcolonial' world. Racism works against struggles aimed at pushing for the 'will to live' and setting afoot new and genuine postracial humanism. Invisible racism continues to underpin a modern world that is comfortable with production and reproduction of coloniality long after the dismantling of direct colonialism. Consequently, the invented ontological split created by racism continues to sustain whitism on a world scale in a hegemonic position and blackism on a world scale in a subaltern state of dehumanisation. The invention of blackism in particular threw all those who were designated as non-white into a problematic 'liminal state of being' characterised by a perpetual feeling of being incomplete or in never-ending state of 'becoming' human (Ndlovu-Gatsheni 2013a, 2013b). Philosophically speaking, liminal identity constitutes a long unending transitional state of being – located between dismemberment (separation/fragmentation/denial of humanity) and re-membering (reaggregation/wholeness/unity/re-gaining of denied humanity). Liminality is therefore a state of ontological limbo framed by what William E. B. Du Bois (1903) termed the 'colour line.'

In this chapter, 'postcolonial' politics is re-defined broadly as preoccupied with the dialectics of dismemberment and re-membering as part of a planetary Global South decolonial struggle aimed at transcending the invented ontological split. Blackism on a world scale is understood at two broad levels in this chapter. The first level is that of 'dismemberment,' that is, the very process of ontological splitting resulting in pushing of all those people designated as black out of the human family (Maldonado-Torres 2007; Ndlovu-Gatsheni 2015). This ontological splitting of humanity lies at the foundation of Euro–North American-centric modern world. Race worked and continues to work as an organising principle.

Historically speaking, the fossilisation, unfolding and expansion of Euro–North American-centric modernity took the form of what Valentin Y. Mudimbe (1994: xii) described as the submission of the world to European memory through exploration, surveying, 'discovering', mapping, conquest, colonisation, naming, dispossession, and claims of ownership of everything in the modern world. On the one end was invented a self-defining Cartesian subjectivity claimed and monopolised by emerging European male bourgeois. Mobilising and deploying unfounded claims of scientific racism, early European philosophers and scientists justified, naturalised and routinised the Cartesian self-definition European subjectivity. At the other end, was invented blackness as a sign and symbol of incomplete and disabled humanity (Ndlovu-Gatsheni 2013a, Ndlovu-Gatsheni 2013b).

Geographically speaking, blackism on a world scale emerged at a time that continents were being invented not only through cartography but also through the spreading of the exploitative and inhuman capitalist economic system across the human globe and the nascent unfolding of global colonial division of labour. How the invention of blackism on a world scale was inextricably intertwined with the unfolding of the capitalist economic system is articulated by C. L. R. James (1982), who argued that the eighteenth-century slave-society in San Domingo (later Haiti) connected Europe, Africa and the Americas, as the wealth generated through slavery in the Americas resulted in the rise of capitalist bourgeoisie in Europe as well as a new civilisation underpinned by capitalist world economy. The abolition of the slave trade was succeeded by the invention of indentured labour as a new form of enslavement, this time bringing Indians and Chinese into the nexus of evolving capitalist Euro–North American centric and modernist civilisation. Building on this background, it becomes clear that blackism on a world scale, materially speaking, articulates the global emergence not only of 'a modern racial division of labour' but also a new world social order underpinned by racial hierarchisation and social classification of human species in accordance with race as an organising principle (Lowe 2006: 192–3).

What is also clear is that from the very beginning of the construction of the modern Euro–North American-centric world system and its global orders, imperial technologies of dismemberment always locked horns with resistant forces of re-membering. Therefore, the concept of blackism on a world scale is used in a second sense in this chapter, which is that of 're-membering.' Re-membering encapsulate the consistent and complex contestations, resistances and struggles against dismemberment that took the format of not only initiatives aimed at counter-self-creation, self-definition, recovery and restoration of denied humanity, but also systematic self-re-writing of black people back into human history. These struggles and initiatives ranged from Garveyism, Ethiopianism, Negritude, African Personality, Pan-Africanism, African nationalism, African humanism, African socialism, Black Consciousness Movement, Harlem Renaissance to African Renaissance.

The two terms: 'dismemberment' and 're-membering' are borrowed from the leading African novelist and intellectual Ngũgĩ wa Thiong'o (2009a, 2009b). He understood 'dismemberment' as 'An act of absolute social engineering, the continent's dismemberment was simultaneously the foundation, fuel, and consequence of Europe's capitalist modernity' (Thiong'o 2009b: 5). For Thiong'o (2009b: 35) 're-membering' is 'the quest for wholeness, a quest that has underlain African struggles since the Atlantic slave trade.' Thus at the centre of 'dismemberment' and 're-membering' is the politics of modern humanism that are accurately articulated by Lisa Lowe (2006: 206) in these revealing words:

> In this sense modern humanism is a formalism that translates the world through an economy of affirmation and forgetting within a regime of desiring freedom. The affirmation of the desire for freedom is so inhabited by the forgetting of its conditions of possibility, that every narrative articulation of freedom is haunted by its burial, by violence of forgetting. What we know as 'race' or 'gender' are the traces of this modern humanist forgetting.

As part of contributing to the so-called 'postcolonial' politics, this chapter commences with a brief engagement with how decoloniality theory differs from postcolonial theory to enhance understanding of the core interventions of this chapter to the comprehension of the problematic 'postcolonial' on a world scale. It proceeds to trace the complex genealogies of politics of invention of non-beings and their symbolisation by blackism on a world scale, highlighting in the process the equally complex and brutal and specific technologies of dismemberment such as genocides, epistemicides, linguicides as well as infantilisation, inferiorisation, dehumanisation, feminisation, conquest, dispossession, peasantisation and proleterianisation. It proceeds to document the politics of 're-memberment' that are constitutive of what Nelson Maldonado-Torres (2008a) termed the 'Third Humanist Revolution.' This 'third humanist revolution' as noted by Maldonado-Torres (2008a: 115) 'has existed alongside the Renaissance and the Enlightenment, always pointing to their constitutive exclusions and aiming to provide a more consistent narrative of the affirmation of the value of the entire human species.' But, decolonially speaking, 'postcolonial' politics is not simply about inclusion of blackism into whitism. It is about transcending, innovation and creation of new humanism where both blackness and whiteness as binary state of being are dead.

Dismemberment and the colonial death project

Enrique Dussel (2011) identifies six interrelated discursive and instrumental technologies of dismemberment. These are Hellenocentrism, Westernisation, Eurocentrism, Secularism, Periodisation and Colonialism (Dussel 2011: xv–xviii). Hellenocentrism is not only an invented myth of foundation of Europe but is also the father and mother of what James Blaut (1993) termed 'the colonizer's model of the world.' Hellenocentrism's declaration is simply that 'All starts in Greece' according to Dussel (2011: xv). Hellenocentrism is a central leitmotif of usurpation if not outright beginning of what the anthropologist Jack Goody (1996) described as 'theft of history' by Europe. Hellenocentrism gave birth to Eurocentrism and Westernisation as part of consolidation of the projection of Europe as the centre of the world.

Taken together, Hellenocentrism, Eurocentrism and Westernisation amounted to what David Marriott (2012) termed 'inventions of existence,' with Europe playing the role of a 'discoverer' of other human species – almost claiming the place of the 'Creator'/God. Such a historian as John M. Headley has been so blinded intellectually by the unfounded claims of Hellenocentrism, Westernisation and Eurocentrism to the extent of writing a book revealingly entitled *The Europeanization of the World* (2008), which valorises Europe as the progenitor of values of humanism, democracy and human rights. The consequence of this enchantment by Hellenocentrism, Westernisation and Eurocentrism is clearly exemplified by Headley's unproblematic acceptance of the imperial and colonial 'paradigm of discovery' as laying the basis for common humanity rather than coloniality.

Headley's defence of Westernisation and its so-called unique gifts reveals obliviousness to coloniality – particularly how the unfolding of Euro–North American-centric modernity unleashed not only mercantilism, enslavement of black people and colonialism but also how it was predicated on racial hierarchisation of human species for purposes of exclusion of some from the common human race. Decolonially speaking, human rights are not derived from European Renaissance, natural law and Protestant Reformation. Rather, they are products of resistances and struggles of those who were written out of the human ecumene. The Haitian Revolution, rather than the Renaissance and Protestant Reformation or even the French and American Revolutions, constitutes a better base for human rights because at the centre of the struggle is those whose humanity was denied proclaiming their humanity to the world.

So to argue as Headley does, that no other human civilisation in human history has bequeathed so sustained a tradition of universalising aspirations as Western civilisation is to ignore two issues. The first is that modern Western civilisation has been predicated on a paradigm of difference that systematically denied humanity of non-European people across the human globe (Ndlovu-Gatsheni 2016). The second is that modern Western civilisation has been predicated on a paradigm of war and fetishised notion of politics as the 'will to power' rather that the 'will to live' (Dussel 2008). These dehumanising constitutive elements of the Western civilisation and its mode of spread across the world through conquest, enslavement, colonising, exploiting and racial hierarchising of human species led Aimé Césaire (2000: 31–2) to describe it as a decadent, sick and deceitful and indefensible civilisation.

The very act of stealing history and denying others humanity is the highest form of barbarism. Eurocentric secularism became predicated on imperial reason and what Lewis R. Gordon (1999) articulated as 'bad faith.' Bad faith is to endlessly proclaim tenets of humanity of all rhetorically while practically killing the humanity of others everywhere. Bad faith is claiming humanity for a particular race and denying all other human species humanity. Bad faith is a central leitmotif of Eurocentrism. Eurocentrism is founded on another problematic concept that Dussel (2011: xvi) terms 'periodisation' in which human history is cut into a linear chronology of 'Ancient, Middle and Modern Ages.' In this periodisation, all other civilisations are dismembered and pushed into the category 'Ancient' and Europe claims the category 'Modern.' This is part of the broader technology of dismemberment called 'theft of history' through 'colonisation of time itself.' Colonisation in its theoretical, intellectual, political, social, cultural and economic constitutive character has mutated and metamorphosed into global coloniality underpinned by invented asymmetrical power relations, hegemonic knowledge and particular articulations of human ontology based on race.

What has emerged from all this is the foundational dismemberment of black people taking the form of denial of their very humanity. Christopher Columbus's questioning of the natives of Latin America as to whether they had 'souls' – a discourse that sparked the historic Valladolid Debates (1550–1) in Latin American history, pitting Bartolome de Las Casas against Juan Gines De Sepulveda over the ontological question of the humanity of the natives – is illustrative of the genesis of the 'colonial death project' that eventually engulfed Asia, Africa and the rest of the world that experienced modern colonisation (Castro 2007). Julia Suarez-Krabbe (2016: 3) defined the 'death project' as reference 'to the exercise of violence in coloniality, which targets the actual processes of life and the conditions for existence: in short, polarity.'

At the centre of the death project is what Achille Mbembe (2003: 11) termed 'necropolitics' and Maldonado-Torres (2008b: 4) understood as the 'ethics of war.' These two levers of the 'death project' determined those who 'may live' from those 'who must die.' Outright denial or questioning of the humanity of non-European people was a deliberate technology to enable the 'death project' of coloniality. When it became increasingly difficult to deny outright the humanity of non-Europeans, there was a shift to the imperial/colonial logic of racial hierarchisation and social classification of human species in accordance with assumed and invented differential ontological densities. In this scheme of things, those people with black pigmentation were pushed to the lowest echelons of the invented pyramid of human species.

Ramon Grosfoguel (2013) building on the expansive work of the Argentinean philosopher, historian and theologian Enrique Dussel, identified what he termed the 'four genocides/epistemicides of the long sixteenth century' that are foundational to the politics of dismemberment and the modern colonial death project. These being the conquest of Al-Andalus, the enslavement of Africans in the Americas; the killing of millions of women accused of being witches through burning them alive in Europe; and the extermination of natives of Latin America (Grosfoguel 2013: 74). The conquest of Al-Andalus in 1492 targeted the Muslims and Jews and was propelled by the logic of 'purity of blood' as a form of dismemberment. At that time, colour was not yet used as a criteria of exclusion. Purity of blood and religion were the key technologies of dismemberment. Here lies the origination of the fundamentalist ideas of 'one identity, one political authority, and one religion' (Suárez-Krabbe 2016: 54).

The next group to experience dismemberment, this time taking the form of physical extermination (genocide/ethnocide) were the indigenous peoples of the Americas, Caribbean, Asia and Africa. This dismemberment began in 1492 with the arrival of Christopher Columbus in the Americas. The black people of Africa did not only experience genocides but more specifically enslavement, with what became known as the 'transatlantic slave trade' naturalising 'the colonial criteria of inferiority, linking racism and capitalism' (Suárez-Krabbe 2016: 56). Du Bois traces the genealogy of the terms 'Negro' and 'black' as racial inferiorising categories to the time of the enslavement of black people and their shipment as cargo across the Atlantic Ocean into the Americas. He argued that:

> The word 'Negro' was used for the first time in world history to tie colour to race and blackness to slavery and degradation. The white race was pictured as 'pure' and superior; and the black race as dirty, stupid, and inevitably inferior; the yellow race as sharing, in deception and cowardice, much of this colour inferiority. Mixture of races was considered the prime cause of degradation and failure of civilization.
>
> (Du Bois 1965: 20)

One of the ironies of the shifting European discourses of the human is that by the time they acknowledged the native people of America's humanity, even though maintaining that they were inferior; they did so at the expense of the black people of Africa who were then shipped from Africa into the Americas. Sylvia Wynter (2003: 297) correctly captured what the enslavement of black people created: 'a model for the invention of a by-nature difference between "natural masters" and "natural slaves."' When the abolition of the slave trade came, it was replaced by indentured labour, which brought Chinese and Indians into the nexus of a new form of enslavement. The historian Moon-Ho Jung (cited in Lowe 2006: 202) correctly observed that the indentured labour of Chinese and Indians constituted 'a transitional figure, mid-way between slavery and free labour, used both to define and to obscure the boundary between enslavement and freedom.'

With specific reference to Africa, Thiong'o (2009a: 5) argued that 'dismemberment' of Africa unfolded in two stages. The first stage is traceable to the enslavement of black people and their shipment as 'cargo' across the Atlantic into the Americas and the Caribbean. The second form of 'dismemberment' of Africa identified by Thiong'o took place at the Berlin Conference of 1884–5. This second level 'dismemberment' took the literal format of fragmenting and reconstitution of 'Africa into British, French, Portuguese, German, Belgian, and Spanish Africa' (Thiong'o 1999a: 5). Thiong'o further argues that those black people who were physically removed from the continent experienced 'an additional dismemberment' in the form of separation 'not only from his[/her] continent and his[/her] labour but also from his[/her] very sovereign being' (Thiong'o 1999a: 6).

For those who remained on the continent but who experienced the 'scramble' for and 'partition' of Africa, were also subjected to further 'dismemberment' in the form of dispossession of land: 'The land is taken away from its owner, and the owner is turned into a worker on the same land, thus losing control of his natural and human resources' (Thiong'o 2009a: 6). But it is in his celebrated book entitled *Decolonising the Mind* that Thiong'o provides a most revealing summary of how colonialism not invaded the African mental universe but consolidated dismemberment:

> But the biggest weapon wielded and actually daily unleashed by imperialism against that collective defiance is the cultural bomb. The effect of a cultural bomb is to annihilate a people's beliefs in their names, in their languages, in their environment, in their heritage of struggle, in their unity, in their capacities and ultimately in themselves. It makes them see their past as one wasteland of non-achievement and it makes them want to distance themselves from that wasteland. It makes them want to identify with that which is furthest removed from themselves; for instance, with other people's languages rather than their own. It makes them identify with that which is decadent and reactionary, all those forces which would stop their own springs of life. It even plants serious doubts about the moral rightness of struggle. Possibilities of triumph or victory are seen as remote, ridiculous dreams. The intended results are despair, despondency and a collective death-wish. Amidst this wasteland which it has created, imperialism presents itself as the cure and demands that the dependent sing hymns of praise with the constant refrain: 'Theft is holy'.
>
> (Thiong'o 1986: 3)

The school, the church and the university play an active role in the colonial and even 'postcolonial' process of 'dismemberment.' This is so because 'cultural subjugation was a necessary condition for economic and political mastery' (Thiong'o 1997: 9). Colonial education is identified by Thiong'o as the most important force for 'dismemberment' and alienation because it invades and takes control of the mental universe in order to produce a distorted consciousness among the colonised (Thiong'o 2012: 28). Highlighting the alienating consequences of the colonial process in general, Thiong'o posited that:

> The colonial process dislocates the traveller's mind from the place he or she already knows to a foreign starting point even with the body still remaining in his or her homeland. It is a continuous alienation from the base, a continuous process of looking at oneself from the outside of self or with the lenses of a stranger. One may end up identifying with the foreign base as the starting point toward self, that is from another self towards one-self, rather than the local being the starting point, from self to other selves.
>
> (Thiong'o 2012: 39)

In summary, one can identify six forms of 'dismemberment.' The first is what I have termed 'foundational dismemberment' involving the very questioning of the very humanity of black people as well as the very invention of blackness (Ndlovu-Gatsheni 2015; Ndlovu-Gatsheni and Zondi 2016: 5). The second is enslavement, which resulted not only in reduction of black

African people into a commodity but also in fragmentation of African personhood into continental and diaspora. The third is the scramble and partition of Africa that took place in Berlin resulting in the fragmentation of the continent not only into various colonies but also invented contending ethnicities enclosed within colonially crafted boundaries. The fourth is theft/usurpation/erasure/silencing of African history so as to deny its very existence and to establish the Hegelian notion of a people without history and a continent of darkness and emptiness. The fifth is production and reproduction of dismemberment by the 'postcolonial' state under the leadership of colonially produced black bourgeoisie who are trapped in neo-colonialism/coloniality. The final is continuation of reproduction of patriarchy so as to dismember women from power, knowledge and being itself.

At the centre of all these forms of 'dismemberment' are clear technologies of the colonial 'death project', namely genocides (physical killing of colonised peoples and black peoples in general even after the so-called end of enslavement and colonialism, e.g. the rising white police shooting of black Americans today); epistemicides (killing and appropriations of knowledges of the colonised); and linguicides (killing of languages and cultures of the colonised) (Ndlovu-Gatsheni 2015). Mbembe provides us with another technology of the colonial 'death project' known as 'conversion.' He argues that:

> [T]he act of conversion is also involved in the destruction of worlds. To convert the other is to incite him or her to give up what she or he believed. Theoretically, the passage from one belief system to another ought to entail the submission of the convert to the institution and the authority in charge of proclaiming the new belief. [...]. A test or ordeal of defamiliarization and disorientation, conversion distances the convert from family, relatives, language, customs, even from geographical environment and social contacts – that is, from various forms of inscription in a genealogy and an imaginary. This distancing is supposed to allow the neophyte to situate himself or herself within an absolutely different horizon – a horizon that paganism, in its horror, can no longer attain or recuperate.
>
> (Mbembe 2001: 228–9)

Since Euro–North American-centric modernity unfolded as a combination of enslavement, genocides, conquest, colonisation, epistemicides, conversions, and linguicides; the major challenge facing 'ex-colonised' people is how to 'recuperate.' This difficult and complex process of recuperation is called 're-membering.' The complexity is partly to do with the fact that 'blackness does not exist as such' but is constantly reproduced as a 'social link of subjection and a body of extraction' (Mbembe 2017: 18). Blackness is according to Mbembe (2017: 18) also 'the name of a wound' that is festering and is not healing. Blackness speaks to 'a mutilated humanity' and the present day stateless migrant and the Muslim suffering the brunt of Islamophobia – are clear representations of the black condition as a state of being on a world scale. Mbembe (2017: 6) articulated what he termed 'the becoming black of the world' as a 'new norm of existence and expanded to the entire planet.'

Re-membering/re-humanisation

Because dismemberment was implemented through usurpation and theft of history, re-membering of necessity involves recovery of history. Indeed without 'dismemberment' there would be no need for 're-membering.' Archie Mafeje (2011: 31–2) captured this point very well when he argued that 'we would not proclaim Africanity; if it had not been denied or degraded; and we would not insist on Afrocentrism, if it had not been for Eurocentric negations.' Following

Mafeje's logic, one can safely argue that such re-membering initiatives, ideologies and movements as Garveyism, Ethiopianism, Negritude, African Personality, African Socialism, African Humanism, African Renaissance and many others emerged within a context of realities of 'dismemberment' and existed as props developed by the dismembered across time to help in the 're-membering' process. For example, Leopold Sedar Senghor explained the circumstances that led him and Césaire to launch the Negritude Movement:

> In what circumstances did Aimé Césaire and I launch the word negritude between 1933 and 1935? At that time, along with several other black students we were plunged into panic-stricken despair. The horizon was blocked. No reform was in sight and the colonizers were justifying our political and economic dependence by the theory of the *tabula rasa* [...]. In order to establish an effective revolution, our revolution, we had first to divest ourselves of our borrowed attire – that of assimilation – and assert our being, that is to say our negritude.
>
> (Senghor quoted in Ba 1973: 12)

It is clear from Senghor's words that the Negritude Movement was part of the broader search for identity within a context of dismemberment. Therefore, Wole Soyinka's widely quoted critique of Negritude from the perspective that a tiger does not articulate its 'tigritude' was misplaced as it ignored the context of dislocation and alienation. Negritude is one of the earliest re-membering initiatives. Cheikh Thiam (2014) correctly understood Negritude as part of an early expression on 'Afri-centred' conception of the human that was consistently critical of Western universalisation of human that however excluded those with black pigmentation. Negritude was propelled by what Césaire termed the 'tormenting questions, who am I? Who are we? What are we in this world?' (Césaire quoted in Thiam 2014: 2). The best articulation of the logic behind re-membering initiatives came from the leading Nigerian novelist and intellectual Chinua Achebe:

> You have all heard of the African personality; of African democracy, of the African way to socialism, of negritude, and so on. They are all props we have fashioned at different times to help us get on our feet again. Once we are up we shall not need any of them anymore.
>
> (Achebe quoted in Moore-Gilbert 1997: 179)

Historically speaking, one can legitimately posit that the Haitian Revolution (1791–1804) occupies a place of pride at the centre of black people's 're-membering' struggles aimed at transcending the 'colonial' and can legitimately be credited for setting the stage for the 'post-colonial.' In the first place, it defied the Eurocentric, colonial and imperial and even Western philosophical idea of denial of the humanity of black people. It turned upside down the racist myths of a people who were naturally slaves and were said to be unable to develop any notions of fighting for freedom simply because they were not considered to be rational human beings. When enslaved blacks revolted on a large scale in the form of the Haitian Revolution, it became one of those events that were 'unthinkable' for those who had convinced themselves that black enslaved people were naturally slaves and had no capacity to rebel. The second significance of the Haitian Revolution is that it was not only part of the unfolding modern history of slavery, racism and colonisation but the revolt of the enslaved challenging 'the iron bonds of the philosophical milieu in which it was born' (Trouillot 1995: 74). On the paradigmatic importance of the Haitian Revolution in human history, Trouillot noted that:

> The Haitian Revolution did challenge the ontological and political assumptions of the most radical writers of the Enlightenment. *The events that shook up Saint-Domingue from*

> *1791 to 1804 constituted a sequence for which not even the extreme political left in France or in England had a conceptual frame of reference.*

They were 'unthinkable' facts in the framework of Western thought (Trouillot 1995: 82 emphasis in the original).

Any acceptance of the fact that enslaved black people were up in arms against the system of slavery amounted in Western thought to acknowledgement of the humanity of black people. Europeans in general and speculative plantation owners in particular were not prepared to concede that they were faced with a people claiming their denied humanity. This is why Trouillot (1995: 88) argued that:

> The Haitian Revolution was the ultimate test to the universalist pretensions of both the French and the American revolutions. And they both failed. *In 1791, there is no public debate on the record, in France, in England, or in the United States on the right of black slaves to achieve self-determination, and the right to do so by way of armed resistance* (emphasis is in the original).

The Haitian Revolution indeed posed a difficult philosophical and intellectual problem for Western thought: how to think about and conceptualise black revolution in a world in which black people were not considered to be rational and humans in the first place? This is why even 'international recognition of Haitian independence was even more difficult to gain than military victory over the forces of Napoleon' (Trouillot 1995: 95). The most important but silenced significance of the Haitian Revolution is that it led to the collapse of the entire system of slavery and constitute a major chapter in the history of 're-membering' of black people. It was truly an anti-systemic revolution that occupies a place of pride in the anti-systemic resistance marked by the definitive entry of the enslaved and colonised into modern history as human beings opposed to all forms of 'dismemberment.'

The Haitian Revolution forms an important base from which to articulate what Thiong'o (2009a) underscores as the importance of 're-membering visions.' What preceded the Haitian Revolution were numerous re-membering initiatives including Ethiopianism and Garveyism. Thiong'o (2009a: 35) noted that at the centre of Ethiopianism and Garveyism lay 'the quest for wholeness, a quest that has underlain African struggles since the Atlantic slave trade.' He elaborated:

> Though Ethiopianism and the like preceded these struggles, Garveyism and Pan-Africanism are the grandest secular visions for reconnecting the dismembered. Garveyism, with its Caribbean roots, unfolded on the terrain of America, but its vision – embodied in the title of Garvey's organization, the Universal Negro Improvement Association – was focused on the continent and its diaspora. 'Africa for Africans, those at home and abroad' was the chorus of Garvey's speeches and plans. The name was meant to 'embrace the purpose of all black humanity': to be free and equal members of the community of nations and peoples. For behind the rhetoric of blackness was also the universalist-humanist vision of using the Universal Negro Improvement Association to inspire African peoples 'with pride in self and with the determination of going ahead in the creation of those ideals that will lift them to the unprejudiced company of races and nations. There is no desire for hate or malice, but every wish to see all mankind linked into a common fraternity of progress and achievement that will wipe the odour of prejudice, and elevate the human race to the height of real godly love and satisfaction'.
>
> (Thiong'o 2009a: 36)

Since the time of the Haitian Revolution and Marcus Garvey, those human beings that have been designated as black have continued to fight for freedom and recovery of their denied humanity. Pan-Africanism emerged as one broad re-membering initiative dating back to the times of Martin, Delany, Edward Blyden and William Sylvester, who planned and hosted the first Pan-African Congress in 1900, to William E. B. Du Bois's series of Pan-Africanism, to Kwame Nkrumah's struggle to unify Africa into a Pan-African Nation. In the United States, black people launched the civil rights movements as part of re-membering initiatives. The re-membering initiatives have taken intellectual and political forms. At the centre of re-membering initiatives has germinated the African idea as opposed to the idea of Africa – 'the African idea as the quest for freedom on a Pan-African scale extended from the diaspora to the continent and back again' (Thiong'o 2009a: 75). The African idea captures the efforts of Africans defining themselves, as opposed to the idea of Africa invoked by Mudimbe (1994) that spoke to external definition of Africa and the Africans.

Scaling the question of blackism on a world scale to specific re-membering activities on the African continent, the period from the 1950s to the late 1960s were dominated by struggles for political decolonisation and the emergence of 'postcolonial' states. Re-membering took the form of:

> Country after country in Africa reclaimed their independence, announcing themselves as players on the modern stage – and, in the process, reshaping that stage, or at least the colour of it. Each country may have emerged as a nation-state, territorially speaking, but beneath their national colours all of their people saw themselves as Africans. The journey of the African idea, beginning in Haiti and championed by Pan-African congresses, reached its climax in the independence of Angola, Guinea Bissau, and Mozambique and the liberation of South Africa in the 1980s and 1990s.
>
> (Thiong'o 2009a: 77)

The major challenge to re-membering initiatives continues to be the active global imperial designs (Mignolo 2000; Ndlovu-Gatsheni 2013a, 2013b). As noted by Grosfoguel (2007) political decolonisation amounted to what he terms 'the most powerful myths of the twentieth century' because the withdrawal of direct colonial administrations and juridical apartheid did not 'amount to the decolonisation of the world.' Grosfoguel elaborated that:

> This led to the myth of a 'postcolonial' world. The heterogeneous and multiple global structures put in place over a period of 450 years did not evaporate with the juridical-political decolonization of the periphery over the past 50 years. We continue to live under the same 'colonial power matrix.' With juridical-political decolonization we moved from a period of 'global colonialism' to the current period of 'global coloniality'.
>
> (Grosfoguel 2007: 219)

The admission of the so-called newly 'independent states' into the United Nations, simply symbolised accommodation into an existing and un-decolonised Euro–North American-centric world system and un-deimperialised global order. This was not what re-membering entailed. The so-called newly 'independent states' occupied the lowest echelons in an asymmetrical world system. The New World Economic Order (NWO) that was demanded by those who fought against colonialism did not materialise. As noted by Nkrumah (1965), neo-colonialism as a form of coloniality emerged in which the so-called independent states became entrapped in global coloniality.

At the internal level, the African leaders who had spearheaded the anti-colonial struggle displayed deep-seated 'pitfalls of national consciousness', to borrow a term from Frantz Fanon (1968), and the consequences were what Basil Davidson (1992) terms the 'black man's burden' of just reproducing what was invented by colonialism and imposing it on Africa. To be more specific, they imposed the Westphalian template of nation-building on Africa. The consequences of this are well-captured by Liisa Laakso and Adebayo O. Olukoshi:

> [A]t the heart of the modern nation-state project was the idea, flawed from the outset, of tight correspondence between the nation and the state whereby each sovereign state was seen as a nation-state of people who shared common language or culture [...]. This notion of the nation-state stood in direct contradiction to the reality that most states were, in fact, multi-cultural, multi-lingual, and multi-religious and that not all ethnic groups (however defined) were sufficiently large or powerful or even willing to achieve a state of their own. [...]. At independence, most African governments set themselves the task of undertaking a vigorous process of nation-building with the aim of welding their multi-ethnic, multi-lingual, multi-cultural, and multi-religious countries into 'one-nation.' [...]. The nation-building project was, therefore, state-driven from the outset, often relying on a top-down approach that carried far-reaching centralising implications. In time, the unity project increasingly took the form of a unitary project which sometimes rested on a narrow ethnic base around which a system of patronage networks was then built linking other groups and their elites. Another key element of nation-building project was the assumption that the diversity of ethnic identities was inherently negative and obstructive and that it was a requirement of successful nation-building that different identities be eradicated, submerged under or subordinated to the identity of the group(s) that dominated state power.
>
> (Laakso and Olukoshi 1996: 11–13)

The nation-building project as a re-membering initiative failed. It failed partly because the leadership that took over the state at the end of direct colonialism were products of the same colonialism they claimed to be fighting against, and partly because of mimicry involving the imposition of external templates as policy on Africa. The African leaders were all entrapped in global coloniality. It was not nation-building only that failed. The pan-African project failed as territorial sovereignty was privileged over pan-African unity. The inherited economies collapsed by the beginning of the 1970s. Taking advantage of this desperate situation, agents of coloniality such as the World Bank (WB) and the International Monetary Fund (IMF) presented themselves as the cure for the African problems, and they literally took over the policy space as they prescribed Structural Adjustment Programmes (SAPs) (Cheru 2009).

The 1980s and 1990s became dominated by experimentation with what was imposed and prescribed by coloniality. Such re-membering initiatives as the *Revised Framework for Implementation of the New International Order in Africa* (1976), the *Lagos Plan of Action 1980–2000* (1980), the *Africa's Priority Programme for Economic Recovery, 1986–1990* (1986), the *African Alternative Framework to Structural Adjustment Programme for Socio-Economic Recovery and Transformation* (1989), the *African Charter for Popular Participation for Development* (1990), and the *United Nations New Agenda for Development of Africa in the 1990s* (1991) 'were opposed, undermined, and jettisoned by the Bretton Woods institutions and Africans were impeded from exercising the basic and fundamental right to make decisions about their future' (Adedeji 2002: 4). Adebayo Adedeji (2002) who worked as the Executive Secretary General of the United Nations Economic Commission for Africa (UNECA) described the colonial matrices of power at play in imposing exogenous ideas and policies on Africa in 1980s and 1990s as 'development merchant system' (DMS).

Africa entered the 2000s limping and still dismembered. The African Renaissance was formulated by President Thabo Mbeki of South Africa as another initiative aimed at re-membering Africa. This initiative witnessed the conversion of the Organisation of African Unity (OAU) formed in 1963 to the African Union; the adoption of the New Partnership for Africa's Development (NEPAD), the launch of the African Peer Review Mechanism (APRM) and the opening of the Pan-African Parliament (PAP) in South Africa (Ndlovu-Gatsheni 2013a). All these initiatives were premised on the pan-African agenda. The optimism which accompanied these initiatives was based on a false idea that the developed and industrialised Euro–North American states were now partners of Africa not dominators of the world. There was false hope that the invented predicament facing black people across the world would now be resolved through financing from the Global North. Coloniality was somehow forgotten, particularly the facts that the existing asymmetrical power relations between the Global South and the Global North were deliberately created and that the economic success of the Global North is still very dependent on the underdevelopment of the Global South. There was apparent forgetfulness of racism as an organising principle of the modern world.

Conclusion

If the 'Black slave, in his dark splendor' was the first invented 'racial subject,' then Mbembe (2017: 179) is correct to argue that the advent of capitalism invented blackism on a world scale. Today, the stateless and victimised 'migrant' and the hated 'Muslim' who is the target of Islamophobia are today's symbols of blackness on a world scale. As long as capitalism exists as an organiser of the world economy dependent on what Mbembe termed 'racial subsidies', then re-membering will continue to elude those who have been dismembered. The difficult y is compounded by the fact that 'for those who have been subjected to colonial domination, or for those whose share of humanity was stolen at a given moment in history, the recovery of that share often happens in part through the proclamation of difference' (Mbembe 2017: 183).

The reality is that the 'postcolonial' is yet to be born. Rather, what looms on the horizon is what Mbembe termed 'a Becoming Black of the World.' Historically speaking, this is clearly demonstrated by the fact that at the African continental level, almost sixty years after celebrations of 'political decolonisation,' the African Union, is still speaking of building and achieving a prosperous, united, self-defining and peaceful Africa in 2063. This is an admission that the long-standing racist, colonial, imperial, capitalist and patriarchal technologies of global power have not yet been broken, defeated and dismantled. They continue to actively foreclose any possibilities of a postracial world in which new humanism will be allowed to flourish.

Indeed new humanism can only emerge within a decolonised, de-patriarchised, de-imperialised, detribalised, de-corporatised and genuine democratised world. Such an envisaged postcolonial and postracial world has to be pluriversal in character rather than universal. This is the demand of such movements as Black Lives Matter in the United States, where coloniality continues to devalue lives of those designated as black, and the Rhodes Must Fall and Fees Must Fall Movements in South Africa – a country where not only intersections of race and racial capitalism continue to generate deep inequalities, exclusions and alienations, domination and oppressions, exploitation and dehumanisation, but also a country that Richard Pithouse (2016: 120) correctly characterised in these revealing words: 'South Africa is a colonial creation that has not fully escaped the iron cage in which it was born.' In short, 'postcolonial' politics remains fundamentally that of suffering and dehumanisation at the hands of predatory racial capitalism and anti-colonial but never decolonial local elites at the helm of the neo-colonised states of the Global South in the service of coloniality.

Bibliography

Adedeji, A. 2002. 'From Lagos plan of action to the new partnership for African development and from the Final Act of Lagos to the Constitutive Act: whither Africa?' (Unpublished Keynote Address for presentation at the African Forum for Envisioning Africa, Nairobi, Kenya, pp. 1–26).

Ba, S. W. 1973. *The Concept of Negritude in the Poetry of Leopold Sedar Senghor*. Princeton, NJ: Princeton University Press.

Bhabha, H. 1994. *The Location of Culture*. London: Routledge.

Blaut, J. M. 1993. *The Colonizer's Model of the World: Geographical Diffusion and Eurocentric History*. New York and London: The Guilford Press.

Broeck, S. and Junker, C. (eds.). 2014. *Postcoloniality–Decoloniality–Black Critique: Joints and Fissures*. Frankfurt and New York: Campus Verlag.

Castro, D. 2007. *Another Face of Empire: Bartolome de Las Casas, Indigenous Rights and Ecclesiastical Imperialism*. Durham and London, NC: Duke University Press.

Césaire, A. 2000. *Discourse on Colonialism*. Translated by Joan Pinkham. New York: Monthly Review Press.

Cheru, F. 2009. 'Development in Africa: the imperial project versus the national project and the need for policy space.' *Review of African Political Economy*, 120, pp. 275–8.

Comaroff, J. and Comaroff, J. L. 2012. *Theory from the South or, How Euro-America Is Evolving Towards Africa*. Boulder and London: Paradigm Publishers.

Davidson, B. 1992. *The Black Man's Burden*. London: James Currey.

Du Bois, W. E. B. 1903. *The Souls of Black Folk*. New York: Dover Publications, Inc.

——1965. *The World and Africa: An Inquiry into the Part Which Africa Has Played in World History*. New York: International Publishers.

——2001. *The Negro*. New York: Dover Publications.

Dussel, E. 2008. *Twenty Theses on Politics*. Translated by George Ciccariello-Maher. Durham and London: Duke University Press.

——2011. *Politics of Liberation: A Critical World History*. Translated by Thia Cooper. London: SCM Press.

Fanon, F. 1968. *The Wretched of the Earth*. London: Penguin.

Goldberg, D. T. 2015. *Are We All Postracial Yet? Debating Race*. Cambridge: Polity.

Goody, J. 1996. *The Theft of History*. Cambridge: Cambridge University Press.

Gordon, L. R. 1999. *Bad Faith and Anti-Black Racism*. New York: Humanity Books.

——2009. *Existentia Africana: Understanding Africana Existential Thought*. New York: Routledge.

Grosfoguel, R. 2007. 'The epistemic decolonial turn: beyond political-economy paradigms.' *Cultural Studies*, 21(2–3), (March), pp. 211–336.

——2013. 'The structure of knowledge in Westernised universities: epistemic racism/sexism and the four genocides/epistemicides of the long 16th century.' *Human Architecture: Journal of the Sociology of Self Knowledge*, XI(1), (Fall), pp. 73–90.

Headley, J. M. 2008. *The Europeanisation of the World: On the Origins of Human Rights and Democracy*. Princeton and Oxford: Princeton University Press.

Hoppers, C. O. and Richards, H. 2012. *Rethinking Thinking: Modernity's 'Other' and the Transformation of the University*. Pretoria: UNISA Press.

James, C. L. R. 1982. *The Black Jacobins: Toussaint L'Ouverture and the San Domingo Revolution*. New York: Vintage Press.

Laakso, L. and Olukoshi, A. O. 1996. 'The crisis of the post-colonial nation-state project in Africa.' In A. O. Olukoshi and L. Laakso (eds.), *Challenges to the Nation-State in Africa*. Uppsala: Nordic Africa Institute, pp. 7–39.

Lowe, L. 2006. 'The intimacies of four continents.' In A.L. Stoler (ed.), *Haunted by Empire: Geographies of Intimacy in North American History*. Durham and London: Duke University Press, pp. 191–211.

Mafeje, A. 2011. 'Africanity: a combative ontology.' In R. Devisch and F. B. Nyamnjoh (eds.), *The Postcolonial Turn: Re-Imagining Anthropology and Africa*. Bamenda and Leiden: Langaa and African Studies Centre, pp. 31–44.

Maldonado-Torres, N. 2007. 'On coloniality of being: contributions to the development of a concept.' *Cultural Studies*, 21(2–3), (March/May), pp. 240–2070.

——2008a. 'Lewis Gordon: philosopher of the human.' *CLR James Journal*, 14 (1), pp. 103–37.

——2008b. *Against War: Views from the Underside of Modernity*. Durham and London, NC: Duke University Press.

—— 2011. 'Thinking through the decolonial turn: post-continental interventions in theory, philosophy, and critique – an introduction.' *Transmodernity: Journal of Peripheral Cultural Production of Luso-Hispanic World*, 1(2), pp. 1–28.
Marriott, D. 2012. 'Inventions of existence: Sylvia Wynter, Frantz Fanon, sociogeny and the 'the damned.' *CR: The New Centennial Review*, 11 (3), pp. 45–90.
Mbembe, A. 2001. *On the Postcolony*. Berkeley, LA: University of California Press.
—— 2003. 'Necropolitics.' *Public Culture*, 15 (1), pp. 11–40.
—— 2006. 'What is postcolonial thinking?' http://www.eurozone.com/articles/2008-01-09-membe-en.html (Accesses 15 October 2016).
——2017. *Critique of Black Reason*. Durham and London: Duke University Press.
Mignolo, W. D. 2000. *Local Histories/Global Designs: Coloniality, Subaltern Knowledges, and Border Thinking*. Princeton, NJ: Princeton University Press.
—— 2014. 'Further thoughts on (de)coloniality.' In S. Broeck and C. Junker. (eds.), *Postcoloniality–Decoloniality–Black Critique: Joints and Fissures*. Frankfurt and New York: Campus Verlag, pp. 15–33.
Moore-Gilbert, B. 1997. *Postcolonial Theory: Contexts, Practices, Politics*. London: Verso.
Mudimbe, V.Y. 1994. *The Idea of Africa*. Bloomington and Indianapolis: Indiana University Press.
Ndlovu-Gatsheni, S. J. 2013a. *Empire, Global Coloniality and African Subjectivity*. Oxford and New York: Berghahn Books.
—— 2013b. *Coloniality of Power in Postcolonial Africa: Myths of Decolonisation*. Dakar: CODESRIA Books.
—— 2015. 'Decoloniality in Africa: a continuing search for a new world order.' *Australasian Review of African Studies*, 36 (2), December), pp. 22–50.
—— 2016. *The Decolonial Mandela: Peace, Justice and the Politics of Life*. Oxford and New York: Berghahn Books.
Ndlovu-Gatsheni, S. J. and Zondi, S. 2016. 'Introduction: the coloniality of knowledge: between troubled histories and uncertain futures.' In S. J. Ndlovu-Gatsheni and S. Zondi (eds), *Decolonising the University, Knowledge Systems and Disciplines in Africa*. Durham, NC: Carolina Academic Press, pp. 3–24.
—— 1997. *Writers in Politics: A Re-engagement with Issues of Literature and Society*. Oxford: James Currey.
—— 2009a. *Something Torn and New: An African Renaissance*. New York: Basic Civitas Books.
—— 2009b. *Re-membering Africa*. Nairobi: East African Educational Publishers Ltd.
—— 2012. *Globalectics: Theory and the Politics of Knowing*. New York: Columbia University Press.
Nkrumah, K. 1965. *Neo-Colonialism: The Last Stage of Imperialism*. London: PANAF.
Pithouse, R. 2016. 'Frantz Fanon: philosophy, praxis, and the occult zone.' *Journal of French and Francophone Philosophy*, XXIV (1), pp. 116–38.
Santos, B. de S. 2007. 'Beyond abyssal thinking: from global lines to ecologies of knowledge.' *Review*, XXX(1), pp. 45–89.
Suarez-Krabbe, J. 2016. *Race, Rights and Rebels: Alternatives to Human Rights and Development from the Global South*. London: Rowman & Littlefield International Ltd.
Thiam, C. 2014. *Return to the Kingdom of Childhood: Re-Envisioning the Legacy and Philosophical Relevance of Negritude*. Columbus: Ohio State University Press.
Thiong'o. 1986. *Decolonising the Mind: The Politics of Language in African Literature*. Oxford: James Currey.
Trouillot, M-R. 1995. *Silencing the Past: Power and the Production of History*. Boston: Beacon Press.
Wynter, S. 2003. 'Unsettling the coloniality of being/power/truth/freedom towards the human, after man, its overrepresentation – an argument.' *New Centennial Review*, 3 (3), pp. 257–337.

PART II

Popular postcolonial imaginaries

8
INTRODUCTION

The sustained Eurocentric conception of global politics has produced and popularised a set of political concepts and imaginaries, a political lexicon that does not only populate academic scholarship on global politics but also affects the layperson's common-sense of politics. Democracy, security, cooperation, terrorism, migration, development, human rights, civil society, minority rights: given the great diversity of human experience, ideally these issues would be open to hermeneutic contingency, given meaning according to time, place and purpose, and debated on as such. The postcolonial critique argues that in fact these issues carry Eurocentric dispositions that have fixed their conceptualisation within particular contexts and with particular normative connotations. In the process, the often-violent colonial contexts and purposes for which certain concepts have been deployed are obfuscated, especially when the concepts themselves speak of a putatively universalist normative agenda that few would want to question.

In this section, we confront the naturalisation of these Eurocentric imaginaries, especially as their everyday usage injects global politics with a lexicon of coloniality. Indeed, it is our provocation that colonial principles survive most strongly when their associated imaginaries are made common-sense for understanding and enacting contemporary global politics. This being the case, alternative understandings and enactments of global politics are then attenuated or even ignored. Hence, we have ordered this section to come after the reader's engagement with alternative points of departure into global politics so that the stakes at play in accepting the facticity of postcolonial imaginaries can be clearly recognised.

One further point is noteworthy here. The chapters in this section clearly indicate that the lexicon of global politics owes as much – if not more – to fields of inquiry that are not the provenance of political science. This is not only the case in terms of the sustained influence of cognate fields such as development studies, which shares an intimate genealogy with modernisation theory. There is also the heavy implication of anthropology – theoretical and applied – in the formation of these popular imaginaries, which stands as testimony to the deep imbrication of colonial science in the making of our understandings of global politics.

In the first chapter of this section, Nivi Manchanda takes on perhaps the most popularised and misused concept of colonial anthropology – the tribe. One would be hard pressed not to notice that this concept is almost exclusively deployed to depict non-western societies or to derogatively refer to antiquated communal ties. Manchanda not only points to the fact that the 'tribe' is profusely used in the study of Afghanistan, but also that it has developed into a shorthand to describe the whole of Afghan society. The chapter begins by engaging with the so-called 'founding father' of modern Afghan studies, Mountstuart Elphinstone (1779–1859), as well as the writings of later colonial 'adventurers' such as Campbell, Bellew and others. Manchanda demonstrates how this written material about the 'tribe' is mobilised for an increasing essentialisation of Afghan society in the twentieth century, culminating in the wars and interventions that followed 9/11. Manchanda argues that the deployment of the popular imaginary of the 'tribe' serves a particular colonial function of control and legitimating domination, as well as the perpetuation and reproduction of the colonial state of affairs into the present. Conceiving of Afghanistan as a 'tribal' land makes of it an 'intervenable object', that is, a place in which it is 'fair game' to intervene, invade and impose nation-building.

The Afghanistan war (2001–14) was, of course, the first instillation of the US-led Global War on Terror. While 'terror' and 'terrorism' are terms that have a long genealogy in global politics, 9/11 has pushed this particular imaginary firmly into the spotlight once again. Academics have responded to a putatively new kind of war on terror by developing the field of 'terrorism studies'. In Chapter 10, Swati Parashar takes issue with the premises of this field, especially in terms of its focus on the security of the modern nation-state. This focus – an implicitly normative one – identifies the threat of terror to emanate mostly from religious fundamentalists and extremists who are averse to embracing Western secular democracy and modernity. Parashar draws attention to the critique of such premises by 'critical terrorism studies', which addresses, amongst other issues, the prosecution of 'state terror'. Nonetheless, Parashar argues that critique of the terrorism imaginary is still missing an engagement with its postcolonial determinants. Parashar illuminates these determinants by turning to the history of India's Maoist violence since the 1968 Naxalbari Revolt. She demonstrates how violent resistance by citizens (not necessarily seeking a separate statehood) is looked at only from the terror lens that threatens the postcolonial ideal of the nation-state.

A key consequence of the Global War on Terror (and the various political ruptures that have followed in the wake of its prosecution such as the Arab Spring) has been the mass uprooting of peoples living in or nearby the many arenas of conflict. Presently the Mediterranean is one of the deadliest sea crossings in the world, and in much right-wing commentary the sea has come to mark a tragic frontier of civilisation. In Chapter 11, Emilio Distretti critically engages with this popular imaginary of the Mediterranean as a frontier of civilisation. Many of the deaths of migrants and refugees making the crossing have occurred between the Italian Island of Lampedusa and the northern coasts of Libya, a route mostly used by smugglers. The identity of most of the victims stays unknown, and most of the retrieved human remains have been buried anonymously in unmarked graves in local cemeteries in Sicily. Rather than imagining the Mediterranean as a frontier, Distretti re-envisages the sea as part of a colonial history of 'anonymisation'. In this respect, Distretti pays attention to Italy's colonial history, investigating anthropometric materials and human remains from early colonial practices which produced racial taxonomies up to the most contemporary technologies used for limiting migrant mobility in the Mediterranean.

Against the brute prosecution of war and its various anarchical effects, scholars of international relations have traditionally turned to the pacifying qualities of diplomacy and treaty making. Diplomacy – regardless of its success – is most often portrayed as a rational pursuit of the balancing of interests. But might this popular imaginary of diplomacy also be deserving of a postcolonial critique? In Chapter 12, Deep Datta-Ray explores the roots of this imaginary in the Christian mission to provide temporal unity and the transmission of this faith into a linear understanding of the expansion of civilisation into savage and barbarous lands. Datta-Ray argues that, in this imaginary, the diplomacy of postcolonial states must be lacking in all judgment and its diplomats must only follow faithfully the injunctions and practices of their already-civilised European and Western counterparts. Alternatively, Datta-Ray investigates the practices of Indian diplomacy in its own terms and unveils coherences at the levels of diplomat, the Ministry of External Affairs and the state. As commentators ponder the relative decline of influence exerted by the Global North, Datta-Ray turns our attention to the limitations of imagining diplomacy solely through the logics proclaimed by its political actors.

Datta-Ray's challenge to the popular imaginary of diplomacy resonates with a wider critique of Eurocentrism in terms of the assumption that normative values and practices are only ever created in the imperial centre and subsequently diffused through local actors across the world. A growing critique of such assumptions, as they pertain to human rights, is evident in scholars of international law. Key, in this regard, has been an engagement with women's rights and the question as to whether postcolonial critique requires a defence of 'local' cultural practices that are oppressive of women. In Chapter 13, Soumaya Mestiri addresses such issues and the popular imaginary of Arab feminism. In Tunisia, white and secular feminism was traditionally promoted by the postcolonial and anticlerical elite who worked, for decades, on implementing a state feminism, until the Revolution of 2010. Mestiri argues that the new pluralism and democracy ushered in by the Revolution enabled the emergence of Muslim feminism, a 'cultural' or a 'differentialist' response to the French variant. However, Mestiri argues that secular and Muslim feminisms are not so different. Both fail to imagine an alternative project, as both share the same will to essentialise the condition of women. Mestiri agitates for a more radical re-imagination of feminism in the contemporary Maghreb.

Since the end of the Second World War, Eurocentric narratives of the normative expansion of human rights into an un-civilised world have been tangibly connected to the project of 'international development'. The development imaginary constitutes one of the most powerful conceptions of global politics as a normative project rather than as an eternal game of pursuing powerful self-interests. In Chapter 14, Althea-Maria Rivas examines the ways in which international development reproduces and reinforces racialised and gendered subjectivities and how these identities are constructed through everyday encounters where development takes place. Working within a postcolonial feminist framework, Rivas explores these issues both historically and in contemporary times, and draws upon a collection of narratives from six women of colour that currently work in, or have worked in, the development industry. The narratives highlight the intersection of race and gender in the construction of identity and experiences of these subjects as they operate within transnational spaces as part of the international development architecture. Rivas's investigation demonstrates that the development imaginary is constitutively colonial, especially in terms of how it relies upon hierarchies of normative competency constructed along lines of race and gender.

In Chapter 15, Christine Klapeer turns our attention to recent shifts in the perceived relationship between human rights and development aid. While women's oppression has long been imagined as a clear rational for sustained political, social and economic intervention into the Global South, presently such rationales have shifted towards issues of sexuality, specifically, LGBTIQ rights. While these policy changes have been welcomed by various LGBTIQ advocates and organisations all over the world, a number of postcolonial, queer and race critical scholars and activists have also questioned the growing attention to LGBTIQ rights in the field of foreign policies, particularly by pointing to racialised undercurrents and colonial genealogies of those developments. Klapeer examines problematic implications of current LGBTIQ rights diplomacies and development frameworks, and elucidates the (im-)possibilities of queer agency and resistance within these configurations, particularly focusing on discussions and policy interventions related to the African context. Klapeer therefore calls attention to the way in which the popular imaginary of development has increasingly incorporated sexuality – alongside race and gender – as part of the calculus for deciding who is worthy of aid and who is needy of intervention.

9

THE IMPERIAL SOCIOLOGY OF THE 'TRIBE'

Nivi Manchanda

The 'tribe' has become a notion intimately connected to the study and understanding of the people of Afghanistan. We in the 'West' are routinely confronted with images, popular accounts and media reports that depict Afghans (and also oftentimes Libyans and Yemenis) as fundamentally 'tribal'. However, there appears to be no accepted definition of 'tribe'. The term has been largely forsaken by anthropologists or used in very specific instances to delineate particular modes of social organisation and political formation, and never to refer to an entire nation's social structure. Indeed, in his seminal text *The Notion of the Tribe*, prominent anthropologist Morton Fried analysed the birth of the concept and its subsequent application.[1] Fried problematised the common assumption that tribes both pre-date and stand in opposition to the state through a detailed examination of American Indian 'tribes', and then proceeded to deliver a swift blow to the understanding of tribes as groups that possess a shared ideology.[2] The crux of Fried's argument was that the prevalent notion of the tribe is profoundly misleading and has little expository value. He argued that as early as 1975 cultural anthropologists had long abandoned the idea of 'tribe' and so should all other anthropologists and political scientists.[3]

So why has this problematic concept of tribe become shorthand for 'Afghan society'? Where has it come from and what are the implications for our study of Afghanistan in particular but of 'other' places more generally? This chapter undertakes a genealogy or intellectual history of the tribe to address some of these questions. It posits that this notion of 'tribe' can not only be added to the indefinite number of terms that are (essentially) contested and contentious, but also to the list of terms that have been specifically 'mined' for dubious political purposes; most often in the service of empire. This notion has become so widely accepted that it could be blithely remarked in 2010 that '[t]o be a Taliban today means little more than to be a Pashtun tribesman who believes that his fundamental beliefs and customary way of life, including the right to bear arms or defend the tribal homeland and protect its women, are threatened by foreign invaders.'[4] Not only do statements such as these risk simplifying and over-determining the politics of the region but they also actively contribute to the production of Afghanistan as a certain type of 'intervenable object'; that is, how Afghanistan through recourse to a discourse of tribalism has become 'fair game' for intervention, invasion and nation-building.[5]

The chapter shows that what was initially a particular (ill-defined and fluid) construct with which the early East India Company administrators made sense of the alien people they were encountering, 'the tribes' soon became the irrefutable marker of Afghan society, polity and culture.

The 'tribe', as a generic signifier for most relations and identities in Afghanistan appears to have displaced the need for a deep theoretical engagement with the changing political and social configurations in the country. This concept, widely used in the British Empire and initially deployed to capture a specific network of relations at a given historical juncture, has become increasingly de-historicised, losing any conceptual purchase and clarity it may once have had. Even today it remains a dominant trope in the Western analysis and understanding of Afghanistan.

In the chapter, I map the way in which the term 'tribe' has been deployed in the Afghan context, further problematising the notion of the tribe and showing how a monolithic and unreflective body of work has become the norm in reference to Afghan social organisation. Specifically, the chapter follows the evolution of the concept from its use in the early nineteenth century by the influential Mountstuart Elphinstone, and on to his most significant successors writing in the late colonial period. It traces the conceptual hardening and reification of the term during the twentieth century and its particular deployment in the literature on Afghanistan in the twenty-first century, wherein the 'tribes' seem to have acquired a newfound importance. Drawing on scholarly literature on Afghanistan, the chapter argues that the 'tribe' has become a familiar and accessible idiom – another expedient shorthand – used to make sense of Afghanistan's diverse and complex social structure, but that in the process the term has veered far from the context in which it was originally conceived and utilised. The term has not only become more thoroughly racialised; it now amounts to a conceptually vapid word that has paradoxically been credited with ever more importance in 'understanding Afghanistan'. Through the articulation of this concept over time we can see old colonial logics reproduced. In this sense, the tribe belongs to a family of concepts used to make sense of the Other, to render him/her legible. What is exceptional is the manner in which this particular concept has become fossilised, and the complete erasure of the colonial legacy that has led to this fossilisation.

Mountstuart Elphinstone and the invention of Afghan 'tribes'

In more ways than one, Mountstuart Elphinstone (1779–1859) was the first real scholar of Afghanistan, and his work was to be so pivotal that it would not be a stretch to call him the 'founding father' of modern Afghan studies.[6] Elphinstone was appointed through family interest to the East India Company and arrived in India in 1796, where he learned Persian and developed a keen interest in Indian history and politics. In 1808 Elphinstone was appointed the first British envoy to the court of Kabul under Shah Shuja by Indian governor-general Lord Minto. Elphinstone's mission was the inceptive British diplomatic mission to what was to become Afghanistan.[7] Although Elphinstone failed to secure a friendly alliance with Shuja, who was deposed shortly thereafter, his mission generated a wealth of material which he turned into a detailed report. This text – Elphinstone's enormously influential *Account of the Kingdom of Caubul and its Dependencies*, was first published in 1815. It was his report of the first modern British contacts with the Afghan country, a voluminous exposé of all that he encountered and observed in the country. Elphinstone's work was vastly influential in other nineteenth century literature on Afghanistan. From Sir Alexander Burnes[8] to the last governor, Olaf Caroe, Elphinstone's thought has had a profound impact on the work of an entire legion of Anglophone Afghan specialists.[9] In Jon Anderson's words, Elphinstone's *Account* provided 'the most synoptic and in some ways integrated account of Afghanistan and Pakhtun society, history, geography, tribal organisation, government, and more briefly, economic life.'[10]

What then are the major hallmarks of Elphinstone's work? First, Elphinstone himself based his understanding of 'the tribe' on his own personal experience as a Scotsman. The notion of tribe for him was analogous to that of the Scottish notion of clan, and he argues that the Afghan kingdom was remarkably similar to ancient Scotland in its social and political organisation:

> the situation of the Afghaun country appears to me to bear a strong resemblance to that of Scotland in ancient times; the direct power of the King over the towns and the country immediately around; the precarious submission of the nearest clans, and the independence of the remote ones; the inordinate power and faction of the nobility most connected with the court; and the relations borne by all the great lords to the crown, resemble each other so closely in the two states that it will throw light on the character of the Douraunee government to keep the parallel in view.[11]

Elphinstone was trained in land survey practices and focused primarily on the village as a unit of analysis. This training and his Scottish background gave form to his 'republican' interpretation of Afghan social organisation. Indeed, Elphinstone's intellectual universe was delineated by the Scottish Enlightenment: 'both his conceptualisation and understanding of Afghan society were mediated by that universe';[12] and the first British contacts with Afghanistan were a largely Scottish enterprise.[13]

Scholars have since pointed out that Elphinstone was quite mistaken in the connections that he was making – the Scottish clan system was markedly different from the Afghan tribal code or *pashtunwali*.[14] As has now been verified by historians and ethnographers, the differences Elphinstone discerned between what he called 'republican' tribes and 'monarchial' ones were based on an amalgamation of hearsay evidence; his involvement not only with the Edinburgh Enlightenment but with 'a Scotland of clearances' in which clan leaders regularly exchanged kinship for proprietorship; and an affinity for the tribes who were resisting the Afghan monarchy at the court to which he was the company's envoy.[15] His noted preference for 'republican' tribes – those who preserved patrilineal institutions and deployed them to ensure their leaders were emasculated, or were entirely acephalous – to 'monarchial' ones – in which genealogical ties lose importance relative to the more exigent demands of territory and chieftainship – was thus an inescapably political one, combined with perceptive observation, first-hand acquaintance and a 'classicist formalism that has a decidedly eighteenth-century ring'.[16] Thus, Elphinstones's starting premise was misguided, as well as based strongly on personal (political) preference.

Second, his work is characterised by an uneasy tension between nuance and sophistication on the one hand and a lack of rigour on the other. As intimated above, and given that his embassy's reach extended only to Peshawar, much of what was written by Elphinstone was based on rumour and an 'intuitive understanding' of the 'Afghaun culture'. Large parts of the *Account* are anecdotal: in effect, the musings of one person's inescapably situated experience that has only retrospectively been granted the status of having laid the intellectual groundwork for the ways in which Afghanistan would be interpreted, known and acted upon for many years to come.[17] For instance, it was through his conversation with a local tribesman on the latter's opinion on strong government that Elphinstone based his generalisation about the tribes' innate vehemence towards central authority.[18] The Pathan allegedly said: '[w]e are content with discord, we are content with alarms, we are content with blood but we will never be content with a master', and in response, Elphinstone perfunctorily asserted that there is a 'reason to fear that the societies into which the nation is divided, possess within themselves a principle of revulsion and disunion, too strong to be overcome, except by such a force as, while it united the whole into one solid body, would crush and obliterate the features of every one of the parts.'[19]

In spite of such statements, Elphinstone had the political perspicacity to locate this innate republicanism in some of the particular tribes he encountered and in their equally particular history and geography – those on the southeast of Afghanistan, along the 'scientific frontier' bordering India. Elphinstone was circumspect about the scope of his work; his tome, nonetheless, has been understood as the key to apprehending all of Afghanistan.[20] Moreover, his arguments were more often than not explicitly contextualised and anchored to his particular frame of reference. For instance, he observed that the Pashtun tribes most directly under the rule of the Afghan king were likely to have a hierarchical structure and hereditary leaders.[21] The minutiae of his rich work have been largely lost in the two hundred years since.

Finally, Elphinstone's work developed the notion of 'clan' or 'tribe' in a manner which was vastly different to the ways in which it was picked up and comprehended by future generations of East India Company and colonial administrators. *Account* lacked any explicit racialisation of 'tribe' that sets apart Elphinstone's work from that of his successors. Writing at a time before the 'white man's burden' was fully formulated and internalised by European travellers in distant lands, Elphinstone's account of the Afghan tribes displayed a fresh intellectual curiosity, and drew upon notions of similarity (to an ancient Scottish past) as much as it did upon notions of difference.[22] Although stadial theory was central to the Scottish Enlightenment,[23] and Elphinstone's text is a 'conjectural history' built upon ideas of sociocultural evolution, the 'stagist' notion of progress that underpins his work is based more on the mode of production or subsistence of the society in question than on the colour of the skin of its inhabitants.[24] It was, therefore, relatively unburdened by the dramatic shift in British and French ideas about empire and civilisation that took place from the end of the eighteenth to the mid-nineteenth centuries, where theories of human progress became increasingly triumphalist, less nuanced and less accepting of cultural difference.[25]

Elphinstone's work still provides the touchstone for much of the academic work done on Afghanistan. Louis Dupree, the foremost scholar of Afghanistan of the Cold War era, said as recently as 1982 that anything articulated in reference to Afghan 'peoples' and 'cultures' since Elphinstone is merely a 'footnote'.[26] Benjamin Hopkins speaks of the 'Elphinstonian episteme' and credits him with the 'tribalization of Afghan society', by which he means that Elphinstone's writings gave 'the concept [of the tribe] an acceptable permanence which was taken up not only by subsequent imperial administrators, but also by later academics'.[27] In 2001, *Account* was described as 'arguably the best book on Afghanistan today';[28] in 2012, his understanding was said to be 'intact and unassailable'.[29] In sum, therefore, we are to have an entire intellectual edifice constructed upon one man's (mammoth) study of the land, people, flora and fauna he encountered in the early nineteenth century.[30] Our present-day understanding of Afghanistan as a predominantly tribal society can be traced back to him. Elphinstone's 'high spirited republics [...] ready to defend their country against a tyrant' have since become widely acknowledged as the basis of Afghan 'tribal culture'.[31] Meanwhile, the socio-political context of the Elphinstone's writing has been largely forgotten; in its stead we are presented with a timeless image of Afghanistan as a country of tribal *dis*order and corruption.

The colonial era and its stereotypes

In the period after Elphinstone, knowledge of the Afghans became increasingly instrumentalised to serve British interests in the region. Elphistone's scions were (semi-official) colonial administrators wrestling with the problem of how to work with and/or control the Afghan population. These contingencies resulted in the development of stereotypes which were each aligned with two opposing courses of action. The first aspect of the colonial literature was therefore the concomitant development of two different stereotypes, each with its attendant policy, as personified in the opinions and work of two high profile British authors: administrator Sir

George Campbell, and his contemporary, the political agent and prominent Afghan expert, Sir (Dr) Henry Walter Bellew. A second aspect of the colonial literature, seen particularly clearly in Campbell, was a further exacerbation of the trend, first developed in Elphinstone, to attribute differing and even contradictory character traits to different Afghan tribes. Below, I examine these different trends and their associated stereotypes.

Sir George Campbell (1824–92) was the lieutenant-governor of Bengal and a leading figure in the energetic 'Punjab School' of British Indian administrators who saw themselves as 'looking to the happiness and welfare of the masses'. He said of himself that he was 'in heart almost a Panjaubee' and was criticised for being of a 'revolutionary kind' by his British peers in India. He published widely on ethnological subjects.[32] Campbell acknowledged a significant intellectual debt to Elphinstone.[33] But he nonetheless warned of the dangers of applying Elphinstone's Scottish analogy to the Afghans, especially in a military context: 'I have heard Afghanistan compared to our Scotch Highlands. I have heard it said, "You put down those troublesome Highlanders and turned their hills into delightful recreation and shooting grounds – why should not you put down the Afghan tribes in the way?"'[34] Instead, Campbell argued that the problem of Afghanistan was of an entirely different scale: that the country was bigger, the mountains higher, and the people less acquiescent when faced with authority. Highly critical of the British equivocation with regard to taking a decision about Afghanistan, he believed that Britain 'must either go back or go forward'.[35] However, he asserted on more than one occasion that to 'go back' – that is, a 'close' policy – was the best option, in order to avoid a veritable hornet's nest:

> [m]y experience is, that if you have to deal with hornets only two courses are possible – one, not to stir them up or aggravate them, the other to smoke them out and take the nest. To stir them up, put your hand into the nest and keep it there is not what a wise man would do; yet that is what I am afraid of, if our present position is maintained.[36]

In keeping with his advocacy of a cautious policy towards the frontier, Campbell emphasised the 'ungovernable' nature of the Afghan tribes, borrowing selectively from sources available to him. For instance, he offered what has now become a banality:

> [W]e know by painful experience that the Afghans are a people of a totally different character – turbulent – bred from infancy to the use of arms – and with a passion for independence in which they are exceeded by no people in this world. This love of independence is such as to make them intolerant, not only of foreign rule, but almost of any national, tribal or family rule. They are a people among whom every man would be a law unto himself.[37]

'These traits', he wrote,

> are not of a passing kind; the Afghans are not to be tamed by subjection and peace; nothing induces them to surrender that love of independence which seems to be the *essence* of their nature [and the][...] *character* of the people occupying so difficult and inaccessible a country.[38]

Ironically enough, the conclusion he draws from these connate Afghan characteristics is that Afghans are inherently 'democratic' and that 'indigenous self-governing institutions' form the 'ancient law of the Afghan race'.[39] Campbell contended that the Afghans are not easily manipulated and are astute *political* actors rather than *religious* fanatics. He claimed of the Afghans that 'their religion sits very lightly on them. They are more governed by their own customary laws than by the Mahommedan Code, and seem just as ready to sell their swords to an unbeliever as to anyone else, even though it is to fight against believers.'[40]

The writings of Campbell can be instructively read in opposition to those of Henry Walter Bellew (1834–92). Bellew was an army medical officer born in Nusserabad, India. As a civil surgeon in Peshawar he became 'well-known among the Frontier peoples, whose language he spoke and with whose manners and feelings he was familiar.' Bellew allegedly belonged to 'the school of dedicated Anglo-Indian officials who helped to build up and consolidate the British Empire in India by acquiring a thorough knowledge of indigenous customs and modes of thought.' [41] H. W. Bellew was considered to be a leading expert on Afghanistan, his work extolled as some of the finest on the region.[42] His famous *Races of Afghanistan,* first published in 1880, has been called the first real ethnography of the country and he is said to have been intimately familiar with the language, culture and politics of Afghanistan at a time when Afghanistan was still the land of mystery for most British officials. Bellew himself wrote in 1867 that '[t]he officials with the British force who could claim any acquaintance with the Afghan languages were to be counted on the digits.'[43] To rectify this inadequacy, he went on to write the *Pushto Instructor*, which became the primary linguistic guide for British officers in Afghanistan. [44]

Bellew was more sanguine than Campbell about the prospect of taming the wild Afghan tribes, insisting that everything could be 'put right' by rectifying the frontier. He writes:

> But what does the reconstruction of the frontier imply? By reconstruction of the frontier is implied the subjection of the border tribes, and the embodiment of schemes for their employment. We must now no longer pursue the course we have hitherto followed. We must now change our policy entirely; we must now alter our tactics altogether. Instead of, as heretofore, settling our border quarrels by expeditions against the offending tribes, we must now, and for the future, take advantage of them to settle our border line. We must, in future, wage war with each offending tribe. We must annex their hills, disarm the people, and reduce the clans to subjection. We must tell them that they are bad neighbours, not fit to be free; that we have tried them for twenty years, and found them habitually abusing their independence; that they are no longer tolerable as neighbours; and that we now come to take their country under our rule, and to reduce them to subjection.[45]

Bellew was explicit in his desire not merely to hold the passes but to occupy and control the entire country. He therefore constructed the Afghans as unruly but not ungovernable, arguing that once civilised they would be grateful to be ruled by a legitimate authority. Bellew's conviction about the urgent need to bring the frontier under British rule and the relative ease with which this could be achieved was not all that set him apart from Campbell. He also ascribed prime importance to the religiosity of the Afghan tribes. Bellew said of the Pathans in *Races of Afghanistan*, that '[t]he only common bond of union among them is that of religion, and to this their devotion is of a fanatic kind, owing to the blindness of their ignorance and the general barbarism of their social condition.'[46]

The contrast between Campbell and Bellew illuminates Paul Titus' argument about how the British vacillated between two competing policies in Afghanistan – a 'close border' and a 'forward policy'. Those administrators who confronted tribal groups whilst enforcing the more antagonistic 'forward policy' developed a negative opinion of the tribes. In contrast, the administrators following the 'close border' policies granted the tribes more autonomy and had friendlier relations and therefore a better perception of them.[47] Both Bellew's and Campbell's texts are politically motivated statements, each championing a particular strategy to deal with the frontier peoples. One stressed the Afghan's love of independence and democracy as evidence in favour of a less ambitious policy towards the tribes, the other accentuated the urgent need to bring civilisation to an intractable but not unmanageable people.

As Anderson argues, the British were equally guided, and divided, by 'taken-for-granted, literally common-sense ideas' that defined the racialised worldviews of high Victorian imperialists.[48] Even as they arrived at opposing conclusions, Campbell and Bellew's descriptions of the Afghans draw upon a familiar stock of stereotypes mostly inherited from their Scottish predecessors and reworked to align with Victorian preoccupations with 'character' and 'human nature'.[49]

The literature on the Afghan tribes in the post-Elphinstone nineteenth-century era saw an increasing reification and stereotyping of the Baluch and the Pashtun as the two dominant tribes on the North-West Frontier. Elphistone was the first to draw a distinction between the Pakhtun (or 'Afghan') tribes and their Baluch compeers.[50]

Later nineteenth-century work further reified the Beluch/Pathan distinction and was quicker to attribute distinctions between these groups in terms of inherent character. Sir George Campbell himself notes: 'I may say of the Belooches generally, that it is well known to our political officers that they are in their character materially different from the Afghans, being much less rabidly independent [...] and more amenable to be dealt with through their chiefs.'[51] He also added 'and though not free from predatory habits, the Belooches are much more tractable and easy to manage than the Afghans. In fact, we have already both by treaty and by occupation complete access to the Belooch country.'[52]

The contrasting stereotypes of the Baluch and the Pashtun resulted from differences in the social organisation of the two peoples, differences which predated the colonial era but were crystallised and internalised thereafter.[53] The British preferred to interact with the Baluch over the Pathan, because the former were thought of as honourable men with a 'tribal organisation', and the latter were perceived as 'shrewd and unethical' – stereotypes usually associated with what Titus calls 'stranger communities and middlemen minorities'. [54] Homi Bhabha's understanding of the stereotype as a 'form of knowledge and identification that vacillates between what is always "in place", already known, and something that must be anxiously repeated', can be seen at work in the British interaction with, and management of, the Pashtun and Baluch people.[55]

Nevertheless, there was still a tendency at this time to account for differences between tribes and the political, economic and social backdrops against which these tribes operated. In an instructive passage on Pathan tribes, Campbell claimed that '[t]hey have the character of being avaricious, mercenary, treacherous, and predatory'. He, nonetheless goes on to explain in considerable detail how each of these characteristics developed – as a result of 'nature', 'necessity' and 'situation'.[56] Moreover, even as, over time and with enough anxious repetition, British assessments of the people of the frontier began to harden, on the whole, the tribes were not written off as beyond the pale of civilisation. The British in the colonial era still operated with the assumption that 'their [the tribes'] faults were caused by their institutions and could be alleviated by humanitarian reforms.'[57]

The twentieth century: the increasing essentialisation of the tribe

Campbell and Bellew represent a kind of intermediate step between a very fluid conception of tribes under Elphinstone and an essentialising discourse on the tribe that took hold in the twentieth century. In the late nineteenth and early twentieth century, these significant differences between how the British dealt with the Southern and the Northern tribes, and between the Pashtun and the Baluch, while periodically registered by nineteenth-century observers, gradually stopped playing a role in explaining why these tribes were so different from one another.[58] Over this period, the theme of cyclical or countervailing manifestations, one frequently analysed by anthropologists, gave way to more 'innatist' understandings of character.[59] The increasing fossilisation of the discourse by the early twentieth century is best exemplified in Thomas Holdich's, account of his twenty-year career as surveyor and military officer on India's western frontier.[60]

Holdich distinguishes between the Baluch and the Pathan on the basis of their way of fighting, their organisation and their 'character'. The Pashtuns are portrayed as entrepreneurial, religious and treacherous even towards their relatives, while the Baluch are portrayed as forthright, honest and especially concerned with honour. Holdich echoes the observations of many other colonial officials, missionaries and journalists before him, albeit in an ever more essentialist fashion, insisting that the Baluch is far easier to 'deal with' and to 'control' than the Pathan because of his 'tribal organisation, and his freedom from bigoted fanaticism or blind allegiance to his priest' On the other hand, '[t]he Pathan is a republican of the worst type. He is a law unto himself, and although he is very much under the influence of the Mullah, he has always an eye to business even in his most fanatical outbursts.'[61] While he keeps this distinction between the Baluch and the Pashtun alive, Holdich's statements lack the subtlety that characterised Elphinstone's work[62] and are even less nuanced than Campbell's. He continues: '[t]he Pathan will make use of any stratagem or subterfuge that suits his purpose. He will shoot his own relations just as soon as his enemy, possibly sooner – and he will shoot them from behind.'[63]

If Holdich represents the culmination of the shift in colonial writing by focusing on the inherent 'character' of the Afghan people with its 'natural' locus in tribalism, then Olaf Caroe's *The Pathans*, written in 1957, represents its apogee. The last British governor of the North-West Frontier, Caroe's exemplary text, part memoir, part cultural historiography, ostensibly covers the period from 550 BC to AD 1957 and claims to document the life and times of the Pashtun people through the ages. His descriptions are in no way wholly negative,[64] but they typify the uniformity with which the Afghans, and the Pathans in particular, came to be viewed by their British overlords. Caroe's extended metaphorical references to the tribesman as wild predatory creatures have been instrumental in carrying forward and cementing the allegorical construction of Afghanistan as the land of beasts that either need taming or are unsalvageable.[65] Not unsurprisingly, the period also saw the development of the political use of 'tribe' in the 'pacification' and control of the frontier and its population. The operationalisation of 'tribe' by frontier officers shows the ways in which colonial knowledge impacted on the genealogy of the term and its subsequent use.

After the three Anglo-Afghan wars and with the dismemberment of the British Empire in the mid-twentieth century, Afghanistan was either forgotten by the Western world or used as a laboratory for experiments with 'modernisation' theory.[66] From the time of the British withdrawal to the early twenty-first century, Afghanistan was largely considered a blip on the world map, except for the brief interlude that was the Soviet intervention. This second burst of Pashtuns onto the world scene as freedom fighters battling imperialism and communism in the guise of the Soviet Union was preserved in popular memory through films such as the 1988 blockbuster *Rambo III*. Although much of the fighting was conducted by non-Pashtuns in Afghanistan, including Tajiks, Uzbeks and Hazaras, and the Pashtuns who were most vocal in opposition to the occupation were in fact in Pakistan, the image of the Pathan as ferocious defender of the homeland endured.[67] Not only does this one-dimensional image mistakenly conflate all Afghan identity with Pathan identity,[68] it also completely bypasses an entire strand of non-violent Pashtun tradition embodied by the Khudai Khidmatgar, or the Red Shirts. As

Mukulika Banerjee explains: 'between 1930 and 1947 the Pathans, quite against their wild and martial reputation, had employed not rifles and guerrilla tactics but rather the method of disciplined non-violent civil disobedience against the British. Moreover, belying their reputation for feuding and factionalism, they had remained united for almost two decades.'[69]

The latter half of the twentieth century found the tribes placed, if momentarily, on a pedestal, lionised as holy warriors in the United States, in accordance with the logics of the Cold War. The Soviet Union was vilified, and Afghan 'freedom fighters' became romanticised in Anglophone public discourse. Thus, on what was celebrated as the second 'Afghanistan Observance Day', 21 March 1983, Ronald Reagan, then President of the United States, could remark '[T]o watch the courageous Afghan freedom fighters battle modern arsenals with simple hand-held weapons is an inspiration to those who love freedom. Their courage teaches us a great lesson – that there are things in this world worth defending.'[70] Whilst the collapse of the USSR saw Western interest in Afghanistan dissipate, the events of 11 September 2001 brought the country firmly back on the 'map'. This led to a resuscitation of the dualisms and stereotypes discussed above, albeit buttressed by a new grammar of difference and enunciated by different vocabularies of power.

'Tribal' Afghanistan post 9/11

In a post 9/11 world, writings that focused on the 'difficult' or obdurate nature of the Afghan 'tribes' came to be favoured because they helped to devise a cogent programme of action to deal with the abiding 'problem of the tribes'. In recent times, there has been a return to the literature on these 'tribes' and a focus on tribal structure as the key to understanding Afghanistan's social, political and economic organisation that borrows from but also caricatures the experience of the British administrators. In the twenty-first century, Afghanistan is still an object of inquiry about which definitive claims are made by political administrators without the benefit of a rigorous scholarly apparatus dedicated to the study of the country. The problem is compounded by the fact that the work of these modern-day administrators relies heavily on the scholarship of their predecessors, which was either written close to two centuries previously or is presented in the form of travelogues and personal memoirs.[71] This is especially the case with the literature on the tribes in Afghanistan, but eventually influences the way in which all aspects of the country are studied, contributing to what Hanifi, with regard to work on Afghanistan, has called the metaphorical black hole or Bermuda Triangle that 'absorbs much and produces little'.

So, as recently as 2009 the aforementioned Major Jim Gant could assert that: 'the central cultural fact about Afghanistan is that it is constituted of tribes. Not individuals, not Western-style citizens – but tribes and tribesmen', and that 'the answer to the problems that face the Afghan people, as well as other future threats to US security in the region, will be found in understanding [...] the tribal system of Afghanistan.'[72] The fact that these words have been written by a US Army Major who wields significant influence in the country is not incidental. Gant's paper, titled 'One tribe at a time: a strategy for success in Afghanistan', has been circulated widely within the US military, the Pentagon and Congress, and, in the words of the *Washington Post*, 'lays out a strategy focused on empowering Afghanistan's ancient tribal system'. Gant has been described as none other than the 'Lawrence of Afghanistan'.[73]

Gant had been assigned to deploy in Iraq, but with senior military and civilian leaders, including Defense Secretary Robert M. Gates, General Stanley McChrystal (the top US commander in Afghanistan at the time) and General David Petraeus (the head of the US Central Command) expressly endorsing Gant's views, he was instead sent back to Afghanistan in 2010 to 'work on tribal issues'.[74] McChrystal distributed a copy of 'One tribe at a time' to all the commanders in Afghanistan, while Petraeus similarly claimed 'Major Jim Gant's paper is very impressive – so impressive, in fact, that I shared it widely.'[75] We are told that '[i]ntellectually, Gant is driven by a belief that Special Forces soldiers should immerse themselves in the culture of foreign fighters', and that in Afghanistan's case this 'culture' is overwhelmingly, even exclusively, 'tribal'.[76]

In a similar vein, Dr Mike Martin, former British Army Officer, whose self-proclaimed intention was to write a 'non-Orientalist' account of the war in Helmand, can write without a trace of irony: '[t]he early adoption of Islam has generated an exceptional degree of interwovenness between religion and culture that is an enduring theme of Pushtun politics and identity. This feeds into the sense of superiority felt by the Pushtun, particularly those who inhabit the south-west of Afghanistan.'[77] Equally unselfconsciously, Thomas Johnson, director of the culture and conflict studies programme at the Naval Postgraduate School in Monterey, California, and 'a leading expert on the Pashtun tribal areas', declares: '[t]he problem of course is finding people willing to negotiate. Pashtuns generally will not negotiate when they sense they are winning. Hence, you see that the Taliban are "willing" to negotiate, but only after international forces leave the country.'[78] These ideas have been most notoriously mobilised in counter-insurgency doctrine, especially in shape of the US Department of Defense's Human Terrain System (HTS).

The HTS is a United States Army, Training and Doctrine Command (TRADOC) support program employing personnel from the social sciences – disciplines such as anthropology, sociology, political science, regional studies and linguistics – to provide military commanders and staff with a particular and instrumentalised understanding of the local population (i.e. the 'human terrain') in the regions in which they are deployed. The Human Terrain Teams have come under intense criticism because they have deployed anthropological knowledge for dubious (neocolonial) violent ends. This 'weaponisation of knowledge' is crucial to understanding how information and knowledge has been used to control, influence and depict certain peoples as 'alien others'. This has led to a highly racialised and unequal postcolonial world order that is reproduced through our subconscious biases and ingrained prejudices. The HTS, which resorts to 'social science's' purportedly 'authentic' claims about Afghan society and culture, reaffirms our biases and prejudices, and revivifies the colonial episteme in the War against Terror. The capstone of this colonial episteme is none other than the discourse of 'tribe' configured and utilised as a fixed marker of Afghan identity and society.

Even those critical of the US-led intervention and the foreign policies of most Western states on Afghanistan, use the 'tribe' as a crutch or as a way to describe Afghan socio-political organisation in its entirety. Professor Akbar Ahmed, hailed by the BBC as 'the world's leading authority on contemporary Islam',[79] is one singularly prolific example of the sympathetic (to Afghans) group. Much of his sizable oeuvre has been dedicated to the study of the population straddling the Afghanistan–Pakistan border and, as Political Agent of Waziristan in the 1970s, he has had the benefit of considerable first-hand experience in the region. He is a fervent proponent of interfaith dialogue and a dedicated critic of the US drone programme. However, despite all this, Ahmed nevertheless frames his strident denunciation of US foreign policy vis-à-vis Afghanistan as a defence of the long-standing tribal systems in place in the country.[80] Of the recent drone offensives he writes: '[f]or a Muslim tribesman, this manner of combat was not only dishonorable but also smacked of sacrilege. By appropriating the powers of God through the drone, in its capacity to see and not be seen and deliver death without warning, trial, or judgment, Americans were by definition blasphemous.'[81]

More problematically, Ahmed's writings consciously and perhaps subconsciously draw on the imperial literature which this article has catalogued. He cites British colonial administrators including H. W. Bellew and Olaf Caroe on multiple occasions to make a case for 'the Pathan's' fine appearance and indomitable spirit.[82] Ahmed makes a distinction between *nang* (honour) and *qalang* (rent, taxation) Pashtuns, which is strongly reminiscent of Elphinstone's report of hearsay to the effect that remoter tribes were more 'republican' than those he had encountered directly.[83] Moreover, Ahmed's reification of the Pakhtun into these two types is strangely based on an old

Pashtun proverb: 'Honor (*nang*) ate up the mountains, taxes (*qalang*) ate up the plains', which in his own words 'sums up the historical divide well.'[84] Ahmed maintains that *nang* Pashtuns represent tribal purity and that the *qalang* are examples of the inevitable corruption of an idyllic tribal lifestyle by the rapacious modern state.[85] He postulates:

> [M]ore than anything, the *nang* prize their freedom. Even under British rule, the authority's jurisdiction rarely exceeded more than 100 yards on either side of the main roads. In the most profound sense, the *nang* people were probably among the freest in the world.[86]

Ahmed also invokes the popular trope of Pashtun people as inherently revenge-seeking. On Ahmed's account, the United States is perceived as being on 'the warpath against Islam', and therefore has activated 'the code of revenge' against itself. As evidence adduced to support this argument, Ahmed makes recourse to an old Pashtun saying: 'I took revenge after 100 years, and I took it too soon.'[87] Ahmed, the great defender of the Pashtun people, ends up essentialising them by reducing them to tribal, unassuming, god-fearing, simple men. In romanticising the lifeways of these 'tribal' peoples, he merely reproduces the fissure between 'us' and 'them', even while claiming to be on 'their' side. As is the norm in traditional 'Orientalist' narratives, 'their' worlds are accessed through antiquated traditions and their thoughts deciphered through anachronistic proverbs and dubious aphorisms.[88]

There are other 'sympathisers' whose writing on Afghanistan is equally problematic. In his *Wars of Afghanistan*, historian Peter Tomsen describes Afghanistan's political community as a 'tribal incubator',[89] uncritically regurgitating the taxonomies that were devised to make Afghanistan's diverse social structures legible in the colonial era. In his diplomatic history, Tomsen posits that violence was 'an accepted and expected option in Afghan tribal politics when consensus was out of reach',[90] claims that the country is 'the land of the blood feud',[91] frequently invokes references to Afghanistan's 'tribal fighters' and goes as far as to argue that 'fragmented, tribal Afghanistan' exists in a 'Hobbesian state of chaos'.[92] Stephen Tanner, who similarly identifies the 'tribes' as the major obstacle to Afghan nationhood, argues:

> In the early 1800s the tribes fell away from the concept of Afghan nationhood that had once seemed so promising under Ahmad Shah Durrani. At the beginning of the nineteenth century, the people actually devolved back into local tribal government, blissfully unaware of how the rest of the world was evolving.'[93] For him the 'tribes' – and how to manage them – remains Afghanistan's 'enduring problem.

While the British ex-Foreign Secretary David Miliband can hardly be said to command the authority and expertise of the authors cited above, he nevertheless advances an argument strongly redolent of colonial scholarship in his 2010 article for *The New York Review of Books*. Citing lessons from Britain's experience in the nineteenth century and the Soviet Union's in the twentieth, he dwells on the vital importance of 'working with the tribes'.[94] As I have sought to show here, this has increasingly become the standard story: 'working with the tribes', 'engaging the tribes' and 'understanding tribal matters' are the *sine qua non* of a 'successful Afghan strategy'. To this end, the *New York Times* extolled the Afghan tribes as America's 'new hope', providing a number of 'infographics'. These include a self-proclaimed guide to 'understanding Afghanistan's tribes', boasting exhaustive knowledge but curiously focusing solely on the Pashtuns, which, according to the article itself, make up about 38 per cent of the Afghan population. *Pashtunwali*, 'a traditional unwritten code of conduct that has governed tribal affairs for thousands of years', is credited with '[u]nifying the whole structure of tribal authority'.[95]

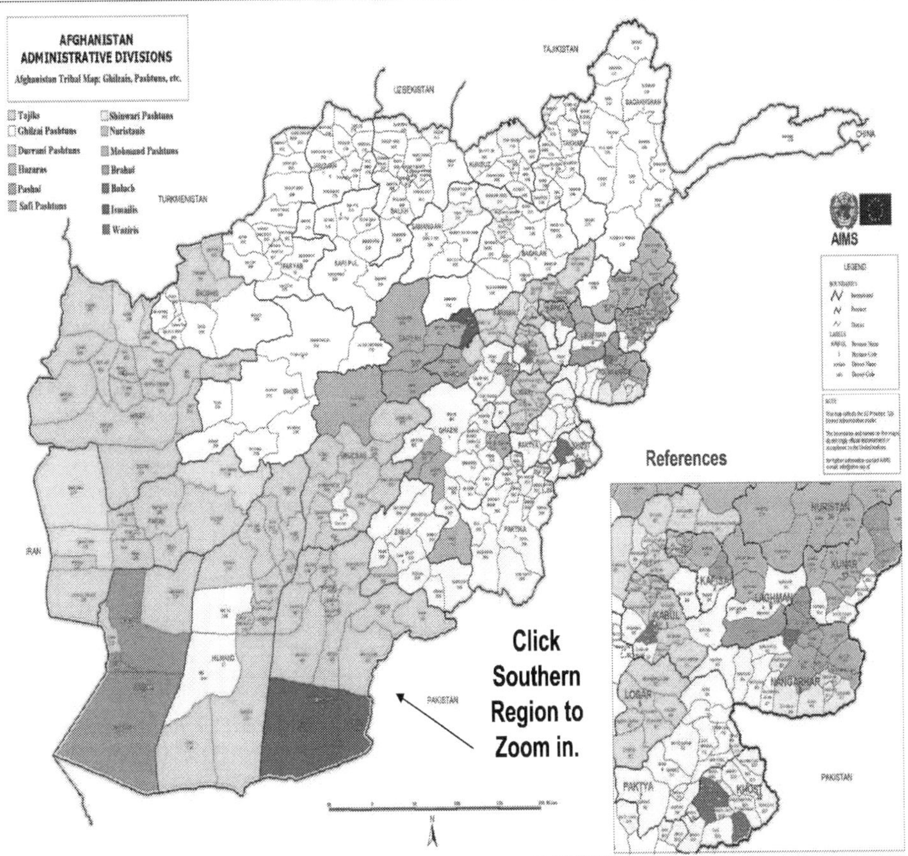

Figure 9.1 Afghan tribal map.

This has fed into visual representations of Afghanistan as a country divided along tribal or ethnic lines. 'Ethnic maps' now proliferate and figure prominently in country reports published by the World Bank and USAID, among other organisations. The US naval postgraduate school in its programme on 'culture and conflict studies' uses many of these maps to help its students navigate social difference in its courses on Afghanistan, one of which is reproduced (see Figure 9.1).[96] Not only are these maps unavoidably arbitrary political acts, but, in an effort to render Afghanistan legible, they also serve to reify difference on the basis of categories that may have little resonance on the ground.[97] And while (neo)colonial practices of cartography are problematic for a number of reasons, and continue to be the subject of critique,[98] given the lack of sustained surveys and data in Afghanistan, even the nominal accuracy of these 'tribal' maps is disputable.

Conclusion

Through the particular articulation of the concept of 'tribe', this paper has shown that the discourse on Afghanistan is both typical and atypical of imperial modes of thought. It is typical in that the notion of 'tribe', not unlike those of 'race', 'caste' and 'ethnicity' found elsewhere in the colonies, has been mined and instrumentalised in the service of empire.[99] Tracing the genealogy of 'tribe' in Afghanistan, however, also reveals the ways in which Afghanistan as a discursive regime is exceptional. It is distinctive in the way it has been carved out in accordance with the cadences of colonial interest in the region. Unlike colonial India, imperial interest in Afghanistan ebbed and flowed, alternating between long periods of apathy and short concentrated bouts of intense concern and involvement. As such, this has led to a sort of 'emergency episteme' of the Afghan tribe, a familiar convocation of alterity at the behest of empire, but without the intellectual, economic and emotional energies that were expended in the construction of other idioms of difference such as race, caste and ethno-nationalism. Moreover, the colonial genealogy of this concept has been largely forgotten, not least because of the manner in which Afghanistan has been studied.

There has been a distinct paucity of resources devoted to studying the region, a lack of any profound academic engagement with the country, and most importantly, a lack of any consistent and sustained interest in the area. Even at the height of imperial involvement in Afghanistan, there were no monographic studies of tribes, few or no income and production surveys, and no colonial ethnography on religious leadership and other networks of the kind that were vital in mobilising armed resistance to the British.[100] Consequently, the imperative to churn out massive amounts of 'knowledge' and be acquainted with the 'facts' about Afghanistan – in a compressed period of time, for immediate political purposes – has become an enduring feature of 'scholarship' on Afghanistan. As Anderson has indicated, nearly all the colonial ethnography that emerged on the Northwest Frontier of British India, and Afghanistan more generally, was gathered, sifted and culled for political intelligence. In his own words: 'in direct service of imperial design, it [the ethnography of the frontier] was a genuine handmaiden of imperialism by comparison to the camp follower of anthropological ethnography'.[101] Anderson characterises the change in the literature from a state of multiplicity to one of conformity.[102]

Over time and with repetition, any nuanced appreciations of social relations, intuitive and incomplete as they may have been, gave way to a generalised and abstracted understanding of tribal or Afghan 'character' that in effect was 'a list of traits that only restated the problem'.[103] The abstracted conception of Afghan character came to figure prominently in the official colonial institutional memory, and by the time the British Empire collapsed, all understanding of Afghanistan came to rely heavily on this trope, as a 'common-sense' crutch for the necessary articulation of difference.[104] As Bhabha reminds us, the processes of subjectification that these tropes and stereotypes unleash always affect both colonial subjects – coloniser and colonised.[105] But while the practices of citation, reusing and rehashing old material, have led to a less subtle, more slipshod understanding of Afghan social relations, they have also unwittingly compounded a problem that has plagued the study of Afghanistan from the outset: that of limited data and weak scholarly engagement. We now inhabit an intellectual world in which 'Afghan tribes' are studied and acted upon unproblematically – paying no heed to the fact that both those terms have contestable and profoundly complex histories.[106] The Human Terrain Teams and counterinsurgency doctrines are contemporary manifestations of colonial knowledge and current practices in the arsenal of (neo)imperial power that have reinvigorated these forms of knowledge.

It should thus come as no surprise that these hastily applied and decontextualised notions of 'tribal character' have continued to obscure more than they reveal. Based on an outdated paradigm and utilised to signal difference, distance and alterity they dangerously masquerade as a guide to practice. Against the politically charged backdrop of war and an invasion in which foreign forces are committed to an avid restructuring of the Afghan polity, albeit in a way that is sensitive to prevailing cultural mores and customs, any new account of Afghanistan that overlooks the shaky architectures of colonial power/knowledge – built around personal memoirs, travelogues and hearsay – that have given shape to the claims about Afghan 'tribalism', constitutes a lapse that is bound to have a mighty material fallout. Whilst all traditions are 'invented' intellectual projects buttressed by political (imperial) power, the increasing racialisation of 'tribe' has enacted problematic 'actionable' policies, rendering Afghanistan a country of backward peoples and thus an object of intervention.

The implications of this problematic historical and contemporary understanding of the 'tribe' in Afghanistan extend much beyond the country itself. The 'tribe' as a concept emerged as a legacy of colonial knowledge but now functions as part of the wider grammar of imperial power. Contemporary practices of (neo)imperial power have reinvigorated these forms of knowledge, something we can see in the bolstered and racialised dynamics of the 'far right' in Western Europe and North America and in counter-insurgency doctrine and interventions in the Middle East. In order to overcome these provincial colonial knowledges and the violence they perforce engender in the Global South, our task as academics is to broaden and deepen our own understanding of what constitutes legitimate knowledge and authority and to not fall foul of the multiple and layered prejudices, violences and erasures that structure the lives on the 'wrong' side of the colonial equation. Decolonising the concept of 'tribe' and its irresponsible application in Afghanistan would be a good place to start.

Notes

1 Morton H. Fried, *The Notion of the Tribe* (Menlo Park, CA: Cummings Publishing Company, 1975), 10–12.
2 Ibid, 11, 47, 74. See also Elizabeth Colston, 'Political Organizations in Tribal Societies: A Cross-Cultural Comparison', *American Indian Quarterly* 10, no. 1 (1986), 5.
3 Ibid, 11.
4 Scott Atran, *Talking to the Enemy: Violent Extremism, Sacred Values and What It Means to Be Human* (London: Penguin, 2011), 262.
5 This 'history of the present' is opposed to what George Lawson has called 'scripture' or 'the mining of the past in order to support suppositions about the present', which is both how the literature on tribes in Afghanistan is used and is the standard practice in the discipline of International Relations. See George Lawson, 'The Promise of Historical Sociology in International Relations', *International Studies Review* 8, no. 3 (2006), 404.
6 This patriarchal designation is rather fitting given the subsequent paternalistic nature of the study of Afghanistan.
7 C. A. Bayly, 'Elphinstone, Mountstuart (1779–1859)', *Oxford Dictionary of National Biography* (Oxford: Oxford University Press, 2004); online ed., Jan 2008 [http://www.oxforddnb.com/view/article/8752, accessed 4 Feb 2014]. Sir Thomas Edward Colebrook's *The Life of Honourable Mountstuart Elphinstone*, 2 vols. (Cambridge: Cambridge University Press, 2011), written in 1884, provides a detailed introduction to Elphinstone's life and work, commemorating his role in British pre-colonial history. For a summary of his mission and its significance, see Bakshi, 'Elphinstone's Mission to Cabul'.
8 Burnes (1805–41) was an explorer and political officer in India who also travelled extensively in Afghanistan. Burnes's memoir *Cabool: Being a Personal Narrative of a Journey to, and Residence in that City in the Years 1836–38*, which was published posthumously in 1842, draws heavily on Elphinstone's work and continues to be cited in contemporary work on Afghanistan. On Burnes's enduring impact on Afghanistan studies, see Peter Hopkirk, *The Great Game: The Struggle for Empire in Central Asia*.
9 See for example Colebrook, *The Life of Honourable Mountstuart Elphinstone*; Olaf Caroe, *The Pathans*.
10 Jon W. Anderson, 'Poetics and Politics in Ethnographic Texts: A View from the Colonial Ethnography of Afghanistan', in Richard Harvey Brown, (ed.), *Writing the Social Text: Poetics and Politics in Social Science Discourse* (New York: Aldine Transaction, 1992), 96.
11 Elphinstone, *An Account of the Kingdom of Caubul*, 173–4.
12 Ibid, 14. See also Jane Rendall, 'Scottish Orientalism: From Robertson to James Mill', *The Historical Journal* 25, no. 1 (1982).
13 Anderson, 'Poetics and Politics in Ethnographic Texts', 102.
14 Hopkins, *The Making of Modern Afghanistan*; Rendall, 'Scottish Orientalism: From Robertson to James Mill'; and Martha McLaren, *British India and British Scotland, 1780–1830: Career Building, Empire Building, and a Scottish School of Thought on Indian Governance* (Akron, OH: University of Akron Press, 2001).

15 Ibid, 102; cf. S. R. Bakshi, 'Elphinstone's Mission to Cabul', *Journal of Indian History* 15 (1967).

16 Anderson says that such sensibilities 'virtually disappeared by the end of the nineteenth century': see Anderson, 'Poetics and Politics in Ethnographic Texts', 103.

17 In Hopkins's words: 'For its European audience, including company officials it [the *Account*] set the bounds of what could be known about the Afghans' *(The Making of Modern Afghanistan*, 13).

18 Stephen Tanner has called this propensity for warfare Afghanistan's 'enduring problem': see his *Afghanistan: A Military History from Alexander the Great to the Taliban. The Examiner*, in an article titled 'U.S. Should Focus on Afghanistan's Tribal Balance', also cites the Elphinstone quote, advocating a 'focus on developing the Afghan tribal balance and let[ting] history run its course' [http://www.examiner.com/article/u-s-should-focus-on-afghan-tribal-balance, last accessed 9/02/2014].

19 Cited in the article above.

20 Hopkins argues: '[b]asing their larger generalizations about Afghan society on the limited knowledge of these *peripheral* tribes, Company servants mediated their understanding of Afghanistan through them' (*The Making of Modern Afghanistan*, 19; emphasis added).

21 Elphinstone, *An Account of the Kingdom of Caubul*, 163.

22 It could be claimed that Elphinstone's account was an *Orientalist* one but not an explicitly racist one. Or alternately, that the category of tribe was reified but not essentialised in his writing. The strategy of Othering through notions of temporality, where the Other always exists in both a different space and a different time from us, is best expounded by Johannes Fabian in his abovementioned *Time and the Other: How Anthropology Makes Its Object*.

23 Indeed, arguably, stadial theory was the main and the single most important theoretical contribution made by the Scottish Enlightenment. See Silvia Sebastiani's *The Scottish Enlightenment: Race, Gender and the Limits of Progress* (London: Palgrave Macmillan, 2013), 55–7.

24 Jane Rendall, 'Scottish Orientalism: From Robertson to James Mill'.

25 See Jennifer Pitts, *A Turn to Empire: The Rise of Imperial Liberalism in Britain and France* (Princeton: Princeton University Press, 2009); Uday Singh Mehta, *Liberalism and Empire: A Study in Nineteenth-Century British Liberal Thought* (Chicago: University of Chicago Press, 1999); and Sankar Muthu, *Enlightenment Against Empire* (Princeton: Princeton University Press, 2009).

26 Louis Dupree, 'AFGHANISTAN iv. Ethnography', *Encyclopaedia Iranica*, online edition, 1982, available at http://www.iranicaonline.org/articles/afghanistan-iv-ethnography, accessed 9 March 2014.

27 Hopkins, *The Making of Modern Afghanistan*, 20.

28 Nigel Allan, 'Defining Place and People in Afghanistan', 547–8.

29 Hanifi, in Shahzad Bazir and Robert Crews (eds.), *Under the Drones: Modern Lives in the Afghanistan–Pakistan Borderlands* (Cambridge, MA: Harvard University Press, 2012).

30 See also Charles Lindholm, 'Images of the Pathan: the Usefulness of Colonial Ethnography', *European Journal of Sociology* 21, no. 2 (1980); Edward Ingram, *In Defence of British India: Great Britain in the Middle East 1775–1842* (London: Routledge, 2013); Nabi Misdaq, *Afghanistan: Political Frailty and External Influence* (London: Routledge, 2006); and Richard Tapper, *The Conflict of Tribe and State in Iran and Afghanistan* (London: Croon Helm, 1983).

31 Elphinstone, *An Account of the Kingdom of Caubul*.

32 G. Le G. Norgate, 'Campbell, Sir George (1824–1892)', rev. David Steele, *Oxford Dictionary of National Biography* (Oxford University Press, 2004) [http://www.oxforddnb.com/view/article/4499, accessed 4 Feb 2014].

33 George Campbell, *Afghan Frontier: The Substance of a Speech not Delivered (1879)*: see 'Digitized Afghanistan Materials in English from the Arthur Paul Afghanistan Collection', University of Nebraska-Lincoln, 2010, 20, 22, 23.

34 Ibid, 57.

35 Ibid, 80.

36 Ibid, 6. This metaphor is reminiscent of the one Sir William Kaye used when he referred to the Afghans as 'wild horses' that could not be reined in by 'silken braids'. In spite of this, Campbell on the whole was more positive about the tribes and also more cautious in dealing with them.

37 Ibid, 12.

38 Ibid, 2, emphasis added.

39 Ibid, 69–70. This does not prevent him from dwelling upon his naïve, even faintly ludicrous idea of establishing a 'porter's lodge' at the foothills of the Khyber which would grant admittance on the basis of British diktat. In Campbell's own memorable words: 'I threw out for consideration that possibly we might establish an easily-garrisoned hill fort at the mouth of the Khyber – a sort of 'Porter's Lodge', as

I described it – where would be kept the key of the gate, and admittance given or refused as we should desire' (40–41).

40 Ibid, 25.

41 Bellew published widely and his works include the *Journal of a Political Mission to Afghanistan in 1857* (1862), *A Grammar and Dictionary of the Pukkhto or Pukshto Language* (1867), *Afghanistan and the Afghans* (1879), *A New Afghan Question, or, Are the Afghans Israelites?* (1881). See D. A. Power, 'Bellew, Henry Walter (1834–1892)', rev. James Falkner, *Oxford Dictionary of National Biography* (Oxford University Press, 2004); online edn, May 2008 [http://www.oxforddnb.com/view/article/2052, accessed 4 Feb 2014].

42 Christine Noell, *State and Tribe in Nineteenth-Century Afghanistan: The Reign of Amir Dost Muhammad Khan (1826–1863)* (London: Routledge, 2012).

43 Henry Walter Bellew, *Races of Afghanistan* (Calcutta: Thacker Spink and Co., 1880), vii.

44 Written as a corrective, Bellew's *Pushto Instructor* paradoxically used only 20 of the 40 Pashto characters and relied on English transliteration. Setting aside matters of philology, this is a chilling testament to the nature of knowledge generated about Afghanistan: the first real textbook on Pashto was authored by a person who was only partially versed in the language. Hanifi, *Beyond Swat*, 71; see also Henry George Raverty, *Notes on Afghanistan and Baluchistan* (Quetta: Gosha-e-Adab, 1976).

45 Cited in Campbell, *Afghan Frontier.*

46 Bellew, *Races of Afghanistan*, 12.

47 Paul Titus, 'Honor the Baloch, Buy the Pashtun: Stereotypes, Social Organization and History in Western Pakistan', *Modern Asian Studies* 32, no. 3 (1998).

48 Anderson, 'Poetics and Politics in Ethnographic Texts', 105.

49 For the Victorian preoccupation with character, see Stefan Collini, 'The Idea of "Character" in Victorian Political Thought', *Transactions of the Royal Historical Society* 35, 5th ser. (1985); and Peter Mandler, *The English National Character: From Edmund Burke to Tony Blair* (New Haven, CT: Yale University Press, 2007).

50 For him, the distinction was loose, with the former being agricultural and the latter pastoral Pashtuns. It is telling that his discussion of the Baluch was rather limited; Elphinstone focused on the Pashtuns because of his affinity for their acephalous tendencies.

51 Campbell, *Afghan Frontier*, 30–1.

52 Ibid, 61.

53 Paul Titus, 'Honor the Baloch, Buy the Pashtun: Stereotypes, Social Organization and History in Western Pakistan', *Modern Asian Studies* 32, no. 3 (1998).

54 Ibid, 674

55 Bhabha, 'The Other Question', 18.

56 Campbell, *Afghan Frontier*, 24.

57 Titus, 'Honor the Baloch, Buy the Pashtun', 663; see also Malcom Yapp, *Strategies of British India: Britain, Iran and Afghanistan 1798–1850* (Oxford: Clarendon Press, 1980), 471.

58 Akbar S. Ahmed, 'The Colonial Encounter on the North-West Frontier Province: Myth and Mystification', *Economic and Political Weekly* 14, no. 51/52 (1979); Holdich, *The Indian Borderland 1880–1900*, 186; Caroe, *The Pathans 550 BC–AD 1957*, 276.

59 Titus, 'Honor the Baloch, Buy the Pashtun'. See also Anderson, 'Poetics and Politics in Ethnographic Texts'.

60 Thomas Holdich, *The Indian Borderland 1880–1900* (London: Methuen & Co., 1909).

61 Cited in Titus, 'Honor the Baloch, Buy the Pashtun', 663.

62 See for instance, Elphinstone, *An Account of the Kingdom of Caubul*, 162–3 and 247–53.

63 Holdich, *The Indian Borderland 1880–1900*, 185.

64 This is equally true of the work of those cited above. Elphinstone, Bellew, Campbell and Caroe all speak of the racial superiority of the Afghan in comparison to Indians, for instance. A telling example is an old British Army field manual which states: 'The Afghan character is a strange blend of virtue and vice', and peremptorily concludes that '[t]he race in short is a mass of contradictions which are accentuated by the strong individuality of the people'. See General Staff of India, *Handbook of Kandahar Province* (1993), 7.

65 Olaf Caroe, *The Pathans 550 B.C.–1957 A.D.*, 393; see also Evelyn Berkeley Howell, *Mizh: A Monograph on the Government's Relations with the Mahsud Tribe* (Karachi: Oxford University Press, 1979), 89.

66 See Nick Cullather, 'Damming Afghanistan: Modernization in a Buffer State', *The Journal of American History* 89, no. 2 (2002).

67 Richard Tapper, 'Studying Pashtuns in Barth's Shadow', in Benjamin Hopkins and Magnus Marsden, (eds.), *Beyond Swat: History, Society and Economy Along the Afghanistan–Pakistan Frontier* (London: Hurst, 2013).

68 The historical discussion below, however, uses 'Afghan' interchangeably with 'Pashtun' or 'Pathan' in order to remain consistent with the historical archive in which it is located. This may appear confusing, but the Persian word 'Afghan' was first employed to refer to the Pashtun tribes, which predates the creation of the Afghan state.

69 Mukulika Banerjee, *The Pathan Unarmed: Opposition & Memory in the North West Frontier* (Santa Fe, NM: School of American Research Press, 2000), 3.

70 University of Texas archives: http://www.reagan.utexas.edu/archives/speeches/1983/32183e.htm.

71 For example: Martin Ewans, *Afghanistan: A New History* (London: Routledge, 2002); Ahmed Rashid, *Taliban: The Story of the Afghan Warlords* (London: Palgrave Macmillan 2001); Tanner, *Afghanistan: A Military History*.

72 Jim Gant, 'One Tribe at a Time: A Strategy for Success in Afghanistan', http://www.globalsecurity.org/military/library/report/2009/2009_one_tribe_at_a_time.pdf, last accessed 30 May 2014; see also, Dan Green, 'Going Tribal: Enlisting Afghanistan's Tribes', *Small Wars Journal*, http://www.smallwarsjournal.com, last accessed 19 September 2014.

73 Ann Scott Tyson, 'Jim Gant, the Green Beret Who Could Win the War in Afghanistan', *Washington Post*, January 17 2010. Note that, as a Green Beret, Gant is part of a long tradition of unconventional warfare.

74 Ibid.

75 Ibid.

76 Ibid.

77 Mike Martin, *A Brief History of Helmand* (n.p.: Afghan Coin Centre, 2011), 14. Martin was instrumental in designing and implementing the UK's Culture and Human Terrain Capability and is also author of *An Intimate War* (London: Hurst, 2014).

78 Cited in *The Mail and The Globe*, 'Graeme Smith: Portrait of the Enemy', 22 March 2008; see especially Ehsaan Entezaar's *Afghanistan 101: Understanding Afghan Culture* (Bloomington, IN: Xlibris, 2007), a widely disseminated text that at its core functions as a long list of stereotypes about Afghanistan couched in academic jargon.

79 As stated on his faculty webpage: http://www.american.edu/sis/faculty/akbar.cfm, last accessed 30 May 2014.

80 His most recent work, *The Thistle and the Drone: How America's War on Terror Became a Global War on Tribal Islam* (Washington, DC: Brookings Institute, 2013), is the single best example of this argument.

81 Ahmed, *The Thistle and the Drone*, 2.

82 See, for instance, ibid, 16; and also Akbar S. Ahmed, 'Colonial Encounter on the North-West Frontier Province: Myth and Mystification', *Economic and Political Weekly* 14, no. 51/52 (1979), 2093, 2096.

83 Akbar S. Ahmed, 'Tribes and States in Waziristan', in Tapper, (ed.), *Conflict of Tribe and State in Iran and Afghanistan*; Akbar S. Ahmed, 'The Code of the Hills', *Foreign Policy*, 6 May 2011. This distinction also finds echoes in Frederick Barth's work, where he contrasts *bar* (upper, remote) and *kuz* (lower, toward the government centre) Pashtuns. Other observers have made similar distinctions: for example, Peter Mayne's essentialist and rather confusing one between the Pathan as 'settled' and Pakhtun as 'independent'. See Mayne, *Journey to the Pathan* (New York: Doubleday, 1955). Also Anderson, 'Khan and Khel: Dialectics of Pakhtun Tribalism', in Tapper, (ed.), *Conflict of Tribe and State in Iran and Afghanistan*, 128.

84 Ahmed, 'The Code of the Hills'.

85 Akbar S. Ahmed, 'Tribes and States in Waziristan'. See also Tapper and Anderson in the same volume.

86 This is evocative of James Scott's argument about the Malay peasantry in his *Weapons of the Weak: Everyday Forms of Peasant Resistance* (New Haven, CT: Yale University Press, 1987).

87 Ahmed, 'The Code of the Hills'.

88 One of the recurring quotes in Ahmed's work belongs to the Pakistani leader Wali Khan, who in the early 1970s purportedly claimed: 'I have been a Pathan for 6,000 years; a Muslim for 1,300 years; and a Pakistani for 25'. Ahmed has argued that this is testimony to the fact that tribal identity is supreme for Pashtuns in Afghanistan and Pakistan. However, in a research poll conducted in 2009, 72 per cent of the population identified as Afghan first and then with other ethnic identities. Whilst this does not necessarily prove that Afghans are a 'nationalistic' people, 'nationhood' as 'imagined community' is certainly as salient in Afghanistan as other competing identities, just as in other parts of the world. The

poll can be accessed at: http://abcnews.go.com/images/PollingUnit/1083a1Afghanistan2009.pdf, last accessed 19 September 2014.

89 Peter Tomsen, *The Wars of Afghanistan*; incidentally, a book review in *Foreign Policy* claims that 'the tribal situation in Afghanistan is clearly defined' in the text. See: http://www.foreignpolicyjournal.com/2012/11/30/book-review-the-wars-of-afghanistan/last accessed 30 May 2014.

90 Tomsen, *The Wars of Afghanistan*, 5

91 Ibid, 214

92 Tanner, *Afghanistan: A Military History*, 130, 326.

93 Tomsen, *The Wars of Afghanistan*, 127.

94 David Miliband, 'How to End the War in Afghanistan', *The New York Review of Books*, April 29 2010.

95 Ruhulla Khapalwak and David Rhode, 'A Look at America's New Hope: The Afghan Tribes', *The New York Times*, 30 January 2010.

96 This and the rest of the maps are available here: http://www.nps.edu/programs/ccs/Docs/PDF%20 Maps/RCSouthTribalmap07.pdf, last accessed 28 August 2014.

97 See, for instance, Nancy Lindisfarne, 'Exceptional Pashtuns', in Hopkins and Marsden (eds.), *Beyond Swat*, 123.

98 John Pickles, *A History of Spaces: Cartographic Reason, Mapping and the Geo-coded World* (New York: Routledge, 2004); Geoff King, *Mapping Reality: An Exploration of Cultural Cartographies* (London: Palgrave Macmillan, 1996); Christian Jacob, *The Sovereign Map: Theoretical Approaches in Cartography Throughout History* (Chicago: University of Chicago Press, 2006).

99 Nicholas Dirks's abovementioned *Castes of Mind* is an excellent example of a work similarly dedicated to the evolution of a concept: that of caste in British India. He demonstrates that caste, in the way it is presently conceived, was the product of a concrete historical encounter between the colonisers and the colonised. His contention is not that caste was invented by the British but that it was under the British that the vocabulary of caste became the only one capable of imagining the Indian political universe(s). Although literature on the inadequacy of the concept of caste as a 'guide' to Indian culture continues to proliferate, there is no equivalent work on the notion of tribe. But see Charles Tripp, *A History of Iraq* (Cambridge: Cambridge University Press, 2002), for an account of how the British handled and literally 'made up' tribal difference with their Mandate in Iraq, based on their experience in Afghanistan, and often implemented policies to align with their notion of 'indigenous tribal authority'.

100 Anderson, 'Poetics and Politics in Ethnographic Texts', 103.

101 Ibid, 89.

102 Ibid, 106–7. Unfortunately, most contemporary students of Afghanistan have failed entirely to engage with his work, especially in the field of political sociology and international studies, which has precluded any attempt to gauge the continuing relevance of Anderson's research. Crucially, none of the critical, theoretically sophisticated work cited in this paper has been done by IR scholars.

103 Ibid, 92.

104 Charles Lindholm explores the prominence of this trope and its increasing control over British institutional memory, and also shows how these stereotypes reflected British concerns and anxieties (if not quite in these words) in his 'Images of the Pathan: The Usefulness of Colonial Ethnography', *European Journal of Sociology* 21, no. 2 (1980). Recently, Shah Mahmoud Hanifi has argued that Afghan elites have 'uncritically absorbed and reproduced colonial frameworks of reckoning' about themselves and their homelands ('Quandaries of the Afghan Nation', 86); while in *The Making of Modern Afghanistan*, Hopkins contends that the colonial state only partially penetrated the Afghan (self) imaginary, and that even this only happened many decades after 'Afghanistan' was thought up by the British.

105 Bhabha, 'The Other Question', 18–20.

106 The Tribal Engagement Workshop, sponsored by Small Wars Foundation, the U.S. Joint Forces Command Joint Irregular Warfare Center, the U.S. Marine Corps Center for Irregular Warfare, the U.S. Army/U.S. Marine Corps Counterinsurgency Center, and Noetic Group, conducted 24–5 March 2010, which assessed the value of a 'tribal engagement approach to Afghanistan', is one particularly egregious example.

10
TERRORISM AND THE POSTCOLONIAL 'STATE'

Swati Parashar

Introduction

> The danger inherent in the normative definition (of terrorism) is that it verges on the polemical. If 'terrorist' is what one calls one's opponent (regardless of whether or not one's friend is a freedom fighter), then the word is more of an epithet or a debating stratagem than a label that enables all who read it, whatever their ideological affiliation, to know what terrorism is and what it is not.
>
> Martha Crenshaw (1983, 2)

'Terrorism studies', since 9/11, has developed into a sub-discipline of its own, focusing on the security of the modern nation-state and terror threats to it from mostly religious fundamentalists and extremists who are averse to embracing Western secular democracy and modernity. Although 'critical terrorism studies' has challenged this dominant perception about terrorism and in particular has addressed 'state terror', entrenched historical factors including colonialism and imperialism which can inform the terrorism discourse are still found missing. Very little attention has been paid to terrorism as a product of and contributor to discourses around political violence.

There are two points that this chapter seeks to make. The first is that terrorism imaginaries continue to normalise the Euro-centric nation-state, its vulnerabilities and violence as a universal model of political existence. Even the 'terrorist vs. freedom fighter' debate does little to move away from the nation-state as the object of desire or resistance in the postcolonial context where collective political and cultural identities are predominantly imagined in various other ways. The second is that the history of India's Maoist violence since the 1968 Naxalbari Revolt, demonstrates how violent resistance by citizens (not necessarily seeking a separate statehood) is looked at only through the terror lens that threatens the idea of the nation-state. The erasure of postcolonial histories of class, caste and gender marginalisations is made possible through an affective allegiance to the nation-state where any dissident voice can be simultaneously constructed as a 'terrorist' or 'deviant citizen' who must be either obliterated or rehabilitated into the 'mainstream'. The chapter thus problematises the prevalent terrorism discourse and asks that the gaze be turned inwards to understand the legacy of colonial control and marginalisations, which legitimises territorial nation-states and challenges alternative ways of collective political and cultural existence.

Definitions of political violence are always complex and contested. For the purposes of this reflection on terrorism as a form of political violence, it becomes imperative to engage with the latter as collective ideologies inspired by one or more objectives and leading to violent acts. Ted Honderich has defined political violence as a considerable or destroying use of force against persons or things, a use of force prohibited by law, directed to a change in the policies, system, territory of jurisdiction, or personnel of a government or governments, and hence directed to changes in the lives of individuals within societies (cited in Merkl 1986). This kind of definition exempts the state and governments from engaging in acts of political violence, recognising only violence by non-state actors. As Peter Merkl (1986) argues, to be taken seriously, political violence has to not only violate the taboos of the prevailing order but also has to give the impression of an attempt not just to nudge, but to overwhelm some persons or objects symbolic of that order. Though ideologies may not necessarily lead to political violence, there is a strong correlation between extremist ideologies and violence. The combination of religious extremism and nationalism has often provided the most enduring basis for political violence and terrorism, but most of these are directed either towards the creation or the protection of the territorial nation-state.

'Terrorism' as one kind of political violence has within its conceptual ambit most forms of politically motivated violent attacks targeted at unarmed civilians or security actors outside a regular war. Largely associated with modern French and Russian histories and anti-colonial struggles where political terror was used to resist colonial regimes, terrorism has acquired a pejorative meaning. The 'ism' attached to terror seems misleading because 'terrorism' is not an end in itself nor a set of ideas or belief system on its own. It is in most cases a means to an end, which can range from the domination of particular political ideologies to religious and ethnic sovereignties. Just as the Second World War was against Nazism and not Blitzkrieg, there can be no war against 'terrorism', which is merely a strategy or tactics used in support of an ideology. 'Terrorism' in a pejorative sense, also takes away the sense of rational purpose that governs the violent activities of certain political actors. It also fails to distinguish between violence or the threat of violence sanctioned by states and non-state actors. I argue that in order to understand violent political and religious groups as important actors within the international system, 'terrorism' must be understood within competing and contested discourses with particular genealogies and contexts.

Terrorism produces discourses as much as it is discursively produced, and that remains the main concern of this paper. I am interested in a discursive reading of terrorism, its ruptures and continuities with the colonial pasts in the context of postcolonial states. I am particularly drawn to the idea of revolutionary terrorism which has been an important method deployed to resist both the colonial and the postcolonial state. At the heart of the postcolonial project and its core discourse, 'is a focus on the relations of domination and resistance and the effect they have had on identity, in, through, and beyond the colonial encounter.' (Darby and Paolini 1994, 375). The terrorism discourse has largely determined the self-perception of postcolonial nations and their anxieties around their statehood; they in turn continue to develop specific genealogical narratives about terrorism (and revolutionary terrorism in particular as this paper explores further) and its encounter with postcolonial modernity and its violences.

Discourses, terrorism and (post)colonial encounters

> Terrorism is not the complete revolution and the revolution is not complete without Terrorism. This thesis can be supported by an analysis of any and every revolution in

> history. Terrorism instils fear in the heart of the oppressors, it brings hope of revenge and redemption to the oppressed masses, it gives courage and self-confidence to the wavering, it shatters the spell of superiority of the ruling class.
>
> Manifesto, Hindustan Republican Association (1929)[1]

Ashis Nandy suggests that the word 'terrorism' was a colonial import that entered Indian public life in 1860 and gained significance after the Bengal Partition of 1905 (2003, 134). The first moral debate Nandy alludes to was focused around the legitimacy of those using violent methods to fight the British Raj to be called freedom fighters and revolutionaries; these people were stigmatised as terrorists by the colonial regime. The second debate was about the legitimacy of political terror in the Indian traditional way of life. (Nandy 2003, 134). Nandy's further insight that (with terrorism) 'there is a latent clash between the dominant language of the nation-state system and the residual traditional language of rebellion,' (1995, 25) and that terrorism is discursively produced through the media for the consumption of the middle classes, is widely evidenced in the modern usage of the term. His observations can be mapped on to the treatment of Bhagat Singh in postcolonial India and the public discourse around the Naxalite/Maoist movement, as discussed further.

In 2016, amidst all the debates taking place in India over the Government's right-wing disposition and its meddling with policies and institutions, one stood out in terms of its far-reaching implications on the public discourse on terrorism. ***India's Struggle for Independence***, a textbook widely used in university curricula to teach Modern Indian History and authored by eminent historians, Bipan Chandra, Mridula Mukherjee, Aditya Mukherjee, K. N. Panikkar and Sucheta Mahajan came under scrutiny by the Human Resources Ministry of the Government of India. The book was attacked in public debates in the media and its Hindi translation was withdrawn from Delhi University on the grounds that it addressed the legendary freedom fighter and national hero, Bhagat Singh[2] as a 'revolutionary terrorist'. In a country where outrage over all and sundry is becoming common and where books have been banned at the first opportunity,[3] this was a noteworthy political moment for various reasons. Under a right-wing regime, protests were raised against calling a widely acclaimed and respected freedom fighter a terrorist. Moreover, Singh, like Che Guevara, enjoys a cult status among communists and radical revolutionaries in India, including among the erstwhile Naxalites and present-day Maoists, all of whom have challenged the State.

Then there was always admiration for him from the neighbourhood. The LTTE (Liberation Tigers of Tamil Elam), the militant group in Sri Lanka which will be remembered for its successes in suicide bombing operations, looked up to Singh as a hero. LTTE's iconography and popular culture representations included the veneration of Singh who had challenged the might of the British Raj with the help of the bomb and who was eventually hanged by the colonial justice system. After the LTTE supremo, Velupillai Prabhakaran, was killed by the security forces on 19 May 2009, the President, Mahinda Rajapaksa, delivered his victory speech as an address to the parliament. Speaking the first few sentences in Tamil, he remarked, 'Our heroic forces have sacrificed their lives to protect Tamil civilians. The victory we have gained by defeating LTTE is the victory of this nation, and the victory of all people living in this country.'[4]

Rejecting any notion of legitimacy in the LTTE's struggle for an independent Tamil homeland, the President's speech in Sinhalese made it clear that the LTTE was a 'terrorist' group and an enemy because it sought to challenge the sovereignty of the country, and sought to divide the motherland. He equated winning the war against the terrorists as the liberation of the Tamil people and the restoration of national pride and dignity which was lost with the 1815 fall of the

Kandyan Kingdom and the advent of British colonial rule in Sri Lanka. The victory against the LTTE was seen as the ultimate moment of freedom and national revival which finally ended the remnants of colonial politics and control.

In a complex picture that emerges about Singh's ideology and its appropriation by various groups in the postcolonial context, the Indian Government has argued that labeling Singh as a revolutionary 'terrorist' disrespected his legacy and his contribution to the national movement. The same government remains quite opposed to and even at war with those radical groups who have co-opted Singh in their armed resistance. A close scrutiny would establish that Singh as an atheist and communist would be ideologically opposed to the current right-wing political disposition of the ruling class in India. The key questions that emerge from the 2016 protests are about the sudden discomfort and anxiety around 'terrorism' and its genealogy which can be traced back to the anti-colonial struggle against the British Raj. In both these instances, of the history text book protests in India and the military defeat of the LTTE in Sri Lanka, a certain continuity is visible in the colonial and postcolonial state and the terrorism discourse.

Terrorism qualifies as any kind of violence that threatens the modern state, in both Western and non-Western contexts. Terrorism imaginaries continue to normalise the Euro-centric nation-state, its vulnerabilities and violence as a universal model of political existence. Even the 'terrorist vs. freedom fighter' debate, as in the Singh or LTTE cases mentioned above, does little to move away from the nation-state as the object of desire or resistance in the postcolonial context where collective political and cultural identities are predominantly imagined in various other ways. Those who draw from Singh's ideology are modern-day terrorists and extremists, like the Indian Maoists or the erstwhile Tamil Tigers in Sri Lanka, whom the state seeks to obliterate, and who in turn wish to carve out or create new states for themselves. Singh, the hero of these modern 'terrorists' is an icon of the anti-colonial freedom struggle for the creation of the independent nation-state of India, based on the European model of territorial sovereignty and nationality. However, his terrorism becomes acceptable as revolutionary violence.

Nation, statehood and terrorism

> The idea of the state that dominates modern India is that of an imperial state run, naturally enough now, by modern Indians well versed in Anglo Saxon theories of the state.
>
> Ashis Nandy (2003, 113)

The idea of nation as a shared community has been the most important inspiration for the resistance of colonial societies against imperial control. Prominent scholars of nationalism have envisaged the concept of 'nation' as an 'imagined community' (Anderson 1983, 15), but the relevance of the nation-state as the principal representative of a cohesive socio-political-cultural collective is entrenched in postcolonial societies. One may attribute some prophecy to Benedict Anderson's claim that 'nation-ness is the most universally legitimate value in the political life of our times' (Anderson 1983, 12) as postcolonial societies have adopted the Euro-centric conception of nation-state as the ultimate goal of their national independence. They continue with their obsession with the idea of nation-state in their postcolonial existence. Partha Chatterjee (1993) highlights the centrality of the idea of nation in the case of postcolonial societies as virtually inseparable from political consciousness. Interestingly, the awakening of this political consciousness is achieved though the conception of the Indian nation as a cultural unit, predating the colonial rule (Kaviraj 1994). This imagining allows the anti-colonial political movement to claim that 'the nation is already sovereign, even when the state is in the hands of the colonial power' (Chatterjee 1993, 6). The anticolonial movements then deployed this rationale to seek political sovereignty from colonial rule for an already sovereign cultural nation.

The pre-eminence of the idea of nation and nationality during anti-colonial movements and its prevalence in postcolonial societies has been challenged by some of the most iconic figures of the anti-colonial movements. Frantz Fanon framed the anti-colonial struggle as based upon 'cultural nationalism', and defined national culture as 'the whole body of efforts made by a people in the sphere of thought to describe, justify and praise the action through which that people has created itself and keeps itself in existence' (Fanon 1994, 44). However, Fanon had the foresight to warn against the dangers of nationalism, such as the national bourgeoisie replacing the colonial bureaucracy while maintaining the colonial power structure, imposing a rigid national identity, and enforcing a coercive view of national commitment. Gandhi had warned against the monopoly of the nation on violence and stated 'I have recognised that the nation has the right, if it so wills, to vindicate her freedom even by actual violence. Only, then India ceases to be the land of my love, even though the land of my birth' (Gandhi 1927, 382). It can be argued that some of the most eminent anti-colonial nationalist leaders were concerned about the inherent violence in the political structure of the nation-state.

Independent nationhood in postcolonial societies is considered the next stage of progression of the struggle for self-rule against colonial subjugation. Anti-colonial nationalisms are based upon the premise that 'while the colonial nation-state can only confer subjecthood on the colonised, the projected postcolonial nation-state holds out the promise of full and participatory citizenship' (Gandhi 1998, 118). However, several leading scholars like Benedict Anderson (1991), Edward Said (1993), Bernard Cohn (1983), and Partha Chatterjee (1993) have described the anti-colonial nationalism as a derivative discourse of the Eurocentric conception of enlightenment, modernity, liberty and nationalism. Chatterjee (1993) expounds the concept of 'liberal dilemma' in the context of Indian anti-colonial nationalism; on the one hand it promises liberty and universal suffrage, while on the other it is complicit in undemocratic forms of government and domination of a few.

Indian socialist leader Jayprakash Narayan censured the state machinery of postcolonial India for 'its continued adherence to the British imperialist theory that it is the duty of the people to obey first and then to protest' (Narayan 1971, 5). Narayan believed that in post-independent India, the indigenous bureaucracy had refused to engage with any peaceful protest until popular action was withdrawn or coercively put down. Consequently, the concerned people are 'driven to violent action, after which government usually surrenders or makes a compromise' (Narayan 1971, 5). Dharmapal associated the Indian bureaucratic trait of utter contempt towards public protests to their colonial inheritances (1971, 51). The British colonial rule in India derived its sanction and legitimacy from military strength, and by creating the 'impression of invincibility'; the British could not afford to make any concessions in order to protect the infallibility of the state structure.

Anti-colonial nationalism, thus, transferred power to the bourgeois elite in the independent postcolonial nation-state of India, where the Western-educated indigenous ruling class replaced the Western colonial ruling elite. It has long been argued that the indigenous elite seems to speak on behalf of the people but functions to keep them disempowered, by privileging elite consciousness over subaltern consciousness and highlighting only the elite contribution in the history of anti-colonial struggle (Guha 1983). The movement for self-rule in colonised societies is not one homogenous, monolithic, acquiescent movement; rather it encompasses several distinct, contradictory, conflicting counter currents within the umbrella of anti-colonial nationalism(s). Elitism in anti-colonial nationalism not only marginalises the contribution of the subaltern but also ignores the conflictual relationship between elites and subaltern groups (Guha 1983). Narayan describes this conflictual relationship as between 'the people-who-comprise-the-nation and the State-which-represents-the-nation' (Gandhi 1998, 119).

In postcolonial societies, the formation of the independent state is supposed to be the generic closure of all the different strands of nationalism. The anticolonial nationalist movements evolve into an overarching umbrella for several parallel movements reflecting subnational, ethnic, social, cultural, labour, gender, caste and class diversity. The indigenous successors to colonial rule assume that the formal declaration of independence brings all these parallel movements to their conclusion.

The new rulers of independent India desperately needed and hoped for the complete closure of all the other movements in order to focus on their state-building exercise. However, rather than providing for a generic closure, the success of one part of the movement unleashed the dissent of the people-who-comprise-the-nation against their new rulers. This led to the conflict between two different political imaginations of those who believe in the inviolability of the state-structure and those who reject the pre-eminence of the State. The primacy of the State-structure 'not only keeps intact the distrustful, hostile and alien stance of the state-system *vis-à-vis* the people but also makes the latter feel that it is violence alone which enables them to be heard' (Dharmapal 1971, 51). The principle of the infallibility of state structure established by the British has been adopted *in toto* by the post-independent Indian state. It is important to note that the Indian state has occasionally condescended to seek rapprochements with protestors, but mostly as a circuit-breaker to end violent protests.

Despite the widely-held view that 'there is something rotten in the state of the state' (Nandy 2003, 14), no alternative approaches have captured the imagination of the public. However, as Nandy powerfully reminds us, 'no system becomes morally acceptable merely because human imagination has failed to produce an alternative to it at any given point of time.' (2003, 14). The state is here to stay because it has 'acquired immense institutional power and a wide base within global mass culture' (Nandy 2003, 7); it remains aspirational and desirable with a quality of redemption even for those who wish to challenge the existing state and then establish their own version. Yet the state contains within it, conceptual and material anxieties related to its legitimacy and purpose that not only makes it violent but also inspires violent resistance or acts of terrorism against it. (Parashar et al. 2018, forthcoming).

Postcolonial states have demonstrated more faith in the nation-state than their Western counterparts. This has typically been the case in the light of their fraught transition from colonial rule to self-rule and a degree of optimism that emerged with the embracing of modernity. The state was seen in an 'idealized form – as an impartial, secular arbiter among different classes, ethnicities and interests' (Nandy 2003, 3). All types of political arrangements in the postcolonial world had to conform to the European 'nation-state' model. Pre-modern versions of states were written out of contemporary accounts on the notion that these ancient systems of governance were neither universal in their legitimacy nor adequate for addressing structural inequalities in society (Kaviraj 2000). The postcolonial state, which replaced the colonial one, practises the same politics of 'othering'. Armed challengers to postcolonial states are seen as violent terrorists who need to be obliterated to not just reclaim territorial sovereignty but also national honour and pride. The anti-state rhetoric by Marxists and Maoists is also rooted in the notion that the European nation-state must first be established in an ideal form, before the state withers away (Parashar in Parashar et al., 2018 forthcoming). It is the absence of governance and the failure of state institutions to bring social justice and equality that has led to deepening identity politics and armed resistance in the postcolonial world. We next look at the case of the Naxalite or Maoist Movement in India which started as peasant revolts in colonial India.

Revolutionary 'terrorism' in India

> Here in India, as in other countries in the past, terrorism will develop into the revolution and the revolution into independence, social political and economic.
>
> Hindustan Socialist Republican Association.[5]

The history of peasant rebellions during the British colonial period in India started with the onset of colonialism; at an estimate, 'no less than 110 violent peasant uprisings have been recorded between 1783 and 1900' (Guha 1983, 6). The subsequent colonial rule in the twentieth century also witnessed several rebellions in various parts of India. The most prominent Communist-led violent peasant uprising in India were the Telangana revolt in the state of Andhra Pradesh and the Tebhaga revolt in the state of West Bengal around the time of the British transfer of power to India. Independent India inherited the colonial era land tenancy system, which granted ownership of land to local landlords in return for their collection of land revenue. The landlords subleased their lands to landless peasantry (sharecroppers) and collected a proportion of the yield (typically 50 per cent). These sharecroppers worked for the landlords for generations without any tenancy rights to the land. The inherent inequity in land distribution and exploitation by the landlords led to disaffection among the rural poor. A major portion of India's poor population is formed of dalits (untouchable castes) who have been deployed as landless peasants and bonded labourers in the rural economy. The legal abolition of untouchability has done precious little to address the social evil and has not liberated the dalits from the oppressive caste regimes in India since independence (Kunnath 2006).

The other oppressed group within Indian society is the tribal population or the *adivasis*.[6] The British colonial administration categorised the numerous disparate indigenous communities that were not part of the mainstream Brahmanical order as tribes (Pathy 2000). There were a number of significant tribal revolts against the colonial state during the nineteenth and early-twentieth century (Kennedy and King 2013). The British administration labelled the tribal insurgents as criminals and suppressed these insurgencies with state power. However, it must be underlined that the Constituent Assembly of independent India recognised the grim situation of the *adivasis* and framed a new social contract between the Indian State and Tribal India in the form of the Fifth Schedule.[7] This new schedule provided for constitutional rights and special financial privileges to protect the livelihood of and land alienation amongst the tribal population. However, it is important to highlight that 'the postcolonial Indian state inherited the res nullius principle adopted by the British, along with its Orientalist undertones' (Malreddy 2014, 597). Furthermore, despite the constitutional provisions, the postcolonial Indian state has been largely absent in the tribal areas or has been in active collusion with the oppressors and exploiters of the tribal population (Guha 2007). A report commissioned by the Planning Commission of India estimated that between 1947 and 2004, of the total displaced population for various development projects, 40 per cent are of tribal origin, while tribals constitute 8.08 per cent of country's population (Government of India 2008).

The Marxist-inspired peasant revolt is traced to the year 1967 to a small village, Naxalbari in the state of West Bengal, and to a political outfit called Communist Party of

India (Marxist-Leninist). These CPI(M-L) revolutionaries were inspired by the Chinese leader Mao's ideology and were popularly known as 'Naxalites' or 'Naxals'. In the early days this revolutionary movement attracted a large number of idealistic urban middle-class and upper-caste activists to fight on behalf of the subalterns, especially for the peasants and tribals in eastern and central India (Gupta 2007). However, the postcolonial Indian nation-state crushed the Naxal insurgency quite brutally, and it must be underlined that the political parties harboring socialist or communist ideology were equally vicious towards these Communist-inspired rebels.

The present-day Maoist rebels are considered to be the natural successors of the erstwhile Naxalites of 1960–70: a replica of their twentieth-century predecessors in ideology, strategy, objectives and their support base. It is quite important to underline that despite overwhelming similarities of ideology, strategy and purpose, there are some fundamental differences in the two incarnations of the rebel group. The top leaders of the 1960's–70's Naxalites such as Charu Mazumdar and Kanu Sanyal believed that India was ripe for a massive uprising and the single spark that would start the proverbial prairie fire against an oppressive social and political system. The Naxalites believed that the peasants could be convinced that by killing their oppressors, such as the landlords and moneylenders, class hatred would lead to popular uprising against the Indian state and society (Gupta 2007, 169).

However, the Naxalite's focus on unleashing a terror campaign instead of a mass movement did not receive popular support, and state repression ultimately crushed their campaign. The Naxalites assumed the tribal population largely based in the forested areas to be exactly the same as the rural peasants based in the Indian plains, overlooking the inherent differences in the socio-economic needs and political aspirations of these two diverse groups. Furthermore, there was a disconnect between Naxalites' goal of establishing the people's democratic state while the average peasants were more focused on the immediate economic and social benefits like 'a plot of land, a home, higher returns from labour, improvement in civic facilities, schooling for their children, better medical services, an end to casteist discrimination and oppression' (Banerjee 2009, 263). The Naxalite movement was controlled by the educated, urban youth from middle- and upper-middle class families rather than the poor peasants or tribal people who were the bulk of the constituency (Gupta 2007).

It is significant to highlight that the 1970s was a period well before the events of the 9/11 attacks and the 'Global War on Terror'; Naxalites were quite candid in flaunting terror tactics as authentic tools to further their movement. They made no efforts to downplay the violent and horrific aspect of their revolutionary activities. Using 'peasants' and 'the people' as euphemism for party cadre functioning as guerrilla hands, the Naxalite party journal, *Liberation*, regularly catalogued such violent incidents. Sample these: 'The people's hatred and anger found expression when they painted slogans with his blood and hung his head from the roof of his house' (*Liberation*, August 1969). 'The hatred of the peasants was so intense that they cut the landlord's body into pieces' (*Liberation*, October 1969). A key leader of the Naxalites, Charu Mazumdar, openly advocated the annihilation of the class enemy through terrorist tactics (Mehra 2000).

> The method of forming a guerrilla unit was to be wholly conspiratorial. The petty bourgeoisie intellectual comrade must take the initiative in this respect as far as possible. He should approach the poor peasant, who in his opinion has the most revolutionary

> potentiality, and whisper in his ears, 'Don't you think it is a good thing to finish off such and such jotedar'. This is how the guerrillas have to be selected.
>
> Charu Mazumdar, CPI(ML) leader, in *Liberation*, February 1970.

Conversely, the Indian state characterised the Naxalites as terrorists and believed extermination of Naxal terror as their natural obligation to the people of India (Mehra 2000). Chaudhary Charan Singh, the central Home Minister in the first non-Congress government (1977–79) in independent India, offered the most imperial-colonial explanation to justify state coercion as the most effective tool to crush any rebellion. 'Rebels cannot be won over by sermons. Do you think violence has not solved problems in this country, in this world? Where are the American Indians today? Crushed out of existence and now North America belongs to Europeans. Where are the original inhabitants of Australia? Where are they today? To say that violence will never solve anything is wrong. In the ultimate analysis, the state is an apparatus of coercion.'[8]

The state oppression in 1970s forced several of the Naxalites to go underground and work in the remote forested areas inhabited by the tribals; thus the Maoists' area of influence continues to be concentrated in the regions of Eastern and Central India. The brutal force of state violence managed to quell the Naxal revolution in the 1970s, but the state did not make any meaningful attempts to address the fundamental inequalities and structural violence in major parts of rural India. In 1992 India shed its quasi-socialist economic policy and introduced neoliberal economic reforms under the direct supervision of international funding agencies such as the World Bank and the International Monetary Fund. These structural changes to the Indian economic system created major problems for the already struggling population and thereby provided inspiration to the various revolutionary groups to reinvigorate their violent activities against the state (Kunnath 2006; Guha 2007).

The reincarnation of the Naxalite movement under the banner of the Maoists occurred in 2004 and unlike in earlier times, the revolutionaries believe in undertaking a 'protracted people's war' in order to eventually overthrow the existing state' (Chandra 2014, 415). In 2004, the two major revolutionary groups, the Maoist Communist Centre (MCC) and the CPI (M-L) People's War Group (PWG) merged to establish the Communist Party of India (Maoist), as the umbrella organisation of Maoist rebels. The CPI (Maoist) considers the postcolonial Indian state as 'reactionary' and 'autocratic', and seeks to establish a 'people's democratic state under the leadership of the proletariat' that will 'guarantee real democracy for the vast majority of people while exercising dictatorship over a tiny minority of exploiters' (Chandra 2014, 414).

The unification of different insurgent groups as CPI-Maoists has provided for a more coherent strategy and a cohesive organisational set-up. The centralised control of the politburo guides and strategises the movement, while the regional and district committees have autonomy in decision-making at the local level. The armed militia of the Maoists, the People's Liberation Guerrilla Army (PLGA), has an estimated strength of around 40,000, with over one million sympathisers (Malreddy 2014, 596). Like the Naxalites, most cadres of the Maoists hail from the dalits (untouchable castes) and *adivasi* (tribal) communities. The top Maoist leaders have almost invariably been men from upper- or middle-caste backgrounds; men and women from subaltern backgrounds have yet to assume top leadership posts in the party (Chandra 2014, 416). The Maoists have managed to effectively control certain territories within the Indian nation-state, mostly the regions inhabited by the most deprived sections of the Indian rural poor, including tribals. These areas have been largely ignored in state-sponsored development programs and the Maoists have set up parallel administrative units in their 'liberated zones' to govern them.

The Maoist idea of setting up a parallel administration can be seen as tentative steps towards the seizure and control of state power. In this instance, the Maoists are engaged in 'a process of competitive state building rather than simply an instance of collective action or social contention' (Kalyvas 2006, 219). This challenge to the state's monopoly of violence can be defined as alternative sovereignties or dual sovereignties (Tilly 1978, 191). In the case of Maoist-controlled territories, dual sovereignty operates more like contested sovereignties where two political organisations, namely the insurgents and the State, 'compete to claim and establish legitimacy' (Kennedy and King 2013, 9). The Maoist rebels deploy a dual approach of offering selective incentives to generate support from certain sections of the local population and enforcing selective sanctions to discipline the local population. It is argued that the local population's 'obedience is determined by highly robust motives of fear and hope' (Weber 1991 [1948], 79).

The Maoists have demonstrated unwavering commitment to overthrow the current Indian state, its democratic institutions, its security and bureaucratic infrastructure; and ultimately usurp political power. However, these rebels have also shown remarkable commitment to the idea of the nation-state of India. In 2009, Pakistan-based Taliban insurgents threatened to attack India once their objective of turning their own country into a hardline Islamist state was achieved. Koteswara Rao, alias Kishenji, who was the second-in-command of the combat forces and a politburo member of the Communist Party of India (Maoist), in an interview to the Indian newspaper *The Hindustan Times* stated, 'If the Taliban attack India, we will stand with the people and rally against the attack.' Kishenji repeated a similar commitment to fight the Taliban in another interview to the Indian magazine *The Week* in 2010. In the same interview, Kishenji supported Kashmir's aspirations for self-determination but put a condition that this self-determination must include the whole of Kashmir (including the part which is administered by Pakistan). Kishenji's claim of including the whole of the Kashmir in the process of self-determination instead of just the Kashmir Valley is quite close to a number of mainstream discourses from the Indian establishment. It is important to underline that while the Indian state terms the Maoists/Naxalites as terrorists and 'left-wing extremists', these rebels echo certain narratives of the same state against which they continue to wage war.

One of most iconic official events in the yearly calendar of the postcolonial nation-state of India is the celebration of its Independence Day on 15 August. On this much-celebrated occasion, the Indian Prime minister unfurls the national flag and addresses the nation from the ramparts of the Red Fort (Lal Qila).[9] The Maoists believe in armed struggle against the Indian nation-state with the ultimate objective to capture state power being disclosed through their slogan 'Lal Qila par Lal Jhanda' (Red Flag on the Red Fort) (Sundar 2011). The dyad of 'terrorist versus freedom fighter' is at play in these pronouncements: on the one hand, the Maoists/Naxalites claim to replace the Indian state structure, while on the other, they seem quite keen to first capture and then sustain the same state structure. The ambition of the Maoists, thus, is to preserve the idea of the nation-state while supplanting the current state apparatus with their own model of the state. The framing of their ultimate goal further reinforces their obsession with the construct of the nation-state and with usurping state power.

> The JS (Janathana Sarkar)[10] shall be the newly formed People's Democratic State and the power of a government. This power shall attain a complete character and a form with the formation of countrywide People's Democratic Republic federation. Depending on the common minimum program prepared by the Party the Janathana

> Sarkars forming in the process of development of revolutionary struggle in DK[11] shall make efforts to implement the people's government power as the new state power.
>
> Policy program of Janathana Sarkar, CPI Maoist document, 2004, (Sundar 2014, 472)

The next section addresses the Indian state's responses to this armed rebellion, labelled as left-wing extremism or terrorism that challenges the territorial sovereignty and integrity of India.

State responses to Maoist terror

> Should we react only after the attack? We should be proactive. We should have aggression in our thoughts, development, security, infrastructure development. Foundation principle of fighting the Left-Wing Extremism is through financial choking. I am sure that attempts to stall development and to throttle democracy at gunpoint will not be successful ever. There is need to depute shadow intelligence officers to track prominent targets associated with Left Wing Extremism (LWE).
>
> Rajnath Singh, Home Minister, Government of India[12]

The Maoists unified as one group in 2004 and their challenge to the Indian state has acquired threatening proportions to the extent that in 2006, the then Prime Minister, Manmohan Singh, referred to Naxalism as 'the biggest internal security challenge' to India.[13] In 2010 the Ministry of Home Affairs in India claimed that the Maoist violence had spread to ten separate states of India and over 200 individual districts. The geographical spread of what is also perceived as Left-Wing Extremism or Red Terror has also brought financial and military benefits and powers to the rebels, resulting in a significant rise in violent attacks on security forces and the general population by the Maoists. In certain parts, the parallel Maoist system has gradually obliterated the Indian state, and has replaced the state with 'structures that look similar as well as different, the Indian state is trying to force its way back in' (Sundar 2014, 478).

The Indian state has adopted a two-pronged approach of expanding security operations to fight the rebels while offering developmental assistance to the erstwhile neglected areas and population. There is increasing realisation that development measures are needed to address the issues of extreme poverty and exploitation of the local population, which draws people towards the insurgents' propaganda (Goswami 2013). In this context, the Indian government has implemented an ambitious scheme called the 'Integrated Action Plan' to provide a generous financial package to address the development deficiencies in Maoist insurgency-affected districts. The Indian state has also implemented Mahatma Gandhi National Rural Employment Guarantee Programme (MGNREGA), National Rural Health Mission (NRHM), The Scheduled Tribes and Other Traditional Forest Dwellers (Recognition of Forest Rights) Act, National Food Security Act among others to ameliorate the dire economic situation faced by a large population within the country that prefers to join the Maoist armed rebellion.

It can be argued that while these new initiatives have brought in much-needed investments to improve the overall socio-economic deficiencies in certain parts of India, there have not been many changes in the deeply flawed governance model. More importantly, the Indian state strategy places securitisation as the precondition for implementing these developmental assistance programs and thus is driven by the objective of bringing the conflict-ridden area under complete government control. The Indian government has deployed a very large number of security personnel armed with better equipment and weaponry to bring the areas under Maoist control under their purview (Parashar in Parashar et al. 2018, forthcoming).

The expansion of security operations by the Indian state has occurred not only in the administrative and organisational levels but also at the discursive and socio-political levels. It can be claimed that while the 'Global War on Terror' may have gained universal recognition after 9/11, it has also allowed the state apparatus to declare an indiscriminate war on its detractors, dissidents and nonconforming citizens. The Indian state has embraced the global discourse on terrorism as defined by the United States (and its allies) and has adopted similar discursive, legal and operational practices and strategies to construct its counterinsurgency framework. It can be argued that these global discourses on terrorism are nothing 'but a militant form of Orientalism' (Malreddy 2014, 592). The contemporary portrayal of 'terrorist' is rooted in the colonial legacies of understanding of the cultural differences between 'us' and the 'other' (Talabani 2016). The legal framework of India's anti-terror laws such as the Prevention of Terrorism Act (POTA) and the amended Unlawful Activities (Prevention) Act (UAPA) has been compared with the United States' Patriot Act, which allows labelling of an entire section of the population as terrorists, whether armed militants or dissident common citizens (Malreddy 2014).

Nandni Sundar (2014, 470) describes the othering of Maoists through linguistic practices aided by a compliant media; 'when something as ordinary as hand pumps or solar panels is discussed, the setting for it is always 'Maoist-hit districts'. The label 'Maoist' functions metonymically for everything that is wrong in these areas.' Author-activist Arundhati Roy (2010) had described the official and media depiction of 'Naxal infected areas' as a 'disease zone which must be cured, contained, or wiped out'. The concentration of Maoist insurgents was limited to certain areas dubbed the 'Red Corridor' by the Indian government, and these were subjected to a virtual economic blockade which prevented the entry of basic supplies such as salt and malaria medicine (Navlakha 2012; Malreddy 2014).

The most intriguing aspect of the Indian state's militaristic response was the launch of armed vigilante groups via the recruitment of mercenaries from among the tribal population to counter the Maoists (e.g. the Salwa Judum in the state of Chhattisgarh). The phrase Salwa Judum can be roughly translated as 'purification hunt' or as the more benign peace campaign' (Sundar 2014). In the initial phase Salwa Judum was 'touted as a grassroots movement, spontaneously cropping up in response to the excesses of the Maoists' (Gupta 2007, 176). However, the Chhattisgarh state government proceeded to employ and arm groups of local tribals to fight against those within their own community who were suspected of supporting the Maoists. This led to an 'unprecedented internecine warfare with far-reaching consequences for the daily life of the tribal population' (Banerjee 2009, 266). The campaign, launched in 2005, lasted for about four years, and involved several brigades of a civilian army of 18,000 to 20,000 (Myrdal 2012, 220). These pro-government militias were responsible for indiscriminate violence against the local tribals and have inadvertently helped the Maoists gain wider support in the local population of Chhattisgarh. Sundar claims that the state security personnel tend to imitate the guerilla tactics of the Maoists and hence have outsourced their monopoly over violence and power to the vigilantes (2014, 470). In 2009 from the orders of the Supreme Court of India, the Salwa Judum campaign was abandoned only to be replaced by a fully-fledged militaristic campaign under the banner of 'Operation Greenhunt', with more troop deployment and direct involvement of the state security forces. [14]

The postcolonial state of India has followed its colonial predecessors when faced with direct confrontation with its subjects. The overall complex of the development–security narrative and the policy frameworks to bring the tribals, dalits and other marginalised groups to the mainstream tend to mimic the 'civilising mission' campaigns of its colonial masters. Thus, the responses to the Maoists is rooted in the idea of the preservation of the nation-state at all costs.

Conclusion

> There are daily exhortations in the national newspapers, to the police and other security forces, to be tough and ruthless with the terrorists....As if the main function of the agencies was not the containment of terror but the containment of the anxieties about terrorism that plagued a section of citizens.
>
> Ashis Nandy (2003, 142)

The Indian state's understanding of 'terrorism' and its responses to the Maoist rebellion offers two kinds of generalisations to emerge. On the one hand, the 'freedom fighter vs. terrorist' discourse gets messier with the recognition that the same person can be perceived differently depending not on the action or intent itself or the ultimate goal, but by the kind of 'state' being challenged. Bhagat Singh was a 'terrorist' for the colonial state and a 'revolutionary' for the postcolonial state; his Maoist admirers continue to be treated as 'terrorists' and 'extremists'. On the other, militant groups like the Naxalites/Maoists fighting the Indian nation-state do not aim to replace the political entity of a nation-state; rather, they strive to change the governance model alone without altering the basic structures of the nation-state.

The story of Ananta Singh sums up the main arguments of this chapter. In 1920s and '30s, several revolutionary youths/militants/terrorists in colonial India undertook daring raids in Chittagong on the two main armouries, the telegraph and telephone office, and the European Club. One of the leaders of these raids was Ananta Singh who was sent to the Cellular Jail in the Andamans in 1932. During his prison term he became a die-hard communist and upon his release returned to Calcutta and joined the Communist Party of India (CPI). In the 1960s, Singh ventured into commercial activities and dabbled in film production and the transport business. In the meantime, he planned another revolution and formed the ultra-left Revolutionary Communist Council of India (RCCI).[15]

The Naxalite armed rebels made their appearance in West Bengal in 1967 and a series of daring bank robberies were reported during this time in Calcutta, possibly to fund the rebels. The robberies followed a common pattern: the gunmen would shout that they were not dacoits but revolutionaries and would not harm anyone unnecessarily. They would hand out leaflets detailing RCCI's agenda to terrified employees and customers. The state government arrested Singh as the prime suspect behind these robberies. Singh and the other accused spent seven years in jail. However, the lack of evidence and pressure from human rights bodies like Amnesty International led to their release.

In 1977, a leading Indian weekly, *India Today* published a feature on Singh titled 'Profile of a terrorist: The perennial revolutionary'.[16] The write-up claimed that Singh 'personifies the enigma of terrorism over five decades' and described him as the 'perennial revolutionary' for political scientists; 'the immortal man' to his followers; and 'nothing short of a Dacoit' by his detractors.[17] A celebrated freedom fighter and hero regarded for his daring acts against the colonial state becomes a terrorist in postcolonial India for the same act of opposing the state. Bhagat

Singh would have possibly met the same fate in contemporary India. Such is the power, control, charm and romance of the modern nation-state in the postcolonial world.

Bibliography

Anderson, B. 1983, *Imagined Communities: Reflections on the Origins and Spread of Nationalism*, Verso, London.

Banerjee, S. 2009, 'Reflections of a One-time Maoist Activist', *Dialect Anthropol*, vol. 33, 253–69.

Chandra, U. 2014, 'The Maoist Movement in Contemporary India, Social Movement Studies', *Journal of Social, Cultural and Political Protest*, vol. 13, no. 3, 414–19.

Chatterjee, P. 1993, *The Nation and Its Fragments*, Princeton University Press, Princeton, NJ.

Cohn, B. 1983, 'Representing Authority in Victorian England', in *The Invention of Tradition,* eds. E. Hobsbawn and T. Ranger, Canto/Cambridge University Press, Cambridge, 165–210.

Crenshaw, M. 1983, 'Reflections on the Effects of Terrorism', Martha Crenshaw ed. *Terrorism, Legitimacy and Power,* Wesleyan University Press, Middletown, CT.

Darby, P. and Paolini, A.J. 1994, 'Bridging International Relations and Postcolonialism', *Alternatives: Global, Local, Political*, vol. 19, no. 3, 371–97.

Fanon. F. 1994, 'On National Culture' in Patrick Williams and Laura Chrisman (eds.), *Colonial Discourse and Postcolonial Theory: A Reader*, Columbia University Press, New York, 36–52.

Gandhi, L. 1998, *Postcolonial Theory: A Critical Introduction,* Oxford University Press, New Delhi.

Gandhi M.K. 1927, 'On Trial', *Young India*, S. Ganeshan, Madras, India.

Government of India 2008, 'Development Challenges in Extremist Affected Areas: Report of an Expert Group', *Planning Commission of India*, New Delhi.

Goswami, N. 2013, *India's Internal Security Situation: Present Realities and Future Pathways*, Monograph Series No. 23, Institute of Defence and Security Analyses, New Delhi.

Guha, R. 1983, *Subaltern Studies II: Writings on South Asian History and Society*, Oxford University Press, Delhi.

——— 2007, 'Adivasis, Naxalites and Indian Democracy', *Economic and Political Weekly*, vol. 32, 3305–12

Gupta, D. K. 2007, 'The Naxalites and the Maoist Movement in India: Birth, Demise, and Reincarnation', *Democracy and Security*, vol. 3, no. 2, 157–88.

Hoelscher, K., Miklian, J. and Vadlamannati, K.C. 2012, 'Hearts and Mines: A District-level Analysis of the Maoist Conflict in India', *International Area Studies Review*, vol. 15, no. 2, 141–60.

Kalhan, A. et al., 2006, 'Colonial Continuities: Human Rights, Terrorism, and Security Laws in India', *Columbia Journal of Asian Law* 20.1, 98.

Kalyvas, S. 2006, *The Logic of Violence in Civil War*, Cambridge University Press, Cambridge.

Kaviraj, S. 1994, 'On the Structure of Nationalist Discourse' in TV Sathyamurchy (ed.), *State and Nation in the Context of Social Change*, Volume I, Oxford University Press, New Delhi.

——— 2000, 'The Modern State in India' in Zoya Hasan (ed.), *Politics and the State in India*, Sage, New Delhi.

Kennedy, J. and King, L. 2013, 'Adivasis, Maoists and Insurgency in the Central Indian Tribal Belt', *European Journal of Sociology*, vol. 54, 1–32.

Kunnath G.J. 2006, 'Becoming a Naxalite in Rural Bihar: Class Struggle and Its Contradictions', *The Journal of Peasant Studies*, vol. 33, no. 1, 89–123.

Malreddy, P.K. 2014, 'Domesticating the "New Terrorism": The Case of the Maoist Insurgency in India', *The European Legacy*, vol. 19, no. 5, 590–605.

Mehra, A.K. 2000, 'Naxalism in India: Revolution or Terror?', *Terrorism and Political Violence*, vol. 12, no. 2, 37–66.

Merkl P. H. (ed.) 1986, *Political Violence and Terror: Motifs and Motivations*, University of California Press, Berkeley, CA.

Myrdal, J. 2012, *Red Star over India,* Imprinta, Kolkata.

Nandy, A. 1995, *The Savage Freud and Other Essays on Possible and Retrievable Selves,* Oxford University Press, New Delhi.

——— 2003, *The Romance of the State: And the Fate of Dissent in the Tropics*, Oxford University Press, New Delhi.

Narayan, J.P. 1971, 'Foreword', in Dharmapal, *Civil Disobedience in Indian Traditions*, Sarva Seva Sangh Prakashan Varanasi, India, 1–5.

Navlakha, G. 2012, *Days and Nights in The Heartland of Rebellion*, Penguin, London.

Parashar, S., Tickner, A., True, J. 2018 (forthcoming). *Revisiting Gendered States: Feminist Reimaginings of the State in International Relations*, Oxford University Press, London/New York.

Pathy, J. 2000, 'Tribe, Region and Nation in the Context of the Indian State', in Sharma S. L. and T. K. Oommen, (eds.) *Nation and National Identity in South Asia*, Orient Longman, New Delhi, 97–111.

Roy, A. 20 March 2010, 'Walking with the Comrades', *Outlook India*. www.outlookindia.com/magazine/story/walking-with-the-comrades/264738, accessed 7 May 2017.

Sundar, N., 2011. 'At War with Oneself: Constructing Naxalism as India's Biggest Security Threat', *India's Contemporary Security Challenges*, Woodrow Wilson International Center for Scholars Asia Program, Princeton, NJ.

Sundar, N. 2014, 'Mimetic Sovereignties, Precarious Citizenship: State Effects in a Looking-glass World', *Journal of Peasant Studies*, vol. 41, no. 4, 469–90.

Talabani, K. 2016, 'Defining a Terrorist: A Critical Examination of the Discourse of Terrorism', *Inquiries Journal*, 8(09). Retrieved from <http://www.inquiriesjournal.com/a?id=1452> Accessed 4 December 2016.

Tilly, C. 1978, *From Mobilization to Revolution*, Addison-Wesley, Reading.

Weber, M. 1991 [1948]. *From Max Weber: Essays in Sociology*, Gerth Hans and C. Wright Mills, (eds.), Oxford University Press, New York.

Notes

1 The manifesto of the HSRA can be read at: <http://www.shahidbhagatsingh.org/index.asp?link=bomb> Accessed 21 December 2016.

2 Bhagat Singh (28 September 1907–23 March 1931) was an Indian freedom fighter with socialist revolutionary leanings. He committed acts of terror against the British in India and was executed at the age of 23. While debate rages about his revolutionary vs. terrorist status, he is considered a hero of the Indian independence movement by those of all ideological persuasions.

3 India was the first country to ban Salman Rushdie's *Satanic Verses*. Since then banning books from public sales and university curriculums, and burning and pulping them have been part of the political trend in the country. Most recent bans have been on Wendy Doniger's, *The Hindus: An Alternative History* and Rohinton Mistry's *Such a Long Journey*.

4 The full speech of Rajapakse can be read at <http://www.satp.org/satporgtp/countries/shrilanka/document/papers/president_speech_parliament_defeatofLTTE.htm > Accessed 23 December 2016.

5 See details about the HSRA at <http://www.shahidbhagatsingh.org/index.asp?link=bomb > Accessed 23 December 2016.

6 The upper caste Hindus claim their origin to the fair-skinned Aryans, who, according to one theory, settled in India in prehistoric times and took over the land from the indigenous people, many of whom, much like the Native Americans in the US, were pushed to the remote forests and other badlands. They are often the poorest of the poor and are collectively called the 'tribals' or the *adivasis*, which literally translates as the 'original inhabitants.'

7 B. G. Verghese, *Causes and Cures of Left Wing Extremism* <http://www.bgverghese.com/ExtremeLeft.htm> Accessed 20 January 2017.

8 See Charan Singh's interview in *India Today* <http://indiatoday.intoday.in/story/rebels-cannot-be-won-over-by-sermons-charan-singh/1/435734.html> Accessed 21 January 2017.

9 The Red Fort in Delhi has been the symbolic seat of India's power from the Mughal period onwards and hence the continuity of symbols of power and statehood.

10 A Janatana Sarkar is a parallel government set up by the Maoists who provide the people with facilities in education, health, security and other sectors. For more details see: <https://revolutionaryfrontlines.wordpress.com/tag/janatana-sarkar/> Accessed 07 May 2017.

11 DK or Dandakaranya is a vast region with deep forest cover in Central India where majority of the Indian tribal population lives. See: < https://revolutionaryfrontlines.wordpress.com/2010/03/28/maoist-development-in-the-dandakaranya-region/ > Accessed 7 May 2017.

12 For responses from the Indian Home Minister after the Maoist attack in Sukma in April 2017, in which 25 military personnel were killed, see: <http://indianexpress.com/article/india/should-we-react-only-after-the-attack-we-should-be-proactive-rajnath-singh-on-naxal-violence-4645594/> Accessed 7 May 2017.

13 See<http://www.thehindu.com/news/national/Naxalism-biggest-threat-to-internal-security-Manmohan/article16302952.ece> Accessed 23 December 2016.
14 <See http://www.thehindu.com/opinion/op-ed/Green-Hunt-the-anatomy-of-an-operation/article16812797.ece> Accessed 3 September 2017.
15 See <http://indiatoday.intoday.in/story/profile-of-a-terrorist-the-perennial-revolutionary/1/435744.html> Accessed 7 May 2017.
16 Ibid.
17 See <http://indiatoday.intoday.in/story/profile-of-a-terrorist-the-perennial-revolutionary/1/435744.html> Accessed 7 May 2017.

11
THE COLONIAL MEDITERRANEAN, ANONYMITY AND MIGRATION CONTROL

Emilio Distretti

Introduction

With over 5,000 deaths at sea borders, the International Organisation for Migration (IOM) has estimated that 2016 was the deadliest year for migrants and refugees crossing the Mediterranean trying to reach Europe. Many of these deaths occurred between the Italian island of Lampedusa and the northern coasts of Libya, a route mostly used by smugglers. The identity of most of the victims stays unknown and most of the retrieved human remains have been buried anonymously in unmarked graves in local cemeteries in Sicily.

This chapter argues that these unidentified human remains are the final phase of a lasting process of identity loss which sees its inception in the modern timeless and spaceless relation to the 'black body' which colonialism was built upon. The proliferation of nameless border deaths on the Mediterranean frontiers seems to echo past colonial practices when the bodies of the 'others' and their remains were used to construct anonymity, where plaster masks and skulls were presented as museum specimens, and human remains anonymously disposed of in mass graves as a means to erase the native from historical narratives. This chapter reads these constructions of anonymity as 'anonymisation'. The focus within the chapter is placed on the Italian context by investigating anthropometric materials and human remains from early colonial practices which produced racial taxonomies up to the most contemporary technologies used for limiting migrant mobility in the Mediterranean. In so doing, the chapter presents 'anonymisation' as originally a colonial narrative and practice that shapes the understanding of postcolonial politics within the global order of mobility and specifically with regards to the Mediterranean.

Moreover, the chapter argues that the total loss of identity of both colonial and postcolonial bodies marks the inception of a new path where de-identified human remains enter a public sphere, questioning the 'anonymisation' practices that have generated them and providing the tools to fight it. In this respect, the chapter brings human material residues into dialogue with the larger fields of knowledge (geopolitics, human rights and material culture) that assimilate and re-articulate these experiences. Here, human remains stand as epistemic objects bearing witness to present and past forms of violence, and serve as traces of missing identities. Examining the struggles for identification and repatriation that reclaim the right of identity, the chapter shows how the bones turn into public 'things' producing evidence and justice, and opening up the possibility of posthumous repatriation.

Here, 'anonymisation' enters the sphere of Achille Mbembe's description of the transition from the colony to the *postcolony* as the interval that preserves the ex-colonial subject under the yoke of the Western stigma of 'absence', 'non-being' and 'nothingness' (Mbembe, 2001: 4). Following Mbembe's scheme, the chapter unveils the way in which anthropometric materials and human remains embody such an 'absence' and represent the continuity between the colonial and the post-colonial eras.

'Anonymisation' usually belongs to media and computer science terminology where it is applied with regard to privacy and security concerns to contexts where personal identifying elements, information and data are removed from databases and media storage. 'Anonymisation' techniques perform the complete removal of personal identifiers from data and disassociate them permanently from the individual. It is therefore the process of destroying tracks. In other words, 'anonymisation' and 'de-identification' define the long process of the cancellation of nuances and details from the individual history and records of a given subject. The outcome is an artificial estrangement of the 'individual' from the 'subject'. In this chapter, 'anonymisation' operates through the body and functions throughout distant but symmetrical historical and political phases. Starting from colonial anthropometric artefacts and unidentified African skeletal remains preserved on the shelves of Italy's natural history museums this chapter widens the focus to the case of the human remains of Libyan freedom fighters who have been imprisoned and died in Italy's penal colonies in the 1930s. This chapter ends by arguing that today's 'anonymised' and 'de-identified' others are constantly present within the contemporary post-colonial discourse as undocumented migrants, refugees and asylum seekers who often die at sea borders.

Plaster masks and Italy's anthropology of race

Italian colonialism stretched from the period starting at the end of the nineteenth century, with the purchase of East African strips of land on the Red Sea (present-day Eritrea and Somalia), through the early occupation of Libya in 1911 and its re-conquest in 1932 operated by Mussolini, up to the fascist occupation of Ethiopia and the birth of the Empire in 1936. In this lapse of time, Italian colonial anthropology developed and became particularly concerned with African human skulls and physiognomy, and this was often manifested (as in many other European colonial countries) through colonial plunders of African bones and anthropometric experiments on the living bodies of African natives (producing casts in plaster to immortalise African faces).

The case of plaster masks and African skulls purloined at the time of colonial occupation and their persistence on the dusty shelves of Italian anthropology museums demonstrates how the process of 'fossilising' natives points to nineteenth-century European anthropology's creation of the dogma of native timelessness. The museum space became the ideal repository for these objects. Timothy Mitchell argues that the colonial museum has introduced mechanisms of representation, which have shaped human diversity and otherness as natural rather than historically constructed (Mitchell, 1989). Thereby the opposition between modern and traditional, or natural forms of human existence, divided humanity into two halves, living in two different times.

Thinking of constructed 'timelessness' leads us also to anthropologist Johannes Fabian's understanding of colonialism, which he investigates through the conflation of time and space in terms of *chronopolitics*. Fabian claims that colonial power relies on an ontological separation and distance between the Western subject and its other, based on the following assumption 'what makes the savage significant [...] is that he lives in another time' (Fabian, 2002: 27). According to that idea, the archetypal construction of otherness in modern times expresses the spatialisation of time, as the real premise for the distribution of humanity in the geographical space, where the discourse on civilisation, evolution and development starts with classification through spatialised temporal slopes.

How then is anonymity deliberately constructed? Revolving around death, either as pre-mortem or post-mortem practices – the production of plaster masks on living bodies or the studies of dead human crania – colonial anthropometric measurements were able to realise 'immobility' on human faces, and hence immortalise natives' absence from history and celebrate it on the shelves of colonial anthropology museums. After Pierre Broca in 1866 introduced anthropology as a positive science inquiring into the classification of human groups, the scientific reconstruction of human life focused more on the material dimension of diversity, and the human face became a paradigmatic anthropological object able to set fixed indices for racial taxonomies. Anthropologically and ethnographically, museums represented the stage where colonial subjects, being removed both temporarily and spatially, could experience an ultimate degree of reification, turning into objects under the privileged observation of the scientist.

Lidio Cipriani is considered to be the Italian anthropologist whose work relied the most on the production and use of plaster masks to analyse human diversity. Cipriani travelled extensively in Africa during the 1920s and 1930s and was the leading figure of Italian anthropology at the time of fascism (Cipriani, 1932). He was actively involved in the creation of the 'anthropology of race' (Chiozzi, 1994: 91–4; Sorgoni, 2002) and he believed that human psychical functions and cultural behaviours depended on the morphology of skulls and brains. According to this understanding, racial inferiority was due to underdeveloped brain sections, such as the parietal and the frontal lobes (Cipriani, 1932: 589). Hence, human groups were classified by calculating and comparing their proportions across evolutionary cycles, and individual development, maturity and decline were seen as being merely due to biological reasons (Dore, 1981).

The justification of fascist racism was always at the centre of Cipriani's production of plaster masks. From his extensive travels across Ethiopia, Eritrea and Somalia, Cipriani brought back hundreds of masks. The most important collections of these are still held today at the Museum of Natural History within the section of Anthropology and Ethnology in Florence – founded by scientist Paolo Mantegazza in 1862 – and the Giuseppe Sergi Museum of Anthropology at La Sapienza University in Rome.

Anecdotes from Cipriani's diaries and archival photos show that from a technical point of view, taking a facial cast was a rather simple task (Cipriani, 1932: 21). The native was laid down on the ground, tied and liquid gypsum was poured onto his or her face. In this manner, a matrix was produced and the negative cast could be used to produce an infinite number of copies. As historian Andrew Zimmerman explains, 'making a plaster cast of a face took about forty minutes, during which time even pure gypsum plaster often began to irritate the skin. If the plaster was adulterated with lime [...] the process could cause serious burns'. But in this way 'plaster casts gave anthropologists a virtual human body, which, once taken, could be studied without having to deal with a resistant subject' (Zimmerman, 2003: 165).

When walking through the rooms and seeing the archives at the museums in Florence and Rome, the visitor will notice how Cipriani's collections today serve mainly to illustrate anthropology's history of racism (Zavattaro et al., 2011). However, the casts represent the trace, the embodiment of the absence of the subject's flesh and whole body, and reveal a subtext that discloses the preliminary steps of modern physical anthropology in constructing natives' identity, pushing the colonial subject towards an eternal and a-historical anonymity. The moment of the cast's production, through the pouring of the gypsum, discloses one of the preliminary forms of contact between the manufacturer/anthropologist and the native subject in the colonial context. In a context where mimesis entails dramatic contact, the coloniser discovers the corporeal dimension of knowledge.

Therefore, like Michael Taussig's sorcerers who make a copy of what they want to affect by acquiring the properties of the original, the masks of the natives' faces imply the colonisers' mastery and power over the object (Taussig, 1993: 26). In this sense, the organised control of mimesis aimed at representing racial types and *de facto* leads to the deliberate demolition of any trace of subjectivity and individuality. In relation to this, Kelly Gates in her study about biometric technologies highlights how in the late nineteenth century the proliferation of humanoid replicas through the techniques of plaster masks created the 'phantasms of the living' (Gates, 2011: 12).

The visual power and epistemological burden expressed by the masks at the museums Mantegazza and Sergi inspire to make a difficult, dual assumption: if on the one hand, the mask, as if it were a proper snapshot marking the instant in which the colonial subject undergoes the passage between life and death as a last testimony to the native's subjectivity, embodies the aesthetics of colonial domination, on the other hand, its material production corresponds to and symbolises the abandonment and departure from individuality and identity that the colonial subject is forced to undergo. In this sense, the epithet 'phantasm' cited above perfectly describes the corporeal volatility of the subject under colonial manipulation and reification. This process eventually achieves the aims of colonial anthropology: the construction of otherness through practices of de-personalisation, 'anonymisation' and negation.

The next section shifts the focus to the objects that best symbolise the power of 'anonymisation' practices: human remains. Human remains, unlike the 'phantasms' created by plaster masks, are instead a more complex and special category of museums' holdings, as ontological and epistemological issues concerning the identity of bones and skulls question the immobility they are forced into. Human remains can indeed give rise to disputes, demands and conflicts that might lead to breaking such immobility.

The postcolonial paleontological present

Since the nineteenth century, the exhibition of human remains has been used as evidence for the 'objective' scientific demonstration of racial difference. Bernard McGrane suggests that the emergence of anthropology and the proliferation of evolutionary museums institutionalised the 'necrology practiced on the living' (McGrane, 1989: 111). African bones, skulls and corpses were ideal for displays in museums to support Darwinian genealogies, where the 'ground zero' of human development finally gained an alternative aesthetic representation. The proximity of contemporary African bones to ancient human specimens belonging to our prehistoric ancestors allowed for the presentation of a gradual paleontological continuity, which was essential to immortalising otherness behind the glass of a showcase.

Through the exhibition of linear sequences of skulls and skeletal remains, scientific speculation – entangled with colonial domination – created new relations of space and time. The museum space, as the result of the denial of the agency of colonial subjects, indeed became the best stage to give representation to this 'frozen history' (Bennett, 2004). The looting of the bones introduced a *paleontological* influence in the form of prevarication of the 'material over textual evidence' (Ibid: 74). The crucial anthropological evidence offered by a 'naked' skull, emptied of its flesh, 'meant for anthropologists a human body without the subjective history of tissue'. In this way 'the corpse was in many ways a perfection of anthropological evidence voided of subjectivity' (Zimmerman, 2001: 86). In a more sophisticated and complex way than plaster masks, the captive skull became the ultimate device for the negation of any trace of agency and subjectivity of African natives, indeed becoming the symbol of direct ownership of the subject populations. Even if still speculative to scientific analysis, naked skulls devoid of history today present a problem for historical research.

The Giuseppe Sergi Museum of Anthropology in Rome holds a large collection of unidentified human skulls from colonial times currently stored in its dark back rooms. These human remains are mainly adult specimens that were collected and prepared since the beginning of the twentieth century. Many of them originally came from Italy's former colonies, Libya, Ethiopia, Eritrea and Somalia, but without relevant information about their status at the time of their taking. According to the testimony of Sergio Sergi (the son of the founder Giuseppe), in 1912, the human skeletal remains and the skulls held at the museum represented 'the most beautiful collection of Abyssinian crania after the one exhibited at the Society of Anthropology in Berlin' (Sergi, 1900). However, rare direct testimonies of travellers were sometimes able to provide a little description about the colonial acquisitions: often retrieved and collected along caravan routes at the time of European explorations and the colonisation of Africa, the bones were often the remains of Abyssinians, who, while migrating because of the drought affecting the Horn of Africa in 1894, succumbed to cholera spread during their exodus (Duchesne-Fournet, 1908).

The lack of precise labels has frequently prevented scientists and anthropologists from providing sufficient critical taxonomic information about the skulls. Today, epidemiological surveys, population biology, human palaeontology and forensic sciences still see these bones plundered a century ago to be their main objects of inquiry in explaining evolutionary origins (Bruner and Manzi, 2004: 51–6). As a matter of fact, due to the absence of relevant information (archival material and historical research) around the identity and the details of colonial collections (poor catalogues, empty archives, missing information around collectors and the missions which brought the specimens to Italy), the anonymous piles of African human skulls from ancient to more contemporary epochs *de facto* seem doomed to be permanently excluded from a public sphere capable of questioning colonial 'anonymisation' practices. Moreover, the absence of any public sphere built around them can also be explained from the perspective of law: if on the one hand it is true that the status of skulls as stolen artefacts might introduce legal debates around the illicit trafficking and restitution of cultural property, on the other hand it is also difficult to speak in terms of restitution when there is no actual request of return.

Unlike the Italian case, in the last decade the question of the repatriation of human remains previously plundered at the time of colonialism has stood out: disputes are constantly proliferating between Western institutions and governments from the ex-colonial world with differing results and ends. For instance, in Germany in 2011 a collection of Namibian skulls originally looted at the beginning of the twentieth century during the genocide of the Herero and Nama populations in German West Africa, was unexpectedly brought back into the spotlight. After Namibian pressure to revisit the dark chapters of its colonial history, Germany eventually agreed to return twenty of those skulls belonging to victims of the genocide a century ago, as a symbol of posthumous justice.

Alternatively, in the dispute between the Aboriginal community of Tasmania and the British Natural History Museum concerning human remains claimed by the former, the Museum had intended to conserve the remains in order to take DNA samples as material of scientific interest for future use. Similarly, the skull of Hintsa, the macabrely preserved Khoisan heads which were taken from the Cape Colony (South Africa) by the British in the early-mid nineteenth century, are still the object of disagreement. On the contrary, the famous Hottentot Venus, Saartjie Baartman, who was taken from South Africa around 1810 and died in France in 1816, and whose skeleton was displayed in the Musée de l'Homme until 1976, was returned to South Africa (Cornu and Renold, 2010: 10).

Human remains indeed allow us to re-think colonial legacies, reconnecting former empires to the ex-colonial world: retrieved routes and backward trajectories of colonial objects disclose entangled political struggles around cultural heritage and reparations, calls for political subjectivity and autonomy. There, human remains answer to the most complex questions around memory and colonial violence: what is the testimony for colonial atrocities? What is representation without oral testimonies? The scarcity of oral sources and data around early necro-political practices have always constituted a problem of assessing the crimes of European colonialism.

On the contrary, the bones, formerly abstracted from their conflict-ridden contexts and thereby undergoing the neutralisation of any emotional and political allegations, can eventually abandon their instrumental role of 'narrative device' which they were forced into by modern anthropology and medicine, either to describe evolutionary chains or to justify biological racism. Now they constitute a counter-power. Unlike plaster masks, which seem resembling more Michel Foucault's definition of *simulacra*, namely an anomalous type of materiality with only surface and no depth that 'dissipates the density of matter' (Foucault, 1977: 169–70), human remains are the embodiment of a human material transmutation from flesh to bones. Such a transition while introducing the idea of the co-existence of organic and inorganic matter as constitutive of the human body, preserves traces of identity and individuality. Human remains can be considered the ultimate epistemic trace for history telling.

On the one hand, remains can be considered the prime objects around which technologies of representation have evolved throughout history, shaping images of otherness as natural and therefore alien to the discourse of history, culture, progress and civilisation. On the other hand, human remains stand as epistemic objects and as perfect natural–cultural artefacts bearing witness to present and past forms of violence and traces of missing identities. It is therefore possible to understand how the ontological and epistemological value of human remains informs the politics of repatriation in the post-colonial era. As objects of reclamation for posthumous identification and justice from their aboriginal communities and descendants in the ex-colonial world, human remains, while dealing with the right of identity and repatriation, address questions of human rights and international humanitarian law.

Following these parallel trajectories, human remains are the 'historical manure which legitimates power and helps create social bonds as well as history' (Domanska, 2005: 120). They are both evidence of a crime and the reference point to what Thomas Keenan and Eyal Weizman define as a 'theatre of mourning' (Keenan and Weizman, 2012: 67). In spite of the old 'spatial arrangements' and certain 'epistemic ordering' (Roque, 2011) of the anthropology of colonialism, human remains while seeking identity, evidence and justice enter the sphere of public truth. Such events can be considered as the mementos that inaugurate an effective decolonisation of science, where both the tools of violence and their objects experience a radical inversion of trajectories. From embodying an ultimate stage of anonymity, bones turn into epistemic tools for seeking identity, while science now acts on behalf of postcolonial justice.

The next section expands this debate to historical events where postcolonial disputes have been generated around the question of repatriation of human remains from colonial era cemeteries/mass graves, and have deeply changed the relations and cooperation plans between Italy and Libya in the postcolonial present.

Libyan legacies in the Mediterranean

Unlike the German/Namibian case, the 'immobility' of the bones in Italy still marks the same spatialisation and temporalisation of bodies that were constructed a century ago. However, the temporal and spatial 'immobility' experienced by the African human bones described above is, nevertheless, not exclusive to such a context. The presence in Italy of human traces of African natives from colonial times is a reality that cannot be historically confined to the showcases and archives of anthropology museums. Traces on the Italian ground of colonial human remains also come from the times of deportation of Libyans and Ethiopians who had been exiled to Italy, as part of the Italian strategy to break anti-colonial resistance under both liberalism and fascism. Therefore, while some human remains have been found as such, gathered and then taken to Italy and placed behind glass, the colonial wars also presented Italy with an opportunity to collect 'living' people and force them into exile in Italian penal colonies erected on islands and little archipelagos in the Mediterranean.

Since the early stages of Italy's liberal colonisation of Libya in 1911, the Mediterranean has been the crossing place and privileged site for exercising control over and policing the bodies of colonial subjects. Many of the exiled rebels died on these islands and were buried in mass graves, becoming *de facto* nameless victims of Italian deportation.

In the early 1990s, Colonel Muammar Qaddafi forwarded a request to the Italian authorities to allow a delegation of 200 Libyan citizens to enter the island of Ustica in Sicily to visit a charnel house hosting the remains of 132 Libyans who were deported and then died on the Sicilian island in 1911 and 1912. After the 1911 battle of Shara Shatt in Libya, which saw Italian troops heavily challenged by Libyan resistance, the liberal government of Giovanni Giolitti started to deport suspected fighters who were put onto boats heading towards Italy (Del Boca, 2006). Many of them were piled in the sheep hold, and some died because of asphyxiation while crossing the Mediterranean. Many prisoners also died a short time after their disembarkation: 500 Libyans who arrived in October 1911 in the Tremiti archipelago in the south-eastern Puglia region did not survive their first month of captivity, and a mass grave was arranged on the small island of San Nicola. According to a rare testimony of an old inhabitant of the island 'every day, 10 to 12 Libyans were dying. Their remains are preserved in the most desolate part of the island' (L'Unità, 2011).

Like Tremiti and Ustica, other Italian archipelagos and islands such as Favignana and Ponza, as well as the gulf of Gaeta, are also sites that are known for having been used as penal colonies for Libyan rebels and other Ethiopian notables and freedom fighters. Many of the prisoners who were not repatriated died over the years because of the spread of tuberculosis, smallpox, typhus and other epidemics caused by the harsh conditions of imprisonment, life and hygiene on the islands.

According to the work of the Centro Studi e Documentazione Isola di Ustica, the few reports retrieved from some municipal archives of Ustica's town hall and Palermo's police headquarters display how the taxonomy of death made by Italian authorities was very superficial and approximate: the deceased were catalogued with numbers, and only vague indications were given regarding their age and origin. The causes of death were generally left blank. The bodies were then piled up and buried in a mass grave. Up to the present day the Favignana and Tremiti archipelagos also preserve the remains of Libyan prisoners who still lie in mass graves that were only recently converted into mausoleums.

Only after Qaddafi and the Italian Prime Minister Silvio Berlusconi signed an historic agreement in 2008 – the Treaty of Friendship, Partnership and Cooperation between the Italian Republic and the Great Socialist People's Libyan Arab Jamahiriya – did the requests for exhumation, repatriation and compensation for Libyan deaths cease. The agreement around colonial reparations between Italy and Libya emerged around important economic and political reciprocal exchanges. Most importantly, Libya and Italy built a strong partnership over the fight against undocumented immigration. Italy and other EU countries for years sought the cooperation of

Colonel Qaddafi's Libya – a non-state party to the 1951 UN Convention relating to the Status of Refugees – to stem the flow of people arriving in Europe from Africa, which resulted in serious violations of the human rights of refugees, asylum-seekers and migrants.

Since 2008, Italian/Libyan deals around migration have become the object of a huge public debate, raising criticism and condemnation from Amnesty International and the European Court of Human Rights. According to Human Rights Watch, the agreement around the Italian/Libyan joint operations for border protection known as 'push backs' – namely the interception of undocumented migrants and asylum seekers in Italian territorial waters and returning them to Libyan ones – was set up in complete defiance of international humanitarian law (Human Rights Watch, 2009). The recent militarisation of the Mediterranean and its transformation into an open space of policing, rather than the discouraging of the movement of people, has rendered these crossing trajectories more and more perilous, causing a dramatic increase in the death toll since 2011 after the collapse of Qaddafi's regime (UNHCR, 2012).

The case of dead bodies and human remains of unidentified African migrants from the Maghreb, Sub-Sahara and the Horn of Africa, who drown in the Mediterranean en route to Europe, represent for this chapter the ultimate examples of 'anonymisation' practices. The number of migrants who die on the marine frontiers because of shipwrecks, severe weather conditions or asphyxiation is high but remains 'unknown, as are the identities of many – perhaps most – of those who have died' (Grant, 2011: 136). Most of the retrieved bodies remain anonymous, unless possible survivors or relatives are willing or able to participate in the identification process. Loss of identity is the most common peculiarity of irregular travel, where small boats used by smugglers have no passenger lists and migrants move without identity documents because of the threat of immediate forced repatriation to their country of origin. Since one frequent consequence of undocumented migration is the loss of personal identity – name, nationality, religion, home country and family – establishing the identities and then marking the graves of these people are extremely difficult operations, due to the complications caused by the same process of denying entry into Italy in the first place. In most of the cases, despite humanitarian international law and the International Committee of the Red Cross guidelines regarding the right of the dead to be identified, individually buried or returned to their family if possible, the bodies of migrants from the boats or waters still belong to a realm of anonymity and to an indistinct and undefined space and time, devoid of name, origin and state.

Apart from the survivors, as a matter of routine, those who undergo a definitive loss of identity are those who vanish in blue water and those whose dead bodies are dragged by tidal currents and washed up onto the shores. After forensic analysis to understand the causes of death, the bodies are stored with catalogued numbers that hold all of the collected information for future identification. In many cases after shipwreck around Lampedusa or in the eastern/southern coasts of Sicily, the burial procedures then commonly take place in those villages on the Sicilian coast that are willing to host unidentified dead migrants within their cemeteries.

But as shown before, the occurrence of death interrupting the travel of undocumented migrants is just the last moment of a forced 'anonymisation' process that starts much earlier, an event that does not strictly depend on death for its own realisation. In fact, as reported by Stefanie Grant describing Caroline Moorehead's collections of some very compelling testimonies from the island of Lampedusa, for many smuggled migrants who have safely reached the Sicilian coasts, the loss of identity is a voluntary act in response to the fear of detection: their refusal to tell even the villagers who have welcomed and supported them who they are or where they have come from, seems to be a recurring scene which, beyond death, proves the liquidity of the mechanisms of production of anonymity (Moorehead, 2005: 70).

Nevertheless, since the early 2000s when new EU and national policies and technologies of government have been implemented to tackle undocumented migration, the evidence of nameless graves on Italian soil emerges as a consequence of an increasing number of anonymous deaths at sea. While sometimes it is possible to detect the country of origin of the unknown migrant, in most cases this is a difficult task. In some cases, like for instance in the cemetery of Canicattì in Agrigento, Sicily, there are three graves that are marked with *Cittadino Liberiano* or Citizen of Liberia, with a single letter of the alphabet to distinguish one from the others, because none of the survivors was able or willing to name the bodies.

But in many other cases, even this is an unrealistic expectation. At the cemetery of Scicli, 80 unidentified dead migrants are buried in unmarked graves. The bodies were retrieved from the waters near the coastal boroughs of Donnalucata, Sampieri and Cava d'Aliga under the municipality of Scicli in Ragusa, Sicily, between 2004 and 2011. The rudimentary gravestones are made of thin marble plates that are covered by a wooden tablet and a leaf. On the paper is written *Cadavere di persona sconosciuta* or 'cadaver of unknown person' and *Cadavere N. 5* or 'cadaver number 5', followed by *Sbarco di clandestini* or 'disembarkation of illegal immigrants', to explain the cause of death, after which the location and date of the body's retrieval from the coast are indicated. It is indeed the *illegal* condition of being an undocumented traveller that is the last mark of the identity of this dead individual. In this way, the conditions that determined his/her loss of identity, namely a restricted regime of mobility, leave the last markers on the body – a body turned into 'phantasm'.

Entangled 'anonymisations'

In his essay *Walter Benjamin's Grave,* Michael Taussig describes the atmosphere of Port Bou's cemetery in Spain, where the body of Benjamin lies. In 1940, after being refused entry to Spain while escaping from Nazi Germany, Benjamin committed suicide with a high dose of morphine. His body was then disposed of with other dead refugees and Spanish republicans into *fossa communes*. While cemeteries represent and exist to keep a direct bond between name and body, the living and the dead, mass graves are commonly perceived as the home of absence, namelessness, secrecy and disappearance. In Taussig's words, the Port Bou's lost remains look like 'the princess in the fairy tale awaiting the kiss of the prince' (Taussig, 2006: 19).

In the post-colonial era, the story of Benjamin's desperate final act has been inspirational for global border narratives and struggle for the right to escape. Moreover, the deep sense of absence embodied by Benjamin's story reinforces the ties with the questions around 'anonymisation', death and post-mortem invisibility at the time of postcolonial migrations, currently centring around the Mediterranean route of escape.

Between October 2013 and 2016, the most dramatic shipwrecks in the Mediterranean took place. On 3 October 2013, 350 refugees and migrants died in a shipwreck off the Italian island of Lampedusa, while a week later, on 11 October, an additional 200 passengers died in the same place. In April 2015, more than 800 people drowned in the central Mediterranean during an operation of rescue operated by a private cargo. IOM estimates at least 3,771 deaths in the Mediterranean Sea in 2015, while UNHCR calculates that 'an average of 14 people have died every day in the Mediterranean Sea during 2016, the highest number ever recorded' (UNHCR, 2016). Again, most of these deaths remained anonymous.

There are several aspects that should be considered in order to understand how the 'militarisation of the Mediterranean' (Fekete, 2003) functions as the pre-condition of the increase of death tolls in it (Spijkerboer, 2007: 132).

After the collapse of Qaddafi's regime, and the Syrian exodus caused by the civil war, new practices forbidding migrants to reach Europe have been implemented. Lorenzo Pezzani and

Charles Heller with the project of Forensic Oceanography have described and focused on how the 'war against migrants' (Migreurop, 2007) functions through 'mechanisms of illegalisation, militarisation and refusal to assist' (Heller and Pezzani, 2014). The project offers a detailed documentation (made of extensive investigations built on interviews, mapping, modelling, satellite images, animations and visual reconstructions of the crime scene) of those practices of 'non-assistance' that too often lead to the deaths of migrants at sea.

Firstly, 'illegalisation' functions through the increase of visa restrictions by EU states towards the non-Europeans. Accordingly, travellers are forced to 'resort to dangerous means of crossing and rely on smuggling networks, which usually provide boats in poor condition' (Ibid.). Secondly, the militarisation via more or less legal means (again the case of the illegal pushbacks or direct physical violence by border guards) and the creation in 2005/2006 of Frontex, the European Agency for the Management of Operational Cooperation at the External Borders of the Member States increased surveillance, interceptions and patrols of the routes of migration. These made the crossing routes in the Mediterranean more perilous and eventually increased the human cost. Lastly, the criminalisation of assistance: too often coastal states, potentially in charge of processing the asylum requests or for deporting migrants, have become progressively unwilling to assist migrants in danger.

In 2014, the Italian government launched a massive military–humanitarian operation called *Mare Nostrum* aimed at the rescue of migrants at sea which inverted the trend described above. While the operation constituted a considerable break with the practices of non-assistance, it did not last long. Its conclusion in November 2014 led to the more limited operation *Triton*, which inaugurated a new phase: rather than being grounded on proactive patrolling, *Triton* relies on the loose coordination between Frontex, the Italian Coastal Guards and private cargos (Heller and Pezzani, 2016). As border controlling constitutes *Triton*'s main priorities, the situation came back to the status quo where the militarisation of the sea – together with the politics of non-assistance – would not prevent border crossings but rather cause more deaths.

In this scenario, the sea itself emerged as the crime scene. There, the forced invisibility is produced on a mass scale completing *de facto* the process of 'anonymisation'. Not only names, faces, and families are vanishing but also the testimonies, tales and memories of transnational migration and global economic inequality. While border language uses a terminology of deterrence focusing on the responsibility of smugglers only as a way to justify the policies' unintended consequences of increasing the number of deaths, the sea becomes the most effective tool of boundary enforcement. Jason De León's description of the desert at the American/Mexican border as the most efficient killing machine, emphasises how the raw physicality of the environment complements state power. Bare spaces swallow their victims, while the environment erases traces of state violence. Across deserts – as much as in blue waters – there are no executioners anymore as 'nature civilizes the way government deals with migrants' (De León, 2015: 68).

Here, the sea, like deserts, generates liquid mass graves, where human bodies in their slow process of decomposition are returned to a state of bare nature and timelessness. 'Anonymisation' is again produced through space and time, while namelessness – as if we were in colonial times – constitutes the epistemic foundation of necro-violence. Across different epochs and cases, it has been possible to trace a continuous and seemingly endless sense of obscurity built on the legacy of human traces in multiple nameless contexts and from across different temporalities: human specimens in anthropology museums, exiled Libyans buried in mass graves in former Italian penal colonies, and unidentified migrants in unmarked graves in Sicily.

The contact point between the human specimen, exiled freedom fighters and migrants is indeed defined around them being subject to being forced through artificial and cyclical 'anonymisation' phases where the ultimate stage is represented by the dissolution of human tissues into mineral traces, whose only fragment of identity relies on the type of petrified human remains that early modern anthropology used as ultimate evidence to deny subjectivity.

Nevertheless, in spite of the constructed limbo that human remains seem forced to experience, the hermeneutics of bones and skulls relies on the assumption that such artefacts are considered to be the major trace of physical evidence. Indeed, it is the notion of this *trace* itself that brings back to the fore a lasting debate around the ontological status of the past and its influence on the present. Skeletal remains, while holding traces of inter-connected historicities (tying victims to perpetrators, the colonised to the coloniser, and shaping temporal continuities along the axis of colonialism/decolonisation/post-colonialism), can open up the possibility of unexpected individual or collective acts of mourning, post-colonial demands for emancipation, and struggles ranging from questioning the illicit trafficking of cultural properties, shedding light on the possession of others' cultural heritage, to the struggle for recognition for those who 'vanish' at sea borders.

Indeed, this parallelism is founded on a shared origin that is marked by the total loss of identity. Nevertheless, this same condition is to be the inception of a new path, designing a symbolic kinship between the bones – the ones kept on museum shelves, in mass graves and nameless burial chambers and unidentified remains after death at sea. In all cases the struggle is for identity and return. The case of the Namibian bones illustrated before clearly opens to the possibility of new directions. Against the same techniques which impose upon the subject a forced 'anonymisation' that is, to reach a stage of inanimate materiality, it is the materiality itself of the human subject and its mineral tissues that allows us to trace the lost elements of human subjectivity. In this sense, the bones set the aesthetics of law serving a dual purpose: collective mourning for the benefit of the memory of the dead, and then justice, awarding compensation for a crime or loss. Hence the retrieved identity of the skulls symbolises and leads one to think of decolonising objects, towards the dismantling of an old-fashioned colonial matrix of power grounded on mechanisms of 'anonymisation'.

Since 2014, the research centre LABANOF – Laboratorio di Antropologia e Odontologia Forense – based at the University of Milan, operates to give identity to those unidentified bodies retrieved at Italy's sea borders. Cristina Cattaneo, forensic pathologist and director of the lab, explains how the project intends to rescue the identities of the victims in order to 'reconcile the living with their dead loved ones' (Piscitelli et al., 2016: e512). In so doing, LABANOF, in a joint effort with the Italian Office of the Commissioner for Missing Persons and other Italian academic institutes and NGOs (but without the financial support of the Italian Government), have started to build a database to help identify the scores and names of the dead: DNA comparisons are made and 'much of the data is culled from autopsies: tattoos, surgery scars, dental records and other biological remains' (*New York Times*, 2015).

Stressing the importance of 'improving the forensic analysis, documentation and identification of dead migrants' Cattaneo recalls the 'previous challenging experiences in humanitarian forensic action to identify the dead, including from the tsunami but also from countries affected by armed conflicts and other forms of violence, such as South America and the Balkans' (Cattaneo et al., 2015: e2). Technically the identification process requires the comparison between ante-mortem and post-mortem data: scientists and doctors need to find and coordinate family members, who might hold 'fragments of the lost lives — photographs, ID cards and photos or videos, clinical and dental records and personal effects like toothbrushes or combs — to help make a match' (*New York Times*, 2015).

The development and the success of such practices confirm the intuition of Keenan and Weizman that forensics turns out as the practice that encompass more than just death, revealing an agency of skeletal remains and corpses. They place human remains at the centre of humanitarian, political, scientific, symbolic and cultural intersections, within the sphere defined by Bruno Latour of forms of non-human agency: through the calculations of performed actions, produced effects and altered situations, life, history and politics are performed by and around material things as much as by human agents (Keenan and Weizman, 2012: 29; Latour, 1999: 303).

In 2015, the Italian government started to recover the 800 bodies from the largest shipwreck that has ever occurred in the Mediterranean, dated 18 April 2015. This event can be considered the first state-driven process of exhumation of migrants' remains from the Mediterranean Sea. From South America to the Balkans and Rwanda, exhumations have always been part of humanitarian processes. This usually starts when conflict is over and times are mature for reconciliation and reparation. While it is difficult to understand at which stage in history the war against migrants is, these exhumations seem to be leading to the Plaza de Mayo's Grandmothers' model and struggle in post-dictatorship Argentina: the creation of a genetic database to store the genetic information of the families looking for the disappeared and the missing children of dissident families (Arditti, 1999). The database offers a model for scientists working on behalf of justice and human rights, with the right of identity being at the core of the struggle. In 2016, LABANOF working on the case of the 18 April 2015 shipwreck pursued a similar agenda, addressing questions of memory, justice, publicness and trauma.

Conclusion

In this chapter, practices of 'anonymisation' have been presented as a complex and sophisticated aspect of the penetrative power of both colonial and post-colonial technologies of government: through the reading of human remains and anthropometric replicas it is possible to unveil the ultimate stage of colonial subjection, namely the transformation of colonial subjects into real objects. This investigation inspires at the same time a reflection around today's necro-political violence at sea borders, outside and beyond the frameworks of law and memory. The recognition of the victim's identity necessitates the recognition of the level of violence perpetrated and the mechanism that generates it. In the same way, we interrogate the facial expressions of those plaster masks held in anthropology museum since the time of colonial explorations; it is possible to investigate what the grimaces of pain and the bloated faces typical of drowning victims can say about the mechanisms and ideology that have 'made' them.

Against the same techniques which impose upon the subject a forced 'anonymisation' that is, to reach a stage of inanimate materiality, it is the materiality itself of the human subject and its mineral tissues that allow us to trace the lost elements of human subjectivity. As Derek Gregory comments while thinking of Foucault, 'power is productive, constitutively involved in the double process of *assujetissement*: subjection and subjectification' (Gregory, 1994: 191). Accordingly, power dynamics are performative in this double sense and are themselves inceptive of new 'subjectification' that may lead to the elaboration and creation of new counter-powers or practices of resistance.

From the museums' shelves, through unnamed gravestones to the Mediterranean's blue waters this currently happens around disputes of reparations and around the identification process. In all these cases, legal and civil battles carried out by descendants, relatives and families, activists, lawyers, academics and aid workers aim to reclaim these bodies and their identities, which have become invisible while technologies of government in both colonial and post-colonial times become operative and effective.

Aimé Césaire, while describing colonialism not as a mere form of exploitation but as a real practice aiming at the dehumanisation and objectification of the colonial subject, has offered the equation 'colonisation = thingification' (Césaire, 1972: 21) as a preliminary premise to understand the colonial logic of domination. While as we have seen, mechanisms of 'thingification' cannot be temporally and spatially confined to museum spaces, it is through this ultimate stage of human reification or 'thingification' that the colonial scheme of subjection can be reversed. With the support of science and forensics, it is specifically on the basis of the material and seemingly inanimate status of the postcolonial subject that new discourses on agency and resistance are ready to develop.

Bibliography

Arditti, Rita. 1999. *Searching for Life: The Grandmothers of the Plaza de Mayo and the Disappeared Children of Argentina*. University of California Press.

Bennett, Tony. 2004. *Pasts Beyond Memory: Evolution, Museums, Colonisation*. New York: Routledge.

Bruner, Emiliano and Giacomo Manzi. 2004. Variability in Facial Size and Shape among North and East-African Human Populations. *Italian Journal of Zoology*, 71 (1): 51–6.

Cattaneo, Cristina, M. Tidball Binz, L. Penados, J. Prieto, O. Finegan and M. Grandi. 2015. The Forgotten Tragedy of Unidentified Dead in the Mediterranean. *Forensic Science International,* 250: e1–e2.

Césaire, Aimé. 1972. *Discourse on Colonialism.* Translated by Joan Pinkham. London: Monthly Review Press.

Chiozzi, Paolo. 1994. Autoritratto del Razzismo: le Fotografie Antropologiche di Lidio Cipriani. In *La Menzogna della Razza. Documenti e Immagini del Razzismo e dell' Antisemitismo Fascista*. Edited by the Centro Furio Jesi. Bologna: Grafis.

Cipriani, Lidio. 1932. *In Africa dal Capo al Cairo*. Firenze: Bemporad.

Cornu, Marie and Marc-Andre Renold. 2010. New Developments in the Restitution of Cultural Property: Alternative Means of Dispute Resolution. *International Journal of Cultural Property*, 17: 1–31.

De León, 2015. *The Land of Open Graves: Living and Dying on the Migrant Trail*. University of California Press.

Del Boca, Angelo. 2006. *Italiani, Brava Gente?* Milano: Neri Pozza.

Domanska, Ewa. 2005 Toward the Archaeontology of the Dead Body. *Rethinking History*, 9 (4): 389–413.

Dore, Giovanni. 1981. Antropologia e Colonialismo nell' Epoca Fascista: il Razzismo Biologico di Lidio Cipriani. *Annali della Facoltà di Lettere e Filosofia di Cagliari*, 2 (XXXIX): 285–313.

Duchesne-Fournet, Jean. 1908. *Mission en Ethiopie (1901–1903)*. Paris: Masson et cie.

Fabian, Johannes. 2002. *Time and the Other: How Anthropology Makes Its Object*. New York: Columbia University Press.

Fekete L. 2003. *Death at the Border – Who Is to Blame?* London: Institute of Race Relations.

Foucault, Michel. 1977. Theatrum Philosophicum. In *Language, Counter-Memory, Practice. Selected Essays and Interviews*. Edited by Donald F. Bouchard. Ithaca: Cornell University Press.

Gates, Kelly A. 2011. *Our Biometric Future. Facial Recognition Technology and the Culture of Surveillance*. New York: New York University Press.

Grant, Stefanie. 2011. Recording and Identifying European Frontier Deaths. *European Journal of Migration and Law,* 13 (2): 135–56.

Gregory, Derek. 1994. *Geographical Imaginations*. London: Blackwell.

Heller, Charles, Lorenzo Pezzani and Situ Studio. 2012. Forensic Oceanography. Report on the 'Left-To-Die Boat'. *Forensic Architecture.* http://www.forensic-architecture.org/wp-content/uploads/2014/05/FO-report.pdf.

Heller, Charles and Lorenzo Pezzani. 2014. Time to End the EU's Left-to-Die Policy. *openDemocracy*. https://www.opendemocracy.net/can-europe-make-it/charles-heller-lorenzo-pezzani/time-to-end-eu%E2%80%99s-lefttodie-policy

—— 2016. Ebbing and Flowing: The EU's Shifting Practices of (Non-)Assistance and Bordering in a Time of Crisis. *Zone Books. Near Futures Online*. http://nearfuturesonline.org/ebbing-and-flowing-the-eus-shifting-practices-of-non-assistance-and-bordering-in-a-time-of-crisis/

Human Rights Watch. September 2009. *Pushed Back, Pushed Around. Italy's Forced Return of Boat Migrants and Asylum Seekers, Libya's Mistreatment of Migrants and Asylum Seekers*. http://www.hrw.org/sites/default/files/reports/italy0909webwcover_0.pdf

Keenan, Thomas and Eyal Weizman. 2012. *Mengele's Skull: The Advent of a Forensic Aesthetics*. Berlin: Sternberg Press.

Latour, Bruno. 1999. *Pandora's Hope. Essays on the Reality of Science Studies*. Cambridge, MA: Harvard University Press.

L'Unità. 14 November 2011. *Ustica 1911, Il Lager della Vergogna*. http://archiviostorico.unita.it/cgibin/highlightPdf.cgi?t=ebook&file=/golpdf/uni_2001_11.pdf/14CUL29A.pdf&query=Kabul
Mbembe, Achille. 2001. *On the Postcolony*. Berkeley: University of California Press.
McGrane, Bernard. 1989. *Beyond Anthropology: Society and the Other*. New York: Columbia University Press.
Migreurop. 2007. *Guerre aux Migrants: Le Livre Noir de Ceuta et Melilla*. Edited by Emmanuel Blanchard and Anne-Sophie Wender. Paris: Migreurop.
Mitchell, Timothy. 1989. The World as Exhibition. *Comparative Studies in Society and History*, 31 (2): 217–36.
Moorhead, Caroline. 2005. *Human Cargo, a Journey among Refugees*. London: Chatto & Windus.
The New York Times. 2 October 2015. *Italian Lab Battles 'Not to Lose the Dead' from Migrant Ships*. http://www.nytimes.com/2015/10/03/world/europe/italian-lab-battles-not-to-lose-the-dead-from-migrant-ships.html?_r=0
Piscitelli, Vittorio, Agata Iadicicco, Danilo De Angelis, Davide Porta and Cristina Cattaneo. 2016. Italy's Battle to Identify Dead Migrants. *The Lancet*, 4: e512–e513.
Roque, Ricardo. 2011. Stories, Skulls, and Colonial Collections. *Configurations*, 19: 1–23.
Sergi, Giuseppe. 1900. *Specie e Varietà Umane. Saggio di una Sistematica Antropologia*. Torino: Bocca.
Sorgoni, Barbara. 2002. Racist discourses and practices in the Italian Empire under Fascism. In *The Politics of Recognizing Difference. Multiculturalism Italian-style*. Edited by Ralph Grillo and Jeff Pratt. Aldershot: Ashgate.
Spijkerboer, Thomas. 2007. The Human Costs of Border Control. *European Journal of Migration and Law*, 9: 129–39.
Taussig, Michael. 1993. *Mimesis and Alterity. A Particular History of the Senses*. London: Routledge.
——. 2006. *Walter Benjamin's Grave*. Chicago: University of Chicago Press.
UNHCR. 31 January 2012. *Mediterranean Takes Record as Most Deadly Stretch of Water for Refugees and Migrants in 2011*. http://www.unhcr.org/4f27e01f9.html
——. 23 December 2016. *Mediterranean Sea: 100 People Reported Dead Yesterday, Bringing Year Total to 5,000*. http://www.unhcr.org/news/briefing/2016/12/585ce804105/mediterranean-sea-100-people-reported-dead-yesterday-bringing-year-total.html
Zavattaro, Monica, Maria Gloria Roselli, Cataldo Valente, Anna Maria Bedini. 2011. Il Valore Della Diversita: Suggestione Estetica E Coinvolgimento Del Pubblico Sui Temi Della Biodiversita' Umana. *Museologia Scientifica -- Memorie*, 8: 201–3.
Zimmerman, Andrew. 2001. *Anthropology and Antihumanism in Imperial Germany*. Chicago: University of Chicago Press.
——. 2003. Adventures in the Skin Trade: German Anthropology and Colonial Corporeality. In *Worldly Provincialism: German Anthropology in the Age of Empire*. Edited by Glenn Penny and Matti Bunzl. Ann Arbor: University of Michigan Press.

12
VIOLENCE, HERMENEUTICS AND POSTCOLONIAL DIPLOMACY

Deep K. Datta-Ray

Introduction

India's Foreign Secretary (FS, top diplomat), who became National Security Advisor (NSA) and is a third generation member of the Ministry of External Affairs (MEA), once stated:

> strategic discourse is not yet developed enough to describe what we face as reality around us. The use of concepts from other situations and interests bear little relationship to our unique circumstance. We need to develop our own concepts (Menon 2007).

Implicit in the explicit call to rethink international relations (IR, the discipline) for Indian reality, is the denial of universal concepts. The import is astounding, for undermined is the hegemonic story of how *European* diplomacy became diplomacy, and the general narrative it arises from: modernity and modernisation.

Clearly, the investigation of bureaucrats can result in two possible outcomes: dismissal, which amounts to a charge of either trickery or insanity; or taking the individual at their word and probing. Even if at issue is the minor one of the functionary's morality, determining it requires examining the official. Following this bureaucrat into the proverbial rabbit hole then, is unavoidable. To do so is to map the Anglosphere's substance and limits, and to exceed them, by engaging the postcolonial not only as a temporal and spatial entity, but also capable of politics. Evidently politics is manifest in everyday practices. To interpret them in terms of practitioners, might reveal Indian politics to be generated by a rationality altogether different. Precisely that makes Henry Kissinger list the multitude of ways in which Indians are Westernised, only to bemoan: 'Americans have great difficulty in coming to grips with the way Indian leaders approach foreign policy' (2001: 154).

To lay bare the rationale for postcolonial diplomacy, in this case in India, requires first baring diplomacy's rationale, which will form the first part of this chapter. Conflated with a peculiarly Anglo-Saxon and modern practice, its origins are Christian. Replicating Christianity's mission of delivering us to unity, diplomacy sanctifies itself as uniquely capable of doing so. This linear understanding of time is history, and it manufactures automatons lacking in *judgement*, for actors are only expected to unthinkingly progress through history. In the postcolonial world, modernity claims to have already replicated this process. Yet this violence of conversion continues, and its vanguard is composed of *arriviste* analysts from the Global South who wage analytic-violence to convert the very rationality of postcolonials.

Yet this campaign actually suggests Indian diplomacy is altogether alternate. The next section therefore fabricates a heuristic capable of moving in a neutral fashion between rationalities, to avoid confirmation bias: Producer-Centred-Research (PCR). Inoculated against modernity, PCR eschews diplomacy's rationality by both recognising the postcolonial's ability to conduct politics and calculating this in their terms to produce not a modern analysis, but exegesis. PCR then, does not rely on the 'foundational knowledge of what constitutes IR': history. Rather, PCR upon 'creating alternative sites of knowledge construction', investigates them 'with an alternative set of tools and resources' (Behera 2007: 358).

The following section concerns the MEA, its denizens, and the extant analysis of nuclear diplomacy, for this topic is the only aspect of Indian foreign policy to be subjected to two analytical tools: Realist and Postcolonial. Deploying PCR makes palpable the entwinement of analytics in analytic-violence, by presupposing subjects to be ignorant and therefore denying them subjectivity. This is 'not a simple antithesis of knowledge. It is a state people attribute to others and is laden with moral judgement' (Hobart 1993: 1). Underpinning it is modernity's history, which is revealed to be a fabrication. Yet it still stands by ignoring Indians, denying them their practices, and denigrating them as irrational. Absurdly, the result is a vanishing subject, which warrants the contention: the metric for explicative success cannot simply be analytical coherence, for it pivots on analytic-violence.

Excavating their practices, and on their own terms, unveils coherence at the levels of the diplomat, the MEA and the state, which solidifies the claim for alterity. Moreover, these practices, when understood in practitioner terms, are pregnant with a plethora of scintillating possibilities unavailable to modernity. Alarmingly, also divulged are intimate relations, characterised by intensity, between all the elements of Indian diplomacy, and violence.

Modern diplomacy and the postcolonial

Violence is coded into modern diplomacy because it is the internationalisation of European diplomacy and its axioms are anarchy and binarism. For IR, anarchy is 'the central fact of the international system and the starting place for theorizing about it.' (Bull 1966: 35). The presumption that there is no unity obligates modern diplomacy to pursue an end diametrically opposite: utopian unity. This is binarism and it makes of history the overcoming of anarchy, that is, emancipation from violence. To move towards this is to progress-through-history. History then is unilinear and it:

- restricts progress thereby making it mono-directional and arterial;
- denies diplomats judgement by confining calculations of interest within pre-set origins and ends.

The prime explicator of this is James Der Derian who replicates centuries of European thought to conclude that diplomacy is the mediation of alienation (1987). 'European diplomacy's logical frame of reference is that unity is the natural condition of social order, which should be restored through proper mediation among its divided parts' (Feldman 2005: 223–4). European diplomacy's frame is alienation because lodged deep in Western society is Christianity. It pre-sets alienation as origin in the Old Testament with the fall of man, that is, estrangement from God. This is universalised as the 'brotherhood of man' in the New Testament, the semantic shift making one man's origin everyone's. Hence we are all dependent on God's mediator: Christ (Der

Derian 1987: 51–9, 69). He legitimises the Papacy, uniquely imbuing it with the power to unify us with God. With the end also pre-set, mankind has no need for judgment so no calculations of interest need be made. All that is possible is to unthinkingly move through linear time: history. To move forward is to progress-through-history and it has just one meaning: unity with God.

The word 'progress' itself derives from the Christian *profectus*: perfecting the soul by unifying with God (Koselleck 2002: 235). The Papacy progresses enough to establish spiritual unity in medieval Europe, because people believe. Its demise is the Reformation, which marks the rise of judgement because the Papacy is undermined by the belief in man's direct ability to negotiate unification with God. Significantly, the will to unify remains, despite the fracturing of Christianity into Catholicism and Protestantism. This new-found belief in man's ability to unify results in Christian society fragmenting into states as they usurp the Church's role in delivering unity (Der Derian 1987: 51–66, 105–16).

Nevertheless, this is a splintering which necessitates the modern diplomatic system, and it is sealed by the Treaty of Westphalia's appropriation and reproduction of spiritual unity as an intellectual contract; i.e. an admonition to accept Westphalia's assumptions in order to mitigate violence. Embarrassingly, this heralds a new technology to realise unity – diplomacy – but also obliterates unity because diplomacy regularises a religiously and politically fragmented Europe. This delusive notion is 'second order mediation' (Der Derian 1987: 127–8). In short, Europe displaces God, but not his logic: a pre-set origin and end remain. It means that the dawn of European judgement – the belief in man – is short-circuited by the maintenance of unilineal time. Though spirituality is abandoned because it failed to deliver unity as oneness with God, the idea of unity continues as an intellectual and diplomatic project. Its success makes for the 'culture of modernity' and it is, given its history, the 'culture of the dominant Western powers' (Bull 1977: 39).

Moreover, modern culture is 'rationality in the sense of action that is internally consistent with given goals [and] the modern diplomatic tradition embodies an attempt to sustain behaviour on this model.' Modern diplomacy then is a rationality. Its legatees are an 'elite culture, comprising the common intellectual culture of modernity' (1977: 39; 1984: 122). They are an exclusive club, a '*corpus Christianorum* bound by the laws of Christ' (Wight 1977: 128). His laws remain the 'essence of diplomacy … unchanged [because diplomacy is] always … promoting and justifying states' interests' (Berridge, Keens-Soper and Otte 2001: ix). Its calculation, in turn, remains insulated from judgement, for interest is simply a function of history. The calculation of interest is no more than the violence of assimilating all into the *corpus Christianorum*, that is, Westphalia.

Though anarchy is the origin for only Europe, its history demands an end predicated on incorporating all: unity. In short, the internationalisation of history. If the 'mutual estrangement of states from Western Christendom gives rise to an international diplomatic system' then 'the Third World's revolt against Western "Lordship" precipitates the transformation of diplomacy into a truly global system' (Der Derian 1987: 23). Hence, the seminal authors of diplomacy are, from Machiavelli to Kissinger, all from Christian societies. They have to be, because 'the modern world system … came into being in the Italian peninsula and reached its full expression in Europe'. As for diplomatic theory, it 'appeared at the same time as diplomacy began to assume its distinctively modern form in the late fifteenth century' (Berridge, Keens-Soper and Otte 2001: 1–2). Or so we are led to believe, for underscoring modernity's 'facts' is the tale of Europe as 'master' encountering the postcolonial and its restriction to four forms of mimicry which inexorably prove modernity's subjugation of postcolonial time. The forms are:

- outright capitulation;
- 'hybridity', introduced by anthropologists describing the 'mixture' of 'pure races' as mongrelised 'hybrids' (Duvernay-Bolens 1993; Kapchan and Strong 1999);

- 'cross-contamination' or the postcolonial's failure to mimic (Delanty 1995: 45–6);
- 'acculturation' or the postcolonial choosing to convert itself to protect itself from the West's violence (von Laue 1987: 43–5).

The capitulation thesis is dominant. Presumed is the casting of all postcolonial societies from a Western mould, making for an 'international cultural grammar of nationhood' (Löfgren 1989: 21–2). In one fell swoop, modern time is legitimised at the expense of all precolonial times and the practices they generate. Sequestering the past secures the present: diplomacy is born in Europe and internationalised, so nothing exists beyond history. The result is the globalisation of diplomacy as no more than the means to conduct violence now to free us from violence in the future. The abject submission and conversion of postcolonial India is most ably conducted by recent *arrivistes* to modernity. From India there is Dipesh Chakrabarty, for whom comprehending the postcolonial is 'impossible' without first taking on 'the burden of European thought and history' (2000: 4). Perhaps the vast amount of self-transformation required by Chakrabarty in taking on the 'burden' explains why he is limited to unearthing in terms of diplomacy, variations in anarchical-binarism (2002: xxi–xx). A variant of this is proffered by another Indian migrant, Dilip Gaonkar (2001: 14). Sudipta Kaviraj makes a similar argument for 'reflexivity' (2000: 138–40).

Less widespread is Charles Taylor's 'hybridity' thesis which destabilises the West's pre-eminence by removing Eastern deviancy. The postcolonial organically subsumes itself to become 'modern' (1999: 169–73); in practice this is 'cross-contamination' or the intermingling of two masters understood as dense cultures. Investigated in India, via an 'interactional perspective' (van der Veer 2001: 3–8), it maintains modernity's diplomatic rationale but permits the postcolonial a role in crafting it. Reinforcing this is 'acculturation': the world is not made Western but chooses to be so. The West, exceptional thanks to its Christian roots (Parsons 1971: 29), discovers military technology which makes its diplomacy. The only way to challenge Western domination is to auto-assimilate or Westernise oneself. The result is 'Western political ambition and competitiveness become universal' (von Laue 1987: 4–6). In short, even when choice is permitted, postcolonial India cannot escape modernity as 'master', for its time organises the world.

The locating of the 'practice of the analysis of Indian diplomacy' within these paradigms of dependency (Datta-Ray 2013) is, however, belied by modernity's rearguard invention of 'cultural diversity' or the problem of precolonial remnants to be assimilated at a later date (Luhmann 1997: 151). Modernity's hubris is further undermined by its errors, as noted by a former FS (Srinivasan 2014). Most significant is how analysts miscalculate on their own terms when they encounter postcolonials. India possesses a rationality at the least different from that of Pakistan, claims an analyst, paradoxically, by recourse to the totalising rationality of Realism to explain both Islamabad's and New Delhi's foreign policies (Ganguly 2001). In short, the claim to difference is stillborn for both are understood as followers of Realism! Another analyst makes the error of transforming Jawaharlal Nehru, India's first Prime Minister (PM) and architect of foreign policy, into being both Liberal and Realist. Astounding, for the two are ontologically incompatible (Chacko 2011). These mongrel arguments cannot suffice, because they impose modern time at the expense of their own analytic. Yet analysis persists.

Producer-centred-research

A hypothesis about why Indian migrant scholars and those resident in India, enclose India in modernity is offered from a much earlier migrant scholar. Thorstein Veblen sensed US academics assume their tiny group's way is universal, 'although it is evident to any outsider that it will take its character and its scope and method from the habits of life of the group, from the institutions with which it is bound in a web of give and take' (1918: 4). In short, migrants buy acceptance in their new homeland by containing peoples left behind. Immigrant insecurities about their ability to mimic to integrate into the host nation feeds the assimilative project. As for those in India striving to cage Indians, the 'web of give and take' has extended itself, since Veblen's time, into the postcolonial space. In India, the most comprehensive productions of modern knowledge germinate in Western academies or arise from Western financial charity.

Avoiding the ruptures that scar the doxology that is analysis and its foundational notion of time as history would necessitate an alternative hermeneutics. Its success rides on eschewing modernity's lexicon because it promotes narratives founded on a compromised time, regarding both postcolonial data collection and its interpretation. Such a method does not rule out of court, even before the trial has begun, the possibility of the postcolonial not being a function of modernity, yet is aware that despite Bull's *diktat*, rationality is no more Western than perception, thought or language (Ganeri 2001: 4). Contemplating such a possibility is to approach modernity's limits, which is precisely the threshold crossed via an altogether new hermeneutic: producer-centred-research (PCR). Its defining insight and practice are:

- postcolonials may be made sense of in postcolonial terms; and
- that the objects most directly connected to the subject must be engaged, not silenced.

To take these in turn, PCR's insight makes for a style of searching devoid of the paternalistic sentimentalism that is Liberal, Marxist, Realist and Global History; the egocentric fantasia of the postcolonial and postmodern; or mechanistic notions of the world as a self-organising and regulating ecosystem (Prakash 2000a, 2000b; O'Hanlon and Washbrook 2000; Barlow 1991). The failure of all three cliques to transcend history is evident in their politics, including the politics of research. The first set's categories apply to all to make for a politics of trusteeship that is really the imposition of European order. Postcolonial and postmodern analysis swings to the other extreme to make for a politics of hopelessly individuated subjects constantly sparring with one another (Lyotard 1984, 1988). The violence intrinsic to both camps is removed in 'Gaia' theories by rendering us apolitical by making us part of an automatically regulating ecosystem, cogs in a machine beyond our comprehension, let alone control. In short, the first flattens all politics to Europe's, the second returns us to Europe's political origins or anarchy, and the last takes us out of politics.

What this means in terms of India as subject, is exemplified by Ashis Nandy (1995). Commendably, he avoids the first error and transcends history by recognising Indians can only be made sense of in their own politics and he does so without rendering them apolitical. Nevertheless, Nandy undermines the very purpose of explaining Indians in terms of their own politics, by making his heuristic something totally alien to Indians until the 1920s: psychoanalysis. En masse, Nandy erases the 'superabundance' of textual and other political resources accumulated over at least 2,500 years and consistently utilised at every level of Indian society (Ganeri 2008: 553). Replacing them is a Western metric born at the tail end of colonialism and one limited to a tiny section of the population.

Like Nandy, PCR's insight does not deny politics, only the fact that it may be possible to move beyond modernity's history and all that that entails. Moreover, PCR also anticipates that political theory is not a craft exclusive to a handful of Westerners, but evident in postcolonial practice. Unlike Nandy then, PCR views postcolonials as 'authoritative sources', using them to interpret their practices instead of relying on Western intellectuals and their metrics, for instance, Sigmund Freud and psychoanalysis (Halliburton 2004). The failure to do so is analysis. '[W]hen shit happens – events that defy conventional language, fit no familiar pattern, follow no conception of causality – I [Der Derian] reach for Virilio's conceptual cosmology' (2000: 215). He will not reach out to the people who make shit happen, because that tacitly admits modernity is not 'master'. In other words, Der Derian and his *gurus* are 'shit'. Therein lies the precise recognition of practices that disclose a rationality altogether alternate: alterity. Its existence renders delusive the compelling and absolutely obvious nature of an all-time modernity as no more than pretence.

Deploying PCR is to engage the subject in terms of its rationality. Understood as 'an ideas toolkit' (Wilkening 1999: 705–6), rationality is not only 'a phenomenon to be accounted for' but also 'one that accounts' (Friedman 1994: 27). These 'macro' categories are expressed in real life micro-sociological situations (Durkheim and Mauss 1971: 812). Modernity then, is operationalised by its own 'tool kit', and if used by postcolonials, then proves their containment in history. It, of course, cannot order a PCR that might deal in different times. It is to inoculate PCR against history, that its characteristics have been delineated. Hence, the question is not Max Weber's, 'Why has only the West produced cultural developments of "universal significance and value"?' (1958: 13–31) that propels PCR, but the reverse: What is the postcolonial present and has it been sequestered by history?

The answer lies in micro-sociological research which is consistently made sense of in terms of the producer's rationality. The objects for research are naturally determined by the subject. Since this PCR seeks postcolonial diplomacy's rationality, the objects are all that comprise such a state's diplomacy. In other words, PCR truly entertains the possibility that the postcolonial may not be a capitulation to, or a hybrid of, modernity, but may be animated by a different time altogether. Indian diplomacy may therefore play a politics incalculable in modernity's lexicon, in a manner unencumbered by its certainties and to realise goals indecipherable. Determining them requires research not in terms of modern metrics – in any way or form – but in terms of the practitioners themselves. This is what makes the conduct of PCR not analysis, but exegesis, for what might be unearthed in terms of rationality is alterity.

Hermeneutics beyond modernity

Deploying PCR in the postcolonial, in the first instance, clarifies the analytic-violence lodged at the empirical core of modern analytics: Realist and Postcolonial. Both parrot the same linear history: an immature India learns the costs of its idealism and matures to mimicking modernity by imperfectly speaking the West's language of nuclear diplomacy, Mutually Assured Destruction (MAD) or deterrence. This is sometimes termed '*ad hocism*' (Kumaraswamy 2004). India began 'mimicking the once-derided big powers' (Perkovich 2001: 505). This popular story is regurgitated by Indians in modernity's employ (Raja Mohan 2003: xxii). For Realists then, India's capitulation to their analytics and its replication, is progress-through-history. Yet Indian practice defies categorisation, and so Indian permutations of Realism are sought (Paul 2010). In other words, ruptures in Realist analysis turns them to account for India in terms of 'hybridity', 'acculturation' and 'cross-contamination' and condemn India for being no more than an incompetent simulacrum.

Indian diplomacy is also subject to analytic-violence by postcolonial analysts, despite their 'ambivalence' heuristic. It politicises the material to argue that meaning cannot be fixed. The position was first deployed by Itty Abraham (1998) who tried to further corral Indian diplomacy into 'ambivalence' a decade later with an edited volume (2009). Around the same time appeared Karsten Frey's monograph on Indian nuclear policy (2006). All three works utilise 'ambivalence' to argue that the atom is for development or security. The result is that what for Realists leads to an inept maturity becomes for Postcolonials, regress. New Delhi is disdained as infantile and incapable of managing the atom, for Indians succumbed to the atom's violence. In short, and just like Realists, Postcolonial claims ride on imprinting history on India. However, 'ambivalence' makes Postcolonials decry India's mimicry as irrational.

PCR not only illustrates how analytic-violence is used to commandeer Indian reality, but also how modernity's claims are at best tenuous at a foundational level: history. A hint of history's unravelling lies in modernity's self-proclaimed history in India. The claim – a subset of the modernisation thesis – that diplomacy was imposed upon India by the British, is ironically undone by their own records. These illustrate that the British, far from imposing themselves, sought to tessellate into the existing order, the Mughal Empire. The precursors of the British state in India, the East India Company (EIC), achieved this in 1717. Tessellation continued till 1857, when the EIC's Indian troops mutinied in favour of the Emperor and as a result, the British wrested away his sovereignty. The proclamation of the British Queen as Empress of India in 1877 completed the process (Datta-Ray 2016).

The intervening years saw the British appropriate wholesale Mughal diplomatic systems and personnel. Both were undoubtedly modified and globalised, but this was in keeping with the tenor of processes from Mughal times. The only authentically British contribution was to sequester, on the basis of 'race', all executive positions. Only in 1918 was a token 'native' (the word Indian being reserved for whites in India) permitted to become an executive – for one year. Racial manipulation meant that at independence, natives had almost no experience of modern diplomacy (Fisher 1984, 1990, 1993; Hogben 1981). The newly founded state's diplomatic apparatus was thus populated by a *milieu* which only knew diplomacy at a remove. In short, British-India's model was not diplomacy as invented in Europe and in any case, it was unfamiliar to Indians.

While the turn away from this compromised history of modernisation is facilitated by PCR, its true import lies in the immediate abrogation of Europe's role in ordering Indian diplomacy now. An inkling of history's, and hence modernity's, irrelevance are the multiple narratives of the MEA, by the MEA and for itself. There are three parsimonious origin stories. For probationers – new entrants, nearly all of whom will become ambassadors – there is an 'introduction' which claims the origins in the 'Secret and Political Department' in 1842 (Ministry of External Affairs n.d., slide). For the public, the date is 1783 when the 'Foreign Department' was created (Ministry of External Affairs n.d., Indian Foreign Service). For researchers, the date is pushed to 1756 by the institution's Historical Division, to a 'Secret Committee' of the British East India Company (EIC) established in Bengal (IFS Officer 2; Ministry of External Affairs n.d., documents).

It is at this juncture that PCR's aim of treating Indians as capable of not only politics, but also understood on its terms begins to be realised. Analysts, no doubt, will be exasperated by a people aspiring to modernity for so long still being confused by history. On the other hand, PCR is blasé, for it is inoculated against presuming everything is modern. Nevertheless, all three stories deposit the MEA in modernity, which enhances the incongruity of origins (as opposed to origin, even if its history was truthful) so important to modernity. Rather than dismiss this as error as modernity does by presuming history, PCR turns to the subjects to explain. A probationer, upon being pressed, unscrambled the narratives, but in terms of a purpose, and means, inexplicable to modernity's history. What it amounts to is a glimpse of alterity:

> You see, we are secular. So a secular history cannot create a timeline going back further. We are so riven with all kinds of things but we are here. This kind of story then

becomes the best way of ... you know ... maybe of not causing any problems [today]. ... So for the purposes of an introduction it worked' (IFS Probationer 2).

Similar comments were made by others (IFS Probationer 4, 5, 7, 9, 12, 15, 16 and 20). To view the past as they do converts the MEA's pronouncements from a morass of confused steps into history, to a balm soothing the multitude of differences within the MEA including, but not limited to, racial, religious and social. This is also the moment where modernity's hubris is exposed, for it is no more than a technology to further alterity. This is because Indians employ modernity's secularism. An outgrowth of Christianity, secularism is homogeneity and of the same order which leads to diplomacy: both restrict difference by an underlying intellectual contract (Connolly 1999: 19–25; Taylor 2007).

The MEA in appropriating this modern tool shears away the contract. Instead of assimilative violence flattening all intellects into history, secularism is employed to instead manage a present whose hallmark is a variety of intellectual categories and tangible differences from the past. Pre-modern categories do not just persist; they are perpetuated to proliferate at the very centre of a state presumed modern. Moreover, the probationer's progress rejects history, by making the field of reflection and action the present. Despite utilising modernity, it manifestly is not promoted. Combined, these throw into disarray Realism for the very history upon which it posits Indian learning is refuted by modernity's history, and then by it being altogether ignored, for a diplomat's purpose is to calculate in terms of the present to delete violence now. Finally, that this is achieved by an annexation from modernity but to promote another purpose indicates a motivating rationality altogether different: alterity.

The case for alterity is reinforced by the diplomat's very unmodern use of secularism being replicated at an institutional level, by the MEA itself. Rather than being distracted by the past or future, the MEA, like the diplomat, is also engrossed by the present. Hence, the MEA does not reproduce its past and so foregoes the security of insulating itself from the challenges of the present. The MEA began as an elite organisation, but now hazards itself by incorporating people from the bottom of global society, and is castigated for lacking diplomatic, read Western, qualities. The MEA's metamorphosis is measureable in longstanding policies of positive discrimination. Founded on classifications of destitution, the state lowers barriers to entry for, literally, the other half (Indian Constitution: Article 340; Mandal Commission 1980; Supreme Court 1992).

Accordingly, the MEA is no longer the playground of former princes and the *Ingabanga* or the *crème de la crème* of the Anglicised elite, as it was following independence in 1947 (Datta-Ray 2005). Then, royalty – the very pinnacle of the colonial regime – sought the IFS because it was invested with the capacity to replace lost royal status. The IFS was the 'last bastion of the brown *sahib*' where the non-Anglicised were 'despised and kept at a distance to avoid offending the prime responsibilities of their masters' (Laiq 1999). Knowing this, Nehru slotted royals into the IFS to provide 'psychological and political rehabilitation for erstwhile rulers,' wrote the man tasked with dissolving the princely order (Menon 1956: 204). By the 1960s, numbered were the days of royals like the *Maharajah* of Alirajpur. As High Commissioner to Singapore, he acquired a reputation for 'messing things up', according to Singapore's former Chief of Staff (Datta-Ray 2009: 125–9).

Alirajpur's kind and the *Ingabanga* were substituted by the beneficiaries of positive discrimination. In 2014 the latter constituted 37 per cent of MEA staff (Kaur 2014). Their growth is attested to by the Parliamentary Standing Committee on External Affairs chastising the MEA's incompetence in English (2016). This is a truism. In 2010 the *Times of India* published a report titled: 'Lessons in English for today's diplomats' (16 January 2010). It is testimony to the success of the institutional use of secularism in a way unimagined by modernity, that the MEA continues to function in the face of such dramatic and self-inflicted change.

Appreciating the risk, and the magnitude, of the change the state willingly inflicts upon itself by eschewing a monochrome elite to instead actively incorporate India's technicolour diversity, obliges the contemplation of a non-Westernised diplomatic biography. Its consonance with the MEA's practices makes for a coherence indicative of rationality alternate. Both are exemplified by the biography replicating the MEA's risk-taking to overcome a *leitmotif* of unspectacular violence by spectacular incitements to violence that play havoc with the self. In contrast to modernity's outward violence, Indians direct it inwards, into themselves, like the MEA. Similarly, purpose is directed not by history, but to terminate the everyday suffering scarring the biographies of nearly all Indian diplomats.

Typical is an officer whose parents' combined monthly salary in the mid-1990s, was 'around Rs. 5,500 [USD 130]' (Reserve Bank of India Historic Exchange Rates n.d.). This supported four people, putting them at the *World Bank's* poverty line of one US dollar per day. The reality of hovering around the poverty line is discernible in their abjuring luxuries, such as bus travel, unless absolutely necessary. His deprivation was also geographic, linguistic and educational. His grandparents were forest nomads, but his father lives in a village. Born in the 1980s, his district remains scarred by insurgency: 50,000 out of 1,200,000 live in concentration camps. He first watched television aged 18 in the third town he lived in and accessed despite near impenetrable forest, via a road built in the late 1980s, which remains 'impossible' to traverse during the monsoons. He attended three schools as only primary education was available at his village. His mother, who was 'very special' for being literate and from 'a better, plains family where there were schools,' brought formal education to her husband's village. Before her arrival, the 'school [was] on paper' [that is, no school existed because state funds for building and running the school continued to be illegally siphoned away]. He continued: 'Only 10 or 20 per cent' of the village's primary schoolchildren transition into secondary school because there are no teachers for the alien language of instruction: Hindi. He gambled his family's scant resources on secondary school, but failed: there were no teachers. Hence the third school, which only lacked science teachers. 'My area was a punishment post. … There was violence.' Aged 13, '10 to 30 policemen died' there. Out of 90,000 people in his 'home-place', he was 'the sixth person' to complete school. He graduated because he taught himself while living as a 'paying guest in the house of a friend of a friend.'

Next he wanted to enrol at university, which required an application form. He asked the bus driver (who drove a bus once a day to the nearest town, 12 hours away) to get the form, but the driver kept on changing so he never got it. This uncertain route was also the way to get books. Having saved earlier state scholarships – Rs. 6,600 [USD 156] per annum, for three years, and a Rs. 1,500 [USD 35] book grant – he could afford university. This despite knowing that racial or caste violence would be wreaked upon him. Inevitably, physical abuse followed, culminating in his ejection from the hostel. Intriguingly the violence incited him to seek it out. 'I decided to take it as a challenge,' he said and paid the price: loss of 'self-esteem' because his racist compatriots ostracised him. Finally, he got a job, but spurred on by a will to eradicate his suffering, he gained admission to a postgraduate course. Yet again, he gambled all and lost. Having to pay the fees in advance, combined with his position near the bottom of global society meant he, 'needed a loan and had to apply from my home-place. That meant taking leave from work. So I went to my village and was told that to apply … I had to go to the district HQ; there they didn't know anything. But having exceeded my leave, I lost my job' (IFS Probationer 21).

The intriguing enigma of diplomats and the MEA putting themselves in harm's way, is neutralised by PCR for it recognises that actors may, contra modernity, possess judgement. Moreover, PCR identifies that the field for calculation is resolutely the present as the sum total of everything, and the purpose is to overcome violence now. Its calculations do not ignore the past, only history; do not repose faith in the future, but the present; and do not generate more violence by countenancing violence, but rather seduce it to quell it by internalisation. To license Postcolonials to theorise themselves permits another discovery: an uncommon courage. Its extent is only indicated in this biography, for to become a diplomat involves an altogether different scale of violence and hence amplified courage, in that it is generated by the weakest members of global society (Datta-Ray 2015: Chapter 2). Courage accounts for such people's successful incorporation into the MEA since at least 1964 (Haksar 1992, 1994), and is also testimony to the institution's mettle. Such courage, unavailable to modernity's automatons, gives further credence to the case for alterity.

In addition to modernity's analytic-violence being used to prop up a compromised history and the practices inimical to modernity that PCR unearthed, are the practices which totally refute modernity by altogether eradicating history. One such impossible possibility is progress as return. New Delhi's Regional Passport Officer – in charge of issuing passports – briefing probationers spoke frankly in advising:

> a lot of you will come from ... real India not Delhi, and will want to go back. A lot of the work you will do will be ... quite pointless. But becoming a Regional Passport Officer can give you something real. You don't have to go abroad. You can be posted in your part of India. You can actually help people from your place (IFS Officer 19)!

What is refuted is progress-through-history. Indicative is Western anthropology's claim that progress is to move from rural to urban (Osella and Gardner 2003). This officer reiterates the widely held notion that progress is without doubt movement, but it involves returning to one's origins albeit in a new form (an officer) and to help one's fellows – understood as a linguistic group rather than 'Indian' – realise their desire to migrate away from India. In doing so, the officer discards the entire rubric of history.

Given the MEA's and diplomat's multivalent and omnidirectional practices of progress predicated on overcoming tangible violence by embracing it, it is hardly surprising that this makes for the Indian state's negotiation style. The state's mobility is also geared by progress calculated and realised in the present. This frees mobility from its modernist cage of moving towards a terminal, but transforms it into bringing the terminal to the origin. Unaccountable by history, such mobility demands alterity. Only it explains India's nuclear negotiations in 2007 with the US. The purpose was freedom from the violence of energy deprivation, and at stake was assimilation which in matters nuclear amounted to becoming a part of the international nuclear community. Preventing it was an infrangible condition amounting to exceptionalism and established by Indian PM Dr Manmohan Singh: some reactors had to be beyond IAEA inspections (2006: 471; 2006: 446). In keeping with Dr Singh's directive, his negotiators successfully limited IAEA surveillance to civilian, not military, reactors and secured the right to build new military reactors (Ministry of External Affairs Vienna 2008). The creation of India-specific IAEA safeguards stymied assimilation into the international nuclear community, by readjusting it to the already existing Indian self.

This is baffling for history, because it makes the terminus contingent on transmuting one's original self. India did not progress-through-history towards the international nuclear community, and so did not partake of Realism's learning curve. Yet the purpose of ending the violence of energy deprivation by providing Indians with energy was realised with the 123 Agreement, and it was achieved without outward violence. Indeed, that was proscribed (Foreign Secretary's Note 2007). In its absence Dr Singh and hence the state, resorted to immense courage because

India risked engaging the lone superpower in not acquiescing to its power but demanding an exception, and in so doing, aggravated the global nuclear architecture crafted since the Second World War. Compounding the danger was the risk of failure internationally and its consequent, political humiliation for the PM at home. In short, the MEA's and its diplomat's quotidian calculations founded on the present and for the present were repeated by the state. So too was the tempting of violence upon oneself to eradicate violence.

That such practices are manipulated into history by Realists undermines the discipline of IR, but perhaps its death knell is sounded by Postcolonials actively retreating from what they seek to illuminate: the state. Postcolonials presume the state a result of history and hence modern, and use this as an excuse from actually researching practitioners (Abraham 1998: 4–5). Lofty claims to 'understand nuclearisation through the lens of socio-cultural and historical analysis' are hollow because precisely that is denied to the state (Roy 2009: 114). Instead, bureaucrats are rendered 'protagonists of rationality', inexplicably presumed Western. This is phenomenal, for the claim is either that bureaucrats are impervious to the logics, thoughts and practices of their society, or that they totally divest it every time they begin work (Kaur 2009). In short, the political culture of the state is *a priori* presumed disconnected from the society that produces it.

The result are claims that necessarily must silence practitioners, for they cannot be contained by history. Hence, India's nuclear diplomacy supposedly oscillates between security concerns (or materialism) and 'moral exceptionalism' (Frey 2006: 197) and the 'major casualty of the nuclear dream shared by India and Pakistan is peace' (Ramana and Rammanohar Reddy 2003: 23). Both claims are astounding. The first eliminates Nehru's writings on the morality of nuclear security and his foundational role in combining security and morality to the extent of not selling nuclear material to the US for food, in the midst of famine, because it would further global insecurity (McMahon 1987: 374; Datta-Ray 2015: chapter 6). Deleted too is the entire sequence of peaceful overtures spanning decades by the tag 'unrealistic', rendered irrational then is the work of an entire MEA section, DISA or Disarmament and International Security Affairs (Frey 2009: 195–212).

The proactive misconstruing of the state abounds, even when it comes to mundane practices such as secrecy. Common to any state's nuclear program, secrecy is an uncontested subject for Realists and India must practise it to become modern (Morgenthau 1967: 142–143). Since India does, Realists are silent about it. Postcolonials are not, because 'ambivalence' adds to secrecy the dimension of being detrimental. In India, Postcolonials find secrecy weakens the very ideal that nuclear weapons safeguard: democracy (Ramana 2009: 41–67). For Realists secrecy is intrinsic to deterrence, but for Postcolonials, secrecy is the succumbing to the atom's violence. Both subsume postcolonials to history, but does it hold?

The answer lies in a range of sources that present, not mould, practitioners. Sunanda K. Datta-Ray inadvertently sheds light on the question. Conversing with a top general, the FS and the PM, Datta-Ray concludes that secrecy can only be made sense of in terms of broader sensibilities that manifest themselves in issue-based practices (2002: viii–ix). The entire state is certainly not secrecy-obsessed. Dr Singh repeatedly spoke for 'declassification' and critiqued bureaucratic secrecy as PM (*Indian Express* 18 April 2006). In conversation, he recounted with admiration American openness. President George W. Bush introduced him to White House staff including some of Indian origin. Rhetorically, Dr Singh asked: 'If they can be so open, why cannot we?' (12 October 2009).

Patently at work in the corridors of power is not Realism's obsession with secrecy. Meanwhile, Postcolonial's ordering secrecy as a threat to democracy cannot explain the continuing contest between Dr Singh and his bureaucrats. Nor can either tool account for Dr Singh's audacity, for what openness amounts to is a temptation to the violence of investigations of his very self. Escaping these awkward impositions requires permitting the practitioners of secrecy their rationality. Doing so lets slip that the practice of secrecy is not inimical to democracy but delivers it. One of my encounters with secrecy was to be denied travel with diplomats to Bombay. FS Shivshankar Menon's email explained, 'some of these programs [were] only open to government servants' (2007). On their return, in conversation innocuous to the point of banality, I wondered about their stay, sightseeing, the ocean [I knew some had never seen it]. I also asked if they visited the nuclear facility, limiting my inquisitiveness to 'what it was like?' No replies were forthcoming. One muttered 'national secrecy', as if that were an explanation. Another expanded, bureaucrats take an oath, which they embrace as the denial of some Constitutional rights – such as free speech (IFS Probationer 16; Indian Constitution: Article 309). This wall of silence was however punctured by another probationer. She giggled, 'they don't want to talk about it because it gives them status(!)' and added:

> I was talking to one of the [nuclear] scientists and he was saying ... "Why for all this secrecy? It's just to hide incompetencies here. And as for this national security business ... we use all these private contractors and all their records are public. If any Chinese want to find out what we do, all they have to do is go look at the private company's records!" These peoples' [the probationers] heads are spinning now with all this secrecy (IFS Probationer 23)!

The quote provides an avenue to interrogate the state by illuminating a hidden metre. Possibly a Weberian attempt to insulate oneself from critique (1958), secrecy is certainly a means to display bureaucratic status. Secrecy becomes a technology of differentiation from the bulk of the citizenry, to negate the violence of low status which engulfs the MEA's denizens from pre-bureaucratic times. Low racial and economic status is only partially managed by newly acquired job status. It requires bolstering, and bureaucratic secrecy does the job by enabling and empowering, by deleting violence, which is, after all, democracy's purpose. Neither Realist nor Postcolonial accounts suffice, because secrecy's purpose is neither to safeguard nor undermine democracy, but to deliver it.

Modernity's self-inflicted misunderstandings, silencing and branding of the postcolonial state as irrational, motivated by the will to order the globe, in actuality imperils itself. Analytics cloak what ought to concern those engaging India: the diplomat's, the MEA's, and the state's licentious soliciting of disaster. The temptation of violence might well be an escalating seduction, evocative of the diplomat's gambles, which ultimately risks, and loses, everything. To court disaster at the level of the state raises the policy issue of how modernity ought to engage India in a responsible manner? The answer demands determining India's appetite for violence. Instead, there are frivolous debates, and they occur even when modernity's and the state's categories coincide.

Two such categories are status and prestige. Realists state 'prestige and status' have nothing to do with India's nuclear programme, which arises from a long lesson in *real politic* (Ganguly 1999: 171–2). In other words, Indians learnt superpower deterrence to manage its own region, that is, China and its proxy, Pakistan. Both had been aggressors, and Beijing, which weaponised the atom prior to India, subsequently also clandestinely proliferated the technology to Pakistan (thereby violating the Non Proliferation Treaty). 'Beijing has consistently regarded a nuclear-armed Pakistan as a crucial regional ally and vital counterweight to India's growing military capabilities,' testified the CIA's Director in 1993 (Datta-Ray 2009: 41). In contrast to Realists, Postcolonials chasten India for being awed by a 'nuclear myth' (Frey 2009: 196): nuclear weapons are totems of status, obligatory signifiers for 'legitimate, modern states' (Sagan 1996: 74). Myths of course are irrational, and when connected to the nuclear, abhorrent.

Yet obstinate reality remains – which is that which is excluded, misrepresented or silenced by modernity's readings – as policies resolutely about status but inimical to modernity's nuclear status. Its status is defined by the Mutually Assured Destruction (MAD) policies of the superpowers, but India's policies are No First Use (NFU) and Credible Minimum Deterrence (CMD). These make for a different status altogether, because NFU and CMD deliberately imperil over a billion people by exposing them to the threat of a pre-emptive nuclear assault which no country has hazarded since the advent of the bomb. This throws modernity into disarray. Realists cannot account without analytic-violence: repeating that without Western style deterrence, Indians remain improper moderns. Meanwhile, Postcolonials cannot explain why India seeks status but uses it in ways that are different from what Postcolonial scholarship views as legitimate. Remarkably, both renditions miss the Indian habit of tempting violence on the grandest scale imaginable by choosing to live in the shadow of nuclear *power politics* without the security of MAD and all that it entails for global security.

A consequence of the conduct of exegesis then are possibilities that might invigorate both the academy and the practice of diplomacy. These include:

- the negation of history and progress-through-history but not at the expense of the past or progress;
- progress as the exercise of judgment to calculate interest and in terms of the *present* to relieve it of violence;
- discerning progress' borrowings from modernity, but not to promote it;
- limiting violence by recognising that progress' hand-maiden are the temptations to a violence unlike modern violence. It is directed outwards, whereas Indian violence is directed inwards, which nevertheless risks practitioners and those they engage; and
- renewing the discipline by surmounting Realism's intellectual dead-ends and Postcolonial work's closure.

In short, modern narratives are riddled with fissures which a fraying discipline disciplines with analytic-violence. In contrast to the discipline's undermining, by its own analysts, PCR recognises analytic-violence as moments of analytic failure arising from the cry of mimicry and as impossible to manage via hybridity, cross-contamination or acculturation. Rather than annihilate practices that cannot fit history, PCR ejects modernity altogether to perform micro-sociology, which crucially, is interpreted in subject terms. The implications are not limited to restoring the subject, identifying risks to the international community, and renewing the discipline, but catalyses the academy. For instance, PCR challenges sociology's foundational claim, propounded by Area Studies, that India's political dynamo is primordial or instrumental nationalism (Smith 1986; Chatterjee 1986). Undercutting the first is the MEA not projecting an artificial cultural unity into the past, present or future. Nor are the MEA's denizens manipulated by an elite; instead they escape everyday and unspectacular violence, to improve their present.

Conclusions

In tracing modernity's rationality apparent is unending violence against the postcolonial from the imposition of a fabricated history to its maintenance via various technologies of control. This violence continues because, though a *bona fide* member of the diplomatic system and internationally engaged, India's calculations, conduct and purposes are redolent of alterity. It is pedestrian to say so, but only if the postcolonial conduct of politics is measured on postcolonial terms. Instead, the assault by a sententious modernity seeking to reform a recalcitrant India renders it subaltern for it is 'denied the lines of social mobility' (Chakravorty Spivak 1988). These are unambiguously not modernity's, but moderns actively choose to misunderstand India's mobility as failures on the road to modernity. It cannot be so, for the moves by diplomats, the institution and ultimately the state are all iterative of each other. Not only are they all treading the same path, but it is patently devoid of predestination, for progress arises from the same space it seeks to convert: the here and now, and not history. It is this that vouchsafes the notion of an alternate judgement, for interest is calculated not linearly as is the case for moderns, but contextually.

The preponderance of such practices at every level of Indian foreign policy buttresses the position that New Delhi's foreign policy is propelled not by modernity but an altogether different rationality. Its contours need further gauging for they may disclose further possibilities beyond history. Unearthing these opportunities calls for not censorious modernity, but many more deployments of PCR to grasp alterity. Doing so revives the academy and reduces global insecurity for, as PCR also discovered, all the elements of Indian diplomacy knowingly imperil themselves. This remains an untheorised risk within and without: citizens depend on the state to relieve them of violence now, while modernity depends on the nation-state construct as a means to relieve all violence in the future. Beyond contention for both rationalities then, is caring for the nation-state. It is precisely this that makes it imperative to know specifically how adept New Delhi is at internalising the consequences, and the extent, of its taste for violence.

Bibliography

Oral sources

IFS Officer 2, 19.

IFS Probationer 2, 4, 7, 9, 12, 15, 16, 20, 21, 23.

Singh, M., Conversation, 7 Racecourse Road, New Delhi, 12 October 2009.

Documents and newspapers

Foreign Secretary Shivshankar Menon, 2007, email, 27 July 2007.

Haksar, A.N.D., 'Shine off the Foreign Service,' *Hindustan Times*, New Delhi, 16 August 1992.

Haksar, A.N.D., 'Mandalisation and the Foreign Service,' *The Pioneer*, New Delhi, 4 Sept. 1994.

Indian Constitution, *Article 340*.

Kaur, P., 2014, Lok Sabha Unstarred Question No. 4201, 19 February 2014 from http://www.mea.gov.in/lok-sabha.htm?dtl/22943/Q+NO+4201+SC+ST+AND+OBCs+IN+FOREIGN+SERVICES

Laiq, J., 1999, 'Diplomatic Impunity,' *The Outlook*, 27 September 1999, New Delhi from http://www.outlookindia.com/article.aspx?208153

Mandal Commission, 1980, from http://www.ncbc.nic.in/User_Panel/UserView.aspx?TypeID=1161

Menon, S. 2007, Foreign Secretary's Note, Document No. 9475/FS/2007, 27 July 2007.

Menon, S., 2007, 'Speech by Foreign Secretary Shivshankar Menon at the Observer Research Foundation on "The Challenges Ahead for India's Foreign Policy"' in Avtar Singh Bhasin' (ed.), *India's Foreign Relations – 2007*.

Ministry of External Affairs Vienna, 2008, Communication dated 25 July 2008 received from the Permanent Mission of India concerning a document entitled 'Implementation of the India-United States Joint Statement of July 18, 2005: India's Separation Plan,' INFCIRC/731, 25 July 2008 from https://www.iaea.org/sites/default/files/publications/documents/infcircs/2008/infcirc731.pdf

Ministry of External Affairs, n.d., Slide on Evolution. The slide is from a database which is used every year to induct probationers.

Ministry of External Affairs, n.d., 'Indian Foreign Service, a Backgrounder' from http://meaindia.nic.in/mystart.php?id=5002

Ministry of External Affairs, n.d., Documents.

Parliamentary Standing Committee on External Affairs, 2016, Minutes.

'PM: To aid research, may consider declassification,' *Indian Express*, 18 April 2006 from http://www.indianexpress.com/news/pm-to-aid-research-may-consider-declassification/2732/

Reserve Bank of India Historic Exchange Rates, n.d., from https://www.rbi.org.in/scripts/referenceratearchive.aspx

Singh, M., 2006, 'Statement of Prime Minister in Rajya Sabha on the India-US nuclear agreement' [17 August 2006] in Avtar Singh Bhasin (ed.), *India's Foreign Relations – 2007*, New Delhi: Geetika Publishers.

—— 2006, 'Implementation of the India-United States Joint Statement of July 18, 2005: India's Separation Plan Tabled in Parliament on May 11, 2006' in Avtar Singh Bhasin (ed.), *India's Foreign Relations – 2007*, New Delhi: Geetika Publishers.

Srinivasan, K., 'Special Bond', *The Telegraph*, 31 January 2014 from https://www.telegraphindia.com/1140131/jsp/opinion/story_17876883.jsp#.WJCH40navIU

Supreme Court, 1992 from https://indiankanoon.org/doc/1363234/

Secondary sources

Abraham, I., 1998, *The Making of the Indian Atom Bomb: Science, Secrecy and the Post-Colonial State*, London: Zed Books.

Barlow, C., 1991, *From Gaia to Selfish Genes: Selected Writings on the Life Sciences*, Cambridge, MA: MIT Press.

Behera, N.C., 2007, 'Re-imagining IR in India,' *International Relations of the Asia Pacific*, 7(3).

Berridge, G.R., M. Keens-Soper and T.G. Otte, 2001, *Diplomatic Theory from Machiavelli to Kissinger*, New York: Palgrave.

Braudel, F., 1958, 'Histoire et sciences sociales. La longue durée,' *Annales E.S.C.*, 13.

Bull, H., 1966, 'Society and anarchy in International Relations,' in H. Butterfield and M. Wight (eds.), *Diplomatic Investigations, Essays in the Theory of International Politics*, London: Allen & Unwin.

—— 1977, *The Anarchical Society*, New York: Columbia University Press.

—— 1984, *Intervention in World Politics*, New York: Oxford University Press.

Chacko, P., 2011, 'Srinath Raghavan, war and peace in modern India: A strategic history of Nehru years,' *Indian Economic & Social History Review*, 48(2).

Chakrabarty, D., 2000, *Provincializing Europe: Postcolonial Thought and Historical Difference*, Princeton: Princeton University Press.

Chakrabarty, D., 2002, *Habitations of Modernity: Essays in the Wake of Subaltern Studies*, Chicago: University of Chicago Press.

Chakravorty Spivak, G., 1988, 'Can the subaltern speak?' in C. Nelson and L. Grossberg (eds.), *Marxism and the Interpretation of Culture*, Chicago: University of Illinois Press.

Chatterjee, P., 1986, 'Nationalism as a problem in the history of political ideas,' in P. Chatterjee, *Nationalist Thought and the Colonial World: A Derivative Discourse*, Tokyo: United Nations University.

Connolly, W.E., 1999, *Why I Am Not a Secularist*, Minneapolis: University of Minnesota Press.

Datta-Ray, S. K., 2002, *Waiting for America: India and the US in the New Millennium*, New Delhi: Harper Collins.

—— 2005, 'The Last Ingabanga,' in *First Proof: The Penguin Book of New Writing from India*, New Delhi: Penguin.

—— 2009, *Looking East to Look West: Lee Kuan Yew's Mission India*, Singapore: ISEAS Press.

—— 2013, 'The analysis of the practice of Indian diplomacy,' in N.C. Behera (ed.), *India Engages the World*, New Delhi: Oxford University Press.

—— 2015, *The Making of Indian Diplomacy: A Critique Of Eurocentrism*, New York: Oxford University Press.

—— 2016, '"Inverted history": Diplomacy, modernity, resilience,' Caliban: *French Journal of English Studies*, 54.

Delanty, G., 1995, *Inventing Europe: Idea, Identity, Reality*, Basingstoke: Macmillan.

Der Derian, J., 1987, 'Mediating estrangement: A theory for diplomacy,' *Review of International Studies*, 13(2).

—— 1999, 'The conceptual cosmology of Paul Virilio,' *Theory Culture Society*, 16(5–6).

Durkheim, E., M. Mauss, 1971, 'Note on the notion of civilization,' (trans.), B. Nelson, *Social Research*, 38(4).

Duvernay-Bolens, J., 1993, 'Un trickster chez les naturalistes: la notion d'hybride,' *Ethnologie Francaise*, 23(1).

Feldman, G., 2005, 'Estranged states: Diplomacy and the containment of national minorities in Europe,' *Anthropological Theory*, 5(3).

Fisher, M.H., 1984, 'Indirect rule in the British empire: The foundations of the residency system in India (1764–1858),' *Modern Asian Studies*, 18(3).

—— 1990, 'The resident in court ritual, 1764–1858,' *Modern Asian Studies*, 24(3).
—— 1993, 'The office of Akhbār Nawīs: The transition from Mughal to British forms,' *Modern Asian Studies*, 27(1).
Frey, K., 2006, *India's Nuclear Bomb and National Security*, London: Routledge.
—— 2009. 'Guardians of the nuclear myth: politics, ideology, and India's strategic community,' in I. Abraham (ed.), *South Asian Cultures of the Bomb: Atomic Publics and the State in India and Pakistan*, Bloomington: Indiana University Press.
Friedman, J., 1994, *Cultural Identity and Global Process*, London: Sage.
Ganeri, J., 2001, *Philosophy in Classical India: The Proper Work of Reason*, London: Routledge.
—— 2008, 'Contextualism in the study of Indian intellectual cultures,' *Journal of Indian Philosophy*, 36.
Ganguly, S., 1999, 'India's pathway to Pokhran II: the prospects and sources of New Delhi's nuclear weapons program,' *International Security*, 23(4).
—— 2001, *Conflict Unending: India-Pakistan Tensions Since 1947*, New York: Columbia University Press.
Gaonkar, D.P., 2001, 'On alternative modernities,' in Dilip P. Gaonkar (ed.), *Alternative Modernities*, Durham, NC: Duke University Press.
Halliburton, M., 2004, 'Social thought & commentary: Gandhi or Gramsci? The use of authoritative sources in anthropology,' *Anthropological Quarterly*, 77(4).
Hobart, M., 1993, 'Introduction: the growth of ignorance?' in M. Hobart (ed.), *An anthropological Critique of Development*, London: Routledge.
Hogben, W.M., 1981, 'An Imperial Dilemma: The Reluctant Indianization of the Indian Political Service,' *Modern Asian Studies*, 15(4).
Kapchan, D.A., P.T. Strong, 1999, 'Theorizing the hybrid,' *The Journal of American Folklore*, 112(445).
Kaur, R., 2009, 'Gods, bombs and the social imaginary,' in I. Abraham (ed.), *South Asian Cultures Oof the Bomb: Atomic Publics and the State in India and Pakistan*, Bloomington: Indiana University Press.
Kaviraj, S., 2000, 'Modernity and politics in India,' *Daedalus*, 129(1).
Kissinger, H., 2001. *Does America Need a Foreign Policy? Towards a Diplomacy for the 21st Century*, New York: Free Press.
Koselleck, R., 2002, *The Practice of Conceptual History: Timing History, Spacing Concepts*, trans. Todd Samuel Presner *et al.* (Stanford University Press).
Kumaraswamy, P.R., 2004, 'National security: a critique,' in P. R. Kumaraswamy (ed.), *Security Beyond Survival: Essays for K. Subrahmanyam*, New Delhi: Sage.
Löfgren, O., 1989, 'The nationalisation of culture,' *Ethnologia Europaea,* 19.
Luhmann, N., 1997, *Die Gesellschaft der Gesellschaft, Erster und Zweiter Teilband*, Frankfurt am Main.
Lyotard, J-F., 1984, *The Postmodern Condition: A Report on Knowledge*, (trans.), G. Bennington and B. Massumi, Minneapolis: University of Minnesota Press.
Lyotard, J-F., 1988, *The Differend: Phrases in Dispute*, (trans.), G. Van Den Abbeele, Minneapolis: University of Minnesota Press.
McMahon, R.J., 1987, 'Food as a diplomatic weapon: the India wheat loan of 1951,' *Pacific Historical Review*, 56(3).
Menon, V.P., 1956, *The Story of the Integration of Indian States*, London: Longmans, Green.
Morgenthau, H., 1967, *Politics Among Nations*, New York: Knopf.
Nandy, A., 1995, 'History's forgotten doubles,' *History and Theory*, 34 (2).
O'Hanlon, R., D. Washbrook, 2000, 'After Orientalism: culture, criticism and politics in the Third World,' in Vinayak Chaturvedi (ed.), *Mapping Subaltern Studies and the Postcolonial*, London: Verso.
Osella, F., K. Gardner, 2003, 'Migration, modernity and social transformation in South Asia: an overview,' *Contributions to Indian Sociology*, 37(1–2).
Parsons, T., 1971, *The System of Modern Societies*, Englewood Cliffs, NJ: Prentice-Hall.
Paul, T.V., 2010, 'Integrating International Relations studies in India to global scholarship,' *International Studies* 46(1–2).
Perkovich, G., 2001, *India's Nuclear Bomb: The Impact on Global Proliferation*, Berkeley: University of California Press.
Prakash, G., 2000a, 'Writing post-Orientalist histories of the Third World: perspectives from Indian historiography,' in Vinayak Chaturvedi (ed.), *Mapping Subaltern Studies and the Postcolonial*, London: Verso.
—— 2000b, 'Can the "Subaltern" ride? A reply to O'Hanlon and Washbrook,' in Vinayak Chaturvedi (ed.), *Mapping Subaltern Studies and the Postcolonial*, London: Verso.
Raja Mohan, C., 2003, *Crossing the Rubicon: The Shaping of India's New Foreign Policy*, New Delhi: Penguin.

Ramana, M.V., 2009, 'India's nuclear enclave and the practice of secrecy,' in I. Abraham (ed.), *South Asian Cultures of the Bomb: Atomic Publics and the State in India and Pakistan*, Bloomington: Indiana University Press.

Ramana, M.V. and C. Rammanohar Reddy, 2003, 'Introduction,' in M.V. Ramana and C. Rammanohar Reddy (eds.), *Prisoners of the Nuclear Dream*, Hyderabad: Orient Longman.

Roy, S., 2009, 'The politics of death: the antinuclear imaginary in India,' in I. Abraham (ed.), *South Asian Cultures of the Bomb: Atomic Publics and the State in India and Pakistan*, Bloomington: Indiana University Press.

Sagan, S. D., 1996, 'Why do states build nuclear weapons? Three models in search of a bomb,' *International Security* 21(3).

Smith, A., 1986, *The Ethnic Origins of Nations*, Oxford: Basil Blackwell.

Taylor, C., 1999, 'Two theories of modernity,' *Public Culture*, 11(1).

—— 2007, *A Secular Age*, Cambridge, MA: The Belknap Press of Harvard University Press.

Van der Veer, P., 2001, *Imperial Encounters: Religion and Modernity in India and Britain*, Princeton: Princeton University Press.

Veblen, T., 1918, *The Higher Learning in America: A Memorandum on the Conduct of Universities by Business Men*, New York: BW Heubsch.

von Laue, T.H., 1987, *The World Revolution: The Twentieth Century in Global Perspective*, New York: Oxford University Press.

Weber, M., 1958, 'Bureaucracy,' in H. Gerth and C. Wright Mills (trans. and eds.), *Essays in Sociology*, New York: Oxford University Press.

Wight, M., 1977, *Systems of States*, (ed.) Hedley Bull, Leicester: Leicester University Press.

Wilkening, K.E., 1999, 'Culture and Japanese citizen influence on the transboundary air pollution issue in Northeast Asia,' *Political Psychology*, 20(4).

13
ARAB FEMINISM
Between secular and Islamic models

Soumaya Mestiri

Introduction

The feminism that is defended, valued and studied nowadays in Tunisia, since the independence of the country, is broadly speaking the feminism that one could have found in France in the 1970s. Then, the Mouvement de Libération des Femmes (MLF), which can be translated as 'Women's Liberation Movement', was struggling for sexual equality.[1] At that time and for a long time, Tunisia was the first and only Muslim country to promulgate a specific Code, the CSP (Code on Personal Status) which established the basic rights of women (abolition of polygamy, creation of a legal proceeding for divorce, etc.). But it was and still is a white and secular feminism that was promoted by the postcolonial and anticlerical elite who worked for decades on implementing a state feminism. They exhibited a kind of ornamental concern for women designed to reassure Western partners: 'we are a dictatorship but we are obviously feminist so we can't be that bad.'

However, the sparkle of the Arab Spring, i.e. the Tunisian Revolution of 2010, changed things. The new pluralism and democracy enabled the emergence of a real opponent: a Muslim feminism, a 'cultural' or a 'differentialist' one, to use Nancy Fraser's word, whose self-proclaimed aim is to rehabilitate the femininity (or so-called femininity) through a(n) (involuntary) deconstruction of the androcentrism at work in white and secular feminism, which is accused of transforming women into men.[2] One could say that there is nothing surprising here: Tunisian feminism demonstrates a classical opposition between equality and difference, which can be easily understood in the very light of the history of Western feminism as a first phase of an evolving process.

Nevertheless, Tunisian feminism has its own specificity. The first feature of this originality is that the anti-essentialism promoted by progressive feminists appears as a relatively basic one: there is no real will to deconstruct group identities. This stands in contrast to what Western feminists do when saying that those identities are never given and fixed, which is another way to affirm that they can be understood as the result of the cultural processes that inform them. Thus, liberal Tunisian feminism is content with reproducing a clearly Western-centered MLF feminism which has conditioned these women both historically and ideologically, but it remains very careful to present a kind of light version of such a feminism which fits with a genuinely conservative society. The second original feature of Tunisian feminism is, quite unfortunately, that Muslim feminism does not represent a livable alternative to its secular opponent. Indeed, if Muslim feminists ride the differentialist wave towards the promotion of the value and positive content of femininity, this 'gender identity', supposed to apply to all women, seems to be in fact fundamentally exclusive. Muslim feminists' sorority cannot be understood as an ecumenical project.

With these issues in mind, the aim of this chapter is to suggest that Tunisian feminism has missed its *rendezvous* with history. To this end, I will focus on Muslim and secular activism, pointing out their common androcentric nature, which is clearly visible in what I call the 'political maternalism' of progressive feminists but also in the Muslim conception that essentially sustains this androcentric orientation.

The first section will investigate the oppressive elitism of secular feminism especially in the political sphere where women embody a kind of reverse paternalism. Here, there exists a sort of mimicry of MLF feminism, convincing subaltern elites, more or less directly, to incarnate white values without. I will then, in the next section, move to the failure of Muslim feminism regarding both its essential inability to address the ordinary believer's issues and the lack of personal and more generally, normative ambition: there is a noticeable lack of even a vague desire to enter into a reformist process to break up with the oppressive religious orthodoxy. This double reflection will finally lead me to the conclusion that secular and Muslim feminisms are not so different. This is the case not only because they both fail to suggest an alternative project, but also because they share the same will to essentialise, the same generational gap that makes their renewal difficult, and the same false and oppressive logic of hybridisation.

Secular feminism

Let us begin with progressive feminists' 'political maternalism'. Here, we will focus on the political dimension of the phenomenon. It is very important to note that the Tunisian Revolution exhibited, and made more visible, a long-standing situation in the socio-political landscape: the very strong impact for almost twenty-five years of 'white' and Western-centered feminism. It is as if what had been called into question by non-Western and non-white feminists since the 1970s did not affect Tunisian feminists, who were only concerned with mimicking an MLF feminism with a fidelity that even Simone de Beauvoir would probably not dare to show nowadays.[3]

The monopoly position of MLF's universal feminism was only superseded by its rejection, as demonstrated by the result of the Constituent Assembly's elections in October 2011.[4] And indeed, the progressive feminists were totally disavowed: nearly all of them were defeated. A certain kind of paternalism was sanctioned, and this paternalism was embodied by the vast majority of women who engaged in politics immediately after the Revolution.

The pedagogical difference between *vulgis* and mere propaganda is very small. Take the following example. A famous plastician artist, politically engaged and number one on the electoral list of a little party in the district of Tunis 2,[5] explained that she always defended the rural women. She taught them as an artisan how 'to adapt Tunisian patrimony [...] to the requisites of modern society', and so it seems very natural today to 'go on' in this 'very direction' as a political woman elected in the Constituent Assembly. 'Politics', she affirms, 'is based on concept and projects. I am above all a creative artist so that I feel able to give new ideas that would be helpful for Tunisian people' (Zbiss, 2011). Such a way to understand the situation displays both a tendency to mix things that obviously don't mix, and a genuine misunderstanding concerning the political commitment: are artistic and 'political creation' proceeding from the same vein?

It seems very hard to accept this kind of reasoning. Nonetheless, we need to be careful here. We are not calling into question the honesty of this woman's commitment: what is at stake is both the power relationships implemented at this level and the problematical nature of the qualitative leap we're facing here, a leap which is, in addition, understood as natural and obvious.

The 'scientific' and 'civic knowledge' must not be placed on the same level, especially when the latter is clearly imbued with ideological considerations.

It has to be said that when presenting themselves as holding a specific knowledge – a democratic one – these political women are immediately considered to embody a power whose implementation creates a feeling of mistrust, if not rejection, in 'ordinary' women's hearts. 'Democratic' here, means 'ideological': that is to say a knowledge that asserts domination through an attractive discourse on rights and freedom. And indeed, one can read the resistance of the rural feminine population in the election's result. Rural women displayed a very strong rate of abstention, especially the younger ones; while the elder cast a punishment vote against the activism and modernism of the new social project, considered both as opposed to the Islamic values and totally disconnected from their own reality.

What is remarkable about this rejection is the fact that the Tunisian Revolution was launched by these 'indigenous' women, that is to say the subaltern ones who live in the marginalised regions of the country swept aside from all development strategies not only since the independence of the country but also during colonisation. It was as if those subalterns had given to the elite the opportunity to finally live in a democracy but had, by this very fact, denied to themselves the right to choose freely how to live their own life. Indeed, without these women, the initial insurrection in December 2010 would never have become a revolution. As such, the testimony of one women from Kasserine, in the middle of the country (one of the towns which gave the most important number of its sons to the Revolution between December 2010 and January 2011), is of significance:

> Since the beginning, women were leaders of the movement and when the Committee of the Defence of the Revolution was created, women were side by side with the syndicalists to maintain this structure alive [...] They went out, the progressive ones and the others... We used all possible means to make our voices heard.
>
> (Mahfoudh 2011, 83)[6]

We have now gathered all the elements with which to understand why those activists arriving from the city were seen as an intrusion and regarded as a quasi-colonial force intent upon saving 'indigenous people' from themselves by stripping them from their millenary victim's status. This judgment, made by a feminist elite of a Third World society, mimics a certain Western feminism opinion of Third World women. This situation reminds us Spivak's formula, which one can parody by saying that 'some white women decided to protect and save colored women from colored men.'

None of this is to infer that 'colored men' are saints: rural women are over-exploited, working in the fields (in Kasserine, for example, they provide more than 70 per cent of the agricultural labor), and looking after the home, without any financial, moral or even symbolic compensation. The point here is rather that this 'rhetoric of salvation' is motivated by ideological considerations which are themselves based on a particular epistemology: the question is to promote a specific knowledge in order to serve a given power. Moreover, it is indicative that both the urban-associated activists and their fellows engaged in politics were taught the kind of knowledge just mentioned – which is a supplementary proof regarding the implementation of paternalism, a paternalism which obviously doesn't spare any woman. In effect, the 'women of power' were reproducing the paternalist pattern that the socially disadvantaged women suffered from.

The Summer School organised in 2011 by the UNDP, the National Democratic Institute, the UN Women, the Iknow Politics network and the Center of the Arab Woman for Training and Research, demonstrates the pervasiveness of an effective authoritarian pattern in the relationships between women. This project's aim was to teach women how to run an election campaign and to work with civil society, but also to help organisers identify the specimen that could become, as one of the moderators put it, 'women leaders' and therefore able to 'network' at both local and regional level.

And indeed, fifty Tunisian women, coming from different horizons and supervised by international experts, took part in training workshops on how to create a campaign team, how to build and deliver a message and how to communicate with the electors and the media – this is exactly the 'democratic knowledge' we talked about above. Incidentally, it is revealing to note that nobody thought about organising a mixed-gender summer school. Obviously, the lack of political culture is gendered.

Synthesising these considerations, we can understand why secular feminism in Tunisia did not manage to reach 'ordinary' women: their maternalism and elitism (which are two sides of the same coin) embody hegemony and oppression, which are exactly the opposite of the so-called emancipation that secular feminists pretend to implement.

Muslim feminism

Neither has Muslim Tunisian feminism managed to gather together the women of the country. The reasons for this failure are numerous and interconnected. However, it is essential to understand that Muslim feminism is fundamentally *political*. Those who speak in the name of Muslim women are members of the Islamist Party; we are therefore talking about an Islamist feminism – if we are allowed to use such an oxymoron – rather than a Muslim one.[7] This basic observation points towards the different features of the problem.

To begin with, Tunisian Islamic feminism never had any normative ambitions, contrary to what exists, for example, in Iran, Pakistan, Egypt or even in the United States. There is neither a will to deconstruct the Koran's principles nor the disposition to offer the result of this alternative reading to the public. Neither is there a concern to undermine the religious orthodoxy's power, nor to work on minimising the gap between Islamic and secular feminists in terms of the 'universalistic turn' of Muslim feminism.[8] This in turn explains why Islamic feminism has no female leader promoting its ideas, that is, a woman who can be, more a less, a mirror for them. This religious feminism is articulated as a voice of a political party, a party managed by and considered for men.

This is typically Tunisian. The situation has been quite different in other Muslim countries such as Kuwait, Jordan and Palestine. The increasing participation of women in both local and parliamentary elections with movements linked to the Muslim Brotherhood was an incredible force for change within the party during the 1990s and 2000s. Most of these women never hesitated to run counter-current and orthodox views and sometimes to affirm very bold positions, a fact which enables us to clearly notice the real influence of Muslim feminism on political Islam.[9]

But in Tunisia we evolve within the field of allegiance, which, unlike mere partisanship one cannot easily be freed from. What is at stake here is an allegiance to the exclusive religious principles whose roots are fixed at the core of political Islam. Of especial importance is the principle that any norm and value determined by the government at any point in time cannot be challenged. Hence, expressed dissent will be considered as heretical. This structural allegiance explains why we must not be disappointed by these Islamist political women's behavior when they militate against their fellows rather than struggle for implementing their rights.

An example will help to illustrate this situation. During the summer of 2012, the Islamist party Ennahdha proposed to replace 'sexual equality' by 'complementarity' in the first draft of the Constitution (article 28).[10] This was clearly an attempt to validate a hierarchy and therefore to utilise an inequality principle to protect what is considered as the 'equilibrium' of society.

This was a strategy to impose a content and not merely a framework upon Tunisian society by sacrificing the individual on the altar of communitarianism: family becomes the supreme norm.

But to really understand the strength of what was not just a legal controversy, it is essential to consider the propensity for defending so harshly the complementarity ideal as a direct extension of a pre-modern conception of the world, where equality is thought of as geometric and not arithmetic. The Muslim Middle Ages was the heir of the Ancient conception of the world wherein individuals, *stricto sensu*, do not have the same value because they cannot be considered interchangeable. Therefore, to do someone justice is to give him what he deserves, that is to say, what he can lay claim to as a 'complement' to social harmony. To use a vulgar example, the carpenter will be given a saw and the farmer a spade with the understanding that their status will of course not be subject to any change: we are all complementary, but everybody has to remain at his place without hope of change. Because they are firmly rooted in this conception of the world, the Islamist feminists of the Ennahdha Party can hardly be part of a process of lasting empowerment.[11]

One can therefore understand why Muslim association is more successful than political association. With the Revolution, approximately ten Muslim associations have emerged that are headed by women. The number is small, considering the whole Tunisian associative landscape.[12] They are conservative associations since they seek to implement traditional family values. This issue is more or less clearly mentioned in the name of the associations themselves (they present themselves as associations 'for the woman and the child'). One can also easily notice the existence of a charitable dimension.

Consider, for instance, the association 'Kahdija, Mother of the Believers for Caring and Support', headed by a lawyer close to the Islamist Party Ennahdha (dismissed for the Bar for non-respect of deontology). The association aims to help poor families, on behalf of the 'Muslim and creative woman', to 'spark people's interest in religion', and to develop relationships between the female/feminist associations with the idea, clearly mentioned in the status, to 'regulate' such groups. The core of the project is to 'anchor both individual values of creation and Islamic values and principles which promote progress and creativity'. This notion of a 'religious awakening' is sometimes expressed with more 'energy' when it comes to a perceived lack of religious culture in society. This is exactly what the association 'Read and Raise' seeks to address.

Perhaps more radical is the Nour association 'for the Woman and the Child', which is tightly linked with the Islamist charitable association '2Justice and Piety' (*El birr wal ihsên*) and whose explicit aim is to 'guide the woman towards the ways to the Good Life' (sic). This is also the case for the association 'Free Women for the Good', whose first goal is to 'encourage the learning of the Koran, the Sharia and the learning of life'. These 'ways to the Good Life' are also promoted by the 'Association for the woman and the family's image in the media', which aims to fight for an 'objective image' of the woman against 'stereotypes' (all this is quite confusing) and to implement 'programs thought to develop and anchor good habits' (sic). And finally, the association 'The Muslim Woman', undoubtedly the most explicit regarding its name and goals, seeks to 'defend the rights and the interests of the Muslim woman in Tunisia' especially for women who wear the *niqab* and *hijab*.

It is not immediately evident how these associations work, but it seems that we can affirm that the aim of the so-called Muslim associative feminist field is not to fight to change the current order. Indeed, the reformist spirit is patently lacking: these Muslim feminist associations have nothing to do with the Muslim feminism we find in the different diasporas or in other Muslim countries such as Iran, Pakistan or Turkey. Moreover, Muslim associative feminism in Tunisia continues to favour the charitable dimension, which is shared by all the groups, as the tradition requires. Boldness is not the main feature here, to say the least.

There are nevertheless two associations which seem to separate themselves from the crowd – 'Muslim and Creative Woman' and 'Muslim Woman'. The first one, however, oscillates between an obvious will for emancipation (talking about creativity leads clearly to this interpretation) and an unwillingness to decry the need to regulate the activities of feminist associations. Meanwhile, the second association aims at defending the rights of the women wearing *niqab* and *hijab* but in a very *infra* way, which is very different from what one can see to, for example, the Malaysian 'Sisters in Islam', which always fought against religious orthodoxy by subverting it from the inside. Indeed, the idea that Muslim women can dispose of more than what they actually have and that it is possible to have it *from the Muslim framework itself* (which is the principle of Muslim feminism) is totally missing from the Muslim feminist associations in Tunisia.

To sum up, neither the political Muslim Feminism nor the associative one can pretend to take into account the interests of the ordinary believer. The failure is therefore not only the failure of secular feminism, but also the failure of religious feminism. Both political and associative fields in each pattern have not succeeded in providing solutions to women's problems in Tunisia. This is not so surprising given that secular and Muslim feminisms are in fact two faces of the same coin, as I will now try to show.

Beyond secular and Muslim feminism

Secular and Muslim feminism share at least three essential features.

Firstly, they are talking from the same *locus* because none of them has achieved what the Moroccan thinker Abdelkebir Khatibi (1985, 1990) calls the 'double criticism' (*double critique*). Indeed, taking diversity into account requires both criticising one's own tradition, in a deconstructive way, and criticising the Western tradition, in the decolonial sense. This is the *sine qua non* condition for a real understanding of others. But one has to notice that this is far from being the case: Muslim feminism is content with the second criticism whereas secular feminism focuses only on the first one.

Hence, we are facing two central feminisms, in the geopolitical sense, which feed from the hegemony they are working to settle. Both are feminisms *at* the border, which means that although they pretend to take difference into account, they inhabit this border as a sacred refuge. Indeed, because they did not take advantage of the Revolution to renew their references, they remain connected to a fantasised East and an idolised West. This positionality strengthens separations instead of fighting against them. Unable to project themselves *from* the border, both secular and Islamic work to essentialise the border. In doing so, they think of the border as a limit and a closure, whereas feminism should view the border as a boundary (in the Kantian sense of the word *Grenze*), that is to say, as a limitation which can always be overridden, at least potentially, due to its essential contingency.

For example, when the Franco-Tunisian writer Fawzia Zouari explains that 'there is nothing such as Eastern or Western feminism', she fixes an existing border instead of deconstructing it because she is moved by the desire to replicate, using another way, the MLF feminism's hegemony. Indeed, she argues that there is no such thing as colonial and white feminism and that focusing on this kind of denunciation is both bad and dangerous since it sets the stage for 'green feminism' (i.e. a Muslim feminism) which is, in her opinion, profoundly hostile to freedom. This is why, she explains, it is more than natural to stretch towards the 'classical feminism' which is essentially peaceful. Therefore, people who criticise the West and 'its' feminism lack what she calls 'mind sovereignty' since they always play the victimisation card by considering the Western world as solely responsible for all the world's misfortunes:

> I dismiss the word 'colonial' because this feminism initiated the biggest struggle of all time without shedding a single blood drop. I call for vigilance against all these new theories which defend 'a postmodern dimension of the religious' considered as a 'source of re-enchantment' and a 'new opportunity for feminism'![13]

Similarly, when Férida Labidi talks about 'things we can't do', she is speaking from within a specific cosmology, thus greatly contributing to essentialising borders. Labidi is an Islamist political woman elected at the Constituent Assembly and also the President of the Rights and Liberties Commission in the Assembly. She argues that 'one cannot talk about equality between man and woman *stricto* because he runs the risk of breaking the familial equilibrium and disfiguring the social model we live in.' She adds that 'this is about the paternity question, the surname giving and the matter of inheritance. If man and woman are equal, this means that the woman will have to pay the alimony, exactly as the man does! Now this is definitely against our social way of life.'[14] If there are 'things that shouldn't be done', this is because roles and tasks have always been distributed, and such a distribution has proven itself. That is why every attempt to introduce change in the system by giving, for example, a saw to the farmer and a spade to the carpenter, will deteriorate the functioning of the whole machine. This is obviously another way to fix borders.

In this manner, secular and Muslim feminisms fail to defend both equality and difference. The former only defends equality, considering difference as a potential threat to freedom, whereas the latter only fights for implementing difference, but a difference exclusively thought of as complementarity. We are then facing a dilemma: on the first side: equality without difference; on the other side: difference without equality.

Secondly, both feminisms suffer from a generational deficit. The rearguard retains the media and decision-making monopoly, even if young people try to make themselves heard. One cannot speak of the existence of young iconic figures who emerge in the public sphere to sing a different tune. Some have seen Amina Sboui, born in 1994 and known as 'Amina Femen', as incarnating such an alternative vision when defending LGBT rights in Tunisia. But she is far from being taken seriously. Similarly, one might consider Saïda Ounissi, born in 1987, member of the Islamist Party Ennahdha, former vice-president of the *Forum of European Muslim Youth and Student Organisations* and currently Secretary of State in charge of Private Initiative, ensuring the succession of the Women of the Party. But embodying a break in the profile should not be mistaken for engaging for women. We are still far from that.

Thirdly, both feminisms defend an understated logic of hybridisation secular feminism rides the wave of 'Tunisia, an historical melting pot of cultures and civilizations' in order to explain that the country is not simply an Arabo-Muslim one, but also Berber, Vandal and Phoenician. A survey suggesting that Tunisia is populated by only 4 per cent of Arabs has strengthened the concept of cultural mixing, the aim of which is not so much to celebrate difference as to dismiss an Arab-Muslim identity that is considered by certain elites to be insulting. Secular feminism is seen by 'ordinary people' as relaying such a discourse and is therefore considered a threat to what they believe to be the core of their personal identity.

Muslim feminism's philosophy is also easily soluble in hybridisation and mixing categories: the promotion of the complementarity ideal, which is, I insist once more, totally unfair, can be read as a variation on the difference paradigm and, for example, as a free interpretation of Western theories of care. This is not so surprising as such a literature is well-known by a certain academic public and the translation into Arabic of the philosopher Virginia Held's (2006) book, *The Ethics of Care*, cannot be seen as simple chance.

I would suggest, then, that secular and Muslim feminism are not as opposed as they appear. They both reject diversity, which is considered as a potential threat to the privileges of the elite, on the one hand, and to the religious identity of the society, on the other.

Conclusion

The Revolution could have been the chance (even the excuse) of Tunisian feminism to drop the equality–difference debate and move to another stage of awareness of 'the difference between women', to quote Nancy Fraser. There were reasons, at the beginning of the movement, to dream of such a movement. Indeed, the Revolution, since its beginning in December 2010, was not only initiated and driven by women but also by the 'ordinary' folk, the subalterns of the marginalised cities of the country and the poor suburbs of the capital. It looked as if we had entered a new era where the monolithic vision of the feminine promoted by Tunisian feminism for more than fifty years could at last be discredited. Objective conditions prompted us to think 'at the intersection of plural differences', by crossing gender and other specificities like regional loyalties, ethnical features (in the sense of tribal ones), social and professional categories. Tunisian feminism could have taken a decolonial approach, that is, to have taken seriously the position of the speaker and Audre Lorde's (1984) credo for whom the master's tools will never dismantle the master's house.

But unfortunately, this goal has not been achieved; in fact, the *status quo* is being maintained. Neither secular nor Islamic feminism can put an end to the domination existing in Tunisian society. We need now to look beyond and learn how to live at the border and not only to go across. It seems to me that the condition *sine qua non* to achieve this task is to break up with the Manichean vision of two opposing feminisms; after all, we have explored how secular and Muslim feminisms are not so contradictory. The key lies in understanding that we have to work together because we have no other choice. Taking this point seriously requires moving from Khatibi's double criticism to what Miriam Cooke calls a 'multiple critique', that is to say, an awareness that we are triply oppressed: firstly, as women (gendered oppression); secondly as subjects of coloniality, sharing this condition with men (generic oppression); and thirdly as women trying to fight against the identity that Muslim orthodoxy tries to assign to us (religious oppression):

> First, and like women elsewhere, they are victims of gender relations which benefit men. Second, and like their male counterparts, they are struggling with the problems and challenges left behind by colonial rule. The European colonizers may have left Arab soil, but they also left behind a burden of colonial legacies that link different Arab nations vis-à-vis a global system that may or may not include them in its purview. Women are peculiarly vulnerable where their men are most threatened. Finally, the growing prominence of Islam in world politics has drawn attention to the ways in which Islamist groups use women as passive cultural emblems. Women's responsibilities and images in the new Islamic systems are symbolically foregrounded and then pragmatically relegated to the political margins (Cooke 2000, 100).

To parody Sade, addressing republicans in the nineteenth century: 'Tunisian women, just one more push to be feminists!'

Bibliography

Abdallah, Stéphanie Latte. 'Féminismes islamiques et postcolonialité au début du XXIème siècle', *Revue Tiers-Monde*, 2010.

Abou-Bakr, Omaima. 'Le féminisme islamique et la production de la connaissance: perspectives dans l'Egypte post-révolutionnaire', in Zahra Ali (ed.), *Féminismes islamiques*, Paris, La Fabrique, 2012.

Cooke, Miriam. 'Multiple Critique: Islamic Feminist Rhetorical Strategies', *Nepantla: Views from South*, I, 1, 2000.
Fanon, Frantz. *Sociologie d'une révolution*, Paris, Maspero, 1968.
Fraser, Nancy. 'Mapping the Feminist Imagination: From Redistribution to Recognition to Representation', *Constellations*, 2005, 12 (3), pp. 295–307.
—— *Fortunes of Feminism: From State-Managed Capitalism to Neoliberal Crisis*, Verso, 2013.
Held, Virginia. *The Ethics of Care: Personal, Political, Global*, Oxford University Press, 2006.
Khatibi, Abdelkébir. 'Double Critique: The Decolonization of Arab Sociology', in Halim Barakat (ed.) *Contemporary North Africa: Issues of Development and Integration*, London: Croon Helm, 1985.
—— *Double Critique*, Rabat, Oukad Publications, 1990.
Lazreg, Marnia. 'Féminisme et difference', *Les Cahiers du CEDREF*, 2010.
Lorde, Audre. 'The Master's Tools Will Never Dismantle the Master's House', in *Sister Outsider: Essays and Speeches*, Crossing Press, 1984.
Mahfoudh, Dorra. *Le Maghreb Magazine*, Tunis, no. 2, October 2011.
Zbiss, Hanen. 'Femmes têtes de liste: qui sont-elles … que veulent-elles?', no. 1344, 2011, pp. 46–9.

Notes

1 Regarding the story of Western feminism and especially what she calls 'feminism of the second wave', see for example Fraser (2005) and Fraser (2013).

2 Although Tunisian secular feminists view themselves as such, Muslim Women do not see themselves as feminists *stricto sensu*. They often say, as Meherzia Labidi (deputy of Ennahdha and vice-president of the Constituent Assembly in 2011) does for example, that Islam and feminism are not incompatible, that engaging in a process of emancipation as a woman isn't contradictory with Islam. But they never clearly mention that they are feminists.

3 Marnia Lazreg (2010) makes the same diagnosis: 'The Algerian and middle-eastern feminist project takes place within a frame of reference which is imposed on it from outside and according to norms which are also imposed from outside.'

4 After the Tunisian Revolution, a choice was made to write a new Constitution to break definitively with the Ancient Régime. The results of the elections were obviously in favour of the Islamist Party, Ennhadha.

5 Involved, more precisely, in the political party called 'Parti de l'Union Populaire' and head of its electoral list in Tunis..

6 One can find here some real fanonian reminiscences, especially in the excerpt where Fanon (1968, 93) describes the struggle against colonisation led by the Algerian woman, arguing that she makes the 'unresponsible word where she lived explode' and therefore 'participate both to the destruction of colonialism and the birth of a new woman', *Sociologie d'une révolution*, Paris, Maspero, 1968.

7 Of course, these women never consider themselves to be promoting an *Islamist* feminism.

8 Regarding the mediatic and normative presence of Islamic feminism's key-figures, both of the two pioneers of the Arab Spring, Tunisia and Egypt, did not follow the same process, In Egypt, scholars had a substantial presence in the media such as So'ad Saleh, Amina Nusayr Malakah Zirar Nadia 'Imarah, whereas such a profile was totally absent in Tunisia. For the Egyptian case, see Omaima Abou-Bak (2012, 180).

9 See for example the case of the Jordanian Nawal al-Fa'ouri, detailed in Abdallah (2010, 63).

10 The State commits to protecting woman's achieved rights and works to promote and develop them as a real partner of man in the construction of the homeland and [as a partner] for whom complementarity of roles inside the family [is guaranteed]. The State shall guarantee equality of opportunity for woman in the bearing of all responsibilities and in all fields. The State shall take the necessary measures to eradicate violence against women, whatever it can be.

11 In support of this idea is the fact that on the 19th February 2014 we can find five women among the eleven Islamist deputies who wish to abolish the decree-law 103 concerning the CEDAW convention due to articles 2, 9, 16 et 29 regarding the right of the Muslim woman to marry a non-Muslim man, the right to inherit, the right to give children the name of the mother, the right to move around freely the perfect equality in the possession of goods and regarding the law..

12 All the information and data that will follow are taken from the 'Guide des ONG tunisiennes', published by the CREDIF, http://www.credif.org.tn/images/livres/Guide%20des%20ong's%20Tunisie.pdf.

13 See http://www.liberation.fr/auteur/13018-fawzia-zouari

14 Interview given to Express FM Radio, 6/08/2012.

14
THE EVERYDAY PRACTICES OF DEVELOPMENT

Althea-Maria Rivas

Introduction

The colonial history and legacy upon which international development discourse and practice is built continues to produce and reinforce asymmetrical power relations in new and complex ways. This chapter examines the ways in which the international development paradigm reproduces and reinforces racialised and gendered subjectivities and how these identities are constructed through everyday encounters where development takes place. Working within a postcolonial feminist framework, the chapter explores these issues both historically and in contemporary times and draws upon a collection of narratives from six women of color who currently work in, or have worked in, the development industry. The narratives highlight the intersection of race and gender in the construction of identity and experiences of these subjects as they operate within transnational spaces as part of a particular power structure, in this case the international development architecture. The interviews were carried out in 2012 and 2013 with six female aid workers, ranging in age from 30 to 50, from the Caribbean, North America and the Pacific.

The chapter unfolds in three sections. First, it firmly locates the architecture of aid as one of power, borne from the colonial project. In doing so, it calls for recognition of the importance of historical projects, which utilised discourses of race to justify their existence, therefore challenging assumptions that development takes place outside of racialised and gendered histories. The second section questions who we see as relevant actors in development spaces by exploring the literature on two relevant communities: aid workers and diaspora communities. It also draws linkages between postcolonial and black feminist thought as a basis for developing deeper understanding of the complex realities arising from new global–local moves. Lastly, the bulk of the chapter examines what can be considered a postcolonial interaction within the Global South, but does not place its focus on the engagement between the former colonised and colonisers. Rather, this section presents an exploration of the narratives and contradictions that play out in the experiences of the female aid workers. The subjects are taken to be transnational actors who move swiftly between many different spaces in the Global South all the while attached to an architecture of power.

The chapter aims to complicate the ways in which we understand development to be intertwined with and reproduce certain historical and global processes and power relationships. Ultimately, it disrupts dichotomous development imaginaries and critiques to expose the nuanced circulation of constructions of race and gender for the diverse group of actors who live and work in locations targeted by development institutions.

Racialised and gendered histories: colonialism and development

In the colonial imaginary, the territories encountered during exploratory journeys were prime opportunities for exploitation and settlement. The non-European societies in Africa, Asia and the Caribbean that provided the basis for European development and capitalist expansion, both through slavery and colonial extraction, were constructed in opposition to Europe. Upon encountering 'the natives', Europeans adapted racial constructions that would justify their actions. The racial categories used to legitimatise conquest and exploitation generated forms of social relations based on hierarchy and superiority. Categories were authoritative and acted as signifiers of power that associated, among other things, blackness with backwardness and acknowledged the existence of colonial nations but without their own history or importance. Kipling's white man's burden suggested 'trusteeship' as a means to control these societies, constructed as dark and stagnant in the case of Africa, and declining but exotic in the case of Asia (Wilson 2011, 316). As Grovogui (2001, 435) points out, 'once it conquered and colonized the rest of the world Europe imposed its own ontology…that displaced all others'. The *others* signified separateness, primitivism and difference, yet were also entirely known and visible. It was only through their relationship with Europe, therefore, that the colonies became visible and acquired the potential to become less primitive.

At the beginning of the post-Second World War era, colonial powers embarked on extensive 'development' programs throughout Africa and Asia. Cooper (2002) and Leys (1996), among others, have documented the history of development thought and practice beginning with the nineteenth century, and its literal translation into development theory in a postcolonial world conjoining forces with racisms, the population bomb and untrustworthy masses. Though not explicitly named 'development' until the 1940s, during the nineteenth century similar ideals were contained in the French policy of *constructive exploitation*[1] or the British Empire's *constructive imperialism* policy.[2] According to British Colonial Secretary, Oliver Stanley, the 'opportunity of setting the Colonial Empire on lines of development' could not be missed due to its low-cost and potential to keep the colonies close and loyal to the former imperial power (HC Debates 1943). Such policies suggested a *softer* form of imperialism where extraction was not the only task but occurred alongside more altruistic social programming. The constructed divisions that justified the colonial project were reproduced in development discourse as the primitive and backwards, mapped on to the new development-speak, and became the underdeveloped, the Third World and the poor. Unsurprisingly then, development, just as colonialism and slavery, depended upon the reproduction of racial and gendered hierarchies that mapped on to dichotomous thinking about the West and the rest.

Historically, black and colonised women's experiences of sexual violence, exploitation and dispossession were portrayed in ways which intensified women's subordination (Wilson 2011, 316–17). Third World women formed the epitome of the underdeveloped, poor victim. They were seen as being backward and unproductive members of society, and these experiences, and the resistance they generated, were made invisible by the colonial discourse. When they did appear, it was often in relation to the perceived need to be rescued from their men and/or backward societies. As Spivak (1985) contends in her now famous essay on the British interdiction of the Sati in colonial India, colonial discourse was framed around 'white men saving brown women from brown men'. This representation of women in the Global South as terrified, passive and needing to be spoken for continued into the post-1940s' development project (Rajan

1993) and also informed the Western feminist critique contributing to black and Third World feminist resistance against what they saw as continuities between the white feminist approaches of the 1970s and colonial discourse.

Development discourse and practice articulate racialised forms of knowing (Biccum 2002, Mohanty 2003) language and representations (Cornwall, Harrison and Whitehead 2007, Cornwall 2010) that emerged out of colonial imaginaries. The racialised tropes that are central to contemporary development representations are easily conjured up in one's imagination as they have become part of the everyday scenery, both in the Global North and South. A staple within the development portfolio for decades has been the poor dark-skinned child; hungry, desperate and alone. Countless aid agencies have extensive media campaigns around these types of images as part of fundraising drives. In fact, the notoriety of such frames is inextricably linked to certain aid agencies. If one thinks of World Vision or Save the Children, the immediate image that comes to mind is that of the helpless black child.

These development advertisements served not only to represent the Third World as being in need, but also confirmed the identity of those in the developed world as being able to provide that assistance. The helping hand that reaches out to sooth those dark, poor, sick and dying bodies is almost always a white one. More recently, the frames around these images have shifted as the increased neo-liberal footprint on aid agencies led to a recent repackaging of aid images. The image of the dark-skinned child continues to be resistant, but alongside them now are more 'popularised' text and imagery (Biccum 2002, 2005). The new aid billboards are filled with Western celebrities, young dark-skinned girls who can 'just do it' (Cornwall and Rivas 2015), smiling African boys playing soccer, still poor but no longer naked. The stereotypes that accompany these new campaigns, however, remain unchanged.

An irony of development is the continuous stripping of complexity from women in the Global South through development policy and practices, which ironically are framed to empower them (Kabeer 2003, 2008, 2010; Cornwall, Whitehead and Harrison 2007; Kothari 2005). Aid campaigns, like Nike or the Girl Effect, juxtapose gendered and racialised tropes against material expressions of neoliberal individualised agency. Such ads, which have become increasingly popular with development agencies, tend to feature a dark-skinned woman or girl 'just doing it' and becoming aware of their own power and agency through the gift of development assistance. The seduction of the promotions, however, is in their recognisable message which allows the viewer to feel like they have the power to save the women in the ad. The agency and empowerment of those women and girls is dependent upon the willingness of the Western viewer to provide assistance. This 'pornography of poverty' (Cameron and Haanstra 2008, 1477) reconstitutes familiar scenery. Colonial dreams, based on racialised and gendered dichotomies, still act as a signifier for the development industry everywhere.

This section has highlighted the ways in which development is borne from racialised and gendered histories by briefly tracing the colonial origins of development thought, and providing examples as to how its anxieties have been copied onto a postcolonial world. Rather than transforming the way the world was organised, as some scholars have suggested, what emerged as decolonisation began to unfold was a new efficient approach to achieve the dual goals of civilising the population enough while building the means to explore 'the unexplored areas of the colonies' (Rist 1997). Much, however, remains to be said about the people located in matrices of intersectional inequalities, and the lived and embodied experience of these processes of governance and control. The next section interrogates how the constructions of race and gender reproduced through development discourse and practice have shaped our understanding of the relationships that take place within areas targeted by development institutions. It suggests that pushing the boundaries of work on aid workers, diaspora communities and postcolonial and black feminisms can open a space for deeper understanding of these experiences.

Complicating relationships

Aid workers and diasporas

There are dizzying arrays of actors that converge within postcolonial development spaces. Though the existence of these multiple actors in development spaces is rarely contested, the approach to understanding and researching these actors varies considerably. Considerations, which only speak of the development paradigm as one characterised by interactions between white aid workers and dark aid recipients, while important, leave much unsaid. Much of the work on the everyday of development encounters has been located in scholarship about the lives of aid workers and more recently on diaspora communities. Both bodies of work are relevant for our discussion here, but in divergent ways; the first for what it leaves out, and the second for what it suggests is possible.

The study of the lives of aid workers is a growing field of scholarship. Several scholars have utilised 'the everyday' as a lens, which tends to be practice-focused, to examine interactions between various actors in development spaces. A common trend here is the coining of different terms to describe the spaces which they are investigating. A growing body of scholarship examines the lives of aid workers in 'Aidland', a term coined by Mosse (2011). Austerre (2014) uses the term 'Peaceland' to investigate the failure of Western intervention in the Congo through an everyday lens. Loftsdóttir (2009), building upon Arjun Appadurai's (1996) idea of globalisation consisting of different 'scapes', attempts to coin the term 'Developscape' to examine white affect, identity and racialised development practices and representations. Several practitioner-scholars have reflected on their own development experiences and the rituals in which they observed, infused with racial stereotypes (Sylvester 1999, White 2002, Fernando 2006, McKinnon 2011), the power of the aid gift that is bestowed upon and wielded by white development workers and the constructed notion of capacity and conflictions journey of the Western expert (Eyben 2006, 2007, 2014). Indeed, development as with colonialism, depends upon clear divisions between the holders of knowledge and expertise and the receivers as it touts certain political, economic and social values, which frame the problems and identify the solutions for local populations (Escobar 1992, 1997). While often adopting a critical and sometimes practice-oriented, lens, these bodies of work also reinforce the binary distinctions which are at the foundation of development thinking between white Westerners and dark-skinned others.

A great number of these critiques have focused on challenging the power of whiteness in the aid industry, and indeed, much more remains to be said about these relationships. The aid worker in this literature, however, is invariably a white one. In some ways, therefore, the critique reinscribes the binary relationships propagated by development discourse itself, rather than attempting to disrupt it. This imagery reinforces stereotypes of the darkness of the developing world and the whiteness of the aid industry. Falling victim to the assumption that power and whiteness run alongside each other and understanding development power relationships can only happen through this lens. Therefore, Eurocentrism is investigated through a centering of whiteness and its linkage with power. The relationships examined in these bodies of work reflect colonial legacies of the development project. While it is essential to critique global hierarches of power, it is also essential to disrupt them by challenging the framing of the critiques themselves. Considerations which only speak of the development paradigm as one characterised by interactions between white aid workers and dark aid recipients, while important, leave much unsaid.

Deconstructing the manner in which racialised representations resonate and control those working and living in contemporary development spaces, however, requires not only exploring the truth of the *local* or of the *Western* but moving beyond the tendency to essentialise through categorisation. A less interrogated issue, however, is what this means for the lived experience of development workers who are part of racialised communities. As Kothari (2006) points out, 'development [is] an industry that is founded upon relations between West and the rest but also articulates relationships within these spheres, managing a critical "contact zone" between them'. In fact, many development organisations are maintained by large numbers of staff from Africa, Asia, the Middle East and Latin America. Therefore, the complexity of racial constructions becomes evident not only through interrogation of the colonised/coloniser dichotomy reproduced by development practices but also by exploration of the other relationships and actors.

The diaspora, while a contested term, has proved to be resilient, and is suggested to be a space where, through differentiated forms of difference and new revelations, new forms of consciousness are produced. Extensive work which details the diversity of black subjectivities and experiences has come from scholars focusing on the diaspora, and the Africa diaspora specifically. More recently, this body of work has broadened to delink theorising about the diaspora from the trans-Atlantic slave trade to broaden the terms of inclusion. The complexity of these diverse interactions has been taken up and explored by Gilroy's (1993) work on the Black Atlantic, Fikes' (2009) and Sawyer's (2006) investigation of Black Europe, Brown's (2005) work on black GIs in Liverpool, Clarke's (2010) analysis of the humanitarian diasporas, Edwards's (2003, 2015) use of Senghor's concept of articulation to explore the diaspora through different spacetimes, and Shilliam's (2015) work on the Black Pacific and spirituality. Khan's (2004, 2015) work on Islam, Hosay and Obeah maps the history and intertwining of religion, gender and race among different diaspora groups in Latin America and the Caribbean. More recently, Naber (2012) and Lesser and Klich (2007) have provided insights into gender relations, activism and sexuality among Arab and Jewish diaspora communities in different parts of the world. Each of these works tries to complicate the ways in which we understand the diaspora and the ways in which they interact with other communities and global processes.

The discussion below, however, does not focus specifically on the diaspora as an organising principle for the analysis. Rather, the subjects are taken to be transnational actors that move swiftly between many different spaces in the Global South: women from the Caribbean working in South East Asia, Chinese women working in East Africa, Latina women working in Central Asia and Eastern Europe. Therefore, while diasporic ontologies come into question, they are less central to the chapter. Nevertheless, diasporic literature is useful for our analysis here as it highlights the possibilities that emerge from new forms of recognition and consciousness revealed by and through fractious encounters (Lowenhaupt-Tsing 2005) and mutual recognition (Hintzen and Rahier 2010).

Intersections and positionality

Intersectionality is a concept that emerged in the late 1980s as part of critiques by black and Third World feminists. It aims to expose the interconnection of different identities and forces of oppression in shaping one's lived experience. The term, coined by Crenshaw (1991), rejects the idea that class, race and gender are essentialist, divisible categories (Davis 1981; Lourde 1984; Hill-Collins 2008) by highlighting their interdependence and the ways in which discrete multiple forms of oppression shape, and are shaped by, one another. While Crenshaw is credited with advancing the concept in the 1980s, calls for intersection recognition can be found as far back as the writing and speeches of Sojourner Truth (1851) who muses in *Ain't I a Woman* over the multiple axis of oppression that black women were facing.[3]

The postcolonial feminist frame makes room for an intersectional understanding of experience, oppression and resistance. Women in the Global South had different experiences from women in the West because of context, but also due to the fact that those experiences themselves are shaped by various politically, socially and culturally rooted identities. Their analysis therefore opens up an intersectional space by highlighting the complex realities of women in the Global South and the importance of cross-cultural feminist work being attentive to the micro-politics of context, struggle and choice (Mohanty 2003). While intersectionality, as a concept developed by black feminists, and postcolonial feminism emerged from different places, the two provide complementary and related, rather than exclusive and divisive, points for analysis. Both agendas see the universalist claims of global sisterhood as too often communicated through the construction lens of the dominant discourse rooted in white, Western, middle-class, heterosexual experiences. They both also reinforce the need to focus on the spaces where women have been marginalised and silenced and unravel the intertwined realities of categories of identity that circulate in structures of dominance and subordination.

Mainstream Western feminists had resisted attempts to destabilise gender as the main category of analysis for broader feminist claims. They argued such changes would be divisive and would weaken the 'global sisterhood' (Wieringa 1995). In doing so, however, they failed to recognise that the *global* feminist agenda they purported was shaped through the white, middle-class Western women's lens and therefore already shaped by class and race claims. Black feminists, mainly in Europe and North America, pushed back against the privileging of those experiences and interests in the feminism movement (hooks 1989, Hill-Collins 2008); a phenomenon that Amos and Parmar (1984) referred to as 'imperial feminism'. Women who struggled to locate themselves in mainstream feminist discourse challenged these ideas and argued for a more inclusive feminist vision. They challenged the supremacy of gender over other forms of oppression in feminist discourse and highlighted the heterogeneity of women's experiences.

This frame centered on the experiences of those who had been excluded from the mainstream feminist movement through an analysis that focused on how gender, race, sexuality, ability and class intersect simultaneously to produce different experiences (Nash 2008). Black feminists, though mainly communicating their claims from Western locations, focused on reflexivity, diversity of experience and oppression as the core of their arguments. The movement itself was diverse and included immigrant women, many of whom came from the Global South, and the arguments were not just articulated by black women, but also by women from other marginalised groups struggling to carve out a space that spoke to their own experiences. For these women, the intersection of their various identities formed multiple and shifting sites of oppression and privilege which speak to the uniqueness of their experiences and gave clues about their choices for political action. Activist-scholar Angela Davis takes this up and explores the overlapping nature of groups in *Women, Politics and Culture* (1990), where she reflects on her visit to Egypt and highlights the importance of reflecting upon positionality as a means to understand women's experiences globally.

This section has suggested a framework that adopts the interstices of postcolonial feminist thought and pushes at the intersectional space that black feminists have carved out. Ultimately, the marginalisation of women in the Global South, and of black feminist thought, has meant that both the mainstream development representation and practice, and feminist critiques reproduced racial and gendered power inequalities. Black and Third World feminist movements have attempted to destabilise essentialist notions of privilege and oppression (hooks 1989; Valentine 2007). This approach forms an adequate basis upon which to examine a unique site of *inbetweenness* where these narratives are located and which have not been explored sufficiently. It provides a platform for rethinking gender, race and development and for potentially powerful critiques. The narratives in the next section demonstrate the multiple ways in which development takes place in racialised and gendered spaces as it interacts with diverse histories and localised meanings in different parts of the world.

Racialised and gendered spaces

Juanita: development double speak and talking about race

A common sentiment among the participants of my study was that it was hard to address issues of racism within work environments because their colleagues refused to even consider the possibility that their behavior reflected racist attitudes. The response was often, how could that be possible, I am here and working every day with poor black or Asian people, how could I be racist? At the level of practice among those who do development, race and racism are often perceived as being of little importance or relevance to the achievement of development objectives. This is because race is often viewed as being a slippery concept that may be secondary to other forms of social differentiation, such as class, ethnicity or religion, in helping us to understand social stratification and injustice (Kothari 2002; Petierse 2007). In fact, development is sometimes seen as occurring outside of racialised histories. Meaning that, though race may have made an appearance in colonial discourse and practice, those historical events no longer matter for the development project that emerged after decolonisation. Clearly, as discussed above, this is not the case. However, resistance to interrogate these issues further has obstructed our understanding of the prominence of racialised discourses in development, and specifically the embodied experience of race for those who operate within the aid architectures.

A disturbing account was given by Juanita about her first month of work in Pakistan, where she had witnessed the white British logistics officer drag an elderly local staff member from a car. Juanita said she was shocked by the incident, as she would have been witnessing any type of violence, but what was more disconcerting was that no one said or did anything. It was just something that was allowed to happen and unproblematic. The incident made her feel unsafe and made her wonder where she fit within the hierarchy that characterised the development project which she was part of. She explained:

> There is something strange that happens to people when you work overseas doing development. I don't know how else to say it but it is strange and ironic because in principle all of these people belong to organisations aimed at helping people globally and respecting their rights. So you would think the people that work for these organisations have certain principles but sometimes it is the opposite. Development people come to these places and give in to all of their racist and sexist ideas all at once and for some reason think it is okay in this space as if being here and being an expat or expert gives them some impunity. There is something about the industry and these organisations that facilitates this kind of behavior. There is the constant double speak…

Lisa and Teresa: race, gender and sex

The first issue that came up in almost all of the interviews was the intersection of race, gender and sexuality in social spaces. Lisa, who was from the Caribbean originally, explained:

> The social activities and events are highly segregated. If you belong to a group that has enough numbers, sometimes you can organise side events, but most of the time you end up being in places that are expat dominated, and even the local places you go are local expat places. These places and events are usually dominated by white American and European men, and if you are working in a conflict area this is even more the case. As a woman you have to be careful in those environments and as a woman of color even more so. Having a romantic relationship or even close friendship with a local woman is taboo. Actually, in some places that I have worked, certain institutions will evacuate or fire you for such a crime. But as an expat woman of color you are simultaneously familiar and civilised enough yet still somewhat exotic. You are the unknown in a cleaner package.

All of the participants agreed that this intersection of race and gender made romantic relationships and friendships difficult in development spaces.

One of the consequences of the development industry is the impact on the political economy of the local environment. The aid industry injects money into the economy of the place where interventions are being made and this happens in a few ways. There are development interventions themselves, which create infrastructure and sometimes seek to create new markets; they create jobs for local citizens through employment with various agencies and organisations and this creates industries not only through the interventions but also to support the needs and desires of the aid workers themselves. Several of the women described the direct relationship between development interventions and the sex industry in the missions where they worked. They explained that if a sex industry already existed, the presence of foreign aid workers would inevitably expand it. In places where this was not the case the development industry would create it.

Teresa, who was of Chinese heritage, spoke candidly about her last posting in a country where the local women were not accessible to foreign men. As a result, and to meet the market created by the large-scale international intervention that was taking place there, women were trafficked from East and Central Asia to work as prostitutes and domestic workers for international guesthouses who were also supposed to provide sexual services to the residents and the large numbers of expat men that had arrived there as part of the international development assistance mission. The places where they were housed, regardless of the services provided, were referred to as Chinese restaurants. The wide range of men who used the restaurants and the nature of their presence there and the amounts of money that changed hands seemed to make all of this normalised, not only among the aid workers but also within the society as a whole. She said that initially she made a clear distinction between herself and these women. She explained:

> Throughout the city there was an explosion of Chinese restaurants. My mind had a schizophrenic conversation between the questions: How do I create a distance between myself and these women? I felt disgust? Pity and pain.

Teresa was there for a different purpose, but as time went on she began to understand things differently. She recounted a number of incidents where she was called derogatory names on the street, groped by guards and propositioned by colleagues. The things that were written on her body had constructed her in this space as an object to be sexualised and disregarded. Ironically, it was the dynamics and economy of the international aid mission which she was a part of which had not only facilitated, but created this situation. All of the participants agreed that this intersection of race and gender made romantic relationships and friendships difficult in development spaces.

Helen, Kathleen and Serena: the power of representation

The dynamics between the participants and local staff members and communities were also complex. There were spaces of solidarity and understanding carved out between some of the participants and the local communities and staff, based on a joint understanding of being marginalised or othered at different times and in global and local spaces, and around common discourses of rights and resistance. Helen explained that this commonality assisted her to develop friendships with local staff and citizens and experience community life and events which gave her a deeper understanding of where she was. Interestingly, in some cases, exactly the opposite was true. For example, Kathleen worked with local governments and much of her work involved speaking with local decision-makers and leadership. She said:

> Most of the places I work in are very patriarchal societies, at least in public life. So usually all of the local leadership will be men. Sometimes this is a challenge because they will refuse to speak to me, or ignore me. But I have to say in the majority of cases my race and gender has been a powerful tool. Because often these local leaders will consider me such a non-entity because of the color of my skin and the fact that I am a woman that the dynamics of the meeting totally change. They will be much more open and relaxed with me than one of my white male colleagues. In the end it is a useful strategy.

Both Helen and Kathleen felt their raçe and gender provided them with deeper access to local communities, discourses and the opportunity to develop a better understanding of local dynamics than their white male counterparts, but for very different reasons. In both cases, however, the meaning given to race and gender within these contexts were used as tactics to gain power and knowledge.

Another common theme was the privileging of whiteness among the local staff members. Local staff were recalled as being visibly upset when they learned that the participants being placed in positions of authority were non-white, and in some cases non-male. A racial hierarchy existed that placed white managers at the top, and then Asian and then black managers, intersected with a gendered hierarchy. Kathleen explained that she did not feel that this was because the local staff disliked her or felt that white people were smarter, though at times it was, but rather because the staff felt their white managers had access to power that she did not, as well as access to others with power, and therefore were better placed to influence decisions over resources and to communicate interests. Therefore, the disappointment lay in having to work with a female manager who was not white and therefore might not be able to successfully achieve program objectives and generate financial or political support which would be needed for the staff to keep their jobs.

Others, however, had more negative experiences with local staff and the result of this was various levels of frustration but also disbelief. The feeling of entitlement to that power, by virtue of being members of this structure, was very strong for Serena. Therefore, when they entered these spaces but were faced with attitudes which sought to diminish or question their role as experts and their claim to power, they became quite angry. Serena said she felt shock and wondered – how could these people consider me inferior to them? This anger was manifested in a determination to wield power over the other in ways that belonging to these international aid organisations and political missions allowed. This often took the form of controlling of resources, knowledge and jobs.

At the foundation of these emotions was a sometimes unacknowledged 'othering' of the local actors and staff. This was based on a perception of the local as backwards and primitive. These aid workers were in these spaces because of the fact that they belonged to the international aid architecture, a structure whose existence is both historically, and in current times, rooted in representations of the uncivilised other and the expert self and particular global hierarchies of power. It is a structure that supposes the ownership of certain expertise, deeming those who belong to it as expert and as having the solutions to assist others to emerge from their troubled situations of poverty, insecurity and ignorance.

The narratives presented in this section come from a diverse group of women. The actors are shaped not only by the sum of their experiences within their own countries but also by the context in which they work and live, which is often the postcolony. Race and gender intersect to shape the experiences of the women in this chapter. They also locate themselves within spaces where they are not local but where local, non-white women have historically been viewed as victims lacking complexity. They arrive in these spaces as part of the international development architecture, which is a structure of power borne from a colonial past.

The site of the postcolony is one characterised by the distinctive ways identities are multiplied, transformed and put into circulation. Mbembe (2001, 104–5) suggests that in these sites people live out their lives and encounter one another in overlapping domains and realities as each person has their own logic that becomes tangled with the musings of others. Interrogating these subtleties allows us to uncover some of the nuanced and undiscussed contradictions and power inequities within development discourse and practice today around race and gender. The relationships these women form are reflections of their own identity and the obstacles they face, and are shaped by these multiple forces. Their experiences unfold in a nuanced manner, which recognises the fluidity of movement between identities of different actors in different spaces as racial and gender constructions are embodied and resisted.

Conclusion

This chapter challenges claims that development occurs outside of racialised histories and spaces but also critiques of development, which though important, can also re-center the whiteness of the aid industry and perhaps the academy as well. It begins by mapping out the close relationship between colonialism and development and demonstrates the centrality of racialised and gendered constructions to both endeavors. It then moves on to interrogate how these constructions have shaped our understanding of the communities and relationships that populate development spaces. It explores what insights in literature on aid workers and diaspora communities might afford to us about the complexity of these relationships and also gaps in our knowledge. The postcolonial and black feminist lens of the chapter recognises the intersection of different forms of identity, oppression and resistance and the complexity of experiences of those who inhabit development spaces. Finally, the chapter draws attention to the underplayed significance of race and gender in development work through an exploration of aid worker narratives.

Three key themes resonate throughout the narratives. Firstly, the everyday development encounters build upon racialised and gendered assumptions, however much denied, that become complicit in the reproduction of various racist, and gendered stereotypes. Secondly, the narratives demonstrate how race and gender become markers of boundary but also erasers of boundary. In the everyday life of the aid workers, social constructions and power relationships manifested themselves in private, public and professional spaces and relationships, and were reproduced and negotiated in the locations where the development project takes place. The six female aid workers in my study were constrained and constructed by these racial formations but also manipulated and participated in them. This constant drawing and redrawing is necessary as race and gender signal powerful hierarchies globally and locally. These expat women of color, however, also disrupt those hierarchies.

Finally, these testimonies unravel the mechanisms of the assumed power distance between development agencies and the local people by looking at the intersectional inequalities among development workers themselves. The mutual recognition that takes place between the women and the local staff produces spaces of solidarity and of anger. The women tell stories of moral indignation, as they feel in-between the subject and objects of development because of their race and gender. These latter stories speak to the ways in which power circulates through the structures of aid. All of the actors recognise the power-laden development project; however, perceptions of expertise, access and rights to that power are rooted and closely tied to racialised and gendered inequalities which reveal the presence of colonial legacies and the fluidity of positionality of the women themselves.

Development, race and gender are contested sites that constitute a global historical phenomenon while at the same time intertwine with different histories and boundaries within particular given local contexts. As lived activity, it is an important site of encounter between individuals from the developing world and the West (Lottisdiur 2002), but also both intersects with and produces movements of people, products and images, conceptions and desires, the realities of which are translated by and influence localised contexts and the actors who find themselves there.

Bibliography

Amos, V. and P. Palmer. 'Challenging Imperial Feminism.' *Feminist Review* 17, Autumn, 1984: 3–19.

Appadurai, A. *Modernity at Large: Cultural Dimensions of Globalization*. Minnesota: University of Minnesota Press, 1996.

Austerre, S. *Peaceland Conflict Resolution and the Everyday Politics of International Intervention*. Cambridge, Cambridge University Press, 2014.

Biccum, A. R. 'Interrupting the Discourse of Development: On a Collision Course with Postcolonial Theory.' *Culture, Theory & Critique* 43, 1, 2002: 33–50.

——— 'Development and the "New" Imperialism: A Reinvention of Colonial Discourse in DFID Promotional Literature.' *Third World Quarterly* 26, 6, 2005: 1005–20.

Brown, J. N. *Dropping Anchor, Setting Sail: Geographies of Race in Black Liverpool*. Princeton: Princeton University Press, 2005.

Cameron, J. and A. Haanstra. 'Development Made Sexy: How It Happened and What It Means.' *Third World Quarterly* 29, 8, 2008: 1475–89.

Clarke, K. 'New Spheres of Transnational Formations: Mobilizations of Humanitarian Diasporas.' *Transforming Anthropology* 18, 1, 2010: 48–65.

Cooper, F. *Africa Since 1940: The Past of the Present*. Cambridge: Cambridge University Press, 2002.

Cornwall, A. *Deconstructing Development Discourse: Buzzwords and Fuzzwords*. London: Practical Action Publishing, 2010.

Cornwall, A., E. Harrison, and A. Whitehead. 'Introduction.' In *Feminisms in Development: Contradictions, Contestations and Challenges*. London and New York: Zed Books, 2007: 1–20.

Cornwall, A. and A. M. Rivas. 'From "Gender Equality" and "Women's Empowerment" to Global Justice: Reclaiming a Transformative Agenda for Gender and Development.' *Third World Quarterly* 36, 2, 2015: 396–415.

Crenshaw, K. 'Mapping the Margins: Intersectionality, Identity Politics, and Violence against Women of Color.' *Stanford Law Review* 43, 6, 1991: 1241–99.

Crewe, E. and P. Fernando. 'The Elephant in the Room: Racism in Representations, Relationships and Rituals.' *Progress in Development Studies* 6, 1, 2006: 40–54.

Davis, A.Y. *Women, Race, and Class.* New York: Random House, 1981.

——— *Women Culture and Politics.* New York: Vintage, Reprint edition, 1990.

Du Bois, W.E.B. *The World and Africa.* (Original work from 1946). New York, International Publishers, 1990.

——— *The Souls of Black Folk. In Three Negro Classics.* (Original work from 1903), New York: Avon Books, 1965: 207–389.

Edwards, B. H. *The Practice of Diaspora Literature, Translation, and the Rise of Black Internationalism.* Boston, Harvard University Press, 2003.

Escobar, A. 'Imagining a Post-Development Era? Critical Thought, Development and Social Movements.' *Social Text* 31/32, 1992: 20–56.

——— 'The Making and Unmaking of the Third World through Development'. In *The Post-Development Reader.* eds. M. Rahnema and W.V. Bawtree. London: Zed Books, 1997: 85–93.

Eyben, R. 'The Power of the Gift.' *IDS Bulletin* 37, 6 2006: 88–98.

——— 'Harmonisation: How Is the Orchestra Conducted?' *Development in Practice* 17, 4/5, 2007: 640–6.

——— *International Aid and the Making of a Better World: Reflexive Practice (Rethinking Development).* London: Routledge, 2014.

Fanon, F. *Black Skin, White Masks.* Translated by C. L. Markmann, [Original Title, Peau Noir, Masques Blancs]. New York: Grove Wei Press, 1967.

Fikes, K. *Managing African Portugal: The Citizen-Migrant Distinction.* Durham: Duke University Press, 2009.

Gilroy, P. *The Black Atlantic: Modernity and Double Consciousness.* Cambridge, MA: Harvard University Press, 1993.

Green, E. H. H. 'The Political Economy of Empire'. In *The Oxford History of the British Empire: The Nineteenth Century, Volume 3.* ed. A. Porter. Oxford and New York: Oxford University Press, 1999: 346–70.

Grovogui, S. N. Z. 'Come to Africa: A Hermeneutics of Race in International Theory.' *Alternatives* 26, 4 (2001): 425–48.

Hill-Collins, P. *Black Feminist Thought: Knowledge, Consciousness, and the Politics of Empowerment.* New York: Routledge, 2008.

Hintzen, P. C. and J. M. Rahier. 'Introduction: Theorizing the African Diaspora: Metaphor, Miscognition, and Self Recognition'. In *Global Circuits of Blackness: Interrogating the African Diaspora.* eds. P.C. Hintzen and J. M. Rahier. Urbana Champaign: University of Illinois Press, 2010, xi – xxvi.

Hoodge, J. and G. Hodl. 'Introduction'. In *Developing Africa: Concepts and Practices in Twentieth-Century Colonialism,* eds. J. Hoodge, G. Hodl and M. Kopf. Manchester and New York: Manchester University Press, 2014, 1–34.

hooks, b. *Talking Back: Thinking Feminist, Thinking Black.* Boston: South End Press, 1989.

Hull, A., P. Bell Scott and B. Smith. *All the Women Are White, All the Men Are White, but Some of Us Are Brave.* New York: Feminist Press, 1982.

Kabeer, N. *Mainstreaming Gender and Poverty Eradication in the Millennium Development Goals.* London: Commonwealth Secretariat, Ottawa: International Development Research Centre, 2003.

——— 'Passion, Pragmatism and the Politics of Advocacy: A 'Gender and Development' Perspective on Nordic Approaches to Gender Equality.' In *Global Perspectives on Gender Equality: Reversing the Gaze.* eds. N. Kabeer, A. Stark and E. Magnus. London: Routledge, 2008.

——— 'Women's Empowerment, Development Interventions and the Management of Information Flows.' *IDS Bulletin,* 41, 2010: 105–13.

Khan, A. *Callaloo Nation: Metaphors of Race and Religious Identity among South Asians in Trinidad.* Durham, NC: Duke University Press, 2004.

——— *Islam and the Americas.* Miami: University Press of Florida Press, 2015.

Klich, I. and J. Lesser. *Arab and Jewish Immigrants in Latin America: Images and Realities.* London: Routledge, 2007, Original printed 1998.

Kothari, U. 'An Agenda for Thinking about "Race" in Development.' *Progress in Development Studies* 6, 1, 2006: 9–23.

Leys, C. *The Rise and Fall of Development Theory*. Indiana: James Currey, 1996.
Loftsdóttir, K. 'Landscapes of Whiteness and Racial Identity in International Development.' *Anthropology Today* 25, 5, 2009: 4–7.
Lourde, A. *Sister Outsider: Essays and Speeches.* Berkeley: Crossing Press, 1984.
Lowenhaupt-Tsing, A. *Friction: An Ethnography of Global Connection.* Princeton , NJ: Princeton University Press, 2005.
McKinnon, K. *Development Professional in Northern Thailand: Hope, Politics and Practice.* Honolulu: University of Hawai'i Press, 2011.
Mbembe, A. *On the Postcolony.* Berkley and Los Angeles: University of California Press, 2001.
Mohanty, C. '"Under Western Eyes" Revisited: Feminist Solidarity through Anticapitalist Struggles.' *Signs* 28, 2, 2003: 499–535.
Mosse, D. *Adventures in Aidland: The Anthropology of Professionals in International Development.* New York and Oxford: Berghahn Books, 2011.
Naber, N. *Arab America: Gender, Cultural Politics, and Activism.* (New York and London and Oxford: New York University Press, 2012.
Nash, J. 'Re-thinking Intersectionality.' *Feminist Review* 89, 1, 2008: 1–15.
Rajan, R. S. *Real and Imagined Women, Gender, Culture and Postcolonialism.* Routledge: London, 1993.
Rist, G. *The History of Development.* London: Zed Books, 1997.
Sawyer, L. 'Racialization, Gender, and the Negotiation of Power in Stockholm's African Dance Courses'. In *Globalization and Race. Transformations in the Cultural Production of Blackness.* eds. K. M. Clarke and D. A. Thomas. Durham, NC: Duke University Press, 2006: 316–34.
Shilliam, R. *The Black Pacific: Anticolonial Struggles and Oceanic Connections.* London, Bloomsbury Academic Press, 2015.
Spivak, G. 'The Rani of Sirmur: An Essay in Reading the Archives.' *History and Theory* 24, 3, 1985: 247–72.
Sylvester, C. 'Development Studies and Postcolonial Studies: Disparate Tales of the 'Third World'". *Third World Quarterly* 20, 4, 1999: 703–21.
Truth, S. *Ain't I a Woman.* Women's Convention in Akron, Ohio. (1851)
Valentine, G. 'Theorizing and Researching Intersectionality: A Challenge for Feminist Geography.' *The Professional Geographer* 59, 1, 2007: 10–21.
White, S. 'Thinking Race, Thinking Development.' *Third World Quarterly* 23, 3, 2002: 407–19.
Wieringa, S. *Subversive Women: Women's Movements in Africa, Asia, Latin America, and the Caribbean.* London: Zed Books, 1995.
Wilson, K. '"Race", Gender and Neoliberalism: Changing Visual Representations in Development.' *Third World Quarterly* 32, 2, 2011: 315–31.

Notes

1 Constructive exploitation replaced expansion and plunder as official French colonial policy in the 1890s. See Hoodge, J. and G. Hodl. 'Introduction.' In *Developing Africa: Concepts and Practices in Twentieth-Century Colonialism.* eds. J. Hoodge, G. Hodl and M. Kopf. (Manchester and New York: Manchester University Press, 2014).

2 Constructive imperialism was a response to the decline of the empire, which envisioned building one progressive, united empire. See Green, E. H. H. 'The Political Economy of Empire.' In *The Oxford History of the British Empire: The Nineteenth Century, Volume 3.* eds. A. P. William et al. (Oxford and New York: Oxford University Press, 1999) 346–70.

3 For earlier writings on intersectionality see A. Hull, P. Bell Scott and B. Smith. *All the Women Are White, All the Men Are White, but Some of Us Are Brave* (Feminist Press, 1982).

15

LGBTIQ RIGHTS, DEVELOPMENT AID AND QUEER RESISTANCE

Christine M. Klapeer

Introduction

> Resistance is not always saying no to power.
>
> Nikita Dhawan

In 2009 the drafting of the Anti-Homosexuality Bill in the Ugandan parliament incited an unprecedented level of 'public'[1] diplomatic interventions and global interest in the 'West' for sexual and gender dissidents 'abroad'. Major political actors and international institutions, as well as human rights/social justice organisations from the Global South/East and North, condemned the bill as a violation of the fundamental human rights of Lesbian, Gay, Bisexual and Transgender (LGBT[IQ]s[2]) people in Uganda and were calling upon Ugandan political actors not to approve this new legislation. While the draft was off the table until 2011, the re-introduction of the bill in the Ugandan parliament once again produced a wave of harsh international critique.

In October 2011 former British Prime Minister David Cameron suggested, also reacting to pressure from (some) British LGBTIQ groups urging him to tackle LGBTIQ rights at the Commonwealth Heads of Government Meeting, to make aid conditional upon 'proper' adherence to human rights for LGBT(IQ)s (Cameron 2011). Such attempts to link development aid to LGBTIQ rights were not exclusive to Britain; the Obama administration took a quite similar approach when advising US diplomats to consider how countries treat LGBT(IQs) when making decisions about the allocation of foreign aid (Encarnacion 2016). The question of how 'Western' governments and donor institutions should use their economic, diplomatic and normative power as aid-givers in favour of LGBT(IQ) populations became a highly debated topic in foreign and development politics as well as among queer scholars and organisations, and in particular, against the background of the signing of the controversial Anti-Homosexuality Bill by President Yoweri Museveni in February 2014 (Abbas 2012; Statement on British Aid Cut Threats 2011; Laskar 2014; Anguita 2012; Rao 2012). The annulment of the bill by Uganda's Constitutional Court in August 2014, however, caused less international attention.

While aid conditionality has been widely criticised in the 1990s, it nonetheless gained new credibility as a 'progressive' tool of diplomacy in the promotion of human rights and the rights of 'vulnerable' groups, such as LGBTIQs. Some countries and international institutions, including the US, Sweden, the Netherlands, Denmark, Norway and the World Bank also suspended or redirected (some of) their financial aid (temporarily) in response to the passing of the 'Anti-Homosexuality Act' in Uganda. Furthermore, the 'official' condemnation of human rights violations based on sexual orientation and gender identity by the UN Human Rights Council[3] has further contributed to the acknowledgment of LGBTI(Q) rights as an intelligible topic of development cooperation and diplomatic relations. And with the historical speech of Hillary Clinton, in Geneva in December 2011, claiming that 'gay rights are human rights, and human rights are gay rights' and that 'we must [...] work here and in *every region of the world* to galvanise more support for the human rights of the LGBT community' LGBTIQ rights moved to the center of diplomatic and foreign politics (Clinton 2011a, emphasis added; see also Encarnacion 2016). An increased number of bilateral and multilateral development agencies and development organisations, including the EU[4] and the World Bank, have made substantive institutional policy commitments regarding the 'promotion' of LGBTI(Q) rights through aid policies and development cooperation and started to address LGBTI(Q) rights more explicitly in their (public) diplomatic efforts. Traditional donor agencies, such as those in Sweden, Norway, the Netherlands, the UK, Denmark, Finland, Germany, the (pre-Trump) US and to a lesser extent France, are recently also aimed at implementing (or extending[5]) LGBTI(Q) 'inclusive' development frameworks and aid policies (Bergenfield and Miller 2014; Gosine 2015; Lind 2010a).

While these policy changes have been welcomed by various LGBTIQ advocates and organisations all over the world, a number of postcolonial, queer and race critical scholars and activists, including myself, have also questioned the growing attention to LGBTIQ rights in the field of foreign policies, particularly by pointing to racialised undercurrents and colonial genealogies of those developments. Postcolonial researchers have been at the forefront in examining the wider implications of growing attention for the situation of LGBTIQs in global politics, thereby provoking critical questions about entanglements between transnational LGBTIQ rights policies and 'homonationalist' (Puar 2007; Haritaworn, Erdem and Tauqir 2008), 'homotransnationalist' (Bacchetta and Haritaworn 2011; Laskar 2014), 'homodevelopmentalist' (Klapeer 2016) and 'modernisation' (Petzen 2012; Rahman 2014, 2015) agendas and frameworks (see also: Nichols 2012; Rao 2015).

However, while these works are critical for understanding contemporary shifts with regard to transnational LGBTIQ rights policies, much research on that subject is predominantly focused on (high-level) politics or discourses *from* and politics *in* the Global North, and, as a consequence, often disregard the (strategic) involvements, complex entanglements and transnational struggles of those sexual and gender dissidents who ought to be 'supported' by development interventions and diplomatic efforts (Thoreson 2011, 2014). Besides the growing significance of the 'development industry' for transnational LGBTIQ rights policies, engendering particular perceptions of sexual and gender dissidents and LGBTIQ activism in the Global South (and East), still remains an under-researched topic (I deliberately used the term 'sexual and gender dissidents' here because of the contentious nature of the terms *lesbian, bisexual, gay, trans(gender)* and *inter(sex)*.

Postcolonial scholars, and activists from the Global South and East in particular, have pointed to an increased invisibilisation of 'local' sex/gender systems and identifications through a 'globalisation' of LGBTI. This is also the reason why I always add the 'Q' to the internationally used acronym LGBTI, since the 'Q' stands for 'queer' and 'questioning', indicating that the author is aware of the historical and political contingency and situatedness of sexual and gender categories and related social identities. I am therefore not presupposing that LGBTIQs exist 'everywhere' in the world, but I am, nevertheless, also taking account of the 'traveling' implications and transnational flows of sexual identifications and categories. The terms LGBTI(Q) have been re-articulated, appropriated, re-defined and transformed by sexual and gender dissidents in many different spaces and contexts around the world.

By critically interlinking findings from the field of postcolonial and decolonial theory with transnational queer studies, 'radical' development studies and international relations (IR), this chapter aims to illuminate some of the complexity and ambivalences regarding LGBTIQ 'inclusive' development frameworks and (public) LGBTIQ rights diplomacy. I will examine problematic implications of current LGBTIQ rights diplomacies and development frameworks and elucidate on the (im-)possibilities of queer agency and resistance within these configurations, particularly focusing on discussions and policy interventions related to the African context.

The chapter proceeds in four sections: First, I will situate LGBTIQ rights diplomacies and development strategies within the sexualised and gendered coloniality of the international system and shed light on some of the colonial and racialised genealogies of political agendas aimed at 'supporting' LGBTIQ rights in so-called 'developing' countries. Second, I will provide a more detailed postcolonial analysis of these agendas and illustrate how they are based on (racialised) ideas of sexual modernisation which are aggravating, even hindering, the aim of 'promoting' LGBTIQ rights through diplomatic interventions and aid policies. Third, I will elaborate on how the diplomatic terrain, particularly the field of development, is nevertheless an arena that is constantly being challenged, coopted and instrumentalised by sexual and gender dissidents and LGBTIQ-identified activists. And finally, by focusing on responses against/to diplomatic interventions and the 'tool' of aid conditionality that have been articulated by LGBTIQ, human rights and social justice activists in/from Sub-Sahara Africa, the chapter concludes with some rumination about whether the (Western) 'desire' for development and the modernisation of 'others' can be, and already is, turned against itself.

LGBTIQ rights diplomacies and the sexualised coloniality of the international system

Decolonial theorist Anibal Quijano coined the term 'coloniality' as a global hegemonic model of power based on the imposition of racial, ethnic, and gender classification of the global population as the cornerstone and defining element of the modern international (world) system (Quijano 2000; see also: Shilliam 2011). Coloniality therefore 'refers to long-standing patterns of power that emerged as a result of colonialism, but that define culture, labour, intersubjective relations, and knowledge production well beyond the strict limits of colonial administrations. Thus coloniality survives colonialism. [...] In a way, as modern subjects we breathe coloniality all the time and everyday' (Maldonado-Torres 2007: 243). Postcolonial and decolonial feminists have particularly shown how gender and sexuality have played, and still play, a pivotal role in maintaining, (re-)producing and actualising the 'coloniality' of the international (world) system (Lugones 2007; Weber 2016).

However, by following a feminist and queer approach, 'coloniality' does not only have a gendered and sexualised dimension but is *contingent upon* colonial constructions of gender and sexuality (Lugones 2008; Weber 2016). By examining the sexual and gendered implications of colonial politics, Anne McClintock (1995) and Ann Laura Stoler (2002) have particularly revealed how non-European 'others' have consistently been constructed as 'sexually deviant', as 'promiscuous' and 'violent animals', as 'sexually backward' and 'uncivilised' with regard to their gender performances, sexual practices or family organisation (see also: Kapoor 2015; Lugones 2007). María Lugones (2007: 195), for instance, emphasises that the colonisers of the Americas imagined 'the indigenous people [...] as hermaphrodites or intersexed, with large penises and flowing milk' whereas 'gender dimorphism', heterosexuality and a clear socio-political distinction (and hierarchy) between 'men' and 'women' was considered 'a mark of civilisation' (Lugones 2010: 743). In the light of these sexualised and gendered implications of colonialism, McClintock also coined the term 'porno-tropics' in order to describe how Europeans envisaged the 'far-off lands' as highly sexualised places full of sexual aberrations and 'forbidden sexual desires' (McClintock 1995: 22). Critical development scholars have likewise shown how development programs have further contributed to an actualisation of 'porno-tropics' and racialised notions of 'sexual deviance' (Wilson 2012; Gosine 2009). Andil Gosine (2009: 6) argues that '[i]nternational development theory and practice have long been fixated upon [...] dissident sexual subjects' that provided 'a rationale and impetus for the pursuit of development', thereby ensuring 'that sexuality is one of its primary components.' Racialised constructions of the 'overly reproductive Third World woman' and the 'sexually violent' and 'promiscuous Third World man', still evident in many development programs concerned with health, reproduction, and sexual rights, are particularly contributing to reinstitute colonial tropes of sexuality and gender.

An alleged 'sexual promiscuity', 'backwardness' and 'abnormality' of the 'Non-West' (or the 'Third World') has therefore been key in legitimising colonial violence and exploitation and various developmental interventions, including forced sterilisations on women *of color* (Wilson 2012; Kapoor 2015). From this follows that a (sexualised) dichotomy between the (sexually) 'normal' and the 'perverse', between the 'civilised' and the 'barbaric', between the 'sexually developed' and 'sexually underdeveloped/undevelopable' served, and continues to serve, as a constitutive element of (the coloniality of) international orders. This is also why Cynthia Weber speaks of 'sexualised orders of international relations' (Weber 2016: 6).

However, the irony is, of course, that while 'proper' (white) heterosexuality has long been seen as an indicator of 'civilisation', 'modernity', 'development', the exact opposite has become the case in the contemporary context. Jasbir Puar (2007) refers to the contemporary context as a specific historical moment, that is characterised by an increased inclusion of (white, 'proper', homonormative) LGB(TIQ) subjects into (Western) national imaginaries at the expense of the partial and full expulsion of (racialised, non-normative, Muslim) 'others' (see also: Haritaworn, Erdem and Tauqir 2008). Due to (new) entanglements between (Western) LGBTIQ rights policies, nationalism(s) and imperial politics, Puar speaks of a 'homonational time' (ibid.). Against this background, particular notions of 'sexual diversity' and 'homotolerance' have increasingly assumed a key role on the configuration and self-constitution of (some) nationalism(s) in the US and Europe. Homonationalism, also an ambivalent outcome of the (relative) success of LGBTIQ and feminist movements in 'mainstreaming' LGBT(IQ) rights, is thus intrinsically interrelated with a growing 'geopolicisation' of LGBTIQ rights (Lavinas Picq and Thiel 2015a: 1). LGBTIQ rights have begun to play an important role in international politics; they shape foreign policies, development strategies and diplomatic relationships and are increasingly being framed as 'the' new markers of 'civilisation', of 'modernity' and 'development' (Lavinas Picq and Thiel 2015b; Nichols 2012); or, in the words of Hakima Abbas:

> LGBTI issues have gained ground in the international arena as a barometer to determine who the 'good liberal' countries versus the 'bad backward' ones are. With racist undertones about the 'barbaric' and 'uncivilized', it has been written that the 'cultures' and 'traditions' of the Black and Brown peoples of the world have not yet been civilized enough to tolerate gay and lesbian people.
>
> (Abbas 2012)

'The West' is, once again, being constructed as (sexually) exceptional, as model of and for 'sexual development' and 'homotolerance' while all (internal or external) 'others', such as 'migrants', 'Muslims', and 'fragile' and 'developing states' are rendered as 'backward', 'uncivilised' and 'sexual underdeveloped', and without knowledge about LGBTIQ rights (Weber 2016: 10; see also Puar 2007; Haritaworn, Erdem and Tauqir 2008; Nichols 2012; Rahman 2014; Rao 2015; Klapeer 2016). According to Momin Rahman (2014a: 279), sexual exceptionalism has even become 'the' privileged marker of civilisational exceptionalism itself, which means that LGBTIQ rights are 'not simply located within the space of the West', but rather positioned as the 'apex of Western exceptionalism' itself. That means, in turn, that the colonial binary between a 'sexually underdeveloped rest' and a 'modern West' remains unchanged, and even becomes actualised through the unquestioned 'progressivity' of LGBTIQ rights diplomacies.

The transnationalisation of LGBTIQ rights and the rerun of modernisation frameworks

From the previous section follows that violence against LGBTIQs and (homo-)tolerance are increasingly being 'located' in certain spaces and places of the world, and attitudes towards sexuality, and sexual and gender dissidents become 'markers of belonging to particular places' (Rao 2014a: 181). The most prominent and most cited 'location of homophobia' is the Lesbian, Gay and Bisexual Map of World Laws[6] provided by the International Lesbian, Gay, Bisexual, Trans and Intersex Association (ILGA), which frequently appears in policy papers promoting LGBTIQ 'inclusive' development strategies and frameworks. The Map uses a traffic light system in order to depict the status of lesbian and gay rights in the world (Rao 2014a). According to Rao (ibid.: 170), the way states are color-coded implies a 'ranking impulse' and produces 'a Western – more specifically, northern European – temporal narrative' of sexual modernisation: A society/nation moves from 'decriminalisation' to 'anti-discrimination' and finally to the institutionalisation of 'partnership rights', preferably same-sex marriage. Hence, only a certain type of 'rights', 'development' or 'liberation' is being read as 'progress' and 'development' (such as same-sex marriage). Those, who are not able to 'develop' these patterns are, according to this logic, not only 'lagging behind' but are necessarily seen as 'inferior' and/or 'less developed' due to their 'inability' to reach an 'advanced' stage of sexual modernisation (see also: Rahman 2014b). Hence, these spaces become, due to their 'backwardness', the main targets of 'external' interventions and diplomatic efforts.

Therefore, the 'responsibility' and 'authority' to intervene 'externally' in order to promote LGBTIQ rights 'abroad' is suffused with, and being legitimised through, temporal tropes. When examining contemporary international debates on LGBT(IQ) rights diplomacy,[7] aid conditionality and LGBTIQ rights, and by exploring concrete policies and policy documents including speeches, action plans, policy programs, manuals and instructions, and media articles concerned with the role of LGBTIQ rights in foreign policy and development cooperation, it becomes evident that processes of social change towards (more) 'sexual diversity' and 'homo-tolerance' are framed as a 'journey through time', or in the words of David Cameron in his pledge for aid conditionality:

> They [countries, which criminalise homosexuality] are in a different place from us on this issue. [...] I think these countries are all on a journey and it's up to us to try and help them along on that journey.' (Cameron 2011).

This quote perfectly demonstrates that global inequalities and the economic and epistemological hegemony of the 'West', including the 'West's' self-authorisation as bearer and supervisor of homotolerance and LGBTIQ rights, can be disguised through temporal tropes and a geopoliticisation of time (see: Nichols 2012; Hoad 2000). McClintock already highlighted in her analysis of the discursive tropes and rationalities of British colonialism how 'time became a geography of social power, a map from which to read a global allegory of [...] social differences' and (McClintock 1995: 37). In other words, non-European 'cultures' and people have been, and continue to be, considered as 'living anachronisms', as relicts from the (West's own) past, *à la* 'we were like them, but have developed, they are like we were and have yet to develop' (Rao 2014a: 174). Thus, (political) homo- and transphobias become not only spatialised and associated with certain geopolitical places (in the non-West) but are also temporalised and projected into an 'anachronistic space' (ibid.). LGBTIQ rights are increasingly being applied as temporal 'indicators' to define the 'developmental stage' of a societies, regions or countries. However, this also means that, temporality and hierarchy are being bound together, since a movement forward in 'time' ('sexual modernisation') is, according to this logic, necessarily a movement 'upward' on the scales of ('civilisational') development. From this follows, that 'time' (and related concepts, such as development and modernisation) itself functions as political apparatus of regulation (Rao 2014b).

Furthermore, constructions of 'anachronistic spaces' also allow, or rather, assume the possibility of 'time travel'; diplomatic and development efforts from the West aiming to 'support' LGBTIQ rights in the so-called development countries become rendered as 'temporal interventions', as time journeys to previous temporal stages (of the West), in order to 'help'/'urge'/'force' those ('barbaric', 'premodern', 'traditional') people to find the route to (sexual) modernisation. The international arena therefore seems to be a battleground and/or an encounter zone of and for different temporalities but nevertheless, already presupposing which (temporal) direction is entailing 'progress' and 'more' homotolerance. Despite the fact that developmentalist models and modernisation theory are often perceived as to have lost credibility in recent years, a spatialised global hierarchy is once again turned into a temporalised (putative) historical sequence. Even though the term 'modernisation' has disappeared, social transformations regarding LGBTIQ rights are, nevertheless, mainly being framed as manifestations of a process of 'modernisation' with the 'West' as model and goal of development.

Besides, what is even more important, LGBTIQ rights are themselves presented as a 'solution' to a lack of modernity (Rahman 2014b: 95; Rahman 2014a), or in the words of Katyal (2010: 1434): 'LGBT advocates' stress the 'homophobia of third-world traditions,' implying that 'modernisation' will make the non-Western world more liberated for queers.' Hence, very different forms and manifestations of violence and discrimination against sexual and gender dissidents are increasingly turned into 'universal' signs of '(under-)development', which can be 'measured' and 'compared'. In consequence, resistance *against* violence and discrimination, for instance, exhibited *by* sexual and gender dissidents, tends to be interpreted as a desire *for* 'modernisation' and a movement *towards* an (alleged) universal modernity. In her famous speech on LGBT(IQ) rights in Geneva, Hillary Clinton made perfectly clear that there is only a single history - 'the right side of the history', and only '[t]hose who advocate for expanding the circle of human rights [to LGBTs] were and are on the right side of history, and history honors them' (Clinton 2011a; see also: Weber 2016). However, according to this logic, 'the West' has already proven to 'be on the right side of history' due to its 'advanced' stage of sexual development regarding LGBTIQ rights and 'homotolerance'. Therefore, drawing on Gayatri Spivak (2004), Western (donor) states have, also in cooperation with NGOs from the Global North and South, to carry (again) the (humanist) 'burden of the fittest' and consequently engage themselves in transnationalising LGBTIQ rights and developing the 'rest'. Thus, LGBTIQ rights can, according to Sara Ahmed, be 'exercised as if they are political gift', that has to be forced upon others: 'what we have, what we give them, what we must force them to have' (Ahmed 2009).

Public diplomacy and development institutions are increasingly becoming associated with an 'observation' of how these 'gifts' are treated, whether they are rightly employed, and thus monitoring processes of sexual modernisation. They can 'measure', 'compare' and 'support' processes of development through a transnational apparatus, while at the same time claiming a 'panoptical point of view' from which the 'time journeys' of 'others' can be watched (and what Spivak would also call 'wronged') as an anachronistic 'spectacle' (McClintock 1995; Spivak 2004). According to this logic, this means that 'the fittest must shoulder the burden of righting the wrongs of the unfit' (Spivak 2004: 524). The role of the 'queer' or 'LGBTIQ-friendly' diplomat, the 'modern' and 'homotolerant' political actor or state, or the (international) LGBTIQ or human rights organisation, is therefore not only to carry the 'burden of the fittest', but also to wrong those '[p]athological states [...] that deny human rights and state protection to the "LGBT"' (Weber 2016: 138). This is also why Spivak (2004) problematises human rights policies because they contribute to the production of a problematic global divide 'between those who right wrongs and those who are wronged' (ibid.: 563).

International arenas and spaces of queer resistance

Temporal framings have important implications and very real effects on *how* diplomatic actors and development institutions read LGBTIQ movements, organisations and activists in 'recipient countries', and consequently, how donor institutions and Western governments frame their policies aiming to 'promote' LGBTIQ rights abroad (Klapeer 2017 forthcoming). LGBTIQs from the Global South (and East) are being perceived as mainly demanding 'things' and 'rights' that have already been 'achieved' in the West, and donor organisations are being perceived as 'providing' the necessary (financial) assistance and knowledge to 'promote' 'catching up'-processes (see: Klapeer 2017 forthcoming). Moreover, while sexual and gender dissidents have long been seen as unproductive to development, LGBTI(Q)s in recipient countries are now constructed as 'temporal' and 'cultural brokers', as democratic change agents who are able, due to their (alleged) embodied connection to modernity, to break with their 'time' and 'culture'. They are read as cultural mediators, as 'integrable others', who, in contrast to 'non-integrable others', *want* to take part in the project of modernity since modernity is being equated with 'homotolerance' and LGBTIQ rights (Weber 2016; see also: Nichols 2012). The revival of modernisation frameworks with regard to transnational LGBTIQ rights policies, thus, implicates and produces, particular constraints for LGBTIQ organising in the international system, and contributes to an invisibilisation and delegitimisation of 'other' (queer/sexual) frameworks or strategies, including translocal appropriations, re-articulations, re-framings and re-definitions of concepts and models that have been developed in the 'West', such as 'alternative' understandings of LGBTIQ justice, LGBTIQ rights or queer liberation (Dhawan 2013; Rahman 2014).

However, due to all these problematic implications of current transnational LGBTIQ rights policies, the inter- and transnational sphere can easily be misconstrued as an arena where power is predominantly enacted by 'Western' states *towards* postcolonial states or/and aid receiving countries, and power is then mainly understood in a Weberian or realist sense. While a critical understanding of coloniality and global power asymmetries continues to be indispensable for a postcolonial analysis of transnational LGBTIQ policies, it is, nevertheless, important to not reduce power to a monolithic flow from the 'West' to the 'Rest' and to consider the Global South merely as 'passive recipient' of dominant perceptions of LGBTIQ rights, sexual modernisation and development (Dhawan 2015; Rao 2010; Thoreson 2011, 2014; Lind 2010a; Rahman 2014b). Such a perspective risks to invisibilise the political agency, and the multi-faceted engagements with the international arena enacted by sexual and gender dissidents and LGBTIQ identified subjects, movements and organisations. By analysing transnational sexual politics and sexual flows, Inderpal Grewal and Caren Kaplan, for instance, demonstrate how 'local', or 'domestic' spheres are not merely sites where global (sexual) norms and impulse, or in our case, diplomatic efforts and development interventions, are simply being 'negotiated' (Grewal and Kaplan 2001). They are, despite global asymmetries, rather appropriated, transformed, reconstructed and recirculated.

Therefore, I share some of the criticism related to the influential work of Joseph Massad (2007), particularly the arguments offered by Rahul Rao (2010) and Momin Rahman (2015). Joseph Massad accuses Western LGB(TIQ) rights policies, as for instance exemplified by the transnational work of organisations such as the International Lesbian, Gay, Bisexual, Trans and Intersex Association (ILGA) or the former International Gay and Lesbian Human Rights Commission (now OutRight Action International) of cultural imperialism. According to Massad, these organisations – or what he calls the 'Gay International' – are imposing a Western sexual epistemology on Arabs (his research focus), thereby obliterating 'indigenous' forms of sexual subjectivity and, moreover, inciting massive violence due to the new 'visibility' of 'out' LGB(TIQ) subjects. Although I share Massad's problematisation of an increasing and hegemonic universalisation of LGB(TIQ) as the *only* possible categories, terms and identities for sexual and gender dissidents, I am also in line with Rao's argument, asserting that it is a 'denial of the agency and subjectivity of Arabs who are appropriating and reworking Western identities in their struggles for sexual self-determination' (Rao 2010: 176). LGBTIQs from the Global South/East are, as Rao states, 'far from being simply "native informants" to the Gay International as Massad would have us believe' but rather holding much more 'complex and conflictual' relationships with the international sphere and transnational LGBTIQ movements (ibid.: 192). He stresses that '[a]lthough many have begun to appropriate Western identities in their struggles for sexual self-expression, this has not always amounted to a slavish endorsement of everything that emanates from the Gay International' (ibid.; see also: Rahman 2015; Thoreson 2014).

A number of studies from the field of transnational/global queer studies and queer IR have also revealed how and in what ways the international terrain and related norms, institutions and organisations (such as development agencies, transnational LGBTIQ organisations or the UN), are, and have been, playing a vital and rather *enabling* role in the formation of several LGBTIQ movements and activisms in the Global South and East, particularly by providing material resources, normative support and cultural capital for 'local' and 'domestic' LGBTIQ rights struggles (see: Binnie 2004; Lavinas Picq and Thiel 2015b; Ayoub and Paternotte 2014; Currier 2012; Rao 2010; Thoreson 2014; Rahman 2015; Ekine and Abbas 2013; Kollmann and Waites 2009). LGBTIQ and queer advocates, organisations and activists from the Global North, South and East, which are part of 'local' as well as transnational ties and networks, have begun to play an increasingly important role in international politics, thereby also strategically utilising, and probably also coopting diplomatic arenas and the field of development. The effort to bring LGBTIQ rights into international arenas, including development, therefore has necessarily to be seen as 'a paradoxical process from the start, one that is imbued with hegemonic as well as oppositional forms of knowledge, consciousness and experience' (Lind 2010b: 7).

Queer mimicry on the international stage and other decolonising maneuvers

Recent developments in Uganda and Nigeria have particularly shown that 'external' interventions and LGBTIQ rights diplomacies have not solely been initiated and shaped by political actors *from* Europe or the US (Thoreson 2011). For instance, during the drafting of the 'Anti-Homosexuality Bill', as well as after the signing by Museveni, several LGBTIQ and social justice/human rights activists based in Uganda and beyond, were calling for international solidarity and support from Western donor countries, also welcoming *certain* diplomatic interventions, but, however, harshly criticising (neo)colonial language and general aid conditionalities. In 2011, shortly after David Cameron was considering making aid conditional upon adherence to human rights for LGB(TIQs), around 50 African social justice, human rights and LGBTIQ organisations and activists based in Uganda, Kenya, South Africa, Burundi, Liberia, Cameroon, Zimbabwe, Nigeria, Tanzania, Algeria, Burkina Faso, Namibia, Egypt, Mozambique, Côte d'Ivoire, the Democratic Republic of Congo, Rwanda, Botswana and Ghana published a statement that condemned aid conditionalities as a probate instrument to support and protect the rights of LGBTI(Q) people (Statement on British Aid Cut Threats 2011). The statement emphasises, that '[d]onor sanctions are by their nature coercive and reinforce the disproportionate power dynamics between donor countries and recipients' and highlight the role of colonialism in producing (African) 'homophobia' (ibid.). According to the undersigning LGBTIQ and social justice/ human rights activists, such aid conditionality is 'based on assumptions about African sexualities and the needs of African LGBTI people' (ibid.):

> *The history of colonialism and sexuality* cannot be overlooked when seeking solutions to this issue. *The colonial legacy of the British Empire* in the form of laws that criminalize same-sex sex continues to serve as the legal foundation for the persecution of LGBTI people throughout the Commonwealth.
>
> (ibid., emphasis added).

However, by pointing to the colonial histories of African homo- and transphobias as well as problematic neocolonial implications of aid conditionalities, these activists are, in my reading, calling upon an active (sexual) decolonisation of the project of development, and more particular the diplomatic terrain itself. They are demanding that donor countries truly devote themselves to, what Troy A. Richardson (2012) conceptualised as a 'decolonial diplomatic project'. In this specific context, that would imply a critical engagement with the sexualised and gendered coloniality of the political and international terrain itself, including the racialised/sexual framing of those 'conflicts' and 'differences', which should be solved *through* diplomatic efforts or aid conditionalities. The above statement, on the one hand, interrupts a sexualised and racialised reading of 'cultural difference' and 'geopolitics', e.g. the perception that LGBTIQ rights can be seen as a 'marker' or 'barometer' of 'development' and/or a certain 'stage' of modernisation; on the other hand, it also radically dismantles the coloniality, racism and underlying asymmetry of such interpretations and sexual modernisation logics themselves. In this case, the participating activists and organisations are not only challenging the production of neo/colonial and racialising frames of 'Third World' (homo-)sexualities in the context of development and diplomatic policies, they also demand a complete *decolonisation* of aid relationships, but not their abolition.

Aid and diplomatic interventions were not completely rejected, and resistance against the Anti-Homosexuality Bill was not located 'outside' the arena of international development and diplomacy. In 2014, the Civil Society Coalition on Human Rights and Constitutional Law

(CSCHRCL), a political coalition between different organisations and activists aiming to fight the Anti-Homosexuality Bill, released concrete 'guidelines on how National, International and Regional partners can support Ugandan LGBTI Persons and their allies' (CSCHRCL 2014). According to these guidelines, the Coalition called upon partners, friends and allies to '[g]et more foreign leaders in foreign governments to say something about the Act as they have not come out strongly as it was expected', to 'contact your own embassies in Uganda to voice your concerns' (ibid.). The coalition was also supporting 'strategic aid cuts to specific sectors': 'We encourage urgent review of aid to organisations and government institutions that have failed to demonstrate respect for Human Rights and those that have been actively supporting this bill.' (ibid.; see also: Thoreson 2011). However, all statements made perfectly clear, that the 'local' LGBTIQ and human rights movements are, and must be, the main carrier of social change.

LGBTIQ movements operating in countries where sexual and gender dissidents are heavily persecuted and criminalised have, however, strong incentives to frame their protests in transnational terms, not only in order to strengthen their 'domestic' claims and ensure their actual safety through international attention[8] (or pressure), but also in order to gain substantial economic[9] resources. Sexual and gender dissidents and LGBTIQ activists from the Global South/East have not only started to engage with the 'requirements' and 'languages'[10] of development, most literally by seeking aid for their projects and initiatives, they have also provided intersectional critiques directed towards the *organisation*, structures and rhetoric of international interventions aid policies from the very beginning (Lind 2010b; Currier 2010; Statement on British aid cut threats 2011). On the backdrop of my discussion above, I therefore propose to read the increasing number of critical interventions, in which aid is being 'rightly' demanded, as an interrogation of 'Western' conceptualisations of aid (and LGBTIQ rights) as a 'political gift'. I would even go so far as to argue that claims *for* aid are being conceptualised, or turned, into claims for *reparations* due to the effects of colonial *and* anti-colonial politics for sexual and gender dissidents. Aid and the development apparatus are thus used to strengthen and articulate claims for 'alternative' understandings and non-heteronormative visions of *decolonisation*, or what Ashley Currier termed as 'sexual decolonization' (Currier 2011). Or in the words ofVal Kalende (2014), an Ugandan self-identified lesbian/trans scholar and activist:

> What needs to happen in Africa is an honest discussion on human sexuality in the African context *before, during and after the colonial period.* [...] The pushback against Western interventions such as aid cuts is usually informed by an African resistance to neocolonialism. However, there is no going back. More than ever, what Africa needs is a pan-African uprising for LGBT rights.'

Against the backdrop of heteronormative decolonisation discourses, LGBTIQ movements and social justice organisations such as those in Uganda, Namibia, Malawi and Nigeria are instrumentalising development politics to challenge 'antigay, state leaders' monopoly on decolonisation' (Currier 2011: 19). Particularly with regard to LGBTIQ and human rights activism against the Anti-Homosexuality Bill in Uganda, it became evident, that activists are trying to *reclaim* the (decolonial) state and are challenge the 'homosexuality-is-unAfrican' discourse by using the field of international diplomacy and development aid (Nyanzi 2013; Ekine and Abbas 2013). These efforts remain, however, a balancing act, since the vast number of diplomatic interventions have been criticised as worsening rather than improving the situation of sexual and gender dissidents.[11]

However, my reading does also not suggest an uncritical romanticisation of queer engagements within the constraints and arrangements of the development apparatus and the diplomatic terrain. But these arenas can be interpreted as a spaces of 'failure' which can be, and already are, being utilised for multiple forms of resistance and subversion, thereby producing a complex interplay between mimicry tactics, strategic alignments and complicities. Thus, it remains essential to engage, analytically and politically, with the manifold political maneuvers which might derive from, or are being enabled, *by* the (Western) 'desire for development' as well as by the 'desires' and 'expectations' generated *by* the 'promise' of development, such as funding to strengthen LGBTIQ advocacy. If we consider, as Pieter de Vries (2007: 26) states, 'development [...] as a desiring machine' what happens, when the desire for development is being 'played back'? What if the desire of 'the West' to constantly re-affirm its 'superiority' through development interventions and modernisation narratives, or what Gabriele Dietze also called the Western desire for an 'occidentalist self-ascertainment', is (already) being appropriated and coopted by LGBTIQ activists from the Global South (Dietze 2010)?

One important 'promise' evoked by developmentalist and modernisation frameworks is, for instance, the promise that LGBTIQs (in recipient countries) are already 'part' of the project of modernity. Due to the fact that within a sexual modernisation framework homosexuality and 'sexual diversity' can mainly be read as 'signs' or 'achievements' related to a universal idea of 'modernity', LGBTIQs in 'developing countries' tend to be interpreted – in contrast to women – as sexual subjects who already 'embody' (some) elements of modernity (Klapeer forthcoming 2017; see also: Bracke 2012). According to this logic, they already are, recounting Clinton's famous speech, on the 'right side of the history', and they want, in contrast to 'non-integrable others', to take part in the project of modernity and (universal) progress (Nichols 2012). This idea of a 'natural' connection to 'modernity' and 'Western' notions of progress becomes particularly evident in Clinton's reaction to the assassination of David Kato, a famous Ugandan gay activist, in 2011:

> Everywhere I travel on behalf of our country, I make it a point to meet with young people and activists – people like David – who are trying to build a better, stronger future for their societies. I let them know that America stands with them, and that their ideas and commitment are indispensible to achieving *the progress we all seek*.'
>
> (Clinton 2011b)

On the backdrop of Homi Bhabha's (1994) discussion of (colonial) mimicry, I am therefore suggesting to read LGBTIQ-related development strategies as political practices which are producing their own 'slippages', thereby opening up spaces for 'ironic compromise[s]' and queer mimicry (Bhabha 1994: 86). While mimicry is, according to Bhabha, the most elusive and effective strategy of colonial power, it is, nevertheless, also a position of subversion. Bhabha asserts that mimicry does not refer to mere imitation, nor does it assume assimilation into the dominant culture; to him, mimicry is rather an exaggeration of a copying of the ideas, language, manners of the dominant culture that differentiates it from mere imitation: it is repetition with *difference*, difference which may destabilise 'the dominant' itself, particularly by revealing its inherent ambivalence. Regarding LGBTIQ rights, mimicry therefore means that developmentalist and diplomatic strategies that are based on a notion of 'Western sexual exceptionalism' might also produce an 'immanent threat' and a loss of power, because notions of ('cultural') difference are themselves destabilised through the 'promise of modernisation' for non-Western LGBTIQ subjects.

The claim, enunciated on 'both' sides, that to be able to 'be' LGBTIQ is not only to become 'the same', but to be (already) 'modern', thus decenters the modernity of 'queerness', 'homosexuality' and Western sexual exceptionalism itself. Uncritically condemning current diplomatic interventions from the Global North as 'only' neocolonial ventures invisibilises the complex engagements, negotiations, appropriations of these arenas and the resources allocated. In light of Spivak's concept of human rights as 'enabling violation' (Spivak 2004: 524) we have to consider in what way these policies have the potential to enable sexual and gender dissidents to strategically invoke and demand these 'promises' without necessarily sharing the visions, norms or goals articulated by many international actors. From this follows that we, as researchers, have probably also to look *beyond* an alleged authority of sexual modernisation narratives when analysing 'resistance' in the international terrain, in order to *see* the 'affirmative sabotage' of dominant frameworks and to take account of the manifold operations of power exhibited by the mimic subject, thereby probably also disrupting 'the West's' authority, and imperial fantasies. (Spivak 2012; Dhawan 2014).

Conclusion

In this chapter I have tried to illustrate some of the complexity of transnational LGBTIQ rights policies, by particularly drawing attention to the field of development aid and LGBTIQ rights diplomacies. While I do not want to deny that solidarity and 'real' interest in the lives of sexual and gender dissidents shapes and motivates many political actors, particular many LGBTIQ organisations, to lobby and fight for LGBTIQ rights 'abroad', I have, however, illuminated, how the coloniality of the international system complicates, hinders, and endangers political struggles against myriad forms of homo- and transphobias. Sexual and gender dissidents and LGBTIQ identified activists in 'recipient' countries are, on the one hand, confronted with an actualisation of (racialised) sexual modernisation frameworks, temporal narratives and Western sexual exceptionalism (co-)produced by development institutions and diplomatic actors. On the other hand, they experience social and/or state sponsored violence and discrimination, which is precisely being legitimised by the argument that homosexuality and LGBTIQ rights are 'un-African', and a Western, neocolonial imposition.

However, there is a strong movement to navigate between these different political appellations and to claim 'substantive' solidarity from 'Western' donor countries and international institutions, but concurrently demanding a *decolonisation* of the diplomatic terrain itself. LGBTIQ activists are making (strategic) use of the potential enablement of development aid and LGBTIQ rights diplomacies while at same time also scrutinising and challenging hegemonic and neocolonial implications of development aid and/or diplomatic interventions. LGBTIQ rights diplomacy, including development aid, might therefore be analysed, drawing on Spivak (1993), as something that 'we cannot not want', even though it cannot provide what we want, or what is being wanted. But we, nevertheless, 'engage in a persistent critique of what one cannot not want' (ibid: 284). In line with Puar (2013: 23), I am therefore not claiming that homo(trans)nationalism as a specific historical moment can be transcendent by the tactics I have been discussing in this chapter, since 'we are all conditioned by it and through it', but it can be resisted, re-signified and probably also turned against itself.

Bibliography

Abbas, H. 'Aid, Resistance and Queer Power'. *Pambazuka News*, Apr 05, 2012. Accessed July 26, 2012. http://www.pambazuka.org/governance/aid-resistance-and-queer-power

Ahmed, S. 'Problematic Proximities, Or Why Critiques of "Gay Imperialism" Matter'. Accessed July 22, 2016. http://www.alanalentin.net/2009/11/09/problematic-proximities-or-why-critiques-of-gay-imperialism-matter/

Anguita, L. A. 'Aid Conditionality and Respect for LGBT People Rights.' *Sexuality Policy Watch* (2012). Accessed August 14, 2016. http://sxpolitics.org/we-recommend-134/7369

Ayoub, P. M., and D. Paternotte. *LGBT Activism and the Making of Europe: A Rainbow Europe?* Basingstoke: Palgrave Macmillan, 2014.

Bacchetta, P., and J. Haritaworn. 'There Are Many Transatlantics. Homonationalism, Homotransnationalism.' In *Transatlantic Conversations: Feminism as Travelling Theory*, edited by K. Davis, and M. Evans, 127–44. London: Routledge, 2011.

Bergenfield, R., and A. Miller. 'Queering International Development? An Examination of New "LGBT Rights": Rhetoric, Policy, and Programming among International Development Agencies.' *Harvard Kennedy School LGBT Policy Journal* (2014). Accessed May 31, 2015. http://www.hkslgbtq.com/wp-content/uploads/2014/11/Queering-International-Development_-An-Examination-of-New-_LGBT-Rights_-Rhetoric-Policy-and-Programming-among-International-Development-Agencies-1.pdf

Binnie, J. *The Globalisation of Sexuality*. London: Sage, 2004.

Bracke, S. 'From 'Saving Women' to 'Saving Gays': Rescue Narratives and Their Dis/continuities.' *European Journal of Women's Studies* 19, no. 2 (2012): 237–52.

Cameron, D. 'Interview with David Cameron on BBC.' October 30, 2011. Accessed Feb 15, 201. http://www.youtube.com/watch?v=lYhEkB0AOQs.

Civil Society Coalition on Human Rights and Constitutional Law (CSCHRCL) 'Updated Guidelines on How National, International and Regional Partners Can Support Ugandan LGBTI Persons and Their Allies.' March 3, 2014. Accessed July 20, 2016. https://76crimes.com/2014/03/04/lgbt-ugandans-heres-how-you-can-help-us/

Clinton, H. 'Clinton on Gay Rights Abroad: Secretary of State Delivers Historic LGBT Speech in Geneva (Video and Full Text).' Delivered December 6, 2011a. Accessed July 20, 2016. http://www.huffingtonpost.com/2011/12/06/hillary-clinton-gay-rights-speech-geneva_n_1132392.html

——— 'Murder of Ugandan LGBT Activist David Kato: Press Statement.' January 27, 2011b. Accessed July 20, 2016. http://www.state.gov/secretary/20092013clinton/rm/2011/01/155520.htm

Council of the European Union. 'Guidelines to Promote and Protect the Enjoyment of All Human Rights by Lesbian, Gay, Bisexual, Transgender and Intersex (LGBTI) Persons.' Luxembourg, 2013.

Currier, A. 'Decolonizing the Law: LGBT Organizing in Namibia and South Africa.' *Studies in Law, Politics and Society*, no. 54 (2011): 17–44.

——— *Out in Africa: LGBT Organizing in Namibia and South Africa*. Minneapolis: University of Minnesota Press. 2012.

——— 'The Empire Prays Back: Religion, Secularity, and Queer Critique.' *Boundary 2* 40, no. 1 (2013): 191–222.

——— 'Affirmative Sabotage of the Master's Tools: The Paradox of Postcolonial Enlightenment.' In *Decolonizing Enlightenment: Transnational Justice, Human Rights and Democracy in a Postcolonial World*, edited by N. Dhawan, 19–78. Opladen: Budrich, 2014.

Dhawan, N. 'Homonationalismus und Staatsphobie: Queering Dekolonisierungspolitiken, Queer-Politiken dekolonisieren.' In *Femina Politica*, no. 1 (2015): 38–51.

Dietze, G. '"Occidentalism", European Identity and Sexual Politics.' In *The Study of Europe*, edited by H. Brunkhorst and G. Grözinger, 89–116. Baden-Baden: Nomos, 2010.

Ekine, S., and H. Abbas, ed. *Queer African Reader.* Oxford: Pamabazuka Presee/Fahamu, 2013.

Encarnación, O. G. 'The Troubled Rise of Gay Rights Diplomacy.' *Current History*, no. 1 (2016): 17–22.

Funders for LGBT Issues. *A Global Gaze: Lesbian, Gay, Bisexual, Transgender and Intersex Grantmaking in the Global South and East*. 2011. Accessed May 5, 2013. http://www.lgbtfunders.org/files/A_Global_Gaze_2010.pdf

Gosine, A. 'Monster, Womb, MSM: The Work of Sex in International Development.' *Development* 52, no. 1 (2009): 25–33.

Gosine, A. 'Rescue, and Real Love: Same Sex Desire in International Development.' *IDS Sexuality and Development Programme* (2015). Accessed May 31, 2015. http://opendocs.ids.ac.uk/opendocs/bitstream/handle/123456789/5891/Resue%20and%20Real%20Love.pdf?sequence=1

Grewal, I., and C. Kaplan. 'Global Identities: Theorizing Transnational Studies on Sexuality.' *GLQ – Journal of Lesbian and Gay Studies* 7, no. 4 (2001): 663–79.

Haritaworn, J., E. Erdem, and T. Tauqir. 'Gay Imperialism: The Role of Gender and Sexuality Discourses in the War on Terror.' In *Out of Place, Queerness and Raciality,* edited by A. Kuntsman, and E. Miyake, 9–34. York: Raw Nerve Books, 2008.

Hoad, N. 'Arrested Development or the Queerness of Savages: Resisting Evolutionary Narratives of Difference.' *Postcolonial Studies* 3, no. 2 (2000): 133–58.

Ilesanmi, Y. 'LGBT Rights in Africa: Interview on SkyNews.' Accessed April 5, 2016. https://www.youtube.com/watch?v=t8bRjAR5Y0Q&feature=youtu.be

Kalende, V. 'Colonial Legacies of Africa's Homophobia: Finding a Narrative That Works for African LGBT Movements.' In Pambazuka Press (2014). Accessed September 13, 2016. https://www.pambazuka.org/gender-minorities/colonial-legacies-africa%E2%80%99s-homophobia-finding-narrative-works-african-lgbt

Kapoor, I. 'The Queer Third World.' *Third World Quarterly* 36, no. 9 (2015): 1611–28.

Katyal S. K. 'The Dissident Citizen.' *UCLA Law Review* 57 (2010): 1415–76.

Klapeer, C. 'LGBTIQ-Rechte als "Entwicklungsbarometer"? Ambivalenzen einer Sprache und Politik der sexuellen Menschenrechte im entwicklungspolitischen Kontext.' In *Feministische Kritiken und Menschenrechte: Reflexionen auf ein produktives Spannungsverhältnis*, edited by I. Leicht, C. Löw, N. Meisterhand, and K. Volk, (2016): 95–112. Opladen: Barbara Budrich.

——— 'Queering Development in Homotransnationalist Times. A Postcolonial Reading of LGBTIQ inclusive Development Agendas.' *Lambda Nordica* (Special Issue on Postcolonial Queer Europe), forthcoming 2017.

Kollmann, K., and M. Waites 'The Global Politics of Lesbian, Gay, Bisexual and Transgender Human Rights: An Introduction.' *Contemporary Politics* 15, no. 1 (2009): 1–17.

Laskar, P. 'The Illiberal Turn. Aid Conditionalis and the Queering of Sexual Citizenship.' *Lambda Nordica*, no. 1 (2014): 87–100.

Lavinas Picq, M. and M. Thiel. 'Introduction: Sexualities in World Politics.' In *Sexualities in Sexualities in World Politics. How LGBTIQ Claims Shape International Relations*, edited by M. Lavinas Picq and M. Thiel, 1–22. London: Routledge, 2015a.

——— *Sexualities in Sexualities in World Politics. How LGBTIQ Claims Shape International Relations*. London: Routledge, 2015b.

Lind, A., ed. *Development, Sexual Rights and Global Governance*. New York: Routledge, 2010a.

——— 'Introduction: Development, Global Governance, and Sexual Subjectivities.' In *Development, Sexual Rights and Global Governance*, edited by A. Lind, 1–19. New York: Routledge, 2010b.

Lugones, M. 'Heterosexualism and the Colonial/Modern Gender System.' *Hypatia* 22, no. 1 (2007), 186–209.

——— 'Toward a Decolonial Feminism.' *Hypatia* 25, no. 4 (2010): 742–59.

Maldonado-Torres, N. 'On the Coloniality of Being.' *Cultural Studies* 21, no. 2 (2007): 240–70.

Massad, J. A. *Desiring Arabs*. Chicago: University of Chicago Press, 2007.

McClintock, A. *Imperial Leather: Race, Gender and Sexuality in the Colonial Contest*. New York: Routledge, 1995.

Melissen, J., ed. *The New Public Diplomacy: Soft Power in International Relations*. Basingstoke: Palgrave Macmillan, 2005

Nichols, R. 'Empire and the Dispositif of Queerness.' *Foucault Studies*, no. 4 (2012): 41–60.

Nyanzi, S. 'Unpacking the [Govern]mentality of African Sexualities.' In *African Sexualities: A Reader*, edited by S. Tamale, 477–501. Cape Town: Pambazuka Press, 2011.

Puar, J. *Terrorist Assemblages: Homonationalism in Queer Times*. Durham: Duke University Press, 2007.

——— 'Rethinking Homonationalism.' In *International Journal of Middle East Studies* 45, no. 2 (2013): 336–9

Quijano, A. 'Coloniality of Power, Eurocentrism, and Latin America.' *Nepentla* 1, no. 3 (2000): 533–580.

Rahman, M. 'Queer Rights and the Triangulation of Western Exceptionalism.' *Journal of Human Rights* 13, no. 3 (2014a): 274–89.

——— *Homosexualities, Muslim Cultures and Modernity*. Basingstoke: Palgrave Macmillan, 2014b.

——— 'Sexual Diffusion and Conceptual Confusions: Muslim Homophobia and Muslim Homosexualities in the Context of Modernity.' In *Sexualities in Sexualities in World Politics. How LGBTIQ Claims Shape International Relations*, edited by M. Lavinas Picq and M. Thiel, 92–107. London: Routledge, 2015.

Rao, R. *Third World Protest: Between Home and the World*. Oxford: Oxford University Press, 2010.

——— 'On "Gay Conditionality", Imperial Power and Queer Liberation.' *Kafila.org*, Jan 1, 2012. Accessed Feb 3, 2012. http://kafila.org/2012/01/01/on-gay-conditionality-imperial-power-and-queer-liberation-rahul-rao/#more-11088

——— 'The Locations of Homophobia.' *London Review of International Law* 2, no. 2 (2014a): 169–99.

——— 'Queer Questions.' *International Feminist Journal of Politics*16, no. 2 (2014b): 199–217

——— 'Echoes of Imperialism in LGBT Activism.' In *Echoes of Empire. Memory, Identity and Colonial Legacies*, edited by K. Nicolaïdis, B. Sèbe, and G. Maas, 355–72. London: I.B.Tauris, 2015.

Richardson, T. A. 'Indigenous Political Difference, Colonial Perspectives and the Challenge of Diplomatic Relations: Toward a Decolonial Diplomacy in Multicultural Educational Theory.' *Educational Studies*, no. 48 (2012): 465–84.

Samelius, L., E. Wagberg, and SIDA. *Sexual Orientation and Gender Identity: Issues in Development. A Study of Policy and Administration*. Stockholm: Swedish Ministry for Foreign Affairs, 2005.

Shilliam, R. ed. *International Relations and Non-Western Thought: Imperialism, Colonialism and Investigations of Global Modernity*. London: Routledge 2011.

Spivak, G. C. *Outside in the Teaching Machine*. London: Routledge, 1993.

——— 'Righting Wrongs.' *The South Atlantic Quarterly* 103, no 2/3 (2004): 523–81.

'Statement on British Aid Cut Threats to African Countries That Violate LBGTI Rights.' *Pambazuka News*, Oct 27, 2011. Accessed Feb 2, 2012. http://pambazuka.org/en/category/advocacy/77470

Stoler, A. L. *Carnal Knowledge and Imperial Power: Race and the Intimate in Colonial Rule*. Berkeley: University of California Press, 2002.

Thoreson, R. R. 'The Queer Paradox of LGBTI Human Rights' *Interalia – A Journal of Queer Studies*, no. 6 (2011). Accessed April 5, 2015. http://www.interalia.org.pl/en/artykuly/2011_6/06_the_queer_paradox_of_lgbti_human_rights.htm

——— *Transnational LGBT Activism. Working for Sexual Rights Worldwide*. Minneapolis: University of Minnesota Press, 2014.

Weber, C. *Queer International Relations: Sovereignty, Sexuality and the Will to Knowledge*. Oxford: Oxford University Press, 2016.

Wilson, K. *Race, Racism and Development: Interrogating History, Discourse and Practice*. London: Zed Books, 2012.

Notes

1 Jan Melissen (2005) draws attention to the rise and growing importance of 'public diplomacy' after 9/11 in contrast to more 'traditional diplomacy', mainly concerned with relationships *between* representatives of states, or other international actors. Public diplomacy, in contrast, targets the *general public* and also 'non-official' groups, organisations and individuals, such as NGOs, and the media.

2 Many international documents, policy paper, media articles and political actors are using the abbreviations LGBT or LGBTI. In order to signify the absence of Q(ueer) and I(nter*), I decided to put the IQ or Q in brackets when I am not referring to a specific quote or organisation.

3 Human Rights Council Resolution 17/19, July 14, /2011.

4 In 2013 respect for LGBTIQ human rights entered European foreign policy prominently by becoming an integral part of European foreign external and diplomatic relations. The Council upgraded its 'toolkit' on the human rights of LGBTI(Q) persons into a binding guideline that aims 'to provide officials of EU institutions and EU Member States, with guidance to be used in contacts with third countries and with international and civil society organisations [...] in order to promote and protect the human rights of LGBTI persons within its external action' (Council of the European Union 2013).

5 The Swedish Development Agency, SIDA, for instance, already started in 2005 to deal with questions of sexual orientation and gender identity in development and how to make development more inclusive for LGBT(IQ)s (Samelius, Wagberg and SIDA 2005). SIDA and the Norwegian Ministry of Foreign Affairs are among the ten 'top' funders of projects or programs tackling LGBTIQ issues in the Global South/East (Funders for LGBT Issues 2011).

6 For the ILGA world map, see: http://old.ilga.org/Statehomophobia/ILGA_WorldMap_2015_ENG.pdf. Accessed September 30, 2016.

7 See the international discussion on LGBTIQ rights diplomacy hosted by the Atlantic Council in the US: http://www.atlanticcouncil.org/events/webcasts/lgbt-diplomacy-securing-a-more-inclusive-future (Accessed August 12, 2016).

8 See for instance the discussions on LGBTIQ diplomacy at the Pride World Forum 2016 https://www.youtube.com/watch?v=1ZudWGPlreQ (Accessed Sept 1, 2016).

9 Yemisi Ilesanmi, an activist and scholar from Nigeria, for instance, demands in an interview on 'LGBT Rights in Africa', aired on SkyNews in August 2014, that 'governments like the UK and the US

government' should 'back their swift action and walk their talk [...] when it comes to enforcing LGBT rights and practicing the rights of sexual minorities in those countries' (Ilesanmi 2014). She furthermore questioned the self-affirming rhetoric of Western donor states, arguing that there have to be economic consequences of their diplomatic announcements. Ilesanmi along with other LGBTIQ activists and advocates particularly called for substantive financial support in order to support 'local' resistance against homo- and transphobic laws. This is a particular relevant regarding the fact, that LGBTIQ related organisations receive, despite 'official' rhetoric, only very little funding from development organisations.

10 Such, as for instance, the AIDS/HIV discourse, or the recent rise of human rights-based approaches (HRBA) (Gosine 2005; Lind 2010b; Theron, McAllister and Armisen 2016; Currier 2010).

11 Human rights and LGBTIQ organisations have reported a spike in violence toward sexual and gender dissidents in the very places, including Uganda and Nigeria, that have been the main targets of Western interventions and diplomatic critique.

PART III

Struggles over the postcolonial state

16
INTRODUCTION

The independence and liberation movements following the Second World War ultimately established the state as the almost-universal form of governance. However, this state was configured by and large – and not without the pursuit of other experiments such as federation – as an ideal-type of that produced in European history. The 'proper' state would be framed by hard and impermeable borders that cut through existing social formations and migratory routes; it was to govern from a central and singular point, and project political power only from there; and it was to distinguish an impersonal public realm from private lives and enterprises. Such organisational predicates were always more the ideal in Europe (and North America) than a historical reality. But in the postcolonial world, the state was erected on arguably even more uneven ground, especially, the bifurcated systems of colonial rule that distinguished between governing citizens and a multitude of governed subjects, often along invented racialised, ethnic and religious lines. The chapters in this Part all engage with the various contestations that have accompanied the imposition/importation of state rule within imperial constellations and colonial contexts.

However, these constellations and contexts can be markedly different. And in this respect, we might imagine the state to be postcolonial in two respects. Firstly, for a number of polities, the state is postcolonial in terms of locking in many of the hierarchies and exclusions that colonial rule depended upon as that rule came to a formal end. But secondly, in some situations the state is postcolonial in so far as polities and peoples that had only briefly, partially or derivatively been under colonial rule have paradoxically become even more affected by the logics of that rule with the arrival of the modern state accompanied by political-economic and cultural arrangements that rely upon principles of coloniality. In fact, many of the chapters in this Part investigate struggles over the state that are far less intuitively or straightforwardly 'postcolonial'. Therefore, one of the key points that we wish to convey is that the coloniality of the modern state exceeds the geographical borders of historical colonialism.

In Chapter 17, Gurminder Bhambra provides a salient conceptual discussion of the modern state as constitutively colonial. Many classical political and sociological theories treat colonialism as entirely external to the consolidation of the modern European nation-state or, at best, a process that was derivative to this consolidation. Hence, discussion over the 'postcolonial state' is usually directed towards those polities that were once-colonised. Alternatively, Bhambra utilises a 'connected sociologies' approach to turn attention back towards the imperial heartlands. There, she argues that, in fact, even the so-called 'original' modern states were less nationally contained and far more imperially delineated. This acknowledgement significantly challenges mainstream theories of the formation of the modern nation-state. In fact, Bhambra's argument proposes that even the historical ideal-type of the state must be refigured as colonially-constituted. And this consideration has ramifications for political struggles in our era of global migration that seek to address who counts as a 'citizen' and who does not.

In Chapter 18, Desiree Poets takes us to South America, a region that holds some of the oldest postcolonial states, having gained independence from European rule mostly in the first part of the nineteenth century. Focusing on Brazil, Poets' chapter details the great efforts that postcolonial states go towards managing and organising the diversity of peoples within their borders. This is especially the case in terms of the contemporary impact of historical categorisations that accompanied settler colonialism and plantation slavery. Poets focuses especially on the Quilombo, communities formed by the escaped enslaved. More recently, the Brazilian constitution has granted collective land rights to members of these communities. However, Poet demonstrates how these rights remain complicit with settler colonialism in so far as the state manages their possible profusion in a neoliberal context via the notion of authenticity – i.e. exactly who and what a Quilombo should be, ethnically and culturally.

Dilar Dirik's chapter takes us to the post-Ottoman Middle East, a region defined by various nationalist responses to European imperialism, responses which themselves consisted of colonial premises in terms of imagining states that racialised, ordered and dominated diverse peoples within their borders. One of the abiding issues, in this respect, has been the so-called 'Kurdish question', that is, the possibility and desirability of constructing a polity that provides self-governance to Kurdish peoples spread across Turkey, Syria, Iraq and Iran. Dirik turns to one response: Abdullah Öcalan's project of 'Democratic Confederalism' that has evolved into an anti-patriarchal, anti-statist and anti-capitalist project. Dirik demonstrates how the women of Rojava (the West of Kurdistan) have been remarkably pursuing this project even in the mist of militarily arresting the expansion of ISIS near the Syrian-Turkey border. Dirik's account demonstrates how struggles over the postcolonial state – that is, coloniality as the principle of political rule – are taking centre-stage in global politics and in what, on first glance, appear to be unlikely arenas.

In Chapter 20, Eiichi Hoshino turns to another region where European imperial expansion was historically challenged by and mediated through cognate regional projects. Japan is often pointed to as a historical example of non-European imperial expansion within the era of global European imperial administration. However, Hoshino's concern is with Okinawa, the southernmost set of islands in Japan, and its governing through a 'postcolonial complex' - first as a victim of Japanese imperialism and then as a victim of US occupation through the San Francisco Peace Treaty of 1951. Ever since, Hoshino argues that Okinawans have suffered from – and struggled against – 'human insecurities' from the Japanese government's support of US military bases on their islands. To this effect Hoshino documents some of the serious crimes, accidents and environmental pollution that have accompanied this military presence. Hoshino's chapter demonstrates how struggles over the postcolonial state are complexly layered at local, national and global levels.

Calvin Xin Liu, in his chapter, seeks to account for the recent rise of nationalism in Hong Kong, as demonstrated by the Umbrella Movement in 2013. These sentiments have sought to disrupt Beijing's compromise of 'one country two systems', guaranteeing a certain level of local governance when Hong Kong was returned to China in 1997 after the end of its colonially-induced ninety-nine-year lease to the British Empire. Liu argues that Hong Kong's current predicament does not fall easily into most narratives of the formation of the postcolonial state. Hong Kong's geo-cultural position between China and Britain encouraged a sense of in-between-ness that positioned the island territories as a space of alterity rather than a site of opposition between East and West. Liu argues that the current rise of nationalist sentiments also play on this alterity, albeit in a contemporary context wherein neither Britain nor China are invested in retaining Hong Kong's in-between-ness. Liu's chapter demonstrates that postcolonial critique must be challenged – and broadened – to account for the many 'a-typical' contexts wherein the postcolonial state is being forged and struggled over.

17
THE STATE
Postcolonial histories of the concept

Gurminder K. Bhambra

Introduction

Our contemporary political landscape is organised around the idea of the nation-state and, as Habermas (1998) (among many others) has argued, this idea is seen to have its origins in the system of sovereign states that came into being in Europe in 1648 with the Treaty of Westphalia. The history of the modern nation-state is then understood to be further shaped by the American and French Revolutions in the late eighteenth century. Within Europe, there are seen to be two routes to modern statehood. The first was the evolution of nation-states 'within the boundaries of existing territorial states' (Habermas 1998: 397), as was the case for most North and Western European states. The second was in establishing a nation and then a state, as exemplified by the projects of Germany and Italy in the late nineteenth century and the subsequent formation of states in Central and Eastern Europe in the twentieth. These initial formations, he continues, were followed in the period of mass decolonisation in the mid- to late-twentieth century by the establishment of 'postcolonial' states. A final moment in the history of nation-states is then presented as the secession of states from the Soviet Union in the aftermath of its collapse in the late twentieth century.

This brief historical outline of the emergence of modern states is commonplace within the social science literature, and it is this that I take issue with in the chapter; in particular, the odd elision that posits a 'postcolonial state' without addressing the process of colonisation itself as part of state formation. Specifically, I argue that the period that is seen to give rise to the emergence of the modern state is precisely a period of colonial expansion that saw some European states consolidate their domination over other parts of the world. Yet, this 'external' domination is rarely theorised as a constitutive aspect of the 'modern state' which, instead of being understood as an imperial state, is presented in 'national' terms. The period from, at least, 1648 onwards, for example, is a period of the dominance of Spain and Portugal primarily in the southern half of the Americas and of Britain, France, Belgium and the Netherlands (among other European countries) of conquest and domination in the Americas and across Africa and Asia. The forms of domination were varied; from actual conquest followed by settlement (in the Americas, Southern Africa, New Zealand and Australia) to the establishment of colonial and dependency status elsewhere, for example in India, the Caribbean and across Africa and Asia.

The issue in this chapter is not so much with the forms of domination, but with the wholesale erasure of that (external) domination from the theorisation of the modern state as it is seen to develop within Europe. As such, this chapter focuses on what is included within the standard historical genealogies, and what is omitted, and how this structures our conceptual understandings of the state. Overall, I argue that a more adequate conceptual understanding requires us to take seriously the imperial histories that were constitutive to the formation of modern states. Not to do so is not only an intellectual error, but has profound consequences for the nature and possibilities of politics in the present. In sum, I take issue with the standard social scientific conceptualisations of the modern state and offer an alternative way of thinking about it.

In what follows, I especially address the inadequacy of the historical record used to support such conceptualisation and argue, instead, for a connected sociologies approach that would take into account the imperial histories of European states. As such, I first set out the standard social science conceptualisation of the state, before going on to discuss how a connected sociologies approach enables us to better historicise the emergence of the state. Connected sociologies, as I have argued at greater length elsewhere (Bhambra 2014), is an approach that draws on historical sociology and postcolonial theory. What is at issue in such an approach is not simply a matter of substance (of the historical record), but how the configuration of that substance is linked to the methodological underpinnings of comparative historical sociology.

While postcolonial arguments have been useful in challenging the limitations of historical narratives and historiographical traditions, the issue is not simply one of a failure to extend the range of analysis. What is needed is an analytical approach that structures the 'inclusion' of any new, additional objects, such that they work also towards the (re)construction of pre-existing understandings by providing new interpretations, explanations and solutions in the process. As such, as I seek to demonstrate in this chapter, a connected sociologies approach puts forward a distinctive way of understanding the history of the modern state and opens up new avenues for thinking through the implications of this politically, and for the social sciences more generally.

The Westphalian system of sovereign states

The Treaty of Westphalia brought to an end the Thirty Years' War between Protestant and Catholic powers in Europe and has been often cited within the social science literature as the harbinger of the system of modern states. As Blaney and Inyatullah argue, the Treaty is often seen as representing 'a movement from the religious to the secular, from the idea of Europe as unified by Christianity to a European system of independent states, and from a web of overlapping and competing authorities to a modern state system based on the demarcation of exclusive territorial jurisdictions' (Blaney and Inyatullah 2000: 39). Similarly, Krasner presents the place of the Treaty within the discipline of International Relations as inaugurating 'the modern international system composed of sovereign states each with exclusive authority within its own geographic boundaries' (Krasner 2001: 17). This has led to the Westphalian sovereign state model, he suggests, that is 'based on the principles of autonomy, territory, mutual recognition and control' (2001: 17).

While there have been critiques of this model – for example, for its failure to account properly for difference and the place of the 'other' in understanding questions of sovereignty (Blaney and Inyatullah 2000) or contesting the idea of 1648 as a marked watershed in the development of international relations (Teschke 2003) – few of these critiques address what I would regard as the central issue. Namely, that while Westphalia is the byword for the establishment of sovereignty and the political equality of states, European states did not simply exercise their sovereignty within the territorial bounds assigned as those of the national state. They also exerted power over territories and populations elsewhere and yet this is rarely addressed within the literature.

Even where the 'Westphalian thesis' is critiqued for offering a deficient account of the historical processes at work, this critique is, for the most part, turned inwards rather than seeking to account for the colonial endeavours of European states. For example, Krasner (2001) points to the European Union and to Andorra as examples of how the sovereign state model is violated in territorial terms, but he has nothing to say about settler colonialism or the establishment of colonial rule. To the extent that he does address issues of coercion and imposition, this is done primarily in legalistic terms. The examples given by Krasner are of intra-European negotiations in the nineteenth century or the use of economic sanctions in the twentieth century. There is no discussion of the imposition and coercion used against populations in other parts of the world that involved bringing their land, labour and resources under the control of European powers and for their benefit. In a similar vein, Osiander (2001) criticises the centrality of the Treaty of Westphalia to the discipline of International Relations by arguing for the inadequacy of the historical narratives at the centre of its theorisations of the state. However, his critique is primarily oriented to the failure of IR theorists to acknowledge the complexity of the treaties rather than to account for the broader territorial ambitions of those states.

One of the substantial critiques that has been made of the Westphalian thesis in the context of its failure to address the realities of colonialism is by Antony Anghie (2006). He argues that within this model, sovereignty is seen to be the primary concept in terms of determining the nature of relations among states and determining the fact of being a modern nation-state. While this model is based on the historical examples of European states, it ignores the exercise of power of those states over other societies. This is deemed not to be a problem for the theoretical framework as those other societies and states are not regarded as being sovereign. As such, they can be unproblematically incorporated into the ambit of the modern nation-states (through imperial conquest) and not contest the claim to nationhood that is otherwise being made (they are simply subjugated and elided territories of no empirical or ideological consequence).

However, as Anghie asks, it is unclear how it was 'decided that non-European states were not sovereign in the first place?' (2006: 741). Indeed, he continues, it is the doctrine of sovereignty itself that sets up the non-European world as excluded from its understanding and 'then proceeds to legitimise the imperialism that resulted in the incorporation of the non-European world into the system of international law' (2006: 741; see also Kayaoglu 2010). It is not until decolonisation that non-European states are seen within the standard literature to emerge as sovereign states, as noted by Habermas above, and thus enter the international system of nation-states. They are presented as utilising a pre-existing idea of sovereignty, notwithstanding that this pre-existing idea of sovereignty was previously articulated in the context of their subjugation. If colonisation was taken seriously, however, then the modern *nation*-state would *only* be seen to emerge in the period of decolonisation as previous states would be more appropriately understood as *imperial* or colonial states (see, for example, the work of Gary Wilder 2015).

The nation-state in imperial times

The failure to acknowledge the realities of imperialism as central to the emergence of what are conceived as nation-states within Europe has a long conceptual history. The Westphalian thesis is one aspect of this, and another is Weber's commonly accepted definition of the modern state, as that entity which secures the legitimate exercise of coercive power within a given territory. While this definition does not necessarily originate with Weber (1980 [1895]; 1949 [1904]), it has been most powerfully illustrated in his work and in the work of those who cite his influence (see Bhambra 2016a). From the early collaborative projects associated with comparative politics and modernisation theory to later iterations of cultural historical sociology, for example, the focus has primarily been on the emergence, in Europe, of what were seen to be sovereign, territorial states organised along national lines (see Almond and Coleman 1960; Tilly 1975, 1994;

Steinmetz 1999). Such an understanding associates a particular population with a given territory and makes the state responsible for and responsible to that population. This, however, fails to take into account the actions of the state upon populations outside its self-defined parameters and towards whom there is no relationship of emerging equality, only of domination (though, of course, domination also defined the relationship to some subjects of rule within given territories, such as Poles and Jews in the emerging German state, and formal equality was also hierarchically ordered in terms both of class and gender).

As I have argued at greater length elsewhere (Bhambra 2016a), Weber's conceptualisation of the modern state was based upon the contemporary German state as defined by its national boundaries. However, the construction of the 'national state' was concurrent with, and indeed constituted by, its associated imperial activities. The establishment of the German state in 1871 was followed by the intensification of processes of 'de-Polonisation' and 'Germanification' at the borderlands of the new state. In his inaugural lecture in Freiburg in 1895, for example, Weber outlined an economic policy that would prevent the displacement of German peasants by Polish labourers and thus would strengthen the power of the newly established German state. 'Our state is a *national state*,' he asserted, 'and it is this circumstance which makes us feel we have a right to make this demand' (Weber 1980 [1895]: 436, italics in original). Note how the claim for legitimacy is undertaken in terms of the incorporation of territory beyond that associated with the German 'Ethnie', *while at the same time asserting that ethnic identification over Poles (and Jews).*

Further, within 13 years of unification, the German state had begun the process of acquiring 'the fourth largest colonial empire at the time' (Conrad, 2013: 544). At the same time as establishing itself in Europe, the incipient German state was consolidating its hold over external territories through a variety of violent colonial expeditions, including in South-West Africa (where the Herero and Nama people were dispossessed and effectively exterminated in the desert regions), Samoa and Qingdao in China (see Steinmetz 2005, 2007). There is little consideration, however, of this colonial activity in most discussions of the formation and development of the German state. Similarly, apart from the work of Mommsen (1974, 1984 [1959]) on 'economic imperialism', there are real lacunae in Weberian scholarship in examining the relationship between Germany's colonial activities and Weber's conceptualisation of the modern state.

The nation-state, for Weber, is defined in ethnic terms. It is defined against the (Jewish and) Polish people who may have lived within the borders of the Prussian and then the German state for centuries and it is defined against all other nations and peoples. This understanding of the nation is simply naturalised within Weberian scholarship – there is no recognition of historical complexity or contemporary contradiction – and it is established as the fundamental value within which social science should operate (despite the call for social science, otherwise, to be value-free). Mommsen suggests that the 'nature of Max Weber's concept of the nation is central to his political value system' (1984 [1959]: 48); I want to argue that it is perhaps better to reverse this formulation and, instead, see Weber's political value system as central to his conceptualisation of the nation. It is only this reversal that enables us to account for his concept of the nation-state failing to take into consideration his commitment, otherwise, to Germany being a world power, that is, an imperial state.

What we commonly understand as the nation – and as the concept of the nation bequeathed to historical sociology by Weber – was actually an imperial state. While Weber elides the concept of the nation with imperial power, what enables the concept to gain traction in its own terms is the omission of German imperialism from what are presented as 'national' histories. The state, as standardly defined, then, did not simply lay claim to a monopoly of the legitimate use of violence within a given (national) territory, but extended that violence into other territories and in support of non-state actors (such as trading companies and the appropriations of settlers).

Indeed, the techniques of violence that were used 'externally' were then frequently applied to 'national' populations (see Cohn and Dirks, 1988; Elkins, 2005; Shilliam 2013; Dunbar-Ortiz, 2014). Yet, it is the state defined nationally that comes to be the focus of social scientific understandings as will be discussed in the following section.

Contemporary conceptualisations of the state

The standard conceptualisation of the modern state sees it as emerging through a process of institutional differentiation whereby, as Gianfranco Poggi outlines, 'the major functional problems of a society give rise in the course of time to various increasingly elaborated and distinctive sets of structural arrangements' (Poggi 1978: 13). While he thinks that such an account, based on a general theory of social change, cannot adequately identify and delineate the origins and nature of the state, it is nonetheless able to trace 'the diffusion of the state as an existing entity from its European heartland to outlying areas' (1978: 15). At the very outset of his analysis of the modern state, then, Poggi's call for a more complex historical understanding to inform such conceptualisations is already, itself, predicated on the ahistorical assumption of a qualitative difference between Europe and the rest of the world. Further, the period that is seen to give rise to the emergence of the modern state is precisely that period of expansion that saw these states consolidate their domination over other parts of the world. Yet, this 'external' domination is not theorised as a constitutive aspect of the state which, instead of being understood as an imperial state, is presented in 'national' terms. This (mis)understanding continues to be reproduced in more recent social scientific accounts of the state.

Bob Jessop's latest book on the state, for example, focuses in the main on 'the genealogy of the state, the periodisation of state formation, contemporary states, and likely future trends' (Jessop 2016: viii). His seemingly comprehensive study covers varying conceptual definitions of the state, different understandings of the state as a social relation, as well as thinking about the state in terms of issues of power, interests, and domination. These themes structure the chapters in this first part of his book and are followed by discussions on notions of territory and population, with the final part looking at the future of states and statehood. Jessop's discussion of the variety of understandings of the state acknowledges that the majority of the theories used within the social sciences rely on an examination of European and Western states. He points to the significance of also looking at other state forms beyond Europe, but these are not given much consideration in the overall analysis.

While this is a significant issue, there is another that I take as more serious in terms of determining the adequacy of the concepts we use to understand the state. This is the fact that Jessop takes as the primary formation the idea of the nation-state even when the states under consideration were not actually national states, but rather, imperial ones. Jessop agrees that Weber's classic definition of the state – as having a monopoly on the legitimate use of violence within a territory – provides one entry point into thinking about the state and suggests two further elements (though, in truth, each is bound up in Weber's original conceptualisation). One is 'the territorial organization of political authority' (Jessop 2016: 29) and the other is the population associated with the state. He distinguishes territorialisation – 'the division of the earth into more or less clearly demarcated areas that are governed by a political authority' (2016: 29) – from its more generic association with *terra*, that is, land in its broadest sense. As such, he sees the Westphalian demarcation of states within Europe as a significant moment in the genealogy of their conceptualisation. Interestingly, he notes the concomitant presentation of the New World as *terra nullius*, to be colonised and divided between Portugal and Spain, but fails to address the implications of extending political control over territories where there were not only other populations, but also existing political structures.

The problems identified by Jessop with the Westphalian underpinning of the modern state fail to address the key problem even though it is implicit within his text. He suggests that the Westphalian system involves 'the systematic division of a potentially global political system into a series of exclusive territories controlled by mutually recognizing, mutually legitimizing states that are not *legally* subject to the authority of another state' (2016: 32). This works so long as the focus is on European states within the geographical territory standardly associated with the European landmass. As soon as we broaden our horizons to take into account the lands and populations over which European states exercised their political authority a problem emerges that requires address.

In his discussion of populations, Jessop again notes the difficulties with reconciling 'the relations between a colonial or settler state's plenary power and the rights of indigenous peoples to (partial) sovereignty' (2016: 35). However, he sees the problem as resting in the need for indigenous peoples to use colonial/settler laws and discourses to contest the occupation of their land and to assert their own claims for recognition. There is no comment on the foundational problem of colonial/settler states in that, if they are recognised as distinct from nation-states, then that can only be based on the fact that a political authority located in one part of the world is seeking to exercise its power over land and populations over whom it does not have the legitimacy (in its own terms) to do so. Instead of factoring this into his analysis, Jessop simply repeats the familiar (and supposedly anthropologically sensitive) claim that indigenous people had no cognate concepts of nation or sovereignty with which to protest their colonisation (for critique of this general position, see Veracini 2010; Byrd 2011).

Further, even though Jessop mentions 'the right to national self-determination' as one of the key issues associated with thinking about populations in relation to the modern state, there is no discussion of the legitimacy, or otherwise, that would put populations into the position of having to struggle for that; that is, there is no discussion of colonisation and the establishment of imperial rule over other territories and populations that necessitated struggles for national self-determination. And, more significantly, no discussion of the implications of these processes for how we think conceptually about the modern state.

This three-element approach, drawing on and developing Weber's foundational conceptualisation of the modern state, is the basis for Jessop's general account of the state. He acknowledges that, as with all general theories, qualifications of these elements may be required. In particular, he points to the necessity of recognising that 'the territorialization of political power and the creation of the population over which such power is exercised are historical accomplishments grounded in struggles' (2016: 41) and that a comparative-historical approach is useful in determining the conceptual boundaries under discussion. The historical accounts alluded to by Jessop throughout the book relate either to the period of the Middle Ages or to the mid-twentieth century onwards. This enables him to displace colonialism from consideration of the emergence and formation of the modern state form and discuss the modern state only in terms of its earlier antecedents or in its consolidated form after the era of decolonisation. Colonialism to the extent that it is mentioned, is devolved to capitalism or elided with empire and the imperial projects of formations such as the Ottoman and Habsburg empires. There is little to no discussion of modern European imperialism and its implications for thinking about the emergence and formation of modern European states.

One of the key issues here is that the national state is assumed to *have* an empire, rather than to *be* an empire or imperial state. The possession of colonies is not regarded as making a difference to how the national state is understood and, indeed, it is believed that the national state can be understood and adequately theorised separate from any consideration of its constitution as an imperial state. Elisabeth Clemens (2016), for example, argues that there are two distinct political forms that have dominated the modern world order: empires and nation-states. The main difference between them, she argues, 'can be captured by the relationship between the character of rule (direct or indirect) and its relationship to group membership or identity' (2016: 25). While she accepts that a number of European states extended their powers beyond national boundaries through imperial activities – that is, by establishing empires – recognition of this co-extensive and overlapping activity does not call into question the categorisation of 'nations' and 'empires' as separate entities. Given that the empires of the modern world are recognised as having nations at their heart, it is unclear why they are presented as separate entities, at least as far as the dominant nation-state is concerned. The nation-states that emerge through struggles for self-determination and decolonisation are necessarily understood in relation to their previous colonisers and their previous subjugated position within a larger imperial state.

Implications of misidentifying the imperial state as a national state

While my focus has been on social scientific conceptualisations of the state, a similar problem also exists within the discipline of history. Stefan Berger (2015 [2007]), writing about the power of national pasts in nineteenth- and twentieth-century Europe, fails to mention colonialism as significantly implicated in such processes. His edited volume, *Writing the Nation: A Global Perspective*, emerges out of a five-year European Science Foundation project on representations of the past. Neither his introduction to the volume as a whole nor his stand-alone chapter fully addresses the fact that the point at which European states are constructing national histories for themselves, is precisely the point at which they are most appropriately understood as imperial states and not nation-states. He acknowledges that the impact of postcolonial criticism to history writing has meant that historians can no longer 'present the history of empire as an extension of a glorious national history' (2015a: 53), but does not go on to reassess what it means to construct and propagate a *national* history of states which were, in fact, *imperial*.

Further, as Drayton has argued in the context of Britain, even when empire was discussed by British historians, it was usually done on the basis of maintaining a belief 'in the inner virtue of British empire as an engine of emancipation and justice' (Drayton 2011: 677). This separation of the nation from the broader imperial endeavour has many consequences, not least that, in Drayton's words, it enables 'the British nation to escape the scene of the crime' (2011: 678). That is, not only is the state conceptualised without address of the violence necessary to institute imperial rule, but it is also never held to account for that violence as it is not represented as integral to the national past of the state (see also, Lowe 2015).

This definition of the state – in terms of its contemporary boundaries and historical constitution – is central to our understandings of the configuration of politics in the present, especially in terms of defining who belongs and, perhaps more importantly, who has the right to belong. The boundaries of the political community and the associated rights of citizenship, for example, are usually imagined to be congruent with the territorial boundaries of the state as understood in national terms. Yet most states in Europe were imperial states as much as they were national states – and often prior to or alongside becoming national states – and so the political community (or constituency) of the state was much wider and more stratified than is usually now acknowledged.

The standard histories of the British nation-state, for example, usually start with the Act of Union in 1707 – which brought together the kingdoms of England and Scotland – and its political development is predominantly seen in terms of events and processes that took place within the territorial bounds of the new nation. However, both England and Scotland had acquired colonies prior to Union, and continued their colonial conquests after Union, and so they were already imperial states prior to becoming a conjoined nation-state – and alongside this process (Bhambra 2016b, Colley, 1992, 2002). Refusing to take into account this broader history has many implications including misidentifying British citizens as migrants.

British citizenship was delineated formally for the first time in the British Nationality Act of 1948. The primary forms of citizenship outlined here were 'Citizens of the United Kingdom and Colonies' and 'Citizens of independent Commonwealth countries' (Karatani 2003). At the very moment that the British government first sought to clarify what British citizenship meant, then, people in the colonies were formally stated to share citizenship with people in Britain and populations of the former colonies and dominions were also regarded as citizens of the wider Commonwealth. This meant that they continued to have rights to travel to, and to live in, Britain by virtue of remaining within the Commonwealth. Notwithstanding the standard association of citizenship with the nation-state (see Baubock 1994), then, British citizenship emerged in – and was configured by – the multiracial and ethnolinguistically plural context of empire and Commonwealth. This history, however, rarely informs contemporary discussions of belonging or of understandings of citizenship. In part, this is as a consequence of the subsequent history of immigration control which effectively restricted citizenship of the UK on the basis of race.

Migration from the darker nations of Commonwealth to the UK from the 1940s onwards led to increasing concerns about the impact of 'coloured migration' on the domestic polity. This led to a series of immigration Acts – the Commonwealth Immigration Acts (CIA) of 1962, 1968, and 1971 – that began the process of differentiating citizenship effectively on the basis of race. The Commonwealth Immigration Acts of 1962 and 1968, for example, were enacted precisely to restrict the freedom of movement of darker citizens and to enable those of the Old Commonwealth (Australia, Canada and New Zealand) continued access. The British government presented its concern over movement into the country by New Commonwealth citizens as an issue of numbers and the fact that they 'were entitled to claim all citizenship rights once inside the United Kingdom, and to be treated on an equal basis to those British who were born' here (Karatani 2003: 132). However, no similar concern was expressed about Old Commonwealth citizens about whom the same was true. Instead, the CIA 1962 was enacted on the premise of maintaining favourable relations with Old Commonwealth (OCW) countries and restricting the rights of New Commonwealth (NCW) citizens by now grouping them as OCW *citizens* and NCW *immigrants*. In this way, as Hampshire argues, 'the development of immigration controls in post-war Britain was governed by a racial demographic logic' (2005: 77; see also Bhambra 2017).

Conclusion

How we understand the histories of the state is crucial for how we go on to develop our conceptual understandings of the same. As Sheehan argues in the context of German history (and with broader implications) scholars have 'too often allowed the political sovereignty of the nation-state to become the basis of the conceptual sovereignty of the nation' (Sheehan 1981: 4). This, in turn, has consequences for the organisation of politics in the present, particularly, as I have argued, in terms of our understandings of citizenship. The standard accounts of political citizenship align it with the contours of the nation-state where non-citizens, 'aliens', are (or can be) admitted to citizenship (see Baubock 1994).

In the British context, however, the defining of British citizenship has been predicated on the basis of making citizens into immigrants on the basis of an explicit racial hierarchy (Karatani

2003). This legislative removal of citizenship rights from darker citizens occurs alongside the constriction of understandings of the country's past in national terms, rather than in imperial terms. Recognising the imperial history of Britain would entail an inclusive understanding of darker citizens; focusing instead on the erroneous national history places darker citizens outside of that history and with no rights in the present. This is not simply an issue of historical adequacy, it is a matter with profound implications for how we understand the present and act, politically, within it.

Bibliography

Almond, G. A. and J. S. Coleman (eds) (1960) *The Politics of Developing Areas*. New Jersey: Princeton University Press.

Anghie, Antony (2006) 'The Evolution of International Law: Colonial and Postcolonial Realities,' *Third World Quarterly* 27 (5): 739–53.

Baubock, Rainer (1994) (ed.) *From Aliens to Citizens: Redefining the Status of Immigrants in Europe*. Avebury: Aldershot.

Berger, Stefan (2015 [2007]) (ed.) *Writing the Nation: A Global Perspective*. Basingstoke: Palgrave Macmillan.

Berger, Stefan (2015a) 'The Power of National Pasts: Writing National History in Nineteenth- and Twentieth-Century Europe' in Stefan Berger (ed.) *Writing the Nation: A Global Perspective*. Basingstoke: Palgrave Macmillan.

Bhambra, Gurminder K. (2014) *Connected Sociologies*. London: Bloomsbury.

——— (2016a) 'Comparative Historical Sociology and the State: Problems of Method,' *Cultural Sociology* 10 (3): 335–51.

——— (2016b) '"Our Island Story": The Dangerous Politics of Belonging in Austere Times' in Stefan Jonsson and Julia Willen (eds.) *Austere Histories in European Societies: Social Exclusion and the Contest of Colonial Memories*, 21–37. London: Routledge.

——— (2017) 'Locating Brexit in the Pragmatics of Race, Citizenship and Empire' in William Outhwaite (ed.) *Brexit: Sociological Responses*. London: Anthem Press.

Blaney, David L. and Naeem Inayatullah (2000) 'The Westphalian Deferral,' *International Studies Review* 2 (2): 29–64

Byrd, Jodi A. (2011) *The Transit of Empire: Indigenous Critiques of Colonialism*. Minneapolis: University of Minnesota Press.

Clemens, Elisabeth S. (2016) *What Is Political Sociology?* Cambridge: Polity Press.

Cohn, Bernard and Nick Dirks (1988) 'Beyond the Fringe: The Nation-State, Colonialism, and the Technologies of Power,' *Journal of Historical Sociology* 1 (2): 224–9.

Colley, Linda (1992) *Britons: Forging the Nation 1707–1837*. New Haven: Yale University Press.

——— (2002) *Captives: Britain, Empire and the World 1600–1850*. New York: Pantheon Books.

Conrad, Stephen (2013) 'Rethinking German Colonialism in a Global Age,' *The Journal of Imperial and Commonwealth History* 41 (4): 543–66.

Drayton, Richard (2011) 'Where Does the World Historian Write From? Objectivity, Moral Conscience and the Past and Present of Imperialism,' *Journal of Contemporary History* 46 (3): 671–85

Dunbar-Ortiz, Roxanne (2014) *An Indigenous Peoples' History of the United States*. Boston: Beacon Press.

Elkins, Caroline (2005) *Imperial Reckoning: The Untold Story of Britain's Gulag in Kenya*. New York: Henry Holt.

Habermas, Jürgen (1998) 'The European Nation-State: On the Past and Future of Sovereignty and Citizenship,' *Public Culture* 10 (2): 397–416

Hampshire, James (2005) *Citizenship and Belonging: Immigration and the Politics of Demographic Governance in Postwar Britain*. Palgrave: Basingstoke.

Jessop, Bob (2016) *The State: Past, Present, Future*. Cambridge: Polity Press.

Karatani, Rieko (2003) *Defining British Citizenship: Empire, Commonwealth and Modern Britain*. Frank Cass: London.

Kayaoglu, Turan (2010) 'Westphalian Eurocentrism in International Relations Theory,' *International Studies Review* 12 (2): 193–217.

Krasner, Stephen D. (2001) 'Rethinking the Sovereign State Model,' *Review of International Studies* 27 (5): 17–42

Lowe, Lisa (2015) *The Intimacies of Four Continents*. Durham: Duke University Press.
Mommsen, W. J. (1974) *The Age of Bureaucracy: Perspectives on the Political Sociology of Max Weber*. Oxford: Basil Blackwell.
——— (1984 [1959]) *Max Weber and German Politics 1890–1920*, translated by Michael S. Steinberg. Chicago: University of Chicago Press.
Osiander, Andreas (2001) 'Sovereignty, International Relations, and the Westphalian Myth,' *International Organization* 55 (2): 251–87.
Poggi, Gianfranco (1978) *The Development of the Modern State: A Sociological Introduction*. Stanford: Stanford University Press.
Shilliam, Robbie (2013) 'Intervention and Colonial-Modernity: Decolonising the Italy/Ethiopia Conflict through Psalms 68:31,' *Review of International Studies* 39: 1131–47.
Steinmetz, George (1999) (ed.) *State/Culture. State-Formation after the Cultural Turn*. Ithaca: Cornell University Press.
——— (2005) 'The First Genocide of the 20th Century and Its Postcolonial Afterlives: Germany and the Namibian Ovaherero,' *The Journal of the International Institute* 12 (2): winter. Permalink: http://hdl.handle.net/2027/spo.4750978.0012.201
Steinmetz, George (2007) *The Devil's Handwriting: Precoloniality and the German Colonial State in Qingdao, Samoa, and Southwest Africa*. Chicago: University of Chicago Press.
Teschke, Benno (2003) *The Myth of 1648: Class, Geopolitics and the Making of Modern International Relations*. London: Verso.
Tilly, Charles (1975) (ed.) *The Formation of National States in Western Europe*. Princeton: Princeton University Press.
Tilly, Charles (1975a) 'Reflections on the History of European State-making' in Tilly C. (ed.) *The Formation of National States in Western Europe*. Princeton: Princeton University Press, 3–83.
——— (1994) 'States and Nationalism in Europe 1492–1992,' *Theory and Society* 23 (1): 131–46.
Veracini, Lorenzo (2010) *Settler Colonialism. A Theoretical Overview*. Basingstoke: Palgrave.
Weber M. (1949 [1904]) *The Methodology of the Social Sciences*, translated by E. A. Shils and H. A. Finch. New York: Free Press.
——— (1980 [1895]) 'The National State and Economic Policy (Freiburg address)'. Translated by Ben Fowkes, *Economy and Society* 9 (4): 428–49.
Wilder, Gary (2015) *Freedom Time: Negritude, Decolonization, and the Future of the World*. Durham: Duke University Press.

18

RACE, ETHNICITY AND THE STATE

Contemporary *quilombos* in Brazil's settler colonial present

Desirée Poets

Introduction

Lagoa is a neighbourhood located in Rio de Janeiro's touristy southern side. It surrounds a beautiful lagoon, the Lagoa Rodrigo de Freitas, which offers a privileged view of the Corcovado Christ statue on one side and quick access to the famous Copacabana, Ipanema and Leblon beaches on the other. Lagoa illustrates how racism and class in Brazil are expressed socioeconomically and spatially. The IBGE (2010) census revealed that the neighbourhood has the highest average income in Rio, and that 91 per cent of its residents are white. It is a prime real estate site with the third most expensive square metre in the city (Fipezap 2016). Lagoa, nevertheless, is also the home of the *quilombo* community Sacopã. Contemporary *quilombos* are communities of Afro-Brazilian slave descendants who, much like indigenous peoples, have collective territorial rights since Brazil's 1988 Constitution. Quilombo Sacopã's community comprises the c.30 members of the Pinto family who have been living in Lagoa's Rua (street) Sacopã since the start of the twentieth century.

The Pinto family migrated to Lagoa before it became a prime real estate area, when it still belonged to the city's semi-urban periphery and several *favelas* formed its landscape. In the second half of the twentieth century, the neighbourhood's urbanisation led to its gentrification, and since then the *quilombo* has resisted repeated attempts to be removed. However, the many residents of their neighbouring *favelas* were forcefully relocated in the 1970s during a period of extensive *favela* removals in Rio's southern side. As part of the Pintos' struggle to remain in Lagoa, they initiated the process of collective land titling as a *quilombo* in 2005. They opted for this title as a last resort after their special adverse possession process stagnated. The Pintos at Rua Sacopã are legally recognised as a contemporary *quilombo* for being a family of slave descendants whose territory has been inseparable from their struggles of resistance and cultural survival. The community was a thriving cultural hub for *samba* and *pagode* music in the 1970s and 1980s, and they still organise one of Rio's most traditional *bloco de carnaval* (street carnival group), the Rola Preguiçosa.

Growing up in Rio, my school was located in the adjacent neighbourhood of Humaitá. I passed the community's area every day on my way to school, and had friends who lived two streets down from Quilombo Sacopã. Despite this, I was completely unaware of their presence in Lagoa. While I knew of historical *quilombos*, such as the well-known Quilombo dos Palmares (c. 1580–1710), the existence of contemporary *quilombos*, especially in urban centres, was completely unknown to me. I only learned of the Sacopã community when I developed an academic interest that drew me in their direction. The invisibility of contemporary *quilombo* communities is not specific to my experiences at home, but a widespread problem. The main aim of this chapter is to explore the reasons for this invisibility. How, when and why do certain groups become visible or invisible to us and the state? The 'prejudice of authenticity', this chapter contends, is a helpful starting point to begin unpacking this question.

Common-sense depictions conceive *quilombos* in the image of Quilombo dos Palmares. They are imagined as communities of escaped slaves that were established before the abolition of slavery (1888) and that, due to their status as fugitive slaves, lived in complete isolation in the wilderness. As a result, such groups were supposedly homogeneous and preserved a certain level of cultural distinctiveness or African-ness. Contemporary *quilombo* communities break from this imagery. They have been emerging since the 1988 Constitution, which was passed in the context of a regional turn to multiculturalism, social mobilisation, neoliberal reform and an established international regime of human rights. The Constitution contained a profound shift in civil rights and recognised Brazil's ethnic diversity. In this context, Article 68 of the Constitution's Ato das Disposições Constitucionais Transitórias (Temporary Constitutional Provisions, ADTC) granted collective land rights to those 'remaining from *quilombo* communities'. In its aftermath, this Article enabled the ethnogenesis of contemporary *quilombo* communities *as a political movement for land rights*.

Through the story of the Pinto family and the emergence of Quilombo Sacopã, this chapter begins with the current anthropological consensus on the definition of *quilombo* in Brazil. As we will see, this consensus was the outcome of a resemantisation or expansion of the term to include a great variety of experiences besides communities of strictly runaway slaves. The chapter then places the ethnogenesis of those 'remaining from *quilombos*' since 1988 in parallel with the ethnogenesis of those 'remaining from indigenous groups' in Brazil's Northeast region since the c.1920s. Within this, it explores under what circumstances the Sacopã community has been able to remain in Lagoa. Sacopã's trajectory raises the following questions: Why could a *favela* not remain in Lagoa, but a *quilombo* can? Why and to what extent did ethnic rights 'work' in this case? To what extent are Brazil's inequalities thereby challenged, and to what extent are new inequalities created? What is transformed within the possibilities of multiculturalism, and what is further entrenched within the accepted social norms and forms?

I argue that the Sacopã community's success in remaining in Lagoa derives from their ability to prove that they are not 'mere' Afro-descendants, but instead an ethnic community in the anthropological sense. In addition, their 'ethnicisation' has been a process of becoming 'like indigenous' (Hooker 2005, 296), which approximates race, ethnicity, blackness and indigeneity. Similarly to the emergent indigenous communities of the Northeast, in order to not be mere descendants, Sacopã had to counter what the Brazilian anthropologist Marcos Albuquerque (2011) has labelled the *prejudice of authenticity* and its three categories of assimilated, acculturated and de-territorialised. This prejudice renews the museum model of native culture that attempts to keep ethnic communities temporally, geographically and socially 'in their place'. Despite the expansion of the definition of *quilombo*, an important limit of multiculturalism in Brazil therefore is the way that it imagines ethnic communities.

These communities' claims to ethnic collective rights and citizenship necessitate claims to authenticity, which is in turn tied to notions of ancestral land and cultural alterity. One facet of ethnic communities' struggles for rights is the simultaneous abiding to and challenging of such expectations of location, historical continuity with pre-colonial groups and cultural difference or exoticism. As a result, only a minority of groups are visible and recognisable to the wider public and the state as legitimately ethnic. This minimalist conception of multiculturalism carries its own inequalities. It makes a concession to groups that are successful in fulfilling the criteria of an institutionalised ethnicity, while capping more radical, structural transformations. Multiculturalism emerges as a way of granting historical reparations, but only insofar as they do not question the legitimacy of the settler colonial state. Brazil, after all, is not an indigenous country.

Within this context, I argue that multiculturalism and ethnic rights are complicit with settler colonialism, and that this complicity is managed through authenticity. Multiculturalism is a seemingly more benevolent stage of settler colonialism, ultimately legitimising and expanding the 'still-settling state' (Simpson 2014, 20). Groups like Quilombo Sacopã and indigenous communities in various postcolonial contexts have been forced to imagine their politics outside of the settler state while being forced to exist within its physical and ideological boundaries – in the present context, within neoliberal multiculturalism. Ethnic categorisation, recognition and self-identification form a space in which power is negotiated. These categories not only emerge out of historical relationships of power, but also distribute power such as rights, legitimacy, resources and authority. In its critique of the possibilities of multiculturalism, nonetheless, this chapter does not aim to provide conclusive answers but, instead, to raise questions that only the communities themselves have the authority to address in their negotiations with the postcolonial state and its authenticating desires.

Bringing a category to life: the emergence of the remainders of *quilombos*

The Constitution's (1988) Article 68 states merely:

> The remaining members of the Quilombo communities are hereby recognised as the legitimate owners of the lands they occupy, for which the State shall issue the respective title deeds.
>
> (Author's translation)

Much in consonance with the aforementioned common-sense about *quilombos*, the constituent assembly assumed that such communities were remnants (*remanescentes*) of historical *quilombos* that had been founded before 1888 (Arruti 2009, 102–11; Almeida 2002, 47).[1] They consequently expected only a very limited number of *quilombos* to exist in Brazil in 1988 (Boaventura Leite 1999, 135). Arguably, this explains the decision to make the Article temporary, placing it in the Constitution's ADTC. Once those remaining communities had been titled, Article 68 would become obsolete. In this way, the constituent assembly evaded a deeper agrarian reform (Arruti 2009, 110) by denying such land rights to the majority of Brazil's rural and urban Afro-descendant populations (Fiabani 2007, 5).

While the postcolonial state created the legal category of *quilombo* in response to civil society demands, this simultaneously provided a strategy of managing difference and containing change by *conceding exceptions* to 'minority' ethnic groups. I return to this point later on. The recognition of *quilombo* communities since 1988, however, has led to a significant resemantisation of the term. The current consensus on the definition of *quilombo* is captured in Decreto (Decree) 4887/2003, which regulates the process of *quilombo* titling. It defines them as:

> ...ethno-racial groups, according to criteria of self-identification, that have a *unique historical trajectory* and *a particular relationship with their territory,* and that have a *black ancestry that is linked to their resistance* to the historical oppression that such groups have suffered.
>
> (Author's translation, emphasis added)

As we can see, the current consensus moved away from narrow expectations of historical continuity with pre-abolition communities of runaway slaves. It 'unfroze' the definition, bringing it back to life by making it relevant for the political struggles of Brazil's contemporary Afro-descendant communities. *Quilombo*, in the present context, is not a mere reference to a slave past, but a future-oriented legal category that enables struggles for citizenship, land and cultural survival. As Boaventura Leite (1999) put it, '[t]he expression "*remanescentes de quilombos*" [...] reappeared at the end of the 1980s not only to describe a *process* of incomplete citizenship, [but also] to systematise a set of demands for change by parts of Brazilian society' (130).

Since 1988, a diversity of communities has been recognised as contemporary *quilombos*, many of which were only founded after the abolition of slavery. This expansion was an outcome of the political alliance forged between anthropologists, especially the Associação Brasileira de Antropologia (Brazilian Anthropology Association, ABA) and the Afro-descendant communities whose land titles required official anthropological reports. For the ABA:

> Contemporarily, the term *quilombo* does not refer to residues or archaeological remains of temporal occupations or biological proof. They are also not isolated groups or a strictly homogeneous population. In the same way, they were not always founded through insurrectional or rebellious movements, but, above all, consist of groups that have *developed everyday practices of resistance in the maintenance and reproduction of their characteristic ways of life in a particular territory.*
>
> (Cantarino O'Dwyer 2012, 293; author's translation, emphasis added)

The Quilombo Sacopã emerged in this context, and their trajectory illustrates the definitions above.

The family arrived in Lagoa at the start of the twentieth century from a coffee farm in Nova Friburgo, where their ancestors had been slaves. Upon arrival in Lagoa, Manoel and Eva Pinto, the community's founders, settled in Rua Sacopã, which was part of the vast estate of the Darke de Mattos family. Manoel became the family's housekeeper, and the family's matriarch, Astréia, verbally conceded to the Pintos the territory of their contemporary community. From the outset, the Pintos derived their subsistence from this territory. They planted vegetables, herbs and fruit trees as well as kept a small variety of farm animals. These were initiatives of Eva, who was also a healer and a midwife. She assisted in the birth of many of the children of the neighbourhood's *favelas* of the time, and in times of sickness applied her traditional healing practices to them and her own seven children (interview with C. Torres, 17 Dec 2014).

Between the 1940s and 1970s, the city of Rio began to expand towards its now touristy and privileged Zona Sul (South Zone), leading to Lagoa's urbanisation, verticalisation and gentrification. These changes not only altered the neighbourhood's landscape but also deeply affected the family's way of life. At first, it created opportunities for them, but in the long run it threatened their cultural practices and physical presence in Lagoa. Their strategies of survival stand as evidence of their resilience to the negative impacts of these changes, while protecting the Atlantic Forest that makes up most of their territory and which forms an important part of their history and identity.

In the initial stages of Lagoa's urbanisation, the older male family members were employed in the opening of the neighbourhood's streets and avenues. Later, in the 1970s, the construction of Rua Sacopã's current luxurious residential buildings attracted migrant workers from the poorer Northeast region. During this period, the family started serving lunch and refreshments to those construction workers, a tradition that they maintain to this day. Later, in the 1980s, Luiz, the community's current leader, and his sister *tia*Eném, who were both singers, musicians and composers, expanded the family's economic ventures by hosting weekly *samba* and *pagode* events (the so-called Pagode do Sacopã). The Pagode do Sacopã made the community famous throughout Rio, giving origin to the carnival block Rola Preguiçosa that the family continues to organise every year. When the Pagode do Sacopã peaked in popularity, the family was in the midst of their land conflict.

Lagoa's urbanisation was also a process of social cleansing. It included plans to relocate the neighbourhood's *favela* residents to Rio's industrial western side. The Favela da Catacumba, for example, was forcefully removed and transformed into a park, the present-day Parque da Catacumba. A similar fate awaited the residents of Rua Sacopã, part of which became a city park, the Parque Municipal José Guilherme Merquior (Rodríguez Cáceres 2013). The residents to be removed included the Pintos and some of the construction workers who frequented their boarding house and who had decided to settle around them, building informal houses. In 1975, at the height of *favela* removals, these settlements were identified as the 'favela do Sacopã'. For the family, however, such a *favela* never existed, and the houses around them were nothing but separate families who lived informally in that area.

Categorising the Pintos and their neighbours as a *favela* was therefore a strategy of the local government to justify their removal. The first eviction attempt took place in March 1975 (*Jornal do Brasil* 1975, 6), a month after a newspaper article identified the residents of Rua Sacopã as a *favela* (*O Globo* 1975, 11). Most of the family's neighbours agreed to relocate to the city's peripheries, accepting a small sum of money in exchange. The Pintos, however, refused to move. Especially for the younger generations, it was unthinkable that they would have to move away from where they had been born. They hired a lawyer and initiated a special adverse possession process. During this time, Brazil was still under military rule. Their lawyer, was fortuitously married to a military official, who attended the evictions of Rua Sacopã and protected the family from relocation. The Pintos are the only ones who have remained to witness their street's radical transformation since the departure of their previous neighbours.

Over time, the weekly Pagode do Sacopã was forced to become a fortnightly *feijoada* (a traditional black bean stew) and *samba* event until it was completely prohibited. As Lagoa gentrified, their new neighbours began to report their weekly events as well as their other subsistence activities, filing noise and disorder complaints. After a number of police interventions in their territory, which the neighbours still instigate from time to time, the family was forced to give up their traditional activities that derived from their land. In the present context, most of them have taken up employment in domestic and other services around the neighbourhood. These losses have been painful for the community. They not only limit their sources of income, which forces many family members to move away from the community and look for employment elsewhere, but they also de-legitimise their claim to a 'different way of life' or cultural alterity.

As previously explained, the family initially attempted to remain in Lagoa through an adverse possession process, which is ongoing to this day. The Pintos had won this process in the first instance, but lost it in the second instance in 2005. Tired out by the tardiness and bureaucracy of this process, Luiz learned from a family friend who used to frequent the *pagode* events that the family was eligible for a collective land title as a *quilombo* community. Soon after, he went with *tia* Neném to the Fundação Cultural Palmares (Palmares Cultural Foundation, FCP) and registered the family for a certificate of self-identification as a *remanescente de quilombos* (remainders of *quilombo*). This marked the first stage of their titling as a collective *quilombola* land, which by 2017 was in the final two stages (INCRA 2009)[2] and seemingly approaching a victorious ending for the family.

While the Pintos have always been aware of their slave past, they only began to openly talk about it and to self-identify as a *quilombo* after they initiated the titling process (interview with M. Arruda, 14 Dec 2014). It is in this way that contemporary *quilombos* did not exist before 1988. Usually, their emergence as *quilombos* is inherently tied to a political struggle around access to land (Cantarino O'Dwyer 2012, 12). As such, *quilombo* land titles are a way of securing the survival of such communities in the present and future. Sacopã's trajectory resonates with the Decree 4887's and the ABA's definitions of *quilombo*. The Pinto's identification as a contemporary *quilombo* community emerged out of their more recent history of resistance to dispossession, out of their black ancestry – including their Afro-descendant cultural activities of the *samba*, the *pagode* and *feijoada* – and out of their particular relationship with their territory.

Contextualising the emergence of the remainders: authenticity, mixture and purity

As a *quilombo* community, Sacopã has been able to remain in Lagoa, but as a *favela*, they would not have been. They could remain in Lagoa because they had proved that they were not 'mere' Afro-descendants, but an ethnic community in the anthropological sense.[3] To this end, Sacopã established an ethnic boundary between themselves and Rio's *favelas*. On a related note, I had a conversation with a long-standing activist during my research with urban indigenous movements in São Paulo that elucidated the problematic of the differentiation between 'descendants' and 'full members of an ethnic community'. Indigeneity, he argued, was a cultural identity that required 'ties to and memory of the ancestral community' (anonymised personal communication, 17 Jul 2015). The forced diaspora of African slaves, on the other hand, had led to their de-territorialisation and thereby de-ethnicisation. As an outcome of these different historical trajectories, the contemporary indigenous movement could not accept descendants in the same way that the black movement can recognise all Afro-descendants as black. Otherwise, 'anyone' could claim indigenous identity and the benefits reserved for indigenous peoples, for so many Brazilians have indigenous descent.

When the indigenous communities of the Northeast emerged as *remanescentes* in the 1920s, they too had to prove that they were not only 'mixed' descendants of indigenous peoples, but authentic indigenous communities. By the end of the nineteenth century, the states of the Northeast had declared all of the region's indigenous settlements as extinct (Carneiro da Cunha 1992). Their extinction was justified by the fact that they were 'too mixed' and therefore no longer recognisable as distinct from the wider mass of peasants (*caboclos*) in the region. In the 1920s, these officially extinct communities experienced severe land conflicts with non-indigenous settlers, including recently freed slaves and white settlers. In order to protect their territory, they contacted the state's official *indigenista* organ, the Serviço de Proteção aos Índios (Service for the Protection of the Indians, SPI, 1910–67), asking for recognition and land demarcation as indigenous communities (Arruti 1996).

As a growing number of Northeastern groups contacted the SPI, it faced the need to determine who would count as indigenous (Arruti 2009, 112), or, to put it differently, to define the criteria for indigeneity. Based on the work of anthropologists in the region, the SPI defined the dance of a ritual, the *toré*, as the regional marker of indigeneity. Those communities who could dance the *toré* would be eligible for indigenous status. A network of ethnogenesis emerged as an outcome of this 'requirement', through which community leaders taught each other the *toré*. Through the dance of the *toré*, the communities proved their exoticism, or their *authenticity* as fully ethnic, culturally distinct communities. The SPI recognised those 'mixed Indians' (Pacheco de Oliveira 1998) as 'legitimate remainders (*remanescentes*) of those old inhabitants of the extinct [settlements]' (Arruti 1996, 9). In this way, the communities of the Northeast invented a cultural tradition that both served a clear political purpose and carried valuable normative as well as affective meaning for those involved.

Arruti (1997, 26–7) notes that in all cases of indigenous emergences of the Northeast, the recovery of indigenous identity – which simultaneously produced this same indigenous identity

– was linked to the discovery of indigenous land rights. As previously stated, '*quilombo*' also emerged as a legal category or 'status' that guarantees land rights. The need to differentiate between 'descendants' and 'members of an ethnic community' also arose in the trajectory of Sacopã to draw a distinction between the *quilombo* and the city's *favelas*. Ethnic self-identification and recognition, therefore, is inherently political. It is always tied to the communities' political struggles as well as to national projects – from the assimilationist projects of previous centuries to neoliberal multiculturalism – which ethnic groups must negotiate. The disadvantaged position of ethnic groups in this process of negotiation is a serious limitation to the transformative power of multiculturalism. This will be explained in more detail below.

Expectations on *authenticity* regulate the difference between descendants and ethnic groups. The Brazilian anthropologist Marcos Albuquerque helpfully labelled these expectations the *authenticity prejudice* (Albuquerque 2011). Expanding on his work, this prejudice shapes the struggles for rights of ethnic communities generally, including indigenous peoples who live in urban centres as well as *quilombola* communities. Marcos Albuquerque identified three categories of this prejudice, namely that 'inauthentic' groups are perceived as *assimilados* (assimilated), *aculturados* (acculturated) and *desaldeados* (without a village or ancestral land, 'de-villaged' or de-territorialised). The content of what counts as *authenticity* may vary in each group, but the authenticity prejudice remains structurally similar. Here, I apply these categories to contemporary *quilombo* communities.

The first (assimilated) is a phenotypic prejudice, which demands that ethnic groups fit the physical stereotypes of their racial group, or that they 'look black/*quilombola* or indigenous'. The second category (acculturated) refers to the expectation that such groups must be culturally distinct from 'wider society', having a different religion, language and specific rituals. The final category (*desaldeado*) defines the geographical location of ethnic groups. As other scholars have noted (Boaventura Leite 1999, 133; Hooker 2005, 302–3; Ng'Weno 2007, 415), indigeneity is inherently tied to notions of ancestral land in Latin America. 'Real Indians' are expected to live in their traditional territories, or, at least, to have 'ties to and memory of' the community that lives in its ancestral territory. This is also tied to images of specific regions. The Amazon and the Andes function as Latin America's 'authentic' indigenous regions, so that indigenous peoples that are located elsewhere are invisibilised, much like Afro-Latinos in the Amazon or the Andes (Walsh 2007).

Returning to the introduction, this prejudice is one of the reasons why I had never heard of a *quilombo* community that was located so close to my school. Expectations on authenticity renew the museum model of culture (Albuquerque 2011, 19) and its static notions of history, tradition and purity. Ethnic communities are hereby kept 'in their place' geographically (in isolation in the wilderness), socially (as marginalised Others) and temporally (as 'of the past'). The colonisation of Brazil, nevertheless, was a history of forced mixing of 'uncivilised' groups to promote their 'civilisation'/whitening (*branqueamento*) while facilitating their exploitation (Arruti 1997, 10–11; Wade 2010; Augusto dos Santos et al. 2002). By the end of the second half of the nineteenth century, *mestiçagem* or *miscigenação* (mixing) had become the distinctive symbol of the modern nation and informed state practices towards indigenous and Afro-descendant Brazilians (Schwarcz 1994). *Mestiçagem*, in addition, has always been synonymous with whitening.

More specifically, the miscegenation of indigenous and Afro-descendant peoples was understood to advance in 'axes of mutations that were structurally similar to one another' (Arruti 1997, 9), passing through the stages of *Indian/caboclo/civilised* or *black/mulatto/white* (Arruti 1997, 9–10). Mixing and purity, *mestiçagem* and *branqueamento* have always been imbricated with one another in Brazil's history of citizenship. The museum model of culture ('purity') has maintained its grasp in Brazil alongside a history of *mestiçagem* ('mixing'). While the multicultural turn was an important break from previous official homogenising discourses of the nation (Ortiz 1988), the politics of authenticity and recognition renews previous discourses on purity/exoticism. Ethnic groups that have to access collective rights are forced to engage with, negotiate and refract the state's expectations on identity from an asymmetrical position. This inequality is not challenged in *quilombo* titles, which caps its transformative potential.

Becoming 'like indigenous' and 'not a *favela*': old and new inequalities in multicultural Brazil

When Sacopã initiated their titling as a *quilombo*, they underwent a process of ethnogenesis. Much like the Northeastern indigenous communities in previous decades, Sacopã had to prove that they were not only descendants of African slaves, or *favelados* (*favela* residents), but a fully ethnic community. In this regard, they had to become 'like indigenous', as we will see, proving that they were not assimilated, acculturated or de-territorialised. The prejudice that they are assimilated emerges in the family's daily lives, such as in the case of Cláudio, whose mother married a white man. In our conversations, Claudio often told me that outsiders, including journalists, regularly questioned his Afro identity due to his skin colour (interview with C. Torres, 10 Jun 2014). In his refutation of such reductions of his ethnic identity to his appearance, he interpreted them as attempts to de-legitimise his and the family's *quilombola* identity and land claim. Part of the Pintos' struggle, therefore, implies a political work of refracting the categories of the prejudice of authenticity, whereby they simultaneously enforce and counter it.

The family's cultural practices of the *samba*, *pagode* and *feijoada* granted them status as a culturally distinct community (as not acculturated) in the eyes of the official bodies. Nevertheless, the appropriation of Afro-descendant culture as national Brazilian symbols complicates Afro-Brazilians' claims to cultural distinctiveness and thereby to collective rights. Consequently, Afro-Brazilians are commonly perceived as a (non-ethnic) racial group in a class society. Contemporary *quilombo* communities must therefore (re-)invent their traditions as the communities themselves are produced as *remanescentes de* (and not descendants of) *quilombos* (Arruti 1997, 21 and 30). On a related note, scholars writing from other contexts have explored how indigenous groups are upheld in Latin America as the 'ideal' or paradigmatic multicultural subject (Hooker 2005, 302–3; Restrepo 2012). They are perceived as 'inherently pre-modern' (Hale 2004, 20), and therefore more distinct from the 'mixed nation' than black cultures. This produces a hierarchical relationship between indigenous and black communities in terms of access to collective rights.

Only Brazil, Colombia, Ecuador, Guatemala, Honduras and Nicaragua have recognised collective rights for black communities, for instance (Hooker 2005, 298). In this context, Hooker (2005) argues that in those cases where black groups have gained the same collective rights as indigenous communities, as she put it, 'they have done so because they have been able to cast themselves as "autochthonous" groups having an indigenous-like status and distinct cultural identity' (304). Within this context, the association of indigeneity with ancestral lands in parallel to the paradigm 'forced African diaspora/de-territorialisation/de-ethnicisation' implies that black communities such as Sacopã have to counter the notion that they are *desaldeados* (de-territorialised). As already mentioned, the family has always had a special relationship with their territory, and therefore an ethnic territoriality. Their cultural and physical survival has always been inseparable from their territory, countering the notion that they are de-territorialised.

Brazil is not an indigenous country

The current consensus on the definition of *quilombo* was an important expansion of the term. Nonetheless, it still contains the categories of the authenticity prejudice, excluding land claims by Afro-descendant groups that cannot articulate this institutionalised ethnicity. One of the effects of the authenticity prejudice is the minoritisation of *quilombo* and indigenous communities. Out of the almost 200 million Brazilians, only c.1.17 million are *quilombolas* (Agência Senado 2012) and c.890 thousand are indigenous persons (IBGE 2010). In this regard, the Brazilian black movement often argues that Brazil has a black majority, since *pretos* ('black') and *pardos* ('brown') added up to 51 per cent of the population in the 2010 census (IBGE 2010). Urban indigenous movements regularly questioned this assumption during my research. They argued that a large number of those *pardos*, who make up 43 per cent of the population, are indigenous peoples who did not self-identify as or were not recognised as indigenous in the census.

Regardless of which group is correct, the exclusion of descendants from official recognition caps the transformative power of ethnic rights. This exclusion hinders a more significant challenging of Brazil's racist structures, a deeper agrarian reform and profounder challenges to the postcolonial state. The state can thereby manage and contain the extent to which historical reparations are granted to Brazil's black and indigenous populations, ultimately legitimising the status quo. I discussed the debate around the 51 per cent and the fears around the inclusion of descendants into the indigenous movement in a conversation with the indigenous writer Daniel Munduruku (personal communication, 17 Jul 2015). His reply was particularly insightful, for it articulated a question that went to the core of the issue: 'Well, then, Brazil would be an indigenous country! Or is Brazil not an indigenous country?'

To put it differently, the maintenance of indigenous and *quilombola* communities as ethnic minorities legitimises the sovereignty of the *mestiço* (as in, white) settler colonial state. This practice emerges out of two interrelated fears. Firstly, the fear that *if everyone is indigenous, then no one is indigenous*, which would make the rights of indigenous and *quilombola* groups obsolete and 'unjustifiable'. Munduruku's reply turns this fear on its head: What about the possibility that, if everyone is indigenous, then Brazil would be an indigenous country? This links to the second fear, namely that, if historical reparations are not contained, then 'where will we end up?' Potentially, we could end up questioning the legitimacy of the status quo, of the 'still-settling' state and its expansion. Furthermore, the need to prove authenticity empowers the state, its lawyers, and anthropologists, who must 'verify' claims to ethnicity. This renews these historical relationships of power within the specificities of neoliberal multiculturalism. It contains indigenous and *quilombo* struggles as a matter of institutions and of the law in what Eduardo Restrepo (2012) has labelled a 'minimalist conception of multiculturalism' (24–5).

The questions that the aboriginal scholar Irene Watson (2000) raises elucidate this point:

> Native title is seen as a right to take to the negotiating table, but who eats best from the native title industry and who waits in hunger for their native title? Can we negotiate 'rights' when we have an unequal power to that of the state? How do we engage with their law when we have never consented to their stolen title of our lands? In discussing indigenous rights are we conceding or consenting to the authority of the colonial state? (5)

Sacopã's story evinces an additional way in which *quilombo* land titles are unable to deeply challenge the status quo. For the family, titling as a *quilombo* has meant a positive re-signification of their blackness and slave past (interview with M. Nascimento, 17 Dec 2014). Their titling process, nevertheless, simultaneously confirmed the power of their richer and more influential neighbours. Initially, the community's anthropological report identified 23,900 m^2 as part of their territory. This demarcation included properties of some of their wealthy neighbours who had invaded their territory. As an outcome of the neighbours' contestations, the INCRA reduced this initial territory to 6,900 m^2. They explained to the community that such a reduction would speed up their titling process, while the inclusion of the properties would stall it, so that the family was left with no choice but to agree to the reduction. Sacopã's land title is therefore viable as long as it does not force the relocation of Lagoa's elites. Historical reparations are acceptable and viable as long as they remain an exception that does not question real property law (Watson 2007, 25) or the structures of power.

Charles Hale (2004) has named this the 'era of the indio permitido', in which 'reforms have pre-determined limits; benefits to a few indigenous actors are predicated on the exclusion of the rest; certain rights are to be enjoyed on the implicit condition that others will not be raised' (17–18). In this era, ethnic communities' issues are kept, as much as possible, in the realm of culture and away from political-economic empowerment. As such, multiculturalism and the state ideology of *mestiçagem* share 'the same dual quality: in some aspects egalitarian and in others regressive' (Hale 2004, 16). *Mestiçagem* had discarded the conclusions of nineteenth-century 'race science' that equated racial mixing with degeneration, but maintained its hierarchical project of whitening, drawing legitimacy from the nation's Indian Other. Multiculturalism, while distancing itself from such homogenising discourses, is complicit with settler colonialism, allowing only a specific kind of reform that avoids more radical projects. Multiculturalism, too, legitimises the settler state through its recognition of internal ethnic diversity and collective rights within an international context of human rights and 'development'.

Conclusion

Is it possible to occupy the spaces opened up by multiculturalism so as to avoid its pitfalls and deepen its progressive elements? Can multiculturalism create the conditions for a profound challenging of Brazil's unequal structures, and can it, as Watson (2007) put it, provide 'direction in the "road-map" or journey of decolonisation?' (25). These are the questions that the trajectory of the Sacopã community raises, and they speak to the wider challenges of ethnic groups in other postcolonial contexts. Only the communities themselves can address these questions in their negotiations with the 'still-settling' states within which they are forced to be. Sacopã, against all odds, have so far managed to remain in their territory. They arrived in Lagoa when it was part of the city's semi-urban periphery and the location of several *favelas*. They witnessed its urbanisation, verticalisation, gentrification and whitening. Currently, Lagoa contains some of Rio's most expensive square metres.

Sacopã stands as evidence of what is possible within multicultural Brazil. The community was able to resist the mass *favela* removals of the 1970s and, when their special adverse possession process stagnated, initiated the collective land titling as a *quilombo*. Their special relationship with their territory, their history of resistance and their engagement in the Afro-Brazilian traditions of the *samba*, the *pagode* and the *feijoada* granted them status as a *quilombo*. Simultaneously, Sacopã calls for a critical appraisal of these possibilities. In order to access land rights, they had to become anthropologically ethnic or 'like indigenous' and therefore different from the *favelas* and 'mere' Afro-descendants of past and present Rio. In order to fulfil the state's expectations of authenticity, the Pintos had to counter the idea that they had been assimilated, acculturated and de-territorialised.

As we have seen, the ethnogenesis of the remainders of *quilombos* in Brazil is analogous to the ethnogenesis of the remainders of indigenous communities in previous decades. They, too, had to prove that they were not mere descendants of extinct indigenous communities. The complex lived experiences of contemporary *quilombos* blur the lines between race and ethnicity, blackness and indigeneity. Multiculturalism, however, carries old and new inequalities. It upholds the indigenous as its paradigmatic subject, creating a hierarchy between indigenous and Afro-Brazilian groups, and especially excluding Afro-descendants from its policies. In addition, the Pintos' subordinate position in Brazilian society and Lagoa forced them to compromise over a large portion of their territory to accommodate the contestations of the economic and political elites that had invaded it. As such, multiculturalism inherited and reproduces the racist order of Brazilian society, unable to challenge its structures and the prevalence of private property, or 'real property', over collective rights.

Multiculturalism is, in fact, a seemingly more benevolent stage of settler colonialism. It creates its own minorities of 'authentic indigenous and *quilombola* peoples' to which it grants 'special' rights. The still-settling state's sovereignty and authority thereby becomes legitimised and in demand. The state, its lawyers and anthropologists are required to 'verify' the legitimacy of claims to collective rights, while the proportion of the territory granted to ethnic groups as collective lands is contained. Multiculturalism is thus the current solution to settler colonialism's 'racial problem' (Schwarcz 1994), allowing the postcolonial state to manage difference and contain change. The parallels between the emergence of contemporary *quilombos* and of indigenous communities in the Northeast, in addition, show that a preoccupation with the exotic/authentic is not an invention of multiculturalism. It also formed part of previous national and sub-national projects. The official extinction of all indigenous settlements of the Northeast during imperial Brazil and their later recognition and demarcation by the SPI since the c.1920s illustrated this.

In the era of the 'indio permitido', this preoccupation with the exotic is renewed within the specificities of neoliberal multiculturalism. Ethnic groups that need to access native peoples' rights are trapped within the parameters of recognition and authenticity that the state sets, which they refract through their more complex lived experiences. While this state no longer officially promotes the assimilation of such groups, their communal projects run the risk of being contained in what is deemed legitimate and what legitimises the settler colonial state. Yet, far from arguing that the demarcation of indigenous and *quilombola* lands are not important, or that they should be abolished, the reflections contained in this chapter pose the challenge, instead, of imagining ways to inhabit the possibilities of multiculturalism so as to expand them towards more radical futures. If we cannot move in that direction, then what does it mean to talk about decolonisation in Brazil?

Bibliography

Agência Senado, 2012. Brasil tem 1,17 milhão de quilombolas [online]. *Agência Senado*, 5 November. Available from: https://goo.gl/j3XuN7 [Accessed 01 October 2016].

Albuquerque, M., 2011. *O Regime imagético Pankararu (tradução intercultural na cidade de São Paulo)*. Thesis (PhD). Universidade Federal de Santa Catarina.

Almeida, A.W.B., 2002. Os quilombos e as novas etnias. In: O'Dwyer, E.C., ed. *Quilombos: Identidade étnica e territorialidade*. Rio de Janeiro: Editora FGV, 43–81.

Arruti, J.M.A., 1996. *O Reencantamento do mundo: Trama histórica e arranjos territoriais Pankararu*. Dissertation (Masters), PPGAS/MN/UFRJ.

——— 1997. 'A emergência dos remanescentes: notas para o diálogo entre indígenas e quilombolas.' *MANA*, 3 (2), 7–38.

——— 2009. Quilombos. *Revista Jangwa Pana*, 8 (1), 102–21.

Augusto dos Santos, S. and Hallewell, L., 2002. 'Historical Roots of the "Whitening" of Brazil.' *Latin American Perspectives*, 29 (1), 61–82.

Barth, F., 1969. *Ethnic Groups and Boundaries*. Bergen-Oslo: Universitets Forlaget.

Boaventura Leite, I., 1999. 'Quilombos e quilombolas: Cidadania ou folclorização?' *Horizontes Antropológicos*, 5 (10), 123–49.

Cantarino O'Dwyer, E., 2012. *O fazer antropológico e o reconhecimento de direitos constitucionais: O caso das terras de quilombo no Estado do Rio de Janeiro.* Rio de Janeiro: e-papers.

Carneiro da Cunha, M., 1992. *Os povos indígenas no Brasil.* São Paulo: Companhia das Letras.

Cohen, A., 1974. *Urban Ethnicity.* London: Tavistock.

Constituição da República Federativa do Brasil de 1988, Article 68 of the ADTC [online]. Available from: https://goo.gl/3YvSL2 [Accessed 28 September 2016].

Decreto 4887/2003, Artigo 2o. Available from: http://www.planalto.gov.br/ccivil_03/decreto/2003/d4887.htm [Accessed 01 October 2016].

Fiabani, A., 2007. O quilombo antigo e o quilombo contemporâneo: verdades e construções [online]. *Associação Nacional de História – ANPUH XXIV Simpósio nacional de história,* 15–20 July 2007 São Leopoldo. Available from: https://goo.gl/hTjn8X [Accessed 14 September 2016].

Fipezap, 2016. *Índice Fipezap de preços de imóveis anunciados* [online], 5. Available from: goo.gl/4LziHo [Accessed 15 September 2016].

Hale, C.R., 2004. 'Rethinking Indigenous Politics in the Era of the "Indio Permitido".' *NACLA Report on the Americas,* 38 (2), 16–21.

Hooker, J., 2005. 'Indigenous Inclusion/Black Exclusion: Race, Ethnicity and Multicultural Citizenship in Latin America.' *Journal of Latin American Studies,* 37 (2), 285–310.

IBGE, 2010. *Censo Demográfico: Caracteristicas da População e dos Domicílios: Resultados do Universo* [online]. Available from: goo.gl/537GG2 [Accessed 15 September 2016].

INCRA, 2009. Instrução Normativa No. 57. Available from: https://goo.gl/GXqnHC [accessed 01 October 2016].

Jornal do Brasil, 1975. 'Moradores de favela se mudam.' *Jornal do Brasil,* 14 March, 6.

Ng'Weno, B., 2007. 'Can Ethnicity Replace Race? Afro-Colombians, Indigeneity and the Colombian Multicultural State.' *Journal of Latin American and Caribbean Anthropology,* 12 (2), 414–40.

O Globo, 1975. 'Nasce uma favela no Sacopã, os moradores reclamam.' *O Globo,* 27 February, 11.

Ortiz, R., 1988. *Ideologia da Cultura Brasileira.* São Paulo: Companhia das Letras.

Pacheco de Oliveira, J., 1998. 'Uma etnologia dos "índios misturados"? Situação colonial, territorialização e fluxos culturais.' *MANA,* 4 (1), 47–77.

Restrepo, E., 2012. 'El multiculturalismo amerita ser defendido?' In Ferro Medina, J.G. and Tobón, G., eds. *Autonomías Territoriales: Experiencias y Desafíos.* Bogotá: Editorial Pontificia Universidad Javeriana, 19–40.

Rodríguez Cáceres, L.S., 2013. 'Naturezas monumentalizadas, cotidianos politizados: a construção discursiva do lugar no caso do Quilombo Sacopã.' *Sociedade e Cultura,* 16 (1), 91–106.

Schwarcz, L.M., 1994. Espetáculo da miscigenação. *Estudos Avançados,* 8 (20), 137–52.

Simpson, A., 2014. *Mohawk Interruptus: Political Life Across the Borders of Settler States.* Durham: Duke University Press.

von Martius, K.F.P., 1956. 'Como se deve escrever a História do Brasil.' *Revista de História de América,* 42, 433–58.

Wade, P., 2010. *Race and Ethnicity in Latin America.* London: Pluto Press.

Walsh, C., 2007. 'Lo Afro en América andina: Reflexiones en torno a luchas actuales de (in)visibilidad, (re) existencia y pensamiento.' *Journal of Latin American and Caribbean Anthropology,* 12 (1), 200–12.

Watson, I., 2000. 'There Is No Possibility of Rights without Law: So Until Then, Don't Thumb Print or Sign Anything!' *Indigenous Law Bulletin,* 5 (1), 15–32.

——— 2007. 'Settled and Unsettled Spaces: Are We Free to Roam?' In: Moreton-Robinson, A. *Sovereign Subjects: Indigenous Sovereignty Matters.* Crows Nest: Allen & Unwin, 15–32.

Notes

1 This concept of quilombo was prevalent until the mid-1990s and can be traced back to 1740 in a Reply to the King of Portugal by the Ultramarine Council of 1740. See Almeida 2002, 47.

2 *Quilombo* land titling is an administrative process under the responsibility of the Instituto de Colonização e Reforma Agrária (Institute of Colonisation and Agrarian Reform, INCRA) as regulated in Decree 4887/2003 and the Instrução Normativa (Normative Instruction, IN) No. 57 of 2009. Analogous to the process of indigenous lands demarcation, the titling stages are identification, recognition, delimitation, demarcation, non-intrusion of occupants, provision of the land title and land registration.

3 In Brazilian scholarship, the current consensus on the meaning of 'ethnic group' is based on the work of Fredrik Barth (1969) and Abner Cohen (1974).

19

THE REVOLUTION OF SMILING WOMEN

Stateless democracy and power in Rojava

Dilar Dirik

Introduction

The form in which the Kurds re-entered global agendas after a period of perceived invisibility was indeed spectacular: previously remote and unknown to most, the women of Kurdistan became the icons of the fight against the so-called Islamic State. Most notably, the battle for Kobane (Ain al-Arab) at the Syrian–Turkish border in 2014, which resulted in the first victory against ISIS in January 2015, drew attention to the revolutionary momentum in the predominantly Kurdish-inhabited region of northern Syria, which is referred to as 'Rojava' (meaning 'West' in Kurdish, i.e. western Kurdistan).

But not only did they establish themselves as the strongest enemy of ISIS's explicit war on women, the people of Rojava further amazed radical circles and left-democratic forces worldwide, due to their ability to mobilize popular support among the masses for an alternative, progressive and radical political system in the midst of war. Interestingly, this liberation movement does not struggle for the ideal of a post-colonial nation-state, but for an explicitly anti-nationalist, anti-statist, anti-capitalist and anti-patriarchal freedom proposal.

Often referred to as the 'largest nation without a state', the Kurds, a people divided by four powerful states, namely Turkey, Iran, Iraq and Syria, experienced the oppressive nation-state system in decades-long conflicts and wars after the dissolution of the Ottoman empire in the early twentieth century. While nationalisms in the post-Ottoman Middle East, especially pan-Arabism and Kemalism, often emerged in reaction to imperialism and colonialism, they also imported the premises of European nation-states and perpetuated racism and internal colonization of peoples that did not fit in their monist models. In the context of postcolonial politics, the Kurds, especially women, were marginalized and rendered speechless in a multiply layered manner due to their particular position in different intersecting forms of violence as colonized subjects in previous colonies. Ismail Besikci describes Kurdistan as an international colony which has 'not even' been granted the status of being a colony (Besikci, 1990).

However, despite the experience with different colonialisms and multiple layers of violence, combined with the transnationalism of the so-called 'Kurdish question', original freedom proposals also evolved in Kurdistan. The most notable has been Abdullah Öcalan's project of 'Democratic Confederalism', implemented through communes, academies, councils, and cooperatives as practices of 'Democratic Autonomy', based on a 'grassroots-democratic, ecological, women's liberationist paradigm' as an antidote to the statist, capitalist, patriarchal system. This system of a 'stateless democracy' was articulated by a previously Marxist-Leninist party that pursued the aim of an independent Kurdish state, which today advocates overcoming the state in favor of empowering and organizing the community.

In this chapter, I intend to provide a description of everyday politics in Rojava[1] in order to outline the Kurdish freedom movement's critical definition of the state through its ideological discourses and organizational practices. I illustrate a political movement's attempt at comprehensively constructing an alternative vision of polity, belonging and legitimacy which challenges the conventional idea of democracy as representative politics and goes beyond the limits of the power and authority of the nation-state. Rather than appropriating the means of the state, the understanding of any state as being colonialist by nature turns the postcolonial context into a struggle to dismantle the state by rendering it as meaningless for the everyday lives of the people. This includes challenging one's own claims to stateness through radical democracy. The functions and mechanisms traditionally embodied and provided by the state (such as force, administration, economy, education, etc.) are thence re-articulated within a new framework with the purpose of upsetting traditional power relations. Ultimately, the freedom concept that emerges as a result directly impacts its subjects' ability to imagine politics differently and act upon it as rendered necessary for meaningful self-determination and autonomy. As we shall see, the liberation of women is seen as the most defining method through which social administration is sought with a new set of terms.

A revolutionary culture

Before we can adequately discuss the political system in Rojava, it is important to recognize that it is not possible to understand the contemporary Democratic Autonomy project without taking into account the twenty-year-long presence of the Kurdistan Workers Party (PKK) headquarters and its leader, Abdullah Öcalan, in Syria. This will help us understand the nature of the notion of 'politics' that has become a rooted tradition in the region through the influence of revolutionary ideology and practice on the ordinary community and vice versa. The PKK was formed in 1978 as a Marxist-Leninist national liberation party to fight the Turkish 'colonizer state' and to establish a united, socialist Kurdistan that could contribute to the global proletarian revolution. In 1984, the PKK started armed guerrilla warfare against the Turkish state. Anticipating the 1980 military coup d'état in Turkey, large sections of the party cadres and leadership managed to cross into Syria to protect their structures. Drawing its base from the mostly rural masses of Kurdistan, the PKK managed to mobilize solid popular support and is regarded by millions of Kurds as the political force which represents their interests.

When trying to understand the women's revolution in Rojava, the impact of the PKK cannot be overestimated. This is a point that every single woman I have interviewed strongly emphasized. Narîn Afrîn, one of the YPJ (Women's Defense Units) commanders during the historic war in Kobane, told me: 'Everyone has seen the reality of the PKK in the battle for Kobane'. On her trip to Rojava, Anja Flach observed: 'You mustn't forget, the head of the PKK lived here for twenty years'. We were often told this on our May 2014 visit: 'his work shaped the way we think.' In retrospect, fifteen years after the departure of Abdullah Öcalan, his philosophy and methods, and especially his efforts to empower women, seem foundational for the new society and the mainspring of the revolution' (Flach et al., 2016, 63).

It is a commonly maintained idea among PKK supporters that the organization was accepted by the population due to 'the way they sat down and stood up'. This refers to their everyday behavior and habits, manifested in their lack of material values and statuses (including property, sexual relations, family and marriage), twenty-four-hour dedication, and open hostility to Kurdish landlords that were exploiting the rural population and workers. All this left the impression that the PKK are the politicized and brave children of the ordinary and poor people of Kurdistan. The expectations and perceptions of the cadres and guerrilla are especially articulated in contrast to classical Kurdish political leaders or tribal chiefs who symbolize traditional institutions of legitimacy, loyalty and power, and who live in wealth and comfort at the expense of the population (Westrheim, 2008).

Öcalan personally gave many seminars to thousands of ordinary Kurds, especially women, in Syria and was in direct dialogue with the community (see also Demir, 2015). This, combined with his availability to the common people, left a strong impression on the population and shaped their idea of leadership. Stories of encounters with Öcalan are remembered fondly and are gladly shared throughout Rojava. The fact that the PKK practiced what they preached asserted credibility among the skeptical population, but also made them subject to direct scrutiny by the community, which in turn established a mutual system of accountability and responsibility.[2]

Among the women who joined the PKK from Rojava is Zaxo Zagros, member of the executive board of the KCK, based in the Qandil Mountains. She points to the importance of women becoming active in political activities for the first time upon Öcalan's arrival. Before, only men were involved in the public sphere in Rojava.

> At first, the cadres appeared elitist, but while the population was becoming militant, the cadres were becoming more communal. Women were more receptive and supportive of the cadres than men. They opened their doors to the PKK, sometimes in spite of their families. This influenced family relations. Before, there was the impression that only men could be heroes. But masculinity changed over time, what it means to be man and woman – these concepts were questioned.

The man was forced to change due to discussions with the cadres he highly respected, Öcalan's full support for women, as well as through the increasing strength of women, even those in his own house. Hanîfe Husen, coordinating member of Tev-Dem, told me:

> Previously, Kurdish politics in Rojava was characterized by classical parties or by cultural activities.[3] With the PKK, a revolutionary culture arrived. People saw a contrast between the traditional Kurdish parties and the PKK. They were the children of the poor, they had no personal wealth and they were modest. They ate and slept in ordinary people's homes. Women became involved in all kinds of activities; a questioning of male domination began. This philosophy became a culture. The immaterial rewards of this relationship by far exceeded the material. The PKK embraced the community in Rojava and the people protected the PKK in turn. We see the fruits of that time in today's revolution. An organized society is stronger than an atom. We are implementing radical democracy in Rojava today. And this is the project of Abdullah Öcalan.

Naifa Assad was married at the age of fourteen and is now a grandmother and one of the three coordinators of one of the mala jin[4] in Qamishlo. In her late twenties, she visited Öcalan in the Bekaa Valley, Lebanon, with her children and is one of the hundreds, perhaps thousands of 'traditional' women, previously trapped at home, to participate in Öcalan's educations. 'We always say: our women's revolution started with the arrival of Serok Apo[5] in Rojava.'

It is crucial to realize that while the PKK's presence had a big impact on Rojava's population, in turn, two decades of living intimately with the community was also an educational experience for the PKK and shaped cadres' understanding of socio-economic, psychological conditions and internalized mentalities of colonized and oppressed poor people from a traditional context. Conditioned by constant humiliation, degradation, uprooting and loss of historicity, the Kurd, for a meaningful revolution, had to above all be elevated to the status of human. The PKK's approach vis-à-vis its popular base is one with an explicitly 'humanizing' intention, as is evident from early party writings on the need for ethical militancy, which must be considerate of the character of the oppressed Kurd as a sociological phenomenon. Öcalan's description of 'the Kurd' in many ways resembles Frantz Fanon's phenomenology of 'the native'. It is possible to say, as Kariane Westrheim does, that 'the PKK movement proclaims the pedagogy of hope in a Freirian sense' (Westrheim, 2008).

This emotional attachment of the population to the cadres and to Öcalan checked the power relations between the organization and its social base. It laid the groundwork for a paradigm shift away from a hierarchical understanding of power, concentrated in the hands of a state or cadre party, in favor of popular forms of self-management by the community and a new concept of independence, which does not perpetuate statehood, borders and nationalism but draws on self-sustainability and direct, participatory democracy.

Building a non-state polity: forming a revolutionary identity

Although the scope of this chapter does not permit an in-depth discussion of Öcalan's thoughts, especially of the roots of civilization, the emergence of the city-state, its impact on gender relations and its relation to capital, it is notable that his thought focuses especially on the role of ideology in the architecture of certain mentalities that legitimize systems of domination, subjugation and oppression. Thus, he pays special attention to the roles played by mythology, religion, philosophy and science in the human being's interpretation of the world and the implications thereof for freedom (Öcalan, 2015).

Expressing his deep devastation concerning a geography, wherein thousands of years ago the cult of the mother-goddess shaped the social life of the first cultures in the Neolithic age, could then become the site of women's systematic elimination and degradation, he holds that it is crucial to track the ways in which notions of private property, centralist administration through power concentration, and male domination – in other words, today's capitalism, (nation-)statism and patriarchy – were able to establish themselves and each other. Thus, perpetuating yet another nation-state, even if it is a Kurdish one, would only benefit the elites.

An alternative system of self-governance, 'Democratic Confederalism', based on the direct participation of the community through local communes with committees, councils, cooperatives and academies is envisaged to generate a meaningful concept of self-determination. This concept goes beyond the idea of independence in the sense of the state, especially if, as KCK executive committee member and PKK co-founder Duran Kalkan states: 'The state is a system, to be a state means to be a part of the system. This means dependence and collaboration. Small states are dependent on larger states, and they are all dependent on the state system. It is very clear that the state cannot be free and independent. The statist paradigm has no room for independence and freedom.' Such a conceptualization of the state as inherently anti-democratic necessarily contradicts postcolonial projects of 'catching up' with the rest of the world by creating yet another modern nation-state. If the state per se is likened to colonialism, decolonization then means not to resist the existing colonialists or postcolonial nation-states, but to overcome the state as a system altogether. It is therefore telling that the defining factor for freedom, according to the PKK, is women's liberation, as women are considered to be 'the oldest colony'. Öcalan has refereed to feminism as the 'uprising of the first colony'.

Instead of standardized measures to implement social control over an obedient society, conditioned by labor, violence and official ideology, enabled by coercion, intimidation and force, the model of 'Democratic Autonomy' uses direct action to articulate new understandings of independence and freedom through voluntary pre-figurative, spontaneous, creative and diverse modes of political action, emancipated from statism. The idea of politics here is radically different from Marxism–Leninism's high modernist ideas of a state socialism that would render politics redundant. Instead, politics means the seizure of the means to self-organize, self-sustain, and self-defend.

> It is very important not to equate political force with state power. Politics cannot be equated with power and its institutionalised form, the state. Freedom is in the nature of politics. ... The stronger the politics in a society or nation, the weaker the state and ruling powers. The opposite is also true: the stronger the state or ruling power is in a society or nation, the weaker the politics – and hence freedom – in that society.
>
> (Öcalan, 2016, 37)

This understanding shifts the location of power and legitimacy away from centralized administrative systems in favor of communal and popular mechanisms of self-management through everyday politics while re-articulating the very meaning of politics. Akkaya and Jongerden (2012, 11) assert that the PKK's new project 'is drawing a new agenda for self-determination, while simultaneously going beyond the concept of the nation-state.'

In this sense, the Kurdish freedom movement does not analyse the nation-state merely as a political institution, concretized in the form of the existing nation-states, but also as a culture, a mentality, and an 'organization of violence' (Öcalan, 2016, 15). Note the emphasis on the state as a mentality in the words of KCK co-president and PKK co-founder Cemil Bayik:

> The state is more than a mere political institution—it is insinuated into people's consciousness as a mentality, so that the idea of developing a new political model for the Middle East, one that redresses social ills, seems impossible. But consciousness is the only force that can implement a political model. A mentality that remains enmeshed in the hegemonic state will never be capable of solving the region's social problems. By contrast, an ethical mentality, one that strives for freedom, holds immense promise, for it is embedded in communal lifeways.
>
> (Flach et al., 2015, 15)[6]

Nationalism, as the 'religion of the nation-state', therefore has a toxic effect on peaceful coexistence and ought to be replaced with alternative concepts of belonging. To make sure that this local orientation does not translate into parochial, inward-looking or even nationalist outlooks, the grassroots structures relate to each other in a confederal manner and are held together by a set of common values, such as women's liberation, multiculturalism and ecology.

The 'Democratic Nation' concept is Öcalan's attempt at proposing a new imaginary for a sense of social and political cohesion and identity that does not copy the power institutions of the nation-state but stands in flat opposition to it. Rather than justify its existence through an ethnically defined mythical past or glorious future vision, which is the tradition of nationalism, the character of the Democratic Nation is founded on a 'moral-political society'. This 'moral-political society' derives its existence through its ethics-based commitment to social justice, sustainability and equality. Such a society, in order to survive, must have a political character which does not submit its willpower to elites through means of voting and representative politics. This in turn, in a Freirian sense, means political literacy, consciousness and action.

Unlike the PKK's former Marxist-Leninist approach of viewing capitalism as inevitable for the development of socialism and the state as the crucial tool to establish a socialist society, as evident in the 1978 foundational manifesto (Öcalan, 1993), the current paradigm is centered on organizing the community's direct self-determination with the communes as the most fundamental unit and method of democracy. No longer are patriarchy, capitalism or the state viewed as 'fate', as their analysis of history takes a critical approach on hierarchy and domination beyond economic reductionism. As Murray Bookchin claims, 'The emphasis of anarchist and libertarian utopists on choice in history created a radical new point of departure from the increasingly teleological visions of religious and later "scientific" socialisms' (Biehl and Bookchin, 1999, 151). Rather than aiming at exercising efficiency, standardized order, and control over citizens in the statist manner, the point of the grassroots structures is to provide politics with a radically democratic, creative and inclusive character. The commune in Kurdistan is therefore the proactive choice of the consciously and ethically acting, political society to reject the capitalist nation-state and actively defend itself against it.

In this first section, after roughly portraying the historical relationship of Rojava to the PKK, I have outlined the PKK's ideological stance vis-à-vis politics and the state. The next part will consider the ways in which this anti-statist paradigm is reflected in the political practice of everyday life in Rojava.

Radical democracy and women: undoing the state

Elaborating on the history of the Kurdish women's resistance would exhaust the limits of this chapter (see Anja Flach, 2007). But it shall suffice for our purposes here to state that the PKK's paradigm shift away from the state in favor of Democratic Confederalism directly resulted in the strengthening of the autonomous women's system within the movement. Rather than considering women's liberation as a side effect of a perceived general liberation, the Kurdish freedom movement turned it into its core principle or its 'line', as democracy's guarantor and very method. With the deepening of the state critique, and the exposure of the links between state and patriarchy, the mobilization for the dismantling of male domination was accelerated dramatically.

When I interviewed Gulan Gulveda, a YJA Star (PKK's autonomous women's army) guerrilla, her emphasis on the links between different forms of violence and domination was clear:

> In the PKK, there is a return to this oldest of societies, this humanity created by women, which has not died for thousands of years, although it has been claimed to have been suffocated. It is a return to the mother. A return to freedom.[7] The PKK broke these ancient chains. Something that had been nearly eradicated flourished again. For instance, in the Middle East, the relationship of women and men is the first/oldest point connecting all forms of inequality, slavery, and unfreedom. The first oppressed class, the first instance of enslavement happened within this relationship. Everything started there. That is why the solution must be found there as well. In the ideological leadership of Abdullah Öcalan, our women's liberation ideology, and the PKK in general, we say that woman is life. It was fundamental for woman to participate in politics, in revolution, in the fight. She has gained personality, identity. The Kurdistan

> women's revolution created a very active woman in all fields of life, in politics, in the streets. The woman created herself through her own identity. It is the opposite of the patriarchal, hegemonic, monstrous mentality. It is of course difficult to accept, but just as defeating a mentality like ISIS means for a community to learn how to govern itself, to break the chains of domination among all nations, to break the chains of power in one's own brain, it also means to break this male dominated mentality.

Gulan Gulveda was martyred in November 29, 2016, killed by the Turkish state. KCK co-president Cemil Bayik believes that women's liberation is the guarantor of revolution:

> The fact that the Rojava Revolution places women in the foreground guarantees both its survival and its sustainability. Historically the rise of patriarchy was closely tied to the emergence and development of systems of centralized domination. But such centralized systems negate life.
>
> (Flach et al., 2015, 20)[7]

The Democratic Self-Administration (DSA) of Rojava, which announced 'Democratic Federalism for Rojava-Northern Syria' (DFNS) in the spring of 2016 after the three cantons had been announced in January 2014, consists of a complex governmental system that accommodates interests across parties, ideologies and communities. The Democratic Autonomy system from below is facilitated by the Movement for a Democratic Society, Tev-Dem. The former can be characterized as representative, the latter as participatory, direct democracy, and the two reinforce or challenge each other whenever appropriate. Nazan Üstündağ explains that:

> the relationship between the canton government and assemblies is conceived not in terms of representation but in terms of self-defense. In other words, the primary aim is not to achieve the representation of assemblies in the government, although that could be the case. Rather, assemblies, academies, and communes will be the means by which localities maintain their autonomy against canton governments, unmake the latter's claims to state-ness, and eventually appropriate their functions, proving them redundant.
>
> (Üstündağ, 2016, 203)

Central to Rojava's re-articulation of politics is the decentralization of power monopolies by creating democratizing mechanisms such as the communes that can sometimes even serve as internal oppositions to the administration.

For women, the DSA provided an atmosphere of gender equality in all of its mechanisms via legal and structural principles in favor of women as well as strict bans on patriarchal behavior and conduct including the criminalization of violence against women.[8] The preface of women's laws that address topics like violence and abuse, inheritance, divorce, economy, etc. and which were issued by women in 2014, states that 'The burden of the responsibility for the struggle against the logic of male domination rests on the shoulders of every individual in democratic autonomous Rojava' (Demir, 2015, 63).

Yet, it is in the sphere of the communes and councils in which women's participation in the new social and political system extracts the power to transform the society, beyond bureaucratic rights and mechanisms. Not only do women empower themselves and each other through institutionalized solidarity, they also convince the men of their abilities through direct action.

Although women's political activism in Rojava started in the early 1980s with the PKK's arrival, the revolution, starting in July 2012, for the first time enabled open and free action. Yekitiya Star, the women's umbrella movement of Rojava, illegally held its first congress in 2005. In February 2016, one of the decisions at its assembly was to transform itself into a congress (Kongra Star) in order to be more inclusive. The different committees of Kongra Star include: social, political, councils and ecology, self-defense, women's justice, communal economy, culture and art, education and academies, press, democratic relations and alliances. There are different groups, organizations, communes, assemblies, etc. that are affiliated to Kongra Star, while maintaining their autonomy. In its self-description, Kongra Star states:

> Beginning with Rojava and Syria, Kongra Star aims to realize the Women's Revolution across the Middle East. ... Struggling against patriarchy and the given family structure, it aims for the free-union of woman and man and a democratic family based on mutual will. With the free joint-life perspective it aims to overcome, beginning with relations between woman and man, all forms of domination, power, ownership and sexism to unearth the free society founded on a free and joint life.[9]

In every city and village, Kongra Star is represented and closely engaged with the mala jin, which are 'women's houses' that support women escaping violence or seeking shelter, divorce, economic or social support. All activists of Kongira Star must be members of their local communes, which the former defines as 'the moral and political society's and radical democracy's fundamental organizations and decision-making bodies at the street, village and local levels.'[10]

The first people's council structures were formed in 2011 in Rojava (Flach et al., 2015, 134). These start from the neighborhood and go to the levels of village/town, district, cantons, and the federal unit. The women of each commune or council also create their autonomous women's communes and councils, which are not accountable to any men, but can veto the mixed structures' decisions.

In 2012, then Yekitiya Star's economics commission decided to create economy commissions for every city, which have ever since created autonomous women's cooperatives in areas like textiles, small businesses, cheese-making and agriculture, with special support for women who have lost their families and are socio-economically vulnerable (Flach et al., 2016, 200). In 2016 alone, more than 100 new cooperatives have been created across Rojava, including agricultural initiatives run by women only.

Hundreds of initiatives and projects in the field of education, health, politics, culture, arts, sports, defense and economy are supposed to contribute to facilitating women's lives, including academies, kindergartens, training and research centers, media organs, and culture projects, since 2012. Women's centers, which while functioning partly as shelters, are also understood as sites of political consciousness raising, education and empowerment. WarJin is a long-term project of establishing an autonomous women's village, designed, created and administered by women, who, for whatever reason, prefer to live in women-only environments.

From the beginning, non-Kurdish women, especially Arabs and Syriacs joined the armed ranks and administration in Rojava. They organize together as well as separately. Cross-community solidarity projects among the women are increasing and in fact, a lot of the friendly relations between different communities are owed to the women's movement.

Almost all the women whom I spoke to in Rojava, from commune members to cooperative workers to politicians to journalists to fighters, stressed the dramatic changes that have happened in their personal lives since 2012. While criticizing the prevailing patriarchal attitudes of men and society, all of them emphasized the immense difference from their previous containment to the four walls in their homes and male chauvinistic attitudes that kept them in a one-dimensional state of being, as someone's wife, lover, sister, mother or daughter. Women perceive the revolution as an opportunity to be their own agent and subject, without defining one's identity in relation to a man.

I met women who previously were not able to look out their window who are coordinators of their mala jin today, helping other women to emancipate themselves from abusive husbands. Elderly women without formal education have become respected peace-makers in their neighborhood, co-presidents[11] of councils and municipalities, graduates of academies and even know how to handle AK 47s. Young women in their teenage years chose to be film-makers, economists, artists, athletes and even head academics. Some women live their dream of never getting married and feel like responsible members of their community and sustain themselves in cooperatives. Others joined the armed forces and broke the taboo of women reclaiming the ruling symbol of the male. In the words of Arzu Demir:

> Rojava is where the veterinary becomes a chief medic, an old woman with lots of children becomes the judge of a people's court, a housewife becomes a commander in the YPJ (Women's Defense Units), a young woman becomes the head of an academy – in short, where "everyone is everything". [...] Rojava is where the "ordinary" people become "heroes", and where "heroism" becomes "ordinary".
>
> (Demir, 2015, 10)

In everyday conversations in the homes and in public spheres, the strength of the women's movement is considered to be the most successful achievement of Rojava. Whenever I asked men about their views on the women's movement, their answers expressed pride and happiness, especially because they believed this element stressed their difference to other experiences of revolution. Of course, it is possible that these statements do not necessarily reflect their honest thoughts or personal behaviors, but the very fact that men today are in a position in which they know that a commitment to gender equality is a precondition for the new social system and a requirement for political participation, shows that women's liberation has established itself as an undeniable pillar of Rojava's revolution, despite the challenges in the present and future.

Education as self-defense

Far more than 'education', the word 'perwerde', as used in the Kurdish freedom movement, detonates consciousness-raising, politicization and self-reflection rather than formal education, and it is omnipresent in all areas of life in Rojava. As Kînem, a female member of the coordination of the asayîş academy in Rimelan stresses, without a fundamental challenge to the dogmatic authoritarian culture of surveillance, obedience and fear, it is impossible to make fighters and the general population not repeat the harm previously inflicted on them, physically or verbally, especially considering that many of them have been completely traumatized by oppression, war and destruction and thus may be seeking power and revenge.

It is difficult to raise society's consciousness, especially when internalized colonized mindsets are coupled with war conditions, embargoes and deprivation. Power abuses and apolitical mindsets are likely realities. Öcalan believes that one of the failures of Marxism was its inability to raise worker's consciousness in preparation of uprising: 'One of the biggest errors of the Marxian method was that the proletariat, who were already under daily oppression and exploitation, were expected to bring about the new societal construction without the necessary mental revolution having been initiated' (Öcalan, 2015, 40).

Earlier, I explained how education was one of the first and most important activities of the PKK in Rojava. The emphasis on education implied that blaming a perceived Other, a state, an enemy, capitalism, etc., for one's misery leads to self-victimization where one neglects the importance of personal responsibility for empowerment. Self-reliance requires political will and consciousness. Political literacy is a self-defense mechanism against the state and authority. It is a fundamental criterion for democracy. To re-make the self to give up internalized oppression, hierarchical and authoritarian thinking and practices and to develop a free personality become important aspects of the democratization of society.

Although pre-war Syria's literacy rates were relatively high,[12] it is crucial to recognize that the educational system at the time was based on a racist discourse that glorified the Arab nation and denied the existence or importance of other cultures. Kurdish was illegal, as was any form of cultural activity that would express identity. Nazan Üstündağ described how this is perceived as having created a certain character type – 'alienated and self-interested' (Üstündağ, 2016, 206). This is an explanation that I encountered often as well – the idea of the characterless personality rendered without will due to severe intimidation and repression. Zaxo Zagros explains the psychological dimensions of the Arab nationalist and openly racist policies in the education system of Syria. In her view, the regime was after turning the population into agents of the state, while rendering them without will, especially by applying politics of secret service and fear. Violence was often used arbitrarily, while manipulative tactics were used on dissenting views to create an atmosphere of mistrust – everyone could be a spy, even your family member (see Harriett Allsopp, 2015). If the state constructs itself first in mentalities, the biggest revolution, then, is the one of the mind.

When I interviewed Narîn Afrîn, she did not want to speak about her role as a commander in the historic war in Kobane, but chose education as our topic instead. The reason why Kobane did not fall, in her assessment, was because of its political awareness. 'Someone who has no consciousness cannot resist. Education is an act of raising consciousness, to become aware of oneself, to ask oneself, "How is it I ought to live? How can I organize?" Every education creates a certain type of human. Education is self-defense.'

In Rojava, an alternative education system, in the form of academies aims to promote revolutionary values, especially gender equality and coexistence, while self-organization practically reproduces a conscious society by mobilizing it in all spheres of life and encouraging self-sustainability and political expression. As Flach et al. note, the academies are 'centres of "people's education"' which require 'changing educational methods, the use of buildings and tools, and even daily life at academies, based on sharing and companionship' (Flach et al., 2016, 181). Central to this perspective is the valuing and writing down of local knowledge and the re-reading of history from the view of those who have been excluded from it. The creation of countless academies in areas like women, youth, art, culture, economics, politics, diplomacy, film, social sciences, law, health, etc. is an attempt to decentralize knowledge and education for all ages, especially as a standard education system is simultaneously being created at the federal level.

At the same time, a new federal system is being set up for children with the commitment to promote gender equality and multiculturalism. Children are instructed in their respective native languages and later on pick a 'language of the neighboring community'. In order to encourage tolerance and cosmopolitanism, teachers, for instance, take their students on trips to different places of worship.

I had the opportunity to spend a week in the Ishtar women's academy in Rimelan and participate in an ongoing month-long education for women working in the area of justice and peace-making. Among them were commune members, mala jin workers and legally-trained lawyers, the youngest in her early twenties, the oldest in her sixties. While cooking, sleeping, cleaning and celebrating together, they discussed the role of communes, democratic confederalism, ecology, women's history, self-defense, democratic nation, among many other topics. Every night, different women held night watches. The purpose of these educations is to make the population understand the new system and politics in general. Topics like education and democratic nation are communicated pedagogically in a way that speaks to the life experiences of the participants, and special care is placed on the use of accessible language.

Following a suggestion by Öcalan, the women are developing the concept of 'jineolojî' (jin: Kurdish for 'woman') as a new approach for a science of women and life (Öcalan, 2009b, 318). In the academies that are open to all, which also give seminars to men, questions like 'How to re-read and re-write women's history? How is knowledge attained? What methods can be used in a liberationist quest for truth, when today's science and knowledge productions serve to maintain the status quo?' arise in intensive discussions. The deconstruction of patriarchy and other forms of subjugation, domination and violence are accompanied by discussions on the construction of alternatives based on liberationist values and solutions to freedom issues. In the words of Narîn Afrîn: 'Our education focuses very much on how to analyze power. We do not just want to analyze something, we also want to propose solutions.'

Twenty-year-old Nujîn is one of the students at the Mesopotamia Academy for Social Sciences, which was founded in September 2014 in Qamishlo.[13]

> The difference between the approach of the state towards education, which consisted of memorizing nationalist doctrines and forced us to deny our own identities, and our attitudes towards education is that we research and think for ourselves here. It is very exciting to interpret and try to understand our own communities and lives. Dissecting 5,000 years of patriarchy has given more meaning to my life.

As part of the philosophy of the academies, students can be teachers and teachers can be students at all times in an attempt to break the dichotomy and traditional hierarchies of learning. Knowledge is situated everywhere and needs to be constantly exchanged. Wisdom, experience, contemplation and reflections as results of internal struggles are valued more highly than book knowledge. I became a student of Nujîn's jineolojî class. A few years earlier, it would have been unthinkable to listen to a Kurdish-speaking self-confident woman in a previously regime-owned building that criminalized her language and identity, give a lecture to young men and women on women's history, patriarchy and the need for women's pioneership in the new society, at this time in the history of Syria.

The academy is critical of the role the profit-oriented social sciences play in the construction of injustice and politics of violence and exclusion today. Emphasis is put on discussing the value of sociology and history as methods of understanding social issues and resolving them. Thus, discussions on positivism, colonialist history-writing and patriarchal science paradigms are central parts of the curriculum. The mechanism of criticism and self-criticism are applied in the academy, where for instance, the person facilitating a class gets constructively criticized at the end of the session. The person who teaches today can be the student tomorrow, as the hierarchies between student and teacher blur. For a while, a woman in her seventies would recite traditional folk tales here, in an attempt to recover the knowledge that is hidden inside the community and which has historically been appropriated by capitalism and the state, in the name of positivism.

One important element, as Malik, a twenty-four-year-old teacher-student at the academy points out, is the fight against chauvinism and dogma. He refers to the system of 'criticism and self-criticism' especially, which is a tool to encourage internal transformation and revolutionary progress within individuals and in group dynamics. 'In what system is there the possibility to criticize? The silencing of dissent is one of the greatest coups to knowledge production and human emancipation.' He criticizes Hegel for being an apologist of the state and emphasizes the importance of the realization that history is alive and organic. Oppression is not fate. His fellow Xelîl, who studied English in Aleppo previously, is fascinated with ancient history and believes that analyses from a historical perspective can be liberating in the sense that they make us understand how mechanisms of domination gradually established and thus legitimized themselves consciously:

> We are embarrassed when we speak about 5,000 years of patriarchy. We should have raised our voice, we should have risen up. Dominant history writing belittles the Neolithic society and calls it primitive, but thousands of years ago, community was more ethical and centered around women. And now look what happened to the same geography. I am proud to listen to my female friends' classes.

Decentralizing justice and self-defense against militarism and hierarchical power

In many societies in the Middle East, tribal or religious law or customary values are superior to state-imposed ideas of law and justice. As with education and force, the grassroots movement holds the federal level in check to keep it from assuming state-like attributes in the area of justice, while the latter is responsible for outlining general principles by which to abide, while also accommodating different sections of society.

Rufind Xelef is one of the women who drafted the Charter of the Social Contract. She was formerly professionally trained as a lawyer and now serves on the legislative council of the Democratic Self-Administration. In order to achieve a 'moral-political society', the guiding principle for justice should be ethics rather than law, she claims. According to her, the Social Contract, published in January 2014, was a result of countless discussions in the communities and a six-months' long work meeting. Rufind is also one of the people who drafted the women's laws. In both cases, the communes and councils, women, different ethnic groups, religious leaders and youth were consulted in the process.

While I stayed at the Ishtar women's academy in Rimelan, to participate in the education I previously mentioned, I coincidentally had the chance to witness the ways in which such a process was taking place. A committee came to the academy one evening, and proposed that regulations be shared with the members of the education. Each bullet point was read out in Kurdish and Arabic and was afterwards discussed intensively. The women involved in this process were common women, some educated, some without any formal education, some of them mothers of several children, while others were young and unmarried. They all had the opportunity to criticize the content and express their concerns.

However, as Rufind stresses, laws on paper are secondary to society's internalization of certain principles. Many theorists of law and justice believe that the most superior form of justice is one that is universally valid and above all power hierarchies, overseeing a society and outlining behavioral conducts, often with a claim to morality, referencing ideas of equality through the 'blindness of justice'. But while a federalism-wide justice system operates, on the local level, it is the communes that are in charge of implementation. The first peace and consensus committees were formed underground in the 1990s (Flach et al., 2016, 164). Operating openly since 2011, these committees resolve cases of conflict, injustice and violence at the commune, street and neighborhood or village level through mediation. Rehabilitation is preferred over punishment. Women are the only ones in charge of issues related to women, such as domestic violence.

Other instances are the mala gel (people's house) and mala jin (women's house), which serve as sites of solving social issues and providing public services. Ilham, a mala jin coordinator in her sixties from Qamishlo, claims that 6,000 cases were resolved in this way within a year. In her mala jin in Qamishlo, 33 cases were solved in one month. According to Üstündağ, the Mesopotamia Law School claims that 90% of justice-related cases are resolved in community councils and the mala gel (Üstündağ, 2016, 207).

If the problems cannot be solved at these levels, people can go to the tribunals. These consist of a mix of lawyers, elders and peace-keeping committees of ordinary citizens. Rather than legal expertise, people who can adequately represent people's interests are appointed as rotating judges. For questions regarding women, especially violence, only women are in charge of justice. The fact that women are the only authors of law and the only decision-makers in the implementation of justice is a radical stance and to my knowledge, unique in the world. All workers in these areas go through education on the democratic autonomy system, women's liberation, ecology, the democratic nation, etc.

Conditioned to an idea of justice that is universal and hierarchical, executed by state and safeguarded by prisons, it is difficult to grasp the logic of 'communal justice'. Who would prevent power abuses and guarantee identical implementation of justice?

> In spite of the declaration of the social contract, the state logic prevails among many of us. Drafting a social contract is not easy. Questions like "Who gives you rights?" are difficult to answer, especially for lawyers like me who struggle to unlearn memorized concepts and dogmatic ideas about states and justice. We think only those who have studied and got degrees in something are capable of deciding over and understanding things. It is difficult to think differently.

Rufind stresses that their justice concept is against the idea that one is victim and one is perpetrator. Dogmatism and determinism are not compatible with ethics-based justice. That is why the theft by a rich person is handled differently from a poor person's motivation to steal; the community's conscience decides. She communicates why, for instance, in an atmosphere of violence and deprivation, it is not helpful to criminalize theft. Instead, if someone steals, she believes the administration must work harder to eliminate poverty. She also explains why sociology is important to solve issues of justice. While Dirbesiye, bordering Turkey, has a problem of drug trafficking, Derik (al-Malikiyah), bordering Iraqi Kurdistan, has become prominent for smuggling goods, whereas Qamishlo, the largest city, deals with human trafficking. All of these phenomena have socio-economic reasons and causes and therefore need to be addressed specifically.

The question of justice and legitimacy is connected to power and authority. If the premise of the revolution is to be 'not a state', what are the aesthetics of authority?

The Kurdish freedom movement's war conduct rests on the concept of 'legitimate self-defense' and includes establishing social and political grassroots mechanisms to protect society beyond narrow physical defense. In nature, living organisms such as roses with thorns develop their systems of self-defense not to attack, but to protect life. Abdullah Öcalan calls this the 'rose theory.' In order for society to similarly resist without being militarist, it must refrain from imitating state-like concepts of force and instead protect communalist values, deriving its power from the grassroots (Öcalan, 2012, 460ff).

The armed forces in Rojava, the People's Defense Units, YPG and the Women's Defense Units, YPJ, formed in January 2013, as well as the internal security units, asayîş, value ideological education and ethical conduct in war as crucial elements of warfare against hierarchy, control and domination in a very much militarized context. They believe this to be a reason for their military successes against ISIS. According to Mem, coordinating member of the asayîş academy in Rimelan, the purpose of the academies is to communicate to the fighters the different conditions pertaining to self-defense which emerges out of necessity due to the current conditions, and that the current state of war does not legitimize feelings of revenge or abuse. By filling half of the education in the academy with gender equality, including classes on women's resistance history, they intend to democratize the people who will be in charge of security as much as possible. Ideally, through necessary education, the 'moral-political' society should be able to mediate disputes and solve issues without the aid of an asayîş force. 'We want to struggle for a society with an asayîş without arms, who verbally mediate disputes in the neighborhoods with the ultimate aim of abolishing the asayîş altogether.'

The members of the academy actively reject being labeled as police and try to embody non-statism in their performance through behavioral conducts and principles. For instance, none of the asayîş are sent away for placement; instead, in order to keep their proximity to their community, they protect their own towns. The asayîş academy in Rimelan is part of a complex which was previously used as a secret service center of the Syrian regime among other functions. Among the students are people who have once been tortured by the regime in the same building. Üstündağ, who visited the same academy, writes that 'many of them mentioned that being in places and spaces where they had been humiliated and violated before was a constant reminder of what they did not want to become' (Üstündağ, 2016, 204). Two hundred meters away from the asayîş academy is the previously mentioned Ishtar women's academy as well as a literature academy for youth. All of these buildings were previously used by the regime's intelligence services and often hosted high-ranking guests of the Baath party. Today, the gardens have been turned into green areas with children; bomb shells in the women's academy are now used as flower pots.

Almost all adults of Rojava know how to handle a gun, even women well above their sixties. Militarization is an unwanted necessity, as YPJ/G fighters always stress.[14] It is important, they say, to make sure militarism, usually associated with hierarchy, power and violence, is not normalized. Commanders are elected by battalion members based on their experience, commitment and willingness to take responsibility. The hezên parastina cewherî HPC (Self-Defense Forces) are members of communes who normally are not fighters. They take turns in patrolling their neighborhoods. Üstündağ writes, 'While the YPG and YPJ are increasingly internationalizing themselves, the aim of the asayîş is to deeply localize itself' (Üstündağ, 2016, 205). In Tirbespiye, for instance, a relatively small town, the HPC are divided into four logical units, along neighborhood lines in order to keep safety communal and personal, rather than anonymous like the state.

The question of undoing statism and power is also reflected in the expectations of the representatives in the areas outside of the communes and councils. At the time I interviewed Hadiya Yussif, who is now the co-president of the administration of the Democratic Federalism of Northern Syria, she was the co-president of the Cizire canton. Unlike traditional politicians with bureaucratic personalities and no time for the ordinary, I came across her at least once a week during my entire stay. She was completely indistinguishable from the communities she was representing – washing dishes wherever she ate, playing with the children at community meetings, sleeping wherever she had to. I agree with Üstündağ that 'it is not only by means of organizational models but also through everyday enactments that the state is being unmade in Rojava' (Üstündağ, 2016, 208). As Rahila Gupta observes in her travelogues to Rojava: 'The humility and accessibility of people high up in the administration is an aspect of this egalitarian society which never fails to surprise me' (Gupta, 2016). In fact, this is part of the political culture established by the PKK in the early 1980s in Rojava.

The vast majority of people work voluntarily in Rojava. The fact that many of Rojava's achievements at the grassroots are owed to sacrifice (of time, money, energy, resources and ultimately health and life) establishes a silent but vital moral expectation among the people vis-à-vis the administration. Every member of the administration is thus forced to act in the consciousness that if they do not fulfill their duty of doing nothing but serve the people, they can be easily discarded by the people. This moral responsibility, supervised especially by martyrs' families, women, the poor and the youth, is a mechanism of checks and balances and a system of accountability which simply does not exist in the state system.

In this sense, previously monopolized institutions such as justice, education, power and violence are decentralized and thus democratized. Rather than the mere seizure of such means, the aim is to go as far as to create potential moments of tension within Rojava, in order to secure justice.

Conclusion

By providing examples from areas of everyday politics, including spheres such as force, education and justice, I tried to explain the ways in which the Democratic Autonomy project of Rojava tries to decentralize power and articulate new forms of legitimacy and authority through a new definition of politics, beyond the state. In the context of post-colonialism, this suggests a move away from established concepts of replicating the former colonial regimes, in favor of questioning the pillars of colonialism, by deepening the very idea of the colony through locating it in the very concept of the state as a system. This seems reminiscent of Fanon's call to reject European models on the road to humanity's liberation, as 'we must turn over a new leaf, we must work out new concepts, and try to set afoot a new man' (Fanon, 1963, 255) (and woman!).

It is already evident that Rojava's emergence opened a refreshing dialogue among theorists and activists alike. Its experiment with radical democracy defies the state-normativity of conventional understandings of international relations by deriving its legitimacy and creating its identity from an alternative set of values and by re-articulating the meaning and location of power. The nature of the politics that inform the ongoing revolution of Rojava, its self-conception as a democracy without a state, and its ideological, legal and political stance and practice on issues like capitalism, patriarchy, state, religious fundamentalism and nationalism, made it a difficult case for analysts of geopolitical affairs, who are conditioned to utilize nations, states, hegemony and hierarchical power models as referents to make sense of political behavior and the international order and affairs.

Rojava puts self-defense against security paradigms, communal justice above law, ecology over capitalism, democratic nation and people's diplomacy against nationalism, communes over states, women's solidarity above traditional gender norms, and establishes decentralized institutions for politics, defense, justice and education. And most importantly, the revolutionary principles of this liberation process are safeguarded by women.

Bibliography

Akkaya, A. H., and Jongerden, J., 2012. 'Reassembling the Political: The PKK and the Project of Radical Democracy', *European Journal of Turkish Studies*, Vol. 14.

Allsopp, H., 2015. *The Kurds in Syria: Political Parties and Identity in the Middle East*. London: I.B. Tauris & Co. Ltd.

Besikci, I., 1990. *Devletlerarası Sömürge Kürdistan*. Istanbul: Alan Yayıncılık.

Biehl, J. (ed.), Bookchin, M. (author), 1999. *The Murray Bookchin Reader*. Montreal, PQ: Black Rose Books.

Demir, A., 2015. *Devrimin Rojava Hali*. Istanbul: Ceylan Yayinlari.

Fanon, F., 1963. *The Wretched of the Earth*. London: Penguin Books.

Flach, A., 2007, *Frauen in der kurdischen Guerrilla: Motivation, Identität und Geschlechterverhältnis in der Frauenarmee der PKK*. Cologne: Papy Rossa.

Flach, A., Ayboga, E., Knapp, M., 2015. *Revolution in Rojava: Frauenbewegung und Kommunalismus zwischen Krieg und Embargo*. Hamburg: VSA.

Flach, A., Ayboga, E., Knapp, M., 2016. *Revolution in Rojava: Democratic Autonomy and Women's Liberation in Syrian Kurdistan*. London: Pluto Press.

Graeber, David, 2011. *Debt: The first 5,000 years*. New York: Melville House Printing.

Gupta, R., 2016. *Rojava's Commitment to Jineolojî: The Science of Women*. Available at https://www.opendemocracy.net/rahila-gupta/rojava-s-commitment-to-jineoloj-science-of-women [Accessed 01.02.2017].

Kurdish Institute of Brussels, 2017. Rojava-Kurdistan and Northern Syria: A New Life Style - Trajectory of Events in 2016. Brussels: Kurdish Institute of Brussels.

Öcalan, A., 1993. *Kürdistan Devriminin Yolu*. Cologne: Agri Verlag.

—— 2009a. *Kapitalist Uygarlik*. Neuss: Mesopotamya Verlag.

—— 2009b. *Özgürlük Sosyolojisi*. Neuss: Mesopotamya Verlag.

—— 2010. *Jenseits von Staat, Macht und Gewalt*. Cologne: Mesopotamien Verlag.

—— 2011. *Democratic Confederalism*. Cologne: Transmedia Publishing.

—— 2012. *Kürt Sorunu ve Demokratik Ulus Cözümü*. Neuss: Mesopotamya Verlag.

—— 2013. *Liberating Life: The Women's Revolution*. Cologne: Transmedia Publishing.

—— 2015. *Manifesto for a Democratic Civilization Volume I: Civilization – The Age of Masked Gods and Disguised Kings*. Porsgrunn: New Compass Press.

—— 2016, *Democratic Nation*. Cologne: Transmedia Publishing.

Üstündağ, N., 2016. 'Self-Defense as a Revolutionary Practice in Rojava, or How to Unmake the State'., *South Atlantic Quarterly* 115 (1). Durham: Duke University Press.

Westrheim, K., 2008. *Education in a Political Context: A Study of Knowledge Processes and Learning Sites in the PKK*. Bergen: University of Bergen.

Notes

1 My observations and interviews are results of my fieldwork in Rojava briefly in 2014 and for a longer period in the summer of 2015.

2 Harriet Allsopp gives a detailed overview of Kurdish political party activity in Syria from 1957 up to the Syrian revolution and briefly mentions the PKK's role in transforming tribal mentalities and influence in Rojava and its ability to mobilize wide sections of the population, compared to the classical parties (Allsopp, 2015, 141). She confirms that no women were in leading positions in any of the other political parties, but otherwise does not mention women throughout her entire book, although thousands of Rojava women joined the PKK and even more have engaged in illegal political activities in support of the PKK since the 1980s, while today, Rojava's most remarkable element is women's leadership.

3 See Allsopp, 2016.

4 Women's house, see next section.

5 'Leader Apo'; Apo is an abbreviation of Abdullah and nickname used for Öcalan.

6 The first recorded word for the concept of freedom emerged in ancient Sumer in the 3rd millennium BC. "Amargi" means freedom, as well as return to the mother (David Graeber, 2011, 65).

7 Translated from German by Janet Biehl.

8 Translated from German by Janet Biehl.

9 It was one of the first decisions of the early Kurdish umbrella organization in 2012 in Rojava to ban child and forced marriage, bride price and bride exchange and to criminalize domestic violence, especially honor killings. On the Democratic Self-Administration level, article 27 of the Charter of the Social Contract states that 'Women have the inviolable right to participate in political, social, economic and cultural life'; the next article actively commits to the elimination of gender inequality: 'Men and women are equal in the eyes of law. The Charter guarantees the effective realization of equality of women and mandates public institutions to work towards the elimination of gender discrimination'. This commitment to equality within a secular framework is important, especially considering that Shar'ia courts are legitimate for all citizens of the Syrian Arab Republic, alongside a secular legal system, and deal with issues of personal status and rights such as marriage, property, inheritance, etc. The account of one male witness in court was equal to two women's accounts under Shar'ia law. In Rojava, on 8 March 2014, international women's day and a month after the

declaration of the autonomous cantons, a women's legislative committee was formed to draft women's laws written by women, which are also to be implemented and enforced by women only.[215]

10 Kongra Star brochure, 2016.

11 Kongra Star brochure.

12 Another mechanism of democratizing further the alternatives that are being constructed as democratizers to the status quo system is the co-presidency principle that was introduced by the Kurdish freedom movement in 2013, which splits power equally between one woman and one man. Only women get to choose the female co-president. Beyond providing women and men with equal decision-making power, the co-chair concept aims to decentralize power, prevent monopolism and promote consensus-finding. From the smallest commune to the level of federalism, the co-presidency system has been fully established in Rojava. Nobody can challenge women's autonomous decisions, but the women's structures can veto or boycott the general structures.

13 See UNICEF report on the Syrian Arab Republic: http://www.unicef.org/infobycountry/syria_statistics.html.

14 The building was created by the Baath regime in 2011 as a private university, but never put to use, since the war began immediately afterwards. No institutions of higher education existed in the predominantly Kurdish areas of Syria previously, the closest university being in al-Hasakah. This meant that young Kurds who wanted to pursue higher education had to travel to and live in cities like Damascus and Aleppo, which served the Arabization policies of the state to assimilate the educated Kurds.

15 The Sutoro are the equivalent of the asayish, while the MFS, the Syriac Military Council, defends the border areas along with the YPG and YPJ, and in October 2015 became part of the Syrian Democratic Forces. While Christian women were members of the asayish and YPJ early on, in 2015, they decided to organize themselves autonomously in the MFS and Sutoro and established the Bethnarin Women's Protection Units.

20
THE POSTCOLONIAL COMPLEX IN OKINAWA

Eiichi Hoshino

Introduction

Thank you, Mr. Chair. I am Takeshi Onaga, governor of Okinawa Prefecture, Japan. I would like the world to pay attention to Henoko where Okinawans' right to self-determination is being neglected. After World War 2, the U.S. Military took our land by force, and constructed military bases in Okinawa. We have never provided our land willingly. Okinawa covers only 0.6% of Japan. However, 73.8% of U.S exclusive bases in Japan exist in Okinawa. Over the past seventy years, U.S. bases have caused many incidents, accidents, and environmental problems in Okinawa. Our right to self-determination and human rights have been neglected. Can a country share values such as freedom, equality, human rights, and democracy with other nations when that country cannot guarantee those values for its own people? Now, the Japanese government is about to go ahead with a new base construction at Henoko by reclaiming our beautiful ocean ignoring the people's will expressed in all Okinawan elections last year (2014). I am determined to stop the new base construction using every possible and legitimate means. Thank you very much for this chance to talk here today.

(Mr. Takeshi Onaga, Governor of Okinawa,
UN Human Rights Council Meeting, Sept. 21, 2015)[1]

Okinawa, the islands located at the southernmost part of Japan, is a postcolonial complex. Okinawa is frequently framed as a victim of Japanese imperialism, alongside others such as Koreans, Chinese, and Taiwanese. Okinawan people now have full legal status in Japan, but they had much in common with Koreans and Taiwanese in the past (Hein and Selden, 2003). This, however, is only one layer of Okinawan history.

There are more layers of colonial history in Okinawa. Okinawa was once the Ryukyu Kingdom belonging to a Chinese tribunal system. Ryukyu was forcefully annexed to Japan in 1879 as a prefecture of Okinawa. Okinawa was deemed expendable in the Second World War for protecting the national polity under the emperor. The San Francisco Peace Treaty of 1951 legitimated the extension of the US occupation of Okinawa. The indigenous peoples in Okinawa have been repeatedly denied their right to 'free, prior and informed consent.' Even after the reversion of Okinawa in 1972, the excessive concentration of US bases causes a variety of human insecurities in Okinawa, such as serious crimes, accidents, and environmental problems, including noise pollution. These are the results of Japan's national security policy – a case in which a state becomes a threat to people's security.

These complex colonial pasts have left a variety of legacies in Okinawa today. It has had the lowest prefectural income for more than 40 years. Fiscal dependency on central government has persisted. People in Okinawa have been divided in terms of development policy and against discrimination. A majority of Okinawans raise their voices against the burden of US presence, while people are in a double-bind in terms of strategies to be liberated from the current situation: either through more assimilation into or more independence from Japan. There are a certain number of mainlanders who support Okinawan's struggles, while many others are indifferent to 'Okinawa issues' and, further, some look down on Okinawans as second-class citizens.

In order to build a new military base at Henoko, on the eastern side of the city of Nago in the North of Okinawa's main island, and to make Okinawans accept the enduring US presence, the central government utilizes a variety of instruments and colonial legacies for governing this postcolonial society. People in Okinawa were patient in fighting against 'compensation politics', and in 2014 the 'All Okinawa' coalition seemed to stand strong against Tokyo. The central government, however, did not listen to the voice of Okinawans, and now tries to crush Okinawan protests by explicitly utilizing repressive law enforcement, SLAPPs (Strategic Lawsuits Against Public Participation In Protesting) and lawsuits, based on a politics of divide and rule, with the tacit approval and indifference of people in the center. Still, Okinawans responded 'No' to the new base project in a variety of ways: seeking a proper democratic representation, raising voices, exercising rights, and searching for a semi- or even full detachment from Japan.

This chapter introduces the reader to a number of elements of the postcolonial complex in Okinawa. The first part unpacks the layers of Okinawan history and human insecurity caused by US presence; the second part investigates colonial legacies in Okinawa today; the third part explores the government's strategies for governing postcolonial society; and the fourth part turns to the on-going struggles in Okinawa's postcolonial complex.

Layers in colonial history of Okinawa

The Ryukyu Kingdom was an independent kingdom from the fifteenth to the early seventeenth century. It was a part of Chinese tribunal system, and had trading ties with Korea, Japan, and other Southeast Asian countries as well as China. In 1609, the Satsuma Domain of Tokugawa Japan invaded the kingdom with three thousand samurai forces and compelled Ryukyu to send tributes to the Tokugawa Shogunate and to pay taxes to Satsuma. The king and court continued under the Satsuma watchmen. McCormack and Norimatsu (2012) describe the Okinawa/Ryukyu of this period as a Potemkin-like theater state. Since Satsuma's intention was to squeeze Ryukyu of its profit from the tribute relationship to the Ming Chinese court, Satsuma wanted to conceal the fact that Ryukyu was in effect Japan's colony.

In March 1879, the Meiji Japanese government forcefully annexed Ryukyu as a prefecture of Okinawa. Shō Tai, the last king of the kingdom, was forced to relocate to Tokyo. The right to 'free, prior, and informed consent' was not respected. McCormack and Norimatsu (2012) called Okinawa an 'unrecognized colony.' People of the prefecture were forcefully assimilated and discriminated against as non-civilized peoples. The Japanese government introduced public education to Okinawa in order for them to become 'real Japanese.' The culture of Ryukyu, including language and religious practices, were to be eliminated (Uemura, 2003).

The Battle of Okinawa in 1945 was one of the last major battles of the Second World War. Some Okinawans fought alongside Japanese in order to become 'real Japanese', while many ran away from the Americans with Japanese armies when they withdrew to the south (McCormack and Norimatsu 2012). Over 300,000 people, not only American and Japanese soldiers, but also 120,000 local civilians, lost their lives. Okinawa was expendable in the war when it came to protecting the national polity under the emperor. Military strategy had nothing to do with protecting Okinawan people and everything to do with slowing down the US advance against mainland Japan (Hoshino 2016).

In Okinawa, memories of the war are symbolized by the words 'the military does not protect the people.' Being denounced as spies, being thrown out of caves, being forced to supply food, being provoked to commit 'group suicide' - these memories are a mirror which clearly reflects how the safety of Okinawans was sacrificed for the sake of state security (Hoshino 2016).

After landing on Okinawa, the US forces began to convert Japanese military bases into their own and to construct new ones. Even after Japan's surrender, they kept building new bases while they confiscated land at the point of a gun (Hoshino 2016). After the catastrophe of war, the Ryukyu Archipelago was governed by the United States. In 1952, the Government of the Ryukyu Islands was established, while US effective control of Okinawa continued until the reversion in 1972 (McCormack and Norimatsu 2012). Separation of Okinawa from Japan was suggested by the Emperor Hirohito in 1947 (Shindo, 1979), and the San Francisco Peace Treaty in 1951 legitimized the separation and the extension of US occupation. In ratification of the treaty, Okinawan had no representatives in Japan's national assemblies.

The Okinawa Reversion Agreement was signed between Tokyo and Washington in June 1971. Direct American control of the islands was given back to Japanese administration. Again, there was no representation of Okinawan people in Japan's congress when the Agreement was ratified. Okinawa became, under the terms of the US–Japan Security Treaty, the same as any other part of Japan in May 1972. Even after the reversion, however, the excessive concentration of military bases on the islands remained. McCormack and Norimatsu (2012: 8) conclude that 'the American military colony of Okinawa became the militarized, dual-colonial dependency of Japan and the United States.' The US military facilities occupy 10% of the area of the prefecture, and around 20% of the area of the main island of Okinawa Jima (Okinawa Prefectural Government, 2016).

The continuing US military presence causes a variety of human insecurities in Okinawa, and they give constant reminders of the traumatic episodes of the history of Okinawa's colonial complex. According to documents made public in May 2008, both the Japanese and US governments agreed in 1953 to overlook crimes by US military personnel if they were not of 'material importance' (Martin, 2011). In a 2001 paper concerning the Japan–US Status of Forces Agreement (SOFA), Dale Sonnenberg (International Law Department of the US Military in Japan) states that the consent was not public, but the Japanese side even today adheres to the agreement (*Ryukyu Shimpo*, Oct. 22, 2008).

In September 1995, three US servicemen abducted and gang-raped a twelve-year-old schoolgirl. Rape of the young girl prompted immediate powerful Okinawan responses, and 85,000 people gathered to protest at the Ginowan Seaside Park. In February 2008, a young Marine sexually assaulted a junior high school girl in his car, and then threw her out. The case led to a one-month curfew on all US service personnel in Japan, but two weeks later, there was an incident of rape of a Filipino woman by a member of the US Air Force. The number of crimes has fallen lately, while severe crimes are still occurring. In October 2012, a woman was sexually assaulted on her way home by two US navy soldiers on their way to Guam, who were sentenced to 9 to 10 years for robbery and group rape. In May 2016, a 20-year-old Okinawan woman's body, reduced to bones in a suitcase, was found by the roadside in On'na village. A former US Marine postal clerk, a military contractor on Kadena Air Force Base, was arrested for the rape and murder and reportedly admitted to the crime.

According to Okinawa Prefectural Police statistics featured in 'Okinawa's US Military and JSDF Bases,' criminal arrests made due to US military personnel between 1972 and 2016 amount to 5,919 cases – 576 of which being brutal crimes, including rape, and 1,067 of which being violent crimes. These crimes have had a considerable impact on the lives, livelihoods, and property of the Prefecture's residents (Okinawa Prefectural Government, 2017).

According to Okinawa Prefecture's statistics, there were 709 accidents involving US military aircraft (47 of which were crashes) during 1972 and 2016. Of these, as many as 181 incidents occurred outside of bases, causing great unrest among the citizens of Okinawa. Even in the 2000s, between 10 and 60 cases of aircraft-related accidents have occurred each year, setting the scene for the rise of the movement opposing the Osprey deployment (Okinawa Prefectural Government, 2017).

In August 2004, there was an accident in which a US military CH-53D helicopter crashed into the Okinawa International University campus. No life was lost, although many people recalled the children who died at Miyamori Elementary School in 1959. An *Okinawa Times* editorial pointed out important issues that went beyond the damage from the accident: 'Following the helicopter crash inside the Okinawa International University campus, the US military initially evicted local police and fire squads, and took control of the site. With regard to the rules of SOFA, this is a clear infringement of sovereign rights' (*Okinawa Times*, May 3, 2012). In September 2012, a meeting was held of local citizens in opposition to the deployment in Okinawa of new US military transport aircraft, MV-22 Osprey, and tens of thousands of participants gathered in Ginowan Seaside Park. The new-model transport aircraft, called a 'widow-maker', were to be deployed at Futenma, which the US Secretary of Defense Donald Rumsfeld referred to as 'the world's most dangerous base.'

In December 2016, a US Marine Corps MV-22 Osprey aircraft crashed into water near Henoko. It was the first major accident involving a MV-22 Osprey since it was deployed in the Futenma marine airfield in 2012. The accident injured two of the five crew members on board, and the commander of the US forces agreed to suspend flights of Osprey in Japan. The US military, however, fully resumed Osprey operations in Okinawa less than a week after the crash. Governor Onaga called the government's greenlighting of the flights 'outrageous' (*Japan Times*, Dec. 19, 2016).

One of the insecurities that people suffer in their living space and environment is noise pollution. In the areas surrounding Kadena and Futenma airbases, there is noise pollution from aircraft that exceeds the environmental standard levels determined by the Ministry of Environment (MoE). There are concerns about the effects on the daily lives and health of the areas' residents. Education is also being affected, with, for example, lessons frequently being interrupted at schools near the bases (Hoshino 2016).

Despite confirmation that these circumstances are illegal through a lawsuit on 'roaring' noise pollution, corrective measures have not been taken. In February 2017, the Okinawa branch of the Naha District Court ordered the central government to pay 30.2 billion yen in compensation to the 22,000 plaintiffs in the third Kadena 'Roaring' Noise Pollution case. The court, however, turned down a request by these residents to suspend night-time and early morning flights, stating that there was already judicial precedent in the Supreme Court of the Japanese government that it was not possible to interfere with US military flight drills (*Japan Times*, Feb. 23, 2017).

These issues provide an overview of 'human security' damages caused by the excessive US military presence in Okinawa. It is no surprise that negative opinions formed the majority of responses when residents of the prefecture were asked, 'What do you think should be done about the US bases within Okinawa Prefecture in the future?': 49% of respondents answered with 'reduction' and 37% of them with 'complete removal' (*Okinawa Times-Asahi Shimbun* Joint

Public Opinion Survey, 2012). Andrew Linklater (2005) indicates three cases in which a state becomes a threat to the security of the people, one of which being where immigrants, minorities, and original inhabitants may not receive protection according to the rule of law, or where they are not granted the political, economic, or social rights enjoyed by regular members of the state or territory. So it is, especially for the people living with complex colonial legacies.

Colonial legacies in Okinawa today

Colonialism can be defined as 'the forcible takeover of land and economy' (Loomba, 2015: 40), while colonial legacies not only ensue from the appropriation of wealth and obstruction of economic development, but also pertain to damages done in political, psychological, and cultural aspects. Since not only the colonized but also the colonizer are deeply altered by the colonial process, they are also restructured by the decolonization process (Loomba, 2015). The legacies of colonialism can be found at both the center and the periphery.

During the Satsuma period, Ryukyuan not only kept tribunal relations with both the Tokugawa's Edo and the Ming China's Beijing but also was forced to pay a heavy tax to Satsuma. After the Meiji government abolished the Ryukyu Kingdom and incorporated it as the Okinawa Prefecture, the economy of the islands was dominated by mainland Japanese. After the battle of Okinawa, under the US military rule, the currency called 'B-yen' was circulated in Okinawa. The US authority set a very high exchange rate for the B-yen: one US dollar was exchanged for 120 B-yen, or for 360 yen in mainland Japan. This led to today's composition of industry, because it was easier to import things rather than to put things into production. As a result, while the service industry alone has grown after the reversion, the manufacturing industry has been in poor shape, with primary and secondary industries in stagnation (Tominaga, 2003).

According to a prefectural public opinion survey by the *Okinawa Times* (2007), 85% of participants agreed with the following statement: 'There are various disparities between Okinawa and the mainland.' Further, when the participants were asked about what sort of disparities they were aware of, as many as 65% indicated economic disparities, including low income (48%), military base issues (24%), and unemployment (17%). Thus, Okinawa has been seen (and has seen itself) to be backward, in that its per capita GDP and other economic indexes have been below the rest of Japan, therefore it has had to 'catch up.' Even today, the 'closing the gap' slogan from the 1970s may be seen here and there in newspaper pages. Perhaps this demonstrates that a 'developmentalist' tendency remains strong among the people of Okinawa (Hoshino, 2016).

The prefecture's fiscal dependence on central government remains at a high level of 30–40%, showing an unchanging disparity with national levels (24% in 2009). The need for economic independence is strongly called for, while 'development' funds have been seen by state bureaucrats as the best device to foster the 'mendicant mentality' in which the anti-base and environmental movements would lose momentum. 'Development' therefore has tended to be concentrated on infrastructural public works projects that have often been economically retrogressive, ecologically damaging, and debt- and dependence-building (Hoshino, 2016).

People in Okinawa have been divided, in terms of development policy, into those who seek a more independent economic policy and those who prefer a type of economic management that is more dependent on the central government. The latter tends to sacrifice people's autonomy through cooperation with Tokyo's national security policy. Okinawans have also been divided, in terms of ending discrimination against them, into those who prefer political independence from the central government and those who seek to materialize democratic ideals for Okinawans as ordinary Japanese. The former is a small group today, while the voice for the right of self-determination is gaining more support these days.

Hechter (1975) also considered the division among people in an internal colony:

> In the Celtic lands, too, there arose clearly delimited positions for assimilation, on the one hand, and nationalism, on the other. In the early twentieth century, all of the Celtic peoples were torn between these alternatives as solutions to their internal problems: unemployment; poverty; powerlessness in the face of the central government; a sense of cultural inferiority.
>
> (Hechter 1975: xvii)

People in Okinawa are also divided, in terms of cultural identity, into those who identify themselves as Ryukyuan or Uchina'anchu (nationalism) and those who think of themselves as ordinary Japanese (assimilation). The rest have a double identity as both Ryukyuan and Japanese. According to Lim's survey (2007), 42% of respondents identify themselves as Okinawan, 26% of them as Japanese, and 30% of them as both Okinawan and Japanese. However, as Hall (1990) argued that since cultural identities undergo constant transformation, the divisions seen above are far from being fixed even in the near future.

People who identify themselves as ordinary Japanese tend to deny that most people living in Okinawa today are the indigenous people. They see connotations of backwardness and uncivilization in the status of indigeneity. This overlaps with Loomba's description of the colonized who, with the same view as nineteenth- and twentieth-century writers, 'equated the advance of European colonization with the triumph of science and reason over the forces of superstition' (Loomba, 2015: 41).

Since 'the colonial encounter had an impact on the psyche of both colonizer and colonized' (Krishna, 2014: 354), the psychological legacies for mainlanders represent the other side of the same coin as the psychological legacies for Okinawans: 'Colonialism demanded of the colonizer an immense effort to repress thoughts contrary to the enterprise of domination. It required unremitting faith in one's own racial superiority, masculinity and civilizing mission' (Krishna, 2014: 354). For mainlanders who conceive of their superiority and civility, it is easy to legitimize their rule through exploitation, colonization, and discrimination. Those mainlanders who believe that Western civilization represents a certain triumph over that of Asia, like to feel that they belong to, or are accepted by, the Western nations (Dower, 2014). Indeed, the imposition of Japanese models became the tool by which the colonized societies 'were denied any internal dynamic or capacity for development' (Ashcroft, Griffiths and Tiffin, 2013: 161).

Discrimination is one thing, and indifference is another. According to the joint public opinion poll (*Ryukyu Shimpo–Mainichi Shimbun*, May 2012), in response to the question, 'Do you think it is unfair that over 70% of the US military bases in Japan are currently concentrated in Okinawa?', 69% of respondents in Okinawa answered 'unfair'; meanwhile, only 33% of respondents across Japan answered that they agreed.

Governing postcolonial society

The governments of Japan and the US are now trying to construct a new US military base by landfilling the Oura Bay in Henoko. The people of Okinawa, however, are strongly opposing the plan. Furthermore, the Government of Japan has conducted the construction of new US military helipads in Takae, the northern forest area, by overusing the police force to silence the protest activity of civilians. In order to build the new military facilities and to make Okinawans accept them, the central government utilizes a variety of instruments and colonial legacies for governing a postcolonial society, which are similar to techniques used for governing colonial societies.

'Compensation politics' is 'politics directed primarily toward advertising and satisfying demands for material satisfaction between grantors and supporters, as opposed to those politics oriented toward attaining nonmaterial goals' (Calder, 2007: 132). He calls the network of people regularly involved in this distribution of wealth the 'compensation ring,' and indicates the local interest groups which provide various services to military bases – construction workers, military base labor unions, power companies, owners of land used by the military, and so forth – as the beneficiaries thereof.

Looking at the whole of Okinawa Prefecture, the number of payments made to landlords for military land use has grown from 12.3 billion yen in 1972 to 84.5 billion yen in 2014. The income of military employees has increased from 24 billion to 49.5 billion yen, while the 'sale of goods and services to the US military' has increased from 41.4 billion to 90.6 billion yen. Base-related revenue as a whole was 77.7 billion yen in 1972, and this has almost tripled in size to 242.6 billion yen (Okinawa Prefectural Government, 2017).

Multiple schemes exist in municipalities located within base facility grounds: the Defense Facilities and Living Environment Fund, the Special Defense Facility Subsidy, the Adjustment Subsidy for Municipalities within Base Facilities, and the Base Facility Municipality Revitalization Projects (Shimada Panel Discussion Project), which was implemented from 1997 as consideration for compliance with the bases. In addition to the US Military Base Realignment Subsidy, these are typical representations of compensation politics that may be called 'explicit linkage' between the burden of US bases and budget flows from the central government.

Meanwhile, cases in which 'compensation' is not directly related to bases may be called 'latent linkage.' It is latent because the funds may have originally been announced for other purposes or only partially related to responsibility for military bases. Examples include the budgets for Okinawa Promotion (and Development) Plans, the high rate of subsidies of these Plans, and the Northern Promotion Project, for which 100 billion yen was provided over approximately 10 years since 2000. The government indicated that for the Okinawa Promotion Lump Subsidy System from 2012, approximately half of the 300 billion yen budget related to Okinawa would be made into lump subsidies free of usage restrictions (Hoshino, 2016).

After the Special Action Committee on Okinawa (SACO) agreement in 1996, local opinion was severely split over whether or not to comply and accept a further military presence in Nago City, which had surfaced as the destination for relocating the Futenma airfield. Anti-compliance factions were the majority in a 1997 municipal referendum, but with the Northern Promotion Project, and with the Shimada Panel Discussion Project and similar factors also having an influence, candidates from pro-relocation factions were elected in each of the three mayoral elections from 1998.

After the schoolgirl rape case in 1995, then Governor Masahide Ohta revolted against the central government's base policy. Taking account of the rise of anti-base opinions among the people of Okinawa, Ohta refused to act as representative and sign documents regarding land for use by stationed military forces (this is business handled by state commissions). Ohta subsequently lost a court battle and agreed to sign. The flow of public funds from the central government was reduced, however. He received criticism for the 'economic recession in prefectural administration' and was not re-elected. The Governor for the subsequent three terms agreed conditionally to the government's Futenma relocation plans.

Even granted that there was pressure from the central government, the fact that both the Governor of Okinawa and Mayor of Nago City for a long period sought to accept, however with conditionality, the establishment of a new base at Henoko may be considered evidence of the success of compensation politics.

Since 1972, the three Okinawa Promotion and Development Plans (OPDPs) have promoted 'closing the gap with the mainland' and 'maintaining the fundamental conditions for independent development.' The results however, have been far from what Okinawa expected. Despite large amounts of public investment, the income of Okinawa residents remains at approximately 70% of the national average. The unemployment rate also worsened from 4% to 8% in the 1990s, and have remained at high levels of around 8% since. Jun Nishikawa indicates this as the result of a general form of 'promotion' policy below (Nishikawa, 2011: 142).

Until now, 'underdeveloped' or unfortunate people have been shaped as objects of 'promotion' [...] What are the costs of this [treatment]? None other than damage to nature, the supplementation of Japan's foreign relations and economy, public engineering works following investment of vast amounts of financial capital, and, more than anything, the control of regional society by power-holders in collusion with 'the center' (corrupt relations in politics and business), and the contrasting deprivation of residents' independence and right to self-determination. It is not that the indigenous Ainu population and the Okinawan people are 'unable to be independent'; they have been 'made unable to be independent.'

Thus, the on-going development plan and possibilities of the next development plan, with discretionary power in the implementation process, have been the political leverage for state bureaucrats to 'persuade' post-colonial society to endure the heavy burden of human insecurity.

The US Military Realignment Subsidy is a recent example in which 'compensation' is nominally directly related to the bases. Starting in 2007, and until 2015, a total of 7.4 billion yen was paid to 43 municipalities across the country. The Ministry of Defense hands over subsidies to local governments that cooperate with US military reorganization and seek further cooperation, even from cities, towns, villages, and districts.

In January 2010, Nago City witnessed the appearance of a mayor who was opposed to the acceptance of 'Futenma replacement facilities.' Amid the rise of the 'outside the prefecture, outside the country' opinion among the Okinawan public following the change of political power in 2009, the residents of Nago City selected a candidate who appealed for 'development of our city without links to bases.' In order to maintain consistency with the pledge, Nago City stopped budget allocations tied to the Realignment Subsidy for the next year. In December, the Ministry of Defense gave a 'not granted' notification to the portion brought forward from 2009 and for 2010. Nago City was the first to have the subsidy actually withdrawn. A municipal leader declared, 'From now on, we will run municipal government without relying on these sorts of carrot-and-stick subsidies' (*Ryukyu Shimpo*, Dec. 29, 2010).

Local administrations, which were dependent on revenue related to bases (including subsidies and funds from the government), expected that financial outcomes would be linked to regional independence, namely, that this money would stimulate the regional economy, reduce financial obligations, increase independent revenue sources, and lessen the unemployment rate. It has gradually become clear, however, that this approach is not only unconnected to stable economic growth, it actually increases dependency and makes financial management inflexible; the balance of public debt and unemployment rates also increase (Maedomari, 2009: 132–6). Those who expect a typical linkage between 'base acceptance' and 'economic development' in compensation politics are actually becoming a minority.

As previously noted, base-related revenue itself has increased along with the growth of military land use fees; the proportion of base-related revenue in the income of Okinawan residents, however, has fallen from 15.5% in 1972 to 5.7% in 2014. The proportion represented by amounts paid as military land use fees has also fallen from 2.5% to 2.0%. The number of personnel employed by the military was also 19,980 in 1972, but 8,857 in 2016 (56% reduction) (Okinawa Prefectural Government, 2017).

There was a watershed around 2010, after which the opinion that 'the Okinawan economy cannot stand up without the bases' began to be countered with the assertion that 'reduction of the bases will actually bring about economic growth.' A *Ryukyu Shimpo* editorial made the following comment in response to the former opinion:

> This is nothing but prejudice. One need only look at how the economic effect in the new center of Naha has increased more than tenfold between before and after the return of the bases, or similarly how the growth of the Mihama and Hamby area in Chatan Town has exceeded previous figures 170 times. Okinawa is already escaping the base-dependent economy.
>
> (*Ryukyu Shimpo*, May 15, 2012)

Meanwhile, Nago City decided to accept construction of a new base in 1997. While base-related revenue was 200 million yen in 1995, it increased to 900 million yen in 2001. During this period, the proportion of the Nago City budget filled by base-related revenue jumped from 6% to 29%. This did not, however, bring about growth in Nago City. There was no great change in tax revenue from private bodies expected from enterprises, the absolute unemployment rate worsened from 8.7% to 12.5% (2005), and municipal debt increased from 1.71 billion to 2.35 billion yen (2004) (Maedomari, 2009: 135).

With the slogan of 'closing the gap', the people of Okinawa might have become trapped in a 'developmentalist cage'. However, compensation politics will not necessarily continue to function. One sign of this is that in the November 2011 prefectural governor elections, the opposing conservative and progressive candidates were both negatively disposed towards the relocation of Futenma airfield into Okinawa. The governor election was truly a fierce battle between then-incumbent Hirokazu Nakaima seeking re-election and the former mayor of Ginowan City Yōichi Iha; and both candidates announced that they were unable to accept the plan for relocation to Henoko in Nago City. What is important in this context, however, is that Nakaima's side considered that victory was not possible with the assertion that promotion budgets could be acquired in exchange for accepting the base (Hoshino, 2016).

Another, more definite sign is the fact that Susumu Inamine, who opposed the new base construction, was elected again in the Nago City mayoral elections in January 2014. Since the Ministry of Defense had already withheld payment of the US Military Base Realignment Subsidy from the city, it is important to bear in mind that Nago citizens voted with their understanding that the subsidy was not coming. It is as though the residents of Nago City declared, 'We no longer need compensation politics.'

The voices of Nago City residents were also echoed in the 2014 gubernatorial and national elections. In November 2014, the prefectural governor election saw the appearance of Governor Takeshi Onaga, who appealed for 'All-Okinawa' opposition to new base construction. Under the slogan of 'All-Okinawa', former LDP conservatives and liberals and even communists fought together. In the following month's National Assembly Lower House election, the LDP, which proclaimed 'burden reduction through relocation within the prefecture,' lost all four seats in the four single-member constituencies in Okinawa. It is clear that the opinion of the Okinawan people is hostile to new bases being constructed in Hekono or Takae (Hoshino, 2016). As a result of the series of elections in 2014, the following message has been sent out from Okinawa: it will be impossible to 'persuade' the people of the prefecture with compensation politics and construct a comprehensive military base for Marines in Henoko.

Despite of all these clear messages sent from Okinawa, the central government did not listen. Tokyo utilized much harsher instruments to materialize its intent on building an upgraded military facility over the beautiful coral bay of Ohura.

In terms of compensation politics, a series of promotion schemes linked to the bases has been put in place since the 1995 schoolgirl rape case, but there is now a common awareness among the Okinawan people that these schemes have not solved the problems. Chief Cabinet-Secretary Suga's speech failed to gather votes. Notably, in it he stated that the government would give full support if Okinawa wanted the Universal Studio Japan to be opened on the island (*Nikkan Sports*, Nov. 10, 2014). This was reminiscent of LDP Secretary-General Ishiba's announcement of a 5 billion yen regional promotion fund in a Nago City mayoral election support speech (*Asahi Shimbun Digital*, Jan. 16, 2014).

At the end of 2013, Prime Minister Abe promised the government an annual promotion budget of 30 billion yen for eight years to Governor Nakaima. Soon after coming back from Tokyo, he announced that the prefecture had approved the central government's application of landfill in Ohura Bay. This was practically a green light for the new base construction. Since then, there appeared many more LDP members who mentioned the explicit linkage between money flows from Tokyo and Okinawa's cooperation in building a new military base in Henoko (*Okinawa Times*, Aug. 5, 2016; *Ryukyu Shimpo*, Oct. 8, 2016). Since July 2014, the Japanese police (including the riot police from outside of Okinawa prefecture) and the Japan Coast Guard carried out more than 80 cases of arrests, detention, excessive use of force, and verbal abuse against civilians, who were protesting the construction of a new US base in Henoko.

During the last half of 2016, the site of confrontation between central government and the Okinawan people had moved from Henoko to Takae in Higashi village. The Henoko base construction was temporarily stopped from March 2016, while the helipad construction was resumed in Takae in July, just after the LDP government lost the only seat for Okinawa in the upper house election. The National Police Agency sent 500 riot police from the mainland and police oppression of the protest has intensified and accelerated since then. There have been multiple incidents of protesting citizens' injuries caused by forcible evacuation. These law enforcement officers did not respect the freedom of peaceful assembly, while the violation of press freedom was also reported.

Many civil society groups in Japan have been condemning the arrests and detention as arbitrary measures.[2] Amnesty International called for urgent actions against such measures in January and March 2017.[3] The All Okinawa Council of Human Rights (AOCHR) and The International Movement Against All Forms of Discrimination and Racism (IMADR) proclaimed that 'the Government [of Japan] must fully respect the rights of people of Ryukyu/Okinawa to freedom of expression and peaceful assembly'.

The government has used SLAPPs, lawsuits intended to intimidate and silence individuals by burdening them with the cost of a legal defense until they abandon their criticism. This is illegal in the United States but not in Japan. In 2008, the Okinawa Defense Bureau filed a lawsuit with the Naha District Court against 15 residents, including a child, to stop their protests. The government later dropped the charges against the child, while the Bureau filed another lawsuit with the Naha District Court against two residents accusing them of obstructing traffic in 2010 (*Ryukyu Shimpo*, June 25, 2013).

In October 2015, Governor Onaga cancelled the license to reclaim a large portion of Oura Bay that ex-Governor Nakaima had given to the national government in December 2013. In November 2015, the MLITT (the Minister of Land, Infrastructure, Transport, and Tourism) filed a suit against the prefectural government, alleging administrative malfeasance and trying to set aside Onaga's order by adopting a 'proxy execution' procedure (McCormack, 2016a). In November 2015, Okinawa prefecture launched a complaint against the Abe administration with the Central and Local Government Disputes Management Council. When this complaint was rejected on December 24, the prefecture launched a separate counter-suit against the government the next day. Thus, there were also battles in court between the central government and the Okinawa prefecture (McCormack, 2016a).

In January 2016, the Naha Branch of the Fukuoka High Court advised the disputing parties to consider an out-of-court settlement, and the settlement between the national and prefectural governments was announced in March, that temporarily halted the construction in Henoko, but not for long. In July 2016, the Abe administration filed a new suit against the prefecture, seeking a ruling that the Okinawan government comply with the MLITT minister's order and reverse its cancellation of permission for landfill work on Oura Bay (McCormack, 2016b). Tokyo won this lawsuit at the Supreme Court in December. Onaga followed the ruling, and the central government has resumed construction of the new base at Henoko.

In March 2017, when the rally calling for abandonment of the plan to build a new base in Henoko was held in front of the gate to Camp Schwab, Governor Onaga announced in front of 3,500 participants, 'I will absolutely revoke' the approval to reclaim land off the shore of Henoko (*Ryukyu Shimpo*, March 26, 2017). Chief Cabinet Secretary Suga hinted that the government may seek damages from the Okinawa governor if he continues to attempt to impede the 'relocation of Futenma' (*Japan Times*, March 27, 2017). This sounds like SLAPP to Onaga.

'Even though colonial domination was often brutally repressive, recent scholarship has suggested that … colonial regimes tried to gain the consent of certain native groups, while excluding others from civil society' (Loomba, 2015: 49–50). As Ashis Nandy (1983) wrote, the colonized middle classes set out on a venture of modernizing their societies and becoming the new colonial elites. As we discussed above, people in Okinawa display a variety of cleavages in terms of development, self-determination, and cultural identity in their postcolonial society. But there are chances for the national government to introduce an old-fashioned technology for governing colonies in a postcolonial society: divide and rule.

In November 2013, the LDP Secretary-General Ishiba reaffirmed his party's position, which supported 'reduction of Okinawan burden through relocation within Okinawa.' He proudly did so with LDP congresspersons from Okinawa districts, who broke their election campaign pledges. Since the 2009 lower house election had seen the landslide victory of DPJ who promised 'Futenma relocation outside of Okinawa', these LDP members pledged 'relocation outside' when they won in 2010 and 2012 national elections (*Asahi Shimbun Digital*, Dec. 11, 2012). However, they threw their pledges away under strong pressure from the LDP headquarters.

Between the clarity of Okinawan opposition and the central government's strong hand over money and law enforcement, we can find tacit approval to shoulder heavy burdens created by the national security policy. Behind such tacit approvals, there is the discrimination and indifference of mainlanders. These also are useful resources for the central authority to govern the postcolonial society.

In a joint public opinion poll by *Ryukyu Shimpo–Mainichi Shimbun* (May 2012), 69% of Okinawan respondents said that the heavy concentration of US military bases in Okinawa is unfair, while 22% of them accepted them as unavoidable (9% didn't know). Additionally, regarding the relocation of Futenma airfield, 89% of Okinawan respondents answered either return without relocation, outside of Okinawa, or outside of Japan, while 11% agreed with the government plan at Henoko. Since they are less vocal than politically active groups in Okinawan society, it is difficult to pin-point where the 10% to 20% of tacit approvals came from. Complex reasons would include matters of livelihood, psychology, and social surroundings, though these are only speculations. Thorough investigation and analysis, elsewhere, would help answer these questions.

What is clear is that the Abe administration is trying to establish a taken-for-granted-ness among Okinawans, by creating 'seemingly established facts' with the power of money and law enforcement. This tactic could create some kind of unwilling acceptance of the new base by Okinawan people. Discrimination and indifference on the side of mainlanders could help create take-for-granted-ness, and hence tacit approval.

In October 2016, protesters in front of a gate of Takae helipad construction sites were abused with depreciatory crude words, such as 'Dojin (Natives)' and 'Shinajin (Chinks'), by riot police officers from Osaka (*Ryukyu Shimpo*, Oct. 19, 2016). These officers see Okinawan people as backward and uncivilized, although they will usually not enunciate such ideas. But when second-class citizens speak up, especially against the central government, some of these mainlanders turn their ideas into words.

One month after this incident, the Minister of State for Okinawa and Northern Territories Affairs Yosuke Tsuruho said at the Diet: 'From the position of the Minister, it is impossible for me to conclude this remark [concerning "Dojin (Natives)"] as discrimination' (*Ryukyu Shimpo*, Nov. 9, 2016). The government did not ask him to apologize for his comments, and it made a cabinet decision concluding that no apology was necessary, claiming that 'it is difficult to tell unambiguously' whether this term was considered as discriminatory (*Ryukyu Shimpo*, Nov. 22, 2016). It was not clarified that the 'Dojin' remark was discrimination against Okinawans. Hence the cabinet decision is clear evidence that the Japanese government is not trying to stop discrimination in general against the people of Okinawa but is encouraging it. Steve Rabson criticized this 'Dojin' remark, arguing that it is a reflection of the colonial situation in Okinawa, wherein Japanese and US governments are denying democracy and human rights for Okinawa within their colonialist policies (*Okinawa Times*, Nov. 9, 2016).

A joint *Okinawa Times–Asahi Shimbun* public opinion poll (April 2012) posed the following question: 'Is the fact that bases are not being reduced discrimination against Okinawa by the mainland?' Responses to this question differed greatly between Okinawa and the whole of Japan. Half of respondents in Okinawa, yet only 29% of respondents across Japan, answered, 'It is discrimination.' A joint *Ryukyu Shimpo–Mainichi Shimbun* public opinion poll (May 2012) also shows the difference between Okinawans and mainlanders on the issue of Futenma relocation. While 11% of Okinawan respondents agreed with the government plan of building a new base in Henoko, 28% of respondents across Japan agreed. They also showed a NIMBY (not in my back yard) attitude in that 68% of them are opposed to relocate the base to their city or town, despite the fact that 80% of them support the Japan–US Security Treaty that enables US forces to be stationed in Japan.

In April 28, 2013, Abe, back in power, celebrated the 50th year of the San Francisco Peace Treaty, as the year of Japan's recovery of sovereignty. But for people in Okinawa, the day marks the separation from Japan and extension of US occupation, such that the ceremony greatly hurt Okinawan pride. Indifference toward Okinawa among people in the center is a useful resource for the national government to impose an excessive portion of US military bases to a small prefecture in the periphery. Similar strategies were followed by the state in order to impose a nuclear power plant on reluctant local communities elsewhere in Japan (Takahashi, 2012).

Exit, voice, and representation in the postcolonial complex

'Above all, this is a story of the process by which, for the first time in Japan's history, grassroots democratic forces seized the initiative and over a sustained period became the key subject in determining the course of history' (McCormack and Norimatsu, 2012: 12). Against the variety of central government's strategies and tactics described so far, people of Okinawa still respond 'No,' 'No!' to the new base project. Since Okinawa is under attack in the postcolonial complex, its expression and connotation of 'No' varies in at least these three ways: exit, voice, and representation.

Governor Onaga often says that he would do whatever he could do to stop the new base construction. This means whatever he could do within the limit that laws, regulations, and the constitution of Japan stipulates. In other words, he is betting on democracy in Japan. Krishna (2014: 356) characterizes mimicry as 'a strategy of survival, a weapon of the weak, and is in that sense an ethically justifiable response by the native to a situation in which one is structurally disadvantaged.' To become a 'real Japanese' is to take full advantage of being a Japanese so that one could have a proper representation in the political system, and could enjoy human rights and human security the same as other members of the society.

In our case of Okinawa in 2017, this strategy does not look so promising. As we witnessed above, Tokyo won a lawsuit at the Supreme Court in December 2016, and 'All-Okinawa' has not won local mayoral elections lately. Although any governor or congressperson with an election campaign pledge of 'Futenma relocation to Henoko' could not have won the election for the last 10 years, this is not enough to fight against the power of money and law enforcement of the national government.

Hence, when Ashcroft, Griffiths, and Tiffin (2013: 155) describe mimicry as 'the copying of the colonizing culture, behavior, manners and values by the colonized contains both mockery and a certain "menace",' one might consider that Japanese democracy is not functioning as expected. It does not offer a proper protection of human rights and human security in the level of international human rights standards. But it is not enough to say that Japanese democracy is not working. It is necessary for minority groups of the society to make their democracy work. In order to make their democracy work, people need not only to raise their voice but also to exercise their rights and protect their security. Those are the actions that Okinawan people have been engaging in for a long time.

As already mentioned, in October 2015, Governor Onaga cancelled ex-Governor Nakaima's approval of the landfill of Oura Bay in Henoko. However, the government started research for construction, bringing equipment into Camp Shwab and closing access to the sea surface near the site. People had sit-ins and rallies in front of the gate and even on the coral sea, confronting riot police and coast guards. The sit-in in front of the gate of Camp Schwab had run for 1,000 days by April 1, 2017 (*Ryukyu Shimpo*, March 31, 2017).

Governor Onaga often says 'identity rather than ideology.' The 'All-Okinawa' coalition is founded on Okinawan identity, although we already know that it contains cleavages here and there. There also exists a gradation in saying 'No' to the new base construction. Some argue 'Removal of all US bases from Okinawa', others simply say 'No to the Futenma relocation to Henoko', and there are other people who articulate 'Marines out of Okinawa'.

As previously mentioned, in May 2016, a young woman's body was found dead in a suitcase at Onna Village. Charges of murder and rape were made against a US military contractor and former Marine. In June, 65,000 people dressed in black gathered in Naha, mourned the victim, and demanded for Marines to leave the islands. The Prefectural Assembly of Okinawa approved a resolution demanding the US Marines leave Okinawa for the first time (*Okinawa Times*, May 27, 2016). According to the *Ryukyu Shimpo–Okinawa Television* Joint Public Opinion Poll, just after this murder and rape case, 53% of respondents agreed with the demand for Marines to leave Okinawa, while 32% of them answered that a large reduction of Marine Corps was necessary (*Ryukyu Shimpo*, June 3, 2016). Among the US personnel stationed in Okinawa, 60% of them are Marines. In terms of land space of US military bases, 40% of them are for Marines. So if Marines left Okinawa, the burdens on Okinawan shoulders would be dramatically reduced. While it may not be the majority yet, 'Marines out of Okinawa' could become the new voice of Okinawa.

Faced with a tense confrontation between Okinawan people and the national government, McCormack and Norimatsu (2012: 11) pose a question: 'Can that incompatibility be resolved within the existing state system, or is Okinawa headed toward semi- or even full detachment from the Japanese state?' A new prefectural public opinion poll (*Ryukyu Shimpo*, Jan. 4, 2017) has posed a similar question on Okinawa's future status in Japan. Forty-six per cent of respondents replied 'a prefecture of Japan as it is now', 18% of them preferred 'more autonomous handlings in domestic matters', 14% of them answered 'more independent authority in foreign and security policies', and 3% of them said 'independence.' Compared to previous polls, 'a prefecture of Japan' lost its share by 18%, and the average response shifted toward more self-determination. Hence, one third of the people now prefer a certain degree of detachment from the Japanese state.

In 2008, the UN Committee on Civil and Political Rights recognized the Okinawan people as indigenous inhabitants, and the UN Human Rights Committee stated that Japan should 'recognize the Ainu and Ryukyu/Okinawa as indigenous peoples in domestic legislation, adopt special measures to protect, preserve and promote their cultural heritage and traditional way of life, and recognize their land rights'.[4] The government of Japan, however, did not, so that in 2014 'the Committee reiterates its concern regarding the lack of recognition of the Ryukyu and Okinawa, as well as of the rights of those groups to their traditional land and resources and the right of their children to be educated in their language'.[5] The Committee also stated that Japan should:

> take further steps to revise its legislation and fully guarantee the rights of Ryukyu and Okinawa communities to their traditional land and natural resources, ensuring respect for their right to engage in free, prior and informed participation in policies that affect them.[6]

These moves in the international arena do not necessarily advocate the exit option for Okinawa, but at least support Okinawans fighting for a proper representation and for their voices to be heard.

Conclusion

One thing I could not discuss in this chapter is related to Krishna's following observation: 'Decolonization is not so much a political project as it is a slow and multifaceted unlearning of industrial, capitalist modernization itself' (Krishna, 2014: 358). Unchaining compensation politics could be done as discussed above, although in order for the majority of Okinawans to unchain we need to imagine the future of society in a way Krishna suggested. One thing that I made clear in this chapter is that Okinawa is in a postcolonial complex. I would like to add three remarks here to conclude the chapter.

First, as Ashcroft, Griffiths, and Tiffin (2006: 137) point out, 'most post-colonial writing has concerned itself with the hybridized nature of post-colonial culture as a strength rather than a weakness.' The hybridity of Okinawan culture in its postcolonial complex could prove its strength in transnational relations in East Asia to securitize the situation as a 'crisis'. Successfully bridging movements and civil societies across Japan, China, Korea, and the Asia-Pacific could also be one of the most promising tools for a dismantling of neo-colonial and postcolonial authority.

Second, as already mentioned, Okinawan struggles to date highlight that the 'Okinawa Problem' is not only the problem of Okinawans but one that the government of and people of Japan should work upon. Human insecurity in Okinawa is largely the result of the national security policy of Japan, the US–Japan Security Treaty, which is supported by the majority of Japanese mainlanders. As McCormack and Norimatsu (2012: 11) question: 'if … the Japanese constitution's guarantees of popular sovereignty, basic human rights, and peace do not apply to Okinawa, what does that mean for the rest of the country?'

Third and lastly, it is depressing to note that the colonial technology of governance still works well in the postcolonial complex of Okinawa, and in some other parts of the world for that matter. However, it is encouraging to remember that 'modern colonialism was also resisted at every point – from the very first encounters in the New World until the present moment' (Krishna, 2014: 360), and that struggles against the postcolonial state continue in every location on this planet, as we have seen here in the case of Okinawa.

Bibliography

Anderson, Benedict (1991) *Imagined Communities: Reflections on the Origin and Spread of Nationalism.* London: Verso.

Arnold, D. (1994) 'Public health and public power: Medicine and hegemony in colonial India.' D. Engels and S. Marks, eds., *Contesting Colonial Hegemony.* London: British Academic Press. 131–51.

Ashcroft, Bill, Griffiths, Gareth, and Tiffin, Helen (2006) *The Post-colonial Studies Reader.* Second Edition. London: Routledge.

——— (2013) *Postcolonial Studies: The Key Concepts.* Third Edition. London: Routledge.

Bhabha, Homi (1994) *The Location of Culture.* London: Routledge.

Calder, Kent E. (2007) *Embattled Garrisons: Comparative Base Politics and American Globalism.* Princeton: Princeton University Press.

de Alva, J. J. K. (1995) 'The postcolonization of the (Latin) American experience, a reconsideration of "colonialism", "postcolonialism" and "mestizaje."' G. Parakash, ed., *After Colonialism, Imperial Histories and Postcolonial Displacements.* Princeton: Princeton University Press. 241–75.

Dower, John W. (2014) 'The San Francisco system: Past, present, future in U.S.–Japan–China relations.' *Asia Pacific Journal*, Vol. 12, Issue 8, No. 2.

Hall, Stuart (1990) 'Cultural identity and diaspora.' Jonathan Rutherford, ed., *Identity: Community, Culture, Difference.* London: Lawlence and Wishart.

Hechter, Michael (1975) *Internal Colonialism: The Celtic Fringe in British National Development, 1536–1966.* Berkeley: University of California Press.

Hein, Laura and Selden, Mark (2003) 'Culture, power, and identity in contemporary Okinawa.' Laura Hein and Mark Selden, eds., *Islands of Discontent: Okinawan Responses to Japanese and American Power.* Lanham: Rowman and Littlefield. 1–35.

Hoshino, Eiichi (2016) 'US Military bases and Human Security in Okinawa.' Ishihara, Hoshino, and Fujita, eds., *Self-determinable Development of Small Islands*, Singapore: Springer. 3–32.

Krishna, Sankaran (2009) *Globalization and Postcolonialism: Hegemony and Resistance in the 21st Century.* Lanham: Rowman and Littlefield.

——— (2014) 'How does colonialism work?' Jenny Edkins and Maja Zehfuss, eds., *Global Politics: A New Introduction*, Second Edition. London: Routledge. 338–62.

Lim, John Chuan-tiong (2007) '"Henkyo Ajia" Jumin-no Aidentyityi-wo Meguru Kokusai Hikaku Chosa Kenkyu: Okinawa, Taiwan, Honkon, Makao (International Comparative Research on Identity of Peripheral East Asian Residents: Okinawa, Taiwan, Hong Kong, Macau).' <http://ir.lib.u-ryukyu.ac.jp/handle/123456789/17167>

Linklater, Andrew (2005) 'Political community and human security.' Ken Booth, ed., *Critical Security Studies and World Politics.* Boulder: Lynne Rienner.

Loomba, Ania (2015) *Colonialism/Postcolonialism.* Third Edition. London: Routledge.

Maedomari, Hiromori (2009) '"Kichi izon" no jittai to dakkyaku no kanōsei [Current state of and escape from "military base dependence"]' in Miyazato Seigen, Arasaki Moriteru, Gabe Masaaki, eds., *Okinawa 'jiritsu' he no michi wo motomete.* Koubunken.

Martin, Alex (2011) '1953 records on handling U.S. forces released.' *Japan Times*, August 27, 2011.

McCormack, Gavan (2016a) '"Ceasefire" on Oura Bay: The March 2016 Japan–Okinawa "Amicable Agreement" introduction and six views from within the Okinawan Anti-Base Movement.' *The Asia Pacific Journal*, Vol. 14, Issue 7, No. 1.

——— (2016b) 'Japan's problematic prefecture – Okinawa and the US–Japan relationship.' *The Asia Pacific Journal*, Vol. 14, Issue 17, No. 2.

McCormack, Gavan and Norimatsu, Satoko Oka (2012) *Resistant Islands: Okinawa Confronts Japan and the United States.* Lanham: Rowman and Littlefield.

Miyagi, Harumi (2010) 'Okinawa kara no hōkoku: beigun kichi no genjō to beihei ni yoru reipu jiken [Report from Okinawa: current situation of US Military bases and cases of rape by US soldiers.] *Ritsumeikan gengo bunka kenkyuu*, Vol. 23, No. 2.

Miyagi, Yasuhiro (2014) 'Nago shichō senkyo no kekka wo sezoku-teki ni yomu [A grounded reading of the Nago mayoral election results]' (April 22, 2014), <https://goo.gl/YFTceu>.

Nandy, Ashis (1983) *The Intimate Enemy: Loss and Recovery of Self Under Colonialism*. New Delhi: Oxford University Press.

Nishikawa, Jun (2011) '"Henkyō" wo tsukuridasu no wa dare? [Who creates the "periphery"?]' Fujiwara Shoten, ed., *"Okinawa mondai" to wa nani ka*. Tokyo: Fujiwara Shoten.

Nishizato, Kiko (2010) 'Higashi Ajia shi ni okeru Ryukyu shobun.' *Keizaishi Kenkyu*, no. 13 (February 2010): 74.

Okinawa Prefectural Government, Executive Office of the Governor (Military Base Affairs Division) (2017) *US Military and JSDF Bases.*

Okinawa Women Act Against Military Violence (OWAAMV) (2012) 'Sexual crimes against women committed by US soldiers in Okinawa (April 1945–October 2012).'

Onaga, Takeshi (2015) 'Governor of Okinawa condemned Japanese Government at the UNHRC meeting' (2015.09.21).

Said, Edward W. (1993) *Culture and Imperialism*. New York: Alfred A. Knopf.

Shindo, Eiichi (1979) 'Bunkatsu sareta ryodo,' *Sekai* (April 1979): 45–50.

Takahashi, Tetsuya (2012) *Gisei-no Shisutemu: Fukushima, Okinawa* (System of Sacrifice: Fukushima, Okinawa). Tokyo: Shueisha.

Tominaga, Hitoshi (2003) *Zu-de Miru Okinawa-no Keizai (Okinawan Economy in Figures)*. Naha: Ryokufusha.

Tomiyama, Kazuyuki (2016) 'Ryukyu Kingdom diplomacy with Japan and the Ming and Qing Dynasties.' Ishihara, Hoshino, and Fujita, eds., *Self-determinable Development of Small Islands,* Singapore: Springer. 55–65.

Turner, B. S., ed. (1990) *Theories of Modernity and Postmodernity*. London: Sage.

Uemura, Hideaki (2003) 'The colonial annexation of Okinawa and the logic of international law: The formation of an indigenous people,' *Japanese Studies* 23, no. 2 (September 2003): 107–14: 122.

Newspapers and opinion polls

Asahi Shimbun Digital.

Japan Times.

Nikkan Sports.

Okinawa Times.

Okinawa Times, Prefectural Public Opinion Survey, 2007.

Okinawa Times-Asahi Shimbun, Joint Public Opinion Survey, April 2012.

Ryukyu Shimpo.

Ryukyu Shimpo–Mainichi Shimbun, Joint Public Opinion Poll, May 2012.

Ryukyu Shimpo–Okinawa Television, Joint Public Opinion Poll, May 2015.

Notes

1 'Mr. Takeshi Onaga, Governor of Okinawa condemned Japanese government at the UN Human Rights Council Meeting' (Sept. 21, 2015) <http://www.pref.okinawa.jp/site/chijiko/henoko/>

2 'Fierce opponent of U.S. military bases in Okinawa detained for three months': www.washington post.com/world/asia_pacific/fierce-opponent-of-us-military-bases-in-okinawa-detained-for-three-months/2017/01/18/6d7a51bc-5a3f-4e93-a8f5–47b87d12db1f_story.html>

3 'Okinawa activist released on bail after five months' <http://www.amnesty.or.jp/en/get-involved/ua/ua/2017ua023.html>

4 'Arbitrary arrests and detention of human rights defender of Ryukyu/ Okinawa, Japan' (HRC34, 2017, Joint-OS): <http://imadr.org/arbitrary-arrests-detention-humanrightsdefender-ryukyu-okinawa-hrc 34-2017-joint-os/>

5 Ibid.

6 Ibid.

21
'TOO SIMPLE AND SOMETIMES NAÏVE'
Hong Kong, between China and the West

Xin Liu

Introduction

On the 28 October, 2000, the then President of China, Jiang Zemin, was meeting the then Chief Executive of Hong Kong, Tung Chee-Hwa, in the People's Great Hall of Beijing, who was pursuing his second term in office. Having been bombarded by the Hong Kong media with questions such as whether the central government was to anoint Tung as the next Chief Executive, Jiang had a tantrum at the reporters, calling them '*too simple, and sometimes naïve*'. The phrase was soon coined as an infamous idiom that symbolises Beijing's imperial, colonial stance towards Hong Kong: that is, the degree of autonomy Beijing has granted under the constitutional arrangement of 'One Country Two Systems' should not weaken China's sovereignty over a Hong Kong redeemed from British colonialism. China would reject everything that is thought to be imposed by the West before the 1997 handover – including the democratic movement – in a unequivocal way (Chow 2005, 312).

The Chinese leader's outspoken paranoia has clearly pinpointed the contested position of Hong Kong as a postcolonial polity dwelling under Chinese nationalism: Hong Kong's social and administrative structure established in the colonial context would be vulnerable under China's pressures dressed in anti-imperial rhetoric. Such vulnerabilities have not only characterised the hypocrisy of Beijing's 'One Country Two Systems' but also pointed out the direction of Hong Kong's post-handover democratic movement, which is supposed to be a local struggle against China as a new coloniser. However, as this chapter will aim to demonstrate, Hong Kong's current identity formation, as well as its context of social protests, if situated in a wider historical context, would need to be investigated beyond the question of postcolonial state-formation and decolonising movements in order not to be 'too simple and sometimes naïve'.

'Simplicity' and 'naivety' in the conventional understanding of Hong Kong's post-1997 struggle lie in the liberal-democratic thinking held by the first generation of elite-democrats who grew up in the British-colonial middle-class environment. Liberal democratic thinking was a prominent intellectual tradition deliberately planted by the British colonisers incarnated in the emerging Hong Kongese identity, whereas its corresponding political movement has become prevalent since the open split of the British-educated Hong Kongese elites from the mainland authorities. The latter movement could be dated to the early democrats Martin Lee and Szeto Wah's withdrawal from the Basic Law Drafting Committee after the 1989 Beijing Tiananmen bloodshed and the subsequent plethora of patriotic democratic movements. The so-called pan-democratic movement in Hong Kong in both the Legislative Council (LegCo) and wider society has from the outset viewed democracy as a component of China's century-long pursuit of modernity traceable to the 1919 May Fourth Movement. Hong Kong is perceived as hub of democratic reform for both mainland China and the wider global Chinese community.

Democracy as a form of Chinese nationalism has become increasingly unfavourable among the young generation since the Umbrella Movement in 2013, after which a substantial number of 'Hong Kong nationalists', or at least locally oriented groups came to proliferate. The 2016 LegCo election has become a watershed in Hong Kong's constitutional history, in which the so-called Hong Kong independent (*gangdu*) activists have come to the fore by seizing seven seats, not only replacing many veteran Sinocentric democrats such as the Labour leader Lee Cheuk-yan and the Democratic Party leader Albert Ho, but also reframing the democratic movement by rejecting the agenda of 'Building a Democratic China'. A national division has thus been drawn between China and Hong Kong which has cut cross the traditional standoff between pro- and anti-establishment, while the locally oriented students see democracy in China as irrelevant to the perseverance of Hong Kong's lifestyle and a democratic China as equally threatening.

Explaining the recent 'nationalist turn' in the political development of postcolonial Hong Kong has thus become a significant historical as well as theoretical subject. Scripts and texts of nationalist thoughts in Hong Kong have fallen slightly on the simplistic side which do not deserve much scrutiny in themselves. It is however the 'why', rather than the 'what' question that matters. The case of Hong Kong is exceptional especially in the sense that there have been few elements of crisis in conventional postcolonial politics that have factored in Hong Kong's national formation. There have been, for example, no territorial disputes between Hong Kong and its postcolonial neighbours after Britain's exit. No disputes over sovereignty have been inflicted due to China's landslide victory in the negotiation series with Britain in the 1980s. The Hong Kong public has long remained politically lukewarm under the commercial and entrepreneurial atmosphere.

From a postcolonial point of view, the so-called 'universalisation of the nation-state' via post-colonial elites' conscious re-appropriation of historical memory (Chakrabarty 2009; Guha 1997) has never dominated the political forum of Hong Kong. The patriotic tone and the enduring concerns about mainland affairs in the pre-Umbrella democratic movement have all seemed to be reassuring the centrality of Chinese identity (though in an abstract form) in a postcolonial context. In sharp contrast to all that, recent observers have noted that the Hong Kong public is now waving farewell to its past of political indifference by engendering a wider identity-related movement which is nevertheless unprecedented (see Cheng, Edmund and Samson 2014). This historical split, however, is not coterminous with Hong Kong's decolonisation experience, neither does it fall under any patterns of classic national formation (Anderson 1983; Gellner 2006)

This chapter aims at situating Hong Kong's current political struggle, especially 'the nationalist turn' in context. At first blush, Hong Kong's postcolonial identity formation features both universalist discourses of liberal democracy inherited from the colonial past, and the recourse to native-local cultural memories against old and new colonisers (Chow 1992). However, Hong Kong's current nationalist struggle cannot be understood as a simple hybridity of the universal and the local derived from either colonial or decolonial temporalities (Fung 2007).

To think beyond struggle in and under the postcolonial state, this chapter will argue that Hong Kong's recent nationalist turn should be understood *inbetween* different political spaces. It was Hong Kong's geo-cultural position between China and Britain that gave rise to imageries such as China and Hong Kong *per se* not as rivalling identities along the line between Self and

Other. Rather, these cultural imageries have been used interchangeably to pin down a self-recognition by specific political agents predicated upon 'alterity'. Such alterity, during the Cold War, was structurally mediated by the strategic initiatives of both China and Britain. It is the eclipse of that alterity in the current context of the 'rise of China' that has caused the anxiety in Hong Kongese identity which is predicated on Hong Kong's status as an inbetweener with regard to China and Britain. In this sense, the current desinifying, nationalist turn draws upon the same logic as the traditional pan-Chinese democratic movement in expressing nostalgia about the Cold War.

In what follows, I will first review the main arguments of the current nationalist thoughts in Hong Kong just to show that the nationalist/pro-independent movement needs to be understood by reference to Hong Kong's inbetweener status. Then I will outline a multi-spatial framework that explains such inbetweener status which will broaden the understanding of Hong Kong's postcolonial identity. On this basis, I will analyse the evolution of Hong Kong's historical position inbetween China and Britain in different historical stages; and I will also show how such a position has been eclipsed with China's strategic initiative towards Hong Kong being dramatically weakened in the context of the rise of China. This chapter will finally suggest that it is the location of political subjectivities in which they negotiate and proliferate political narratives, rather than the meaning of those narratives themselves that matters in understanding postcolonial states and social movements.

Hong Kong nationalism in the postcolonial context

Media and liberal scholars have understood the subject of 'Hong Kong nationalism' in a rather simplistic view which highlights Hong Kong's political subjectivity in resisting against different colonisers. The recent wave of the nationalist movement is seen as a revolt against Communist China's intensifying attempt to interfere with Hong Kongese affairs and the erosion of Hong Kong's local lifestyle by fostering a capital-driven Hong Kong-Mainland integration. Actions of resistance such as Occupy Central, and the subsequent Umbrella Movement are understood as results of the Communist government's reluctance to allow genuine universal suffrage in Hong Kong, which has broken the promise laid in the mini-constitution of the Basic Law. It is thus commonly believed that the National People's Congress' decision to impose a nomination committee on Hong Kong's 2017 Chief Executive Election was the immediate trigger to the Umbrella Movement and the nationalist turn hence derived (J. Chan 2014; Ip 2016). 'If Beijing continues to wage a hardline policy toward Hong Kong and interfere extensively in the city, such actions could radicalise Hong Kongers and promote self-determination' (So 2015).

Other scholars attempt to understand the constitutional conflict from a class perspective, and it is highlighted that recent changes in the Hong Kong economy have been creating an angry lower class without hope whose interests are systematically undermined by the existing constitutional arrangement. C.Y. Leung, the Chief Executive handpicked by Beijing, is widely viewed as the agent of the mega-capitalists who have been constantly extracting profits from the Hong Kong–Mainland integration (Hui and Lau 2015, 349–51). The fact that such integration does not favour the younger generation has in turn planted a split between the two populations, while mainland tourists, migrants and investors are also pictured as 'locusts' that have encroached on Hong Kong's status granted under the 'One Country Two Systems' arrangement.[1] Stagnancy in constitutional reform and class polarisation are indeed intertwined in forming the context of the Umbrella Movement. The nationalist turn just represents a more 'non-negotiable stance' taken as 'essentially a statement of defiance and audacity, against the moral and political corruption of

Hong Kong leading to post-totalitarianism' (Hui and Lau 2015, 361). However, why does such a defiance against Hong Kong's deterioration need to take up a nationalist stance? A brief outline of the contour of the nationalist narrative is thus in order.

The most active force of the Umbrella Movement were actually student organisations which grew out of the previous movement against the 'moral and national education' imposed by the central government which was commonly understood by the Hong Kong public as a process of brainwashing. Student groups such as Scholarism and the Universities' Student Unions published a series of locally oriented booklets elucidating the outline of nationalist thinking. The Scholarism leader Joshua Wong told the *New Left Review* that legacies of the Tiananmen Square had become obsolete and overestimated, whereas it needed to be invigorated with a new meaning of 'the old should protect the young generation' to remain relevant (Wong 2015).

The student union of the Hong Kong University has taken a more radical step to nullify the liberal democratic movement which promises Hong Kong's moral responsibility for the mainland. In their student magazine *Undergrad*, 'localism' is a result of the current situation that Hong Kong exists as a divided city. 'On one side you've got the graceful face of the city; towers of financial businesses, office buildings, and splendid shopping malls are connected to each other in the kingdom of the landed ruling class, whereas on the other side, shabby allies, narrow social houses line row upon row'.

For the students, a universalist identity of 'world citizen' underlies the graceful face of the city, which is ultimately the corollary of the impoverished, mundane and devastated scene of the other face of it. Though there has been no enunciation of how and why the incompatibility has to be resolved by a nationalist project, the *Undergrad* rejoinder jumped to the conclusion that Hong Kong nationalism is taking the universalist promise of globalisation to task in an audaciously populist fashion. It drew upon the cases of Brexit and Donald Trump to argue that Hong Kong nationalism, like Brexit, is a 'middle finger' pointed to the impervious financial and landed elites who are dressed in the cosmopolitan as well as pan-Chinese rhetoric outlined by both the patriotic democratic movement and the 'One Country Two Systems' (C. K. Chan 2014, 26).[2] The *Undergrad*'s nationalist turn perceives the emergent Hong Kongese identity as a revolt against the totalising force of capitalism by awakening a past that has not been appropriated as capital's 'self-posited forms'.

A more systematic, but also more audacious argument has been made in a broader, but also deliberately biased historical-cultural perspective. Chin Wan-Kan, former linguistic faculty member in the Lingnan University, who is commonly known as the master of Hong Kong nationalist thought, has elaborated the idea of Hong Kong nationalism in the controversial book *Hong Kong as a City-state*. Chin's book has provided a complex reading of Hong Kong's colonial history, and the city's advantageous position to mainland China. Central to the book is a reinterpretation of the Basic Law and 'One Country Two Systems' as the legal basis for preserving Hong Kong's status as a city-state. Chin's historical claim is actually more provocative and ambitious. He argues that the British-colonial period of the city-state should be viewed as the *normal* condition for Hong Kong, whereas the imposition of the Chinese sovereignty is a historical exception. To Chin, the British colonial history did not exert oppression over Hong Kong; instead, it has rebuilt the place as a city-state that flourished in Britain's global network of free trade. Chin has classified Hong Kong together with Singapore, Kuwait and the United Arab Emirates (Dubai *inter alia*) as Britain's 'Asian city cluster', where Britain governed the city-states by promoting free trade and empowering local compradors. Chin glorifies the city-states for becoming engines of modernisation for their regions after the British withdrawal, and he has coined Hong Kong as the 'first Chinese place to achieve modern life' (Wan-Kan 2012, 85–6, author's translation).

Like most of the nationalist activists, Chin places great emphasis on Hong Kong's particular lifestyle and its inner beauty and see all discords with the mainland, such as the milk powder shortage, parallel trading,[3] non-Cantonese speakers, use of simplified characters and the national education etc. as erosion of Hong Kong's city-state culture (Wan-Kan 2012, 86). Chin defines such a culture as a synergy of 'Victorian gentlemanship and Chinese republicanism' (Wan-Kan 2012, 86), which features both entrepreneurial and aesthetic dimensions with which the Hong Kong people were not only able to succeed in business,[4] but also able to retain some of the best traits of both Chinese and Western traditions (Wan-Kan 2012, 86). The Cantonese pronunciation and traditional characters are, for example, what Chin is obsessed with as a symbol of Hong Kong's proper inheritance of Chinese culture. More importantly, Chin suggests that what Hong Kong has preserved is always the finest and most essential part of each formative culture, which has been tarnished or jeopardised by the highly politicised environment in their regions of origin.

Chin's interpretation of the Hong Kongese cultural identity entails a series of circumstantial and selective interpretation of details, while his understanding of Hong Kong's specific geo-political status deserves more attention. Chin sums up Hong Kong's position in world history as being in a protracted 'intermediate' condition. Unlike the traditional identity formation achieved by prioritising a cultural certainty on a territorial basis (Anderson 1983, 2), the intermediate condition has extricated Hong Kong from ideological disputes as well as prolonged policy debates, given that there have been no constraints of rigid national identity. This freedom enabled an 'intricate governance' to be applied in Hong Kong on an issue-specific basis. The Hong Kong governors, especially the London-appointed official elites who were always aloft from local affairs, were thus able to tailor policy packages accurately according to practical scenarios. The practice of British governance in Hong Kong, according to Chin, has achieved a well-functioning, as well as self-stabilising equilibrium among democratic practices in economic, political and cultural terms (Wan-Kan 2012, 109–11). To Chin, this explains why the British-colonial authority was able to juxtapose financial austerity together with a welfare system in public service without inflicting ideological debates, and also why, for example, Governor MacLehose's social democratic policy could coexist with Margaret Thatcher's neoliberalism back in Britain.

Hong Kong's intermediate condition from which the city-state identity has emerged deserves attention not only in a historical, but also a theoretical sense. The theoretical implication of the intermediate status, however, is not that an intricate governance would always follow as a necessity. Rather, this immediate status, which presumed Hong Kong's 'golden age' during the Cold War, has constituted a site where identity narratives proliferated. It is also this particular intermediate status that allowed contested socio-political and cultural practices to coexist in an equilibrium mediated via the specific configuration of power relations of the Cold War. The intermediate condition as a departure for interrogating Hong Kong's particular nationalist identity cannot, however, be accommodated by the frameworks of universalism or localism outlined by conventional postcolonial theories. To resolve this problem in context, this chapter will introduce the idea of 'multiple socio-political spaces' as a lateral field of explanation in the next section.

Political spaces and the location of Hong Kongese identity politics

The 'intermediate' condition positioned by Chin Wan-Kan as the source of Hong Kongese exceptionality is ultimately a *relational* category which can only be made sense of from *between* socio-political entities. A theoretical framework that denotes the inter-societal dimension of social development is thus in order. It is obvious that the inbetweener status is logically a product of multiple social and political spaces, and it is also conceivable that such an inbetweener position would only emerge through the process of interaction and co-constitution among contested social forces in context. As Benedict Anderson has suggested, the concept of 'national state', especially that in the postcolonial context, should be understood by reference to the broad cultural system that preceded its modern form (Anderson 1983, 19). It is, however, more astutely noticed by Michael Oakeshott and Hannah Arendt that modern national space grows from the competition between local conventions, the *societas* and universal appeals, the *universitas*; and it is always a hybridity of the pursuit of private interests and the proclamation of public significance (Arendt 1958; Bhabha 1990, 2; Oakeshott 1975). It is the ambivalence in all nationalist narratives that has made the history of national formation a contradictory process which is full of both progression and regression in the context of uneven development of capitalism (Nairn 1997; Nairn and James 2005).

The above-mentioned ambivalence has produced the greatest analytical difficulties for understanding the meaning of the current 'nationalist turn' in Hong Kong's social movements. It is obvious that both the local-traditional and the universalist discourses have been used interchangeably in constructing the existing nationalist narratives, whereas the relationships between *societas*, *universitas* and Chinese, non-Chinese imageries have been complex and ambiguous. For Joshua Wong's Scholarism, the *Undergrad* and Chin Wan-Kan, it is the negation of China as historically situated realities, rather than any substantive cultural narrative that is categorically against the idea of 'Chineseness' that matters. Homi Bhabha's emphasis on the 'location' of politics is thus of great significance in this regard. Bhabha questions the 'singularities' in concepts such as 'class' or 'gender',

> What is theoretically innovative, and politically crucial, is the need to think beyond narratives of originary and initial subjectivities and to focus on those moments or processes that are produced in the articulation of cultural differences. These 'inbetween' spaces provide the terrain of selfhood – singular or communal – that initiate new signs of identity, and innovative sites of collaboration, and contestation in the act of defining the idea of society itself.
>
> (Bhabha 1994, 2)

Bhabha's formulation of the concept of 'inbetween' space is particularly useful in Hong Kong's case because it has effectively transcended the concepts such as 'colonial' or 'decolonial' identities which are both 'narratives of originary'. These two categories are both inadequately understood in postcolonial Hong Kong in the sense that Hong Kong's subjectivities have been continuously selecting contradictory narratives supplied or imposed by different colonisers to elaborate the protean idea of selfhood (Chow 1992).

It is thus very important to identify the position Hong Kong has occupied in which its self-oriented identities have been negotiated out historically. As Tom Nairn has compellingly argued, theses and antitheses of postcolonial nationalities should both be understood in the context of capitalist development which is fundamentally 'uneven'. Unevenness is further pitched by recent historical sociologists as the defining character of all social movements which are all products of 'heterogeneous interaction'. First, it is the unevenness between multiple socio-political spaces that makes it inevitable for one course of social development to internalise variegated forms of 'concrete labours' and geographically dispersed societal constructions of multiple origins (Matin 2013; Rosenberg 2006, 308); and second, the combination of uneven social developments in certain historical conjunctures makes it necessary for the negotiation of identity narratives and nationhood to take place which is subject to wider geo-strategic initiatives mediated by uneven social developments. In this regard, it is not the contour of Hong Kong's prolific identity narratives, but the historically emerging site that has proliferated those narratives that matters in particular.

Hong Kong as an inbetweener and a site of alterity

Since China's cession of Hong Kong to Britain in the settlement of the Opium War (1840), Hong Kong's international and regional position has been mediated by various strategic initiatives arising from the drastic socioeconomic and political differences between China and Britain. The unevenness between Britain as a 'free-trade hegemony' (Gallagher and Robinson 1953) and China as a self-enclosed agrarian empire necessitated a linkage between the two societies as economic and social interests became increasingly vested in the British regional network of trade.

Britain's global hegemony of the nineteenth century was largely built upon the 'world-wide networks of dependence' in which Britain's economic interests were accrued via a 'global balance of power' among states that encapsulated *haute finance* and liberal ideology. Britain's particular hegemonic model enabled the re-inauguration of imperialism, the *pax Britannica* without overusing coercion – a political stance of 'splendid isolation' was thus globally erected (Arrighi 1994, 56; Polanyi 2001, 14). Hong Kong's administrative order was completely premised upon British trade and financial relations in Asia. The early British-colonial government of Hong Kong was funded on revenues from the opium trade, while it sustained public service and a social welfare system by housing the headquarters of large international firms such as Jardine Matheson and Hong Kong and Shanghai Bank (HSBC), which has in turn connected Hong Kong to London and other major commercial centres of the world (Tsang 2007, 56–8)

The fact that Britain ruled Hong Kong on a non-settlement basis, while 'asserting itself on the basis of superior organisations, logistics and military might' enabled a transcultural formation with Hong Kong being perceived as an *inbetweener*, thus providing a gateway for China to the global trade community (Donald and Vanderwolk 2014). The late imperial China, though interpolated with treaty-ports imposed by western powers, was still largely insulated from the global market due to the imperial government's stiff regulation and monopoly of domestic trade. Chinese merchants thus needed Hong Kong as a 'trans-regional hub' to bypass imperial regulations and 'joined international intermediaries as full partners in trade with China and the rest of Asia' (Tsang 2007, 57).

Notably, the inbetweener position of Hong Kong arising from the unevenness between China and the global market did not necessarily warrant the intermediary condition described by Chin Wan-Kan, which implies 'intricate governance', apolitical administration and a technocratic approach to public affairs. Instead, the early history of British-colonial Hong Kong was plagued by racial inequalities, class conflicts and political upheavals as a result of the complex demographic and societal compositions (Lau 1990). Though the British authority maintained a rather lax control over the Chinese-local population with no official discrimination, it was Hong Kong's inbetweener position that incurred immigration and social reconfiguration as the trans-regional commerce and shipping flourished.

Class formation in Hong Kong has also taken place along racial and ethnic lines as a result of implicit segregation arising from the daily practice of international business at the intersection of cultures. The British, as well as other Caucasian peoples who were engaged in commercial activities had soon occupied the upper-class echelon of the Hong Kong society, whereas the Chinese population, stratified as the compradors parasitic on the British–Chinese trade, were partly admitted to the business community honoured by the colonial authority (M. K. Chan

1996, 14; Tsang 2007, 63–5). The division in living standards, however, created ferocious labour unrests, including the early anti-British boycott, the joint strike with Cantonese workers, and the ground-breaking 'Hong Kongese Cultural Revolution' of the 1967 riot, which all embodied the simple idea of Chinese nationalism in the context of anti-imperialism.

On the other hand, the Westernised universalist image glorified by contemporary Hong Kong nationalists is derived from the early history of segregation and the creo (settler) culture hence formed. The relative independence, openness and lax control in the British-Western merchant community has made Hong Kong an attraction to the mainland elites since 1860s, as:

> Hong Kong increasingly proved itself a positive example of what a reasonably well-administered British territory, inhabited mainly by Chinese people was like to those Chinese intellectuals who had the interest and the critical faculty to take on board this contrast with the situation prevailing in China.
>
> (Tsang 2007, 74–6)

Hong Kong also provided a 'safe haven' for the Chinese reformers who were excluded by the imperial and communist conservatives where a fountain of progressive thought was able to flow.[5] This inbetweener status explains the combination of pan-Chinese-ness and universal liberal-democracy for Hong Kongers as 'Chinese without a Chinese state' (Choy 2009; Tu 2006). However, the meaning of Chinese-ness here certainly deserves a closer inspection in the aforesaid interspatial context.

The 'safe haven' Hong Kong was able to provide to the incoming population has served not only as a crucible of multiculturalism on the surface, but more importantly as a crucial stabiliser of social order, cooling down socio-political upheavals which would hit the business community. For both Western and Chinese expatriates and migrants, Hong Kong was a 'new world' where social baggage from home was jettisoned and the chance offered to 'progress up a social hierarchy imported from the Old World, without the barriers created by the presence of already established elites' (Shilliam 2009, 78). The image of 'Chinese-ness' in this case did not stand starkly against the British-Western image, particularly in the sense that the Chinese-ness of Hong Kong, reconfigured as a creo identity, was articulated in the contour of 'Chinese alterity'; thus, the lifestyle of Hong Kong was envisioned as a 'China in abstract', negating the concrete 'China in reality' the Creos experienced from imperial breakdown to the founding of the People's Republic of China. In this sense, an image of 'cultural China', which includes the appreciation of traditional characters, the antique beauty of Cantonese pronunciation and the daily practice of Confucian etiquette etc. has coexisted comfortably with universalist liberal-democracy, all in the subset of the spatially configured 'Chinese alterity'.

An alternative China, an autonomous Hong Kong

The site of 'Chinese alterity' has enabled proliferation of both particularist and universalist identity-formation to take place along the same line of 'China in abstract'. This geo-cultural position of Hong Kong reached its zenith towards the end of the Cold War as a result of its own course of 'uneven and combined development'. The most significant strategic condition for Hong Kong during the Cold War was that both Britain and China relied heavily on its intermediary position, which in turn perpetuated the social condition underlying the creo identity amongst the Chinese inhabitants. The trajectory towards this formation was, however, never smooth. Hong Kong underwent the most severe social turmoil in 1967 mainly as a result of the widespread influence of the Proletarian Cultural Revolution stemming from the mainland. A small labour dispute in an artificial flower factory sparked a large-scale anti-colonial revolt headed by the pro-communist Hong Kong Federation of Trade Unions; meanwhile, the power struggle in the Communist leadership in Beijing provoked excessively violent actions by workers against the British authority and critics of the Cultural Revolution (Tsang 2007, 185). The movement, which in turn led to substantial casualties and political instabilities in the colonial government, has preluded Hong Kong's transformation into a Chinese-oriented middle-class society where the current constitutional principle of 'autonomy' is rooted.

Key to this transformation is the so-called 'levelling movement' in Hong Kong's Chinese Creo society, through which 'the civic privileges associated with aristocratic elites' – which was previously monopolised by the British-Western community under segregation – became dramatically democratised as Chinese-Hong Kongese citizens were further included in a more extensive middle-class welfare scheme under the reform of Governor MacLehose (1971–1981).[6] However, if the colonial reform, the rise of Hong Kongese middle-class and the associated identity for autonomy are to be contexualised, it was the mainland China's constant demand for Hong Kong's position as an 'inbetweener' that corresponded with the British reform in Hong Kong.

Historical archives have demonstrated that the Communist government's stance towards the 1967 leftist revolt was always outwardly firm but accommodating beneath the surface (Heaton 1970). Between May to August, the CCP's official paper *People's Daily* published a series of commentaries stridently condemning the British-colonial government's violent suppression of the Hong Kong labourers. For example, on 7 August, a commentary titled 'Tighten the Noose on the British Imperialists' called on the workers to 'take every possible action', and another on 20 August declared that 'Hong Kong Is a Chinese Territory'.[7] What was behind this assertive face was the then Chinese premier Zhou Enlai's reluctance to get involved in Hong Kong affairs and a potential conflict with the British authority. In July, Zhou told the Commander of Guangzhou Military Area that Hong Kong needed to be handled with care, whilst it was the Soviet Revisionists' plot to ensnare China to retake Hong Kong. Hong Kong would also become a 'dead port' if the unrest continued. On 23 August, Zhou received the Red Guards in Beijing and criticised their use of violence on the British representative office (Ruxin 2012, 278).

In retrospect, Zhou's sudden brake on the unrest was not unexpected. Later, as the Cultural Revolution came to the end, the Communist government's official reflection on the event contained criticisms of the violent aspect of the movement. Despite the fact that Mao Zedong conceived of a more adventurous project to retake Hong Kong in event of the unrest, the Chinese government's long-term calculation was to make the best use of Hong Kong for China's own development. The guideline of 'planning for the long-term, and making use of to the greatest extent' set the tone at the beginning of the People Republic of China's (PRC's) Hong Kong policy.

The Communist government's long-term calculation over Hong Kong involved a way of further utilising its role as an inbetweener, which was necessitated by the unevenness between a backward China and an advanced-capitalist West, as well as the combined development of the Cold War. It is obvious that China, during most of its postwar reconstruction, was hampered by shortages in funds, technology and knowledge, which were available in the trade networks of Hong Kong. The abundance of capital in Hong Kong as a financial centre has thus become China's 'privilege of backwardness' (Knei-Paz 1978; Matin 2006) in its efforts to 'catch-up' developmentally, a process essential to China's geopolitically mediated industrialisation and national defence strategy. Under the US-imposed embargo during the Cold War, the porous border of Hong Kong made the city one of the few sources for China to access the privileges behind the 'bamboo curtain'. In the meantime, the Cold War rivalry between the two blocs, Britain's relative decline in the postwar era and China's particular stance that occupied the 'intermediate zone' between the Soviet Union and the USSR made it beneficial for both parties to be benevolent towards each other. China was certainly conscious of avoiding any disruption in Hong Kong's sovereignty in order not to unsettle the Anglo-Chinese relationship (Chen 2001, 3–5). Additionally, Hong Kong's relative autonomy during the Cold War was of strategic importance to China's espionage operations not only against the western bloc, but also Taiwan as an unclaimed territory of China (Walton 2013).

The 1967 riot as China's self-inflicted chaos, which in turn unsettled Hong Kong's autonomous status, eventually taught both China and Britain a lesson that porosity in the Mainland–Hong Kong border would push a homogenised Hong Kong towards China, and also erode Hong Kong's inbetweener position. Both sides thus began to tighten up border control. China's Guangzhou Military Area used force against Chinese refugees who attempted to escape to Hong Kong, while in 1980 the British-colonial government closed the residence path allowing illegal migrants to settle in order to discourage a further influx of mainlanders (Tsang 2007, 193–4).

By curbing porosity, Hong Kong's autonomous status was strengthened after the 1967 riots. This has given rise to a more diverse but also increasingly fluid composition of both universalism, localism and Chinese-ness. The Western-oriented liberal democratic thought became salient as a more inclusive constitutional arrangement began to narrow the gap between the local middle class and the British-Western expatriate community, while the image of 'China in abstract' still featured prominently in the composition of identity from the 1980s. This newly formed identity shared 'outlook incorporated elements of the traditional Confucian moral code and emphasis on the importance of the family, as well as modern concepts like the rule of law, freedom of speech and of movement, respect for human rights, a limited government, a free economy, a go-getting attitude and pride in the local community's collective rejection of corruption' (Tsang 2007, 195). The Chinese aspect, instead of being self-contradictory, has actually served as a mutually propelling force to the universal appeal sitting at the root of the autonomous Hong Kongese identity. Hong Kong's 'Chinese alterity', framed in the fashion of 'pan-Chinese-ness' (C. K. Chan 2014), has actually represented a socio-political condition that the mainland development did not espouse, but would strategically endorse as part of the favourable international–regional environment that China's development would require. Such an endorsement underlay Zhou's suppression of the leftist riots, as well as Deng Xiaoping's post-handover constitutional architecture of 'One Country Two Systems'.

Such a strategic relationship achieved by maintaining Hong Kong's autonomous position served to juxtapose the abstract Chinese identity with the middle-class liberal democratic thinking in an equilibrium, so long as the unevenness between China and the West kept creating an initiative for China's continuous appropriation of Hong Kong as an inbetweener. It was also in such a strategic environment that the most critical reform in Hong Kong's history was carried out by Governor MacLehose, whose initiatives included tackling bureaucratic corruption, streamlining the administrative system and releasing more political opportunities to the locals. MacLehose's reform provided the necessary institutional basis for Hong Kong's economic miracle of the 1980s which has produced a handful of self-made billionaires with abstract Chinese identity such as Li Ka-shing, and the 'swelling ranks of middle class' grounded in a professional and managerial culture, which has further separated Hong Kong from the politicised, amateurish environment of mainland China (Tsang 2007, 192).

The eclipse of inbetweener and the de-signifying turn

It has been argued above that the unevenness between China and the West has prolonged Hong Kong's status as an inbetweener of socioeconomic and strategic significance to both China and Britain. Evidently, unevenness as a generic condition that exists between societies will not vanish (Matin 2013; Rosenberg 2012), However, change in the quantitative unevenness between China and the advanced capitalist world is resetting the Chinese government's strategic priorities and its relative position towards Hong Kong, which will in turn unsettle Hong Kong's inbetweener status on which autonomous development as well as the equilibrated identity composition were premised during the Cold War. In other words, if China is no longer as backward as it used to be during the Cold War, Hong Kong will become functionally less relevant to China's pursuit of national strategies. Unlike what many Hong Kong nationalists such as Chin Wan-Kan have argued that Beijing has been taking an assertive position towards Hong Kong because China needs to colonise the city (Wan-Kan 2012, 122), it is actually the waning importance of Hong Kong to the mainland that has removed the Chinese government's incentive to 'seal Hong Kong off' from mainland politics and society.

The redistribution of unevenness between China and the West is first manifest in China becoming an active exporter rather than importer of capital in the event of 'the Rise of China'. China's rapid economic growth into the twenty-first century has caused it a huge pressure of overproduction, compelling the local and central government to find outlets for 'destocking' domestic capital.[8] Hong Kong had been chosen as China's gateway for outbound investment as it had become the world's third largest outbound investor,[9] while now, Hong Kong is only one of the many gateways as part of China's 'Belt and Road' initiative launched under the Xi Jinping authority in 2013.

The Belt and Road initiative, by projecting China's great power status via a global network of Chinese economic existence (Shambaugh 2015) has in turn dramatically undermined Hong Kong's longstanding status as the 'agent for China's progress' by repositioning it at the receiving end of capital. As Xi Jinping's foreign policy becomes more proactive and assertive, China has become more confident and daring in utilising its power, especially the growing absolute material capabilities to advance its overseas interests (Zhang 2015, 6). Hong Kong is thus no longer viewed by the Beijing leadership as China's gateway to the world, and there is much less of an incentive for Beijing to maintain Hong Kong's inbetweener status by taming the nationalist sentiment in China, as Zhou did during the Cultural Revolution.

Conclusion

Let us return to Tu Weiming's understanding of Hong Kong's identity as being formed by its peripheral status in the Chinese world. Tu insists that the Chinese Hong Kong identity embodies a true understanding of Chinese culture 'from a distance', inasmuch as the Chinese diasporic communities in the city inherit the genuine spirit of Chinese culture without identifying themselves with any concrete form of Chinese nation-state, either the Republic or People's Republic of China (Tu 2006). The fact that the diasporic communities are sealed off from the political fluctuation and destroyed spiritual life in the mainland enabled the Hong Kong-Chinese to 'tap indigenous symbolic resources' from the image of China they conjured up in exile.

However, the distance from mainland China is not only significant in the sense that if any genuine cultural understanding about China remains in the abstract, it is also important in the sense that it immunised Hong Kong from the political realities of China which was broadly perceived as intransigent and degenerative. This explains the nature of Hong Kong's current anti-establishment movements: it is ultimately a quest for a geo-cultural position as inbetweener rather than any substantive cultural-political narrative. The current pro-independence or nationalist movements have thus represented a nostalgia about such a position achieved during the Cold War which the postcolonial political arrangements strive to preserve. Obviously seeing Hong Kong as only a political or constitutional matter is 'too simple' if not always 'naïve' since both Britain and China have lost the incentive to maintain and defend Hong Kong's position in the current environment of social development and strategic relationships between the two powers.

The case of Hong Kong's history as an inbetweener has brought to the scene of postcolonial studies a dimension of political spaces for understanding the nature of postcolonial state-formation and its socio-political struggles. Hong Kong has certainly presented a unique experience which would break down binaries of 'tradition' and 'modernity', or 'localism' and 'universalism' in understanding postcolonial identity formation. Though it is arguable that Hong Kong's recent situation, like most other postcolonial state-formation, could be read largely in the context of the contradictory process of universalisation under capitalism (Chakrabarty 2009; Chibber 2013), the meaning of interwoven narratives and their strategic orientation, however, is negotiated in the interstices emerging from overlapping 'domains of differences' (Bhabha 1994, 2–5) which are all strategically carved by agents of uneven social development. Therefore, the location of a postcolonial struggle is far more important than what it proclaims to struggle for.

Bibliography

Anderson, Benedict. 1983. *Imagined Communities*. London: Verso.

Arendt, Hannah. 1958. *The Human Condition*. Chicago: University of Chicago Press.

Arrighi, Giovanni. 1994. *The Long Twentieth Century*. London: Verso.

Bhabha, Homi K. 1990. *Nation and Narration*. London: Routledge.

—— 1994. *The Location of Culture*. London: Routledge.

Chakrabarty, Dipesh. 2009. *Provincializing Europe*. Princeton: Princeton University Press.

Chan, Chi Kit. 2014. 'China as "Other": Resistance to and Ambivalence Toward National Identity in Hong Kong.' *China Perspective* 1: 25–34.

Chan, Johannes. 2014. 'Hong Kong's Umbrella Movement.' *The Round Table* 103(6): 571–80.

Chan, Ming K. 1996. 'Hong Kong-Colonial Legacy, Transformation, and Challenge.' *The Annals of the American Academy of Political and Social Science* 547: 11–23.

Chen, Jian. 2001. *Mao's China and the Cold War*. Chapel Hill: University of North Carolina Press.

Cheng, Edmund and Samson, Yuen, 'Post-Umbrella Movement: Farewell to the Era of Political Indifference.' *Mingpao Daily*, November 29, 2014

Chibber, Vivek. 2013. *Postcolonial Theory and the Specter of Capital*. London: Verso Books.

Chow, Rey. 1992. 'Between Colonizers: Hong Kong's Postcolonial Self-Writing in the 1990s.' *Diaspora: A Journal of Transnational Studies* 2(2): 151–70.

——. 2005. 'King Kong in Hong Kong: Watching the "Handover" from the USA.' In *A Companion to Postcolonial Studies*, eds. Henry Schwarz and Sangeeta Ray. Oxford: John Wiley & Sons.

Choy, Howard Y. F. 2009. 'Schizophrenic Hong Kong: Postcolonial Identity Crisis in the Infernal Affairs Trilogy.' *Transtext(e)s Transcultures* (3): 52–66.

Donald, David C., and Jefferson P. Vanderwolk. 2014. *A Financial Centre for Two Empires*. Cambridge: Cambridge University Press.

Fung, Anthony. 2007. 'Postcolonial Hong Kong Identity: Hybridising the Local and the National.' *Social Identities* 10(3): 399–414.

Gallagher, John, and Ronald Robinson. 1953. 'The Imperialism of Free Trade.' *The Economic History Review* 6(1): 1.

Gellner, Ernest. 2006. *Nations and Nationalism*. Ithaca: Cornell University Press.

Guha, Ranajit. 1997. *Dominance Without Hegemony*. Cambridge, MA: Harvard University Press.

Heaton, William. 1970. 'Maoist Revolutionary Strategy and Modern Colonialism: the Cultural Revolution in Hong Kong.' *Asian Survey* 10(9): 840–57.

Hui, Po-Keung, and Kin-Chi Lau. 2015. '"Living in Truth" Versus Realpolitik: Limitations and Potentials of the Umbrella Movement.' *Inter-Asia Cultural Studies* 16(3): 348–66.

Ip, Eric C. 2016. 'Constitutional Conflict in Hong Kong Under Chinese Sovereignty.' *Hague Journal on the Rule of Law* 8(1): 75–99.

Knei-Paz, Baruch. 1978. *The Social and Political Thought of Leon Trotsky*. Oxford: Clarendon Press.

Lau, Kit Ching Chan. 1990. *China, Britain and Hong Kong, 1895–1945*. Hong Kong: Chinese University Press.

Matin, K. 2006. 'Uneven and Combined Development and "Revolution of Backwardness": the Iranian Constitutional Revolution, 1906–11.' In *100 Years of Permanent Revolution*, ed. Hugo K Radice. London: Pluto Press.

——2013. 'Redeeming the Universal: Postcolonialism and the Inner Life of Eurocentrism.' *European Journal of International Relations* 19(2): 353–77.

Nairn, Tom. 1997. *Faces of Nationalism*. London: Verso.

Nairn, Tom, and Paul Warren James. 2005. *Global Matrix*. London: Pluto Press.

Oakeshott, Michael. 1975. *On Human Conduct*. Oxford: Oxford University Press.

Polanyi, Karl. 2001. *The Great Transformation*. Boston: Beacon Press.

Rosenberg, Justin. 2006. 'Why Is There No International Historical Sociology?' *European Journal of International Relations* 12(3): 307–40.

——. 2012. 'The "Philosophical Premises" of Uneven and Combined Development.' *Review of International Studies* 39(03): 569–97.

Ruxin, Yu. 2012. *Hong Kong 1967: In the Maelstrom of the Cultural Revolution*, Cosmos Books, Hong Kong.

Shambaugh, David. 2015. 'China's Soft-Power Push.' *Foreign Affairs* (June/July).

Shilliam, Robbie. 2009. 'The Atlantic as a Vector of Uneven and Combined Development.' *Cambridge Review of International Affairs* 22(1): 69–88.

So, Alvin. 2015. 'The Making of Hong Kong Nationalism.' In *Asian Nationalisms Reconsidered*, ed. Jeff Kingston. London: Routledge.

Tsang, Steve. 2007. *A Modern History of Hong Kong*. London: I.B.Tauris.

Tu, Wei-ming. 2006. 'Cultural China: the Periphery as the Center.' *Daedalus* 134(4): 145–67.

Walton, Calder. 2013. *Empire of Secrets: British Intelligence, the Cold War and the Twilight of Empire*. London: Harper Collins.

Wan-Kan, Chin. 2012. *Hong Kong as a City-state*. Hong Kong: Enrich Publishing.

Wong, Joshua. 2015. 'Scholarism on the March.' *New Left Review* 92(March, April): 43–52.

Zhang, Jian. 2015. 'China's New Foreign Policy Under Xi Jinping: Towards "Peaceful Rise 2.0?".' *Global Change, Peace & Security* 27(1): 5–19.

Notes

1 See *Financial Times*' coverage on 'Hong Kong's anger at the "locust" Chinese shoppers intensifies', Feb. 16, 2015, https://www.ft.com/content/895bc3de-b5a5-11e4-b58d-00144feab7de.

2 For the legitimacy of the Hong Kong nationalism, see 'Taking Hong Kong Independence Seriously: Chasm between Two Hong Kongs', in *Undergrad*, Aug. 2016.

3 See how the anti-parallel trade protests involved pro-independent movement in 'Hong Kong Anti-parallel Trade Protest Pulled at Last Minute', *South China Morning Post*, http://www.scmp.com/news/hong-kong/article/1940389/hong-kong-anti-parallel-trader-protest-pulled-last-minute, last access 30 April, 2017.

4 This is not only demonstrated by their ability to build up wealth, but also their success in entering the western noble class. See Wan-Kan (2012, 86).

5 In February 2010, Alan Leung Kah-kit, former Civic Party Leader and Chief Executive candidate, emphasised in his dialogue with the pro-Beijing barrister Hu Hanqing in the TV RTHK talk show, 'Solution', that Hong Kong's autonomous status would facilitate China's future democratic transformation.

6 For the same logic in a creo society, see Shilliam (2009).

7 For details of the relevant publications, see Ruxin (2012, 274–6). (The book is published in Chinese and it is the author's translation here).

8 See 'Overproduction Swamps Small Chinese Cities, Revealing Depth of Crisis' in *The Wall Street Journal*, Feb 17, 2016, http://www.wsj.com/articles/overcapacity-swamps-smaller-chinese-cities-revealing-depth-of-crisis-1455738108, last access 1 Oct, 2016.

9 For the data of China's soaring outbound investment, see statistics of the Hong Kong Trade and Development Council http://www.hktdc.com/mis/coi/en/s/overview.html, last access 1 Oct, 2016.

PART IV

Struggles over land

22
INTRODUCTION

As discussed in our main introduction, postcolonial critique first came to prominence in the academy through English and Commonwealth literature and cultural studies. In this respect, some scholars have questioned the postcolonial focus on discourse and representation to the detriment of more 'material' issues of political economy. This is an especially pertinent critique when we consider the long tradition in Marxist thought of analysing the relationship between imperialism and capitalism. Of course, issues of political economy have always been central to the colonial project, especially struggles over land and the appropriation and control of the resources and peoples in, on and of it. These struggles have themselves been folded into key theological, legal and moral disputes in early-modern European thought: from Vitoria, Las Casas and Sepúlveda to John Locke. Moreover, the political economy of colonial expansion and imperial rule must be considered as a global project: the dispossession and enslavement of indigenous and African peoples in the Americas finds echoes in proclamations of *terra nullius* (uninhabited lands) by European colonisers in Australia and the Pacific.

In this Part, we turn postcolonial critique to engage, specifically, with struggles over land. In doing so, we wish to demonstrate to the reader that, at a minimum, postcolonial critique does not need to – and should not – engage only with the representational at the expense of the material articulations of coloniality. In fact, drawing attention to struggles over land enables us to challenge the naturalised distinction made between the material – land, bodies, resources, etc. – and the representational – discourse, identity, etc. – and even the immaterial or spiritual. In this respect, we might wish to consider that the genocide of peoples has always entailed the attempted destruction not only of bodies and built environments but of knowledge systems (termed 'epistemicide' by Boaventura dos Santos) and the profane and spiritual agencies that bind peoples to the land and which these systems document as being of use to humanity.

The economies of the Global North are organised in such a way that land might not appear to be a fundamental vector of contemporary global politics, and certainly not as crucial as property, community, nationalism and citizenship. Yet if we situate our vantage point from within postcolonial critique, then environmental degradation, the financialisation of agriculture, food sovereignty, and physical and spiritual dispossession reveal themselves to be not only key issues for global governance, but also issues that emerge out of long and continuing colonial legacies. It might be, then, that postcolonial critique will be ill-equipped to pursue global justice unless it engages even more rigorously with struggles over land, especially with regard to restitution, repatriation and reparations.

In Chapter 23 A. Haroon Akram-Lodhi sets out a materialist framework for understanding the relationship between land expropriation, colonialism and contemporary neoliberal capitalism. Akram-Lodhi argues that, at its most fundamental, enclosure has historically involved the expropriation of lands in colonised spaces and places controlled by the colonial power. Crucially, such enclosure was predicated upon the coercive power of the coloniser. In so doing, enclosure transformed livelihoods and reshaped the identities of colonial subjects. Akram-Lodhi is at pains to point out that this process is not simply historical but ongoing: enclosure is also intrinsic to neoliberal capitalism. However, Akram-Lodhi argues that land is no longer the principal foci of the drive to enclose. Instead, contemporary enclosures seek to dismantle any barriers to commodification that restrict the development of an ever-more-flagrant law of value that is so central to the operation of neoliberal capitalism. Finally, Akram-Lodhi turns to one of the most influential global actors concerning land issues, La Via Campesina, who have challenged the power of private property, the power of the market, and in so doing, the power of enclosure under neoliberal capitalism.

In considering land and the legacies of colonialism we might be forgiven for ignoring the largest and most distinguishing feature of our global topography: the Pacific Ocean. In Chapter 24, Joy Lehuanani Enomoto and D. Keali'i MacKenzie address the issues outlined by Akram-Lodhi by turning our attention to the vast sea of islands known as Oceania, many of which are experiencing a significant rise in sea levels caused by the global exploitation of resources and contamination of the environment. But Enomoto and MacKenzie also turn our attention to the struggles undertaken by the indigenous peoples of Oceania to address such extreme environmental challenges. They focus especially on the retention of culture and Native-owned information through the embodied archives, that is, those aspects of culture that are often ignored in colonial archives but are carried with peoples of Oceania as they face the future and navigate the sea once more. Enomoto and MacKenzie make a forceful case that it is Native knowledge that has ensured survival so far, and it will be the same knowledge – held in the continuum of collective memory – that will allow for adaptation to the future. Enomoto and MacKenzie write specifically to the peoples of Oceania concerning forced migration, permanent displacement, threats to sovereignty and other irreparable impacts of climate change. However, their words hold general import.

Ajay Parasram and Lisa Tilley write Chapter 25 inspired by the knowledge and practice of indigenous peoples in their confrontation with global environmental harm. Parasram and Tilley argue that to mitigate against planetary environmental harm, the 'protective ontologies' maintained and cultivated by Indigenous communities must be afforded their rightful guiding position at the forefront of global action. In this respect, the chapter argues for a consideration of global environmental harm from the position of the world's 'internal frontiers' in both settler colonial and former franchise colonial countries. Parasram and Tilley argue that such a position affords, first of all, an understanding of environmental harm from the perspective of those most violently impacted by climate change, contamination, dispossession and state-corporate aggression on the frontlines of climate struggles. Secondly, this focus draws attention to the processes of racialisation of frontier populations and to the environmental racism and raced modes of dispossession these processes enable. And thirdly, a frontier focus centralises protective, relational ontologies. The chapter makes the case that planetary solutions for resuscitating our choking world ought to take guidance from the spaces in our world that are not fully indoctrinated into modern, capitalist thinking as espoused by much of the global leadership on climate change.

In Chapter 26 Ijahnya Christian turns our attention to another key aspect of the relationship between colonialism and land: the removal of peoples from their ancestral homelands and the complex politics of repairing such a breach. When addressing colonial legacies, the dispossession of peoples from their land remains as pressing a concern as the exploitation and degradation of those lands. Christian calls attention to the extraordinary situation of Rastafari who have repatriated to Africa, and specifically to the Shashemene Land Grant provided by Ethiopian Emperor Haile Selassie I. Christian explores themes of power and mobilisation, creativity, conflict, contradiction, inhibition, integration and resilience in the quest for formal recognition, meaning legal status, of the people who lay claim to the land grant. Christian paints the context as one of continued struggle with identity, and variously tempered and frustrated by the realisation that freedom of movement within Africa is not a right guaranteed to most Africans. Christian writes with an insider voice, and with perspectives shaped by frequent travel to and from Ethiopia in order to maintain legal status while in residence at the Nyahbinghi Tabernacle Centre on the Shashemene Land Grant.

We have included, as Chapter 27, a (lightly copy-edited) transcript of a speech delivered by Andile Mngxitama, President of Black First Land First (BLF) and former Member of the South African Parliament. The speech was delivered at the University of Johannesburg, 16 March 2016, and in it Mngxitama addresses the call for decolonisation by university students which, as #RhodesMustFall, has made a global impact. The chapter argues that, while the statue is gone, the colonial spirit of Cecil Rhodes has remained. And crucially, whilst discussion is ongoing about the nature of student demands and how they link up to the project of decolonisation, there is consensus that the call is, in the main, university-centred. Mngxitama takes issues with this shift in focus by recounting the development of the student movement. In the first moment, students made discursive attempts to imagine decolonisation as a project beyond the university and centred on the demand for the return of lands unjustly taken by settler colonialism. However, this demand has yet to find practical expression as a point of mobilisation by the movement. The 'back to land campaign' is yet to be integrated into student demands, and in this respect Mngxitama questions whether a decolonised university is ever possible in a still-colonial society.

23

'OLD WINE IN NEW BOTTLES'

Enclosure, neoliberal capitalism and postcolonial politics

A. Haroon Akram-Lodhi

Introduction

Postcolonial identities and politics, both within and between states, have been decisively shaped by the legacies of colonialism and colonial rule, which structurally transformed the material foundations of precolonial societies and in so doing, not only reconfigured their political and economic organisation but also their cultural and social forms. In this way, then, contemporary postcolonial political discourses and their discursive environments must be situated within the material foundations that were so irrevocably transformed. This chapter argues that a foundational colonial transformation, with a clear and ongoing material impact that continues to shape diverse and variegated identities, was that of enclosure. At its most fundamental, enclosure has historically involved the appropriation of land – in this case, lands in the colonised spaces and places controlled by the colonial power. Such enclosure was predicated upon the coercive power of the coloniser, which acted in support of a discourse that legitimised violence in the name of a mission to civilise by forcibly dragging colonial subjects into modernity. In so doing, enclosure transformed livelihoods and reshaped the identities of subaltern colonial subjects.

However, this chapter also argues that enclosure is not just a colonial phenomenon; rather, enclosure is an ongoing process that is intrinsic to neoliberal capitalism. By capitalism, I mean an economic system of generalised commodity production predicated upon a highly asymmetrical distribution of the means of production and which has as its objective the production of surplus-value. By neoliberal, I mean the ongoing intensification and expansion of market relations since 1980, by increasing the number, frequency, intensity, repeatability, and formalisation of transactions, and with the principal role of the state being that of an enabler of market relations.

In an era of neoliberal capitalism contemporary enclosures continue to appropriate land, but land is no longer the principal focus of the drive to enclose. Instead, contemporary enclosures seek to dismantle any barriers to commodification that restrict the development of an ever-more-flagrant law of value that is so central to the operation of neoliberal capitalism. In so doing, enclosures, of both the colonial and the contemporary type, bring about two key material transformations: the creation and expansion of private property and the creation and expansion of markets. Private property must be understood as an often coercively-constructed political project of both the colonial and the postcolonial periods. Markets must be understood as sites of politically-expressed social power that were constructed in the colonial period and which continue to be constructed in the postcolonial period. From these two transformations flow a series of binaries that have become not only central to neoliberal capitalism but have assumed the ideological guise of 'common sense'.

At the same time, the act of enclosing reconfigures cultural, national, ethnic, gender and class-based identities. While these had held varying degrees of social power under colonialism, it is the parameters of their reconfiguration in the postcolonial period that shape the scope and scale of the hybridisation that, through the agency of postcolonial politics, resists commodification, the creation of private property, the establishment of markets, and hence the very drive to enclose. Indeed, as will be seen, it is no coincidence that one of the most important actors in contemporary postcolonial politics, La Via Campesina, celebrates the hybridity of contemporary peasant identity when it challenges the power of private property, the power of the market, and in so doing, the power of enclosure under neoliberal capitalism.

Enclosure, past and present

In precolonial and colonial societies, land was the principle agrarian means of production, and thus a key determinant of social, political, economic, ecological, and cultural relationships and identities. In other words, the way in which land was held affected the capacity of dominant groups – elites, landlords, ruling classes, colonisers and others – to control agriculture. There were thus, in a sense, precolonial and colonial 'agrarian questions of land': who controlled it, how it was controlled, and the purpose for which it was controlled determined and reflected the distribution of power, property and privilege in the countryside and beyond, the capability of dominant groups to overcome any limitations to their control, and the extent to which the subaltern might be able to resist the actions of dominant groups.

In this context, there is a near-global precolonial and colonial history of country-specific transformations in rights over land that has resulted in restrictions in access to it being established by dominant groups. This is what is termed 'enclosure', and these restrictions have been, historically and, in the agrarian political economy literature, analytically, an important condition of the development of capitalism in both the metropole and the periphery. In the enclosure literature, it is important to stress that the key terrain of analysis is not the conditions under which property rights are transferred between individuals and social classes; rather, it is the conditions under which property rights are vested in individuals and social classes. In other words, the creation of property rights precede the creation of markets.

The importance of enclosure to the structure of social relations in the precolonial and colonial countryside was highlighted by Karl Marx when he wrote that:

> in the history of primitive accumulation, all revolutions are epoch-making that act as levers for the capitalist class in course of formation; but this is true above all for those moments when great masses of men are suddenly and forcibly torn from their means of subsistence, and hurled onto the labour-market as free, unprotected and rightless proletarians. The expropriation of the agricultural producer, of the peasant, from the soil is the basis of the whole process. The history of this expropriation assumes different aspects in different countries, and runs through its various phases in different orders of succession, and at different historical epochs. Only in England, which we therefore take as our example, has it the classic form.
>
> (Marx, 1976: 876, orig. 1867)

Marx thus explicitly recognised the possibility that there could be different types of enclosure through which a set of capitalist social relations would be established or consolidated. In Marx's 'classic' example, independent yeoman farmers began to be dispossessed from the land as the enclosure of the commons that were an important part of their social and material reproduction deepened the crisis of the peasant economy and in so doing, facilitated a process of socio-economic differentiation in the late fifteenth century. Within two centuries, a rural labouring class and a class of capitalist tenant-farmers faced each other, beneath the dominant landlord class (Byres, 2003). However, and this must be stressed, this was but one context-specific path of agrarian transition facilitated by enclosure (Byres, 1996; Akram-Lodhi and Kay, 2016).

Although the concept of enclosure resembles the idea of privatisation in David Harvey's (2005) thesis of 'accumulation by dispossession', its use here is different. Enclosure is about more than the privatisation of space-specific assets such as land, in either their physical or geographical aspects, although these dimensions would be critical for people living through the process. Neither should enclosure be considered to be the result of changes in the technical and commercial characteristics of farming. Finally, enclosure is not a consequence of the emergence of capitalist manufacturing and finance in the metropole. Rather, as Wood (2009) has stressed, in understanding enclosure, it is necessary to focus upon how the emergence of capital is rooted in changes in the content and meaning of social property relations. Capital is, in this materialist sense, a social relation, and not a thing, and the emergence of capital through processes of enclosure reflects deeper processes than simply the transfer of the private ownership of material assets such as land at a given point in precolonial, colonial or indeed postcolonial history. Enclosure is about more than just land, and thus needs to be more widely situated.

This proposition has been stressed by Massimo De Angelis (2001, 2004). However, while De Angelis argues that 'the separation of producers and means of production is…the central category…of Marx's critique of political economy' (De Angelis, 2004: 63), separation is not just 'the historical process of divorcing the producer from the means of production': what Marx refers to as the 'so-called primitive accumulation' (Marx, 1976: 874–5) that was a consequence of the enclosure of land. Rather, 'once capital exists, the capitalist mode of production itself evolves in such a way that it maintains and reproduces this separation on a constantly increasing scale' (Marx, 1971: 271). Bonefeld (2001) puts it thus: 'primitive accumulation…is the presupposition and condition of capital's existence'. In other words, it can be suggested that enclosures are not just a relic of precolonial and colonial times. Rather, 'enclosures are a continuous characteristic' of capital: if capital is a social relation, capital accumulation is an 'accumulation of social relations' (De Angelis, 2004: 60. 65) in which 'the silent compulsion of economic relations (that) sets the seal on the domination of the capitalist over the worker' continuously sits side-by-side with the imposition of 'direct extra-economic force' (Marx, 1976: 899–900).

This understanding of Marx's political economy allows De Angelis to present a more general analytical framework to understand enclosures across time, space and place. According to De Angelis, enclosure can take place whenever 'producers set themselves up as an obstacle to the reproduction of their separation from the means of production' in that capital develops 'social processes or sets of strategies aimed at dismantling those institutions that protect society from the market' (De Angelis, 2004: 69). Enclosure is witnessed whenever 'the forcible separation of people from whatever access to social wealth they have' … 'is not mediated by competitive markets and money as capital.'

Two modes of this 'forcible separation' can be observed: those that occur as a result of the deliberate recourse to extra-economic power; and those that occur as a by-product of the process of accumulation in capitalist markets (De Angelis, 2004: 75, 77). Forcible separation is fundamental to the 'transformation of subject into object' and thus 'echoes Marx's analysis of alienated labour' (De Angelis, 2004: 75, 77) and his understanding of commodity fetishism, with extraordinarily strong implications for the formation of identities and meaning among both the dominant and the subaltern, and thus for political agency and resistance. The 'space of enclosure' is predicated upon capital identifying 'a limit in order to transcend it'. Two types of limit are identified: the frontier, defined as 'a space of social life that is still relatively uncolonised by capitalist relations of production'; and political recomposition, defined as 'the need and strategic problem of dismantling' a social barrier to commodification that is predicated upon people having 'access to public wealth without a corresponding expenditure of work' (De Angelis, 2004: 72, 73, 80). Such access constitutes what today would be called a form of social provisioning and is the outcome of social and political struggle (Wuyts, 1992).

De Angelis thus offers a distinction between enclosure that shapes the historical emergence of a specifically capitalist set of social property relations and enclosure that theoretically and politically recognises the contemporary character of a specific variety of capitalism as a means of sustaining, by both reproducing and extending, capitalist social property relations. Intimately entwined in both is commodification: capital 'makes the world through commodification and enclosures' (De Angelis, 2004: 61); and with commodification comes the explicit and clear need on the part of dominant groups to undertake political processes that construct ideologies of private property as well as develop the markets where social power and privilege can be expressed.

De Angelis's account has five important implications. First, and clearly, as an ongoing process enclosure is not restricted to precolonial and colonial societies but can be found in postcolonial societies as well, as part of the normal, everyday and routine functioning of capitalism. Second, however, the implications of enclosure will vary greatly: depending on the mode of forcible separation; depending on the limits to the space of enclosure; and depending on how cultural, national, ethnic, gender and class-based identities shape and are shaped by access to the social wealth that is the principal object of enclosure. Third, it is within the interstices of these trajectories of variation that the identities that drove subaltern resistance to the colonial, and which now drive postcolonial politics, coalesce. Fourth, it is therefore to be expected that postcolonial identities and politics offer substantive diversity across place and space. Nonetheless, fifthly, and critically, notwithstanding the substantive diversity of postcolonial politics that emerges out of significant trajectories of variation, 'the fact that capital encloses … (generates) real social struggles against the many forms of capitalist enclosure' (De Angelis, 2004: 65, 57) and these form the fulcrum of postcolonial politics among the subaltern. Indeed, De Angelis' argument is centrally concerned with trying to understand how 'alternatives to capital pose a limit to accumulation by setting up rigidities and liberating… counter-enclosures, of spaces of commons' (De Angelis, 2004: 73).

Certainly, as will be seen below, recent literature on the postcolonial politics of subaltern transnational rural social movements, while not articulating the language of counter-enclosures, demonstrates the ways in which the power of peasants can pose limits to the accumulation of capital (Edelman and Borras, 2016).

Enclosure and the creation of private property

Enclosure transforms the character of social property relations through the reconfiguration of property rights. There is nothing 'natural' in this process; precolonial, colonial and postcolonial dominant elites used compulsion to seize social wealth from the subaltern and this brought about a reconfiguration of social property relations. In order to understand this non-natural process in more detail, and its importance for subaltern postcolonial politics in an age of neoliberal capitalism, it is useful to more fully understand what is meant by 'property'.

Property rights can be categorised into four distinct rights, usually referred to as a 'bundle' of rights: the right to use a good; the right to earn income from a good; the right to transfer a good to others; and the right to enforce property rights. These rights are socially defined and monitored and have to be enforceable. This means, in turn, that social institutions must emerge to regulate the governance of property rights. These social institutions are often called property regimes, and four can be identified.

The first regime is called open-access property and is found when property is not managed by an individual or a community and when access to the property cannot be controlled by an individual or a community. Thus, there is no formal limitation on anyone using open-access property because no one or no community 'owns' the property. Formally, open-access property is non-excludable, which means that no one can be excluded from using the property, but it can be rival, which means that one person's use of the property will reduce the amount that is available for other users. Historically, open-access property has been extremely important to smallholder peasant farmer livelihood strategies in the precolonial, colonial and postcolonial period, as the use of open-access property can supplement the holding that the farm owns or controls, and in so doing, can sustain individual and household welfare. For example, returning to Marx's 'classic' example, it was open-access property that sustained serfs during feudalism, and which was initially seized by landlords during the English enclosures of the fifteenth century. Open-access property remains important to rural livelihoods in many parts of postcolonial Asia, Africa and Latin America.

The second regime is state property, which is formally owned by all citizens of a specific jurisdiction. However, access to and use of state property is formally or informally regulated by the state. State property may or may not be excludable, depending upon formal legal parameters, and is rival. Land is state property in many postcolonial countries; China, Vietnam and Ethiopia, to name three.

Common property is the third type of property regime. Common property is owned by groups of individuals, often within the context of a specific spatial community. Access to, use of and exclusion from common property is controlled by the collective owners, although this may be managed by certain individuals within the collective ownership who occupy positions of authority: elders, priests or chiefs, for example, whose management of common property results in them becoming a dominant group within the community. Common property may or may not be excludable, depending upon informal community norms or formal legal stipulations, and is rival. Common property remains common, in postcolonial Africa and Oceania in particular.

The final type of property regime is the one with which we are most familiar: private property, in which access to, use of, exclusion from and management of property is controlled by the legally-recognised owner of the property, who may be an individual or a legally-recognised group of individuals. Private property is both excludable and rival.

A key point that emerges from the unbundling of various property regimes is that it should not be assumed that a private property regime is a uniform characteristic of precolonial, colonial and postcolonial human societies; indeed, it should not even been assumed that private property regimes are historically common. Rather, the establishment of private property regimes is a historical process that can be spatially-specific. This process has its origins in precolonial antiquity: in early civilisations in order for non-farmers to sustain themselves, they had to be able to extract agricultural food surpluses from peasant producers in a way that was deemed to be acceptable by society. In order to do this, the food output that was produced by the peasants could not be common property, as was the case in pre-agricultural hunter-gatherer societies; it had to become private property whose ownership rights, even though they might be weak, could be legitimately transferred from the direct producer of the food to another.

Thus, over millennia in precolonial antiquity, what had been common property – food for subsistence – was transformed as rights to use food, rights to earn income from food, rights to transfer food to others, and rights to enforce rights over food; all became privatised, a process that in many places was driven by force. As part of this process, resource governance became the basis by which socially acceptable transfers could take place from the actual producers of food, who were subaltern, to non-producers, who were dominant; claims to the products of the land were on the basis of dominant elites asserting their rights over the land and the subaltern, using force to back up their claims. In this way, levies from individuals such as landlords who did not directly farm or tithes from local religious authorities could impose a transfer of property from the actual producer of food, on the basis of the socially sanctioned authority of those imposing the transfer.

These precolonial forms of private property metastasised during colonialism, as colonial dominant elites were given rights to enclose land and other forms of social wealth, and transfers could be forced from subaltern direct producers through the use of coercion. Thus, as in precolonial antiquity and the transition from feudalism to capitalism, colonial enclosures were a politically constructed project that supported the interests of dominant elites at the expense of the subaltern and which was ultimately sustained by force. As a consequence, in the nineteenth century:

> British subjects began to accumulate considerable assets in the rest of the world, in amounts previously unknown and never surpassed to this day. By the eve of World War I, Britain...owned foreign assets equivalent to nearly two years of national income, or 6 times the total value of British farmland.
>
> (Piketty, 2014: 120)

Colonial states constructed by Britain, France and Germany were specifically constructed so as to ensure that:

> the rest of the world worked to increase consumption by the colonial powers and at the same time became more and more indebted to those same powers ... A fairly significant social group was able to live off this boon.
>
> (Piketty, 2014: 121)

The foundation of the wealth of this 'significant social group' was, of course, a process of state-supported colonial enclosure that deliberately, systematically and definitively seized resources from the subaltern in the periphery and transferred them to metropolitan dominant elites in ways that not only perpetuated but reinforced the position of the dominant elite and which subsequently served as the foundation of much contemporary wealth. As Piketty (2014: 351) notes with regard to Europe:

> the hyperconcentration of wealth in traditional agrarian societies and to a large extent in all societies prior to World War I ... [was because] ... these were low-growth societies in which the rate of return on capital was markedly and durably higher than the rate of growth ... [resulting in] a very high concentration of wealth and a significant persistence of large fortunes from generation to generation.

The foundational basis this 'hyperconcentration of wealth' was enclosure.

The impact of colonial enclosures continue to reverberate in today's period of neoliberal capitalism. Interestingly, there have not been any attempts to estimate the extent of global rural inequalities of income or wealth, or their trends over time. Given that three-quarters of the world's poor and hungry live in rural areas and rely upon agriculture as the principal source of their livelihood (Nwanze, 2015), this might strike some as being rather odd. Having said that, however, it is reasonably clear that in two large postcolonial Asian economies, China and India, rural inequality has been increasing as distributions of wealth worsen under neoliberal capitalism. In China between 1978 and 2002, the rural Gini coefficient, which is a bounded measure of inequality that can range from 0 for total equality to 1 for total inequality, rose from 0.21 to 0.38, a rise of 81 per cent, and '42 per cent of the aggregate income inequality in China in 2002' was driven by 'rural-urban differences ... [in] ... economic inequality' (Ghosh, 2010: 5). Similarly, 'rural inequality ... went up in India between 1993–94 ... and 1999–2000' (Ghosh, 2010: 15). More generally, in the rural areas of postcolonial Asia, Africa and Latin America, access to land is still the single most important determinant of household welfare, and the single most important store of wealth. In this light, comparative estimates of land Gini coefficients are presented in Table 23.1.

It is clear from Figure 1 that land-based inequality is remarkably high; and while it would be interesting to evaluate patterns since the colonial period there can be little doubt that the origins of contemporary rural land-based inequality lie in the enclosures of the colonial period. Moreover, estimates by the International Monetary Fund indicate that, based upon a restricted sample of developing countries, land Gini coefficients globally rose by 7 per cent between 1960 and 1990 (Erikson and Vollrath, 2004: Table 2), prior to the most recent period of neoliberal capitalism, which is strongly correlated with rising inequality (Piketty, 2014). Further, there is evidence of a clear inverse relationship between land Gini coefficients and agricultural productivity, indicating that the more unequal the land distribution, the lower the level of farm yields per unit of land, which has clear implications for rural livelihoods, incomes, welfare and social equity (Vollrath, 2007). Thus, while agrarian questions of land may trace their origins to colonial enclosures, the ongoing reconfiguration of these agrarian questions can have significant implications for the cultural, national, ethnic, gender and class-based identities of the subaltern, and in so doing, may also have implications for postcolonial politics, particularly as rural postcolonial politics often revolve around production and accumulation issues facing the subaltern (Akram-Lodhi and Kay, 2016).

However, as has been stressed, private property remains by no means universal; in many human societies, open-access and common property regimes remained the norm well into the colonial and postcolonial twentieth century, and these societies were notable for having

Table 23.1 Land Gini coefficients for selected Latin American and African countries, various years.

Latin America	
Venezuela	0.917
Argentina	0.856
Colombia	0.829
Bolivia	0.768
Africa	
Madagascar	0.804
Tanzania	0.790
Kenya	0.711
Uganda	0.549

Source: World Bank, 2009: 104.

relatively lesser degrees of inequality – excluding gender inequalities – than societies based on private property regimes. A central objective of enclosures by dominant groups, then, has been a transformation in the property regime through the commodification of goods and services, including, of course, labour services. Moreover, this objective has driven much of the resistance displayed in postcolonial politics of the rural subaltern. Indeed, if anything, neoliberal capitalism has dramatically broadened and deepened commodification as the reification of unceasing economic growth, endless consumption, continual technological change, the unleashing of ruthless entrepreneurialism and market hyperrationality, has fostered a binary cult of demand and supply, price and quantity, wages and profits, employment and unemployment for the supposedly autonomous individual that is 'free to choose'. As a result, in neoliberal capitalism, commodification can be presented as a near moral imperative.

Yet the binaries that underpin the contemporary commodification witnessed in neoliberal capitalism are themselves an outcome of the mode of forcible separation; of the limits to the space of enclosure; and of cultural, national, ethnic, gender and class-based identities that shape and are shaped by access to the social wealth that is the principal object of commodification. Thus, the commodification that results from contemporary enclosures, while they remain socially constructed by dominant groups for their own benefit, are thus mutually constitutive of the subaltern, who resist; each half of the binary requires the other half in order to exist, even figuratively, and in this way relations of dominance and subordination remain contingent and contested within the domain of postcolonial politics.

The social and political contingencies that underpin the political contestation of commodification between the dominant and the subaltern can be better understood if we return to the distinction between goods that are excludable or not and goods that are rival or not, because this allows the identification of four distinct types of goods in contemporary societies and demonstrates once more the unique specificities of private property. These goods are displayed in Table 23.2.

We are, of course, all familiar with private goods, which are those goods to which individuals can be denied access, and the use of which reduces the amount available to other users. However, just as the property regime is not inevitably a private one, goods need not be inevitably private; there are other types of goods. Individuals can be denied access to club goods, but one person's use of that good does not reduce the amount that is available for other users. Examples of club goods include toll roads, private parks and cinemas. Common goods are those in which individuals cannot be denied access to the use of a good but one person's use of the good reduces the amount that is available for other users. Examples of common goods include air, open-access fish and timber stocks, and unpaid care and domestic work within the household. Public goods are those in which individuals cannot be denied access to the use of a good, and one person's use of that good does not reduce the amount that is available to others. Examples of public goods include national security and street lighting.

The characteristics of goods can appear to be rooted in the inherent characteristics of the good, and thus where goods fall within the typology can appear to be a technical question. However, this is not the case. Excludability and rivalry are not technical questions; they are

Table 23.2 A typology of goods.

	Rival	***Non-rival***
Excludable	Private goods	Club goods
Non-excludable	Common goods	Public goods

'socially defined and constructed: the outcome of complex political processes which evolve around the definition of' the private (Wuyts, 1992: 31). For example, in terms of health and education, in some societies these are public goods and non-commodified and in other societies these are private goods and are commodified; this is not merely a technical distinction. This leads to an important point: commodification is about the creation of excludability. In other words, commodification requires the transformation of common goods and public goods into club goods and private goods. Therefore, enclosure is a process that leads to a twin, mutually constitutive, transformation: of open-access and common property into state and private property; and of common goods and public goods into club goods and private goods. These twin transformations were a key part of the colonial experience; but they have if anything become even more centrally implicated within neoliberal capitalism, and as such, reverberate throughout the domain of postcolonial politics.

Let me be clear: what I am suggesting is that enclosure seizes open-access and common property and transforms them into private and club goods that can be bought and sold as commodities. This is a politically driven and coercively sustained process that enriches dominant elites at the expense of the subaltern. Moreover, enclosure is not just a historical observation of the colonial period; it is, as De Angelis stresses, integral to ongoing capitalist development, and as such has become the object of political contestation. The neoliberal capitalism of the past three decades has witnessed, as both an objective and an outcome, the transfer of common goods and public goods provided by state property regimes into private property through processes of privatisation; it has witnessed the replacement of state provision of common goods and public goods and the private provision of private goods; and it has witnessed the state increasingly using private providers to supply common goods and public goods which have become, in effect, private goods. Moreover, particularly since the signing of the Trade-Related Aspects of Intellectual Property Rights Agreement of 1995, the domain of private property has been significantly extended globally, into areas such as genes, water and climate, which would never have been commodified prior to the rise of neoliberal capitalism. Finally, the information and communications technologies that have driven neoliberal capitalism in the last two decades has required the commodification of domains that were previously not commodified.

If this argument is correct, enclosure is a process that cannot but be seen as being intrinsic to neoliberal capitalism as dominant elites seize open-access and common spaces in order to commodify common goods and public goods. Indeed, when considering some of the most powerful capitals operating across the postcolonial world economy today, this is clearly what they have done: the central role of the Apples, the Googles and the Facebooks is not a consequence of the expansion of the so-called 'knowledge-based economy'; it is a consequence of their capacity to politically capture and enclose spaces of social life that had been relatively uncolonised by capitalist relations of production and secure them as a source of private profitability. In this light, capital itself has undergone a metamorphosis as a result of contemporary enclosure. At the same time, however, the reconfiguration of access to social wealth shapes and is shaped by the cultural, national, ethnic, gender and class-based identities that drive the postcolonial politics of dominance and subordination in an era of neoliberal capitalism.

Markets in neoliberal capitalism

As noted, De Angelis (2004: 75, 77) argues that the forcible separation of the producer from the social wealth that can protect them from capital can also occur as a by-product of the process of accumulation in capitalist markets. Of course, this would be denied by neoclassical economists, who argue that in well-functioning markets people meet as equals to mutually and voluntarily agree to a price upon which to exchange a commodity, an exchange that is equally beneficial to both if it is based upon comparative advantage and specialisation. Neoclassical economics argues that 'agents' operating in markets face constraints that are outside their control when seeking to optimise their production and consumption decisions. If markets are unencumbered by state or monopoly, neoclassical economics can easily demonstrate that equilibrium prices must result in the marginal cost of production being equal to the marginal revenue gained from that production by the producer as well as the marginal benefit received by the purchaser of the product. In other words, unencumbered 'free' markets produce the best possible outcome for the two binaries known as the producer and the consumer. Admittedly, this is a simplified view of Adam Smith's 'invisible hand'. Yet neoclassical economists have a strong view of how the world should work, and have sought, through neoliberal policy reforms that have redefined the role of the state into one that enables markets, to make the world more closely mirror that view. In this sense, then, this simple description of neoclassical economics remains accurate.

However, in any system of commodity-based production, in which enclosure results in production for sale dominating production for use, neoclassical arguments are problematic, for four reasons (Akram-Lodhi, 2000). First, the extent to which exchange in markets is voluntary is debatable. In many markets the identity of those conducting an exchange is essential to its terms and conditions, including the price (Evans, 1991). As a consequence, exchange is often not anonymous. A lack of anonymity may however limit the degree to which market transactions are voluntary (Bhaduri, 1986). Indeed, a fundamental correlate of enclosure is force. Second, it is common for commodities and wider market conditions to not be as well understood by the buyer as they are by the seller. Within neoclassical economics, the price contains all the information required by the seller and the buyer. However, prices may fail to give adequate information to the buyer because of an asymmetrical distribution of information regarding the qualities of the product and its place within specific market conditions (Gerrard, 1989). In a sense, then, a principle objective of the seller is to enclose information so as to maximise the benefits that accrue from a sale. Third, in light of asymmetrical information, it follows that in order for markets to operate, there is a need for supplementary non-market institutions to coordinate and control aspects of resource allocation so as to deal with the uncertainty and bounded rationality arising out of enclosed asymmetrical information. Non-market institutions of resource coordination such as the household, the community, the farm, the firm and the state thus become a necessary precondition of exchange (Fourie, 1989). Finally, buying and selling must be logically and temporally preceded by the establishment of private property, the creation of private goods and the production of the commodity, which makes it available for exchange (Sawyer, 1993). This also implies a role for non-market social institutions that coordinate resource allocation in production before any sale.

In short, the neoclassical conceptualisation of markets lacks sufficient recognition that market transactions are built upon non-market institutions that structure resource control and allocation. Thus, markets are embedded within wider social processes and relations, including those of dominance and subordination (Polanyi, 2001, orig. 1944).

An important point that emerges from this unpacking of markets is that the characteristics of markets should not be assumed, as is conventionally done; indeed, it should not be assumed that markets work in uniform ways across precolonial, colonial and postcolonial time, space and place. Rather, markets are constructed within specific contexts. When considering the emergence of capitalism, for example, the process of establishing capitalist markets can be seen as a part and parcel of a broader transformation that enabled the emergence of capital by sustaining enclosure and commodification. As this was context-specific, the characteristics of the capitalist markets that were constructed were not inherent or inevitable; they were contingent. Thus, the establishment of colonial markets under capitalism was a politically constructed mechanism that supported the interests of metropolitan dominant elites at the expense of the colonial subalterns through the enclosure of social wealth and the drain of resources from the periphery, cumulatively generating some of the inequalities contemporarily documented in Figure 1. More recently, under neoliberal capitalism it is not the case that free markets have been unleashed; rather, there has been a profound restructuring of the terms and conditions shaping the operation of markets, in ways designed to enhance the flexibility of capital and its relation to both the state and labour. Otero (2012) calls this, appropriately, 'neo-regulation', and it has facilitated the appropriation of assets by dominant elites through the normal, routine and everyday workings of markets, buttressed by the direct action of the state.

Markets are thus socially embedded and politically constructed, initially by the coloniser and the colonial state, and latterly by the postcolonial dominant elites that have benefited so handsomely from neoliberal capitalism. Mackintosh (1990) has argued that these 'real' markets—as opposed to the 'abstract' markets of neoclassical economics—operate on the basis of four factors. The first factor is the terms of entry into markets. In particular, differences in wealth amongst those who take part in markets mean that not all are equal. As Bernstein has similarly argued, members of dominant elites, controlling disproportionately large shares of the means of production, will be able to enter markets from a position where they can use markets to their advantage (Bernstein, 1996). When markets are used by dominant elites in this way, markets will be organised to buttress the material advantage of the dominant elites at the expense of the subaltern. Second, then, it is necessary to examine the ways in which those with disproportionate shares of wealth seek to influence the conditions under which markets operate. In particular, members of dominant elites may use principal-agent relations with the subaltern to shape the available information, bounded rationality and uncertainty that are witnessed in markets, to their own advantage. Third, it is necessary to understand the central role played by merchant capital in markets, as it plays a critical intermediary role linking a binary structure of production relations with a structure of consumption relations. Finally, it is necessary to analyze the circumstances under which market-based coordination is supplemented or replaced by the direct actions of non-market institutions such as firms or the state that seek to structure resource allocation.

Neoclassical theorists of course accept that markets may be 'imperfect', in that vested interests may seek monopolistic outcomes. The solution is attention to the reform of wider economic policy in order to make markets work better, as well as clearly defined and enforceable property rights. What the ideologists of neoliberal capitalism would not accept is that under a reasonable set of 'ideal-type' economic and governance conditions, it is still possible for dominant elites to shape the definition of property rights and the operation of the market to their advantage, at the express cost of the subaltern. In other words, even with 'good' economic policy, clear legal rights and responsibilities, and apparent transparency, market transactions are not based upon equality; rather, they are based upon the inequality found between the dominant and the subordinate. Indeed, surely if the 2008 United States financial crisis has taught us anything it is that markets are profoundly asymmetrical, and indeed predatory institutions that dominant elites can use to prey upon the subaltern; witness the US housing bubble, the rewards that it produced for a few, and the costs that it created for many. As socially constructed institutions, markets reflect and can exacerbate distributions of wealth, creating and deepening inequalities within and between individuals, households, communities and social classes, which has strong implications for the identities forged on the grounds of culture, nation, ethnicity, gender and class, as well as the politics that such identities can produce.

Enclosure and postcolonial rural politics

Colonial and contemporary enclosures, the establishment of private property regimes that buttress inequalities of power and privilege, and the political construction and impact of markets drive rural postcolonial politics in many parts of the world, which most centrally revolve around the issues of production and accumulation; or, as Henry Bernstein (2010) would put it, who owns what? Who does what? Who gets what? What do they do with it?

Over the course of the last two decades, a new generation of postcolonial rural peasant movements have arisen that focus on these questions and how they can be answered in the explicit material, cultural and social interests of the subaltern. Celebrating the hybridity of contemporary peasant identity and their diverse cultural, national, ethnic, gender and class-based identities, these peasant movements challenge the social exclusion generated for the many by neoliberal capitalism, predicated as it is on: external food trade liberalisation and the resulting increase in externally-subsidised food imports that undermine local food production; internal food trade de-regulation and the resulting elimination of local input and output subsidies for food producers; as well as the privileging of private property-based market-biased strategies for rural development, grounded as they are on facilitating the entry into and dominance of agro-food transnational capital seeking to consolidate privately-shaped food input and food output markets in most developing countries. Indeed, these peasant movements have transformational aspirations for Asia, Africa and, most explicitly, Latin America, with the *Movimento dos Trabalhadores Rurais Sem-Terra* (MST) in Brazil, the Zapatista movement in Chiapas, Mexico, and the *cocaleros* movement in Bolivia as the most prominent examples. As a consequence, it is the peasantry that has led the struggle against neoliberal capitalism, acting as a force for radical, progressive and ecologically sustainable transformative change.

In undertaking this challenge, postcolonial peasant movements have also come to the realisation that national campaigns are not enough; with agro-food transnational capital operating internationally, peasant movements must also come together across frontiers and operate internationally, and in so doing, they have developed a new aspect of their hybridity. This gave rise to the creation, in 1994, of La Via Campesina, which is now, with 200 million affiliated members, the largest social movement in the world. La Via Campesina is a postcolonial transnational rural social movement that seeks to politically alter the terms and conditions governing rural production, distribution and accumulation, and hence rural lives (Edelmen and Borras, 2016) by constructing something that it calls 'food sovereignty'. As developed initially by La Via Campesina and further elaborated at the 2007 Nyéléni Forum for Food Sovereignty (Akram-Lodhi, 2016), food sovereignty is based on the right of subaltern peoples and peripheral countries to define their own postcolonial agricultural and food policy and has five interlinked and inseparable components:

1. a focus on food for people: food sovereignty puts the right to sufficient, healthy and culturally-appropriate food for all individuals, peoples and communities at the centre of food, agriculture, livestock and fisheries policies and rejects the proposition that food is just another commodity;
2. the valuing of food providers: food sovereignty values and supports the contributions, and respects the rights, of women and men who grow, harvest and process food and rejects those policies, actions and programmes that undervalue them and threaten their livelihoods;
3. localises food systems: food sovereignty puts food providers and food consumers at the centre of decision-making on food issues; protects providers from the dumping of food in local markets; protects consumers from poor quality and unhealthy food, including food

tainted with transgenic organisms; and rejects governance structures that depend on inequitable international trade and gives power to corporations. It places control over territory, land, grazing, water, seeds, livestock and fish populations with local food providers, and respects their rights to use and share them in socially and environmentally sustainable ways; it promotes positive interaction between food providers in different territories and from different sectors that helps resolve conflicts; and rejects the privatisation of natural resources through laws, commercial contracts and intellectual property rights regimes;

4. builds knowledge and skills: food sovereignty builds on the skills and local knowledge of food providers and their local organisations that conserve, develop and manage localised food production and harvesting systems, developing appropriate research systems to support this, and rejects technologies that undermine these;
5. works with nature: food sovereignty uses the contributions of nature in diverse, low external input agro-ecological production and harvesting methods that maximise the contribution of ecosystems and improve resilience, and rejects methods that harm ecosystem functions, that depend on energy-intensive monocultures and livestock factories, and other industrialised production methods.

Food sovereignty is thus an expression of subaltern postcolonial politics that is an alternative to food security, as it has come to be used by multilateral development institutions to promote private property-, market- and monetary-based solutions to a lack of access to food, and which says nothing about the inequitable structures and policies that have, through coercive enclosure and market-led appropriation, destroyed the rural livelihoods of the subaltern and their environment, and thus produced food insecurity. Food sovereignty instead offers a political practice that is an alternative to the current world food system, with its proponents arguing that the food system needs to be predicated upon a decentralised agriculture, where production, processing, distribution and consumption are controlled by communities, where markets are controlled by communities and where private property is not assigned unique privileges. So food sovereignty offers a vision of a real utopia rooted in the contemporary praxis of subaltern individuals and movements, and this vision has, in less than 20 years, become a critical component of global food movements.

However, the members of La Via Campesina understand that the localised smallholder farming model that is central to food sovereignty's alternative food system, and which, by continuing to be widespread throughout Asia, Africa and Latin America, might be thought of as an 'incubator' of food sovereignty, cannot be abstracted from capitalist social property relations, which are defined by relations of exploitation between capital and classes of labour (Bernstein, 2010). Smallholder farming is currently subordinated, through a range of mechanisms, to capitalist social property relations (Akram-Lodhi and Kay, 2010). Thus, and as its transformational proponents clearly recognise, food sovereignty is not about trying to reconfigure the existing social conditions and relations of neoliberal capitalism; it requires transcending the social conditions and relations of neoliberal capitalism and developing a post-capitalist agrarian – and non-agrarian – alternative.

So, food sovereignty is about building power within the fissures of capitalist social-property relations in order to transform food systems in favor of subaltern peasants, smallholders, fishers, food system workers, and underserved communities. To that end, La Via Campesina's call for food sovereignty is one that seeks to foster the generation of rural political struggles by diverse rural social forces across a number of different sites of resistance because rural political struggles are, from the standpoint of its members, capable of reshaping production and accumulation by transcending processes of coercive enclosure as well as market-led processes of exclusionary appropriation that have been fostered by neoliberal capitalism. Indeed, the specific objective of such struggles is the resurrection of what can be called 'commons': social forms, processes and institutions that protect society from the capitalist market imperative, through the de-commodification of land, water, food and other resources; the effective 'de-enclosure' of social wealth; and the construction of spaces of hope that would pose limits to the accumulation of capital by re-embedding the market within society (Polanyi, 2001). In so doing, La Via Campesina's campaigning is very much focused upon mobilising communities in order to protect and enlarge the spaces for both open access and common property regimes, as well as the common goods and public goods needed by rural subaltern populations to construct viable livelihoods. In this way, La Via Campesina directly confronts the global inequities of neoliberal capitalism through its robust postcolonial politics, both within the countryside and beyond, recognising cultural, national, ethnic, gender and class-based identities not as markers of difference but as markers of strength.

Conclusion

Land is central to the rural production process. In the precolonial and colonial history of capitalism, the control of land has been obtained through processes of enclosure. However, as has been argued in this chapter, enclosure is not just a characteristic of history. Enclosure is a central aspect of neoliberal capitalism's drive to accumulate, as enclosure reproduces the separation of the direct producer from social wealth and in so doing facilitates the reproduction of capital. Enclosure can be witnessed in the attempts of capital to colonise spaces not under its sway, and in the attempts of capital to reassert through commodification control of spaces that have been, as a consequence of struggle, disconnected from the logic of the market. Enclosure can be imposed directly by dominant elites or their allies in the capitalist state, or can be an indirect by-product of exclusionary appropriations that emerge out of the accumulation process. In either instance, the impact is to facilitate the deepening of social inequalities between the dominant and the subordinate.

However, these same processes have generated robust resistance, as the cultural, national, ethnic, gender and class-based identities of smallholder farmers around the world have been fused into a global hybrid peasant identity that seeks to de-commodify resources, resurrect commons and socially embed the market: a postcolonial politics of the present that seeks to open up spaces of hope. Thus, this chapter has argued that understanding processes of enclosure, commodification and the market-led appropriation of resources also facilitate a better, more well-rounded and fuller understanding of the resistance that has been engendered by those very processes in the postcolonial world.

Bibliography

Akram-Lodhi, A.H. (2000) 'A bitter pill? Peasants and sugarcane markets in northern Pakistan'. *European Journal of Development Research* 12 (1), 206–28.

———and Kay, C. (2010) 'Surveying the agrarian question (part 2): current debates and beyond'. *The Journal of Peasant Studies* 37 (2), 255–84.

———and Kay C. (2016) 'Back to the future? Marx, modes of production and the agrarian question'. In B.B. Mohanty (ed.) *The Agrarian Question in India: Current Debates*. New Delhi: Routledge.

Bernstein, H. (1996) 'The political economy of the maize *filière*'. In H. Bernstein (ed.) *The Agrarian Question in South Africa*. London: Frank Cass.

——— (2010) *Class Dynamics of Agrarian Change*. Halifax and Winnipeg: Fernwood.

Bhaduri, A. (1986) 'Forced commerce and agrarian growth'. *World Development* 14 (2), 267–72.

Bonefeld, W. (2001) 'The permanence of primitive accumulation: commodity fetishism and social constitution'. *The Commoner* 2 September.

Byres, T.J. (1996) *Capitalism from Above and Capitalism from Below: An Essay in Comparative Political Economy*. Houndmills, Basingstoke and London: MacMillan.

——— (2003) 'Paths of capitalist agrarian transition in the past and in the contemporary world'. In V. K. Ramachandran and M. Swaminathan (eds.) *Agrarian Studies: Essays on Agrarian Relations in Less-Developed Countries*. London: Zed Books.

De Angelis, M. (2001) 'Marx and primitive accumulation: the continuous character of capital's "enclosures"'. *The Commoner* 2 September.

——— (2004) 'Separating the doing and the deed: capital and the continuous character of enclosures'. *Historical Materialism* 12 (2), 57–87.

Edelman, M. and Borras, S.M. Jr. (2016) *Political Dynamics of Transnational Agrarian Movements*. Halifax and Winnipeg: Fernwood.

Erickson, L. and Vollrath, D. (2004) 'Dimensions of land inequality and economic development'. International Monetary Fund *Working Paper* WP/04/158. Available: https://www.imf.org/external/pubs/ft/wp/2004/wp04158.pdf, accessed on 12 May 2016.

Evans, A. (1991) 'Gender issues in rural household economics'. Institute of Development Studies *Bulletin* 22, 51–9.

Fourie, F. C. v N. (1989) 'The nature of firms and markets: do transactions approaches help?', *South African Journal of Economics* 57 (3), 142–60.

Gerrard, W. (1989) *Theory of the Capitalist Economy: Towards a Post-Classical Synthesis*. Oxford: Basil Blackwell.

Ghosh, J. (2010) 'Poverty reduction in China and India: policy implications of recent trends'. United Nations Department for Economic and Social Affairs *Working Paper* No 92. Available: www.un.org/esa/desa/papers/2010/wp92_2010.pdf accessed on 12 May 2016.

Harvey, D. (2005) *The New Imperialism*. Oxford: Oxford University Press.

Mackintosh, M. (1990) 'Abstract markets and real needs'. In H. Bernstein, B. Crow, M. Mackintosh and C. Martin (eds.) *The Food Question: Profits versus People?* London: Earthscan Publications.

Marx, K. (1971) *Theories of Surplus-value, Volume 3*. Moscow: Progress Publishers.

——— (1976) *Capital, Volume I*. Harmondsworth: Penguin Books. First published in 1867.

Nwanze, K. (2015) 'It's not just about the money: to change the world we must change ourselves'. Available: http://www.un.org/esa/ffd/ffd3/blog/its-not-just-about-the-money.html, accessed on 12 May 2016.

Otero, G. (2012) 'The neoliberal food regime in Latin America: state, agribusiness transnational corporations and biotechnology'. *Canadian Journal of Development Studies* 33 (3), 282–94.

Piketty, T. (2014) *Capital in the Twenty-First Century*. Boston: Belknap Press.

Polanyi, K. (2001) *The Great Transformation: The Political and Economic Origins of Our Time*. Boston: Beacon Press. First published in 1944.

Sawyer, M. (1993) 'The nature and role of the market'. In C. Pitelis (ed.) *Transactions Costs, Markets and Hierarchies*. Oxford: Basil Blackwell.

Vollrath, D. (2007) 'Land distribution and international land productivity'. *American Journal of Agricultural Economics* 89 (1), 202–16.

Wood, E.M. (2009) 'Peasants and the market imperative: the origins of capitalism'. In A.H. Akram-Lodhi and C. Kay (eds.) *Peasants and Globalization: Political Economy, Rural Transformation and the Agrarian Question*. London: Routledge.

World Bank (2009) *Kenya Poverty and Inequality Assessment, Volume I: Synthesis Report*. Africa Region Poverty Reduction and Economic Management Unit Report No. 44190-KE. Available: http://documents.worldbank.org/curated/en/2009/04/10842664/kenya-poverty-inequality-assessment-executive-summary-synthesis-report, accessed on 12 May 2016.

Wuyts, M. (1992) 'Deprivation and public need'. In M. Wuyts, M. Mackintosh and T. Hewitt (eds.) *Development Policy and Public Action*. Oxford: Oxford University Press.

24
SALTWATER ARCHIVES
Native knowledge in a time of rising tides

Joy Lehuanani Enomoto and D. Keali'i MacKenzie

In the space between climate justice and climate redemption
stands the one-eyed Hikule'o
Her hair an expanse of roots charred black
In her belly live the children of sky brown as the earth is old
Their tears are the ocean in us

Cresantia Frances Koya Vaka'uta (2012),
1AngryNative on Climate Change

The vast sea of islands known as Oceania is in the midst of sea level rise that is caused by first world exploitation of resources and contamination of the environment. There have been many scientific studies regarding the phenomena of sea level rise. There has been even more written about who is to blame for the causes of climate change. However, the point is, we are losing our land now and we do not have time to wait for the first world to be accountable to itself before decisions are made to ensure the survival of our cultures. Therefore, rather than use this space to repeat the same stories about the environment and the endless ways in which neocolonialism has brought us to this moment in history, that many scholars have previously discussed, this chapter will focus on the retention of culture and Native-owned information through the embodied archives, those vital pieces of our culture that are not considered valid records for imperial archives, but that we will have to carry with us as we face the future and navigate the sea once more. We choose the embodied archives because at its core are Native ways of knowing the world. And it is Native knowledge that has ensured our survival to this point and it will be Native knowledge and our continuum of collective memory that we will need to maintain and adapt in the future.

We will also pose a series of questions to those of us within Oceania on how we can best support each other in a time of shifting geopolitics, forced migration and permanent displacement, threats to sovereignty and other irreparable impacts of climate change. We write this chapter for Tuvalu and Vanuatu who are eye-level with the sea. It is for Fiji, devastated by Cyclone Winston. It is for the Carteret Islanders for whom there is already no option of return. It is for Nauru and the Banabans in Kiribati who have already been displaced by phosphate mining, (Teaiwa, 2015) and for the Marshall Islands who have already endured the tide of nuclear testing and who may be forced to migrate again because of sea level rise. This chapter is for all the islands in Oceania that quietly go unnamed and are actively ignored by those who are at the center of their upheaval. This is an essay for Oceania from within Oceania.

We, as Kānaka Maoli (Native Hawaiian), will use words, phrases, and terms throughout this chapter which come from the Native languages of Oceania. We choose not to italicize these words, which might be considered 'foreign' to some readers. However, these words and languages are not foreign to the Pacific; rather these are the languages of the islands we are engaging. This is a political choice, one that we as Kānaka Maoli understand. Rather than othering these words, we invite readers to learn and engage with new ideas or concepts which belong to Oceania. However, this is often forgotten. Many Kānaka Maoli refuse to include ourselves in Oceania except when convenient. We may hold up the beauty and culture of the Maori or Tahitians, while in the same breath continue to perpetuate colonial hierarchies of racism and superiority toward the rest of the Pacific. It is no surprise that Hawai'i has often been written off as simply belonging to America and not part of Oceania. These colonial constructs have done nothing to serve us, but has ensured our division. We hope this is one form of listening to those we have frequently ignored and is a step toward healing the rift between us.

Also, we would like to make it clear that in no way do the authors speak for all Native people of Oceania; we are examining this issue as Indigenous librarians and archivists, spoken word and visual artists, respectively. Therefore, our approach is quite specific and in no way represents the thinking of all Kānaka Maoli on how to preserve culture. We acknowledge we were both born and raised in the diaspora in the continental United States and our position is simply one among a plethora of many who are committed to finding a way forward. We truly understand that no single individual or group can speak to all the complexities and nuances of Oceania. Therefore, we will put away any assumption that we have any answers, but hope we are asking the right questions. We seek to reaffirm and commit ourselves to the genealogical ties Kānaka have to Oceania. We prefer to open the discussion from the position that we are all collectively facing rising tides in a world in which the West has been actively working toward and waiting for our extinction.

> We are not drowning, we are fighting for our islands, our cultures our homes.
>
> 350 Pacific: Climate Warriors, 2013

The ocean is eroding our islands. This is not up for debate. All that one really needs is to see the fallen coconut trees along the shoreline and to see the salt water coming up where swamp taro can no longer grow. Sea walls are failing and the king tides get higher every year. This is the narrative that is constantly told. But, when we stop to listen carefully, there are many other narratives of resistance. It is not valuable in any way to get caught up in what Chimamanda Ngozi Adichie calls the 'danger of the single story' (Adichie, 2009). Currently, we are being told the single story that Pacific Islanders, due to their inability to develop properly, are ill-equipped to defend themselves against climate change. That they will be climate change refugees. The truth is none of us are prepared for this devastation, but there are those with more resources providing more room for denial. A coalition of young activists from fifteen Pacific Island nations, known as 350 Pacific, have come together to educate, empower and raise awareness of the impacts of climate change. They are challenging fossil fuel companies head on. Their slogan, 'We are not drowning, we're fighting,' demonstrates to us that theirs is a story of active resistance. They refused to be called climate change refugees, since this term is essentializing and perpetuates the myth that Pacific Islanders are passive victims.

Ursula Rakova, the clan chief of Huene Island in the Carteret Islands is also the executive director of Tulele Peisa (Tulele-peisa, n.d.), a non-governmental organization whose title means *sailing in the wind on our own.* When faced with the reality that her community was going to have to move, she proactively negotiated with the Bougainville Diocese of the Catholic Church to provide land to create a space for relocation in Bougainville, Papua New Guinea. She is also the founder of the Bougainville Cocoa Net Limited, a company set up for migrating Carteret Islanders to trade in organic cocoa, to ensure community self-reliance.[1] These are the acts of the head of a matrilineal society looking out for her people and unwilling to wait for governments to change.

This current migration of islanders calls to mind Katerina Teaiwa's reflections on the people of Banaba, who were permanently moved by the British Government to Rabi Island, Fiji in 1947. In 1900, high-grade phosphate had been discovered on the island by the British Pacific Islands company, which by 1920 was taken over by the British Phosphate Commission composed of the British, Australian and New Zealand governments. Banaba was systematically mined for phosphate until 1980. By then it was made completely uninhabitable, leaving only spires of coral and no arable land. Teaiwa states that 'if the Indigenous were or are rooted in specific landscapes and seascapes, then Banaban land and Banaban identities have now become coordinates between islands and continents' (Teaiwa, 2014). Although she is referring to displacement of Banabans due to resource extraction, in which the core of her homeland has been distributed among the gardens of the Pacific, I think her words may be applied to those who are now being displaced due to sea level rise. When return to homeland is made impossible, how do we retain our cultures? Where do we place the repositories of our knowledge?

Rakova, while planning the relocation of her people, said this in reference to her home, 'This belongs to us as a clan and we know that we are losing it and having to move away, it basically breaks us. It makes us feel that we are divided people' (Rakova, 2009). How do we prevent sea level rise from breaking our cultures? To answer this question, we must continue to define for ourselves all the aspects of culture that make us who we are. Tongan scholar and fiction writer, Epeli Hau'ofa, once said, 'to deny human beings the sense of homeland is to deny them a deep spot on Earth to anchor their roots' (Hau'ofa, 2000). If our primary identity is rooted in our land, and the land becomes uninhabitable, then to what are we rooted? Perhaps our roots must come from within our bodies, our chants and song, our dance and stories, our language and spoken word, our secrets and our collective memory. The archives we embody. Those aspects of culture that matter to us and for us, then we cannot be broken.

> Like the glass cases of museums, the archives of colonial regimes and their independent successor states have often been described as prisons for the identities of the oppressed.
>
> Evelyn Wareham, 'Indigenous Voices in New Zealand Record-Keeping' (Wareham, 2001)

Historically, what we have come to know as the archives are the repositories that store the organic stuff of empire – population counts and descriptions, land surveys, maps, quiet titles and countless committee minutes, notes and queries, and the transactions of endless bureaucracies. The imperial detritus of exotification and demonizing of the native was found in settler colonial photograph and postcard collections, travel manuscripts and correspondence. And then came the naturalists, anthropologists and linguists with their field notebooks and recorders. They pinned our insects to boards; pressed our flowers into presses; gathered our shells into boxes; killed, stuffed and mounted our animals; measured and stole our skulls; pillaged our ceremonial objects and mistranslated our languages. Afterwards they packed our culture up and sent them to museums to be taken further out of context and colonial misinterpretations were assumed to be truth.

Entire disciplines were created to diminish our ancestors as peoples whose lives existed within a pre-history, or rather outside of history. Their archives and museums became the material used against us as proof of their superiority, their excuse to dispossess many of us from our lands and to determine our inability to govern ourselves. The colonial records throughout the Pacific became one of the leading ways to dehumanize and silence the Indigenous people of Oceania and make us subject, savage and other. The imperial archives quite frankly were created for them about us.

Nevertheless, several Pacific scholars such as Katerina Teaiwa, Whatarangi Winiata, Noelani Arista and Ralph Regenvanu, to name only a few, have been able to unsettle the imperial archives by pushing to expand access, to create records of Native culture by Natives according to community guidelines, and to apply culturally literate readings of the archives that find the missing voice of Native peoples within. The need to redefine, set new standards and interrogate imperial archives continues to be of vital importance for our communities. And as such there are several efforts being made to ensure the survival of these physical repositories of the state.

In an ironic twist of fate, and yet not surprisingly, many leading institutions from the countries that refuse to lower their emissions and were responsible for the colonization and exploitation of the Pacific to begin with, are now offering to digitize and 'save' these now threatened archives. An interesting example is the British Library's Endangered Archives Program (British Library, 2016). The British Library provides grants to local institutions in countries whose archival records are being threatened by their natural environment or war. The goal is to ensure that records are placed in a stable environment, ideally in a local institution and local staff are trained with new equipment to digitize and/or microfilm the threatened material. 'The original archives and the master digital copies will be transferred to a safe archival home in their country of origin, while copies will be deposited at the British Library for use by scholars worldwide' (British Library, 2012).

In the Pacific, the island nation of Tuvalu, which gained its independence from Britain in 1978, has been working with the Endangered Archives Program since about 2005. It has been able to digitize thousands of documents primarily pertaining to former Gilbert and Ellice Islands colonial land commission records, including documents signed by local chiefs accepting the rule of England. Even though over 70,000 image files have been made to date, only 67 were directly relating to Tuvalu language, culture, history, tradition, customs and art. These are being held by Tuvalu National and Library Archives (TNLA). Given the immediate environmental risks to the TNLA, copies of all the digital material has been distributed among TNLA, the British Library and the Australian National University in Canberra. Furthermore, copies of positive prints are also being held by all eleven member libraries of the Pacific Manuscripts Bureau and the master negatives of the microfilms are being held in cold storage in the National Library of Australia.

It appears that the British Library is struck by the pedagogy of benevolence. How kind of them to train local archivists to, in essence, save the records of their former colonial rule, and how considerate to now make that information available to researchers worldwide. Why exactly, do they need to make this material available to researchers? Isn't the priority to save Tuvalu heritage? We do not question or deny the agency of the people of Tuvalu, to want to protect their national records, many of which are records of local council meetings in Tuvalu language, adoption records, etc., but we do question the motives of the British Library and the Australian National Library who seem to be prioritizing access to information for their researchers to continue to study us, more than a genuine concern for Tuvalu cultural memory. How is this different from when they boxed up our objects and carried them away the first time?

There is serious doubt that a former colonizer acts purely out of the goodness of its heart. Ultimately it is an empty gesture to offer equipment to save records on the one hand but refuse to allow those same 'endangered' people entry into your country. Beneath this act of saving, is once again the narrative of the single story – 'you have been unable to thrive since we ceased to rule, let us help you.' Hawaiian scholar Jon Osorio once said, 'Telling themselves that they are doing the world and Indigenous people a tremendous service, they ignore or rationalize the fact that not everyone benefits equally when they share our information' (Osorio, 1999). Oceania can do better than this. We are resourceful people, who put into practice our methods of cultural retention daily, we must continue to trust this knowledge.

However, there is much that needs to be considered. The concern is not simply the use of and access to archives, it's not just digitizing material and hoping it remains stable for the next century, but to remind ourselves that we are capable of constructing our own archives, if and when the imperial archives are suddenly washed away. Archivist, Evelyn Wareham, quotes Palauan President Tommy Remengesau on the environment of their archives:

> In our tropical climate, paper is so fragile, sometimes more fragile than human memory. Our land court proceedings in some of the states have had to rely almost entirely on our old form of 'archives,' personal memories, because most of the paper records of land ownership in those particular states have been lost or destroyed. These paper documents turned out to be more fragile than human memory.
>
> (Wareham, 2002)

The answers we seek often cannot be found in moldy rooms on eroding paper. Repeatedly we see that collective memory and the repetition of that memory can be stronger than the written record.

The embodied archives sit just outside the realm of imperial records. In the imperial archives, embodied knowledge that lives in the voice, in the body and in the collective memory of kinship groups has mistakenly been considered 'that which disappears because it cannot be contained or recuperated through the archive' (Taylor, 2003). This language of disappearance applied to Native knowledge systems is designed to prioritize the value of the written record. The written is a complement to embodied knowledge, but it cannot replace it.

> Our ancestors etched everything into the tides of their tongues.
>
> *Will Giles and Travis Thompson, Oral Traditions* (2015)

Creation chants position the beginnings of our cultures. They are held sacred and certain members of the community were chosen to recite these chants based on the strength of their memory and the honor of reciting these chants was handed down genealogically. Kānaka Maoli scholar and poet ku'ualoha ho'omanawanui refers to Kamakau, in her description of mo'olelo ha'i waha (stories told, not written) stating that 'it was common for lengthy compositions or those related to mo'okū'auhau such as Kumulipo, to be memorized by a hui (collective). Such practices of cultural or ancestral memory helped ensure the composition would be remembered and transmitted' (Ho'omanawanui, 2014). The Hawaiian creation chant, Kumulipo, is over 2100 lines and at its core is a highly-developed structure of knowledge that provides a system for Native Hawaiians to understand our existence in time and space. It is simultaneously an embodied ecology, star chart and genealogy. If each line were chanted by a different orator, each orator would infuse her own character and inflection into the chant and therefore enhance its meaning. There are subtle changes each time a chant is performed. When those conditions change, the memory is changed.

Samoan and Hawaiian spoken word artists, Will Nu'utupu Giles and Travis Ka'ulula'au Thompson's poem, 'Oral Traditions,' is a type of mo'olelo ha'i waha (Ho'omanawanui, 2014) or performance-based orature that is contextual, interactive and open to interpretation and word play. They also incorporate the use of what Hawaiians call meiwi mo'okalaleo (Aha Pūnana Leo, 2003) – traditional poetic and narrative elements that historically were an 'integral part of oral tradition that were embodied in memory and performance' (Ho'omanawanui, 2014). These poetic devices utilize genealogy, repetition, kaona or hidden meaning, personal names, place names, etc., to ensure the retention of several stories at once, such as genealogies, the impact of banned language and foreign diseases and the power and necessity of oral histories. It is easy to see the continuum of the oral elements used in traditional chants throughout Oceania applied to spoken word composed by contemporary Pacific Islanders.

However, there is one key difference, spoken word is now recorded, filmed and placed on the internet. It is not necessarily published in a book, but it is deemed as archived in a virtual space. It is not necessarily passed on through genealogy, unless those within their kinship group are being taught the poem and memorize and perform it. The video captures a moment, but if the link breaks, the server fails or the creators of the video take down the video, then the orality and the power of that performance is lost. In the end, Giles and Thompson are the source. They are the original record until it is once again passed on orally.

> Sea routes were mapped on chants.
>
> Epeli Hau'ofa, 2000

The power of chant as a tool for survival is perhaps best conveyed in navigation and mapping chants. These types of chants provide cartographies of our world view and allow us to see the vision of our navigators. It is worth quoting in full the passage by Epeli Hau'ofa in which he states:

> I once asked a very knowledgeable seaman how people of old knew sea lanes, especially between distant places. He replied that these were recorded in chants that identified sequences of landfalls between points of departure and final destinations. Distances were measured in how long it generally took to traverse them. I believe that the Australian Aborigines did similarly with their songlines that connected places across their continent from coast to coast.
>
> (Hau'ofa, 2000)

A navigator must be able to read the sea, the stars, the weather, the birds and fish. 'He must know his position in relation to his home and destination and adjust his course as necessary' (UNESCO, 2005). The cartographic chants of Oceania and the songlines of Australia remind us that we must continue to find our way. That we must develop new chants and seek new landmarks.

Marshallese navigators, who use a variety of cartographic techniques, know their place in the world, where they are coming from and where they are going. Navigators from Polowat and Satawal use *etak,* translated as 'moving islands', described as 'the technique for calculating distance traveled, or position at sea by triangulating the speed of the islands of departure and destination with that of a third reference island' (Diaz, 2011). Simultaneously guided by stars in the night sky once beyond the land, the navigator can locate himself in time and space without instruments. This type of knowledge reminds us that we can depend on ourselves to find our way. Another mnemonic device is found in Marshallese navigation charts – maps made from coconut palm fronds and cowry – which were passed down from navigator to navigator. The chart was designed solely for each navigator, and memorized and discarded. No other navigator could read this chart, the intention being to prevent the theft of knowledge of the routes to protected and sacred sites. There are three forms: the mattang, the meddo and rebbilib. Each serves a different function and indicates subtle changes in the seascapes and landscapes. Scholar, poet and climate change activist Kathy Jetnil-Kijiner discusses the role of the navigation chart in Marshall Islands navigation history:

> We Marshallese constructed, through materials from our surroundings, and through our own ways of knowing and learning, a model for depicting and preserving our knowledge of 'reading' waves and island locations. And it only makes sense that one of our first texts would be a navigational chart, reflecting our knowledge which helped us survive and thrive.
>
> (Jetnil-Kijiner, 2014)

As migration into the diaspora accelerates, these maps held in memory become vital. We may not know what lies ahead. Currently, the Marshallese living in the diaspora – whether Guam, Hawai'i or California – are finding and utilizing the materials around them to form new navigation charts to adapt as necessary. They must trust in the tools that have been handed down to them to locate themselves in time and space. In the meantime, we will work to stop further departures, but if they must leave, create a pu'uhonua for them to form new homes.

Wayfinding is necessary for our existence. To imagine a world in which there is no physical homeland because it has been removed from the landscape is devastating. So, we must become our own maps. By maintaining and learning our cartographic chants, we can etch the memories of our homelands onto the tongues of our children.

> *There our words*
> *Will find the delicate filaments*
> *That anchor brain to belly or heart*
> *Words to tease other words*
> *And words*
> *That bear unseen*
> *The source*
> *Which we must touch*
> *To see*
>
> Pio Manoa, 1995

From our chants grow many stories. Those stories hold the histories of our gods, royalty and ancestors. They explain our ecologies, astronomy, fish migration, bird song, the names of the winds and the rain. Storytelling has been a central component of our cultures for millennia; without them we have no histories. Storytelling remains one of the few places where our voices are not drowned by imperialist and colonialist discourse. It has served western historians to attempt to reduce our stories to false histories. The lengths that missionaries and other foreigners went to silence our stories and insert their own demonstrates just how powerful our stories are.

Our stories can live within almost any space. They can be told in chant, poetry, spoken word, plays, song and dance. They can be woven into mats, pounded into kapa and carved into stone.

In what ways can we promote our own stories about climate change? What ways can we tell them? How do we preserve and pass on these stories? How do we ensure our stories of survival and thriving remain dynamic elements of our communities?

Talanoa may be one approach to answer these questions. Talanoa is described by Samoan theologian and scholar Jione Havea as three interconnected subjects: story, telling (of stories, memories, longings) and conversation (teasingly and critically, but mainly informally) (Havea, 2010). Talanoa is a way of speaking honestly and without concealment. It is not easily described or always understood because there is not always a destination, but through it relationships are strengthened. Talanoa creates a space of engagement to speak our minds and have open dialogue about the issues facing our communities. It provides several ways to approach problems and conflict. How can talanoa be considered an archive? Through the conversations and in the telling of stories is the sharing of knowledge. This shared knowledge fosters better understanding and a new record is formed. The power of talanoa is that it must exist face-to-face, and although it can be recorded and transcribed, the true record lives in the interactive exchange. Perhaps by engaging in talanoa, we can raise important questions on sea level rise and migration both within our islands and throughout the diaspora. Talanoa may help to not only promote dialogue, but inspire us to develop creative solutions.

It was mentioned that stories exist in many forms and spaces. What this means is that stories can take multiple forms, and be held by more than one person, implying this: many stories have variations which will be different depending on the individual, lineage, family, profession, class or island group to whom the story belongs. While this diversity may not seem to fit in with western concepts of an archive which holds the 'authoritative' story, it is very much something celebrated by the many cultures of Oceania. For example, in Hawai'i we have stories of the demi-god and ancestor, Maui, whose exploits are also recalled to much renown throughout many parts of what we now know as Polynesia. The term Polynesia, literally meaning 'many islands' is a problematic colonial term for a broad cultural and linguistic part of Oceania. We use it here not as a term of separation, or hierarchy, but to show cultural affinity with other Pacific Islanders. While Maui is known for slowing down the sun in most Polynesian islands, in Aoteaora he also attempts to find the secret of immortality, in Hawai'i he pushes up the sky, in Tonga Maui he is the one who introduced breadfruit to the people, to name but a few examples. This diversity is appreciated among Oceanians today, and when we meet there is often pride and joy at exchanging stories and seeing where there are commonalities and differences.

In a similar vein, Papua New Guinean scholar, novelist and literary critic, Steven Edmund Winduo, has written about the narrative structure of the ogre-killing child which 'is well documented in Papua New Guinea. The structure of this story is fixed, but the narrative itself changes from one society to another' (Winduo, 2000). This diversity of stories, the variation upon similar themes and structures, is seen as an asset. The power of stories, in all their forms, are their multiplicity. In other words, our embodied stories encourage interpretation and adaptation. Indeed, ku'ualoha ho'omanawanui in writing about the many variations on the stories of the volcano gods, and the goddesses Pele and Hi'iaka states that 'the presence of multiple writers and narratives of the Pele and Hi'iaka mo'olelo demonstrates the cultural value of makawalu (multiple perspectives); Kanaka 'Ōiwi accept and even appreciate multiple and sometimes conflicting accounts …' (Ho'omanawanui, 2014). Storytelling invites community, sharing, retelling and new interpretations. Thus, even while the imperial archive privileges hegemony and singular points of view, an embodied archive leaves space for different voices to engage stories and grow a wide range of voices.

One of the best and most complicated forms of storytelling is found in dance and song. In Hawaii, there exist halau hula whose kumu hula pass their knowledge through genealogy and through training of students and dancers. One example is Hālau o Kekuhi, school of hula. Hālau o Kekuhi is a classic school of hula and the center of cultural knowledge for the Edith Kanaka'ole Foundation. The Kumu Hula of this halau are genealogically connected to the land they are from and the traditions they teach: hula (dance), oli (chant), mo'okū'auhau (genealogy) and mo'olelo (story/history). They descend from a line of eight generations of Kumu Hula. In this light, the archive is what is taught from one generation to another – the vast lore and knowledge of the Kumu Hula. This knowledge is then contained within the body – literally in the dances and chants memorized and performed by halau members. It is embodied within the skills passed down – the ability to craft implements, instruments and clothing. The vast forms of dance that thrive throughout the Pacific fill volumes of texts, videos and photographs, but because it must be performed, it is an ever-changing record. Its value is undoubtedly enduring.

During the Pacific Festival of the Arts held in May 2016 in Guam, a group of dancers from Pohnpei performed a dance of remembrance about the Second World War. The dance included the cadence of marching soldiers and their song told the tale of the arrival of the Americans during the Japanese occupation of the islands. The choice to perform this dance in the highly-militarized space of Guam, for whom many are seeking decolonization and the removal of the U.S. military, but also a space where many are active members of the military, demonstrates both the impacts of war throughout the region that live in their cell memory and a recognition of the complicated presence of current military occupation. If this dance had been performed in their home islands for each other, it would be a record of an event held in their own collective memory. Once shared among other Pacific Islanders, the record of this memory transforms through new interpretations. The record is complicated even further when onlookers such as tourists and other foreigners apply their interpretations to the performance. These methods of storytelling do not allow a memory or story to remain fixed.

The truth is that dance and other performances designed to record a specific moment or era in history provide all that is required for those descendants to understand their ancestors' relationship to that moment. An outsider's interpretation of this dance is of little consequence, but for those descendants this dance becomes part of the genealogy of stories of their land.

> I am a tongue, only because
> you are the body planting stories with thumb.
>
> Donovan Kūhio Colleps, 2016

We have so far not addressed the archive of names. The power of naming perhaps more than anything else can tell us all that we need to maintain our societies during migration.

Place names inform our locations in time and space, genealogical names inform land tenure or record events or characteristics of a person. The kaona (layers of meaning) that can exist in a name are endless, so our names may be the most powerful archival record available to any of us.

In the Solomon Islands, on the islands of Guadalcanal, Isabel and Makira, landownership is matrilineal. One can claim ownership by 'proving their genealogical link to their original woman settler...Land succession occurs through the descendants of the first-born female, who heads the family clan. Her descendants become responsible for the inheritance and administration of the land' (Stege and Huffer, 2008). Although bought land and patriarchy have interfered with this tradition, this customary practice tells us many things. The sovereignty of the land is tied to its women, the location of a family's customary land lives within the names of its female descendants. Regardless of how the land tenure practice plays out in contemporary society, the names provide a record for future descendants to understand the sovereignty of their matrilineal ancestors.

In Hawai'i, a story is told by Kānaka Maoli composer and mele historian Kihei de Silva about his composition of the mele 'Hanohano Wailea', a song which describes the traditional land names and sites of Ka'Ōhao, O'ahu, now most often referred to as Lanikai, a name 'given' by housing developers of that neighborhood. As de Silva tells the story, he overheard a white settler talking to another white settler about the old place of Lanikai – the pill boxes, the mokes – names which have no history in Hawai'i except as the names settlers and colonizers, unfamiliar with our language, have applied to our landscape in their complete ignorance and arrogance. As a remedy, de Silva composed his song as a remedy:

> My purpose was simple: name the old names of Ka'Ōhao. Put them back in our mouths and ears where they belonged. Ka'Ōhao itself was a lost name, long out of everyday use. It had been swallowed up since 1925 by "Lanikai," a name that –like Smith's, Pillbox, Mid-Pac, and Mokes – was no name at all.
>
> (Kamehameha Schools, 2016)

Because of de Silva's composition, this song has become the new song for Lanikai elementary school and has become the official song for halau Mohala Ilima, his wife Mapuana's halau hula. When colonial and imperial names are overlaid upon our lands, our embodied archives, the archives we share through song, dance, chant and storytelling helps to counteract loss. Although some aspects may be erased, our systems of knowledge preserve what is important and reinforces our memory. So even when names seem to be lost, our embodied archives serve as a guide to reclaim and restore what is true and of value.

'Pā'ele ke lani'

'Ōlelo No'eau, 2565 (Pukui and Varez, 1983)

The last embodied archive that we will mention in this essay is the tattoo, also known by other terms such as pe'a/ tatau/ malu/kakau/eọ/moko. Each term has its own distinct meaning within each culture. The tattoo is literally a living text living within the skin. It is perhaps the most misunderstood and most misappropriated symbol of Pacific identity in history. So, its identity as an archive is delicate. Albert Wendt had this to say about the role of tatau in Samoa:

> tatauing is part of everything else that is the people, the aiga, the village, the community, the environment, the atua, the cosmos... The tatau and the malu are not just beautiful decoration, they are scripts/texts/testimonies to do with relationships, order, form and so on.
>
> (Wendt, 1996)

This quote by Wendt makes plain the significance and role of tatau and malu (women's tattoo) within the Samoan community, but one could argue it gets at the very heart of the embodied archives for Oceania. The inheritance we leave for our children is what dwells in each of us. It may be the text tapped into our skins or the story, song, chant and spoken word that is carried in our voice or the history, humor and tragedy of life's events performed in our dance. All of this exists outside of the political or physical state of the land. Whether our land is decolonized, postcolonial or occupied, our genealogies are ever constant. They are not fixed or static or unadaptable, but constant. The true archives of Oceania live within the knowledge and traditions of its people. Our knowledge can take us anywhere.

Sweeping reef,
sleeping mountain …
do you hear me whisper?

Leilani Burgoyne (Burgoyne, 2006)

Conclusion

Moving into the conclusion, we would like to revisit some of the questions this chapter has raised and attempted to begin to address:

- In Oceania, how do we continue to unsettle and take to task those who are the gatekeepers of imperial archives? How do we continue to assert our agency within a space that has historically held our histories hostage? Is it enough to promote access to historic records, or must we find ways to expand existing archives to include embodied knowledge, so that it cannot disappear? How do we return that knowledge to our bodies?
- How do we remember, reaffirm and reconnect to lands that have been lost? How can collective memory be shared between ourselves and other islanders?
- As physical archives face the threat of disappearance, how do we (re)construct our own archives, collectively on our own terms within new landscapes, without slipping into despair?

We have only touched upon some examples of the continuum of embodied archives available to and being actively used by Pacific Islanders that can lead to an enduring future for our cultures. We have not spoken about many things that are in direct relationship to our embodied archives, such as woven mats, tapa and clothing, carvings, tools and weapons, musical implements and canoe building. We have also not spoken about the aspects of customary practice and protocols involved in ritual ceremony of burial, birth, marriage, gift giving, agriculture, fishing and hunting. It is impossible to truly separate materials and actions from the embodied archives because they are the physical manifestation of our labor, our relationships, our governance and our spiritual beliefs. Our hands can carry and rebuild that which is physical. However, to address these subjects in their entirety would require more thorough explanations than this space will allow.

The primary goals of this essay are to acknowledge the continuing need for the Indigenous peoples of Oceania to assert their agency and develop guidelines around Native knowledge within existing archives, but to also realize that Native embodied knowledge systems can also give us the tools we need to survive the storms that are coming. Embodied knowledge is not static or fixed, it grows and adapts with its owner. With this awareness, we support those who continue to hold the first world accountable to the situation we are now facing and continue to make our demands clear regarding the protection of our islands. Our islands were already addressing many struggles before climate change. There are coups, genocides, challenged economies and many other traumas resulting from capitalism, militarism and exploitation of resources. Collectively, these things put our cultures at risk daily and for many justifiably take priority. The urgency of addressing the issue of sea level rise is that our land, that we are tied to genealogically, that is our blood, may disappear beneath the ocean. But our hope is to find resilience and not sink into despair by trusting our own knowledge systems and our existing tools for survival. In some ways rising sea levels provide us with an opportunity to harness our mana as the peoples of Oceania and retain our cultures regardless of the threats to our physical structures.

Our own archives, our vast and expanding repositories of knowledge, are formed through experience then expressed through any number of ways. While carried in our bodies, our DNA and ancestry, these archives are essential to the continuation and adaptation of our cultures. In what ways do we incorporate new knowledge, foreign knowledge and the experiences we have in new lands? How do we ensure our descendants' stories are woven into the stories we have been telling for generations?

During this time of duress, there will be many with their own agendas who will offer to 'help' and our agency can become muddled. We own our own histories, stories and objects. We therefore have the right to set the parameters and ethical guidelines for access. If we do not do this for ourselves, those on the peripheries of Oceania who have shallow understandings of the complexities of our peoples will once again apply their fictions to our histories, dance and language. Our sovereignty exists not only in our governments but within our knowledge systems. We hope that those of us whose erosion is happening more slowly realize we have the responsibility to provide a pu'uhonua (sanctuary) for each other, both physically and spiritually. It is not the Pacific way to lock borders or restrict movement. Welcoming each other into our homes is perhaps the best way to protect our cultures. We have allowed the discourse of scarcity to interfere with our ability to thrive. We must remind ourselves that the Pacific has always provided a home for us and we will have enough, if we refuse to let the language of despair break our kinship. We will not let our voices or our cultures drown. We are more than our land. We are also the sea.

Bibliography

350 Pacific (2013). 'We Are Not Drowning, We Are Fighting.' Available at: 350pacific.org.

Adichie, C. (2009). 'Danger of the Single Story.' *Ted.com*. Available at: https://youtu.be/D9Ihs241zeg

'Aha Pūnana Leo, KŌmike Hua'Ōlelo, and University of Hawaii at Hilo. Hale Kuamo'o. (2003). *Māmaka Kaiao: A Modern Hawaiian Vocabulary: A Compilation of Hawaiian Words That Have Been Created, Collected, and Approved by the Hawaiian Lexicon Committee from 1987 through 2000.* Honolulu: University of Hawai'i.

British Library (2012). 'Endangered Archives Programme: Home.' Available at: eap.bi.uk.

—— (2016). 'Endangered Archives Programme: Home.' Available at: eap.bi.uk.

Burgoyne, L. (2006). 'Apia.' In *Niu Voices: Contemporary Pacific Fiction 1.* Wellington: Hui Publishers, 173.

Colleps, D.K. (2016). 'Kissing the Opelu.' *Poetry.* Vol. CCVIII, no. 4. July/August 2016.

Diaz, V. (2011). 'Voyaging for Anti-Colonial Recovery: Austronesian Seafaring, Archipelagic Rethinking, and the Re-mapping of Indigeneity.' *Pacific Asia Inquiry,* Fall 2:1.

Giles, W. and Thompson, T. (2015). 'Oral Traditions.' *Button Poetry*. Available at: https://youtu.be/r3psIYJjpDo

Hau'ofa, E. (2000). 'Epilogue: Pasts to Remember.' *Remembrance of Pacific Pasts: An Invitation to Remake History*. Honolulu: University of Hawai'i.

Havea, J. (2010). 'The Politics of Climate Change: A Talanoa from Oceania.' *International Journal of Public Theology,* 2010. 4: 345–55.

Ho'omanawanui, K. (2014). *Voices of Fire: Reweaving the Literary Lei of Pele and Hi'iaka.* Minneapolis: University of Minnesota Press, xxxi.

Jetnil-Kijiner, K. (2014). *Iep Jāltok: A History of Marshallese Literature.* MA Thesis. 28. University of Hawaii Mānoa. Available at: https://scholarspace.manoa.hawaii. edu/bitstream /10125/36868/1/ Jetnil-Kijiner _2014.pdf

Kamehameha Schools. (2016). Hanohano Wailea. Kaleinamanu. Available at: https://apps.ksbe.edu/kaiwakiloumoku/kaleinamanu/mele-hou/hanohano_wailea

Manoa, P. (1995). 'Invitation,' in *Nuanua Pacific Writing in English since 1980.* Honolulu: University of Hawai'i Press.

Osorio, J. (1999). 'Protecting Our Thoughts.' A speech delivered at Voices of the Earth Conference held in Amsterdam, Nov. 10, 1993. In Wood, Houston. *Displacing Natives: The Rhetorical Production of Hawai'i.* Lanham, MD.: Rowman & Littlefield, 53.

Rakova, U. (2009). 'Sisters on the Planet: Carteret Islands.' Oxfam. Available at: YouTube.com, 2009. Available at: https://youtu.be/0XDHMgqlcEU

Pukui, M., and Varez, D. (1983). *'Ōlelo No'eau: Hawaiian Proverbs & Poetical Sayings*. Honolulu, Hawaii: Bishop Museum. Bernice P. Bishop Museum Special Publication; 71.

Stege, K. and Huffer, E. (2008). *Land and Women: The Matrilineal Factor: The Cases of the Republic of the Marshall Islands, Solomon Islands, and Vanuatu*. Suva, Fiji: Pacific Islands Forum Secretariat. Available at: rmicourts.org/wp-content/uploads/ PIFS-Land-and-Women.pdf

Taylor, D. (2003). *The Archive and the Repertoire: Performing Cultural Memory in the Americas*. Durham, NC: London: Duke UP.193.

Teaiwa, K. M. (2014). *Consuming Ocean Island: Stories of People and Phosphate from Banaba*. Bloomington: Indiana University Press,11.

UNESCO (2005). 'The Canoe Is the People: Indigenous Navigation in the Pacific.' Available at: canoeisthepeople.org

Vaka'uta, C. F. K. (2012) '1Angry Native on Climate Change.' *The Personal as Political: 1 A Self-reflective Essay on the Act of Poetry Making and Creating the '1Angrynative' Persona*. University of the South Pacific, 3.

Wareham, E. (2001). 'Our Own Identity, Our Own Taonga, Our Own Self Coming Back: Indigenous Voices in New Zealand Record-Keeping.' *Archivaria*, Fall 52: 27.

—— (2002). 'From Explorers to Evangelists: Archivists, Recordkeeping and Remembering in the Pacific Islands.' *Archival Science*, 2: 187–207.

Wendt, A. (1996). 'Tatauting the Post-Colonial Body.' *Span*, April–October, 42–3.

Winduo, S.E. (2000). 'Unwriting Oceania: The Repositioning of the Pacific Writer Scholars Within a Folk Narrative Space.' *New Literary History*, 601. Available at: https://www.jstor.org/stable/20057621?seq=1#page_scan_tab_contents

25

GLOBAL ENVIRONMENTAL HARM, INTERNAL FRONTIERS AND INDIGENOUS PROTECTIVE ONTOLOGIES

Ajay Parasram and Lisa Tilley

Introduction

At the Globe Leadership Summit on unceded Coast Salish Territories (Vancouver) in March of 2016, the Canadian Prime Minister, Justin Trudeau, set out the need for his country to continue to expand investment in extractive operations and carbon infrastructure in order to fund a low-carbon future (*National Observer* 2016). Trudeau's position – that the most viable route to ecological repair is paved by means of the material expansion of the carbon economy, despite the dispossession and contamination this expansion inevitably exacts – is rooted firmly in the logic of secular modern/colonial science. Yet at the same time, this position is paradoxically demonstrative of what might be described as a mystical faith in an unlikely expectation: that more carbon death can viably lead us directly to a renewable afterlife. The logic behind Trudeau's policy perfectly demonstrates the epistemic problem we wish to draw attention to in this chapter. That is, colonial science[1] alone is ill-equipped to solve colonial problems. Further, to mitigate such colonially-rooted conditions as planetary environmental harm, the protective ontologies maintained and cultivated by Indigenous communities must be afforded their rightful guiding position at the forefront of global action.[2]

The central purpose of this chapter is therefore to argue for a consideration of global environmental harm from the position of the world's internal frontiers in both settler colonial and former franchise colonial countries.[3] Such a position affords, first of all, an understanding of environmental harm from the perspective of those most violently impacted by climate change, contamination, dispossession, and state-corporate aggression on the frontlines of climate struggles. Secondly, this focus draws attention to the processes of racialisation of frontier populations and to the environmental racism and raced modes of dispossession these processes enable. And thirdly, a frontier focus centralises protective, relational ontologies. We make this case because insisting on the continuity of internal 'frontiers' better recognises the enduring resistances along more-than-modern ontological dimensions to the violence of modern colonial life within states (de la Cadena, 2012; Escobar, 2016). We believe that planetary solutions for resuscitating our choking world ought to take guidance from the spaces in our world that are not fully indoctrinated into modern, capitalist thinking as espoused by the Canadian Prime Minister.[4]

Protective ontologies, as understood here, encapsulate more-than-modern ways of being in which nature is not conceived of primarily in its colonial forms as land and commodity to be owned and exploited. Instead, the human is understood as inseparable from nature within which the role of the human should be one of protection and partnership rather than ownership and domination. Most recently, Indigenous groups engaged in pipeline resistance actions at Standing Rock have articulated their wholesale rejection of the 'protester' label, emphasising instead their collective understanding as *protectors* by insisting that: 'the term protestor is a colonised term for standing up for what's right' (Anon 2016). Water protector Kandi Mossett further voiced her community's position in the following words: 'It's so important for people to understand that that label of "protestor" is so small in scope that it could never describe the protectors that are here' (Mossett 2016).

Internal, or interior, frontiers are understood here as locations of enclosure as well as exchange. They are also the meeting place of difference in the form of distinct ontologies where such difference tends to be hierarchised through processes of racialisation. The frontier therefore marks the end of national or imperial subjectivity as Ann Laura Stoler explains:

> When coupled with the word interior, frontier carries the sense of internal distinctions within a territory (or empire); at the level of the individual, frontier marks the moral predicates by which a subject retains his or her national identity despite location outside the national frontier and despite heterogeneity within the nation-state [...] an interior frontier entails two dilemmas: the purity of community is prone to penetration on its interior and exterior borders, and the essence of the community is an intangible 'moral attitude,' 'a multiplicity of invisible ties.'
>
> (Stoler 1997: 199, drawing also on Fichte quoted in Balibar 1990: 4 [emphasis in the original])

The national community is perceived as threatened by the incommensurable ontologies on its frontier, and that world is simultaneously the main inhibition to further resource expansion for the colony or nation.

After a brief overview of global climate change in the present moment, an outline of a selection of existing postcolonial and decolonial approaches to environmental harm will be sketched. We will draw attention to the epistemic problem apparent in the postcolonial work of Dipesh Chakrabarty (2009) in which the comfort of Enlightenment reason is returned to in the search for a solution to ecological catastrophe. After this, we make a call for engagement with protective ontologies as the basis of a decolonial science for a renewable life. We demonstrate protective ontologies in action through examples of Indigenous resurgence, from the settler colonial context of Turtle Island, to the franchise colonial context of Nusantara. Finally, we conclude with reflections on the role of protective ontologies in this present moment of climate urgency, recognising that such ways of being have passed five centuries of endurance against a globalising colonial system.

Climate change, resource frontiers, and black snakes

When the Arctic tundra warms, vegetation grows in place of the previously frozen exposed layer causing the surface to absorb, rather than reflect, heat. At the same time, harmful methane gas is released from beneath the melting snow and ice, contributing further to a warming globe. Changes in the Arctic ecosystem then give rise to planetary changes because of the regulatory function the Arctic performs with respect to global temperatures and weather patterns. A warm Arctic, for instance, leads to subsequent monsoon shifts across Asia and the Central Pacific (Cornell et al. 2016). Therefore, when Arctic temperatures reached a full 20°C above the seasonal average in November of 2016, this immediately led to fears of destructive consequences across the globe (*Guardian* 2016).

The Arctic temperature shock of this season is only the most recent in a series of alarming climate signals which are expected to gather pace as 'Man'-made climate change intensifies. We refer here to capital-M Man precisely because it is the modern over-consumer/investor figure of Man who 'overrepresents' himself as human,[5] as identified by Sylvia Wynter (2003: 260), rather than humanity as a whole, which bears the burden of responsibility for climate change. Hyper-consumerist ways of living in the industrialised, 'developed' parts of the world are disproportionately responsible for the carbon emissions which are altering the ecological balance across our planet which sustains species survival (c.f. Kanngieser and Last 2016; Gunaratnam and Clark 2012). Moreover, those who are most violently affected by Man-made climate change are not its main contributors, but instead those whose ways of being cause little in the way of carbon emissions: Pacific Islanders and South Asians whose homes will be lost under rising seas; impoverished agrarian communities living a precarious land-and-climate-dependent existence in what used to be Europe's formal colonies; and the Indigenous peoples who still live along the world's expanding colonial-resource frontiers who suffer both the violence of corporate expansion and the direct contamination of carbon infrastructure (Dalby 2009; Dalby 2013; *The Hindu* 2009). These latter global Indigenous, racialised, and (post)colonised populations, often situated on the frontlines of carbon and other forms of resource expansion, inspire this chapter's central call for the climate struggle to be guided by the multiple protective ontologies beyond the colonial core.

Our analysis here, as noted, considers parallel responses of Indigenous populations living in distinct settler colonial and franchise colonial settings. The fact should never be diminished that franchise colonies like the Dutch East Indies, today's Indonesia, won their independence through long and arduous anticolonial struggles. However, scholars such as Frantz Fanon and Casanova cautioned that the post-independence nation would allow for the reproduction of colonial dynamics within itself (Fanon 1961; Casanova 1965). Even so, there are limits to be found within the work of critical anticolonial writer/fighters, including Fanon. The precise limit to Fanon's application in the present, argues Glen Coulthard (2014: 153), lies not in a commitment to a teleological understanding of human progress as such, but in the fact that he 'remains wedded to a dialectical conception of social transformation that privileges the "new" over the "old".' Culture, in Fanon's anticolonial reading, is something to transcend. Indigenous struggles along internal frontiers, by contrast, are rooted in dynamic ontological foundations which keep the old alive in the present. It is these protective ontologies of the dynamic 'old' that will lead the world out of the bind of colonial environmental harm.

As we type these words in November of 2016, black snakes are creeping their way across Turtle Island. Harbingers of modern development, these pipelines are understood in the overlapping spaces of settler colonialism and industrial capitalism as productive, practical, and necessary forms of infrastructure to continue the process of transporting oil across contested territories to deliver it to global markets. The most globally famous site of colonial and anti-colonial contestation in the present moment is the Dakota Access Pipeline (DAPL), which is planned to run through Sioux territories. The project is being confronted by an enormous international contingency of Indigenous peoples across and beyond Turtle Island, along with settler-allies with solidarity demonstrations emerging across the continent.

The Standing Rock opposition to the DAPL is only one example of many sites of contestation across the continent, including the Site C dam which was just approved by the Trudeau government despite considerable Indigenous and settler opposition to the mega-project in the colonial Canadian province of British Colombia. In that same contested place (where some 97 per cent of territory is not covered by any treaties) rests the Unist'ot'en camp that practices decolonial politics by continuing to live in accordance with their traditional ways, and in so doing, are opposing multiple pipeline projects that threaten watersheds, rainforests, and more than 1,000 tributaries (Toledano 2014; Omand, 2016; Montsion 2015). The DAPL is a compelling example of environmental racism, as the only reason developers routed it through Standing Rock Sioux territories is because the original plan routed it close to the water reserves of nearby Bismarck, North Dakota – a settler colonial town with a 90 per cent white population (Hayes 2016). Environmental racism is not isolated to places like North Dakota; rather, it has become an everyday practice, accepted by the settler-governments of two of the world's wealthiest countries as necessary, perhaps unfortunate, consequences of modern capitalist development.[6]

Meanwhile, in Europe's former franchise colonies across the Global South, the expansion of resource frontiers is driven by the state-corporate appetite not only for fossil carbons from the subsoil, but also their renewable replicates and other resources for a high consumption existence. The high-yield oil palm, neatly transplanted onto the old colonial plantation estate landscapes of Southeast Asia, is particularly notable for its destructive distension (see Li, forthcoming). Easing this expansion, a similar picture emerges of environmental racism exerted across lines of difference against populations situated along internal frontiers. In fact, while the violent state repression of protectors at Standing Rock drew the keen attention of the alternative media, Indigenous death is repeated across the Global South with very little public recognition. The organisation Global Witness (2016) recently documented rising resource-related violence against rural, and especially Indigenous, environmental protectors across the world from Brazil to the Philippines. During 2015, 185 verifiable killings related to rural corporate activity, especially mining, hydroelectric dams, and agribusiness, took place, but the real figure is likely to be much higher (Global Witness. 2016: 4).

Although there are meaningful differences between the settler and franchise colonial contexts, not least the degree of attention paid to protector killings, this does not preclude the onset of a present global moment of Indigenous resurgence. Increasingly united, although geographically dispersed, Indigenous peoples forge relational solidarities through their common struggles against state-corporate violence and resource-related dispossession and contamination. Most recently, we have seen Standing Rock, the home of the Sioux Nation, become a focal point for global Indigenous resurgence: Māori performed haka at the site (Māori Television 2016), Northern Europe's Indigenous Sami took their own stories of struggles against extractives corporations (Indigenous Network 2016), and Mayan elders also travelled to the camp to demonstrate their gratitude and solidarity (The Free Thought Project 2016).

Such relational Indigenous association demonstrates a commonality across diverse, yet similarly protective, ontologies. This commonality is much more than simply a shared experience of the same forms of resource-related harm and dispossession; it is rooted in a shared understanding of human nature interdependency which marks a sharp distinction with homogenised colonial ways of being centred on land ownership (Rojas 2016). The following section introduces the ways in which such protective ontologies, as decolonial science, unravel the binds of postcolonial thinking on environmental harm, especially those approaches which return habitually to Enlightenment thinking for comfort.

Protective ontologies as decolonial science

Adopting a decolonial lens in the analysis of environmental racism allows us to recognise the historically maligned inequality of multiple systems of knowledge that have always existed alongside the modern/colonial knowledge system with its geopolitical centre grounded in Europe (Mignolo 2011; Grosfoguel 2002). Paying attention to the ontological dimensions of environmental justice brings to light a diversity of ways of understanding nature that is not reducible to the binary categorisations central to Western philosophy, nor reducible to the idea of unilinear development (Escobar 2016; Gudynas 2016). The hegemony of Enlightenment reasoning has re-presented this particular form of knowledge as a universe laying claim to a singular, 'rational', understanding of reality. This reasoning also renders other systems of knowledge to be 'pre-modern' or 'traditional' rather than treating knowledge systems and ways of relating to and with land/nature/one another on terms that are other than, or more-than modern (Rojas 2007; Quijano 2000; Grosfoguel 2007).

Scholars have increasingly described the period of the rise of industrial capitalism from the late eighteenth century onwards as a period in which human beings have become not just historical agents, but geological agents capable of changing the environment at a planetary scale (Chakrabarty 2009). Dubbed the 'Anthropocene,' the term highlights the particularly destructive impact human beings have had on the planet since the early rise of industrial society, though debate continues as to if we have already entered such a stage of planetary history or if we are on the precipice of it (Schmidt et al. 2016). Dipesh Chakrabarty's (2009: 206–7) influential *The Climate of History: Four Theses* offers a thoughtful meditation on the rise of human beings as 'geological agents' beginning around 1750, by which he means humans have collectively gained the ability to affect planetary/natural history as well as human history. He argues in this essay that the division that has separated human and natural histories has necessarily been dismantled in light of humanity's proven ability to have an impact on the planet itself, and comes to the conclusion that 'in the era of the Anthropocene, we need the Enlightenment (that is, reason) even more than in the past' (Chakrabarty, 2009: 211).

This is troubling because within Chakrabarty's analysis, we see at once the truth in the planetary-wide crisis of the Anthropocene, but also the unnecessary privileging of Enlightenment reason as the avenue to escape ecological catastrophe. Chakrabarty argues that the crisis of the Anthropocene has 'no intrinsic connection to the logics of capitalist, nationalist, or socialist identities' but is instead connected to 'the history of life on this planet, the way different life-forms connect to one another, and the way the mass extinction of one species could spell danger for the another' (2009: 217). Framing the Anthropocene as a global problem makes sense and echoes international organisations' and activists' strategies to broker deals like the Paris Climate Agreement. However, while Chakrabarty makes clear that he is not denying the historical role of Western nations in creating the contemporary fossil fuel crisis and the role of industrial capitalism, his attention, like the attention of so many other concerned people, is on the threshold beyond which human life can no longer be sustained. It is in this spirit that the call for modern science is levied. Limiting the scope of ideas and the range of action to modern/colonial reason and its associated ontological assumptions continues the historical fiction that only modern, post-Enlightenment reason is capable of possessing and cultivating crucial expertise about an 'environment' that is a resource.

Chakrabarty's (2000) insistence on the inadequacy but indispensability of 'Europe' gave rise to his famous call to 'provincialise' Europe, which is an important epistemological move. However, we argue that meaningful provincialisation requires the ontological work of decentring Eurocentric philosophy in order to elevate other-than European knowledge systems which are arguably more qualified to diversify and decolonise approaches to addressing the afflictions of the modern world. As Arturo Escobar (2015: 2, italics in original) maintains, '*we are facing modern problems for which there are no longer modern solutions.*' With reference only to systems of knowledge that are centred around Europe, the familiar project of modernity and Enlightenment is visible: a period of intellectual emancipation where new ideas grounded in rational thinking, secularism, and objectivity offer a way of understanding and categorising a single reality. Gurminder K.

Bhambra (2014: 40–4) argues that part of the founding myths of European modernity has been the belief that important events like the Renaissance, the French Revolution, and the Industrial Revolution were somehow endogenous to Europe without regard for the inherent interdependences that demand a global understanding of modernity from the onset. Enrique Dussel has described the totalisation of European knowledge as 'Eurocentrism', which, according to Cristina Rojas (2016: 9), is:

> the narrative of a modernity that emerged in Europe during the Middle Ages as a result of internal dynamics; based on this myth, Europeans claimed to be the 'reflexive conscience' of world history. This myth hides the other side of history: that Europe's centrality was built upon a colonial project premised upon conquest of the Americas (and, of course, Africa and parts of Asia).

The orientation of Western rational thought has been one through which knowledge that emerges from a particular region can be universally applicable without adequate attention to the ontological assumptions about reality upon which knowledge is scaffolded. Part of the blindness of Western epistemology is its investment in the 'ego politics of knowledge' over the 'geopolitics of knowledge' and the 'body-politics of knowledge,' (Maldonado-Torres 2006; Grosfoguel 2013), which brings to light the limitations of Chakrabarty's otherwise compelling discussion of why over-emphasising capitalism as the cause of the rise of the Anthropocene pays limited dividends.

Chakrabarty (2009: 216–17) is correct to warn against attributing to capitalism the cause of planetary ecological distress, because capitalism is indeed merely one of many symptoms of the modern/colonial condition:

> Whatever our socioeconomic and technological choices, whatever the rights we wish to celebrate as our freedom, we cannot afford to destabilize conditions (such as the temperature zone in which the planet exists) that work like boundary parameters of human existence. These parameters are independent of capitalism or socialism.
>
> (Chakrabarty, 2009: 218)

Our issue is not with the diagnosis of the problem so much as it is with the logical prescription that does not leave room for other-than modern leadership. Chakrabarty's juxtaposition of capitalism with socialism, remains ontologically invested in a Eurocentric ego politics of knowledge. It is true that capitalism and socialism share an understanding of the environment as inherently separate from humanity and as a deposit of resources through which to be exploited for human benefit. Socialism and capitalism also share universalistic aspirations predicated on a developmental and colonial logic of gradual linear development. However, folding all of humanity into these two divisions ignores the fact that alternative ways of thinking and acting need not in the past, present, or future, share this assumption of the universal organisation of the world. The problem here is one of mistaking a post-Enlightenment perspective as being universally applicable, and folding all of humanity into the role of co-conspirators in normalising modern industrial life.

It is true that by the time freedom-seeking colonial subjects succeeded in ending colonial rule in Asia, Africa, and the Caribbean in the mid/late twentieth century, generations of modern capitalist development predicated on genocide, slavery, indentureship, and plantations had largely naturalised the structure of modern, satellite states plugged into the formal imperial political economic networks in a way that appeared to be, if not natural, then at least inevitable and with universal validity. But as Fanon (2004 [1961]: 239) reminds us, anti-colonialism was never meant to be a 'crude emulation' of colonial ways of being; rather, the acquisition of the colonial state and its economic structures was meant only as a first step towards a much more radical project of innovation that would build a decolonised future.

Indigenous survivors of colonial genocide have endured and resisted in large part because of the preservation of their knowledge systems that have been grounded to land in ways that are ontologically distinct from the Western tradition. Western understandings of land, whether liberal or socialist, maintain an ontological starting point in which land and humanity are separate, and that land must be worked upon in order to extract value from it. Whether capitalist or socialist, approaches to rapid industrialisation and development have been followed through the nineteenth and twentieth centuries; and both remain firmly grounded in an ontology of land that renders it passive unless improved through human intervention. But as Indigenous scholars have long argued, this ontological starting assumption is not universally held (Coulthard 2014; Corntassle 2012; Hunt 2014; Hill 2008).

The value of taking a decolonial approach to the study of environmental inequality is not in pointing to the obvious fact that Indigenous peoples have been confronting and resisting the interdependent forces of colonialism and capitalism for 500 years, or even in exposing the co-constitutive 'coloniality' of Western modernity (Hill 2009; Mignolo 2011). For readers of this volume, such claims should already be credible starting points for analysis. The value of a decolonial approach to understanding environmental racism is in 'de-linking' from the imperial logic that continues to position 'Western' knowledge and its ontological assumptions about human/nature relations as a universal truth predicated on the representation of other-than European systems of knowledge as 'non-thinkers', 'pre-historical', or otherwise unqualified to enter into the business of knowledge (Mignolo 2009; Maldonado-Torres 2006; Guha 2002). De-linking is, in a way, a strategy for *scholarship* to 'catch up' to what historical survivors of colonialism have been practising since day one by letting go of the Eurocentricity (or ego-politics) of knowledge and coming to terms with the fact that those with the expertise to decolonise and build pathways out of ecological annihilation need not emerge from the fog of modern reason.[7]

Indigenous resistance to ongoing 'development' projects predicated on inherently colonial assumptions about land, nature, and humanity offer a particularly current context to show how even progressive thinking on environmental justice that remains firmly Eurocentric in orientation does not have the conceptual 'chops' for charting decolonial futures. As Kelly Hayes (2016), reporting from the frontlines of the ongoing Standing Rock direct action paraphrases, 'We are not simply here when you see us.' The politics of rendering Indigenous people invisible plays out in terms of seeing Indigenous politics as sporadic and aimed at protecting the environment alone, instead of being part of an uninterrupted 500–year history of ongoing resistance to multifaceted colonial violence (Hill 2009; Corntassle 2012).

Indigenous resurgence 1: Turtle Island

Space does not allow for a comprehensive list of ongoing or historical sites of anticolonial direct actions on Turtle Island, so here we draw illustratively on a few sites of contestation that are less reported internationally. These conflicts speak to various dimensions of resurgent Indigenous politics informed by ontologically distinct starting assumptions that, while encountering modern/colonial power at all times, refuse to be defined by it.

As Cherokee scholar Jeff Corntassle (2012) maintains, the discourse of 'land rights' misses the ontological project at stake in rejecting the modern/colonial terms of dividing and conceiving of land as an object to be possessed, contrasted with land being a relationship that entails obligations and responsibilities. Law, diplomacy, and international relations have a much deeper history on Turtle Island than in Europe. As Mohawk historian Susan Hill (2008) and Algonquin Anishinaabe-kwe scholar Lynn Gehl (2014) clearly show, Indigenous legal principles and conventions were well-developed long before the arrival of Europeans and provide the historical and conventional context for understanding how to interpret relations between nations: both Indigenous and settler. Wampum diplomacy, for example, brokered a lasting peace between the nations who formed the Haudenosaunee confederacy and outlined the manner in which land was to be shared: a practice that continued with the arrival of Europeans. The two-row Wampum belt, that symbolises two peoples travelling along the river of life together without interfering with one another's autonomy has been interpreted through a modern lens to be a call for segregation, but according to Hill, it instead describes the parameters for peaceful interdependency. Two boats travelling together will necessarily move together along a river, because if they stray to one side or the other, they encounter danger and risk ruining their boats. Rather than separation, the two-row wampum is about travelling together (Hill 2008).

Corntassle (2012: 92) characterises colonialism as a 'shape-shifter,' which requires constant attention to the ways through which the colonial settler state attempts to co-opt, disrupt, and pacify Indigenous self-determination. For Corntassle (2012) and other Indigenous scholars working in the resurgence approach, repairing the damage of colonial violence entails reconnecting with the land (Alfred 1999; 2016). One powerful example of decolonial politics is in de-linking from the Lockean principle of 'rights' to exploit land or territory, and instead viewing land as a relationship. Corntassle (2012: 93) discusses Cheryl Bryce and her family's everyday acts of resurgence on their traditional Lekwungen territories on 'Vancouver Island':

> Cheryl continues to harvest kwetlal (camas, a starchy bulb that has been a staple food and trade item for Indigenous peoples in the region for generations) on park lands and private properties, despite threats to her and her family's well-being from settlers attempting to deny her access to Lekwungen homelands.

Bryce and her community also remove invasive plant species, operate a community tool shed, re-draw maps of the area with traditional names, and work with students and community members interested in revitalising traditional food networks on Lekwungen territories (Corntassle 2012). The resurgent politics enacted here is literally de-linking from the framework of rights-based property relations and practising resurgent politics in spite of settler-colonial efforts to control and police these actions.

Across the continent on Mi'kmaq territories in colonial Nova Scotia, the Sipekne'katik First Nation are currently enacting decolonial politics through opposing a large carbon-based project led by Alton Natural Gas Storage LP. The company is attempting to build underground storage facilities which threaten the Shubenacadie River system. According to Andy Crosby (2016), construction of these facilities will involve 1.3 million cubic meters of concentrated salt water brine being 'gradually released into the Shubenacadie River system, which the company claims would not adversely impact the river nor its aquatic life.' Invoking the 1725 Treaty of Peace and Friendship which outlined the parameters of nation-to-nation sovereign relations between equals, the Mi'kmaq are enacting their sovereign rights to blockade, laying eel traps in the waters, which has led to the company offering scholarships and jobs conditional on the removal of these traps so their carbon storage project can continue. It is important that the laying of eel traps is of central concern to the company's attempts, as in doing so, the Sipekne'katik are showing through their practice that their relationship with the land is not one of 'tradition' but rather a continued living practice that existing colonial laws are not able to perceive. At a solidarity march and demonstration on November 5 2016 in K'jipuktuk (Halifax), Mi'kmaq speakers connected the struggle against Alton Gas to the struggle against DAPL through the common and longstanding defence of water for water's sake rather than merely as a commodity to be (mis)used.

Nearby and also on Mi'kmaq territories, the Elsipogtog First Nations recently confronted SWN Resources Canada, successfully blocking them from seismic exploration activity (fracking) for natural gas. More than 285 officers of the Royal Canadian Mounted Police, including tactical units, faced off against hundreds of Mi'kmaq warriors, resulting in six torched police cruisers and 40 arrests (Crosby, 2016). The Mi'kmaq won this battle in terms of blocking the government of New Brunswick's aspirations for a fracking gas industry, but the battle over pipelines continues. [8]

In Algonquin territories in modern-day capital city of 'Ottawa,' Windmill Development Group is attempting to build condominiums over a sacred area known as *Asinabka*, one of the four corners of the world. Citing UNDRIP articles 11, 12, 25, and 32, nine of ten Algonquin chiefs in the area have condemned the project, and groups led by Algonquin grandmothers and elders have been organising teach-ins, demonstrations, and marches that highlight the long history of settler governments breaking legal agreements pertinent to these Algonquin territories since the 1763 Treaty at Niagara (Gehl 2016a; 2016b; 2014). Long before European arrival, the waterways served as an international highway connecting traders, travellers, and diplomats from the west and to the east. The waterfalls were second in size and power only to Niagara Falls, and had strong healing power. Algonquin dispossession began with the arrival of permanent settlements around the turn of the nineteenth century, and the sacred waterfall was dammed in 1908 for a pulp and paper mill. The mill was closed in 2005 and the rights to this sacred land were sold by the settler authorities to Windmill Development Group, which seeks to 'honour' the Algonquins by building condos on the island between the cities of modern Ottawa and Gatineau.[9]

Back across to the west of Turtle Island, the Unist'ot'en clan of the Wet'suwet'en nation have been blocking various pipeline and associated land clearing projects since the colonial Canadian government authorised these projects in 2009 to transport carbon from the Alberta Tar Sands to the port of Prince Rupert for export to international markets. This has taken the form of living on the land of their ancestors and strategically bordering these lands to prevent construction of the pipelines. The community, which has been welcoming allies from other nations (including settlers), has grown over the years, and faced considerable obstacles from law enforcement, corporations, and provincial as well as federal governments. Defying the numerous attempts by police, corporations, and pipeline construction workers to violate their sovereignty, spokeswoman Feda Husan has been particularly clear in explaining to alien trespassers, 'This is Unist'ot'en territory. It's not Canada. It's not B.C. We make our own laws here' (cited in Toledano 2015). Perhaps among the most stunning examples of ontological difference and environmental racism can be seen in a video clip through which representatives from the pipeline project attempt to gain permission to enter the territory with the promise of jobs and offering of tobacco and bottled water as 'gifts' to the community. Husan educated the representatives on the harms of plastic bottles, pointing to the fact that they were currently standing on a bridge above the very running water they drink from and fish in (AJ+ 2015).

In the face of numerous failed attempts to enter the territory by corporations, workers, and police seeking to continue the development of pipeline projects, the RCMP have established checkpoints clearly aimed at frustrating and intimidating the free movement of supporters and Indigenous people alike (Toledano 2015). By engaging in strategic bordering amidst the resurgent politics of living with the land, the Unist'ot'en have been enacting decolonial politics while reconnecting with their lands. Though their territory was never ceded or surrendered, the community has been constantly under threat of violence from the colonial state. Rejecting the hegemony of Canadian law, however, the Unist'ot'en community practises its own law congruent with its traditions in spite of the colonial claim that all territory in Canada falls under the sovereign jurisdiction of the state and its federal police force, the RCMP.

On November 29, 2016, the Trudeau government killed the Northern Gateway project that ran west across Unist'ot'en territory, but approved the Trans Mountain expansion project that would twin existing pipelines moving southwest to Vancouver, as well as the massive Enbridge Line 3 pipeline project that will move carbon east (Tasker 2016). The juxtaposition of what we are loosely calling 'protective ontologies' shared across anti-colonial struggles, with the cognitive dissonance of the Canadian state's mantra of job creation, renewed nation-to-nation relations, and ecological development through carbon extraction demonstrate the ontological significance confronting colonial science. The logic of colonial science enables cost/benefit analyses that facilitate 'good' liberal public policy that render technical the question of acceptable levels of contamination of water. The very framing of this public policy question exemplifies colonial science and the violent history of settler colonialism as it depends on asserting as universally true a Eurocentric ontology of separation rather than relationality. The categorical separation of humanity and nature is an ontological requirement of this colonial science, and conflicts fundamentally with a relational ontology that views humans as part of nature, as well as other forces that exceed the limits of modern reason which we might call in English, rivers, mountains, etc. (cf: Coulthard 2014; de la Cadena 2015).

Some alternative media reports do a decent job of pointing to the obvious environmental racism of American and Canadian governments when it comes to discriminating against Indigenous communities, but the challenge these and other anti-colonial actions pose to colonial science has deeper implications. The environmental racism of the issue is only the modern limit of the ontological violence at play in settler colonialism, beyond which colonial science cannot see. To describe relational ontologies as 'protective' ontologies as we do in this paper is an attempt at translating into English that the challenge of the Anthropocene requires radically reformulating how we understand the problem. This understanding must be drawn from the multiple ontologies that coexist on this shared planet which hold more compelling solutions than digging pipelines in hopes of greener pastures. Colonial science has had its run, and we cannot 'develop' our way out of this problem.

Indigenous resurgence 2: Nusantara

Within the (former) franchise colonies of the Global South, the picture is often more complex than it is within settler colonies with their relatively clearer racialised distinction between settlers and Indigenous peoples. In the case of Indonesia, for instance, of the many hundreds of cosmologically diverse peoples living across the archipelago, many of these are recognised to belong within the state's accepted ways of being which involve adherence to the country's official religions and a sedentarist lifestyle (see Chou 2010: 14–15; Acciaoli 2001). Those Indigenous groups which continue with animist, nomadic, and other non-normalised practices are considered to be outside of this frame and have been subjected to interventions intended to assimilate and acculturate them into the normalised state ways of being. For this reason, the term 'internal imperialism' has been used by Acciaoli (2001) to describe Indonesia's regimes of difference in which 'Fourth World' peoples are subordinated within an independent former franchise colony.

Indigenous groups in Indonesia are, in theory, protected by customary law, or *adat*, which has been fortified in resource politics in recent decades, and forms the central focus of Indigenous struggles. However, *adat* is frequently relegated within a system of legal pluralism and overridden by state law if the case in question is deemed to be in the interests of national development. As such, although Indigenous groups are constantly engaged in *adat* legal struggles to defend their lands and environments, they do so with limited success and continue to combine legal struggles with direct protective action.

In order to understand the kind of protective action Indigenous groups engage in across the world's resource frontiers, it is important to understand that the loss or contamination of land, forest, and waterways amounts to something much more comprehensively detrimental than dis-*possession*. This is because the Indigenous relationship with nature is not accurately described by the concept of possession, instead corresponding more to interdependency and protection, such that nature is central to Indigenous ways of being. Dayak communities of the island of Borneo, recognised as Kalimantan by Indonesia, live according to a cosmology which rests on the interdependence of nature and the human; hence the Dayak concept of *lati tana* sets out the integrated nature of land use with the spiritual and social life of the community (Mulyoutami et al. 2009: 2054–7).

Dayak populations recognise multiple and varying types of forest according to their degrees of cultivation as well as their degrees of regulation by both community and spirits. Dayak forest-dwelling populations in East Kalimantan maintain various forms of *simpukng*, or forest gardens, which may be family-owned or belong to a wider community (Mulyoutami et al. 2009: 2054). *Simpukng* may be cultivated in fallow areas formerly used for growing rice, or otherwise in areas of secondary forest with a mixture of naturally-growing and cultivated plants and trees; therefore, at first glance *simpukng* appear to be wild and unmanaged forest spaces. In reality they are regulated by customary rules to avoid over-exploitation, and traditionally they have been managed by the customary chief of the *lamin* or longhouse, the elevated ironwood structure which serves as a communal dwelling for a number of families. In Central Kalimantan, *Pahewan* is recognised to be a protected forest area which has a spiritual presence. *Kaleka* forests, on the other hand, are used more intensively for cultivation and may be planted on former settlement areas. *Hutan keramat* is a forest from which nothing can be taken and *Tajahan* is the most spiritual form of forest in which a spirit presence acts to protect the trees (interviews in Central Kalimantan 2014).

As oil palm plantations spread across the outer islands of Indonesia, often by means of corporate violence and dispossession, Indigenous communities are compelled to intensify the active protection of their lands and environments. One such community in the village of Semunying Jaya, on the island of Borneo/Kalimantan, has documented its struggle against state and corporation. For this community, the extension of the oil palm frontier has meant the loss of forested areas, rubber trees, and rattan cultivation areas; but it has also meant the destruction of sacred burial grounds and the burning of homes and community buildings by corporate aggressors acting in articulation with the state. The loss of forest, they say, is much more than the loss of the means of self-sufficiency, it amounts to a spiritual loss because without the forest 'life has no meaning' (If Not Us Then Who? 2016). Since 2005 then, the community has been locked in a struggle to protect their forests and cultivation areas in which they have employed a broad range of tools of resistance; from legal cases to direct action against corporate property. When the bulldozers arrived to clear their land for plantation development, they seized the heavy equipment and sabotaged corporate activities. This resulted in the arrest of community members on the grounds of theft; arrests then led to convictions, incarceration, and the inhumane treatment of environmental defenders in jail. But the struggle continues by means of legal cases as well as marches on the capital, in unison with other Indigenous groups from across the archipelago's resource frontiers.

As collective actions gather pace and unite spatially dispersed groups in Indonesia, Indigenous struggles are increasingly framed in the context of a much longer struggle for sovereignty which predates independence struggles and was certainly not resolved by them. The broader understanding is one of continuity in the experience of coloniality well beyond independence from formal European rule. As one Indigenous spokesperson puts it: 'this nation must not let the Indigenous people remain colonised, still discriminated against, remaining the lowest class of citizens' (If Not Us Then Who? 2016).

This picture is repeated across Europe's former franchise colonies of the Global South where Indigenous people make up the paracolonised populations (Casanova 1965) immediately threatened by the expansion of resource frontiers. The protective struggle of Dayak peoples across Borneo illustrates the gravity of what is at stake when Indigenous lands are lost. Although such struggles mark the frontlines of the fight against climate change, they are also a continuation of a much longer ontological battle to maintain a way of being which maintains the integration of the human with nature. As we have shown, the word dispossession is by no means adequate to encapsulate the ontological impact of the loss of land and forest.

Conclusion

The present moment of urgency in the struggle against Man-made climate change and carbon expansion provides the contextual backdrop for the apparent fortification of nation-to-nation Indigenous solidarities across the globe. The water protection struggle against the DAPL oil pipeline at Standing Rock has made more broadly visible that which has been constant at least since the Colombian incursion of 1492: that is, over five centuries of resistance and endurance in the face of genocidal colonisation which itself has taken on geological/planetary implications since the late eighteenth century. Standing Rock and other struggles witnessed today along internal resource frontiers across the globe should not, therefore, be understood as struggles against climate change as such. Instead these are ontological struggles to protect human/nature ways of being by very different Indigenous peoples and nations who have long maintained that modern/colonial society's imagined separation from, and presumed mastery over, nature is leading us along a route to catastrophe.

Our task in this chapter has therefore been to draw attention to protective ontologies across the globe, which, although diverse in their practices, share a long history of resistance to colonialism in its many forms. We engaged with struggles defined within both settler colonial and franchise colonial settings in order to draw attention to the decolonial politics which are lived across the globe in frontier spaces. This frontier focus affords attention to peoples who, despite the assimilative pressure of the global colonial order, maintain ways of being otherwise to the present liberal (or socialist) colonial norm. This focus also centres on various racialised and thus excluded populations across the globe which, despite the geographical distance between them, as well as their distinct settler or franchise colonial contexts, are subject to similar assimilation and acculturation efforts by colonial states. The common condition across the world's resource frontiers is also one of corporate harm and violent dislocation from the nature which is so integral to more-than-modern ontologies.

Although anticolonial and postcolonial thinkers have provided great insight and impetus to scholarship and social action in relation to the colonial question more broadly, the epistemic limits to these approaches are becoming increasingly apparent as we edge ever closer to climate catastrophe. Fanon's anticolonial work, for instance, effectively subjugated more-than-modern ways of being by means of a relegation of the 'old'. Further, Chakrabarty's postcolonial work returns to the comfort of the Enlightenment, precluding engagement with Indigenous ontologies. Decolonial scholarship and politics represents a departure from these modes of engagement with the colonial question which is enacted by following the lead of protective ontologies that have always challenged the environmental destruction reaped from within the global colonial system.

From the Mi'kmaq in colonial Nova Scotia, where the Sipekne'katik First Nation are protecting nature against a large carbon-based project, to the island of Borneo where Dayak populations protect spiritual forests from the spread of oil palm monocultures, we have attempted to draw attention to the condition of more-than-modern peoples globally. They are more than modern because the historical realities of the colonial encounter have never succeeded in erasing Indigenous knowledge systems. Resurgent decolonial politics inhabits the modern/colonial world as 'environmental activism,' but also inhabits worlds that modern reason has never been qualified to understand (cf: de la Cadena 2010; 2015). We acknowledge that the term 'water protector,' by virtue of being part of the English language and an attempt to communicate meaning across worlds of difference to those of us disabled by virtue of our full indoctrination into the universe of modern reason, is itself incomplete. However, to practically engage with the destructive impulses of modern/colonial capitalism, communities are compelled to 'protect' that part of the collective self that is under attack. Diverse and complex nature-based ontologies, illegible to colonial–legal systems, are thus protected in the face of homogenising and expanding liberal–capitalist space.

To return to our original provocation, it should now be clear why PM Trudeau's attempt to expand carbon extraction while seeking to build a greener future is folly. Working purely within a modern, scientific, economic rationality, Trudeau here is representative of state-centric, settler colonial, capitalist modernity and a stark example of the limits of this approach. This form of violent universal reason will not lead to our global salvation; for as long as colonial science holds its ontological dominance, efforts to expand colonial resource frontiers will continue. Yet protective ontologies, working within nature and against the colonial system, have long indicated a more viable route to planetary solutions to colonial problems. In the age of the Anthropocene, as climate change consumes our worlds with alarming haste, a reliance on colonial science alone is not an option.

Bibliography

Acciaoli, G. (2001). 'Archipelagic Culture' as an Exclusionary Government Discourse in Indonesia.' *The Asia Pacific Journal of Anthropology*, 2(1), 1–23.

AJ+ (2015). *Unist'ot'en Camp: Holding Their Ground against Oil & Gas Pipelines*. Retrieved December 19, 2016 from https://www.youtube.com/watch?v=5qUw3bqIHks

Alfred, T. (1999). *Peace, Power, Righteousness: An Indigenous Manifesto*. Toronto: Oxford University Press.

—— (2016). 'Land Claims, Reconciliation and the Resurgence of Indigenous Nationhood.' *Proceedings of the National Native Title Conference*. Darwin, Australia. Retrieved November 7, 2016 from http://aiatsis.gov.au/publications/presentations/land-claims-reconciliation-and-resurgence-indigenous-nationhood

Aman (2015). *2015 Year End Note*. Retrieved December 11, 2016 from http://www.aman.or.id/wp-content/uploads/2016/03/Catatan-Akhir-Tahun-AMAN-English.pdf

Anon (2016). *We Are Land Protectors, Not Protesters*. Retrieved December 15, 2016 from https://www.youtube.com/watch?v=MSE4cH95qlc

Balibar, E. (1990). *Fichte et la Frontière Intérieure. A Propos des Discours à la Nation Allemande*. Le Cahiers des Fontenay: Philosophie et politique en Allemagne, XVIIIe–XXe Siécle Nr. 59, 59, 57–82.

Bhambra, G. K. (2014). *Connected Sociologies*. London: Bloomsbury.

Blaser, M. (2013). 'Ontological Conflicts and the Stories of Peoples in Spite of Europe: Toward a Conversation on Political Ontology'. *Current Anthropology* 54(5), 547–68.

Casanova, P. G. (1965). 'Internal Colonialism and National Development'. *Studies in Comparative International Development*, 1(4), 27–37.

Chakrabarty, D. (2009). 'The Climate of History: Four Theses.' *Critical Inquiry* 35(2), 197–222.

Chou, C. (2010). *The Orang Suku Laut of Riau, Indonesia: The Inalienable Gift of Territory*. London: Routledge.

Cornell, S., Downing, A., and Clark, D. (2016). 'Multiple Arctics: Resilience in a Region of Diversity and Dynamism.' In M. Carson and G. Peterson (eds.) *Arctic Resilience Report* 2016. Stockholm Environment Institute and Stockholm Resilience Centre: Stockholm, 27–61.

Corntassle, J. (2012). 'Re-envisioning Resurgence: Indigenous Pathways to Decolonization and Sustainable Self-Determination.' *Decolonization: Indigeneity, Education & Society*. 1(1), 86–101.

Coulthard, G. S. (2014). *Red Skins White Masks: Rejecting the Colonial Politics of Recognition.* Minneapolis: University of Minnesota Press.
Crosby, A. (2016). 'Natural Gas Nightmare: Indigenous Communities Opposing Canada's Energy Agenda under Increasing Surveillance.' *The Leveller.* 9(2), 8–9.
Dalby, S. (2009). *Security and Environmental Change.* Cambridge: Polity Press.
—— (2013). 'The Geopolitics of Climate Change.' *Political Geography* 37, 38–47.
De la Cadena, M. (2012). 'Indigenous Cosmopolitics in the Andes: Conceptual Reflections Beyond Politics.' *Cultural Anthropology* 25(2), 334–70.
De la Cadena, M. (2015). *Earth Beings: Ecologies of Practice Across Andean Worlds.* Durham: Duke University Press.
Escobar, A. (2016). 'Thinking-Feeling with the Earth: Territorial Struggles and the Ontological Dimensions of Epistemologies of the South.' *Revista de Antropologia Iberoamericano* 11/(1): 11–32.
Fanon, F. (2004 [1961]). *The Wretched of the Earth,* trans. Richard Philcox. New York: Groves Press.
Gehl, L. (2014). *The Truth That Wampam Tells: My Debwewin on the Algonquin Land Claims Process.* Halifax: Fernwood.
Gehl, L. (2016a). 'The Ratification Process for the Algonquin Agreement in Principle Is an Example of What Is Wrong with Canada's Approach in Land Claims and Self-Government Negotiations.' *Policy Options.* Retrieved November 23, 2016 from http://policyoptions.irpp.org/magazines/november-2016/deeply-flawed-process-around-algonquin-land-claim-agreement/
—— (2016b). 'Canada's Interim Comprehensive Land Claims Policy Is No More than Colonial Policy.' *Anishnabek News.ca.* Retrieved December 19, 2016 from: http://anishinabeknews.ca/2014/11/27/algonquin-chiefs-say-tsilhqotin-supreme-court-decision-is-no-more-than-colonial-policy/
Global Witness. (2016). *On Dangerous Ground.* Retrieved July 26, 2016 from https://www.globalwitness.org/en/reports/dangerous-ground/
Grosfoguel, R. (2002). 'Colonial Difference, Geopolitics of Knowledge, and Global Coloniality in the Modern/Colonial Capitalist World System.' *Review (Fernand Braudel Centre),* 25(3), 203–24.
—— (2007). ' Epistemic Decolonial Turn: Beyond Political-Economy Paradigms.' *Cultural Studies,* 21(2–3), 211–23.
—— (2013). 'The Structure of Knowledge in Westernized Universities: Epistemic Racism/Sexism and the Four Genocides/Epistemicides of the Long 16th Century.' *Human Architecture: Journal of the Sociology of Self-Knowledge* 11(1), 73–90.
Guardian. (2016). '"Extraordinarily Hot" Arctic Temperatures Alarm Scientists.' Retrieved December 1, 2016 from https://www.theguardian.com/environment/2016/nov/22/extraordinarily-hot-arctic-temperatures-alarm-scientists
Gudynas, E. (2016). 'Beyond Varieties of Development: Disputes and Alternatives.' *Third World Quarterly* 37(4), 721–32.
Guha, R. (2002). *History at the Limit of World History.* New York: Colombia University Press.
Gunaratnam, Y., and Clark, N. (2012). *Pre-Race Post-Race: Climate Change and Planetary Humanism.* Retrieved December 2, 2016 from http://www.darkmatter101.org/site/2012/07/02/pre-race-post-race-climate-change-and-planetary-humanism/
Hayes, K. (2016). 'How to Talk about #NoDAPL: A Native Perspective.' *Truth Out.* Retrieved November 7, 2016 from <http://www.truth-out.org/opinion/item/38165-how-to-talk-about-nodapl-a-native-perspective>
Health Canada. (2016). 'Drinking Water Advisories in First Nations Communities.' *Health Canada.* Retrieved November 7, 2016 from http://www.hc-sc.gc.ca/fniah-spnia/promotion/public-publique/water-dwa-eau-aqep-eng.php
Hill, S. (2008). 'Travelling Down the River of Life in Peace and Friendship, Forever: Haudenosaunee Land Ethics and Treaty Agreements as the Basis for Restructuring the Relationship with the British Crown.' In L. Simpson (ed.) *Lighting the Eighth Fire: The Liberation, Resurgence, and Protection of First Nations.* Winnipeg: ARP, 23–46.
—— (2009). *500 Years of Indigenous Resistance.* Oakland: PM Press.
Hunt, S. (2014). 'Ontologies of Indigeneity: The Politics of Embodying a Concept.' *Cultural Geographies* 14(21), 27–32.
If Not Us Then Who? (2016). *Semunying, Indonesia.* https://www.youtube.com/watch?v=edzOEO9cl3I&index=3&list=PLyrkxdz3Bgi36uuKIR7-4JtZMX55vc23a
Indigenous Network. (2016). *Sami Indigenous Travel to Stand with Standing Rock Sioux Tribe.* Retrieved December 1, 2016 from http://indigenous-network.com/sami-indigenous-travel-to-stand-with-standing-rock-sioux-tribe/

Kanngieser, A. and Last, A. (2016). *Five Propositions/Critiques for the Anthropocene.* Retrieved December 2, 2016 from http://www.geocritique.org/five-propositions-critiques-anthropocene/
Kauanui, J. K., and Wolfe, P. (2012). 'Settler Colonialism Then and Now. A Conversation between J. Kēhaulani Kauanui and Patrick Wolfe.' *Politica & Società*, 1(2), 235–58.
Li, T. (forthcoming). 'The Price of Un/Freedom: Indonesia's Colonial and Contemporary Plantation Labour Regimes.' *Comparative Studies in Society and History.*
Maldonado-Torres, N. (2006). 'On the Coloniality of Being.' *Cultural Studies* 21/2: 240–70.
Māori Television. (2016). *Māori Risk Safety with Haka at Standing Rock.* Retrieved December 1, 2016 from http://www.maoritelevision.com/news/politics/maori-risk-safety-haka-standing-rock
Mignolo, W. (2009). 'Epistemic Disobedience, Independent Thought and Decolonial Freedom.' *Theory, Culture and Society* 26(7–8), 1–23.
—— (2011). *The Darker Side of Western Modernity: Global Futures, Decolonial Options.* Durham: Duke University Press.
Montsion, J. M. (2015). 'Disrupting Canadian Sovereignty? The "First Nations & China" Strategy Revisited.' *Geoforum*, 58, 114–121.
Mossett, K. (2016). *Dakota Access Pipeline: Protectors Not Protesters.* Retrieved December 16, 2016 from https://www.youtube.com/watch?v=U8Uwo6ZAEG4
Mulyoutami, E., Rismawan, R., and Joshi, L. (2009). 'Local Knowledge and Management of Simpukng (Forest Gardens) among the Dayak People in East Kalimantan, Indonesia.' *Forest Ecology and Management*, 257, 2054–61.
National Observer. (2016). 'Trudeau Says Pipelines Will Pay for Canada's Transition to a Green Economy.' Retrieved December 1, 2016 from http://www.nationalobserver.com/2016/03/02/news/trudeau-says-pipelines-will-pay-canadas-transition-green-economy
Omand, G. (2016). 'Federal Approval for Site C Dam Draws Criticism from First Nations Advocacy Groups.' *Canadian Broadcasting Corporation.* Retrieved November 7, 2016 from http://www.cbc.ca/news/canada/british-columbia/site-c-dam-federal-approval-1.3703527
Quijano, A. (2000). 'Coloniality of Power, Eurocentrism, and Latin America.' *Nepalanta: Views from the South* 1(3), 533–80.
Rojas, C. (2007). 'International Political Economy/Development Otherwise.' *Globalizations* 4(4), 573–87.
—— (2016). 'Contesting the Colonial Logics of the International: Toward a Relational Politics for the Pluriverse.' *International Political Sociology* advanced online access, 1–14. doi: 10.1093/ips/olw020.
Schmidt, J. J., Brown, P. G., and Orr, C. J. (2016). 'Ethics in the Anthropocene: A Research Agenda.' *The Anthropocene Review*, 3(3), 188–200.
Shilliam, R. (2015). *The Black Pacific.* London: Bloomsbury.
Stoler, A.L. (1997). 'Sexual Affronts and Racial Frontiers: European Identities and the Cultural Politics of Exclusion in Colonial Southeast Asia.' In F. Cooper and A. L. Stoler (eds.), *Tensions of Empire: Colonial Cultures in a Bourgeois World.* Berkeley: University of California Press, 198–237.
Tasker, J. P. (2016). 'Trudeau Cabinet Approves Trans Mountain, Line 3 Pipelines, Rejects Northern Gateway.' *Canadian Broadcasting Corporation.* Retrieved December 19, 2016 from http://www.cbc.ca/news/politics/federal-cabinet-trudeau-pipeline-decisions-1.3872828
The Free Thought Project. (2016). *Mayan Elders Go to Standing Rock to Show Solidarity & Give Thanks 'For Lighting a Path for Our People.'* Retrieved December 1, 2016 from http://thefreethoughtproject.com/mayan-elders-standing-rock/
The Hindu. (2009). 'The World's First Underwater Cabinet Meeting.' Retrieved December 19, 2016 from http://www.thehindu.com/news/international/worlds-first-underwater-cabinet-meeting/article35770.ece
Toledano, M. (2014). 'The View from Unist'ot'en: A Camp That Stands Firmly in the Path of Enbridge's Northern Gateway Pipeline.' *Vice.com.* Retrieved November 7, 2016 from http://www.vice.com/en_ca/read/the-view-from-unistoten-a-camp-that-stands-firmly-in-the-path-of-enbridges-northern-gateway-pipeline
—— (2015). 'In British Columbia, Indigenous Group Blocks Pipeline.' *Al Jazeera America.* Retrieved December 19, 2016 from http://america.aljazeera.com/articles/2015/8/20/in-canada-police.html
Wolfe, P. (2013). 'The Settler Complex: An Introduction.' *American Indian Culture and Research Journal*, 37(2), 1–22.
Wynter, S. (2003). 'Unsettling the Coloniality of Being/Power/Truth/Freedom: Towards the Human, After Man, Its Overrepresentation–An Argument.' *The New Centennial Review*, 3 (3), 257–337.

Notes

1 On the distinction between colonial science and decolonial science, see Shilliam (2015: 13): 'Decolonial science seeks to repair colonial wounds, binding back together peoples, lands, pasts, ancestors and spirits. Its greatest challenge is to bind back together the manifest and spiritual domains. For in the latter domain there exist hinterlands that were never colonised by Cook and Columbus, and therein lie the supports of a global infrastructure of anti-colonial connectivity.'

2 We purposely avoid limiting this to global 'environmental' action because, as will be argued within, that categorical separation of nature and humanity itself reflects colonial taxonomies.

3 For clarity of analysis here, we will consider the response of Indigenous populations situated along internal frontiers within both settler colonial and (former) franchise colonial contexts. To make clear this analytical distinction, we understand settler colonial domains to be those with large settler populations and a history of varied policies of extermination against the Indigenous population. White liberal settler colonies include those countries which refer to themselves as the US, Canada, and Australia. Franchise colonies, by contrast, were generally established as extractive economies by European powers. As such, Indigenous populations were largely treated as labour of one form or another, and thus were not subject to extermination policies to the same extent (Kauanui and Wolfe 2012; Wolfe 2013).

4 Neither author claims to be from, or is claimed by, any Indigenous nation in the regions under study in this chapter. Ajay is a multi-generational outcome of British colonisation via nineteenth-century indentureship to Kairi (Trinidad), and has lived and worked across Turtle Island (Canada) in unceded Coast Salish, Algonquin, and Mi'kmaq territories. Lisa was raised in the industrial North of the British imperial metropole and continues to be carried by colonial privilege.

5 Here, Sylvia Wynter claims that the Western-bourgeois 'ethnoclassed' investor-consumer figure of 'Man' represents himself as the normal and proper human, and in doing so works towards the negation of other ways of being human. The act of 'overrepresentation' in this context is therefore a claim upon humanity and a negation of the humanity of others. For Wynter, many of the world's problems, including climate change, other environmental struggles, and the appallingly unequal distribution of the Earth's resources, can all be related to 'the central ethnoclass Man vs. Human struggle'; the struggle of our times, then, is one against the overrepresentation of Man (2003: 260–2).

6 According to the Federal Health Ministry in Canada, as of Aug. 31, 2016 there were 132 drinking water advisories in effect, relating to the water conditions on 89 First Nations communities excluding the province of British Colombia. See: Health Canada (2016).

7 Research in political ontology and decolonial politics draws attention to the fact that multiple ontologies have always interacted and, out of the ensuing conflict, create compelling sites for the creation of meetings between worlds. For distinct approaches to how decolonial scholars practice these relations, see: de la Cadena 2015; Shilliam 2015; Coulthard 2014; Hunt 2014; Blaser 2013).

8 Wayne John, Member of Parliament for Saint John-Rothesay New Brunswick proudly announced to the annual meeting of the Atlantic Provinces Political Science Association on Oct. 14, 2016, that his Liberal government was proud of having approved the controversial Site C dam and was working hard to secure the Energy East pipeline. When, following John's presentation, a member of the audience asked about the Liberal government's promise of 'nation to nation' relations and their recent removal of exceptions to the UNDRIP, he described a vision of 'nation to nation' relationships being one in which Indigenous people are consulted with until they come around to the necessity of pipeline development.

9 Windmill has even named the development project 'Zibi' – the Anishinaabe-moen (Algonquin language family) word for 'water.'

26

NO MIGRATION, REPATRIATION

Spiritual visionings and political limitations of Rastafari repatriation to Ethiopia

Ijahnya Christian

Birth of a nation

> Now I am home, Iyahbinghi seh, Now I am home, I an I still yant Fari, now I am home
> Singing glory halleluJAH, Hail Ras Tafari, Now I am home…
>
> (lyrics of Nyahbinghi chant adapted in Shashemene from the original, 'When I yod/trod home')

In 1948, the same year that land was secured to create the modern day nation of Israel, Ethiopia's Emperor Haile Selassie I granted five *gashas* (approximately 500 acres) of land in Shashemene, Southern Ethiopia, as a gesture of thanks to the Black peoples of the west who had supported Ethiopia during Mussolini's invasion. It remains unique on the African continent, as the only land granted to facilitate the return of the descendants of Africans taken away during the trans-Atlantic trade in African people. Africans in the Diaspora did not return *en masse* and those who hold on tenaciously to what is left of the land grant are mainly Rastafari. There is an Ethiopian proverb which says, 'Do not grow your hair long unless you have been to battle or you have chased and killed a lion.' Rastafari, who have no interest in killing any animal, instead adopted the imago of the lion, the persona of the Conquering Lion, and assumed a power that would overcome all obstacles and propel themselves home from colonized, enslaving lands to a country that had never experienced colonialism.

This chapter calls to attention the extraordinary situation of Rastafari who have repatriated to Africa, with specific reference to those who live in Ethiopia on the Shashemene Land Grant. The complex process of Repatriation (as distinct from event) is infused with what famed educator calypsonian The Mighty Chalkdust, Hollis Liverpool refers to as 'rituals of power and rebellion' handed down from African ancestors. The media by which such rituals are carried out on the Shashemene Land Grant are Nyahbinghi drums and chants as well as popular reggae music. And '… the power to change society and to mobilize the people through song …' (Liverpool, 2001: 450) is consciously recognized by those who survive the odds on a daily basis. The chapter, therefore, reiteratively explores themes of power and mobilization, creativity, conflict, contradiction, integration and resilience in the quest for formal recognition, meaning legal status, of the people Bonnaci (2015: 389) calls 'transatlantic migrants' and who lay claim to the land grant. It also discusses inhibiting factors, all of which are worthy of further exploration.

Though the intent here is to reflect movements and immobilities from the post-colonial era, it should not be assumed that colonialism is a thing of the past. Neither should it be assumed that repatriation is a tidy event in which well-organized masses board ships and planes bound for Africa and a resettlement plan. Some continue to cross the Middle Passage mobilizing resources everywhere to support life in a pan-African family sphere. The context is one of continued struggle with identity and variously tempered and frustrated by the realization that freedom of movement within Africa is not a right guaranteed to most Africans. The writer's is a voice from the colonial present. It is also an insider voice, with perspectives shaped by frequent travel to and from Ethiopia in order to maintain legal status while in residence at the Nyahbinghi Tabernacle Center on the Shashemene Land Grant. This is our story.

On the verge of Jamaica's independence in August 1962, Mortimo Planno, a strong voice from the emerging Ras Tafari Nation in Jamaica, wrote in a Letter to the Editor of *The Gleaner* as follows:

> What provisions will be made within the new constitution for the desire of those who alienate themselves from the Jamaica way of life? I am thinking principally of those whose desire is to be repatriated to Ethiopia. One of the countries of Africa that already granted lands for the sole purpose of resettling people from the Western world. I as one who is claiming by originality (Ethiopian) would like the world to know that our rights must be respected. Because I am of the opinion that respect for man's right is the greatest achievement of peaceful solution to problems which has a temperature of 100 degrees (March 3, 1962).

Planno's letter is significant not only in its assertion of Ethiopian identity but also in its recognition of the Shashemene Land Grant and more importantly, the matter of Repatriation as a right – the Right of Return. Not only were InI called, some were chosen to settle on the Shashemene Land Grant located in the Oromo Region in southern Ethiopia.

Rastafari in the Caribbean Region have therefore had a sense of entitlement regarding the return to Africa, and a sense of mission: fulfillment of purpose defined in themes of African Redemption such as Marcus Garvey's Africa for the Africans, those at home and those abroad. A more recent theme is that of the African Renaissance with Rastafari at the vanguard. But the boundless faith of Rastafari has not been matched by the political work of 'Get Up Stand Up, Stand up for your rights…' (Marley and MacIntosh, 1973). Instead there has been the traditional shying away from politics, especially partisan politics. Despite the trials and tribulations of trying to hold on to land, which is a defining element of nationhood, a contextual analysis of Rastafari in Ethiopia reveals not stagnation but a dynamism bound up in the country's history, culture and the politics of diversity in twenty-first-century globalization. Progress has nevertheless been slow.

In the Caribbean region that gave birth to the Rastafari Nation/Movement, the appearance of these people, terrible and dread, made for instant rejection. An 'otherness' prevailed right from the start as Rastafari rejected options of island nation or regional identity, and instead embraced their identity as Ethiopian. In terms of spiritual direction, more than four decades before the realization of independence in the Caribbean, seers and seekers pursuing knowledge in the 1920s swung the point of the compass eastward to the divine direction of return. The vision of Robert Athlyi Rogers documented in the Ethiopianist text, *The Holy Piby* (1924), generally recognized as the most important theological reference to the foundational philosophy of Rastafari (Hill in West et al., 2009: 140), was clear:

> Then shall the children of Ethiopia return to their own land and there establish a light with [which] no nation shall compare, nor will there be any power sufficient to douse it. For I am the Lord God of Ethiopia.
>
> (Rogers, 1924: 3)

The grand coronation of Crown Prince, Ras Tafari Makonnen, as Emperor Haile Selassie I in Addis Ababa, Ethiopia, on November 2, 1930 is generally considered the birth of the Rastafari Nation. Two years later, the Rev. Fitz Ballentyne Pettersburg of Jamaica, in *The Royal Parchment Scroll of Black Supremacy* (1926), foresaw the precedent set by His Majesty, for His Consort, Her Royal Highness, Itege Menen Asfaw, to be crowned along with him in the Church and not days later in the palace. A few years later, another Jamaican, Leonard Percival Howell, in *The Promised Key* (1935) identified Rogers' God of Ethiopia, as none other than His Imperial Majesty, Emperor Haile Selassie I. The world had also witnessed the anointing of a child in that ceremony, which signaled to these visionaries, in thought, word and deed, that it was time to restore the Mother to the Holy Trinity. Bound up in the mystic revelation of Ras Tafari, whose name the Nation/Movement adopted, was the message of African Redemption necessitating physical return to the African Motherland, the source, the origins – Ethiopia.

Caribbean solidarity with Ethiopia may be marked by the visit of Haitian Ambassador Benito Sylvain's visit to the court of Emperor Menelik II after the latter's victory at the Battle of Adwa in 1896. In the next century, this solidarity was expressed in popular culture decades before the creation of orthodox reggae music in Jamaica. This may have some bearing on the demographics of the repatriated community in Shashemene, which will be discussed later. That solidarity was most strongly expressed in the calypso arena of Trinidad and Tobago during Italy's invasion of Ethiopia in 1936. The calypsonians were conscious of what was taking place in Ethiopia and they, then as now, sang for the common people what a colonized leadership could not speak (Christian, 2011: 1–17).

Songs such as Houdini's (1935) *Ethiopian War Drums*, Lion's *Advantage Mussolini*, Radio's *Abyssinian Lament* and Caresser's *Selassie Held by the Police* in 1936:

> all condemned the invasion of Ethiopia by Italy and called especially upon the Africans in the country to mobilize themselves for possible action against the Italian leader Mussolini and the Pope who, according to widespread rumour, blessed the Italian troops.
>
> (Liverpool, 2001: 452)

Rastafari in Jamaica even appealed to the British government to rescind the law that prevented them as Jamaicans, from joining the Ethiopian army to keep the invading forces out of the 'Promised Land' (Murrell, 1998: 7). Despite the perpetuated notion of the Promised Land – the Shashemene Land was not promised but actually gifted. Eventually even Jamaican society had begun to realize that the idea of Repatriation was not just '…wishful thinking among the uneducated…' (Murrell, 1998: 7), and Rastafari consciousness of their Ethiopian identity could not be diminished by the advent of independence. By the time Jamaica and then Trinidad and Tobago attained independence in 1962, Rastafari in the Caribbean were armed with the spiritual power of an African king in whom they found the example for living and inspiration to take the moral high ground internationally.

Land for a nation of many passports

Man is respected by his utterance; the land is respected by its borders.

(Ethiopian proverb)

The mass movement of Rastafari as envisaged in reggae singer Fredlocks' song, *Seven Miles of Black Star Liner* is yet to be realized. Only a few hundred people are in residence, holding on tenaciously to what is left of the Land Grant. Who are these chosen few?

Among them are those from islands that have not yet tasted the sweets of independence. They are from British Overseas Territories of Anguilla, Montserrat and Bermuda; Bonaire, a Special Municipality of the Netherlands; and the French Overseas Departments of Guadeloupe and Martinique. Persons from these non-independent Territories are holders of European Union passports, though it is generally held that Jamaican passport holders are the largest group on the land. There are also many who are holders of United Kingdom (UK) passports. Many of these brethren and sistren were born to and raised by Jamaican parents in the UK. There are also relatively high numbers of those with passports issued by Trinidad and Tobago. Some came directly from the Caribbean, others via the UK and the United States (US). There are also several US citizens and others who came from Barbados, St. Vincent and the Grenadines. As many as 16 nationalities have been identified, but important as these passports may be to officialdom, many of them have expired and are somewhat irrelevant to Rastafari who came with every intention of staying in Ethiopia, no matter what. Perhaps the biggest irony of all is that in Ethiopia informally, all of the repatriated Rastafari are thought of and called Jamaican. However, there are strong feelings held by some Rastafari of other nationalities who do not accept the Jamaican designation.

Up until 2014 there were also a number of Stateless Persons in the community but the Government of Jamaica made provision for the issue of Jamaican passports to those eligible and interested. It is not clear how many other nationalities may be affected in this way but this response underscored a status as migrants in residence and seemed a regressive step on the path to legal status in Ethiopia.

The size of the repatriated community is often queried but the answer is not so clear. Usually a range of 500 to 800 is given but this has not been verified. It is a fluid community in which people come and go all the time. Among them are those who have established homes there but are concerned to stay on the right side of Ethiopia's Department of Immigration and Nationality Affairs. There are also usually a few Rastafari youths from other African countries – young men from Kenya, Tanzania, Ghana and Zambia who travel to Ethiopia by road, also with the view of repatriating to Holy Mount Zion. Some of them have been temporarily resident in the Nyahbinghi House, usually thought of as a neutral space in the sometimes polarized community.

The Nyahbinghi Order, as the foundation of Rastafari spiritual expression, also employs the musical tradition of gathering and chanting '…to break down barriers… The Nyahbinghi ritual is a Rastafari creation born from resistance traditions…' including retentions of African spirituality in Jamaica and '…layered on an Ethiopian Orthodox philosophical foundation' (Niaah and Christian, 2013: 24).

The Order has its largest tabernacle in Shashemene and a house has been built on the grounds of the Nyahbinghi Tabernacle Center, to serve as the residence of presiding elders. Other Rastafari Churches/Mansions include the Ethiopia Africa Black International Congress (EABIC) aka Bobo Shanti, the Twelve Tribes of Israel and the Ethiopian World Federation (EWF), a black people's organization dominated by Rastafari. Historically, the Shashemene Land Grant was meant to be administered by the EWF.

Youth traveling by road from neighboring Kenya receive their visas at the border town of Moyale and make the two-day journey there annually for them to be renewed. One young man from Ghana incorrectly assumed privilege as a continental African, and fell into the immigration money trap which demands payment of huge sums in foreign currency for persons who have overstayed. Others have sought, and obtained favor through, the Ethiopian Orthodox Tawahedo Church. One Rastafari couple who came to be trained in the duties of the Orthodox faith traveled by road from South Africa with two small daughters. They were provided for by the Church but were eventually forced off land they had acquired independently and on which they had planned to live. Another, a young man who repatriated from the US, graduated as a full-fledged priest of the Church in August 2016. Via the route of his training (during which he was required to cut his dreadlocks), he met the language and other criteria required for citizenship and has successfully attained that status. His passport bears his Ethiopian baptismal name. It would be remiss not to mention that two residents of the community had gained citizenship during the revolutionary years of the Dergue's regime and one Rastafari woman from Ireland who lives in Addis Ababa gained citizenship several years ago.

In order to present the full face of the Rastafari community in Shashemene, mention is made of a few young Ethiopians, some of whom have never left Shashemene but sport dreadlocks, speak with a Jamaican accent and may pretend to visitors that they are Jamaican. There are others who may not have dreadlocks but who faithfully worship with Rastafari in the Nyahbinghi Tabernacle, bringing their families along with them on the high holy days. On such days, particularly the anniversary of the birth of Ras Tafari Makonnen, several members of the wider Ethiopian community also worship with Rastafari. The elders among them refer to the land as 'the Jamaicans' land' in the area commonly called the Jamaican *sefer.* This relationship helps to defend and protect what they call the Ras Tafari Church. It has not, however, protected the repatriated community from the high incidence of breaking, entering, theft and robbery, also experienced by Ethiopians who are born and bred. The ambiguities have been succinctly captured in the following observation:

> Although their culture is sometimes embarrassing to the Ethiopians, they nevertheless build schools and clinics and develop businesses and services. They attract tourists, they invest and they bring up their children in the country. Nevertheless, their contributions remain unrecognized, and their integration is not easy. Bob Marley is now celebrated in the country and adopted as a cultural reference by Ethiopia's youth. Yet there is no government policy to facilitate the settlement and integration of Rastafari. Nor is there any legal or financial assistance from pan-African institutions (Bonacci, 2016: 155).

Multiple forces have diminished access to land in Ethiopia where the more commonly expressed aspiration among Rastafari from the African Diaspora who have settled on the Shashemene Land Grant is the desire to have legal status. The absence of this status disables the holding of federal IDs and acquisition of 'carta' plans for increased security of land use. This Catch-22 situation has severely limited the contributions of repatriated Rastafari to the development of Shashemene and Ethiopian society.

Nevertheless, an article entitled 'Promised Land? Rastafarians Struggle in Ethiopia' published in the *Jamaica Observer* cites Ras Reuben Kush, President of the EWF's Local 14 in Shashemene, thus:

> Ethiopia is our land, for we Blacks in the West ... The Emperor had given us 500 hectares – today we live on six or seven hectares... Today, we have no control over our property.
> (Bould, November 16, 2015)

Bould posits the Rastafari returnees as stateless and hopeless victims of '...Communist-inspired ex-rebels...' but her analysis is accurate only in part. As the following account shows, there are individuals and experiences within the repatriation process that do not quite fit in this narrative.

In a context where land is nationalized and therefore cannot be bought or sold, (though it is), the story of how the original land is occupied by other Ethiopians is well documented. What is acceptable is compensation for increasingly smaller lots of land that have been developed in some way. They may be under cultivation, fruit trees may have been planted, and they may have built structures. But as official demands dictate against larger landholdings, there are stories of land being sold sometimes by the most unlikely persons when hard times hit. Land losses have also occurred through failed conjugal relationships, mainly between repatriated men and Ethiopian women as Ethiopian law is very protective of women and children. Land has also been lost to roads built years after they became part of Shashemene's elusive Master Plan, which includes reports on progress and development objectives. The implementation of such plans has been slow but stories abound about the community having been long-informed of the intent to establish a road network in the part of the city within the bounds of the original Land Grant. Prior knowledge has made these losses no easier to bear when fully-grown trees, fences and more substantial built structures have had to be sacrificed for new roads. Bonacci (2015: 269–79) tells us that the Master Plan of 2000 makes reference to the Jamaica '*sefer*' and the 'Ras Taferians', the first mention in an administrative document after 50 years of Rastafari residence in Shashemene – in acknowledgement of their cultural and touristic value.

The Shashemene Land Grant of the mid-twentieth century was not the only one gifted by Haile Selassie I in Ethiopia. His Majesty had also granted land in the nearby town of Kuyera to the Seventh Day Adventists, who established the Ethiopian Adventist College there in 1947. But there is either no uniformity in arrangements or no provision at all for Africans who have repatriated from the Diaspora to other African countries. Across the continent, the small, West African country of Benin, seems to have gone furthest in ensuring that repatriated Rastafari are relatively secure in terms of land settlement. Administered by Mere and Pere Jah, who repatriated from the French Department of Guadeloupe in 1996, 'Ambassade de la Diaspora' has enjoyed excellent relations with successive Beninese governments, at times being part of government delegations. They were eventually given land designated as a protected area on which they live, engage in educational farming and other sustainable developmental activity. They have not been granted citizenship. There is a larger number of repatriated Rastafari in neighboring Ghana but settlement seems to have been by independent effort with local community support. However, in December 2016, the outgoing John Mahama administration in Ghana went further than any government in Africa in granting citizenship to some persons from the African Diaspora. We will return to this development in the conclusion of the chapter.

At the southern tip, South Africa, reputed to have a Rastafari population significantly larger than even Jamaica's, has at least five instances of lands being secured and held by local Rastafari for the development of Rastafari communities but also with the objective of facilitating repatriation. The oldest of these is the Marcus Garvey Community in Cape Town (unpublished report of the Rastafari Fact Finding Mission aka the Harar Trod, 2009). The experience of persons repatriated to Ethiopia, Ghana and South Africa suggests that no matter how repatriated persons acquire land, if that land is not used, it is lost. It is also clear that the status of returning Africans is one that will be hard won, despite a history of such returns.

The present Constitution of the Federal Democratic Republic of Ethiopia makes provision for a federal arrangement of autonomous and diverse nation states. In fact, one of the regional states is the Southern Nations, Nationalities and Peoples Region (SNNPR). This nomenclature alone, backed by constitutional provision, lends credence to the concept of a Rastafari Nation, though small size and other factors render this unviable. Without that tenuous hold on the Shashemene Land Grant, however, the missing element in the definition of Rastafari nationhood would be land. Without land as a prerequisite, it has been shown that new paths to belonging are being forged. With land, it is, however, conceivable to envision a nation comprising persons of different nationalities, holding different passports and different races.

Race is among the sources of grumbled undesirability seldom openly expressed except in other matters of conflict concerning white people resident on the Shashemene Land Grant. Some of them have been resident for a long time, having come mainly but not exclusively as members of the Twelve Tribes of Israel or as spouses of members. In terms of those non-black nationalities:

> Rastafari from over the world had arrived in Shashemene, sometimes from as far as Sweden, New Zealand, Chile, Japan and South Africa. Rastafari communities had meanwhile developed in Addis Ababa, Bahir Dar, Awassa and Debra Zeit.
>
> (Bonacci, 2016: 155)

There is also the unverified account of the community being criticized by a government official for allowing white people to settle on the land. Except in the EWF, which has been experiencing resurgence over the last three years, Rastafari of European stock have been active in the internal developmental, unification and centralization initiatives of the community. There is a tolerance that speaks to the racial consciousness of Rastafari that is to be clearly distinguished from racism. From the global Rastafari community, some of whose ancestors were the enslavers, are ones who have asserted their presence in the '...land where the gods loved to be...' (Burrell and Ford, 1919). There is no open confrontation but as one attendee at a community meeting in 2012 remarked with reference to this reality, the problem with white people on the land is not one of biology but one of history.

Repatriation and representation

> Woman and earth can handle anything.
>
> (Ethiopian proverb)

Repatriated Rastafari are confronted in many ways with their status as determined by the immigration authorities of Ethiopia. For those who have been in Shashemene longest, this may be no longer relevant, except in the case where children have been born. Others strive to stay legal by any means necessary. Doing so means having the ongoing means of meeting immigration requirements. US citizens can obtain tourist visas that are valid for two years. Tourist visas for other nationalities are valid for three to six months. In the past, those who expressed interest in investment could obtain visas valid for six months, during which time they could secure investment permits from the Ethiopia Investment Commission, along with temporary resident ID cards issued by the Immigration Department. These are valid for one year and are reissued annually once progress could be shown in the area of investment proposed. The end route is a business licence obtained from the Ministry of Trade, but very few of those repatriated and living in Shashemene have been able to attain or sustain this height. Again we hear from Ras Reuben Kush, this time from his perspective as a mechanical engineer, in a joint venture that operates a factory in Addis Abeba's industrial zone in Kality.

There are vast opportunities in Ethiopia that can be exploited with an entrepreneurial spirit. I advise small groups of four or five ones to come together with an investment plan, to work together and live together. Everything hinges on thinking collectively…'

(unpublished interview: 2014)

Those who entered the country with business visas could use them to seek employment if there was no real investment. Business visas are no longer issued except to the actual investor class – evidence of having met investment requirements must now be presented before a business visa can be obtained. In one instance, the holder of a temporary resident ID secured a short-term consultancy with an agency that had diplomatic status and obtained a special ID with diplomatic privileges issued by the Ministry of Foreign Affairs and valid for one year. Those with tourist visas must leave the country upon their expiry but can apply for extended stay, usually of one month at a time. Fees for such extension must be paid in foreign currency, which is scarce in the banking sector. An illegal but thriving parallel foreign currency market operates just outside the premises of the Immigration Department with currency exchange rates that are much higher than bank rates.

Those who have not been able to secure investment permits, business licences or employment and who can afford to do so therefore find it necessary to leave the country every three or six months to return as able. Those who obtained the ID through employment with a work permit must hand these in once contracts are terminated if they are not to be renewed. There is no hunting down and flushing out activity, but those who have long overstayed, from an immigration perspective, are unable to leave the country if they want to as they are unable to pay the carefully calculated immigration arrears or court fines. This is a source of frustration for many on the land and many who are desirous of coming but it does not prevent those spiritually chosen for the mission of physical relocation to Africa from coming. For others, the choice may be to visit and support from outside. As one writer perceives:

The reality is most of our people are not going to emigrate back to Africa. Some of our people have returned but the masses of our people will remain where they are for the rest of their natural lives.

(Stanton posted: July 2016)

Those who have returned may be best represented by one of the community's caregivers, Beverley Stewart, who has lived with her now adult children for over a decade and has built her house in Shashemene. Sister Bev shares the common experience of land insecurity and inadequate representation but ends on an optimistic and persuasive note:

Various organisers spring up to represent us only to peter out. On the ground there are a lot of positive happenings (but individually and not collectively) for economic development. Underneath it all, there are positive vibes… Come with an irit (a spirit) to create, to build on what is already here. Come home soon (unpublished interview, 2014).

Repatriation, however, can be distinguished from either traditional migration or what has come to be known as transnational migration, which refers to the movement of people who relocate from one nation-state to another, who 'live their lives across borders, participating simultaneously in social relations that embed them in more than one nation-state' (Schiller, 2003: 99–128). Other defining characteristics of transnational migrants include the desire to improve their lives, and the sending of remittances from their new countries of residence to those of origin, once they settle (Levitt and Schiller, 2004). While there are some similarities with Rastafari Repatriation, there are also significant differences.

The constraints imposed by lack of legal status, coupled with Ethiopia's financial regulations, mean that they are unable to send remittances back to the countries from which they came – which are not considered 'home'. They left those countries to come home to Ethiopia, and relations with the West are partly maintained out of the need for the support of those left behind. Thus, remittances flow from lands of origin, into the repatriated community. Often, in leaving the country to meet immigration requirements, the opportunity is used to seek employment or to engage in informal fund-raising, to bring money back to the community of returnees. However, there are times when relatives from the more 'developed' world left behind are also in need and unable to give support that may be expected in Ethiopia. Contrary to what may have been true of early repatriates, as reported in the Rastafari Movement Association's (RMA) *Rasta Voice* of September 9, 1971, recent arrivals do not view '... [r]epatriation and self-help organizations such as the EWF and the Ethiopian Orthodox Church as a way out of capitalist-induced poverty, wage labor and unemployment' (Tafari, 2001: 311).

In fact, many Rastafari leave behind in the West what may be to their new neighbors, enviable lives, compared to conditions in which they live in Africa. Others have established substantial to luxurious homes in their repatriated homelands. Yet others pay exorbitant rents for city life. Among those with whom they live in the wider Shashemene community, Rastafari who have returned from the Diaspora are perceived to be wealthy and therefore prime targets for thieves. Under such circumstances, security of home and property are strong concerns. During the Jamaican government-sponsored Mission to Africa in 1961, Haile Selassie I had raised the anticipated challenges of such inequity.

This entire discussion lends itself to the possibility that those on the Shashemene Land Grant who have been there for decades, who have long lost a relationship with the Immigration Department may well be those who can be said to have repatriated. They have no desire to return to the geographical spaces from which they came and are content to live their lives entirely within Ethiopia's borders. Those who prioritize avoiding the inherent risks, despite their best intentions can fit into the category of transnational migrants, with the reverse movement of financial resources in the form of monies brought home from the countries they yearn to leave behind but to which they seem tied. Yet, it must not be imagined that the resources mobilized and brought home by those in motion, flow only from north to south. There is an emerging visibility of repatriated Rastafari women engaging in intra-African trade of cultural items, academic and professional skills. They network successfully to further such activity by invited participation in processes, conferences and festivals in all regions of the continent, including the African Union (AU), and invite others in – a vantage point gained by having an African base. There being a continuation of the legacy of African trading women is worthy of further study. The marriage and family life of repatriated women, to African brothers born and raised on the continent, may also be of gendered sociological interest.

Perhaps with less idealism and grounding in reality, over time the very concept of repatriation has garnered different interpretations. As Ras Ikael Tafari discerns, there has been '...the shift from a millenarianism to... the opening up of new vistas of mass mobilization and power...' (Tafari, 2001: 7). For others, it is the shift from a physical to a psychological and cultural return requiring divine or political intervention (Edmonds, 1998: 31). According to the late Ras Boanerges, a very influential Patriarch of the Nyahbinghi Order:

> the Rastaman is not dealing with the mere physical relocation of a particular group to some part of Africa. His goal is Repatriation, i.e. the overall 'Ransom of Israel [that

> is, the sons and daughters of the black race internationally] by the moral laws of the Almighty Rastafari,' restoring and rightfully returning them to their own national 'vine and fig tree' – Africa.
>
> (Tafari, 2001: 314)

Paradoxically, within the acknowledged weakness in meeting Ethiopia's immigration requirements, there is strength in the continuity of presence that cannot be offered by those who may regularly need to leave the country in the quest to stay legal. Those who are unable to leave because they cannot pay the high immigration arrears are among those who serve some of the leadership needs of informal structures such as Unity in Motion. Without what one may consider the necessary experience in diplomatic or political leadership, they may be late but may well be spearheading the political work and aspirations of the Rastafari Movement, located in:

> the mooted third, unfolding secular cycle of the late 1980s and 1990s, where Rastafari is starting to become the centralized nucleus of a movement for black macro-political liberation and repatriation... [when] the objective conditions within the movement [are] probably ripe for the Rastafari as a unified body to organize and control their political/economic destiny at both the micro and macro/state level ...
>
> (Tafari, 2001: xxxi)

Indeed, the period of the 1990s saw a resurgence of repatriation, particularly following the downfall of the Dergue in 1991 and again during the centenary in 1992, of the birth of Tafari Makonnen.

By 1995–1996, by international effort, the first Nyahbinghi Tabernacle was erected on the Shashemene Land Grant. It is therefore impressed upon visitors to the Nyahbinghi Tabernacle Center in Shashemene, to be mindful of their behavior as they stand on one of the power spots of the Black World. Within the boundaries of this power spot, there has been historical conflict over the legitimacy of representation by one House/Mansion/Organisation or the other with interventions initiated either by the community or by various arms of the government. Much has been made of these differences but careful scrutiny of archival material at the Nyahbinghi Tabernacle Center shows that the Elders of the Nyahbinghi Order have always participated in movements towards centralized representation.

Historically, the responsibility of administering the entire Land Grant was that of the Ethiopian World Federation (EWF), which, by the second decade of the twenty-first century, showed new legitimacy and popularity. However, nothing on record indicates that the EWF ever administered the Shashemene Land Grant in the manner intended. The view that residents on the Land Grant must be members of the organization is contradicted by the fact that non-members have always come and taken up residence as able. Its constituents make it a legitimate organization, but relations between it and the Addis Ababa-based EWF legally registered as a non-government organization (NGO) have been impaired. The registration is a major bone of contention with those for whom the role of EWF is that of a government within a government. Others see the registration as a necessary and helpful step. Given the prevailing spirit of Unity in Motion, a cross-section of the community can be seen at the major social events of the EWF and the Twelve Tribes of Israel whose membership is highest. The only legally registered representative entity in the repatriated community in Shashemene is the Jamaica Rastafari Development Community (JRDC). Issues of credibility and representativeness have caused its influence to wax and wane but it has endured.

Representation of repatriated Rastafari interests has been sporadic at best and the community has not pressed advantage when opportunity has presented itself. Hence, the petition requested by an Ethiopian parliamentary committee, presenting an opportunity to demand legal status in 2012, was not as strongly worded as it could have been and did not bear the maximum number of signatures. Also by invitation was the submission of draft text for the government's Diaspora policy, which focuses largely on Ethiopians who left the country in the twentieth century in search of a better life. Repatriated Rastafari seem to have relied primarily on their resource of unbounded faith. This, combined with a soft power comprising faith, patience and cooperation, contributes to the community's resilience. Several had managed to become permanent residents, but persons who sought such status around 2014 were informed by the Immigration Department that a there was a moratorium on the granting of permanent residence.

Rastafari on the land continue to assert that they are not refugees, people living in exile, internally displaced persons, the type of investors being attracted or any of the existing legal statuses. They represent a category that does not officially exist – returning Africans (Owens, 1976; Christian, 2011; MacLeod, 2014). A former Mayor of Shashemene, Demisse Shito, acknowledged that repatriated Rastafari are different from regular foreigners but:

> they are still not Ethiopians. While he recognizes and values the 'mental and 'spiritual' connection Rastafari have to Ethiopia, his comments point to the enormous difficulty for Rastafari to be fully accepted without government legitimacy. Thus, beyond the current bureaucratic challenges preventing citizenship, the mayor also presents a perceptual problem created by lack of categorization for Rastafari.
>
> (MacLeod, 2014: 226)

MacLeod sees among the options available to Rastafari settlers, the ethnic identity strategy and the African Diaspora strategy. The Rastafari Nation may be a problematic concept but what better time to consider the cultural identity than in the UN Decade for the People of African Descent. It is a problem for consideration in the discourse on the African Diaspora as the 6th Region of the African Union, for in the return home one is no longer in the Diaspora. It is a problem for representation from entities such as the Caribbean Community (CARICOM) in that its citizens, holders of its passports, are demanding to be recognized as Africans/Ethiopians desirous of leaving that space in which their enslaved ancestors sweated, bled and died. The harsh realities of Repatriation may lead one to agree that since the 1961 Mission to Africa:

> apart from fairly limited achievements of the Twelve Tribes and the EWF – no further, single, concrete development on any scale of significance has come from the brethren and sistren, the Jamaican government, or for that matter any African government, following this historic reconnection between Africans at home and abroad which would have sustained or intensified its vital momentum.
>
> (Tafari, 2001: 303)

Conclusion: wielding power with patience

> A property will return to its rightful owners even if it takes a thousand years.
>
> (Ethiopian proverb)

Neither in Ethiopia where Rastafari have been living on the Shashemene Land Grant for over 40 years, nor in any other African country has there been '...facilitation of the welcomed return and resettlement of the descendants of enslaved Africans...' envisioned as a reparatory measure in the UN Durban Programme of Action (2001, Section IV: Article 158). The document coming out of the United Nations World Conference against Racism, Racial Discrimination, Xenophobia and other forms of intolerance was considered groundbreaking as it was the first government documentation to acknowledge repatriation as part of reparations – though neither of these terms was used. Fifteen years after Durban, as the African Union includes the Diaspora Initiative in its journey of implementing Agenda 2063, and as the UN observes its Decade for People of African Descent, Caribbean governments have co-opted the reparations movement and are waging a lukewarm campaign with some level of Rastafari involvement, but the traditional demand of reparations for repatriation seems diminished.

Meanwhile, on the continent, in December 2016 the Republic of Ghana awarded citizenship to 34 persons from the African Diaspora, some of whom were resident, others who were acknowledged for various contributions. Many among the Rastafari Nation repatriated to Ethiopia felt disappointed that Ethiopia had not taken the lead in this regard. Among the new Ghanaians was Dr. Desta Meghoo, Coordinator of the Africa Unite concert, whose country of residence is Ethiopia. It is not clear whether these Ghanaians have full citizenship rights like the generations of those born and bred there. Several years earlier, Bob Marley's widow, Rita Marley, had been granted citizenship following many years of residence.

Ras Shango Baku, writer, publisher and member of the Nyahbinghi National Council (UK), captured the excitement of the new citizenship moment in his emailed notes bearing the subject line, 'Free at last! Ghana Grants Citizenship to Diaspora. Afrikans!'

> Great day in Accra! Wednesday 28th December 2016. Signing of the Diasporan Citizenship Act at the WEB Du Bois Center in the presence of outgoing President John Mahama. Huge gathering in a spacious hall at the Center. At least 400 splendidly dressed African dignitaries and returnees from the Diaspora. Massive Rastafari presence adding color, quality and poignancy to the occasion. Songs of Bob Marley fill the auditorium as the expectant crowd awaits the President's arrival: Redemption Song, Africa Unite, Exodus, etc., setting hearts a-flutter as eyes grow misty with historical remembrance (29 December 2016 21:29).

However, there has been a note of criticism about the process in Ghana, with claims of elitism in the selection made by the Diaspora Coalition which was established to liaise with the government and represent the interest of all Africans from the Diaspora in Ghana. Citizenship had been conferred on only 34 when there were many more who had been resident for much longer. A widely circulated email from Empress Marina Blake, a well-known Rastafari lawyer with interests in Ghana, described the downside like this:

> On January 19, 2017, a meeting of the Diaspora Coalition was held in the offices of the Diaspora Africa Forum (DAF) located at the WEB Du Bois Center in Accra, Ghana. The meeting was well attended, as many people had questions regarding the citizenships granted and what process had been established to facilitate the citizenship of the thousands of remaining diasporans. Many people in attendance were disgruntled and some were outright angry.
>
> (February 5, 2017)

Earlier in 2016, Ghana's announcement that nationals of other African Union Member States could obtain visas on arrival caused no stir of excitement among the Rastafari Nation. Neither did the issue of the African (AU) passport to Heads of Government. Rastafari recalled the announcement made in 2011 that the very first of such passports would be issued to the late stalwart Jamaican pan-Africanist, Elder Dudley Thompson, QC. Sadly, he passed away on January 20, 2012, the day after his 95th birthday. Apparently, the award was never made though plans are afoot to do so posthumously. The intended gesture was symbolically significant, though.

Meanwhile, the repatriated community in Ethiopia continues to be the soul of patience, with individual frustration manifesting more so than communal anger. The community wields a soft power that perhaps contributes to the ongoing accommodation of Rastafari. The best example of this was the successful hosting in 2005 of the mega concert 'Africa Unite' to celebrate the 60th anniversary of the birth of Bob Marley. The Government of Ethiopia closed off the famous city-center landmark Meskel Square for a reggae show that attracted an international audience of some 400,000 (by the highest estimate) reggae and Rastafari lovers. This would obviously have had a strong tourism value and economic impact. Some years earlier, when the press announced the intention of Bob Marley's widow to have his mortal remains interred in Ethiopia, the Jamaican public was loud and fierce in its disapproval. Seated visibly, prominently, perhaps presidentially at the main events of 'Africa Unite', were the Elders of the Nyahbinghi Order of Shashemene, joined by Patriarchs and Matriarchs of the Order flown from Jamaica, along with Mama B, whose repatriation destination was South Africa. On arrival in South Africa, Mama B in her zeal had burned her Jamaican passport. After several years and with great difficulty she was able to obtain a new one and was thus able to travel to Ethiopia to help usher in the Ethiopian New Millennium. Despite years of residence in South Africa, Mama is still unsettled and up to 2017 faced threat of deportation – a fate reserved in Ethiopia only for those who have returned and have been convicted and imprisoned.

Historical tensions surrounding land tenure and development in Ethiopia again escalated in August 2016 with the Amhara nation joining forces with the Oromo in a wave of fatal protests that began in late 2015, and kept resurging, leading to the declaration of a State of Emergency in October 2016. They have not responded to various social media calls for taking a stance on the causal issues, a call echoed by Professor Horace Campbell during his presentation on Bob Marley at the AbiReggae Colloquium in Côte d'Ivoire in April 2017. Rastafari has not protested at all in spite of varied sources of conflict between the repatriated community and the people among whom they have settled. Despite deep anger experienced in late 2015 at the brutal murder of a Rastafari Elder that involved conflict over property he had acquired and lived on for several years, there was no violent response from the community.

Apparently, there has been a limited response by the community to overtures to join an Oromo political party, signaling an element of departure from both the traditional shunning of partisan politics and from strict allegiance to the imperial throne. Though some individuals support political parties and vote in general elections, Rastafari have, in general, shied away from partisan politics, remaining in the realm of non-alignment, affirmative, flexible and using the great strength of moral persuasion, as espoused by Haile Selassie I at the Organisation of African Unity Summit in Cairo on July 21, 1964. It is Bonacci (2015: 389) who explains the relations and affiliations that now seem to be shifting:

> At the local level, in Shashemene, the Rastafari were associated with the emperor, whom the Oromos saw as a coercive central power. In a region still marked by a history of alienation of the land and by economic and social domination, the symbols of imperial power were inevitably despised. At the national level, a group like the Rastafari, which identifies with an imperial, Amhara, and centralized Ethiopian nation, is

> also in contradiction with a national imaginary ... based on ethnic distinction and the autonomy of the federal regions.

But the relationship between the imperial throne and the Oromo had not always been conflictual. At the end of the nineteenth century and beginning of the twentieth century, a class of young people, called by foreigners the Young Ethiopians or Young Abyssinians, mainly educated overseas, who spoke French as a second language, agitated for reform. According to Pankhurst, one of them, an Oromo named Yilma Deressa from Wallaga, thought that the Emperor was educating them to civilize Ethiopia and declared: 'We Young Abyssinians are in duty bound to our country, we are the bridge that the Emperor has thrown across to European culture... ' (2010: 131).

In the twenty-first century, Shashemene, in addition to cases of conflict over land within the perimeters of the Land Grant, the cause of hostility expressed on the part of some Rastafari is based on the claim that the Oromo fought against His Majesty. The passionate justification for that fight is summed up in a personalized account by one of the fighters who took part in the Ethiopian Revolution of 1974, '... with enthusiasm and hope to seek justice for a people [the Oromo] largely expropriated and marginalized by the imperial political system and administration' (Gnamo, 2014: 6). The counterclaim, borne out by Teshale, 1995; Milkias, 2011 and Mekonnen, 2013 is that Oromo blood could be found in the genealogy of both Haile Selassie I and his royal consort, Empress Menen. This may have been the rationale for at least seven of the Land Grant's well-known personalities, acting on the principle of 'by any means necessary', who seem to have found an alternative path to formally becoming Ethiopian.

They have been resident in Shashemene for varying lengths of time and are known to be affiliated with the Bobo Shanti, Nyahbinghi and the Ethiopian World Federation. In 2016–17, these individuals, all born in Jamaica, used their creative genius to make a case based on the sixteenth-century history of a group of Jamaicans originating in Jamma, Werleu, in Ethiopia's Oromo Regional State. The partial account is of 20,000 Ethiopian Christians sold first by Arabs to Iraq, then later to Spain and ending up in Jamaica. A photocopied page of part of the story as documented by an Ethiopian, A. M. Belay, is being circulated in the community by Brother Ayyoono Babu, also known as I Priest Itabarica. He is one of the group of repatriated Rastafarians engaged in a process of 'Oromofication' which, by the traditional Oromo Gada system (recognized by UNESCO), the '... Abba-Gada literally "father of the period"' and by court procedure, enabled them to be issued Oromo names and IDs identifying them as Ethiopian and placing them on an alternative path to citizenship. Those holding such IDs have been told that they can seek employment without the formerly required work permit. Apparently, the new IDs come with the benefit of eligibility to receive 'carta plans', giving their holders the authority to use lands in a context where land is nationalized. In these and other ways they are yet to be tried and tested. However, this phenomenon supports the argument that:

> People in the 21st century will claim multiple political and religious identities, to both national and transnational groups. The critical task is to understand the way individuals and organizations actually operate across cultures, and the costs and benefits of these arrangements. It is to understand how ordinary individuals and organizations ...redefine the boundaries of belonging along the way.
>
> (Levitt, 2004)

Though some in the community have responded with amusement at this development, one concern is the question of where the loyalty of the new Oromos would lie in cases of conflict. The Oromo Nation, the largest in Ethiopia, has been struggling to attain a greater slice of the

Ethiopian political and economic pie. In this quest, violent protest has erupted, resulting in loss of life and property damage. A State of Emergency was declared on October 2, 2016 and this may have impeded outcomes of the most recent engagement between the Ethiopian Ministry of Foreign Affairs and the repatriated community.

The initiative leading up to the meeting with the Ministry had begun several months earlier, when on Sunday, May 29, 2016, having presented his credentials a year earlier, Ethiopia's first Ambassador to Jamaica, Girma Birru visited the island. The media (*Jamaica Observer, the Gleaner, Ethiopian Herald)*, reported his acknowledgement of the historical and cultural affinity between Jamaica and Ethiopia. He further expressed Ethiopia's desire to strengthen ties in the areas of tourism, sports, education, culture and trade (*The Jamaica Observer*, May 31, 2016). Shortly after that, on June 12, Ethiopia's then Minister of Foreign Affairs, Dr. Tedros Adhanom arrived in Jamaica for:

> an historic two-day official visit – the first by an Ethiopian minister of government – to boost long-standing relations between the two countries ... [and] seek support for his country's bid to become a member of the United Nations Security Council next year.
>
> (*Loop News*, June 13, 2016)

It is also felt by the repatriated community that the visit of the Minister to the island was linked to his seeking the Caribbean community's support for his bid to become head of the World Health Organization (WHO). Members of the community quietly reasoned among themselves, raising the concept of reciprocity. The whisper may have been heard in the corridors of power as in July 2016, representatives of the community were invited to a meeting with the Ministry of Foreign Affairs, initiated by the latter. More likely it was the reminder from the government and people in Jamaica about regularizing the status of Jamaicans and other Caribbean nationals living in Ethiopia as repatriated persons. The invitation to the meeting was issued to the Jamaica Rastafari Development Community (JRDC), which then ensured the inclusion of representation from the Nyahbinghi Order and the Ethiopian World Federation (EWF) in Shashemene. Ras Reuben Kush, even before that historic meeting, saw through the nuances and was moved to remark, 'We're here to stay. We haven't been kicked out of Ethiopia after all these years, that means we are accepted,' (Bould, 2015). One outcome of the meeting with the Foreign Ministry, was the formation of a representative task force to work out the details of granting permanent residence to members of the repatriated community.

While that seemed a significant step in the process of that long desired goal, expressed in the passionate cry, 'No Migration, Repatriation!' the aftermath was marked by a competitive air in the behavior of both the JRDC and EWF. The former had begun a process requiring all applicants for legal status to take membership with them. However, at a community meeting called by the EWF in March 2017, several persons expressed dissatisfaction with what seemed like forced membership. The community maturely anticipated the charge of an administration fee to meet expenses and proposed that Shashemene's representation be formally strengthened to include the Nyahbinghi representative who had participated in the meeting with the Minister of Foreign Affairs. The community also advised the EWF that the local team of five should follow up with the government's team of five and that the former should convene the next meeting instead of either the JRDC or the EWF. However, the JRDC had already submitted over 100 applications through its lawyer, and the EWF continues to liaise with various officials and to call community meetings, but at the time of writing there was no alternative process on offer. Up to mid-April 2017, the EWF to the community that among the gains obtained, was an amnesty for those with outstanding immigration arrears.

It is not yet clear how the change in legal status will affect those who remain desirous of repatriation to Ethiopia, but hopefully Ethiopia's long-awaited gesture will reverberate in other countries where there are settlements of returning Africans. After all, though this is another century, the case remains, as it did over fifty years ago, that 'in a real sense, our continent is unmade; it still awaits its creation and its creators' (Haile Selassie I, 1963).

> Man is respected in his native land.
>
> (Ethiopian proverb)

Bibliography

Belay, A.M., n.d. 'Kings of Yesterday Ethiopia', reference book.

Berhan, D. posted on Thursday, December 1, 2016 @ 5:17 am, 'Briefing: What Is Oromo's Gada System?' accessed 20 April 2017 at http://hornaffairs.com/2016/12/01/description-oromo-gada-system/

—— *Exodus! L'histoire de retour des Rastafariens en Ethiopie,* Paris: L'Harmattan.

Bonacci, G. (2015), *Exodus! Heirs and Pioneers, Rastafari Return [t]o Ethiopia* – translated by Antoinette Tijani Alou, Jamaica, Barbados, Trinidad and Tobago: The University of the West Indies Press.

Bould, J. 'Promised Land? Rastafarians Struggle in Ethiopia', in *Jamaica Observer,* Monday, November 16, 2015., accessed 5 September 2016 at http://www.jamaicaobserver.com/news/Promised-land_19238767 -

Burrel J. and Ford, A.J. (1919), 'The Universal Ethiopian Anthem', accessed 19 April 2017 at https://keyamsha.com/2014/08/18/the-universal-ethiopian-anthem-and-how-it-came-to-be-written/

Christian, I. (2011), 'When People Cannot Speak, They Sing', in Baldacchino, G. (ed.) *Island Songs: A Global Repertoire,* Lanham, Toronto, Plymouth, UK: The Scarecrow Press Inc. in collaboration with AIRS (Advancing Interdisciplinary Research in Singing).

—— 2013, *Message to the African Union – A Rastafari Yardstick for Performance Evaluation,* commemorative publication of Haile Selassie I's address at inaugural meeting of the Organisation of African Unity in Addis Ababa, May 1963 for 50th anniversary of the OAU/AU, with Rastafari commentary, Shashemene, Ethiopia, Matriarks Self-Publishers Association.

Edmonds, E.B. (1998), ' "I" In-A- Babylon' in Murrell et al. (ed.) *Chanting Down Babylon – The Rastafari Reader,* Philadelphia: Temple University Press.

Gnamo, A.H. (2014), *Conquest and Resistance in the Ethiopian Empire, 1880–1974,* The Case of the Arsi Oromo. Leiden, Boston Brill.

Haile Selassie I's address at the Cairo Summit of the Organisation of African Unity. accessed 20 April, 2017 at http://nyahbinghi.ca/RasTafarI-speeches/view-speech.asp?word_id=oau_cairo

Hutton, C.A. et al. (ed.), (2015), *Leonard Percival Howell & The Genesis of Rastafari,* Jamaica, Barbados, Trinidad and Tobago: The University of the West Indies Press.

Levitt, P. 'Transnational Migrants: When "Home" Means More Than One Country', *Migration Information Source,* Migration Policy Institute, October 1, 2004, accessed 19 April 2017 at http://www.migrationpolicy.org/article/transnational-migrants-when-home-means-more-one-country

Levitt, P. and Schiller, N.G. (2004), 'Conceptualizing Simultaneity: A Transnational Social Field Perspective on Society' *International Migration Review,* vol. 38, no. 3, pp. 1002–1039. doi: 10.1111/j.1747-7379.2004.tb00227.x Accessed 20 July 2016 at https://www.research.manchester.ac.uk/.../conceptualizing-simultaneity-a-transnational

Liverpool (Chalkdust) H. (2001), *Rituals of Power & Rebellion – The Carnival Tradition in Trinidad & Tobago 1763–1962,* Chicago, Jamaica, London, Trinidad and Tobago: Research Associates School Times Publications Frontline Distribution Int'l. Inc.

Loop News Report (June 13, 2016), 'Ethiopian Foreign Minister Seeks Jamaica Support to Sit on UN Security Council'. Jamaica, accessed 5 September 2016 at https://www.google.com/search?client=firefox-b-ab&btnG=Search&q= Loop+News+Report+%28June+13%2C+2016%29%2C+%E2%80%98 Ethiopian +foreign +minister+seeks+Jamaica+support+to+sit+on+UN+Security+Council%E2%80%99

MacLeod, E.C. (2014), *Visions of Zion: Ethiopians and Rastafari in Search for the Promised Land,* New York: New York University Press.

Marley, R.N. and McIntosh, W.P. aka Bob Marley and Peter Tosh (1973), 'Get Up, Stand Up', The Wailers album *Burnin'*, Recorded: Harry J. Studios, Kingston, Jamaica

Milkias, P. (2011), *Ethiopia*. Santa Barbara, Calif, ABC-CLIO.

Mekonnen, Y.K. (2013), *Ethiopia: The Land, Its People, History and Culture*, accessed 20 April 2017 at https://books.google.com.et/books?isbn=9987160247

Murrell, N.S. et al. (ed.), 1998, *Chanting Down Babylon – The Rastafari Reader*. Philadelphia: Temple University Press.

Niaah, J. and Christian, I. (2013*), What Is Rastafari', Introduction Rastafari – A National Museum Jamaica Exhibition,* Kingston, The Institute of Jamaica, Ministry of Youth and Culture.

Palmer, C.A. (2006), *Eric Williams and the Making of the Modern Caribbean*. Chapel Hill: University of North Carolina Press.

Pankhurst, R. 'Who Were the "Young Ethiopians" (or "Young Abyssinians")? – An Historical Enquiry', *Ethiopian e-Journal for Research and Innovation Foresight,* vol. 2, no. 2 (2010) – Education Issue: pp (121–138), accessed 16 April 2017 at https://www.google.com/search?q=Young+Ethiopians+or+Young+Abyssinians +by +Richard+ Pankhurst &ie=utf-8&oe=utf-8&client=firefox-b-ab

Prunier, G. and Ficquet, E. et al. (2015), *Understanding Contemporary Ethiopia: Monarchy, Revolution and the Legacy of Meles Zenawi'*. C. Hurst & Company (Publishers) Ltd., UK. Accessed 13 September 2016 at https://books.google.com/books?id=wnxeCwAAQBAJ&printsec= frontcover#v=onepage & q &f=false.

Rogers, A. (1924), *The Holy Piby*, Woodbridge, New Jersey, Athlican Strong Arm Company, accessed digitally on 23 May 2013 at the Anguilla Library Service.

Shashemene Profiles (2014), unpublished interviews with Beverley Stewart and Reuben Kush, Shashemene, Ethiopia.

Stanton, J.R. 'The Realities of Resistance and Nationhood', *Current Events and Topical Issues,* posted on TheBlackList Pub. on 7 July 2016, accessed 10 July 2016 at theblacklistpub.ning.com/forum/topics/the-realities-of-resistance-and-nationhood

Tafari, I. (2001), *Rastafari in Transition – The Politics of Cultural Confrontation in Africa and the Caribbean (1966–1988*), Chicago, Jamaica, London, Trinidad and Tobago Research Associates School Times Publications Frontline Distribution Int'l. Inc.

Tibebu, T. (1995), *The Making of Modern Ethiopia: 1896–1974*, accessed 15 April 2017 at https://books.google.com.et/books?isbn=1569020019

United Nations Durban Programme of Action (2001), World Conference Against Racism, Racial Discrimination, Xenophobia and Related Intolerance, accessed 5 September 2016, at http://www.un.org/WCAR/durban.pdf

Vinson, R. (2009), 'Providential Design: American Negroes and Garveyism in South Africa', in West, M.O., Martin, W.G., Fanon, C.W. (ed.) *From Toussaint to Tupac – The Black International since the Age of Revolution,* The University of North Carolina Press, accessed 5 September 2016 at https://books.google.com/books?id=rNxa2v3rz8oC&pg=RA1-PA151&dq

Worku, M. (2007), translated by Ras Abye Tilahun, *The Golden Book of Wisdom from Ethiopia – A collection of Amharic Proverbs & Oral Literature,* Volume I, Shashemene: Author.

27

IS A DECOLONISED UNIVERSITY POSSIBLE IN A COLONIAL SOCIETY?

Andile Mngxitama

South Africa today

The European elite undertook to manufacture a native elite.

(Sartre, in Fanon 1965: 7)

Decolonisation as a political and philosophical question was put back on the South African national consciousness by the student movement almost a year ago. The University of Cape Town (UCT) 'Rhodes Must Fall' (RMF) movement should be credited for making the call, just as the neo-colonial settlement engineered by Nelson Mandela and Desmond Tutu was entering its third decade after proving itself to be nothing but an extension of the colonial settler rule which privileged whiteness at the expense of blackness. The democratic transition has ensured that blacks remain at the bottom of the social, economic, political and cultural life of South Africa (SA).

The past two decades have settled the argument of who democracy actually serves.

Blacks have been rendered a voting powerless black majority. What explains this state of affairs – this positionality of black as permanently marked by exclusion? We argue that the answer is the continuation of colonialism by other means under a non-white administration of the ruling party. Significantly, 1994 did not end colonialism, but more correctly, the political settlement was not meant to end it either. The first hurdle to quickly overcome is the correct characterisation of SA today.

We move from the premise that SA is as it has been for the last 350 years or so. 1994 did not signify a rupture with the past. So, SA is still beset by the problem of white racism as the main defining reality, which operates as colonialism. Steve Biko's injunction for a dialectical conflict as a prerequisite to ending white power has not yet occurred and, therefore, the 'thesis' remains white racism: we haven't yet reached a point of accumulating enough black forces to present an antithesis. There is no new synthesis as we speak. SA is a colony!

It must be remembered that the terms and even rhetoric of the struggle in the last phase (1980s) led by the African National Congress (ANC) through its many proxies under the rubric of the United Democratic Front (UDF) perceived the fundamental problem to be 'apartheid' and, therefore, the fundamental antidote, to be democracy, human rights and in particular 'one man one vote' (we say nothing about the sexist language of the demand itself). The struggle waged by the ANC since its inception has been for inclusion into not obliteration of the colonial reality crafted since 1652 with the arrival of the violent, rapacious, dispossessing Europeans.

It is not an insult to say that the ANC have been fighting for the vote not for the land. But as Pan-Africanists like Sobukwe had warned, fighting for the vote without the land would not give you the land. This blind spot is a direct consequence of the adoption of the Freedom Charter (FC) (or was the FC merely a confirmation of the accommodationist politics of the ANC?). The whole mind-set of the 'congress' tradition is to do things according to the 'law'. (The military wing of the ANC MK found its hands bound by the Geneva Convention – listen to President Zuma or even the Economic Freedom Fighters (EFF) speak about doing things within the constitution, but the constitution is the thing that takes away black people's land rights, or should we say, where is the land? It's the constitution that made the things that made the land not to be there.) This self-limiting political position is ingrained in the DNA of the FC. So according to this 'law is first' logic, you first fight to control the instrument of making law (political power), and then use it to address your problems. This is the old electoral story of, 'vote for us first, then we shall serve you once in power'. It's a fraud! This same logic is at work today even by political formations that purport to be 'radical'.

This mind-set speaks to the two main responses Africans developed with regard to the colonial question, which matured in the Cape's long battles against the invading forces including the hundred years' war of the Xhosa-speaking people against the colonialists. The two ethics developed what was to be known as the Qaba and Gqhobhoka divide. Basically, amaqaba are those who refused western modernity by any means necessary (the children of Okonko of Achebe's *Things Fall Apart*, 1959), and on the other hand, amagqhobhoka, or those who accommodated themselves into western modernity (the first real coconuts). We shall in a moment return to this in some detail.

The new call for decolonisation by university students kick-started a movement that is pegged back to the single symbolic act by Chumani Maxwele of throwing human waste on the statue of the uber-symbol of colonialism, Cecil John Rhodes. This act connected to real and felt frustrations and pain that had been suppressed by the dictates of decorum and respectability of the liberal academic setting at UCT (this is true for all liberal campuses). One had to appear to be 'civil', despite being suffocated by the weight of institutional racism that has become as naturalised as the permanency of the statue of Rhodes. As we know the statue is gone, but the spirit of Rhodes remains.

We also know that some black associate professors have received full tenure, yet the syllabus remains colonial, so too the iconography of the university. In fact, across the white university sphere, there is a sense of 'fast tracking' in process for blacks to be promoted into the professoriate class even if the individuals in question have nothing to profess. The pressure to sort out representivity is on. This is so because representivity is the best mechanism to absorb pressure and continue business as usual. This rhythm has already been tried and tested with the 'Flag Independence Process'.

The call to decolonise the university seems to be operationalised into five demands in the main: firstly, sorting out the skewed race and gender representation in the academic staff; secondly, the transformation of the curriculum from the current Eurocentric version into a more Afrocentric one; thirdly, expanding access to the university by black students (overcoming fees and language barriers); fourthly, the incorporation of workers into the university family or insourcing with benefits they currently do not enjoy; fifthly, and more difficult to define, demanding institutional cultural reform (this may include values and symbols but not limited to those).

Whilst a wide-ranging discussion is ongoing about the nature of these demands and how they link up to the project of decolonisation, there is consensus that the call is in the main university-centred. In the four moments in the movement shortly to be alluded to, we shall show that, in the first moment in the movement, there were discursive attempts to imagine decolonisation as a project beyond the university and centred on the land demand, but this particular move has not yet found practical expression as a point of mobilisation by the student movement. The 'Back to Land Campaign' is not yet part of the decolonisation dance.

The key point is that the decolonisation call by students is a battle based immediately at the university and for the university. This is an interesting turn away from the first generation of black consciousness movement led by Steve Biko in the 1970s through the South African Students Organisation (SASO), which saw itself as a liberation movement, not a student's movement. Its main demands were for societal change, not so much for improvements of life in the university. The university was used as a reference point for the broader society, as we saw with the 1972 powerful and courageous speech by Abram Tiro. We also recall Sobukwe at Fort Hare linking up with the workers' struggle outside the university.

This difference of emphasis comes with the ideological orientation that informs the 1970s and the 2000s. SASO perceived their challenge as a challenge of black people in general, because one was a black before one was a student. The new student movement perceives its challenge (in practice) as one of the university which is not transformed, while the emphasis is on student affairs (the media and ruling party has been pushing this separation of students from the black community outside the varsity gates). For Biko and SASO, the problem was political; for today's movement the problem is in the main policy (admittedly with some important gesturing to politics). This explains why SASO fought for the liberation of black people, and today the call is for the 'decolonisation of the university'.

SASO seems to have appreciated that the university is an instance of the 'colonial superstructure' of the 'colonial economic base' (to borrow and muddy the Marxian rubric). Let us permit ourselves to allow a Marxian framework to help us locate the university, so that we are able to pose the question; 'Is a decolonised university possible in a colonial society?' We need to define more accurately, more or less what is this thing we call university, what is its history, and what is its function in our society and other societies.

It is interesting that the university system in Africa as we know it today is a colonial construct, literally! Of course we note that Africa is the cradle of the university system, but we here now refer to the re-emergence of the university after slavery, specifically, during the 'second coming' which is colonialism. We know they built the church to tame our spirits so that the body can obey the whip and the load of labour on our backs. We know they built hospitals to keep us alive so that we can continue to be a factor of production. Why did they build universities?

We must consider this matter from the perspective of the university builders and also from our perspective, because these are in conflict here. For the coloniser, the university was built to create African managers of the colonial system. The same goes with apartheid South Africa, which went ahead and built the university system for blacks, in tandem with their tribal identities, in order to create a layer of mis-educated Africans to manage white people's affairs while they were on holiday.

It's also instructive that formal Western education was, during colonialism, administered by missionaries (abafundisi). What is the general purpose of education? It was the founding father of Tanzania, Julius Nyerere, who provided a general outline, and he argues: 'education, whether it be formal or informal, has a purpose. That purpose is to transmit from one generation to the next the accumulated wisdom and knowledge of the society, and to prepare the young people for their future membership of the society and their active participation in its maintenance or development.' (Nyerere 1967) This is the general purpose of education in societies which are not oppressed. This is a kind of education for conserving the integrity of the community, its education for the perpetuation of the society's agreed norms and values. But what happens when the education system is not designed for the interest of the community but those of an occupying force? The logic remains the same: 'preservation' of the status quo; therefore, colonial education is for colonial ends.

Nyerere articulates the objectives of colonial education in the context of colonial Tanzania: 'The education provided by the colonial government in the two countries which now form Tanzania had a different purpose. It was not designed to prepare young people for the service of their own country; instead, it was motivated by a desire to inculcate the values of the colonial society and to train individuals for the service of the colonial state. In these countries the state interest in education, therefore, stemmed from the need for local clerks and junior officials; on top of that, various religious groups were interested in spreading literacy and other education as part of their evangelical work' (Nyerere 1967).

The intent and effect was to create a Europeanised African or amaqhoboka, the native who is graphically described by Jean Paul Sartre in the preface to Frantz Fanon's classical work, *Wretched of the Earth* thus: 'The European elite undertook to manufacture a native elite. They picked out promising adolescents; they branded them, as with a red-hot iron, with the principles of Western culture, they stuffed their mouths full with high-sounding phrases, grand glutinous words that stuck to the teeth. After a short stay in the mother country, they were sent home, whitewashed. These walking lies had nothing left to say to their brothers; they only echoed. From Paris, from London, from Amsterdam we would utter the words "Parthenon! Brotherhood!" and somewhere in Africa or Asia lips would open ... "Thenon! ... Therhood!" It was the golden age' (Sartre in Fanon 1965: 7).

Dr Chinweizu takes the discussion further in elaborating on this education for the subjugation process. Sartre's 'Native elite' (in Fanon, 1965) in the hands of Chinweizu (2009) is a 'black colonialist', or better still, 'a rat with the education of a cat'. We have here not education but chains. This colonial education has a function that goes on, beyond the formal ending of colonialism. In fact, it can be argued that the colonialists, by giving the native colonial education, is preparing for another victory in the post-independence era. When colonialism managed by settlers is ended, a new phase of colonialism managed by the 'native elite' begins.

From this point of view, the defeat of the African in the war against colonialism is already guaranteed by virtue of the fact of the native elite who are black only by skin colour. According to Chinweizu (2009):

> On each country's 'independence day', it simply moved from being ruled and exploited for imperialism by white expatriate colonialists to being ruled and exploited for imperialism by black comprador colonialists. There had simply been a changing of the colour of the staff, from white to black, in the same imperialist prison. Consequently, white supremacy remains entrenched everywhere, obscured by black buffer, front office governments.

In this articulation, we see that the problem is deeply political. From the get go, Chinweizu directs us to the fundamental question of power, how it is organised, and the need to imagine change possible only on account of overthrowing the current 'black colonialists' and instituting a new society based on different values.

When Chinweizu was asked, 'The people you have in mind are highly educated, they were exposed?' His response is worth reproducing substantially:

> But educated in what and for what? Were they educated in what C. L. R. James called 'the political intricacies that the modern world demanded'? Certainly not. Despite their university degrees and general exposure, they lacked the appropriate political education. There is an incident reported in Nelson Mandela's autobiography that shows that being 'highly educated' and 'exposed' might even be a handicap in the liberation struggle. Mandela had gone underground to start the military wing of the ANC. At one point, he was hiding in Tongaat, a rural community of black plantation workers: 'Shortly before I was planning to leave, I thanked one

elderly fellow for having looked after me. He said, 'You are of course welcome, but, Kwedeni [young man], please tell us, what does Chief Luthuli want?' I was taken aback but quickly responded, 'Well, it would be better to ask him yourself and I cannot speak for him, but as I understand it, he wants our land returned, he wants our kings to have their power back, and he wants us to be able to determine our own future and run our own lives as we see fit.' 'And how is he going to do that if he does not have an army?' the old man said. [*Long Walk to Freedom*: 330] That incident took place in 1961. By then the ANC was some 50 years old, and it had just come to realize, and reluctantly accept, the necessity for armed struggle to attain its objectives. Now, why had it taken the 'highly educated' leadership of the ANC half a century to realize what was quite obvious to an 'uneducated' rural farm labourer!?'

(Chinweizu 2009)

Chinweizu continues:

so what is the fundamental use and purpose of colonial education? So, everything depends on the education they received, what it moulded them into. If you are educated as a lawyer, your mental framework tends to get limited to what you can do in a law court, or within the existing legal and constitutional arrangements. And if your education is such that you think from the point of view of your conquerors, if it moulds you into a black European, that is miseducation, not education.

(Chinweizu 2009)

The miseducation of a rat

If you take a rat and train it to see the world in the way the cat sees the world, you have not educated the rat, you have mis-educated it for life in a world with rats killing cats. You have actually made it an easier prey for the cats, because the natural instincts of a rat would have told it how to deal with cats, or how to avoid cats. But after you have given the rat the education of a cat, it would lose those instincts. It might even think of itself as a cat! And that is what this colonialist education has done to Africans for the last two centuries. We have been fundamentally mis-educated, and we cannot even see the world from our own point of view, let alone in our own interest.

(Chinweizu 2009)

To present the matter in these stark terms, is not to deny that there is always rebellion from some rats. What must be done?

Ngugi's take:

What should we do with the inherited colonial education system and the consciousness it necessarily inculcated in the African mind? What directions should an education system take in an Africa wishing to break with neo-colonialism? How does it want the 'New Africans' to view themselves and their universe and from what base, Afrocentric or Eurocentric? What then are the materials they should be exposed to, and in what order and perspective? Who should be interpreting that material to them, an African or non-African? If African, what kind of African? One who has internalised the colonial world outlook or one attempting to break free from the inherited slave consciousness?'

(wa Thiong'o 1986)

What must decolonial education do?

> Education is a means of knowledge about ourselves.... After we have examined ourselves, we radiate outwards and discover peoples and worlds around us. With Africa at the centre of things, not existing as an appendix or a satellite of other countries and literatures, things must be seen from the African perspective... All other things are to be considered in their relevance to our situation and their contribution towards understanding ourselves. In suggesting this, we are not rejecting other streams, especially the western stream. We are only clearly mapping out the directions and perspectives the study of culture and literature will inevitably take in an African university.'
>
> (wa Thiong'o 1986)

Nyerere's take:

> The education provided by Tanzania for the students of Tanzania must serve the purposes of Tanzania. It must encourage the growth of the socialist values we aspire to. It must encourage the development of a proud, independent and free citizenry which relies upon itself for its own development, and which knows the advantages and the problems of co-operation. It must ensure that the educated know themselves to be an integral part of the nation and recognize the responsibility to give greater service the greater the opportunities they have had.'
>
> (Nyerere 1967)

What is the condition to attain a decolonised education system? We have presented some elements of what a different education system could look like. But what is clear is that before a new and decolonised education is possible, there must be a process of decolonisation of society itself. This takes us back to the question of the university, if the university, is à la Marx and Althusser, an Ideological State Apparatus, which 'contribute[s] to the same result: the reproduction of the relations of production, i.e. of capitalist relations of exploitation.' (Althusser 1971: 154) If we accept this proposition, then it stands to reason that one could not possibly decolonise the university outside of decolonising society itself. The important point to stress here is that Althusser is one with Nyerere.

Karl Marx is emphatic about the place of ideas and this, we argue, is emblematic of the university. In the German ideology, Marx confirms both Nyerere and Althusser on the place of education (the formal locus of ideas, of intellectual capital) as the preserver of a particular rule for a particular purpose. Marx argues:

> The ideas of the ruling class are in every epoch the ruling ideas, i.e. the class which is the ruling material force of society, is at the same time its ruling intellectual force. The class which has the means of material production at its disposal, has control at the same time over the means of mental production, so that thereby, generally speaking, the ideas of those who lack the means of mental production are subject to it. The ruling ideas are nothing more than the ideal expression of the dominant material relationships, the dominant material relationships grasped as ideas.'
>
> (Marx and Engels 1845)

From here, we can argue that the dominant ideas in colonial society are colonial (we have already established that SA is colonial despite the events of 1994). In a society like ours which is colonial, therefore, the dominant ideas reflect this reality. But where does this domination come from? According to Marx, the class which has the economic power also controls the cultural reproduction (ideas, values, desires, identities, etc.). Here we do not quarrel with Marx, because essentially, the 'means of material production' rest for us in the sin after the original sin (after slavery comes colonialism, but it was slavery which made colonialism possible at the symbolic order level). Basically, we lost more than just land, and our reparations only begin with land. The white man and woman owes us everything they have!

Strategic and tactical dilemmas

We accept Althusser's move and include the university as an instance of the 'ideological state apparatus' which is essentially about the reproduction of the status quo. It's important to note that 'all' institutions of learning fall under this category irrespective of whether they are public or private. This observation presents an immediate tactical and strategic dilemma for the student movement which has been arguing for access as one of the key demands of 'decolonisation'.

This contradiction is based on the reality that the call for access means access to the means of reproducing the colonial status quo. The demand for #AfrikaansMustFall is a perfect example of this dilemma. Black students are pushing for the use of English as part of 'decolonisation', but English linked more closely to Cecil John Rhodes than Afrikaans. We have a bizarre situation where, on the one hand, we are calling for #RhodesMustFall, but on the other hand, we are fighting to force universities to use the language of Rhodes to facilitate our access. This demand, if not properly reflected on, is of dubious value to decolonisation and, can be argued, shows the limitation of decolonising the university in a colonial society.

English is the expression of the economic dominant group/class and therefore to get access to the means of sustenance, one has to hold cultural capital (English) as a key to the house of relative privilege. English is a key to escape blackness in a sense. What has occurred here is that English has expanded itself into a hegemonic position as a language of generalised power (social, political and economic, more importantly as language of knowledge production).

Afrikaans, on the other hand, has maintained the laager mentality of its own affairs and an own identity. (It can be argued with a bit of tilting of the head that English has adopted the 'Indirect Rule' motto towards the end of last century in SA, whilst Afrikaans was trapped in 'Direct Rule'.) That's why we see Orania as a symbol of Afrikaner stubbornness. But English power is diffused, it is everywhere and, therefore, nowhere. The black body and soul has become the carrier of Rhodes' dream.

The first 'multiracial' schools, just before 1994, were part of the assimilation project of the English section of the settler colonialists. Blacks or more correctly, 'Mandela's children' were English-speaking blacks. This idiom grew of course at the back of the 1976 students' uprising in revolt against Afrikaans as the symbolic representation of Afrikaaner arrogance. English presented itself as the friend of the natives. In a hierarchical society based on the values of a powerful minority, for blacks, English became the means to access both the culture and economic spheres of the Anglo-American economic hegemonic forces.

If English gave some access, when one walked into an Afrikaans campus, one was excluded. It didn't help that the Boer children as usual performed more overtly the power of their economic status via belligerent expressions of their 'kultuur'. The English colonise by assimilation; the Afrikaaner has not yet understood the game as they are newcomers. The conundrum of Afrikaans, of course, is that it is an indigenous language which was stolen with land.

Steve Biko shows that both Afrikaans and English have a problematic relationship with Blacks:

> We have a society here in South Africa which recognises in the main two languages, English and Afrikaans as official languages. These are languages that you have to use

at school, at university I mean, or in pursuit of any discipline when you are studying as a black man. Unfortunately, the books you read are in English, English is a second language to you; you have probably been taught in a vernacular especially during these days of Bantu education up to Standard 6; you grapple with the language to JC and matric, and before you conquer it you must apply it now to learn a discipline at university. As a result, you never quite catch everything that is in a book; you certainly understand the paragraph, (I mean I am talking about the average man now, I am not talking about exceptional cases) you understand the paragraph but you are not quite adept at reproducing an argument that was in a particular book, precisely because of your failure to understand certain words in the book. This makes you less articulate as a black man generally, and this makes you more inward-looking; you feel things rather than say them, and this applies to Afrikaans as well.'

(Biko 1978:106–7)

Biko here indicates the power carried by language and the psychosocial impact it has on the outsider to the language. As we can readily see, the black who comes to study any discipline through the medium of English is already disadvantaged. The impact is to make the black feel mediocre/inadequate with negative psychological results. As he says, one is made 'less articulate' in a world where language, naming, speaking is the first act of self-realisation. In the context of the 1960s (before SASO), blacks then would surrender leadership to whites who came across as speaking beings as opposed to blacks who were merely mumbling in a language of the oppressor (so give the task of speaking for us to the sons and daughters of the coloniser). Language exclusion disempowers.

Biko also reconsidered that, whilst the two languages were cultural weapons of the two settler stock, there was, however, a significant difference between the two. For Biko, the alienating impulses of English were much more significant/pernicious than those of Afrikaans, because 'Afrikaans is essentially a language that has developed here, and I think in many instances in its idiom, it relates much better to African languages; but English is completely foreign' (Biko 1978:107). Without going into the economy of numbers (there are more people speaking Afrikaans than English in SA, unconfirmed stats suggest over 50 per cent of the population has some access to isiZulu), the point we wish to highlight is that Afrikaans like land is stolen property. Like the land that we crisscross in this country but which is estranged from us, so too is Afrikaans. It's ours, but no longer of us. Just like land, it's in the hands of the colonisers. The call for decolonisation of land ownership is conterminous with the decolonisation of Afrikaans itself. Like the land, it must be returned! for now, like our land, it is used against us.

So, would calling for indigenous languages be the solution?

It must be remembered that indigenous languages have themselves been used to entrench the colonial project. Today the most 'technically developed' indigenous languages are arguably both isiZulu and Setswana; this is thanks to the apartheid homeland system not a decolonising impulse (Mangope and Gatsha invested in these languages as instruments of white power, to serve tribal pride). Black languages have become languages of subjugation; this is because they are languages of the oppressed. The call for multilingualism and equitable attention to all languages (don't they say there are 12 or so official languages?) – this call is a fantasy that shall never be realised because the under-development of our languages is linked deeply to colonialism. As long as there is colonialism, indigenous languages shall remain marginal like the speakers of those languages.

This makes us pose the question, is the battle for decolonisation, or is it for integration? It would seem, even if it is not the intention of the student movement, any move to decolonise the university outside decolonising society can only lead to integration not obliteration of the colonial university as a colonial construct. In fact, a decolonised university would be a false enclave in the sea of colonial reality, where, if one steps into the University of Johannesburg whether as black student or workers, they would be 'beings with rights'. But as soon as they step outside the gates, they would be part of the black mass without rights or honour. This would be a false universe and deeply unethical. It is unethical because it would be generally resting on the perpetuation of the colonial mayhem just outside of its gates. It would not last.

Black academics want in!

We see the contradiction of decolonisation as integration plays itself out among black academics who are at once outsiders and insiders. As outsiders, they suffer racism and exclusion; as insiders they get their much-coveted professorships with each pressure point the student movement exerts. But this black professoriate is beholden to the university system. They want in, not the end. The consequences are that as in the Black Academics Caucus at UCT, when students sustained the militant struggle after rejecting the treacherous 0 per cent increase, the black academics wrote a petition of denunciation against black students in support of the establishment. Black academics gave Max Price the gift of legitimation and they delegitimised the students' militant struggles. The newly turned professor Xolela Mangcu was one of those who denounced the students (forgetting his professorship was given due to the students he was now denouncing). It felt a little bit like the story of kicking the step ladder away once you are on top.

A similar development occurred at Wits University. Prof Achille Mbembe was outed as a security and public relations advisory to Prof Adam Habib. Basically, the claim said, Mbembe had been advising Habib on how to deal with students through repression without losing face. In other words, how to bring the private security personnel on campus and blame students for it. It was a case of giving private state violence a human face through demonising students as agents of mindless violence (some Fanonian scholars are anti-Fanon). The consequences of these Mbembe moves have been real to students: some of them are suspended as we speak. Mbembe maintains that he stands with the students struggles just like Mangcu.

But their first loyalty is to the preservation of the colonial structure we call university, so any threat to the actual physical existence of the university turns them into soldiers of repression. They are fighting to maintain their false enclave in the middle of a colonial rot. This articulation begs the question: Must we then not struggle for access, etc.?

Here, I want to return to Althusser regarding a different move. First, the struggles for fees falling, ending outsourcing, representivity, syllabi transformation and institutional cultural change must not be seen as an end in themselves. And certainly, these struggles need to strive to transcend the university. These struggles must be seen as instances in the larger societal struggle for change. In other words, the upheaval at the university should not limit its tasks to the 'decolonisation' of the university, but must see the struggle at the university as part of igniting a larger battle for ending colonialism because in any event, there can be no decolonised university in a colonial society. Here, the understanding is that the 'native elite' Sartre spoke about in the 'golden age' is now rebelling against the very system that seeks to subject them. This is possible, but such rebellion is not what the university is about; it is going against the intentions of the ruling classes with regard to the institution of higher learning as an instance of the 'state ideological apparatus'.

A good example of this development is how Forte Hare produced both servants of the system including the leaders of the homeland system and at the same time rebels such as Robert Mugabe, Robert Sobukwe, Oliver Tambo and Nelson Mandela, side by side with the likes of Lennox Sebe,

Kaizer Mathanzima, Mangosuthu Buthelezi, Lucas Mangope, etc. It is instructive to note that these characters were more or less all on the same campus at the same time. They were contemporaries and, therefore, must have been exposed to the same intellectual firmament.

The majority came out as expected, they vied to be administrators of the colonial and apartheid system. However, there was a good layer which chose to go against the teachings of the university and generally rebelling at great personal cost. On his message in celebration of the centenary of Forte Hare, its current Vice Chancellor, chose to acknowledge only one aspect of the truth about Fort Hare, he erased the alumni which were loyal servants of the apartheid monster. You would think from his biased list of alumni he is proud of, that in the passages of that institution never walked the young brilliant minds who became the leaders of the apartheid Bantustans. Here is Prof Mvuyo Tom:

> Known as the 'crucible of African leadership' and the alma mater of anti-apartheid struggle figures such as the great ZK Matthews, Nelson Mandela, Robert Sobukwe, Oliver Tambo and Govan Mbeki, the University of Fort Hare continues to spawn leaders in every sector of society. It is the only southern African university to have produced five heads of states: Nelson Mandela of South Africa, Yusuf Lule of Uganda, Robert Mugabe of Zimbabwe, Ntsu Mokhehle of Lesotho and Sir Seretse Khama of Botswana.'
>
> (Mvuyo 2014)

We see the same pattern of the university being a contradictory zone of producing loyal servants of colonialism, alongside rebels, repeating itself in the early '70s with ASO leaders leaving university in solidarity with Abram Tiro who was expelled for his great speech in 1972 as SRC president during a graduation ceremony at Turfloop University. Tiro's speech (1972) itself shows the general attitude of the student movement towards power. The conditions of the student life were directly linked to the apartheid monster outside the gate of the university.

Tiro's rousing speech is worth referring to, notably his emphatic conclusion. This speech cost Tiro his life, when the apartheid state sent a letter bomb to him in Botswana. Tiro did not come out as the system expected of its products. Listen to Tiro:

> The challenge to every Black graduate in this country lies in the fact that the guilt of all wrongful actions in South Africa, restriction without trial, repugnant legislation, expulsions from schools, rests on all those who do not actively dissociate themselves from and work for the eradication of the system breeding such evils.
>
> (Tiro 1972)

Tiro also has a message to the supporters of apartheid; we must remember this is 1972 and in attendance are the apartheid seconded top management of the university:

> To those who wholeheartedly support the policy of apartheid I say: Do you think that the White minority can willingly commit political suicide by creating numerous states which might turn out to be hostile in the future?
>
> (Tiro 1972)

Then he speaks directly to the graduates:

> We Black graduates, by virtue of our age and academic standing are being called upon to bear greater responsibilities in the liberation of our people. ... The magic

> story of human achievement gives irrefutable proof that as soon as nationalism is awakened among the intelligentsia, it becomes the vanguard in the struggle against alien rule.
>
> (Tiro 1972)

Tiro calls the black graduate to arms:

> Of what use will be your education if it is not linked with the entire continent of Africa? It is meaningless.
>
> (Tiro 1972)

Already, we know that around 1996, big struggles to end outsourcing were had with the specific instance of one led by Prof Adam Habib at the University of Durban Westville. That particular struggle was sufficiently successful in ending outsourcing. But it was not to last. Large-scale struggles by SASCO and allied workers' organisations dominated the discourse of 'transformation' in the early '90s up to the end of that decade. What those struggles ultimately produced were black VCs and now even that trend is being reversed.

What is to be done?

What we need to work out is how the workers, students, unemployed youths, the landless, homeless, victims of racism and black professionals all link up as warriors of decolonial praxis. Chinweizu is very direct about the immediate enemy: 'For independence [decolonisation] to be attained, the struggle needs to be resumed to overthrow the black colonialists – the black comprador managers of what Nkrumah called neo-colonialism' (Chinweizu 2010).

We shall return to this call later, when we lump together the neo-colonialists and their handlers. In the next section, let's deal with the student movement as it is developing, its flow and ebbs, its promises and possible disappointments, its hopes and possibilities in a snapshot.

There are three discernible moments in the student movement which help us make sense of its true nature, limitations and possibilities. These moments correspond to main events which define the movement.

1. The decolonisation moment, at the inauguration of the Rhodes Must Fall movement based at UCT. The decolonisation moment asked fundamental questions about the nature of South African society, without necessarily posing policy directives about what must be done. It was the moment that made radical questioning possible. Soon, the statue of Rhodes dragged the whole thing into the 1994 compromised solution and the place of the figure of Mandela in it. It becomes increasingly difficult to explain the Mandela–Rhodes nexus as acceptable. This moment presented the most promising possibility to pose the question of the nature of South African society now and in the possible future. Suddenly, everything was open to be questioned, and certain actions which a few years back were not possible now become possible.
2. #FeeMustFall (FMF) moment is associated with Wits University and a strange alliance between EFF and the Progressive Youth Alliance (PYA). This moment was a retreat from the big question into the 'bread and butter issues' of fees and of outsourcing. If the first moment

asked the question of the nature of the society, the second moment was about access to what is available – it was more of an economic deterministic moment. 'Decolonisation' opened the possibility of questioning and explaining, the FMF moment was more about meeting certain achievable demands within the system. Many developments that need further elaboration require critical examination, such as how, when the RMF rebels were threatening to enter parliament after having broken the main parameters, the FMF WITS/UJ contingency was found wondering what to do. When the contingency was pointed to Luthuli house, it balked, only giving in when there was a clear break manifesting in the student mass. Then, the amazing development of a mass protest organised by the ruling party to the union building. Anyway, the important question is that the FMF moment was the moment of concrete demands achievable within the current set-up. In a sense 'decolonisation' as a fundamental proposition took a back seat.

3. Imbokodo ANC Doek moment. This moment in many ways facilitated the capture of the student movement through the ruse of 'lack of women representation' in the leadership of the FMF campaign. Of course, unlike RMF which was at its onset much clearer about the question of feminism and queer politics, the RMF at Wits showed little understanding of the dynamics as two male leaders emerged as the symbolic representation of the movement. The women responded to this real issue through facilitating capture of the movement by the ruling party which has been very concerned about how to control and tame the movement.

Decolonisation sans Fanon's chapter 1?

Now we come to the end we must ask the question more directly, what is decolonisation? What are the theoretical contours that help us define its DNA? It has become fashionable to have a whole discussion on 'decolonisation' without reference to Fanon's most important chapter which deals with this matter head on. In fact, Fanon is being mobilised against Fanon. There is little doubt that Fanon is the foremost scholar of decolonisation. But Fanon is broad and complex. Academics associated with 'decolonisation' such as Prof Mbembe have been carefully crafting a perspective of Fanon as a pacifist humanist by selectively reading his last chapter in *Black Skins White Masks* (Fanon [1952] 2008), or in *Wretched of the Earth* (Fanon 1965) we have been subjected to the Pitfalls of National Consciousness.

If we really want to hear Fanon on decolonisation, we have to go back to 'Concerning Violence!' (Chapter 1, Fanon 1965).

Decolonisation needs to be decolonised. The RMF moment has created a new fad. To be relevant one has to associate themselves with 'decolonisation'; it has become the password to legitimation of all manner of things including race denialism. One doesn't have to believe in decolonisation, one just needs to profess it to get a gig. It has been a marvel to watch how – from literature to food – we have been inundated by decolonisation without decolonisation.

I was taken aback when some known race denialist also jumped onto the 'decolonisation' band wagon. People who have been writing books that reproduced racist anthropological type material also turned towards decolonisation. It has been weird and fascinating to see the distance between the literature produced by the new converts to decolonisation and their professed stand on decolonisation. There is no evidence that SA literature post-1994 has contributed in any way to decolonisation. Perhaps we should wait for the next few books.

Anyway, avoiding 'Concerning Violence' is to avoid the meat and soul of decolonisation. So, we are in a situation where we need to separate fake decolonisers from authentic decolonisers. We need to develop some intellectual and praxis protocols to guide us in this venture of exposure. I wish to add to the list two main consideration as a start. First, anyone who speaks about decolonisation without reference or taking a position on the first chapter of *Wretched of the Earth* must be dismissed as a charlatan. Secondly, anyone who writes long tracts on decolonisation without reference to the return of the land is not part of the family. It is in chapter one where Fanon defines more clearly what decolonisation is and links it with the land question.

This takes us back to the university and its function. Land theft and a colonial project driven by violence that accounts only to violence found intellectual justification in the arena of knowledge production and ideas. The university, as we recall à la Marx, is that zone of fortifying the ideas of the dominant class. Crudely, the university plays the same role as the one played by the clergy during the era of Divine Rights of Kings. The oppressed classes were kept oppressed not just by violence but the state ideological apparatus of the Church which said oppression is God's will. Basically, if you believe in God you have to accept his will on earth and not only bear your burden but actually defend serfdom. First is God, then the King, the Nobility, then the Clergy and the masses are down out there in the cold, super-exploited. Things have not changed fundamentally, it is only that bit of sophistication has been added. Just like the 'divine rights of kings', capitalism today, in the plethora of knowledge production sites, is accepted as the natural order of things. The consequence is that we are invited to decolonise so long as capitalism and all its attendant structures remain. This is decolonisation that doesn't end colonialism.

Essentially, accepting this proposition is to accept colonialism and racism because one cannot extricate capitalism from its anti-black foundations. The dominant ideas go to notions of property protection, human rights, democracy, rule of law and a whole raft of ideological schema to avoid addressing the question of freedom as a question of land and violence, because oppression is ultimately a question of violence and land.

So what is Fanon's notion of decolonisation?

The first rule of decolonisation is to embrace 'disorder' or the spirit of Tshwane University of Technology. Fanon teaches us: 'Decolonization, which sets out to change the order of the world, is, obviously, a program of complete disorder' (Fanon 1965: 36). Decolonisation admits or rather is sanctioned by ending dialogue between the colonised and coloniser:

> But it [decolonization] cannot come as a result of magical practices, nor of a natural shock, nor of a friendly understanding. Decolonization, as we know, is a historical process: that is to say that it cannot be understood, it cannot become intelligible nor clear to itself except in the exact measure that we can discern the movements which give it historical form and content. Decolonization is the meeting of two forces, opposed to each other by their very nature.
>
> (Fanon 1965: 36)

Here, the two forces, Black and White are facing each other through a process of hostility and incapacity to communicate across the Manichean divide of the coloniser and the colonised:

> The natives' challenge to the colonial world is not a rational confrontation of points of view. It is not a treatise on the universal, but the untidy affirmation of an original idea propounded as an absolute. The colonial world is a Manichean world.
>
> (Fanon 1965:41)

The contradiction, to borrow from Mao, is 'antagonistic' and can only be resolved by conflict that must play itself out publicly and physically to heal bodies and souls. Sartre understands this; Mbembe is repulsed by it. Fanon celebrates the process of bloody birth: 'Decolonization is the veritable creation of new men. But this creation owes nothing of its legitimacy to any supernatural power; the thing which has been colonized becomes man during the same process by which it frees itself' (Fanon 1965: 36).

What is this process? In the hands of liberals and others who want revolution without revolution, change must happen through dialogue and workshops. This year we have been inundated with 'anti-racism conferences'. In the hands of Fanon and his true followers, there is a task we must face without flinching, a truth hard to swallow, a black blazing flame untold; Fanon gives words to it:

> The naked truth of decolonization evokes for us the searing bullets and bloodstained knives which emanate from it. For if the last shall be first, this will only come to pass after a murderous and decisive struggle between the two protagonists.
>
> (Fanon 1965: 37)

Fanon is pointed about the condition needed to gain victory for the colonised, the native: 'can only triumph if we use all means to turn the scale, including, of course, that of violence.'

No, this is not symbolic violence, this is violence violence. Frank Wilderson says 'Fanon explains everything'; there is some great truth in this, because, there is a period prior to the great reckoning, which operates as an orgy of violence for no reason. The Native against itself. In Fanon, this is a response to the colonial pressure cooker but also a dress rehearsal:

> The settler-native relationship is a mass relationship. The settler pits brute force against the weight of numbers. He is an exhibitionist. His preoccupation with security makes him remind the native out loud that there he alone is master. The settler keeps alive in the native an anger which he deprives of outlet; the native is trapped in the tight links of the chains of colonialism. But we have seen that inwardly the settler can only achieve a pseudo petrification. The native's muscular tension finds outlet regularly in bloodthirsty explosions – in tribal warfare, in feuds between septs, and in quarrels between individuals.
>
> (Fanon 1965: 53)

The first point of the authentic decolonial scholarship, practice and commitment is the acceptance of the violent nature of colonialism and the need to respond to it by any means necessary. It is in this act of emancipation that the deeper aspects of liberation are atoned, the psychological and spiritual wounds. For, it is as Sartre so coldly states, the truth of Fanon, which the SA university-based Fanonian scholars avoid. In the famous preface to *Wretched* he recalls the call of Fanon:

> The rebel's weapon is the proof of his humanity. For in the first days of the revolt you must kill: to shoot down a European is to kill two birds with one stone, to destroy an oppressor and the man he oppresses at the same time: there remain a dead man, and a free man; the survivor, for the first time, feels a national soil under his foot.
>
> (Sartre in Fanon 1965: 22)

The second key index of authentic decolonisation, is land return by any means necessary (excluding any payment for it). Fanon is absolutely clear that the fundamental question of colonialism and decolonisation is *land*: 'For a colonized people, the most essential value, because the most concrete, is first and foremost the land: the land which will bring them bread and, above all, dignity' (Fanon 1965: 44). The goings-on in society, in the boardroom, in the senates and councils, in the lecture room, at church and the media, all of it comes down to the land question. The land was stolen and must be returned! There is no decolonisation outside of this truth. All efforts of decolonisation must of necessity be mobilised towards the resolution of the land question. The first act towards this is to set the terms of the crime straight. Colonialism is essentially a process based on the second crime, land theft.

In conclusion, I invite all black people who really wish to free themselves – those who want to decolonise for real – I invite them to return to Fanon's first chapter in *Wretched of the Earth*: 'Concerning Violence!' It is instructive that the black academics are already withdrawing out of sight of the mere charred remains of pockets of property on their campuses. They are nauseated and embarrassed by the barbarism of violence of black students. Our brothers and sisters are not yet ready for decolonisation.

Bibliography

Achebe, Chinua. (1959). *Things Fall Apart*. New York: Anchor Books.

Althusser, Louis (1971). 'Ideology and ideological state apparatuses.' In: *Lenin and Philosophy and Other Essays* (127–86). London: Monthly Review.

Biko, Steve. (1978). *I Write What I Like*. Johannesburg: Heinemann Publishers.

Chinweizu. (2009). *Black Colonialists: the Root of Africa's Trouble*. Johannesburg: Sankara Publishing. (Frank Talk #4).

Fanon, Frantz. (1965). *The Wretched of the Earth*. New York: Grove.

Marx, Karl, and Frederick Engels. ([1845] 1994). 'Ruling class and ruling ideas.' In: John Storey (ed.) *Cultural Theory and Popular Culture: A Reader, Volume 1*. Harlow: Pearson Education Limited.

Mvuyo, Tom. (2014) *University of Fort Hare: Celebrating 100 Years* [Speech]. Retrieved from: http://www.ufh.ac.za/MediaCentre/News/Pages/UniversityFortHareCelebrating100Years.aspx0

Nyerere, Julius. (1967). *Education for Self-reliance*. Policy Booklet. see: www.swaraj.org/shikshantar/resources_nyerere.html

Tiro, Onkgopotse. (1972). *Graduation Speech at the University of the North*. 29 April 1972. Retrieved from: http://www.sahistory.org.za/archive/graduation-speech-onkgopotse-tiro-university-north-29-april-1972

wa Thiong'o, Ngũgĩ. (1986). *Decolonising the Mind: The Politics of Language and Literature in Africa*. London: James Curry.

PART V

Alternative global imaginaries

28
INTRODUCTION

Part I of this Handbook introduced alternative points of departure that helped to de-normalise the postcolonial imaginaries in Part II that form the quotidian lexicon of global politics. Subsequent Parts focused on the substance of struggles over colonial legacies, especially as they pertained to the uses and abuses of the postcolonial state and the land question. In this last Part we ask: where do we go from here? Some answers have been offered in the different chapters in the previous Parts, providing the reader with glimpses of how global politics can be done and thought of differently with/after postcolonial critique. In this Part, we have curated a set of chapters that explicitly seek to reconstruct global politics beyond postcolonial deconstruction.

In this final Part, we especially wish to foreground the consideration that alternative global imaginaries do – and perhaps need to – take on different forms, even when they are connected via a general anti-colonial ethos. In recent literature, this position has been articulated via the work of Nicaraguan liberation theologist and poet Ernesto Cardenal as a call to dwell in a 'pluriverse', that is, a world where many worlds are possible. We hasten to add, though, that even if different imaginaries are grounded in specific ethics, analytics and even cosmologies, all are disposed towards – and can be oriented towards – commonly received aspects of global politics such as human security, diplomacy, citizenship, solidarity and justice. In other words, an accounting of and dwelling in and between alternative global imaginaries should not be mistaken as a retreat from the political. Rather, we are calling for a radical deepening of engagement via an acknowledgement of the fundamental imbrication of coloniality within the political.

Finally, the chapters in this concluding Part illustrate how the reconstruction of global politics through alternative global imaginaries can – and perhaps must – operate at different levels: in the academic fields that we engage with (or not), in the registers we deploy, the sources we consult, and the varied purposes we imbue knowledge cultivation with. We in no way wish to disavow the utility of the analytical and logical, but at the same time we refute the all-too-easy categorical segregation of those registers from the poetic, literary, artistic and spiritual in the pursuit of rigorous scholarship or teaching of global politics. In this respect, these alternative imaginaries also invoke, along with understanding, outrage, loss, love, healing and repair. Ultimately, then, the chapters in the Part can be read as a call to think despite, against, besides or beyond coloniality. They provide insights and inspirations for orienting towards a global politics upon which the postcolonial no longer has a viable claim.

We start with a chapter that considers alternative global imaginaries within our own teaching and learning strategies. This is especially important in the field of International Relations (IR). For, as many have remarked upon, as anthropology was to nineteenth-century empire, so IR has been to twentieth-century American empire. In other words, and as demonstrated in Part II on popular postcolonial imaginaries, the concepts commonly deployed in IR often confirm and justify the strictures of postcolonial politics, even if – at least after the Second World War – its key interlocutors do not directly speak the language of colonial rule and imperial administration. In Chapter 29, L.H.M. Ling draws attention to these features of IR in the form of a play about Wanda, a first-year doctoral student in IR. Wanda is confronted with a professor who can only conceive of IR through Hobbes' depiction of the State of Nature as 'solitary, poor, nasty, brutish, and short'. Wanda, however, seeks to draw upon alternative resources, which she receives as she dreams. By this story and medium Ling introduces us to a Daoist conception of global politics.

In Chapter 30, Giorgio Shani engages with one of the most influential 'alternative' frameworks with which to conceive of and practice global politics: human security. Shani seeks to work positively with the human security framework in so far as it has sought to mitigate against the worst excesses of state sovereignty in the postcolonial world, particularly in post-conflict societies or transitional democracies. Shani is also, however, attuned to critics of human security who point out that the ideal of 'humanity' cannot be assumed a priori but must be understood from within different cultural traditions. Shani's solution is to work with – rather than against – the role that religion and identity plays. Specifically, he wishes to permit the articulation of different conceptions of human security in vernacular terms, which re-embeds individuals deracinated by the pernicious effects of neo-liberal globalisation and subject to repression by 'secular' authoritarian rule into 'cultural' communities. Shani therefore argues that human security can only be furthered in a multicultural world through a sustained engagement with the 'post-secular', recognising the multiple religio-cultural contexts in which human dignity is embedded. Such a 'post-secular conception' of human security is more suited to an increasingly 'post-western' world where the rise of the BRICS, and the resurgence of political Islam in particular, constitute a powerful challenge to the main institutions and values of an 'international society' dominated by the West.

Chapter 31 addresses another fundamental question, especially for normative IR theory: is it possible to think about non-hegemonic encounters between peoples in a world fraught with inequality, climate crises and rising intolerance of various kinds? Some strands of mainstream IR theory associated with the liberal position have always stressed the need for dialogue and cooperation. Nonetheless, Aparna Devare argues that such approaches often apprehend the 'Other' as a legitimate equal only if she is brought or elevated to a higher temporal scale. In other words, Devare considers the liberal invocation to dialogue across difference to be framed, nonetheless, by the civilisation and racialised hierarchies of coloniality. Plurality is not something to be respected or accepted but becomes a project of the aggrandisement of the liberal Self. Alternatively, Devare turns to Mohandas Gandhi and Rabindranath Tagore, two well-known Indian thinkers, in order to further extend the debate on dialogic cross-cultural encounters in IR. The chapter argues that Gandhi and Tagore were able to glean the violence inherent within the liberal kind of 'transformative' cross-cultural encounter. And their universalist dispositions allowed them to incorporate the colonial experience as not just inflicting violence on the Other through these transformations, but also the violence being done to the Self in the process.

As L.H.M. Ling's chapter suggests, some who work in IR theory have increasingly turned to the power of narrative as a way of framing and making sense of global politics. In this respect, the idea that global politics is fundamentally constituted as an anarchical world of competing states can better be understood less as an ontological claim and more as a cosmological narration of human genesis, found for example, in Thomas Hobbes and, differently, in John Locke. Situating themselves vis-à-vis this 'narrative turn', Rahel Kunz and Archana Thapa devote Chapter 32 to an engagement with a collection of stories, *Telling a Tale*. These stories highlight the diverse ways in which Nepali girls and women from various social backgrounds navigate complex social structures such as gender, caste, religion, marital status and ethnicity and how these have shaped their identities. Kunz and Thapa narrate how their interlocutors resist, subvert and move beyond social norms to create their own alternative ways of knowing and being in the world as they 'move into modernity'. The chapter argues that these stories help to disrupt conventional knowledge on gender in Nepal and fixed notions of the subject of 'the Nepali woman'. While these stories might, at first glance, appear to be located far away from the arenas of global politics, they nonetheless address two key issues at the heart of postcolonial critique: the ways in which coloniality has shaped, and continues to shape, gendered forms of knowledge production and subjectivity formation, even in a country that was never formally colonised, such as Nepal.

In Chapter 33, Hisham Aidi also reconstructs global politics through a narrative of a supposedly 'provincial' site when he recounts the passing through of the musical and literary, scholarly and activist greats in the city of Cairo. Aidi re-imagines the sites and substances of geo-politics by de-centring states and diplomats and placing to the fore an alternative question asked by African-American historian Manning Marable: 'How can the authentic history of black people be brought to life?' Aidi argues that Malcolm X is a powerful figure through which to seek an answer. Indeed, Marable wrote a controversial biography of the famous activist: *Malcolm X: A Life of Reinvention*. And, Aidi points out, if anyone could reawaken an interest in black history and reignite black internationalism it would be Malcolm and his riveting story. The chapter points out that Malcolm's life – and Marable's book – have had a jolting effect among youth beyond America's border. One important prediction that Marable made and, which this chapter dwells on in its journaling of twentieth-century Cairo, is that Malcolm's legacy will be increasingly shaped less by the American nation and more so by Islam.

It is not only through narrative that alternative global imaginaries can be gleaned. Poetic registers and even performance art can yield ways of thinking and doing global politics otherwise. For some years now, Alanna Lockward has been curating a series of meetings entitled Black Europe Body Politics (BEBOP) which bring intellectuals into intimate conversation with performance artists to cultivate ways in which the wounds of coloniality might be healed. In Chapter 34, Lockward turns this healing imperative towards the relationship between Haiti and the Dominican Republic and their respective cultures. The emergence of these two polities has been canonised by their chroniclers in such a way as to assume a natural splitting process: an anarchical and black Haiti differentiated from a more civilised and less black Dominican Republic. And yet, as Lockward is at pains to point out, the two polities are absolutely interdependent, sharing one island. In this chapter, artistic practices are mobilised as resources through which to heal the coloniality of being-sensing and thinking in the island and its diasporas around the seeds of a shared humanity. These seeds are as present as the shared wounds. By re-interpreting socio-political misconceptions across racialised class boundaries and filling historical vacuums using performance art as a medium, Lockward demonstrates how artists can facilitate much needed curative spaces in the island and beyond.

In the final chapter, Denize LeDeatte mobilises her artistic register to address Britain's hypocritical love affair with the memory of its colonial past. For many, reminds LeDeatte, these memories will be different to those of the national narrative. How to make these other memories resonate? The stakes are high. For LeDeatte apprehends transatlantic slavery and the brutal plantation system as everybody's history. Hence, without repairing that shared legacy, the damage to the fabric of humanity will simply continue to deepen. The arts, argues LeDeatte, provide a mechanism to balance the dominant narrative of academic history, which has evolved into 'academic genocide' and in that process, has prohibited a more full rendition of the human story that is exemplary of the Atlantic 'trade'. This chapter narrates the story of 'African Violet', a body of artwork that is LeDeatte's artistic contribution towards the development of a language for debating Africa and its Diaspora *by* Africa and its Diaspora. 'African Violet' explores the historic and contemporary landscape of Britain which gave birth to her very existence. While rooted in circumstances some of which are beyond her control, 'African Violet' nonetheless encompasses aspects of the universal, including how poverty and fear of the unknown impact upon compassion.

29
WANDA'S DREAM
Daoist world politics in five acts

L.H.M. Ling

CAST

(in order of appearance)

WANDA..................................An African-American doctoral student in IR
LIBRARIAN........................... .An ancient with a laughing face
KING.....................................A young man with South Asian features
PRIESTESS...............................A young woman with Himalayan features
SPIRITS..................................Ghosts who had lived as Vietnamese women during the Vietnam/American War
STUDENTS..............................Cohorts in Wanda's IR class
KILLER MILLER.........................Wanda's IR Professor

ACT I:[1]

REACTION

(Yin)

[Wanda, an African-American woman in her late 20s, is sitting in a tiny, book-laden office.[2] It belongs to the ancient librarian with a laughing face. Wanda is drenched from the thrashing wind and rain outside, shown through the library's large windows behind them.

The ancient librarian gives Wanda a steaming cup of tea.]

LIBRARIAN: Here, this will help.
WANDA: Thanks so much. (She shyly takes the cup. The Librarian opens a tin of cookies and offers the contents to her. She takes a cookie and visibly relaxes.) Thanks!
LIBRARIAN: You OK? (He eyes her with concern.)
WANDA: Yeah, sure…

LIBRARIAN: Sure?

WANDA: Well, school could be less…that is, more…(She searches for the right word.)

LIBRARIAN: Ah, intellectual troubles!

WANDA: How'd you know? (Wanda can't help exclaiming through the cookie she's munching. The ancient librarian nonchalantly flicks off the bits that land on his trousers.)

LIBRARIAN: My dear, I'm a librarian. I know *everything*.

WANDA: I – I had a kind of nasty encounter with my professor just now. (She looks down, too full of mixed emotions to look the librarian in the eye.)

LIBRARIAN: Who was it?

WANDA: Miller from Political Science.

LIBRARIAN: Ah, Killer Miller. The graduate seminar on International Relations, right?

WANDA: You know it? (Wanda's eyes open widely.)

LIBRARIAN: Of course! It's famous for being tough.

WANDA: I don't mind it being tough. It's just that…

LIBRARIAN: It's OK. You can tell me. I'm like your local bartender. Everything goes in, nothing comes out.

WANDA: Well, it all started with Hobbes. You know, the one who wrote *The Leviathan*.

LIBRARIAN: Thomas Hobbes.

WANDA: Yeah, *him*. (She sighs.) Miller cited, yet again and without any kind of reflection, Hobbes' famous line about the State of Nature as 'solitary, poor, nasty, brutish, and short.' (She puts on the Professor's ponderous tone.)

'Since there is no world government or Global Leviathan, world politics is like a State of Nature. Those who recognize this are called Realists. They see the world not as they'd like it to be but as it *actually* is: that is, a ceaseless, unrelenting 'war of every man against every man.'

LIBRARIAN: What's wrong with this?

WANDA: It's all crap! (She almost spills her tea.)

Hobbes based his ideas on 17th-century European myths about the New World, written mostly by *conquistadores* and *padres*.[3] And what did they know about native life? All they wanted to do was to *conquer* the whole place and everyone in it![4] (Wanda takes a deep breath.)

In college, I majored in Indigenous Studies with a focus on North and South America.

We studied how life for the First Nations was anything but all about war. Sure, there were conflicts. But, more importantly, people learned how to cooperate with one another to survive – especially with Nature itself – precisely because life was so hard.[5]

But Miller dismissed me out of hand. (Wanda puts on the same tone.)

'This is a class on International Relations, *not* Indigenous Studies!'

(Wanda crumples in her chair.)

LIBRARIAN: Seems to me you have a good argument there. (He smiles kindly.)

You might consider presenting it to Professor Miller. I'm sure it won't be the first time he's faced a tough question in class.

WANDA: But the tough question is to myself (her voice strains thinly): Is this what *I* want? Do I want to put myself through this kind of…this kind of…*violence*?

(The ancient Librarian listens carefully. He turns to his overcrowded desk and fishes out a dog-eared paperback. He tosses it to Wanda.)

LIBRARIAN: Here, this might help. (He picks up a few more books on his desk and piles them on the trolley.) Well, I'd better get going. I'm sure everything will work out! (He waves happily to Wanda, pushing his trolley deep into the library's unknown. Wanda looks at the paperback and reads the title out loud.)

WANDA: *Imagining World Politics: Sihar & Shenya, A Fable for Our Times.*[6] What's this? (A screen over the stage displays the book cover.)[7]

(She turns the book over and reads out loud the blurb on the back cover. The screen overhead highlights these words as Wanda reads them: *non-Western, feminist, transform, Eurocentric, masculinist, non-academic.*)

The book offers a non-Western feminist perspective on world politics and international relations. Creative, innovative, and challenging, it seeks completely to transform contemporary Eurocentric and masculinist IR by re-presenting it in non-Western, non-masculinist, and non-academic terms. This work is a unique and innovative resource for all students and scholars of international relations and world politics.

Hm!

(She flips to the middle of the book and exclaims in surprise.)

One of the characters is a Daoist immortal with a laughing face! (She reads:)

'He jumps from one time to another, one place to another, crossing the human and mythical worlds, playing with people and gods, making the world less predictable but also more fun.'

(Wanda pauses and looks up.)

Sounds like the trickster coyote![8]

(The screen overhead shows this character in animation. A faint beating of drums fills the background. Wanda mirrors the same movements on stage, prancing and mincing like the trickster coyote.

The stage darkens. One shaft of light shines on Wanda. Her voice takes on a dream-like quality.)

There's a Priestess who's an expert on trees.

(A beautiful woman enters. Aged around thirty, she has features indicating she's from the Himalayas. She wears a robe of flowing, white linen tied with three, small knots to one side. Her hair is wrapped atop her head with two, tiny strands of pearls. She holds a twig with leaves and appears to study it. Her gestures and stance evoke ballet.)

And there's a King who rules a small kingdom.

(A handsome young man, with South Asian features and in his late twenties, comes on stage next to the woman. He wears a simple, white riding tunic. He mimes getting off a horse. He is tall and lithe with a thinker's face. They greet each other by folding their hands together and bowing. Wanda continues telling the story.)

Each is *yin* to the other's *yang*.

(The King and the Priestess begin a *pas de deux*. They circle each other, gently and caringly.)

Finding the other within, they resonate with each other even though each is so different from the other.

(The pair begins to dance more vibrantly. Their hands, then their bodies, come into greater contact. The movements flow with their robes. He lifts her at one, exuberant point.)

That's why, also, they fall in love – even when it's forbidden.

(They stop. Her hands are on his shoulders. They look deeply into each other's eyes. Suddenly, wind machines off-stage blow at them strongly, forcing them apart. They try to resist but fail. They exit. Wanda continues the story.)
Karma.
(An ancient woman, with white hair wrapped in a bun, appears on stage with a large, wooden walking stick. She is also robed in flowing white. She recites in a singsong voice.)
When karma comes, it springs from a source eternal.
When karma is spent, that is also a course most natural.
(Lights out. When the lights come back on a second later, Wanda is sitting in the Librarian's chair. She wakes with a start. She had fallen asleep with the book open on her lap. She yawns while giving herself a nice, long stretch.)
Damn, I'm tired! Might as well go home. (She looks out the window.)
Good thing it's letting up. (She opens her backpack and shoves in the paperback.)
He won't mind. Besides, (she speaks to the book) I have a feeling I'll be needing you again.
(She swings the backpack on her shoulder and exits the stage. Lights dim. Curtains fall.)

ACT II

COUNTER-REACTION

(Yang)

Wanda is standing outside her studio apartment. It takes up half a colonial clapboard that has seen better days. She hears her phone *ping* and pulls it out of her purse. She looks at who's sending her a message and exclaims in delight.

WANDA: Auntie Ann![9] (She enters her apartment as the screen overhead shows a video of Auntie Ann with snippets of her life from Vietnam to America.)
(Once in, Wanda takes out her laptop from the backpack and places it on the long, wooden table where she does everything: eat, work, play, nap. The table is piled high with papers and books along with plates of half-eaten food, a jug of wilting flowers, mugs, and unopened bills. An unmade futon bed fronts the room. An old TV faces the bed. Wanda opens the laptop and turns it on as she sits at the table. She clicks on the email from Auntie Ann. The screen overhead lights up. It shows Auntie Ann speaking to Wanda as she reads the email.)

AUNTIE ANN: Hello, Sweetie! How are you? How are your studies? (Wanda groans theatrically.) I came across this computer game and thought you might enjoy it. (Auntie Ann leans in to the screen, speaking conspiratorially.) You need to relax now and then, you know! (She smiles brightly.) Can't wait for Thanksgiving! Will spoil you rotten with your favorite *pho*. Enjoy the game!

WANDA: Yummy...(She grabs a bottle of water from the fridge.)...Now what's this game she sent? (Wanda clicks and the screen overhead lights up.)

COMPUTER: *Empire.* (A deep, male voice with an upper-class British accent comes on.)

WANDA: Hm. Is this what Professor Miller is always talking about? *Real* IR?

(Images flash on screen with sweeping, dramatic music: Egypt's pyramids; China's Forbidden City; Rome's Coliseum; Istanbul's Blue Mosque; Lord Nelson on his horse in Trafalgar Square; the White House. The computer's voice continues.)

COMPUTER: Empires gave us Order and Stability, Civilization and Progress.

(Images: troops neatly lined up, libraries filled with books, researchers in white coats checking vials in laboratories.)

And these have given us what we prize today.

(Images: blindfolded Lady of Justice; children receiving vaccines; people turning on lights in their homes, offices, schools, hospitals; Bell's two-handed phone morphing into the iPhone; the horse-drawn carriage morphing into the latest sports car; astronauts bouncing slowly in outer space.)

But Empire is under assault.

(Images: massive protests on the streets of Seattle against the World Trade Organization; planes flying into the World Trade Center; Osama bin Laden celebrating in his cave; massive protests in Europe against the US invasion of Iraq; huddled, frightened girls kidnapped by Boko Haram; Buddhist monks rampaging against minorities in Myanmar; ISIS militants holding a gun to a hostage with their black flag flying in the background.)

We need to restore Empire! (The computer voice announces dramatically.)

GLOBAL EMPIRE:

A GREAT GAME FOR THOSE WHO DARE!

Do you dare?

WANDA: Yes! (She clicks on the computer eagerly.)

COMPUTER: Whom do I have the honor of addressing?

WANDA: How about 'Empress Wanda'? (She smiles broadly, typing it in.)

Hm, I like it!

COMPUTER: Welcome, Empress Wanda. Ready to conquer the world?

WANDA: Yes! (She types furiously.)

COMPUTER: Excellent. Let us review the rules. The game's goal is Global Empire.

(Screen overhead shows a spinning globe with all the continents on it.)

You win the Great Game of Global Empire by crushing all others through military power (image: fighter jets), economic wealth (image: $ sign), political dominance (image: a Roman eagle), and/or cultural superiority (image: books, computers, movie stars with cars or luxury perfumes).

Supremacy in one area gives you Mach I status (image overhead: small picture of Machiavelli); in two areas, Mach II (image: bigger picture of Machiavelli); in three, Mach III (even bigger picture of Machiavelli); and the ultimate honor, Mach IV (image: giant Machiavelli), when you achieve supremacy in all four areas.

Do you understand?

WANDA: Yes! (She exclaims while typing.)

COMPUTER: Good. The game turns on 'wild cards.' These come from a throw of dice. (Image overhead: a pair of dice.) Evens mean a positive wild card; odds, a negative one. The smaller the number, the greater the impact. A 12, for example, could give you a trade surplus (image: Δ% $); 10, an alliance (image: many flags flying together); and 2, peace accords (image: doves). An 11, on the other hand, could mean a sudden epidemic (image: Rx sign); 7, a financial crisis (image: broken piggy bank); and 1, a civil war (image: many guns firing). Success depends on how well you handle your own wild cards as well as those of your opponents.

Do you understand?

WANDA: Yes. (She is quieter, completely into the game.)

COMPUTER: Excellent. You can play the game with friends or by yourself. It doesn't matter. The logic remains the same. Set your parameters.

WANDA: How about US–India–China relations in the 21st century? (She muses gleefully.) Let's see how the West deals with the rising powers of the East![10]

(Several images show on the screen: Captain America for the US; Ming the Merciless for China; and Ganesh, the Elephant God, for India.

Hours pass. Lights dim in Wanda's apartment. It is now late into night. We see many depleted water bottles, now accompanied by an empty pizza carton and a large, open bag of Twizzlers, beside Wanda's laptop. She slumps back in her chair, raising her arms in celebration.)

Yay, I won! Everyone's destroyed except me. I'm top dog! (Wanda rises from her chair to give herself a nice, long stretch. She shakes a fist intensely at her laptop.) They may not love me but they will *fear* me.

(Image above: a giant picture of Machiavelli confirms Wanda's Mach IV status.)

Take that, Killer Miller!

(But somehow, her triumph rings hollow. Wanda flops onto her bed, staring upwards.)

Guess that's it. The *Great* Game.

(She turns on the TV to distract herself, switching channels with her remote until a movie comes on. The screen overhead shows the opening credits. It's Hollywood's 2005 remake of Graham Greene's 1955 novel, *The Quiet American*, starring Brendan Frazier as the earnest young American, 'Pyle,' and Michael Caine as the world-weary journalist, 'Fowler'. Wanda is impressed and stops to watch.)

The Quiet American! Good movie.

(Soon enough, her eyes grow heavy. They flutter then close. Her breathing rises and falls evenly. Lights out. Curtains down.)

ACT III

CO-IMPLICATIONS

(Yin-within-Yang, Yang-within-Yin)

Curtains rise, lights focus on three female Spirits.[11] Each sits on a large, round, white cushion on the floor. The cushions match the Spirits' flowing white robes but contrast starkly with their long, black hair, parted in the middle and falling straight to their waists. Each Spirit is busy with an activity while sitting on her cushion: one collects books spread around her and stacks them into neat piles; another rolls bandages into a bamboo basket; a third spins cotton yarn onto a loom.

Wanda stumbles in stage left, looking slightly dazed. She sits down and observes the Spirits.

They are watching snippets from *The Quiet American*, projected onto the screen overhead. These scenes flash by as in a broken memory. Finally, one scene settles on screen. It shows Pyle and Fowler holed up with two South Vietnamese snipers in a tower somewhere near the border. Caught in the crossfire, Pyle and Fowler must stay put. During a lull in the shooting, Pyle asks Fowler how Phuong, his mistress (whom Pyle secretly covets), would be spending her day. Fowler answers in tones of hushed reverie:

'This morning, she met a friend for elevenses at La Fontaine. Ice cream and the latest gossip. On her way home, she stopped at the market for fresh fish for dinner. And now, she's flipping through the pages of magazines, looking up photographs of the Royal Family and film stars, listening to Bach's "The Well-Tempered Clavier." I just got her started on Bach.'

Fowler smiles sheepishly but with pride. The scene freezes on this image.

SPIRIT #3: Yiii!! *Bọn Tây*[12] can really fantasize, can't they?

SPIRIT #1: You'd never know a war was on! 'Elevenses', 'La Fontaine', 'ice cream and the latest gossip', 'flipping through magazines', 'listening to Bach'. As if we had time or energy for any of that!

SPIRIT #3: And if we did have the time or energy, why would we care about *their* Royal Family, *their* film stars, *their* Bach? It's sad, really.

SPIRIT #1: I was an anti-colonial guerrilla in my day. (She raises her head proudly.)

SPIRIT #2: I was a doctor. (Her tone is more wistful.)

SPIRIT #1: A bourgeois! (She teases.)

SPIRIT #3: So were you! Of the three of us, I was the only one who came from an ordinary, peasant background.[13]

SPIRIT #1: Remember those early days?[14] Someone could be hanged or thrown in jail simply for coming from a landowning family or speaking French or English.[15] They were all seen as 'traitors.'

SPIRIT #2: But Uncle Hồ spoke French – like many leaders of the resistance![16]

SPIRIT #1: It must have been someone who spoke French *and* supported French rule.

SPIRIT #3: Or had the misfortune of offending someone...probably a former servant, now an officer in the resistance, who always hated the guy's superior ways!

SPIRIT #2: All this bickering about class background is now moot, isn't it? (She sighs.) Today, Việt Nam is united – in making money![17] Former so-called traitors are much needed for their language skills to negotiate with former so-called enemies. Multi-million dollar business deals are at stake!

SPIRIT #3: Ha! Don't think for a minute those class animosities are going away anytime soon. They're always among us, no matter what. The only thing the government can do is distract people with more opportunities to make money – just look at China! Old Mao must be rolling in his grave: 'Ah, I died too early. The Cultural Revolution was incomplete!'[18] (The Spirits nod and laugh at the idea of Mao groaning in his grave.)

SPIRIT #2: I'm sure Uncle Hồ is not far behind! (She jokes wickedly.) He, too, must be suffering from insomnia.

SPIRIT #1: Still (her eyes take on a distant look), I remember the fervor – that unmatched passion of our cause! (She pauses then continues.)

Bourgeois or peasant; man or woman; young, old, or middle aged; with many children in tow or single – we all wanted to free our homeland.[19] Millions of us forged muddy rapids, scaled high mountains,[20] dug tunnels, *lived* in tunnels,[21] not to mention hazarded homelessness, hunger, confinement, and torture. The French had overstayed their welcome by a hundred years. The Americans came for only twenty but managed to change everything with their camps, bombs, and napalm by day and cash, drugs, and sex by night.[22] But just like the Chinese before them,[23] none of these foreigners could last.[24]

SPIRIT #2: Alas, the killings and abuses happened on all sides.[25] No one remains innocent in a war, even after a truce.[26]

SPIRIT #3: And we women suffered the most. The man could be Communist or Republican, Northerner or Southerner, a compatriot or French or American, Catholic-Buddhist-atheist – it didn't matter. He still raped and exploited and abused.

SPIRIT #1: You must admit: such atrocities occurred far more from the US military and its allies than anything the resistance fighters could do. The US military *enabled* such outrage by keeping one eye closed.[27]

SPIRIT #3: But wouldn't you say, for the violated, it makes little difference? She could be a guerrilla fighting in the jungles or a doctor saving lives at a clinic or a simple country girl hauling water for the evening's meal...(her voice cracks slightly). Women are the ones that *got* raped and exploited and abused.

SPIRIT #2: And, one day, the man vanishes. (She speaks as if in a trance.)

Whether it was by death or revolution or worse,[28] the man always leaves and the woman – if she's not with him on the battlefield[29] – must endure *alone* to bear the babies, feed them, raise them, not to mention care for frightened and fragile elders, forever lost in their grief for sons and daughters who will never return.

All the while, society shunned us, rejected us, if we had 'irregular' relations with men. How else could family members survive if we didn't use our bodies to get precious resources? They still exiled us, especially when babies came and the father happened to have dark skin.

SPIRIT #1: Perhaps it was out of shame...This was the only kind of power they had left...

SPIRIT #2: Why not extend a hand? That's another kind of power!

SPIRIT #1: People know only what they know...(she sighs).

SPIRIT #3: Western men were the worst! (She spits on the ground, startling the other Spirits.) What's their excuse? They think they own everything and everyone. To them, a small country like Việt Nam is like a helpless, exotic woman – ripe for the picking![30] Just like in that movie. (She gestures towards the screen above.)

SPIRIT #1: The problems did not end even when the war did! Not only did we nurse the sick and heal the wounded, land and people alike, but we also did so with new patriarchs in power.

SPIRIT #2: Life outside of Việt Nam does not ease these burdens, either. A friend writes from America (reading from a letter):

'[S]econd-generation Vietnamese [have to survive] the upheaval of the "new life" – culture shock, the easy access to drugs, the erosion of traditional values, broken homes (some members left behind, others dead, others still in Vietnamese prisons), divorces, remarriages, single-parent families, parents who cannot speak

English, parents who fail to adjust, parents who lose control of their adolescents – the war after the war.'[31]

(The Spirits dab at tears with their long, flowing sleeves. Spirit #2 tries to rally her sister Spirits.)

There were exceptions, of course...

SPIRIT #1: Of course! *Those* we didn't need to worry about. They behaved the way they should – like human beings! It's the rest that's the problem.

SPIRIT #3: Even so, we managed – didn't we? – whether it was tilling the farm or running a business or keeping the household alive.

SPIRIT #2: I think back on all those lovely young girls in their *áo dài* uniforms, chatting and laughing, sauntering down the street after school, arm-in-arm, maybe stopping to buy a snack here, or a magazine there...

SPIRIT #1: Such happy bourgeois memories!

SPIRIT #3: Don't worry (she turns to Spirit #2). Girls are still sauntering down the street, in *áo dài* or not, and they're still lovely. Only now they can look forward to a job at half a man's pay and retire five years before he does![32] That is, if they don't opt for the usual: marriage and lots of children, especially sons.

SPIRIT #1: You wonder what the revolution was for! (She raises her arms in exasperation.)

SPIRIT #2: What I remember most was where I was stationed. (She turns to the audience.) Every morning, after waking, I would take in a deep breath and drink in its sheer beauty. (She inhales deeply, as if she's back in that place at that time. She continues.)

The rivers plunged daringly from mountains high in the sky straight down into the East Sea.[33] (She makes a swooshing motion with her hands.) The streams always flowed fully, fertilizing large rice paddies shimmering like emeralds under the smiling sun. (She sits back on her cushion, nursing her memories.)

SPIRIT #3: I remember the countryside the most:

In some [places], the dwellings were made of clay and thatch, but others had fine houses with huge polished beams holding up the red-tiled roofs, brick courtyards where the rice was threshed, and outbuildings for pigs, chickens, and water buffalo.[34]

SPIRIT #2: Woman, thy fate is Suffering! (She sighs deeply.)

SPIRIT #1: Thy fate is Suffering...(she thinks out loud) but so is it Triumph!

We are *still* here, struggling every day, but *here*! (She looks upward and stands up. The other Spirits arise, also, looking upwards.)

SPIRIT #2: You're right! After all, who else can emerge like a phoenix, beautiful and strong, ready to soar, despite all the ashes of pain and destruction?

SPIRIT #3: It may not happen today or tomorrow (she raises her fist to the sky) but the phoenix *always* rises!

(The three Spirits begin to sing an ancient Vietnamese melody in three-part harmony. It haunts and reassures at the same time. They start floating upwards, elegantly and languidly, with their long white robes trailing in the air. Hidden wires lift them from their cushions.)

WANDA: But wait! (She also stands up.) Please tell me *more*! What can we *do*? What can *I* do?

(The Spirits smile at our heroine's heartfelt words. But they just continue singing and floating upwards, like wafts of smoke. Wanda tries to catch them but can't.

She falls on stage in despair. Lights on. Wanda is in her bed. The TV is buzzing with static.)

WANDA: Wow, what a dream! (She wakes with a start and rubs her eyes.) What does it *mean*?

(Lights dim, curtains down.)

ACT IV

FLOWING

(The Dao)

A blinking neon sign flashes on the screen overhead, 'Graduate Class on International Relations.' Six students, including Wanda, are seated around a seminar table. A spotlight shines briefly on each student as s/he introduces him/herself to the audience. There's Gary, the eager white guy who spent two years in Africa with the Peace Corps; Melissa, the cynical white feminist who's into labor unions and the world's oppressed; Arjun, the skinny guy from India with the Oxbridge accent; Felicia, the equally skinny girl from Singapore, also with an Oxbridge accent; and Robert, an older white guy who's an instructor at West Point.[35]

The Professor enters the classroom. In his early sixties, he looks like the typical white-male academic in a white-male institution: bow tie, tweed jacket, flannel pants, and a slight air of distraction. The neon light overhead flashes his inner thoughts: *Too busy – Too important!* He sits down at the head of the seminar table and takes out a sheaf of notes from a well-worn, leather satchel.

PROFESSOR: Good afternoon. (Everyone opens a notebook or laptop.)
Last week, we talked about the Founding Fathers of IR: Thucydides, Machiavelli, and Hobbes. We learned from Hobbes that the State of Nature is 'solitary, poor, nasty, brutish, and short.' (Wanda rolls her eyes behind her laptop.) Consequently, it fills the world with fear and anarchy, enemies and murderous competition.
Today, we'll discuss Locke and Kant. The idea is for the world to progress from Hobbesian enmity to Lockean rivalry to Kantian friendship.[36]
Let's begin with Locke…
(The stage darkens. The screen overhead blinks: 'Two hours later.' Lights back on. All the students look a little tired. Their eyes are glazed, postures loose, energy low. Wanda raises a tentative hand. The Professor sits back, remembering last week's confrontation.)
Yes?

WANDA: Um, you said Locke bases his theory of rivalry on the concept of property because it protects us from others while allowing us to secure our interests?[37] (Wanda catches her breath.)

PROFESSOR: Yes. And?

WANDA: Does Locke include people in his concept of property, especially given his time? And if so, does slavery protect the masters in the same way as other kinds of ownership?

(The Professor is about to respond when Gary, the former Peace Corps volunteer, jumps in eagerly.)

GARY: In fact, sir, I read this terrific article on Locke as an undergrad.[38] It talks about his seeming contradiction in condoning slavery while advocating liberty at the same time.

PROFESSOR: Uh, I think I know the article you're talking about. But, please, enlighten the rest of the class.

GARY: Sure. Basically, the article talks about how Locke viewed education as the key to emancipating the body *and* the mind. That is, Locke justified slavery – or any kind of subjugation of 'social inferiors' like women, children, servants, and so on – as a means of educating them in how to become proper stewards of property. So to him, there is no contradiction between slavery and liberty. The former is but a path to the latter, thereby liberating all!

MELISSA: So...the purpose of education is to be more like him? *Right.*

FELICIA: Isn't this the same problem with Kant? He sees a Perpetual Peace in the world only when everybody else thinks and acts just like him. Isn't this what they call Democratic Peace Theory?[39]

ROBERT: In fact, Kant's ideas of peace are highly dependent on his ideas of war.[40] So there could be no peace without war! At least that's what we learned at West Point...

(The Professor looks around and catches eye contact with Arjun, the only student who hasn't spoken so far.)

Arjun, you've been pretty quiet. What do *you* think of all this?

ARJUN: Well, uh, these ideas are all very interesting, sir. To be honest, I've not read much Kant...

PROFESSOR: Not familiar with Kant, eh?

WANDA: Is that a problem? (She feels combative but stops suddenly. She hears the three Spirits singing their song and relaxes. She leans back in her seat.)

ARJUN: Actually, sir, I'm more familiar with the *Bhagavad Gita.*

PROFESSOR: The what? (Everyone perks up.)

ARJUN: The *Bhagavad Gita.* It's from the great Indian epic, the *Mahabharata.*[41]

The *Gita* is about Prince Arjuna who is on the eve of a great battle against another branch of his family. The two armies are evenly matched but grave doubts overwhelm Arjuna. *How can I kill my kin?* he laments.[42]

Lord Krishna, who is disguised as his charioteer, takes Arjuna away to another field so they can take a pause and discuss the matter.

To each of Arjuna's concerns, Krishna answers in terms of a possible scenario. *Is this what you want?* Krishna asks. But Arjuna can't decide – until Krishna finally reveals his true self: a god of gods. (Arjun puts on a godly boom for Krishna.)

I am become death, the destroyer of worlds![43] *Do not worry about whom you kill for that is my domain!*[44] *Nor expect rewards for your labor.*[45] *Just be the best warrior you were born to be. That is your* dharma.

Dharma means 'duty.'[46] (Arjun explains helpfully. He returns to the story.)

	Arjuna trembles humbly before Krishna's blinding light and giant stature. *Please,* he beseeches the god, *return to your mortal self and I will follow your counsel!* So Krishna returns to his guise as a charioteer and drives Arjuna back to the battlefield. Next day, Arjuna vanquishes his enemies and his side of the family regains its honor.
GARY:	So all's well that ends well?
ARJUN:	Not quite. Arjuna's side won but almost everyone is killed. There is no one left to rule the kingdom they had fought so hard to get.
PROFESSOR:	That's quite a story, Arjun. And you're quite the storyteller.
ARJUN:	Thank you, sir. (He feels slightly embarrassed.) But I can hardly claim credit. The story is over five thousand years old.
PROFESSOR:	Oh, uh, yes, of course. But how would you relate it to Kant and what we were talking about earlier: that is, friendship in world politics?
ARJUN:	I guess I would say, sir... (He answers slowly, thoughtfully)... There are many ways to friendship in this world. If we don't recognize *that*, then how could we possibly have a perpetual peace?
PROFESSOR:	Uh, hm, yes. Well! (He looks at his watch.) Our time is up. Next week, we discuss Hegel, Marx, and Lenin. See you then.

(The Professor exits quickly. Everyone readies to leave but they freeze in place as the lights dim and the curtains come down.)

ACT V

CONNECTIONS AND CO-CREATIVITIES

(Reaping the Dao)

The six students are still in the classroom. They unfreeze, continuing to gather their things to leave.

WANDA:	Thank you for that beautiful story, Arjun. It was also kind of reassuring. It reminded me of a dream I had recently...
ARJUN:	Oh, you're most welcome! I don't know what came over me. I guess I get carried away whenever I talk about the *Gita*. My grandmother lives by it.
GARY:	What do you mean that it's 'reassuring'?
WANDA:	Well, the story reminds me that there are many ways to *be* in this world. (Suddenly, Wanda remembers a passage from *Sihar & Shenya*.) It's all about love.
ROBERT:	Say what?
WANDA:	Here, I think this passage says it better than I can. (She pulls out *Sihar & Shenya* from her backpack and opens it to a particular page: The screen overhead flashes these words, some larger than the others, as Wanda reads them: *lacks and talents, RESPECT, meaning and purpose, LOVE, seed => flower, right conditions ↔ right friendship, live WELL with OTHERS.)*

'[W]e live and breathe, laugh and cry, in a much larger, livelier world than our own small corner of lacks and talents. From such appreciation comes respect. Not one thing, even a lack, is without meaning or purpose. And from respect, love grows. We see that everything and everyone in the Universe can turn a lack into a talent, a seed into a flower, once we find the right conditions and the right friendship…[T]hus, we forget the self so as to live well with others…'[47]

GARY: *Ubuntu*! It's just like this philosophy from southern Africa: 'I am here because of you, you are here because of me.'

FELICIA: That sounds a lot like the Buddhist mantra: 'I in you and you in me.'

MELISSA: The Greeks have something like that, too! It's called *poiesis* or 'mutual reverberation.'[48] People come into being through their reverberations with one another.

WANDA: We might be onto something here! (She feels excited for the first time.) Maybe we could 'reverberate' with Old Kant, too…!

ROBERT: Hey, how about if we 'reverberate' with a couple of beers? Meet at the local hang-out?

EVERYONE: Sure thing!

(All laugh heartily and exit together – except for Wanda. She stays behind to close the room.)

WANDA: Thank you, Spirits. (She looks upwards.) I am a phoenix, ready to soar!

(She blows a kiss to them, turns off the lights, and closes the door.

Lights out. Curtains fall. The Spirits' song fills the theatre.)

THE END

APPENDIX 1

Figure 29.1 Front cover from L.H.M. Ling, *Imagining World Politics: Shar & Shenya, A Fable for Our Times* (London: Routledge, 2014).

Bibliography

Agathangelou, Anna M. and L.H.M. Ling. (2005) 'Power and Play through *Poisies*: Reconstructing Self and Other in the 9/11 Commission Report.' *Millennium: Journal of International Studies* 33 (3): 827–53.

Bastian, Dawn E. and Judy K. Mitchell. (2004) *Handbook of Native American Mythology*. Santa Barbara: ABC-CLIO.

Bedford, David and Thom Workman. (1997) 'The Great Law of Peace: Alternative Inter-Nation(al) Practices and the Iroquoian Confederacy.' *Alternatives: Global Local and Political* 22 (1) January–March: 87–111.

Behnke, Andreas. (2012) 'Eternal Peace, Perpetual War? A Critical Investigation of Kant's Conceptualisations of War.' *Journal of International Relations and Development* (15): 250–71.

Beier, J. Marshall. (2005) *International Relations in Uncommon Places: Indigeneity, Cosmology, and the Limits of International Theory*. New York: Palgrave Macmillan.

Crawford, Neta C. (1994) 'A Security Regime Among Democracies: Cooperation Among Iroquois Nations.' *International Organization* 48 (3) Summer: 345–85.

Davis, Peter. (1974) 'Hearts and Minds: A Documentary.' Released by Warner Brothers.

Dienstag, Joshua Foa. (1996) 'Serving God and Mammon: The Lockean Sympathy in Early American Political Thought.' *American Political Science Review* 90 (3) September: 497–511.

Fitzgerald, Frances. (1972) *Fire in the Lake: The Vietnamese and the Americans in Vietnam*. New York: Little, Brown & Co.

—— (ed.). (2007) *Last Night I Dreamed of Peace: The Diary of Dang Thuy Tram*, trans. by Andrew X. Pham. New York: Three Rivers Press.

Flood, Gavin and Charles Martin. (2012) *The Bhagavad Gita: A New Translation*. New York: W.W. Norton & Co.

Hess, Martha. (1994) *Then the Americans Came: Voices from Vietnam*. New Brunswick: Rutgers University Press.

Hijiya, James A. (2000) 'The *Gita* of J. Robert Oppenheimer.' *Proceedings of the American Philosophical Society* 144 (2) June: 123–67.

Ikenberry, G. John. (2011) 'The Future of the Liberal World Order: Internationalism after America.' *Foreign Affairs*, 1 May. (https://www.foreignaffairs.com/articles/2011-05-01/future-liberal-world-order). (Downloaded: 25 July 2015.)

Ikenberry, G. John and Anne-Marie Slaughter. (2006) 'Forging a World of Liberty under Law: US National Security in the 21st Century.' Final Report of the Princeton Project on National Security, Woodrow Wilson School of Public and International Affairs, Princeton University.

Lâm Thị Mỹ Dạ. (2005) *Green Rice: Poems*. Willimantic, CT: Curbstone Press.

Ling, L.H.M. (2010) 'Journeys Beyond the West: World Orders and a 7th Century Buddhist Monk.' *Review of International Studies* (37): 225–48.

—— (2014) *Imagining World Politics: Sihar & Shenya, A Fable for Our Times*. London: Routledge.

—— et al. (2016) *India China: Rethinking Borders and Security*. Ann Arbor: University of Michigan Press.

Milliken, Jennifer and David Sylvan. (1996) 'Soft Bodies, Hard Targets, and Chic Theories: US Bombing Policy in Indochina.' *Millennium: Journal of International Studies* (25) June: 321–59.

Nguitragool, P. (2012) 'God-Kings and Indonesia: Renegotiating the Boundaries between Western and Non-Western Perspectives on Foreign Policy.' *Pacific Affairs* 85 (4): 723–43.

Nguyễn Thị Bình. (2015). *Family, Friends and Country*. Hanoi: Phuong Nam Cultural Corp. in collaboration with Tri Thuc Publishing House.

Nguyễn Thị Định. (1976) *No Other Road to Take: The Memoirs of Mrs. Nguyen Thi Dinh*. Ithaca: Cornell University Press.

Nguyễn Thị Thu-Lam. (1989) *Fallen Leaves: Memoirs of a Vietnamese Woman from 1940–1975*. New Haven: Yale Center for International and Area Studies, Council on Southeast Asia Studies.

Nguyễn Thị Tuyet Mai. (1994) *The Rubber Tree: Memoir of a Vietnamese Woman Who Was an Anti-French Guerrilla, A Publisher and a Peace Activist*. Jefferson, NC and London: McFarland & Co.

Sampson, A.B. (2002) 'Tropical Anarchy: Waltz, Wendt, and the Way We Imagine International Politics.' *Alternatives: Global, Local, Political* 27 (4): 429–57.

Todorov, Tzvetan. (1999) *The Conquest of America: The Question of the Other*. Norman: University of Oklahoma Press.

United Nations Development Program (UNDP). (2010) 'Sexism Rampant in Viet Nam: UN.' (http://www.undp.org/content/dam/vietnam/docs/UNDP-in-the-News/19561_Sexism_rampant_in_Viet_Namx.pdf) (Downloaded: 10 October 2016).

Wendt, A. (1999) *Social Theory of International Politics*. Cambridge: Cambridge University Press.

Notes

1 I am grateful to Ebby Abramson, Fabiola Berdiel, Drew Dockery, John Patrick Lynch, Nicholas G. Onuf, Carolina M. Pinheiro, Patricia J. Robertson, Ignacio Rullansky, and Sara Shroff for reading and commenting on this paper. I especially thank Quỳnh N. Phạm for giving Act III greater accuracy and nuance. I take full responsibility, however, for any mistakes or confusions that may appear.

2 Wanda first appears as a character in Ling (2014). This play resumes where the book ends but also changes some details.

3 Sampson (2002).

4 Todorov (1999).

5 See, for example, Crawford (1994), Bedford and Workman (1997), Beier (2005).

6 Ling (2014).

7 See Appendix 1.

8 The trickster coyote is a character common to all types of native-American lore. See, Bastian and Mitchell (2004).

9 Auntie Ann (Anh) first appears in Ling (2014). She is Wanda's Vietnamese aunt by marriage. A doctor in Saigon (Sài Gòn), she had treated Wanda's uncle when he lost a leg to the conflict there. Later, the two married. More than any class she ever took, Wanda learned about Western imperialism and colonialism in Asia from Auntie Ann and her recollections of French-occupied Indochina. Though stationed in Sài Gòn, Auntie Ann had grown up in the north, the Tonkin area, which had the least colonial influence in the country, thereby giving her a critical eye towards foreign occupation.

10 For a review and critique of the conventional discourse on India and China, see Ling (2016).

11 The spirits represent a composite of characters drawn from memoirs by Vietnamese women and their experiences with the Vietnam War or, what is known in Vietnam as the American War: Nguyễn Thị Thu-Lam (Nguyễn 1989), Le Ly Hayslip (Hayslip and Wurts 1989), Nguyễn Thị Tuyet Mai (Nguyễn 1994), and Dang Thuy Tram (Fitzgerald 2007). These accounts cover the anti-French struggle in the 1950s, the resistance in the 1960s, to the official end of the war in 1975. Oliver Stone turned Hayslip's memoir into a film, 'Heaven & Earth' (1993). Dang died during a shoot-out near her clinic in 1970; in 2009, her story was turned into a film, 'Đừng Đốt' ('Do Not Burn It'). The others managed to immigrate to the US and settle there. Hayslip and Nguyễn Thị Thu-Lam married Americans and had children by them but their marriages ended in divorce after a few years.

12 *Bọn Tây* is a Vietnamese colloquialism for 'these white guys.'

13 Many peasants had joined the war of resistance against the Americans. But many were also caught in-between, innocent of the two ideological sides of the conflict, as conveyed by Le Ly Hayslip's memoir.

14 Here, 'early days' could refer to the anti-colonial struggle against France or the war of resistance against the Americans.

15 Nguyễn Thị Thu-Lam witnessed this hanging and recorded it in her memoir (Nguyễn 1989).

16 'Uncle Hồ' refers to Hồ Chí Minh. Other French-educated leaders of the resistance included Võ Nguyên Giáp and Nguyễn Thị Bình.

17 The American Chamber of Commerce in Vietnam estimates that its middle class will double in size from 12 million in 2014 to 33 million by 2020. See (http://www.amchamvietnam.com/vietnams-middle-class-set-to-double-by-2020-bcg/) According to the World Bank, per capita income in Vietnam has risen from $0 in 1960 to over $2000 in 2015, compared to surrounding neighbors such as Cambodia ($1200), Laos ($1800), Thailand ($6000), and China ($8000). (http://data.worldbank.org/indicator/NY.GDP.PCAP.CD) (Downloaded: 8 October 2016).

18 The Cultural Revolution started in 1966. It ended in 1976, the year when both Mao and his faithful lieutenant, Zhou Enlai, died.

19 'Between 130,000 and 150,000 Viet Minh (Vietnamese who fought against the French), along with many of their family members, migrated north above the 17th parallel. Approximately 800,000 to one million Northern Vietnamese, mainly Catholics and French supporters, relocated to the South within the 300 days mandated in the [Geneva] accords [of 1954]' Fitzgerald (2007: 30, footnote 39).

20 One such climb was on the 'Hồ Chí Minh trail' across the Trường Sơn mountain range.
21 'The Vietnamese dug trenches in the hills encircling the French... Gathering 70,000 Viet Minh troops from all over Vietnam, the Vietnamese hauled and dragged heavy artillery guns to the tops of hills, from which positions they could fire down on French troops and into the sky at paratroopers attempting to resupply them. The French were closed off from the outside world, under constant fire, and taking casualties. They appealed to the Americans, and some American advisers suggested the use of a nuclear bomb. President Eisenhower would not enter into conflict without the British, and Winston Churchill refused, hoping that the Geneva Peace Talks would resolve the situation' Fitzgerald (2007: 57, footnote 65).
22 See Davis (1974).
23 Vietnamese usually see the era of Chinese domination lasting a thousand years (111 BC–938 CE).
24 The Việt Minh, Hồ Chí Minh's revolutionary 'people's army', defeated the French at the battle of Điện Biên Phủ in 1954. Twenty years later, the National Liberation Front (NLF), known as the Việt Cong, drove out the US military. The US could not sustain its stronghold in Sài Gòn after a massive attack by the Việt Cong in what is now called the Tết Offensive of 1968. It boosted North Vietnamese morale and turned the tide of war against the US despite massive casualties and destruction on both sides. 'Washington was estimating that enemy casualties had risen to almost 39,000, including 33,249 killed. Allied casualties were placed at 3,470 dead, one-third of them Americans, and 12,062 wounded, almost half of them Americans... By then, almost 4,000 Americans had died since the start of the lunar year in battles that raged from rice paddies to hilltops to more than 30 of South Vietnam's 44 provincial capitals. The number of enemy dead had climbed to more than 58,000. More than 14,000 South Vietnamese men, women and children also had died'(*New York Times* 31 January 1988: http://www.nytimes.com/1988/01/31/world/tet-offensive-turning-point-in-vietnam-war.html) (Downloaded: 8 October 2016).
25 Discovery of mass graves at Huế, Vietnam's last royal capital, serves as an example. US and South Vietnamese sources claim the North's Communists massacred thousands of civilians after the Tết Offensive in 1968. Others critique that such evidence remains unconfirmed. No doubt the Communists executed hundreds of 'traitors' but not to the scale of thousands; more likely, the other graves resulted from collateral damage (Porter 1987, originally published on 20 October 1987: http://www.nytimes.com/1987/10/29/opinion/l-little-evidence-of-1968-tet-massacre-in-hue-587087.html) (Downloaded: 8 October 2016).
26 'With the defeat of the French in May 1954, France and the Democratic Republic of Vietnam (DRV) signed the Agreement on Cessation of Hostilities in Vietnam (called the Geneva Accords) on July 20, 1954. The accords temporarily divided Vietnam into North Vietnam and South Vietnam at the 17th parallel until mandated elections could be held in 1956 to unify the country... The promised elections were never held. A key provision of the accords was a guarantee against reprisals but in 1959, President Ngo Dinh Diem launched a program to eliminate by killing, jailing, and intimidating southern families with family members who had gone to the North or were connected with the Viet Minh' (Fitzgerald 2007: 30, footnote 39).
27 We do not have statistics to compare incidents of rape, exploitation, and abuse between the two sides of the conflict. However, the former received implicit coverage from the US military and its allies. See, for example, Peter Davis' documentary of the Vietnam War, 'Hearts and Minds' (1974).
28 For example, Frances Fitzgerald (1972) reports on widespread heroin addiction on the part of both Vietnamese and Americans in the South during the war.
29 Plenty of women fought and died on the battlefield. See, for example, Hess (1994), Nguyễn Thị Định (1976), Lâm Thị Mỹ Dạ (2005), Nguyễn Thị Bình (2015).
30 Milliken and Sylvan (1996).
31 Nguyễn Thị Thu-Lam in Fitzgerald (1989: 203).
32 See a 2010 report from the United Nations Development Program (UNDP).
33 Vietnamese refer to the China Sea as the 'East Sea.'
34 Ibid., p. vii.
35 These characters come from Ling (2014).
36 Wendt (1999).
37 '[S]tates comply with sovereignty norms because they think it will advance some exogenously given interest, like security or trade' (Wendt 1999: 287).
38 Dienstag (1996).
39 See, for example, Ikenberry and Slaughter (2006) and Ikenberry (2011).

40 Behnke (2012).

41 The *Mahabharata* is influential not only in South Asia but also throughout Southeast Asia. See, for example, Nguitragool (2012).

42 I am unstrung: my limbs collapse
beneath me, and my mouth is dry,
there is a trembling in my body,
and my hair rises bristling (Arjuna in Flood and Martin 2012: 6).

43 J. Robert Oppenheimer uttered these words when witnessing the first atomic explosion at Los Alamos on 16 July 1945 (Hijiya 2000).

44 In effect, Krishna is saying to Arjuna: 'Act from *dharma* with detachment and God will take care of the rest' (Flood and Martin 2012: xv).

45 Your concern should be with action,
never with an action's fruits;
these should never motivate you,
nor attachment to inaction (Krishna to Arjuna in Flood and Martin 2012: 19).

46 'The Sanskrit term for virtue is *dharma*, whose semantic range includes duty, law, truth, ethics, and the sociocosmic order. It is from a Sanskrit verbal root *dhri*, meaning "to uphold" or "bear up" and so *dharma* points to a power that upholds the universe and to a natural law that constrains the behavior of all beings' (Flood and Martin 2012: xv).

47 Ling (2014: 19).

48 Agathangelou and Ling (2005).

30

CIVILISING PROCESS OR CIVILISING MISSION?

Toward a post-Western understanding of Human Security

Giorgio Shani

Introduction[1]

The retreat from the cosmopolitan notion of Human Security in the face of a populist onslaught in the Anglosphere and beyond, gives us an opportunity to reflect on its relevance to arguably a more unstable and insecure world. Its adoption by the United Nations General Assembly in September 2012 (UN General Assembly, 2012) and its institutionalisation through the United Nations' system through the Trust Fund for Human Security, suggests that Human Security has become part of the global mainstream, a central plank of the post-Cold War 'liberal peace' (Richmond, 2005). The mainstreaming of Human Security, however, has come at a cost. Human Security has lost its critical edge. It is argued that it has failed to contest the hegemony of the 'national security paradigm' which continues to provide the dominant framework for ascertaining and dealing with security threats. Indeed, as the authors of the Commission for Human Security Report (2003) make clear, Human Security *complements* rather than challenges national security.

Human Security has made considerable inroads in providing an alternative to national security by qualifying state sovereignty in the formerly colonised world, particularly in post-conflict societies or transitional democracies, where fragile state structures, deep social cleavages, ethno-religious militancy and pervasive socio-economic problems stemming from underdevelopment have posed challenges to the state's very survival. In some cases, such as Afghanistan, Somalia, Southern Sudan, the Central African Republic, parts of the Democratic Republic of Congo and, most infamously, Rwanda, state structures have collapsed entirely leaving vulnerable populations at the mercy of external assistance. The proclivity of state elites to use violence against their own populations with impunity when faced with challenges to their own authority, such as in Libya and Syria, has furthermore outraged conceptions of 'civilised behaviour' leading to demands for intervention. The recent intervention against the so-called Islamic State (IS) in Syria and Iraq is a case in point. Although not a fully functioning 'state' in a Westphalian sense, IS has – by unleashing a reign of terror against religious minorities (and Western aid workers) – 'necessitated' intervention by the international community.

Human Security, as a key concept associated with liberal peacebuilding, has facilitated the intervention of the 'international community' in the internal affairs of 'post-conflict societies' and governance of many areas of the 'developing world.' For some, this development is to be welcomed as part of a 'civilising process' which seeks to minimise violent harm and the unnecessary suffering of others. The 'civilising process' refers to the process whereby modern Europeans came to regard themselves as more 'civilised' than their ancestors and more 'developed' than other peoples (Elias, 2000; Linklater, 2011). 'Standards of civilisation' (Gong, 1984) were a pre-condition for entry into 'international society' in the mid-nineteenth to early twentieth century and the 'expansion of international society' (Bull and Watson, 1984) after the Second World War was predicated on the acceptance of 'western' notions of state sovereignty, rights and self-restraint as *universal* standards of civilisation. Viewed from the perspective of many of those in the Global South, therefore, Human Security appears as merely the latest instalment of the 'civilising missions' of the nineteenth century which served as a pretext for their colonisation.

However, does not the ideal of human security – a world free from fear and want – remain a universal aspiration for 'humanity'? Humanity, it is argued, cannot be assumed a priori but must be understood from *within* different cultural traditions. It is here that the role of religion and identity, as exemplified by the Arab Uprisings, plays an important role in permitting the articulation of different conceptions of human security in vernacular terms and re-embedding individuals deracinated by the pernicious effects of neo-liberal globalisation and subject to repression by 'secular' authoritarian rule into 'cultural' communities. This chapter seeks to further contribute to the development of a 'critical human security' perspective (Shani and Pasha, 2007; Newman, 2010) by arguing that the project of human security can only be furthered in a multicultural world through a sustained engagement with the post-secular (Habermas, 2008). In my understanding a 'post-secular'[2] conception of human security should seek to recognise the multiple religio-cultural contexts in which human dignity is embedded. For Jürgen Habermas, the term 'post-secular' refers to societies where the continued existence of religious communities in an increasingly secularised environment necessitates, on the one hand, the inclusion of religious-based world-views into the public sphere, and, on the other, the translation of religious-based claims into secular terms in order to guarantee the neutrality of the public sphere.

It will, furthermore, be suggested that such a 'post-secular conception' of human security is more suited to an increasingly 'post-western' world where the rise of the BRICS and the resurgence of political Islam in particular, constitute a powerful challenge to the main institutions and values of an 'international society' dominated by the West. Thirty years ago, Bull and Watson (1984, 433) noted that:

> the most striking feature of international society…is the extent to which the states of Asia and Africa have embraced such basic elements of European international society as the sovereign state, the rules of international law, the procedures and conventions of diplomacy and IR.

Although the main values of international society, and the discipline of International Relations (IR), continue to be articulated in almost exclusively Eurocentric terms, the 'revolt against the West', particularly after 9/11, has created space for the return of religion and identity to IR. While a truly 'post-western' theory of IR still awaits elucidation, the 'secular' values of international society and ontology of IR have been increasingly challenged by the global religious resurgence and a growing interest in the cognitive claims of 'non-western' cultural traditions

(Shani, 2008b). This makes a 'post-western' approach to Human Security not only possible but imperative if it is to claim to be universal.

Human Security: the contemporary civilising mission?[3]

The notion of Human Security is premised on the assumption that the individual human being is the only irreducible focus for discourse on security. Consequently, the claims of all other referents, including the nation-state, derive from the *sovereignty* of the individual (MacFarlane and Khong, 2006, 2). While most advocates of Human Security agree that its primary goal should be the *protection* of individual human lives, they differ as to what the individual should be protected from. Conventionally, a distinction is made between 'narrow' and 'broad' definitions. The first approach conceives of Human Security negatively, in terms of the absence of threats to the *physical* security or safety of individuals. This 'narrow' definition is exemplified in the *Human Security Report* which defines human security as the protection of individuals from 'violent threats' (Human Security Report, 2005, 2011). Furthermore, the narrow approach also informs the concept of the Responsibility to Protect (RtoP) which was adopted by the General Assembly after the World Summit in 2005 and formed the pretext for United Nations Security Council (UNSC) resolutions 1970 and 1971 which authorised the creation of a 'no-fly zone' over Libya in 2011. According to paragraph 138 of the World Summit Outcome resolution, each 'individual State has the responsibility to protect its populations from genocide, war crimes, ethnic cleansing and crimes against humanity' through 'the *prevention* of such crimes' (emphasis mine). Where states, such as Libya in 2011 or presumably contemporary Syria, fail in their responsibility to protect the population under its legal authority, then, under paragraph 139, the 'international community' must assume that responsibility and must be prepared to 'take collective action in a timely and decisive manner, through the Security Council, in accordance with the Charter' (United Nations General Assembly, 2005).

The second approach goes beyond a narrow focus on the responsibility of states to protect their citizens and posits a 'broader' conception of Human Security, which takes into account 'freedom from want, freedom from fear and freedom to take action on one's own behalf' (Commission on Human Security, 2003). A broader approach to HS, one more in keeping with the spirit of the UNDP Report, emerged from the Commission on Human Security (CHS) which was headed by Nobel Prize-winning economist Amartya Sen and former UNCHR Head (and ICU professor) Sadako Ogata. The Final Report stated that the objective of HS was to protect 'the vital core of all human lives in ways that enhance human freedoms and human fulfilment' (Commission on Human Security 2003, 4). However, protection is seen as an insufficient condition to achieve Human Security: it should seek also to 'to *empower* [people] to act on their own behalf' (Commission on Human Security 2003 – emphasis mine). This approach to Human Security appears to have influenced the recent resolution adopted by the United Nations General Assembly (A/66/290) in September 2012, which sought to arrive at a 'common understanding of human security'. The Resolution adopted defined Human Security as the 'right of people to live in freedom and dignity, free from poverty and despair'. 'All individuals', it continued, 'are entitled to freedom from fear and freedom from want, with an equal opportunity to enjoy all their rights and fully develop their human potential' (UN General Assembly, 2012).

The antinomy between the 'narrow' and 'broad' approaches masks the *discursive* continuities between the two approaches which are reflected in the practices of international institutions committed to Human Security. Indeed, it could be argued that the fundamental difference between the two approaches is merely that what advocates of the 'narrow' approach assume to be a social fact – the atomised individual – proponents of the broad approach consider a *project*: the creation of unencumbered individuals out of the culturally differentiated great mass of humanity. As such, there are unmistakable continuities with the 'civilising mission' of nineteenth-century imperialism, which sought to actively impose a '*cultural conversion of non-Western states to a Western civilizational standard*' (Hobson, 2012, 27 – emphasis in the original). The agents of the contemporary 'civilising mission', however, are no longer European empires, private companies such as the East India Company or missionaries, but an 'international community' centred on the United Nations system dominated by powerful Western states (most of which were colonial empires) working in tandem with multinational corporations and selected international non-governmental organisations to institutionalise liberal peacebuilding in 'fragile' post-colonial states.

Critical Human Security[4]

The most persistent criticism of the concept of Human Security is that, in the words of Roland Paris, it tends 'to be extraordinarily expansive and vague, encompassing everything from physical security to psychological well-being, which provides policymakers with little guidance in the prioritization of competing policy goals and academics little sense of what, exactly, is to be studied' (Paris, 2001, 88). For political realists in particular, this broadening and deepening of the concept of security is pernicious in that it distracts states from their primary role in protecting the 'national interest' from external threats. However, from a *critical* perspective it could be argued that the very ambiguity of the concept of HS makes it susceptible to incorporation into the very paradigm it is seeking to replace: the national security paradigm. Critical perspectives challenge the positivist assumptions of conventional approaches to security which they consider to be 'problem-solving' theories designed to promote the smooth functioning of the international state-system (Cox, 1981).

The national security paradigm is premised on the assumption that the state is simultaneously the main instrument of protection for the national community *and* the sole referent object of security discourse. As a sovereign entity, the state gets to decide what constitutes the national interest and the means to pursue it. HS was initially proposed as an *alternative* to the national security paradigm yet it has failed to contest its hegemony within the theory and practice of international relations. Most of the issues it has raised have been incorporated as non-traditional security threats and the power of nation-states has remained undiminished. This can be seen in the UN General Assembly resolution (A/66/290) which categorically states that 'Human Security does not replace State security' and that it is based instead on the principle of 'national ownership'.

On the one hand, Human Security is seen as a 'people-centred approach' marking a significant departure in security studies since it makes the individual and not the sovereign nation-state as the primary referent object of security. Yet on the other hand, the concept of Human Security *reinforces* the doctrine of national security by re-empowering the state through capacity-building so it can protect its populations from a plethora of existential threats, from militant transnational Islamic-based terrorism to contagious diseases such as Ebola. As MacFarlane and Khong (2006, 265) point out, Human Security is 'not about transcending or marginalising the state' but 'about ensuring that states protect their people.' This gives rise to the concern, that Human Security may be sufficiently malleable to allow itself to be used to legitimise greater state control over society in the *name of protection* (Shani, 2007). Human Security, in short, has been 'co-opted and incorporated into statist discourses' (Booth, 2005, 266).

Critically reworked, however, human security has the potential to contest the hegemony of the discourse on national security. Critical perspectives not only challenge the positivist assumptions of conventional approaches to security, but are also concerned with the possibilities for liberation that are immanent within existing political and social relations (Cox 1981, 128). In Booth's words they engage in 'immanent critique: the rejection of utopian blueprints in favour of the discovery of latent potentials on which to build political and social 'progress'. The objective of critical theory is the 'emancipation' of individuals from 'structural oppression suffered on account of gender, class or race' (Booth, 2005, 263).

Recently, Edward Newman has argued that a critical approach to Human Security should adopt the approach pioneered by the 'Welsh School' of Critical Security Studies (CSS) and focus on the emancipation of individuals (Newman, 2010). CSS, as famously defined by Ken Booth, is an issue-area study, developed within the academic discipline of international politics, concerned with the pursuit of critical knowledge about security in world politics. Central to the CSS approach is the re-conceptualisation of 'security as emancipation'. Whilst 'security' means 'the absence of threats', Booth defined emancipation as the 'freeing of people (as individuals and groups) from the physical and human constraints which stop them carrying out what they would freely choose to do'. CSS theorists follow Booth in viewing war, poverty, poor education and political oppression as constraints on 'security'. Emancipation, they argue, 'not power or order, produces true security' (Booth, 1991, 319).

Re-conceptualising security as emancipation, however, as Mustapha Kamal Pasha and I had previously argued, risks leading to a greater 'securitisation' of security; the generic attempt to simply expand the menu of security studies without recognising the insurmountable difficulty of conceptual translation and transmission (Shani and Pasha, 2007). Adopting the idiom of the Copenhagen School, we suggested that critical human security should focus instead on *de-securitisation*, yet the excessive concentration of Copenhagen School theorists on the ways in which political issues become 'de/securitised' from above obscures the very real contributions which people make to the *de-securitisation* of their own lives (see Aradau, 2004; Balzacq, 2010; Buzan, Wæver, and de Wilde, 1998; Huysmans, 2006; Wæver, 1995). They do so, however, not as *individuals* but as part of collective communities with distinct but fluid *cultures*.

In common with the conventional discourses on Human Security they are endeavouring to critique, both 'Copenhagen' and 'Welsh' theorists reproduce the modernist conception of the individual as 'bare life' (Agamben, 1998).[5] Metaphorically denuded of the protective layering of culture through which individuals find meaning, dignity and identity, the abstract individual of conventional Human Security discourse becomes a 'docile body' (Foucault, 1991) to be subjected, used, transformed and empowered by the market. Culture here is not assumed as a 'primordial attachment,' an unchanging ethnic property of territorially-defined groups but is understood in a 'thin sense' as a framework through which individuals attain meaning and identity as part of a community. Culture is, in short, what gives us a *bios*: a life with dignity, endowed with meaning which can consequently be considered 'worthy' of sacrifice (Agamben, 1998). Cultural difference does not stem from mutually irreconcilable core values which inevitably give rise to conflict as some prominent scholars have claimed (c.f. Huntington, 1993, 1996), but must be accepted and understood *in its own terms*. Attempts to negate difference by assimilating 'otherness' to a universal 'self' are not only counterproductive but, it is argued, a fundamental source of insecurity. Universalistic conceptions of Human Security can themselves, therefore, be seen as a type of human *insecurity*.

De-secularising Human Security

The approach taken in this paper does not seek to reject Human Security as merely the latest technique of neo-colonial governmentality (Foucault, 2007) but seeks to reconceptualise it by taking into account cultural *difference* (Pasha, 2013). In keeping with a broadly-defined critical approach which seeks not only to question assumptions but seeks possibilities for liberation that are immanent within existing political and social relations (Cox, 1981), it is argued that Human Security, if critically reworked, can pose a powerful *immanent* challenge to the hegemony of the national security paradigm by using the language of *security* to further the goals of emancipation from fear and want. In order to do so, however, Human Security will need to become *post-secular*. A 'post-secular' conception of HS should, it is argued, permit the articulation of plural claims from a multiplicity of different religio-cultural traditions without prioritising any one 'tradition' as having a monopoly over the definition of what it is to be 'human' and what it is to be 'secure'. Consequently, it contests the ontological underpinnings of both conventional understandings of Human Security and poses a sterner challenge to the hegemony of the national security paradigm.

In modern industrialised societies, a post-secular approach would aim at bringing in the voices of those who have remained marginalised by secular political discourse, particularly those of religious minorities. The aim of such approach, however, would not be to forcibly *translate* political claims emanating from a faith-based perspective into secular claims, as Jürgen Habermas (2008) has suggested, but to try and understand faith-based claims in *their own terms*. To understand, however, is not to accept. Claims which seek to *exclude* others on the grounds of ethnicity, religion, gender and sexual orientation are themselves sources of human insecurity in that they violate the 'vital core' of being. The advantage of a post-secular approach is that it acknowledges that secularism itself can be exclusionary and thus a source of insecurity for faith-based communities. In the post-colonial world, however, the influence of colonial categories of religion has cast a shadow on what constitutes the 'sacred' and 'profane'.

In the post-colonial world, the concept of 'religion' remains an important *marker of difference*. Religion was an imported cultural category imposed upon indigenous societies by the colonising power as part of a regime of colonial governmentality (Chatterjee, 1993). For Tomoko Masuzawa, the rise of the modern social sciences allowed a distinction to be made between the modern, secular West and a mystical East depicted by Orientalist scholarship and historians of religion. Consequently, 'every region of the non-modern non-West was presumed to be thoroughly in the grip of religion, as all aspects of life were supposedly determined and dictated by an archaic metaphysics of the magical and the supernatural' (Masuzawa, 2005, 16).

Following Derrida (1998), it is argued that the Judeo-Christian conception of *religio* is based on a specific cultural tradition that is fundamentally unintelligible to other cultural traditions, yet at the same time it continues to profoundly influence non-western identities through the associated practices of (neo-)colonial governmentality. In particular, modern scientific techniques of classification and enumeration transformed the political landscape of the colonised world and continue to shape its politics today, transforming previously 'fuzzy' and overlapping religious, cultural and political identities into 'enumerated' religious communities through the census. As Bernard Cohn points out, 'what was entailed in the construction of census operations was the creation of social categories' by which colonial societies were ordered for administrative purposes (Cohn, 1996, 8). The Census *objectified* religious, social and cultural difference. In the case of colonial South Asia, the categories of caste and religion became homogenous and mutually exclusive despite the 'fuzziness' of caste and religious boundaries (Kaviraj, 2010). The result is that, for many in the post-colonial world, the concept of 'religion' continues to define subjectivity even though it is alien to the cultural traditions of pre-colonial societies. Religion ceased to be, to borrow Nandy's terminology, a 'faith' and became an 'ideology': a 'subnational, national or cross-national identifier of populations contesting for or protecting non-religious, usually political or socio-economic interests' (Nandy, 1998, 322).

Towards a post-western understanding of Human Security?

In my understanding, a 'post-western' conception of human security should permit the articulation of plural claims from a multiplicity of different religio-cultural traditions without prioritising any one 'tradition' as having a monopoly over what is human security. Secular notions of Human Security, define security in terms of 'freedom from fear and want' and bring into being a universal community of humanity based on birth or our capacity to think which is thought to distinguish us from other sentient beings. However, the genealogy of modern conceptions of human rights and security lie in the Judeo-Christian tradition. The book of Genesis states, 'Let us make man in our image, after our likeness' (Gen. 1: 26–27). Consequently, Christians affirm that all human beings have a 'natural right' to be treated equally since we are all created in the image of God *(Imago Dei)*.[6] Although it could be argued that the end result is the same – equal entitlements to freedom from fear and want – individuals, in the Christian tradition, cannot be the ultimate source of agency and autonomy. Roman Catholicism in particular considers *Imago Dei* to be foundational and grounds its post-Vatican II defence of human rights in the concept.

Similarly, Islam holds that security resides not in individual autonomy and rationality but in our equal submission to the divine will of *Allah*. Those who submit form the *umma*, the universal community of believers. Muslims hold the *Qu'ran* to be the ultimate source of truth and relations between Muslims are regulated by *Shar'ia* Law. Space, however, is allocated in Islamic law for *itjihad*, independent judicial reasoning, and interpretation of the *Qur' an*. However, all Muslims, irrespective of sect,[7] share five fundamental duties: first, all are expected to profess the *Shahada*, their faith that there is no God but Allah and that Mohammed is his Prophet; second Muslims should profess their faith through the *Salat*, a formal ritual prayer uttered five times a day; third, all Muslims are expected to observe the *Sawm* and fast during the holy month of *Ramadan*; fourth, all Muslims must give alms to the poor (*Zakat*); and inally, all Muslims are expected to undertake the *Hajj*, a pilgrimage to Mecca. Faith, and therefore ontological security, comes from observance of these five 'pillars' of Islam (*arkān al-Islām*).

Indic religio-cultural traditions, however, have a different cosmology from the Abrahamic religions of Judaism, Christianity and Islam, and lack a central revealed text such as the *Qu'ran*, *Torah* or Bible. In South Asia, the collection of local faiths subsumed under the term 'Hinduism' have as their central concern the concept of *dharma*. Dharma governs all legitimate world ends (*purushartha*), prescribing different rights and duties for different 'castes.'[8] Ontological security resides in following one's *karma*, the application of *dharma* to individual action. *Karma* in turn determines the cycle of birth, death and rebirth (*samsara*). Brahmans and other 'twice-born' castes have more 'security' than those of other castes as they are nearer to achieving *moksha* (liberation from suffering). There is, therefore, in Hinduism, a 'hierarchy of protection' (Brekke,

2013). In Buddhism as in Hinduism, *dharma* is seen as the provider of protection, and thus, ontological security rests with following one's *karma*. However, *nirvana* (liberation from suffering) is possible through individual meditation or as part of a community, *sangha*. In Sikhism, *dharam* (a variant of *dharma*) guides action, and liberation can be achieved through the recitation of the 'true name' (*Satnaam*). However, the *communal* aspect of religious identity is emphasised through the wearing of the five external symbols of faith making a distinction between the 'religious' community (*Khalsa*) and 'nation' (*qaum*) difficult (Shani, 2008a). Gender equality is particularly emphasised in Sikhism whereas Buddhism extends the principle of equality to all sentient beings while questioning the uniqueness of individual identity through the doctrine of *anatman* (no self).

Although this discussion was necessarily brief and drawn almost exclusively from the traditions with which I am most familiar, it serves to 'provincialise' (Chakrabarty, 2000) secular conceptions of Human Security, and in so doing, illustrate the main point of this paper; that non-western religio-cultural traditions have different notions of human security which cannot be encompassed within a single universal conception of Human Security.

Conclusion: pluralising Human Security

In conclusion, this paper argues that cultural identity remains an important component of human security in our post-global age. Culture, here, refers not to a set of all-engulfing, totalising 'primordial attachments' (Geertz, 1963) but to that which permits the individual to enjoy a life endowed with meaning and dignity as part of a 'community' or collectivity. Consequently, any attempt to enhance human security globally must allow faith-based groups to live in accordance with their beliefs without being forced to assimilate to the seemingly 'secular' values of the state and 'international community'. The project of 'critical human security' can only be furthered, not by a commitment to 'security as emancipation' (Booth, 1991; Newman, 2010) but by engaging with cultural traditions that offer alternative understandings of the 'human' and 'security' than those of secular, liberal modernity.

For the project of 'human security' to be advanced globally, it will need to be based upon multiple culturally-grounded conceptions of the 'human', freedom and security rather than a priori assumptions of a single, universalisable 'secular' human nature which subsumes cultural difference in its totalising desire for emancipation from 'fear' and 'want'. For human security to aspire to 'universality', it needs to be both 'post-western' *and* 'post-secular'. In so doing, it may well contribute to a 'global civilising process' capable of transcending – if not dismantling – the pernicious binaries between the 'civilised' and 'barbaric', 'secular' and 'religious', 'developed' and 'developing' and the 'West' and the 'rest', which have their origins in colonialism and have 'blocked the expansion of an international society consisting of moral equals' (Linklater, 2017).

Bibliography

Agamben, G. (1998). *Homo Sacer: Sovereign Power and Bare Life* (trans. D.Heller-Roazen). Stanford: Stanford University Press.

Aradau, C. (2004). Security and the Democratic Scene: Desecuritisation and Emancipation. *Journal of International Relations and Development*, 7(4): 388–413.

Balzacq, T. (2010). A Theory of Securitization: Origins, Core Assumptions, and Variants. In T. Balzacq (Ed.) *Securitization Theory: How Security Problems Emerge and Dissolve* (1–30). London and New York, Routledge.

Booth, K. (1991). Security and Emancipation. *Review of International Studies* 17: 313–26.

——(2005). Beyond Critical Security Studies. In K. Booth (Ed.) *Critical Security Studies and World Politics* (259–79). Boulder, Col.: Lynne Rienner.
Brekke, T. (2013). Hinduism and Security: A Hierarchy of Protection. In C. Seiple, D. R. Hoover and P. Otis (Eds.) *The Routledge Handbook of Religion and Security* (80–90). London: Routledge.
Bull, H. and Watson A. (Eds.) (1984). *The Expansion of International Society*. Oxford: Clarendon Press.
Buzan, B., Waever O. and de Wilde, J. (1998). *Security: A New Framework for Analysis*. Boulder, CO: Lynne Rienner Publishers.
Chakrabarty, D. (2000). *Provincializing Europe: Postcolonial Thought and Historical Difference*. Princeton, NJ: Princeton University Press.
Chatterjee, P. (1993). *The Nation and Its Fragments: Colonial and Postcolonial Histories*. Princeton, NJ: Princeton University Press.
Cohn, B. S. (1996). *Colonialism and Its Forms of Knowledge*. Princeton: Princeton University Press.
Commission on Human Security (CHS) (2003). *Human Security Now*. New York: Oxford University Press.
Cox, R.W. (1981) Social Forces, States and World Orders: Beyond International Relations Theory. *Millennium: Journal of International Studies* 10(2): 126–55.
Derrida, J. (1998). Faith and Knowledge: the Two Sources of "Religion" and the Limits of Reason Alone' (1–79). In J. Derrida and G.Vattimo (Eds.) *Religion*. Stanford: Stanford University Press.
Dirks, N. (2001). *Castes of Mind*. Princeton: Princeton University Press.
Elias, N. [1978] (2000). *The Civilizing Process*. Revised ed. Oxford: Blackwell.
Foucault, M. (1991). *Discipline and Punish* (trans. Alan Sheridan). London and New York: Penguin Books.
Foucault, M. (2007). *Security, Territory, Population: Lectures at the Collège de France, 1977–1978*. (trans. Graham Burchell). Houndmills, Basingstoke: Palgrave Macmillan.
Geertz, C. (1963). The Integrative Revolution: Primordial Sentiments and Civil Politics in New States. In C. Geertz (Ed.) *Old Societies and New States: The Quest for Modernity in Asia and Africa* (105–19). New York: Free Press.
Gong, G.W. (1984). *The Standard of 'Civilization' in International Society*. Oxford: Clarendon Press.
Habermas, J. (2008). *Between Naturalism and Religion*. Cambridge: Polity Press.
Hobson, J. M. (2012). *The Eurocentric Conception of World Politics: Western International Theory, 1760–2010*. Cambridge: Cambridge University Press.
Human Security Centre (HSC) (2005). *Human Security Report 2005: War and Peace in the 21st Century*. New York: Oxford University Press.
Human Security Centre (HSC) (2011) *Human Security Report 2009/2010: The Causes of Peace and the Shrinking Costs of War*. New York: Oxford University Press.
Huntington, S. P. (1993). The Clash of Civilizations? *Foreign Affairs* 72 (3): 22–49
Huntington, S. P. (1996) *The Clash of Civilisations and the Remaking of the World Order*. New York: Simon and Shuster.
Huysmans, J. (2006). *The Politics of Insecurity: Fear, Migration and Asylum in the EU*. London: Routledge.
International Commission on Intervention and State Sovereignty (2001). *The Responsibility to Protect: Report of the International Committee on Intervention and State Sovereignty*. Ottawa, ON: International Development Research Centre, December.
Kaviraj, S. (2010). *The Imaginary Institution of India: Politics and Ideas*. New York: Columbia University Press.
Linklater, A. (2011). *The Problem of Harm in World Politics: Theoretical Investigations*. Cambridge: Cambridge University Press.
Linklater, A. (2017). *Violence and Civilization in the Western States-System*. Cambridge: Cambridge University Press.
MacFarlane, S.N. and Khong, Y. F. (2006). *Human Security and the UN: A Critical History*. Bloomington and Indianapolis: Indiana University Press.
Masuzawa, T. (2005). *The Invention of World Religions*. Chicago: University of Chicago Press.
Nandy, A. (1998). The Politics of Secularism and the Recovery of Religious Tolerance. In R. Bhargava (Ed.) *Secularism and Its Critics*. New Delhi: Oxford University Press.
Newman, E. (2010). Critical Human Security Studies. *Review of International Studies*, 36 (1): 77–94.
Paris, R. (2001). Human Security: Paradigm Shift or Hot Air. *International Security*, 26 (2): 87–102.
Pasha, M. K. (2013). (Ed.) *Globalization, Difference and Human Security*. London and New York: Routledge.
Shani, G. (2007). Introduction: Protecting Human Security in a Post 9/11 World. In G. Shani, M. Sato and M. K. Pasha (Eds.) *Protecting Human Security in a Post 9/11 World: Critical and Global Insights* (1–17). Houndmills, Basingstoke, Hants: Palgrave Macmillan.

—— (2008a). *Sikh Nationalism and Identity in a Global Age*. London: Routledge.

—— (2008b). Toward a Post-Western IR: the Umma, Khalsa Panth, and Critical International Relations Theory. *International Studies Review* 10(4): 722–34.

—— (2011). Securitizing 'Bare Life': Critical Perspectives on Human Security Discourse. In David Chandler and Niklas Hynek (Eds.) *Critical Perspectives on Human Security: Discourses of Emancipation and Regimes of Power* (56–69). London: Routledge.

—— (2013). De-secularizing the 'Human.' In M. K. Pasha (Ed.) *Globalisation, Difference and Human Security* (64–77). London: Routledge.

Shani, G. and M. K. Pasha (2007). Conclusion. In G. Shani, M. Sato and M. K. Pasha (Eds.) *Protecting Human Security in a Post 9/11 World: Critical and Global Insights* (193–200). Houndmills, Basingstoke, Hants: Palgrave Macmillan.

United Nations Development Programme (UNDP) (1994). *Human Development Report 1994: New Dimensions of Human Security*. New York: Oxford University Press.

United Nations General Assembly (2005, October 24). *World Summit Outcome*. Retrieved September 17, 2012, from. www.unrol.org/files/2005%20World%20Summit%20Outcome.pdf.

United Nations General Assembly (2012, September 10). *Follow-up to Paragraph 143 on Human Security of the 2005 World Summit Outcome*. (A/RES/66/290). Retrieved September 17, 2012, from http://www.un.org/ga/search/view_doc.asp?symbol=A/RES/66/290

Wæver, O. (1995). Securitization and Desecuritization. In R. D. Lipschutz (Ed.) *On Security*, (46–86). New York: Columbia University Press.

Notes

1 An earlier version of this chapter was published at the Social Science Research Institute's international symposium on 'Political Violence, Human Security and the Civilizing Process' and is a summary of the following book: Giorgio Shani, *Religion, Identity and Human Security*. London and New York, Routledge, 2014. A revised version of this chapter was published as 'Human Security at Twenty: A Post-secular Approach' in the *Journal of Human Security Studies* (Autumn 2014) Vol. 3, No. 2: 120–36.

2 For Jürgen Habermas, the term 'post-secular' refers to societies where the continued existence of religious communities in an increasingly secularised environment necessitates, on the one hand, the inclusion of religious-based world-views into the public sphere, and, on the other, the translation of religious-based claims into secular terms in order to guarantee the neutrality of the public sphere. My own view is that the 'translation' of faith-based claims would result in their *secularisation* and that therefore an attempt should be made to understand faith-based claims in their own terms.

3 This section draws on Shani (2011, 2013b).

4 The following section appears in Shani (2013).

5 For Agamben, 'bare life' corresponds to the ancient Greek term *zoe*, which expresses the simple fact of living: *bare life is life which can be killed but not yet sacrificed*. This differed from the term *bios* which denoted a qualified life: a life with dignity, endowed with meaning which was consequently considered 'worthy' of sacrifice (Agamben, 1998).

6 Indeed, in the Christian tradition it is precisely God's love (*agape*) which *constitutes* the subject.

7 A distinction is commonly made in Islam between the orthodox *Sunni* and *Shi'a* Islam. The schism has its origins in the right of succession after the Prophet Muhammad's death. The *Shi'ia* support the claims of the Prophet's cousin and son-in-law, Ali, to have succeeded him rather than his eventual successor, Abu Bakr. Doctrinally, both *Sunni* and *Shi'a* rely upon different *Hadith* (textual traditions) but agree upon the centrality of the *Qu'ran* as the revealed text.

8 The term 'caste' is used to describe the Sanskrit term *varna*, which refers to an endogamous hereditary social group defined by notions of 'purity' and 'pollution' that have their origins in the 'Hindu' sacred texts, the *Vedas*. Society is divided into four *varna*: the *Brahmans* (priestly castes), *Kshatriyas* (warriors), *Vaishyas* (famers) and *Shudras* (slaves). See Dirks (2001) for a discussion of the colonial construction of the 'caste' from Brahmanical accounts and Orientalist scholarship.

31

DIALOGICAL INTERNATIONAL RELATIONS

Gandhi, Tagore and self-transformation

Aparna Devare

Introduction

In this chapter, I wish to take seriously David Blaney and Naeem Inayatullah's (1994, 342) evocative call for the 'possibility of a conversation of cultures that is found in the space bounded by an international society of both common values and commitments *and* diversity.' An appeal made some time ago (in 1994), it remains as relevant in thinking about global encounters between cultures today given increasing global violence. Is it possible to think about non-hegemonic encounters between peoples in a world fraught with inequality, climate crises, and rising intolerance of various kinds? And those that celebrate plurality while also *reasserting the language of universal(s)*? Blaney and Inayatullah (1994, 342) do believe so, arguing that 'this possibility, or hope, must be considered in the face of the serious barriers to conversation posed by a hierarchically ordered international society.' Despite these constraints, how do they propose to undertake such a dialogue?

Bringing the writings of Tzvetan Todorov and Ashis Nandy into International Relations, they suggest one can do this by 'discovering and engaging the other within us, we simultaneously draw the other into a dialogue' (Blaney and Inayatullah 1994, 342), leaving an imprint on both participants in the dialogue. While cultures may vary, what is common to them, they argue, drawing from Nandy, is the language of suffering or co-victimhood. And this 'co-suffering' enables making recessive elements of other cultures 'allies' in the fight against oppression. Thus, the authors (1994, 354) write, 'a dialogical process within the self is coeval with a dialogue between the self and other.' Most importantly, this essay talked about the need for more dialogic Self–Other 'intercultural' encounters that were missing in dominant 'international' relations (henceforth IR). Several others have followed since in focusing on dialogical IR such as more recently, L.H.M. Ling's (2014) work on the Dao in Chinese philosophy which she points out, allows a 'worldist' understanding of IR; and Xavier's Guillaume's (2010) work on identity in world politics, which draws on Bakhtin's conception of dialogism.

I focus on two well-known 'Indian' thinkers, Mohandas Gandhi and Rabindranath Tagore, in order to further extend the debate on dialogic cross-cultural encounters in IR.[1] Although they wrote from their non-western particulars, they thought in universalistic terms about humanity at large. They also borrowed heavily from other traditions, so that one can say that their thinking represented a kind of 'microcosm' of cultural ideas (both western and non-western). Tagore was a poet, writer, artist, thinker and composer (he composed two national anthems – that of India and Bangladesh – and inspired that of Sri Lanka), and founded a university based on his ideals known as *Visva-Bharati*. He wrote extensively in Bengali, his mother tongue, travelled all over the world establishing many friendships, was awarded the Nobel Prize in Literature in 1913 (the first non-European to do so) and died in 1941, just a few years short of India's independence from the British.

One can argue that some strands of mainstream IR such as liberalism have always stressed the need for dialogue and cooperation. In fact, liberals repudiate realist suspicion at the possibility of dialogue as a way of resolving conflicts. IR liberals draw from liberal traditions of political thinking. One of the liberal theorists who aggressively promoted the importance of dialogue was John Stuart Mill. In his chapter titled 'Of Thoughts and Discussion' in his *On Liberty*, Mill (1978, 46) stresses the need for freedom of expression for a plurality of opinions whether these are widely accepted or not in public discourse. As he writes, 'the universality of the fact that only through diversity of opinion is there, in the existing state of human intellect, a chance of fair play to all sides of the truth.'

Mill argues, the minority view point should be heard and not silenced even if one does not agree with it. Thus, he makes a strong case for plurality. This he says, is the morally right thing to do. Reading Mill so far one would think he would extend these views to cross-cultural dialogue as well. But as Uday Mehta (1999) points out, one what sees instead is an 'enormity of silence' in liberal thought with respect to colonial relationships. On the one hand, Mill builds a very persuasive case for the importance of free and fair dialogue between human beings on moral grounds while respecting diversity and on the other hand has nothing to say about the absence of these conditions in the colonies. Rather, Mill goes on to proscribe this dialogue only amongst certain kinds of human beings, who are part of the same civilisational framework. Mill (1978, 67) writes:

> the despotism of custom is everywhere the standing hindrance to human advancement, being in unceasing antagonism to that disposition to aim at something better than customary, which is called, according to circumstances, the spirit of liberty, or that of progress or improvement ... The greater part of the world has, properly speaking, no history, because the despotism of Custom is complete. This is the case over the whole East ...

Mill (1978, 67) suggests that the non-West is unquestioning of traditional authority, 'unless some tyrant intoxicated with power, thinks of resisting.' The Chinese, he argues, have become 'stationary' and 'have remained so for thousands of years' and if they have to be improved it has to be done by foreigners (Mill 1978, 69). He says what makes Europeans superior and not a stationary lot is their individuality: 'they have struck out a great variety of path, each leading to something valuable' (Mill 1978, 69). He goes on, 'But we are progressive as well as changeable: we continually make new inventions in mechanical things, and keep them until they are again superseded by better; we are eager for improvement in politics, in education, even in morals' (Mill 1978, 68). For Mill, other cultures are incapable of participating in a shared dialogue because they do not match up. This allows Mill to justify the colonial project because he believes some societies are 'advanced' enough to move to representative government under overall British rule, whereas in other cases, 'a vigorous despotism is in itself the best mode of government for training the people in what is specifically wanting to render them capable of higher civilisation.'[2] The British are then 'uplifting' non-western people via education and tutelage, and plurality is understood primarily through hierarchy.

Thus, dialogue is hampered if the primary aim of the Self is to convert the Other into an (often inferior) image of itself either through religious or secular terms. In the early phase of European colonialism with Spain and Portugal at the helm, conversions into Catholicism played a big role. In the later years, liberal ideas tied to secular and scientific notions of progress were crucial (which form the backdrop of Mill's ideas). In the latter, a temporal differentiation became very pronounced where, as Walter Mignolo (2007) argues, 'natives' were placed back in history, on a lower temporal scale. Henceforth, these societies could not be defined in any other way but backward. Both the western pre-modern (steeped in traditional Roman Catholicism) and Eastern societies became a traditional, backward people.

According to this mode of thinking, conversation with the Other as a 'legitimate' equal is only possible if she is brought or elevated to a higher temporal scale. Plurality is not something to be respected or accepted but is mapped on this temporal scale and thereby becomes a project the Self must undertake of developing/civilising/liberating/emancipating the Other. Liberals call it 'development/civilising' while Marxists call it 'emancipation/liberation'. As Mehta (1999, 80) puts it, liberalism has a reformist impulse and both Marxism and liberalism 'share in a transformative energy and in a view of the world as something malleable through political effort.' The Other is not recognised and engaged with *as Other* on his or her own terms; rather the project of transformation is inherent to liberalism and Marxism in its dialogue with the Other. The Other's plurality and self-worth is silenced in the process.

I contrast this to Gandhi and Tagore who rejected these 'emancipatory' views and practices towards the Other as fraught with violence and injustices and focused instead on *transforming the Self*. They were able to see the violence inherent to this kind of 'transformative' cross-cultural encounter. And their universality allowed them to incorporate the colonial experience as not just inflicting violence on the Other through these transformations but also the violence being done to the Self in the process (which was expunging the Others within, such as the Jews). Rejecting the language of civilising or emancipating the Other, Gandhi explicitly talked about emancipating the Self. Tagore also was very skeptical of any projects of civilisation or liberation and also discussed self-transformation as an important premise of civilisational dialogue. In the case of Gandhi, one sees a privileging of the Self in which the external Other is recognised and accommodated internally through the notion of self-critique. Self-introspection led to a recognition and acceptance of the Other on its own terms by creating a more humble and plural Self and thereby a more open-ended recognition of the Other. Moreover, rather than inflicting suffering on the Other through various transformative projects, the suffering would be taken upon one's own body through the practice of *satyagraha* (see Chandhoke 2012).

In the case of Tagore, one sees western liberal ideas being used as a basis of self-critique leading to self-transformation much more than Gandhi. Both, however, stress the need to turn inward to understand and digest the presence of the Colonial Other and be open to multiple Selves. However, Gandhi's interventions are in the realm of politics while Tagore's are more metaphysical and philosophical. One is a political/social activist and the other is a writer, poet and novelist; their biggest difference lies in their approach. In the section below, I examine how each explored the Self in order to better understand the Other and ended up with a far more open-ended notion of Self/Other relations and possibility of cross-cultural dialogue.

Gandhi's emphasis on self-transformation as a basis of dialogue

Gandhi's ideas of transformation were entirely focused on the Self. The focus is on persuading the Other, playing on ideas of human conscience, guilt, morality and so on as violent methods are largely eschewed. Violent suffering inflicted on the Self through satyagraha, for instance, can then act as a catalyst to transform the Other (so that the Other in turn will recognise the Self within it through a shared language of suffering). Perhaps, Faisal Devji is not wholly incorrect when he suggests that Gandhi provoked the aggressor to act violently against the non-violent protesters because he wanted to test the efficacy of non-violence. The more the Self suffers, the more likely the Other is going to be roused by this suffering.

Apart from certain elements of Christianity that Gandhi drew upon, I argue that he also drew upon various ascetic traditions of pre-colonial Indian society that highlighted the suffering self as a basis to transform society. But the idea of extending this individual suffering to a collective and then using it to mobilise people against the state in a secular manner is of course a wholly modern formulation. While Gandhi continuously refers to God and a higher being to give the

Self strength to suffer, his concerns are purely rooted in the practicalities of everyday life. Suffering is tied to evoking morality in the Other unlike the ascetic traditions or even Christianity and Islam (for instance, through self-flagellation), which are an attempt to come closer to God. Rather, in Gandhi's case, it is by evoking morality in the Other that one comes closer to God; hence his phrase 'Truth is God' and not 'God is Truth'. This allows, as A. Raghuramaraju (2016, 351) points out, room for both believers and non-believers.

Earlier in mainstream Hindu and many of its dissenting traditions also, individual suffering had to do with metaphysical concerns of trying to liberate the body from the cycle of life and death. It was not oriented towards a collective notion. Therefore, change had to occur at the individual level. Various ascetic traditions and reform movements like Buddhism emphasised this modality of change. The Buddha is the most well-known example of reforming or 'enlightening' the Self in order to change the Other. It is most apparent in the case of Buddha's formidable challenge to existing caste practices such as animal sacrifice, to priestly power and Vedic sources of knowledge. De-emphasising ritual, Buddha talked more about compassionate human conduct in a highly ritualistic society (see Basham 2006, 26).

But in order to bring about a change of attitudes, he undertook great personal sacrifices, took suffering upon his own body (although not extreme suffering such as those prevalent in some yogic and Jain traditions which he did not agree with) and meditated for years in order to transform or gain self-knowledge. Self-mastery and self-knowledge were prerequisites for engaging in dialogue with others. Those who were drawn to these new ideas joined Buddhist collectives known as *sanghas* which were vibrant sites of discussion and debate and membership cut across class and caste (and eventually women were also allowed after one of Buddha's disciples, Ananda, persuaded the Buddha). Buddha's ideas and practices had a tremendous impact on existing society not to mention a worldwide diffusion of those ideas.

While there may be philosophical differences between Gandhi and the Buddha which I will not get into here, I focus on this shared modality of engaging with the Other via the Self. Gandhi claimed that Buddha was also engaging in 'intensely direct action' as he 'fearlessly carried the war into the adversary camp and brought down on its knees an arrogant priesthood.' (quoted in Gier 2004, 51–63) But as Nicholas F. Gier (2004, 59) argues, Gandhi might be making the Buddha more of a political activist than he actually was (B.R. Ambedkar also read him in an intensely political way).

However, I think Buddha's 'political' interventions should be located in the social arrangements of his times. In pre-modern India, social change through the influence of the various dissenting movements over the centuries was generally promoted at the level of society and not the state because the state did not cover all aspects of life. Earlier, the state was a marginal part of people's lives; society was self-regulating through institutions such as caste, religious bodies, village communities and so on. Buddha's response was thus appropriate because it was non-state arrangements such as caste, social attitudes and religious authorities that had to be challenged. Gandhi was dealing with the modern state and knew his response had to be different. Individual suffering had to be connected to collective agency (without foregoing the individual) in new ways and the concerns were less metaphysical even if spirituality remained. The state, he believed, had become all powerful and suffused all spheres of life. He argued skeptically that the modern state affected 'every department of our life. It threatens our very existence' (Gandhi 1987a, 146).

While Gandhi was tapping into various strands of Indian thought that focused on the Self, he argued these ideas were 'universal' and could be found in other religious and spiritual traditions as well. He repeatedly mentioned the example of Christ's life where the suffering Self is given most importance in order to resist injustice: 'He who when being killed bears no anger against his murdered and even asks God to forgive him is truly non-violent. History relates this of Jesus Christ. With his dying breath on the cross, he is reported to have said: "Father, forgive them for they know not what they do"' (Gandhi 1987b, 342). He also mentions other 'spiritual' examples such as Thoreau and Socrates. However, he does say that these ideas were tried and tested over the centuries in India, especially in the ascetic traditions.

While Gandhi was leading one of the biggest anti-colonial movements of the twentieth century against the colonial state, he was also actively withdrawing into the Self through his various practices such as spinning, prayer and silence, which as Uday Mehta (2011, 114) argues, 'represents a withdrawal from the instrumental world of action and politics.' Ironically, while Gandhi was fully immersing himself in politics, he was also constantly stepping away from it by undergoing a spiritualised testing of the Self. The fast was one such practice. Tridip Suhrud (2010, 121) points out, that the fast represented not mortification of self but '*upvaas*' or coming closer to God. Gandhi believed that the things going wrong around him in his last years, such as the Hindu-Muslim riots, were because of his failure of fully controlling his senses, passions and thereby transforming himself through practices such as *brahmacharya* or celibacy. He believed that 'If he could attain perfect brahmacharya ... and unsullied ahimsa, the flames raging around him would subside' (Suhrud 2010, 146). In other words, total mastery over oneself or self-control was important in controlling the violence affecting the Other. For Gandhi, the true meaning of *Swaraj* (freedom) was to rule oneself (Suhrud 2010, 121).

As Mehta argues, Gandhi's practices (such as the fast, prayer, silence, celibacy, spinning) were important primarily because of the effects they had on the Self and fell outside the realm of politics. As he writes (2011, 116), 'In contrast, Gandhi's life is full of the incommunicable, of the singular act, where the self cannot even be represented in words or taken as exemplifying an abstract purpose.' Gandhi's ideas which are inseparable from his practices he suggests, thus cannot be easily rendered into abstract moral principles. Mehta continues, 'Ultimately Gandhi's non-violent practices were not meant to be redemptive instruments for groups or for the realization of political ideas' (Mehta 2011, 119). I think Mehta's claim that Gandhi's practices such as spinning and fasting were not meant to transform the Other downplays the importance of transformation for Gandhi. While these acts may be oriented towards the Self, they were also aimed at having an effect on the Other. Akeel Bilgrami's point about Gandhi as a 'moral exemplar' becomes useful in understanding how he seeks to have an effect on the Other. These practices have an effect on the Other by acting as an example[3] which others can follow (putting it very simply – practicing what one's preaches). As Gandhi states:

> My experience tells me that, instead of bothering about how the whole world may live in the right manner, we should think how we ourselves may do so ... If however, we live in the right manner, we shall feel that others also do the same, or shall discover a way of persuading them to do so.
>
> (Gandhi 1987b, 80)

Here, Bilgrami uses the example of Gandhi to question western moral philosophy's quest for universalisability via abstract moral judgements. He points out that western moral philosophy is based on a cognitive understanding of truth because they are 'predicated on propositions that purport to describe a reality which is distant from our practical and moral experience of it' (Bilgrami 2006, 262). According to Bilgrami (2006, 257), Gandhi, by choosing for himself or through 'exemplary actions', gives less importance to abstract 'principles' as he does not see his actions as obligatory for others to follow. Hence Gandhi's skepticism toward liberal 'emancipatory' projects (so often now found in the language of humanitarianism, human rights, development, etc.) when he responded to a letter from Europe by writing, 'Please do not carry unnecessarily on your head the burden of emancipating India. Emancipate your own self' (Gandhi 1987c, 340). And he would have extended that advice to anyone declaring they wanted to change the world. For Gandhi.

then, 'Truth' can only be based on one's own moral experience even as he believed in universality (see Chatterjee 2006, 90). According to Bilgrami (2006, 261–2), he rejects a notion of 'Truth' that 'intellectualises our relations to the world' and 'views the world as the object of study – study that makes it alien to our moral experience of it, to our most everyday practical relations to it.'

Gandhi the individual, the non-violent satyagrahi, and India as a society experimenting with non-violence then all become Selves being tested or the 'moral exemplars' that must show themselves as mirrors to the world. That is perhaps why Gandhi was often so harsh on himself, his family, the satyagrahis and on those following his movement in the country. As Gandhi puts it:

> We will not inflict suffering on anyone but will try to make others happy by undergoing hardships ourselves. If we do this, we shall be acting not only for the good of India but of the world. Today the world is watching how India is conducting herself' (Gandhi 1987a, 85). India then has to lead by example: 'Through the deliverance of India, I seek to deliver the so-called weaker races of the earth from the crushing heels of Western exploitation in which England is the greatest partner.
>
> (Gandhi 1987a, 255)

However, his claim for India was not in exclusive terms, that somehow Indians had access to moral insights about non-violence that others did not, but to argue that these insights drew from a strong connect between politics/public life and religion/morality and its religious and cultural diversity which in some ways reflected the world's diversity. He talks about this kind of self-understanding or self-knowledge as India's 'gift' to the world (see Skaria 2016).

Yet this self-understanding that comes with self-critique/introspection is not an abstract concept for Gandhi but has to happen at the individual level only. 'One's respective dharma toward one's self, family, nation and the world cannot be divided into watertight compartments. The harm done to oneself or one's family cannot bring about the good of the nation. Similarly, one cannot benefit the nation by acting against the world at large. Thus the purpose is that we must sacrifice ourselves in the interest of the family, the family must do so for the nation and the nation for the world. But the sacrifice has to be pure.' Therefore, it all starts at an individual level (Gandhi 1987b, 81).

The West, in turn, according to Gandhi, had given up these moral insights that were once there in its religious and spiritual traditions because of its quest for modernity that was driven by material greed and wealth seeking. As he put it, 'There is no such thing as Western or European civilisation, but there is a modern civilisation, which is purely material' (Gandhi 1987c, 293). He goes on, 'It is not the British people who are ruling India, but it is modern civilisation, through its railways, telegraphs, telephones… If British rule was replaced tomorrow by Indian rule based on modern methods, India would be no better' especially if it seeks to gain 'American wealth but avoid its methods' (Gandhi 1987c, 359).

Gandhi recognised that any critique of the 'Other' or the West was incomplete without a self-critique. He was acutely aware of the internal deficiencies within Indian society particularly with respect to practices of untouchability pervasive amongst Hindus. He believed the removal of untouchability was even more important than gaining independence from foreign rule and made it a central plank of his campaign, thereby merging social and political concerns. But he did not go far enough in his critique of caste, as his biggest social critic, leader of the 'Untouchables' (later known as Dalits) B.R. Ambedkar forcefully argued. Ambedkar believed that Gandhi, in order to placate upper caste Hindu society, did not denounce caste even if he rejected untouchability, because for Ambedkar these were all interlinked. Moreover, he believed Gandhi treated the Untouchables whom he named 'Harijans' or children of God in a patronising manner, and rejected Gandhi's emphasis on 'self-purification' which he believed did nothing for Dalit's self-assertion and dignity (Ambedkar 2002). Gandhi's views on race have also come under increasing scrutiny with several scholars pointing to very racist statements Gandhi made in South Africa vis-à-vis black Africans (see Roy 2014; Krishna 2015; but see also Kolge 2016). Ashwin Desai and Goolam Vahed's (2015) work combing through Gandhi's writings and speeches in South Africa argue quite forcefully that Gandhi was distinctly racist in his attitudes towards blacks, in the positions he took on several issues and that he regarded South African Indians as superior and closer to whites.

I am not keen to 'defend' Gandhi's positions on some of these issues which are indeed problematic,[4] or argue that there was a 'good' Gandhi that can be salvaged from the 'bad' one; rather I want to emphasise that Gandhi was open to self-transformation through dialogue. Dialogue provided the possibility of a gradual change in attitudes or the recognition of the limits of one's own thinking.[5] Some of his positions did change over a period of time in the process of extended dialogical engagements with others including his staunch critics. While his later statements contradicting his earlier views on Zulus can be read as part of a 'retroactive tidying-up' (Krishna 2015, 145), it can also be read as Gandhi's acknowledgement of his own prejudices. On the caste question, there has been quite a bit of scholarship dealing with what are known as the 'Gandhi-Ambedkar' debates which went on between them from the 1930s onwards. One of the most interesting essays analysing these debates comes from Dalit intellectual D.R. Nagaraj, who argues, that the clash between these two formidable figures left neither untouched.

Gandhi took the position that untouchability was a socio-religious problem and needed self-purification (of the Hindu collective Self to be enacted at the individual level), whereas Ambedkar saw it as an economic-material problem; caste hierarchies were embedded in everyday materiality. Gandhi's emphasis on 'self-purification' to remove the excesses of untouchability for Ambedkar was an upper-caste Hindu problem/solution that removed all Dalit agency and not one that would bring self-respect to Dalits. However, at the end of their intense interactions marked by sharp differences, Nagaraj (2010) writes, 'both Ambedkar and Gandhiji were not the same persons they were when they had set out on a journey of profound engagement with each other. They were deeply affected and transformed by each other.' Ambedkar, who was a rationalist and somewhat skeptical about religion, gradually turned to spiritual concerns particularly in his embracing of Buddhism (officially converting himself and masses of Dalits). It was Buddhist ideas such as *karuna* (compassion) and *maitri* (friendship) that Gopal Guru (2017, 97), a political theorist who also happens to be Dalit, argues, 'constitutes the core ethical principle of Ambedkar's Buddhism' … and 'It is these principles that provide the common moral ground for Ambedkar to find in Gandhi affirmative energies.' Ambedkar's turn to spirituality Nagaraj attributes to Gandhi's influence and in turn, Gandhi's emphasis on regenerating the village economy (which largely impacted Dalits since they were the majority) he attributes to Ambedkar's influence.[6] By the end of his life Nagaraj points out, thanks to Ambedkar, Gandhi was more skeptical about caste.

Tagore's belief in inter-cultural dialogue and humanism through self-transformation

Tagore's notion of self-transformation was very different from Gandhi's. Unlike Gandhi, Tagore was weary of the world of politics and kept his distance from it. Tagore shared the skepticism of many intellectuals towards politics – something that Gandhi fought against in his attempt to extend into the domain of politics the quest for self-realisation and transformation (earlier seen as an individualistic spiritualist goal). At a time when nationalist fervor was at its peak in Europe, India and elsewhere, Tagore spoke stingingly against nationalism, displaying a universalistic attitude toward humanity.[7] He took very unpopular positions and is often described as an iconoclast. This led to his expressing serious reservations about some of Gandhi's political ideas which have now come to be known as the 'Gandhi-Tagore' debates (see Raghuramaraju 2017). Some of these included his opposition to Gandhi's non-cooperation movement, his emphasis on spinning and burning foreign cloth – all which he saw as promoting an exclusivist Indian nationalism (see Prabhu and Kelekar 1961).

For Tagore, western ideas via colonialism did bring about necessary winds of change into Indian society. As he put it, 'Whatever we understand and enjoy in human products instantly becomes ours, wherever they might have their origin' (Bhattacharya 2011, 47). Unlike Gandhi, he was not as critical of modern liberal ideas although a deep skepticism towards the West set in towards the end of his life. Gandhi was very critical of social reformers who were influenced by western ideas unlike Tagore who found their influence to be necessary and favorable. On questions of caste and gender, Tagore was much more strident in his critiques of traditions than Gandhi. In his early years, western liberal ideas could act as the basis of internal criticism, thereby allowing a rethinking and movement toward self-transformation. According to him, the 'one great service the West has done us by bringing the force of its living mind to bear upon our life; it has stirred our thoughts into activity ... We are beginning to know ourselves. We are discovering our own mind' (Tagore 1964).

Tagore used the new liberal ideas to question existing social and religious practices that had become fixed and reified such as caste and gender hierarchies within society. As he says, 'The present civilisation of India has the constraining power of the mould. It squeezes living man in the grip of rigid regulations, and its repression of individual freedom makes it only too easy for me to be forced into submission of all kinds and degrees' (Tagore 2016). He saw the positive impact of these ideas in spurring social reform movements in nineteenth-century Bengal, such as the Brahmo Samaj that began radically questioning caste practices, notions of untouchability, excessive Brahminical emphasis on notions of purity and pollution and so on. The Brahmo Samaj also questioned certain gender exclusions and pointed to the need for women's education. He pointed to his own family as having been greatly influenced by these ideals (his father Debendranath Tagore was a leading member of the Brahmo Samaj).

Tagore's views on how these ideas were being negotiated comes through most clearly in his novels. Tagore operated in a more artistic and literary realm than Gandhi; hence any discussion on Tagore has to move to art, poetry or literature. It is in his novels that one can get a glimpse of new colonial subjectivities. The novel that deals most explicitly with the idea of self-transformation I believe is *Gora* where the main protagonist comes to understand the limits of transforming the Other without first fully realising oneself.[8] The novel is set up in a dialogue form developing 'through interactions between carefully opposed sets of characters with opposite points of view' (Chatterjee 2005, 87), thereby reflecting the different strands of thinking at the time and Tagore's own engagement with these ideas.

The novel is set in nineteenth-century Calcutta, Bengal during the height of the British Raj. The story revolves around two upper-caste Bengali Brahmin families. One is a conservative orthodox Hindu family and the other is a Brahmo family. Brahmos were known to be very Anglicised in their speech, dress and lifestyle. They openly adopted many English mannerisms and customs in their homes and aggressively took to English education. In the novel the women in the Brahmo family are free to come out into their living rooms and interact with young men who visit and are encouraged to express their opinions. The father of the household, Paresh Babu, is a well-known Brahmo reformer and his three daughters, Lolita, Labonya and Sucharita, are encouraged to study, to read and engage in intellectual discussions. This is in contrast to the orthodox upper-caste Hindu household where women are not supposed to mix freely with men and are told to focus on household activities.

The main protagonist Gourmohan Babu or Gora who belongs to the orthodox Hindu family feels the need to defend Hinduism in light of attacks from the British, the Brahmos and the missionaries, including the role of women whom he says belong in the household and are upholders of tradition. But he is shown to secretly start developing an attraction for Sucharita, one of the Brahmo girls, and visits her often. His best friend Binoy, who is also an upper-caste Brahmin but more open-minded, falls in love with another of the daughters, Lolita, who is shown to be strong-willed. It is this love affair between the two, Binoy and Lolita as two partners and equals who have chosen each other, thereby breaking social boundaries between orthodoxy and the Brahmos that Tagore places as one of the most important events in the book. Moreover, they have opted for a 'love marriage' in a society where marriages arranged by families is the norm. A softer, accommodative, gentle and more effeminate Binoy is contrasted to the more hyper-masculinist Gora throughout the story. Tagore's women in the novel are shown to be strong in different ways; Lolita is fearless and feisty; as Niharranjan Ray (1961) points out, Lolita revolts against society, family, religion for love and also gives strength to Binoy, helping him come out of the shadow of a more overpowering Gora. While most people in both families and the society around them oppose the marriage and there is strong censure within the Brahmo Samaj for Lolita marrying a 'Hindu,' there are two people who support the couple against all odds.

It is clear that Tagore admires these two characters the most. One is Lolita's father, Paresh Babu, who though being a Brahmo and is strongly condemned by the Samaj for allowing this marriage says, 'Sectarianism is a thing which makes people entirely forget the simple and obvious truth that man is man – it creates a kind of whirlpool in which the society-made distinctions between Hindu and Brahmos assumes greater importance than universal truth' (Tagore 1949, 42). The other person who defies society and accepts the marriage is Anandamoyi, Gora's mother who belongs to the orthodox family and treats Binoy as her adopted son since he has no mother. Anandamoyi, although seen to be a conventional upper-caste woman, especially from the Brahmo point of view, does not follow caste rules, questions society in her own way and bravely faces all social criticism and ostracism. She says 'marriage is a matter of hearts coming together, what matters what *mantras* (sacred verses) are recited' (Tagore 1949, 42).

The two characters in the novel Tagore is most critical of are Gora and Haran Babu. Gora defends Hindu traditions at any cost including its obsession with purity and ties it to the idea of a nation and the need for national unity above all else. As Gora says early in the novel, 'We must not feel apologetic about the unity of our birth – whether it be about its traditions, faith or its scriptures – neither to others nor even to ourselves. We must save our country and ourselves from insult by manfully bearing the burden of our motherland with all our strength and all our pride' (Tagore 1949, 42). Haran Babu, leader of the Brahmo Samaj (who is supposed to marry Sucharita but she rejects him), opposes Lolita's marriage to Binoy on grounds that it will disgrace the Samaj. He tries very hard to break up their courtship and strongly rebukes Lolita for choosing an 'idol-worshipper'.

Interestingly, Tagore seems to suggest that even the Samaj, while rejecting older notions of hierarchy through Haran, begin to institute new bases of exclusion. Tagore in his rather negative portrayal of the 'reformer' Haran Babu, who rejects all Hindu practices as backward, superstitious and all Bengalis as retrograde, appears to point to the limitations of a liberal rationalist critique.[9] So while Tagore is critical of a defensive Hinduism (as a response to colonialism) which he increasingly sees hitched to nationalism through Gora, he is also just as critical of a dogmatic liberalism which is unable to view others different from itself without placing them within a hierarchy of progressive/backward.

In fact, Tagore seems to suggest that this aggressive rationalist critique (from 'liberal' reformers like Haran Babu) triggers defensive reactions in people like Gora who respond with a hyper-masculine form of nationalism. This is most apparent in the reaction that Paresh Babu's family has to a widowed orthodox woman, Harimohini, who is a relative of theirs who comes to stay with them as she has nowhere else to go. At the insistence of Paresh Babu's wife, Baurasundari or Mistress Baroda (as she is called), the widow is kept in a corner of the house away from the rest of the family where she can worship her idols and follow what are seen as retrograde religious practices and beliefs. She is virtually shunned as a pariah in the house especially by Mistress Baroda and her Brahmo visitors who jeer and laugh at her, viewing her as a lesser human. While later in the book Tagore is very critical of Harimohini's orthodox caste practices and her trying to enforce them on her niece Sucharita, he is clearly not very sympathetic to Brahmo 'orthodoxy' either.

Tagore seems to suggest that 'difference' is not adequately addressed through ways of thinking such as 'rational' liberalism and nationalism. They may posit themselves as 'liberatory' and inclusive but in fact end up instituting new kinds of violence against those who are not seen as measuring up to these values. Tagore suggests that notions of 'purity' get transferred from older notions such as caste to newer ones like nationalism, secularism, liberalism and so on where the boundaries are as strongly policed. In the book, he clearly tries to show that it is easier to denounce the older orthodox practices that may be exclusionary, but the newer ideas cloaked in languages of the 'modern' and 'progressive' conceal exclusions in a more sophisticated manner. Tagore is very weary of any kinds of extremisms including those which speak on behalf of the Other or try to transform the Other in their own image (Mukherji 2011, 93).

The twist at the end of the story is that the patriarchal hyper-masculine, nationalist and caste-practicing Gora finds out that he was born to Irish parents who were killed in the 1857 Revolt and that Anandamoyi had rescued and raised him as her own son despite all societal disapproval. In Gora's 'release' from religion, caste and hyper-masculine nationalism, Tagore suggests he finds true freedom. Tagore shows an inner battle raging within Gora throughout the book whereby he fights injustice irrespective of caste and religious loyalties, such as, for instance, in one incident where he supports Muslim peasants over their oppressive Brahmin and colonial administrator in a village; or his attraction to Sucharita, who is a 'Brahmo' and different from him. However, he fights and suppresses these contrary internal pulls because he wants to remain 'pure' in his ideological positions.

It is only when his ageing orthodox father, Krishnadayal, becomes concerned that his last rites after his death will be conducted by Gora, a non-Brahmin, that he reveals the truth to him, thereby bringing Gora's internal conflicts to an end. Hence, Gora actually expresses great relief when the truth about his origins are revealed to him. He is transformed and feels a sense of freedom from the 'traditions' around which he had woven his own self-definition. One can read this transformation in Gora as a recognition of the Other within the Self which he had been suppressing all along. For Tagore, this recognition allows him to transcend nationalism (although not particularity)[10] and embrace universality. As P.K. Datta (2003, 4) argues, in Gora's coming to terms with his birth, Tagore critiques the idea of a 'pure' national identity but one can extend this to say he rejects the idea of purity (in identity) itself. Or as Rustom Bharucha (2011, 64) puts it, Gora's self-realisation is not the birth of a nation which Tagore actually considers destructive but that of an inner self that is outside the domain of politics.

Tagore suggests that colonial modernity forces one to reinvent oneself in ways that causes great internal conflict (something close to Frantz Fanon's position too) and brings in new forms of exclusions. This is apparent in a dialogue that Binoy, Gora's friend, engages in. Binoy, who is shown to be much more self-aware than Gora says, 'All these religious principles that I have been defending so much all these days, I have been defending, not from the point of religion, but from the point of view of a party ... We do not think of it as religion, but go about fighting for it because it is *our* religion' (Tagore 1949, 302). This indicates that according to Tagore, there are certain postures that one may take even if it goes against one's nature (*svabhava*) and one either becomes aware of this or suppresses it, leading to a kind of internal violence. For Tagore, abstractions can be dangerous especially when they silence individual human suffering and injustice or what he calls 'matters of the heart'.

The three people who Tagore upholds and contrasts with the more rigid characters are Gora's mother, Anandomoyi, Paresh Babu and Gora's friend, Binoy. Tagore, sees these three as suffering from 'no sectarian exclusiveness and are wise enough to place human relations above dogma and communalism ...' (Chatterjee 2005, 193). These are the three that in some ways Tagore suggests provide the most humane alternatives to ideological rigidity (whether religious, national, liberal rationalist, etc.). Anandamoyi is never shown in the novel to be worshipping an idol or reading scriptures and yet is never disparaging of it. She is not accepted in either world but faces her choices with fortitude. As she says, 'Nearly everyone calls me a Christian and whatever else comes to their lips' (quoted in Singh 1997, 10, 9). As Nikky Singh (1997, 10, 2) puts it, 'she feels an affinity to everyone around her' and 'embodies Tagore's expansive vision of India.' Her bond with Gora is a very deep one although as Singh puts it, the two could not look physically more different (she, small-built and dark-skinned; he, tall, big-built and very fair skinned) (Singh 1997, 11).

This process of self-transformation leading to the recognition of the Other within the Self is more explicit in Tagore's essay titled 'Man'. According to Tagore, becoming civilised is gaining a greater awareness of universality based on ethics that apply across time and place. He writes:

> In the words of Christ, he heard that purity lies, not in external commands and prohibitions, but in the sanctifying of the heart. This was the invocation of the universal Personality in the mind of the individual person. The final utterance of this very consciousness is that he alone knows Truth who realises in his own soul those of others, and in the soul of others, his own' (Tagore 1946, 4). For Tagore, 'Man' discovers 'himself' and through that, the Universal, by giving up his self-interest, through his acts of self-sacrifice, self-giving and in promoting love. This, he argues, is seen in innumerable human lives; 'History does not record their names; from their individual lives they pour into the living stream of humanity the immortal energy of Him.
>
> (Tagore 1946, 79–80)

For him, this is the basis of civilisational advancement.

According to him, history is a movement of this greater self-consciousness within the Self. He writes, 'Age follows age in human history, and man continues in his ceaseless search not for the satisfaction of his material needs, but in order to strive with all his might for the revelation of the Universal Man in the world of men, to rescue his own inmost truth from the crude obstacles set up by himself. That is the Truth which is greater than all his accumulated wealth, greater than all his achievements, greater than all his traditional beliefs and knows no death nor decay' (Tagore 1946, 63). And this Universal Man is reflected in, 'Innumerable men in knowledge, in love, in self-giving, in various forms and ways ... revealing the immeasurable within them. History does not record their names; from their individual lives they pour into the living stream of humanity the immortal energy of Him' (Tagore 1946, 79–80).

According to Tagore, this larger universal self-consciousness is gained by looking within: 'This seeking and knowing him is no seeking and knowing outside oneself. It is knowing through becoming, receiving through being true within' (Tagore 1946, 67). This, he argues, is the highest form of knowledge or Self-knowledge which he calls *dharma*. And this, he argues, is what people call 'God' and in devotion to such a notion of a 'Supreme Being' one's self-consciousness is 'enlarged and deepened' (Tagore 1946, 62). For Tagore, divinity can be seen in the divine acts within Man itself and one does not have to look beyond. According to him, the divine is an embodiment of that higher spiritual ideal found within Man itself. That is the self-realisation that Man is always striving for, the actualisation of his dharma or his inner nature by aligning it with the divine beyond. He quotes the Buddha when he says, 'it is through immeasurable love that man reveals the immeasurable truth within himself', highlighting the notion of *maitri* or friendship with all living beings (Tagore 1946, 75).

Given the importance that Tagore gives to individual self-realisation and transformation by seeking a higher spiritual and moral ideal, he is very weary that abstractions such as nationalism run contrary to it and are inherently violent. According to Tagore, the way to fight abstractions like nationalism are not to form counter-nations in response and imitate the West (as he points out militaristic Japan did) but to uphold the 'universal moral law' which goes much beyond the nation. The response in his view should be to 'Be more good, more just, more true in your relation to man, control your greed, make your life wholesome in its simplicity' (Tagore 1918, 31). He is weary of speaking in the language of emancipation on behalf of anyone else as many of his Bengali counterparts were doing influenced by liberal and socialist ideas. He states very clearly that he speaks as an individual only. As he puts it, 'No one can write going beyond his experience...Literature is not produced by acting together ... whatever I write is not for propagating the 'cult of the poor' or the 'epoch' but I write what I alone can say.'

One can see that this view did not provide alternatives in the realm of active politics which required collective mobilisation. Here his difference with Gandhi is quite apparent. For Gandhi, self-introspection had to be channeled into concrete anti-colonial political alternatives which included re-envisioning the nation in a more inclusive and open-ended manner. Tagore saw his own role as a poet who was disinterested and disenchanted by politics. As Rahul Rao (2013, 180) argues, Tagore's inability to capture the public imagination in the same way as Gandhi was partly because he was unable to articulate alternative political institutions to the ones he critiqued. Having said that, however, his setting up of the Visva Bharati centre of learning (which later became a university) in Bengal reflected his effort to create alternative educational institutions. He wanted to make it a truly global university 'in the name of love' (Mukherji 2011, 116) and one that would be a site to develop a 'universal consciousness' (Bhattacharya 2011, 11). He made considerable efforts in the field of education and was also interested in matters related to agriculture.

Tagore's scathing critique of the West which came later in life as expressed in his well-known essays, '*Crisis of Civilization*' and '*Nationalism*', rejected Western conceptions of freedom. For him the conceptions of self-consciousness, freedom and civilisation dominant in the West was a negation of a realisation of universal ethics rooted in *dharma* or the higher ideal of man. Unlike Gandhi who stated that Western civilisation was Satanic and had lost its Christian foundations, Tagore (1918, 11) focused more on the loss of morality/universality as indicated in their embracing ideologies like nationalism and capitalism (he doesn't call it as such but the greed for unlimited wealth and material power), which he stated led to a 'dissolution of humanity'.

He points out that people in the West 'have sacrificed their souls to the passion of profit-making and the drunkenness of power...are constantly pursued by phantoms of panic and suspicion' (Tagore 2012). It is money and organised propaganda that lie behind the notion of nation in the West which he equates with a machine. He sees belief in the nation akin to a 'cult of collective selfishness' and religious fervor. He writes, 'For men are taught by repeated devices the lesson that the Nation is greater than the people, while yet it scatters to the winds the moral law that the people have held sacred' (Tagore 1922, 151). According to him, in the West people had been hypnotised into believing they were free but their 'free choice' was only defined by the aspiration of power and profit (Tagore 1918).

Tagore begins the brief essay '*Crisis of Civilisation*' stating that as a youth he was completely captivated by western liberal universalism. Written in the 80th year of his life shortly before he died, he outlines what he calls the 'tragic tale of the gradual loss of my faith in the claims of the European nations to civilisation' (Tagore 2010–2012). By then he saw liberal universalism as inextricably linked to nationalism, capitalism and colonialism and was totally disillusioned. And yet like Gandhi he continued to make a distinction between the West as ideology and its people, reflected in the extensive travels that he did in the West and the deep friendships he cultivated at the individual level (see Hay 1962). He was 'passionately committed to the interaction of cultures' (Rao 2013, 180) and inter-civilisational dialogue by which we can 'know our own selves through an expansion of sympathies' (see Jahanbegloo 2007, 72).

Conclusion

Both Gandhi and Tagore in their different ways recognised the limits of inter-civilisational dialogue through modern liberal ideas which focused on solely transforming the Other without any kind of self-critique and self-introspection. While both had differences with each other on how this was to come about (Gandhi was trying to bridge the world of politics and spirituality, whereas for Tagore this was not possible), both shared a skepticism towards liberatory or emancipatory projects. It is these forms of transformations (and lack of genuine dialogue) that both believed gave rise to modern forms of instrumental violence. Their colonial location allowed them to see the particularity of the colonial western universal and its using difference as the basis to institute new forms of hierarchies.

Were they also perpetuating internal hierarchies in their conceptions of self-transformation? Were the Selves they talked about located in specific structures of power? It is indeed the case that both did belong to upper castes and Tagore was part of the Bengali urban intelligentsia. Tagore's Gora is set in a privileged middle-class Bengali social milieu. But the Selves that they talk about carry with them as I have argued in the paper, an openness towards self-correction and transcendence of their specific positions through the process of dialogue. These debates (including with each other) were often sharp but did lead to greater self-questioning and changes in their own positions on various issues. It is this openness I argue, which came from debates and dialogues that allows the possibility of plural Selves; it was the Self that had to 'open up' and the various Others within the Self or the plural Self had to be acknowledged.

Returning to Blaney and Inayatullah's call for dialogical inter-national/cultural relations, the act of dialogue is then not just an external process but also internal – to recognise the Others within. This would in turn allow the Other to be recognised as *Other* without rejecting the idea of universality and a shared sense of being human. In this paper, I have argued that Tagore and Gandhi do allow us the possibility of a more 'dialogic IR' that Blaney and Inayatullah hope for, which recognises difference along with universality.

Bibliography

Ambedkar, B.R. *The Essential Writings of B.R. Ambedkar*, ed. by Valerian Rodrigues (New Delhi: Oxford University Press, 2002).

Basham, A.L. 'Traditional Influences on the Thought of Mahatma Gandhi,' in *Debating Gandhi: A Reader* ed. by A. Raghuramaraju (New Delhi: Oxford University Press, 2006).

Bharucha, Rustom. *Another Asia: Rabindranath Tagore and Okakura Tenshin* (New Delhi: Penguin, 2011).

Bhattacharya, Sabyasachi. *Rabindranath Tagore: An Interpretation* (New Delhi: Penguin, 2011).

Bilgrami, Akeel. 'Gandhi's Integrity: The Philosophy Behind the Politics', in *Debating Gandhi: A Reader* ed. by A. Raghuramaraju (New Delhi: Oxford University Press, 2006).

Blaney, David and Naeem Inayatullah. 'Prelude to a Conversation of Cultures in International Society? Todorov and Nandy on the Possibility of Dialogue', *Alternatives* 19(1) (1994), 23–51.

Chandhoke, Neera. 'The Quest for Justice: Evoking Gandhi' in *Indian Political Thought: A Reader* eds. by Aakash Singh and Silika Mohapatra (London and New York: Routledge, 2012), 39–50.

Chatterjee, Kalyan. 'Gora: Tagore's Paradoxical Self', *Indian Literature* 49, 3(227) (May-June 2005), 185–95.

Chatterjee, Partha. 'The Moment of Manoeuvre: Gandhi and the Critique of Civil Society' in *Debating Gandhi: A Reader* ed. by A. Raghuramaraju (New Delhi: Oxford University Press, 2006).

Datta, P.K. ed., *Rabindranath Tagore's The Home and the World: A Critical Companion* (Delhi: Permanent Black, 2003).

Desai, Ashwin and Goolam Vahed. *The South African Gandhi: Stretcher Bearer of Empire* (New Delhi: Navayana Publishing, 2015).

Devji, Faisal. *The Impossible Indian: Gandhi and the Temptations of Violence* (Cambridge, MA: Harvard University Press, 2012).

Gandhi, M.K. *The Moral and Political Writings of Mahatma Gandhi, volume 1*, ed. Raghavan Iyer (Oxford: Clarendon Press, 1987c).

———. *The Moral and Political Writings of Mahatma Gandhi volume 2*, ed. by Raghavan Iyer (Oxford: Clarendon Press, 1987b).

———. *The Moral and Political Writings of Mahatma Gandhi volume 3*, ed. by Raghavan Iyer (Oxford: Clarendon Press, 1987a).

Gandhi, Rajmohan. 'Independence and Social Justice: The Ambedkar-Gandhi Debate', *Economic and Political Weekly* 50:15 (April 11th, 2015).

Gier, Nicholas F. *The Virtue of Non-Violence: From Gautama to Gandhi* (Albany: State University of New York Press, 2004).

Guillaume, Xavier. *International Relations and Identity: A Dialogical Approach* (London and New York: Routledge, 2010).

Guru, Gopal. 'Ethics in Ambedkar's Critique of Gandhi' Economic and Political Weekly, 52: 15 (April 15th, 2017), 95–100, 97.

Hay, Stephen. 'Rabindranath Tagore in America', *American Quarterly* 14, 3 (Autumn, 1962), 439–63.

Jahanbegloo, Ramin. 'Tagore and the Idea of Civilisation', *India International Centre Quarterly*, 34, 1 (Summer 2007), 64–73.

Kolge, Nishikant. 'Was Gandhi a Racist?' *Economic and Political Weekly* 51:5 (January 30th, 2016), 91, 88–93.

———. 'Was Gandhi a "Champion of the Caste System"?' *Economic and Political Weekly*, 52:13 (April 1st, 2017), 42–50.

Krishna, Sankaran. 'A Postcolonial Racial/spatial Order: Gandhi, Ambedkar, and the Construction of the International' in *Race and Racism in International Relations*, ed. by Alexander Anievas, Nivi Manchanda and Robbie Shilliam (London and New York: Routledge, 2015), 139–56.

Ling, L.H.M. *The Dao of World Politics: Towards a Post-Westphalian, Wordlist International Relations* (London and New York: Routledge, 2014).

Mallavarapu, Siddharth. 'Securing India: Gandhian Institutions' in *India's Grand Strategy: History, Theory, Cases*, eds. by Kanti Bajpai, Saira Basit, V. Krishnappa (London, New York and Delhi: Routledge, 2014).

Mehta, Uday Singh. *Liberalism and Empire: A Study in Nineteenth-Century British Liberal Thought* (Chicago and London: University of Chicago Press, 1999).

———. 'Politics and Violence: Gandhi's Ambivalence to Democracy,' in *Democratic Culture: Historical and Philosophical Essays*, ed. by Akeel Bilgrami (London, New York and New Delhi: Routledge, 2011), 104–21.

Mignolo, Walter. 'Delinking', *Cultural Studies* 21:2(2007), 449–514.

Mill, John Stuart. *On Liberty* (Indianapolis and Cambridge: Hackett Publishing Company, 1978).

Mukherji, Gangeya. *An Alternative Idea of India: Tagore and Vivekananda* (London, New York and New Delhi: Routledge, 2011).

Nagaraj, D.R. *The Flaming Fleet: A Study of the Dalit Movement in India* (Ranikhet: Permanent Black, 2010).

Palshikar, Suhas. 'Gandhi-Ambedkar Interface–When Shall the Twain Meet?' *Economic and Political Weekly* 49:13 (March 29th, 2014), 45–50.

Pandit, Lalita. 'Caste, Race, and Nation: History and Dialectic in Rabindranath Tagore's *Gora*' in *Literary India: Comparative Studies in Aesthetics, Colonialism and Culture*, eds. by Patrick Colm Hogan and Lalita Pandit (Jaipur and New Delhi: Rawat Publications, 1997), 207–33.

Prabhu, R.K. and Ravindra Kelekar, *Truth Called Them Differently (Tagore-Gandhi Controversy)* (Ahmedabad: Navajivan Publishers, 1961).

Raghuramaraju, A. 'Ethics of M.K. Gandhi: Non-violence and Truth' in *Bloomsbury Handbook of Indian Ethics*, ed. by Shyam Ranganathan (London: Bloomsbury, 2016), 341–56.

———. 'The Colonized Self's Climb Towards *svaraj*: Revisiting the Debate between Mahatma Gandhi and Gurudev Rabindranth Tagore' in his book, *Modern Frames and Premodern Themes in Indian Philosophy: Border, Self and Other* (New York and London: Routledge, 2017).

Rao, Rahul. 'Postcolonial Cosmopolitanism: Making Place for Nationalism' in *The Democratic Predicament: Cultural Diversity in Europe and India*, eds. by Jyotirmaya Tripathi and Sudarsan Padmanabhan (New Delhi: Routledge, 2013), 165–90.

Ray, Niharranjan. 'Novels of Tagore-"Chokher Bali"-"Gora"-"Yogayoga",' *Indian Literature* 4, ½ (Oct 1960/Sept 1961), 163–81.

Roy, Arundhati. 'The Doctor and the Saint' in B.R. Ambedkar, *Annihilation of Caste: The Annotated Critical Edition* (London and New York: Verso, 2014).
Singh, Nicky. 'Infigurations and Configurations of India: Anandamoyi in Tagore's "Gora",' *Journal of South Asian Literature*, 31/32, no.1/2(1996/1997), 1–31.
Skaria, Ajay. *Unconditional Equality: Gandhi's Religion of Resistance* (Ranikhet: Permanent Black, 2016).
Suhrud, Tridip and Peter Ronald DeSouza, eds. *Speaking of Gandhi's Death* (Hyderabad: Orient Blackswan, 2010).
Tagore, Rabindranath. 'Nationalism in the West' in *Nationalism* (London: Macmillan and Company, 1918).
———. *Creative Unity* (London: Macmillan and Company, 1922).
———. *Man* (Allahabad: Kitabistan, 1946).
———. *Gora* (London: Macmillan and Company, 1949).
———. 'Satyam,' in *Boundless Sky* (Calcutta: Visva-Bharati, 1964), 332–40.
———. 'Crisis of Civilization' in *The Great Speeches of Modern India*, ed. Rudrangshu Mukherjee, (Noida: Random House, 2011), 148–55.
———. 'Spirit of Freedom' in *The Complete Works of Rabindranath Tagore*, available at www.tagoreweb.in, 2010–2012.
———. *The Complete Works of Rabindranath Tagore*, tagoreweb.in, 2010–2012. Accessed on May 1, 2016.
Weber, Thomas. 'Gandhi and World Politics' in *International Relations Perspectives for the Global South*, eds. by Bhupinder S. Chimni and Siddharth Mallavarapu (New Delhi: Pearson, 2015).

Notes

1 Weber (2015) and Mallavarapu (2014) have insightfully discussed Gandhi's ideas in light of mainstream international relations concepts.

2 John Stuart Mill, The Collected Works of John Stuart Mill, Volume XIX-Essays on Politics and Society Part 2 (Considerations on Representative Government), available online at http://oll.libertyfund.org/titles/mill-the-collected-works-of-john-stuart-mill-volume-xix-essays-on-politics-and-society-part-2, accessed on November 11, 2016

3 Hence Gandhi's well-known statement, 'my life is my message'.

4 For a defence of Gandhi on the issues of caste and racism, see Gandhi (2015). Kolge (2017) also defends Gandhi by making a distinction between his writings and lived practices. Gandhi in his lived practice he argues, was very critical of untouchability, caste exclusions, and allowed his son to marry outside caste.

5 I am grateful to Raghuramaraju for pointing me in this direction. A. Raghuramaraju, personal communication, April 30, 2017.

6 Gandhi greatly emphasised physical labour, seen as demeaning in the Hindu caste social order, arguing that everyone should become a 'shudra' (low caste). See Palshikar (2014, 45–50). Gandhi gave a lot of importance to the body and working with one's hands, seen as 'lowly' by Brahmins.

7 Tagore has a very vast corpus of writings including many essays, novels, poems, plays, songs (numbered at 2500). For this paper, I have focused only on some more well-known essays and one novel.

8 Gora means fair-skinned. The character of Gora was said to have been modelled on Brahmabandhav Upadhyay, a firebrand personality who was initially influenced by the Brahmo Samaj, and then converted to Roman Catholicism. He later became a Hindu monk, and eventually a militant Hindu revolutionary. He died tragically in a British prison. Tagore knew him very well and exchanged many letters with him.

9 Lalita Pandit (1997) argues, that the Samaj looked down upon caste and idol worship thereby instituting 'a home-grown variety of imperialist ideology based on differentialist principles. The paradox of Brahmo Samaj was that its members set themselves up as a dissenting group who wished to stand up against the hegemony of traditional Hinduism, but in doing so they adopted a hegemonic point of view identical to that of the imperialist outsider and master'. This she points out, influenced Tagore.

10 When Gora finds out the truth of his birth Tagore suggests, he embraces a universal notion of humanity but within the particular of his locale and situation. He tells his mother Anandamoyi that he will now work for all people living in the land of India, to serve them selflessly and without prejudice since he himself doesn't 'belong anywhere'. And yet he affirms a sense of belonging to the territory, the land and the family he is raised by because he doesn't want to know about his original parents and lovingly embraces his mother as the real truth and to whom he truly belongs.

32

'TELLING A TALE'

Gender, knowledge and the subject in Nepal

Rahel Kunz and Archana Thapa

Introduction

> *I was too hapless to understand the reason for my misery, but miserable I was in my half-Nepali, half-American life. Tortured. ...*
> *I wanted to be a boy. And not just any boy. I wanted to be a freeborn Western boy. Not just any freeborn Western boy. I wanted, specifically, to be Björn Borg, the Swedish tennis star.*
>
> (M. Thapa 2010, 70–2)

How does a Nepali girl come to dream of being a white male Swedish tennis star? Manjushree Thapa's story is part of *Telling a Tale,* a collection of personal narrations about being, becoming and writing as a girl or woman in contemporary Nepal (A. Thapa 2010). The stories highlight the diverse ways in which Nepali girls and women from various social backgrounds navigate complex social structures such as gender, caste, religion, marital status and ethnicity and how these have shaped their identities. The authors also narrate how they resist, subvert and move beyond social norms to create their own alternative ways of knowing and being in the world as they 'move into modernity'. These stories address two key issues at the heart of coloniality and post/decolonial politics: the ways in which coloniality has shaped, and continues to shape, gendered forms of knowledge production and subjectivity formation, even in a country that was never colonised, such as Nepal. In this chapter, we draw on *Telling a Tale* as an archive to explore post/decolonial politics and alternative imaginaries.

You may wonder why a chapter on Nepal would be included in a handbook on postcolonial politics. Even though Nepal officially remained a sovereign country during the colonial era, it was strongly influenced by colonisation. For one, it has been argued that Nepal experienced an 'equally oppressive but noncolonial Rana government' (Des Chene 2007, 215).[1] The broader influence of coloniality and imperialism has been summarised as follows:

> A non-colonial nationalism with deep roots in colonial India, a current political relationship with India that has its roots in Nepal's relationship with British India, a history of labour migration that is similarly rooted in the political-economy of British India. And a vision of the nation premised on the Nepali language, the monarchy and Hinduism as its defining features, a vision forged in contradistinction to colonized India.
>
> (Des Chene 2007, 218)

Moreover, various authors have discussed multiple ways in which coloniality has shaped and continues to shape Nepal, highlighting for instance the 'colonialist aspect of early anthropology in Nepal' (Des Chene 2007, 212) and the 'continuing influence of colonial borders on the ways South Asia is thought about, and of the hold of intra-regional imperialisms' (Des Chene 2007, 209). In this light, Nepal is a particularly interesting site to explore post/decolonial politics, given that it was not formally colonised and yet coloniality has shaped and continues to shape the country (Des Chene 2007).

Gender politics in Nepal has also been influenced by coloniality. Nepali social structures are characterised by a rich diversity of 123 languages, castes, ethnicities, religions and cultures and there is not one single gender regime but many (Mittra and Kumar 2004; Yadav 2016). Yet, a complex combination of influencing factors imposed from outside have shaped and continue to shape knowledge production and social norms about gender in Nepal. Most prominently, these include Hindu nationalism, British imperialism, the arrival of development projects in the 1950s and the 10-year-long civil war (1996–2006). Hindu nationalism has strongly shaped knowledge and norms about gender in Nepal. Particular interpretations of Hinduism and their codification in laws and regulations influenced social norms regarding gender, caste, etc. and promoted particular binary models of heterosexuality and procreation (Sharma 2004; Mittra and Kumar 2004).[2] In this context, marriage is considered a necessary and key event in everyone's life, based on cultural and religious norms, and women are considered to accept their husband's world as their own (Yadav 2016, 47). Despite the fact that Nepal was declared a secular state in 2007 and despite significant policy and legal reforms, these social norms are still widely considered relevant.

With the end of the autocratic Rana regime in 1950, Nepal experienced an influx of large amounts of foreign aid and development experts. In the imaginaries of the international development community, the country was a particularly desirable 'development laboratory' and a 'blank slate' (USAID officials in Nepal, cited in Fujikura 1996, 271), reproducing typical colonial metaphors. Nepal was perceived as a 'small, pure, non-modern country' due to its 'independent' status during the age of colonialism and its insignificance in terms of international politics (Fujikura 1996, 271). The development project created 'a conceptual space of cultural contact, carving into the social complexity of rural Nepal the paths along which nations from the "first" and "third" world can meet' (Pigg 1992, 492). Some have argued that this encounter created similar erasures and silencing of living knowledge traditions as colonialism did in other contexts (Pigg 1992; Tamang 2009). What is certain is that the development project has significantly contributed to shape gender politics in Nepal. It was involved in creating the trope of the 'poor, helpless Nepali women'. This trope remains situated within broader international discourses on gender and development that created the identity of the 'poor third world woman' in its various guises (Mohanty 1984). It continues to dominate mainstream discourses in Nepal and much of the internationally-driven development work in the country.

During the 10-year-long civil conflict in Nepal, knowledge and norms on gender received a makeover. Women and girls constituted an estimated 30–40% of the Maoist political and military wings and were at the forefront of the struggle for intersectional transformations (International Crisis Group 2005, 16). Maoist ideology in Nepal emphasises the importance of the role of women, and includes an explicit commitment to end discrimination against women, but their voices have often been marginalised (Lohani-Chase 2008, 154ff.). This led to a new trope of the fierce combatant that moved grassroot Nepali women from victimisation to empowerment. This trope depicts women combatants as fierce, brave, selfless and willing to be martyrs, carrying guns and fighting alongside their male comrades. Such depictions influenced the perception of women in Nepal, as one Maoist combatant argued that 'today, the image of tired malnourished women carrying children and herding cattle has been transformed into the image of dignified fighting women with gun' (Hisila Yami quoted in Tamang, n.d., 7).

All these elements have influenced not only the political-economic structures of Nepal but also systems of signification within which current forms of knowledge on gender and gendered subjectivity formation are situated. *Telling a Tale*, edited by Archana Thapa, is situated against this background (A. Thapa 2010). This collection of personal narratives of Nepali women illustrates the ways in which coloniality continues to shape gender politics in Nepal. It brings together thirty-one girls and women between the ages of 14 and 60, from various social backgrounds, telling their personal stories related to growing up as women in Nepal, addressing issues such as education, relationships, marriage, sexuality, moving abroad, spirituality and religion, trauma and death. Internationally, there has been a proliferation of such literature of self-writing, especially women writing autobiography, diary, travelogue, memoir and personal narrations. In Nepal, a context where it has been mostly men who write, *Telling a Tale* is the first major anthology of women's personal narrations in English.[3] Some contributors are trained creative or critical writers; for others this is their first publication. The book has been adapted into a play and staged in Nepal in 2012 and 2013. In 2012, Archana Thapa compiled, edited and published the second anthology in Nepali entitled *Swaastitwako Khoj*. The second book is currently being translated into German and adapted for a theatre performance scheduled to go on stage in 2017.

We consider this collection of stories as a legitimate archive to read post/decolonial politics in light of the new importance that storytelling has taken in IR. Storytelling has entered IR within what has been called the 'narrative turn' (Inayatullah and Dauphinee 2016; Jauhola 2015; Dauphinee 2013; Naumes 2015). Stories can make a number of contributions in IR and in social sciences more broadly. They can bring marginalised voices into IR to complete, complexify or disrupt existing pictures. They contribute to challenge established 'truths', to complexify dichotomies and problematise pre-established categories, and to make space for entanglements and contradictions (Naumes 2015, 820). Stories also show alternative ways of being and thinking that do not correspond to prevailing social norms. Bringing lived and embodied experience into international politics, they allow us to bridge the intimate, the local and the global. As a form of contestation and resistance, stories can move beyond zero point writing (Doty 2004, 389). Finally, stories also 'call into question the ability to construct a self that is free from internal contradictions' and show 'a state of being that fuses conflicting identities' (Naumes 2015, 826).

Situating our contribution within this 'narrative turn', our chapter proposes to read the collection of stories *Telling a Tale* as a site of post/decolonial politics. We argue that as explorations into subjectivities, these stories teach us a lot about Nepali society, about the entanglements between the subject and the world, about the imbrications between macro and micro dimensions of power. They contribute to disrupt conventional knowledge on gender in Nepal and fixed notions of the subject of 'the Nepali woman', and they make space for marginalised voices. Listening to these stories, we learn about the multiple and contradictory nature of subjectivity and the various ways in which women in Nepal deal with and resist gendered and other social norms, and develop their own forms of knowing and being. Through their practice of situated knowledge, these stories move beyond zero point writing. Finally, they also show how writing and other forms of art can be a site of contestation and liberation.

The context of the creation of *Telling a Tale* is also intensely political.[4] Archana Thapa recalls that gathering the contributions was a very challenging but also intensely rewarding process. Given that women in Nepal are not used to writing their own life stories and feel that these stories are not interesting to others, this process involved encouraging many of the contributors to write their personal stories for public readership and convincing them that it was okay to publicly share feelings and experiences. The book then is not only a book, it is also a process and project of personal counselling and bonding among the contributors and with the editor, building trust and friendship, and believing in each other. The text came much later. As such, *Telling a Tale* is an example of struggling against social norms and gender discrimination, developing care and solidarity amongst women and alternative ways of thinking and living 'womanhood'. The book has been applauded for constituting a 'plural ecology of knowledge' (Nandy 1989), for its boldness and solidarity, and for a non-androcentric epistemological stance.[5] Thus, we read *Telling a Tale* as a contribution to the decolonial project of promoting alternative ways of knowing and being and opening up the horizon of possibilities for epistemic equality in knowledge production.

In order to analyse gender and coloniality in these women's stories, in the next section we first present the theoretical debates around gender, knowledge production and subjectivity in post/decolonial thinking. Then, in section three, we draw on these debates and on subjectivity as 'a mode of enquiry' (el-Malik 2016) to present how we read *Telling a Tale* as a form of postcolonial politics. We offer some concluding remarks in section four.

Postcolonial politics, knowledge production and the subject

> *I would never be 'I', because I would always be looked at as someone's daughter, sister, would-be wife, and eventually someone's mother.*
>
> (Ojha 2010, 84)

Post/decolonial thought highlights that colonialism not only operates in the realm of material exploitation and military administration, but also in the realm of knowledge production and subject formation (Fanon 1994; Said 1979; Césaire 2000; Spivak 1988; Lugones 2010). Knowledge-making is a fundamental aspect of coloniality, understood as 'the hidden process of erasure, devaluation, and disavowing of certain human beings, ways of thinking, ways of living, and of doing in the world' (Gaztambide-Fernández 2014, 198). Post/decolonial thought focuses on how dominant forms of knowledge came into being historically through silencing or suppressing other forms of knowledge; challenges the epistemological and ontological assumptions of dominant forms of knowledge; and brings to the fore silenced knowledges, non-Eurocentric cosmologies and knowledge traditions. The aim is to unveil the logic of coloniality, to delink from the rhetoric of modernity, and to restitute legitimacy to subaltern knowledges and various visions of life (Mignolo 2012, xvii).

In this effort, post/decolonial scholars have pointed to the problematic implications of modern knowledge practices, such as othering, boundary drawing, and dissecting and boxing people's lives into fixed, narrow subjectivities (Mignolo 2012; Lugones 2010; Allison 2015; Enloe 2015). At the centre of their critique is a challenge of the supposedly objective narrator position occupying 'point zero' that hides itself as being beyond a particular location and claims access to universal knowledge (Castro-Gómez 2005). Describing the 'hubris of point zero' (Castro-Gómez 2005), Doty notes:

> Zero-degree writing is not neutral, but ... an extraordinarily powerful style that is often almost successful in mystifying the fact that it is a style that harnesses desires and intensities in the quest for theoretical progress. The identity of the writing subject as scholar becomes a faceless, formless authority positioned at a removed distance from the human element at stake in what is being written about.
>
> (Doty 2004, 389)

Post/decolonial work on the subject starts with the assumption that the subject is not pre-existing, fixed or natural, but incomplete, flexible and contradictory and cannot be captured by a fixed theory of the subject. As a social construct and product of society, it is a site of the workings of power where social norms are reproduced and instantiated. Thus, 'subjectivity' is not the free and spontaneous expression of our interior truth. It is the way we are led to think about ourselves, so we will police and present ourselves in the correct way' (Mansfield 2000, 10). Analysing processes of subject formation allows us to understand the entanglements between us and the world, and the workings of society, revealing how our daily lives are always already linked to complex political, social and philosophical concerns (Mansfield 2000, 2–3). Focusing on the constitution of subjectivities makes it possible to 'account for how *macrological power* – system forces, authority and governance – and *micrological power* – everyday negotiations and navigations – simultaneously represent the subject and are represented by subjects' (el-Malik 2016, 214). Concretely, such a focus allows us to highlight the ways in which subjectivities are constituted through complex webs of race, gender, class, nationality, religion, etc. that vary across time and space. Importantly, this opens space to consider situated knowledge and to challenge the epistemic violence of modern knowledge practices (el-Malik 2016, 224).

Postcolonial thought is concerned with understanding the ways in which colonial rule and coloniality constituted and continue to constitute particular subject positions. Nandy argues that colonialism colonises minds and bodies and 'helps to generalise the concept of the modern West from a geographical and temporal entity to a psychological category. The West is now everywhere, within the West and outside; in structures and in minds' (Nandy 1983, xi). Fanon sees the subjectivity of the colonised as a direct product of the colonial system: 'it is the settler who has brought the native into existence and perpetuates his (sic) existence' (Fanon 1967, 28). And Césaire emphasises the mutual co-constitution of the subjectivities of the coloniser and the colonised (Césaire 2000). Colonised subjects are perceived as fundamentally 'other' and coloniality produces the marginalising, silencing and dehumanising of the colonial subject. Yet, the subject is also a site of resistance and source of alternative ways of being. For Spivak, this debate takes place around the notion of the subaltern (Spivak 1988). Post/decolonial feminists have called for a conceptualisation of subjects as both victims and empowered agents, both oppressed through, and resisting, the coloniality of gender (Lugones 2010).

Feminists have been at the forefront of the post/decolonial project, highlighting the key role of gender in colonisation and coloniality (Anzaldúa 2012; Lugones 2010; Pérez 1999; Casas 2006; Maese-Cohen 2010). They analyse how the 'colonial imposition of gender cuts across questions of ecology, economics, government, relations with the spirit world, and knowledge, as well as across everyday practices' (Lugones 2010, 742). Post/decolonial feminist research challenges Western (feminist) discourses and the ways in which Third World Women have been portrayed in these discourses (Mohanty 1984). Instead, it asks: what counts as (authoritative) knowledge (on gender), who is (legitimately) involved in producing such knowledge, who gets heard and who does not, what forms of subjectivity are created, and what forms of knowing other-wise exist? It focuses on how relationships between power and knowledge shape women's lives and influence gender and other social dynamics, analysing 'the power to name, the problems of translation and the role of language in the production of subjectivities' (Ali 2007, 192). Post/decolonial feminist highlight how modern knowledge practices tend to produce exclusions and silences, deny agency and voice, and reinforce gendered and racialised structures of global inequality (Tickner 2006; Toulmin 1992).

At the same time, postcolonial feminists also engage in attempts to decolonise knowledge production on gender issues. This has traditionally taken the shape of listening to the subaltern, linked to the famous question 'Can the subaltern speak?' (Spivak 1988). Spivak's provocation prompts us to think about whether we can hear subaltern voices and whether they can be legible in our Western (academic) context and within modernity more broadly, and how they could become heard or are already being heard. This has been accompanied by various efforts to listen and to recover. Yet, feminist scholars have had heated debates regarding the politics and risks of 'recovering silenced voices'. Some have critiqued the project for reinstating the civilisational trope of the 'Western woman helping brown women to get their voices heard' (Spivak 1985; Razack 2004). Instead, the approach of this chapter is one of critical listening and learning. It is inspired by an attitude that has been described by post/decolonial thinkers as 'a subaltern historiography that actually tries to learn from the subaltern' (Chakrabarty 2002, 33).

Within post/decolonial feminist work, this listening and learning has taken various forms. In our chapter, we seek to contribute to this project of decolonising knowledge on gender issues in the context of Nepal. We follow the call to carefully listen to personal narratives to learn about the ways in which people are embedded in a complex web of power structures and how they negotiate contradictions, resistance and alternative ways of being. We draw on the discussions around coloniality, gender, knowledge production and subjectivity to explore the post/decolonial politics of *Telling a Tale*. This collection challenges and moves beyond existing disciplinary boundaries and dominant gender knowledge. Through narrating the self, it highlights the variety of subjectivities and disrupts the idea of the fixed subject, reveals processes of gendered subjectivity formation embedded in coloniality and shows the embracing and negotiating of contradictions and tensions in alternative ways of being and becoming.

The post/decolonial politics of *Telling a Tale*

The stories of *Telling a Tale* are personal, first-person accounts that 'articulate women's feelings and emotions, including their desires, fears, and fantasies: subjective experiences that they passed through as girls and women in our society' (A. Thapa 2010, xx). They are situated knowledge, women's personal truths. Yet, as explorations into subjectivities, they teach us a lot about Nepali society, about the entanglements between the subject and the world, about the imbrications between macrological and micrological power. Here we explore two key dimensions addressed in *Telling a Tale*: knowledge production and subjectivity formation.

Challenging knowledge and beyond

> *We have to ask ourselves, 'WHO ARE WE?' Our struggle isn't going to end until we (women) respect ourselves and believe we are not less. For sharing, we need some mediums. Writing is only one of them.*
>
> (Sheila 2010, 109)

Archana Thapa presents her collection as a 'disruptive interdisciplinary text' that 'explodes disciplinary boundaries' (A. Thapa 2010, xx), mixing various writing styles, such as literature, history, experimental writing, cultural studies and autobiography. The free-flowing writing styles ignore the dichotomies of creative and critical, aesthetic and unaesthetic, serious and surface, sharp and rumbling. Writers simply swing between various borders and manifold emotions, they move in and out of the local and the global, rejoice and then turn sad, tell tales of victimisation and then come out triumphant. They shift as their heart desires and redefine literary sensibility as they like. The tales mix poetry with prose, autobiography with analytical style. Thereby, the contributions challenge disciplinary boundaries established through modern knowledge practices and overcome them through their own ways of mixing and inventing (writing) styles.[6] The sudden shifts in women's stories indicate subjective experiences of out-of-place-ness, shaped by restricted ideals of androcentric styles. They strive to find their own space, style and ideals. The collection is a site of knowledge production that contributes to the disruption of disciplinary boundaries and proposes forms of writing other-wise. The book received mixed reactions for its 'inconstant' style and narration, which testifies to the power of the disciplinary grip.

It is not only the style and form, but also the content of the tales that contribute to challenge existing ways of knowing. Each writer, in her own way, talks about the gender matrices and gender politics of contemporary Nepali society. They critique the dominant knowledge created by powerful formal and informal institutions in Nepal such as religion, law, cultural practices and so on. They challenge dominant Nepali gender tropes and social norms and expose them as one-sided and misleading. They challenge gendered dress codes and norms that discourage women from cutting their hair and that suggest that women should be subservient to family members and dedicate their time to the nurturing of children and work in the household.

Each writer opens a window to let readers have a glimpse of her life. For example, Rashmi Sheila shares her experience of bearing most of the domestic chores because she is a daughter. Her father's explanation is: 'It is daughter's duty to help their mothers at home, not sons. Your brothers will go out to earn when they are grown up. Your practice of helping Mother at home is preparing you for your work that you will have to do at your new home when you get married' (Sheila 2010, 102). She states:

> The major cause of gender discrimination and violence lies in the interpretations of religious scriptures and beliefs. … In the world we live in, the term 'woman' is either a relational term (dependent on the male) or is religiously defined. … Even educated women and girls abide by the gender-biased cultural norms, and if a woman tries to define the social norms in her own way, she is branded as a characterless woman.
>
> (Sheila 2010, 103)

Sheila's narration challenges cultural and religious Nepali norms that render women dependent in various ways. Her story also shows the complex ways in which gender, religion and class intersect in shaping women's lives. As highlighted in the opening quote of this section, writing her story becomes a medium for Sheila to explore her identity, share her experience and affirm her independent personhood, disrupting tropes of the powerless Nepali woman.

In the opening lines of 'Not Being a Fool Anymore', Amrita Gurung writes:

> Growing up as a girl was never easy, and worst of all was the teenage period. … Since the time I passed my School Leaving Certificate, I've been continually bombarded with marriage proposals. Those marriage prospects have been the most nerve-racking experience of my life. … Everyone seemed perfectly assured that they would eventually cajole me into marrying a man I hadn't seen. I would not have married even if I had known the man or if I was in love with him, because I never want to marry without having a career of my own…. My maturity has given me the confidence to live my life on my own terms.
>
> (Gurung 2010, 13–17)

Gurung's narration explains the frustrations she endured during her teenage years because of her gender. She was insistently pressured to get married for various socio-cultural reasons prevalent in Nepali society: her parents wanted to fulfil their parental duties by marrying her off at an early age for – what if she fell in love? Or, eloped! Worse even, lost her virginity! Out of wedlock pregnancy! Gurung suffered as a result of her parents' anxiety, and her story becomes the intervention to subvert the dominant gender knowledge that labels women as emotional and irrational by nature. From Gurung's lively revision and reposition, we learn about Nepali society's norms and beliefs. Her story creates an opportunity for dialogue between parents and teenage girls. She concludes with 'Why did I not have the courage to admit earlier in my life that I was wrong many times? Why did I run without taking a pause to reflect and be myself, instead of joining a rat race and pursuing things that were never of any interest to me?' (Gurung 2010, 17). She posits her own experience as a source of alternative knowledge about gender. Ending her story as a reflexive, empowered subject, she questions her powerless position and prevalent tropes regarding Nepali women.

These stories are both representations of individual experience and of a socio-cultural context that has shaped the writer's subjectivity. Deconstructing androcentric knowledge, the stories in *Telling a Tale* dislodge universal claims concerning gender and reveal the many ways in which gender oppression intersects with class, religion, geographical location, education, marital status, etc. They insist on the fact that gender knowledges are neither value-neutral nor universal. And they highlight that the exclusion of alternative perspectives decreases our chance to have a better understanding and to achieve an epistemic-equal space where all can have equal reciprocal legitimation as knowledge producers. As such, *Telling a Tale* is a site of resistance to zero point knowledge: it is a critique of the supposedly objective narrator position occupying point zero. As Archana Thapa explains: 'the ideal traditional narrator had always been the unified, transcendent (male) subject – the representative of the autonomous self, family, community, society and the nation' (A. Thapa 2010, xxiii). Decolonising this modern knowledge regime, in this collection, women writers have endeavoured to become 'knowing subjects' as first-person narrators (ibid., xxiv). Thereby, they become knowledge producers and contribute to decolonising knowledge on gender in Nepal.

Narrating and negotiating the self

> *In one life, one moment, one can live so many lives as lives are embedded into one another. It's not just my life as I live it, but the interconnections of me, you, and they that make life's memories. If memory is what I am, I see myself as non-existent without the others touching my life. There is no single me but you, you, and you as infinite dots connect to make what I think is my unique, individual self. … I have tried to look deep down inside to unearth the unspoiled, untainted subjectivity … yet what I remember are representations of tainted happenings, moments, impressions.*
>
> (Roma 2010, 115)

One key red thread going through all the stories is the question 'Who am I?' The stories evoke liminal personae, ever-changing identities, a pendulum of being swinging from one side to another, and the feeling of being one thing and its opposite at the same time (see for example Gupta 2010; Mishra 2010). They testify to the difficulty of 'finding oneself' in a context where one is constantly considered as a dependent of someone else (e.g. someone's mother, sister, wife) and not as a person in and of herself. They identify the social structures that influence the forming of subjectivities in Nepali society. They reveal the constraining gendered, religious and caste-based norms regarding marriage that coerce women to get married early, encourage them to give up their education and dedicate themselves to their families instead, and that stigmatise non-married women or widows.

Yet, they are also conscious that one is never completely independent of others, that we are all connected and touching each other's lives (as Roma points out in her story above). In that sense, the stories challenge the idea of 'unchanging and stable feminine selves' and focus on the 'unique cultural locations of individual identities' (A. Thapa 2010, xix–xx). This opens space for contesting essentialist assumptions of the dominant tropes regarding the Nepali woman. Thus, these 'narrations fracture the singularity of the category "women" by rewriting it in terms of plurality and heterogeneity' (ibid., xxi).

The narrations also reveal the continued significance of coloniality in shaping subject creation and its gendered nature. What is a desirable subject continues to be shaped by gendered coloniality, as illustrated most poignantly by the introductory quote to this chapter of a Nepali girl dreaming of being a white male tennis player. Many stories talk about modernity and 'modern woman' and describe processes of 'moving into modernity'. They illustrate the various embodied and gendered processes of 'doing better', 'getting out', 'moving up', 'escaping', associated with understandings of colonial subjects. Implicit in many stories is that in order to move into modernity, one has to leave Nepal behind and move up or abroad. This process of moving into modernity can take various forms, such as moving from the rural to urban areas (Pokharel 2010, 77), enrolling in an English-speaking boarding school in Nepal or communicating in English (Khadka 2010), escaping traditional marriage norms and emigrating abroad (to Canada, the US or the UK) (Pokharel 2010; Shrestha 2010).

Swastika Shrestha tells her story of 'moving into modernity' through going abroad for higher education. Her story helps us understand what 'moving into modernity' can include. She narrates how at home she enjoyed spinning dreams with her father. Following social conventions for obtaining a good education, she left for the US. Yet, her experience of 'moving into modernity' was fraught with contradictions and upon her return to Nepal she found that her father had stopped dreaming and turned bitter:

> Spinning dreams with Baba, I turned twenty-one. My sister was in the US. I decided to go there for further education. 'Don't ever look back thinking about us. We are history', Baba had said. I wanted to be happy in the US. I thought that childhood fear, guilt, and shame would not follow me to a faraway land.
>
> (Shrestha 2010)

Through this move into modernity, Nepal and its cultural traditions are relegated to history as her father tells her when she leaves for the US: 'Don't ever look back thinking about us. We are history'. The tempo-spatial processes at work in this move recalls Chakrabarty's insights regarding how those labelled as 'other' and 'backward' are placed in the 'waiting room of history' (Chakrabarty 2001, 8). Her narration shows how she experiences this as a split within herself, as a feeling of being in-between and a constant fear of departure and loss (Shrestha 2010, 202).

The move into modernity is often experienced as wearing a mask, and writers are conscious that it comes at a cost. Neeta Pokharel's story highlights, for example, the social pressure to 'move up', and the gendered impacts this has on people's identities. She recounts her experience of putting on a mask to be able to move up and her fear of losing herself in the process:

> I have worked continuously to hide my insecurities and complexes of the little town girls from the west of Nepal with no class. So all classed-up now, and with my all-grown-up-been-everywhere and done-just-about-everything self, living in the coolest

> city in America with the coolest job one can find and with all the accolades and assurances that I have made it, one would have thought that all of my masks had merged into my face and my turning art into reality would have disappeared. Nope. Sadly, I feel that I don't even know what is my own anymore. ... Anyway, wrapping up the story, do I feel all is lost now? No. There may still be a saving grace for me in the sense that I don't think I have ever really let go of the little town deep within me. I have hung onto it so tightly – perhaps with the fear of turning into my mother and the imprinted memory of her ever-smiling face with a distant and lightless gaze – lest I lose myself completely, lest when my own children, all born in the 'right' class and beaming with confidence, ask one of these days what my real persona is! Perhaps I can then actually dig it out, however hard it may be. So, all is perhaps not lost.
>
> (Pokharel 2010, 79–80)

While these stories show the continued influence of coloniality on subject formation, they also reveal spaces for resistance and reflexivity. Moving beyond existing tropes of Nepali women as either 'helpless and poor' or 'warrior women', the stories evoke various processes of negotiating, reinventing and being other-wise. For example, some stories narrate the process of breaking away from the severity of gendered Hindu identity and the efforts to make a 'new woman' out of themselves to be able to transcend boundaries and wander across borders as and when they wish (M. Thapa 2010). Others show how they have created a space for themselves 'to be different' (Sheila 2010, 100). As Ashmina Ranjit writes: 'I have reclaimed my own identity and dignity within and outside the prescribed cultural models' (Ranji 2010, 27). These stories represent a radical challenge to the constraining social norms in Nepal.

Conclusion

A collection of narratives of women's situated knowledge in Nepal, *Telling a Tale,* contributes to give voice to gendered realities and alternative forms of knowing and explores possibilities to resist gendered norms. The first-person 'I' in each tale stands out as a knowing self that does not require a man's presence to exist. For Nepali women, to write about the self is a radical act because they break away from prototypes of traditional 'selfless' femininity, take their *ghumto* (veil) off and discard their attributed phantasmic identity. They break taboos in talking publicly about supposedly private issues. The representations of characters, words and expressions, and the language structure contribute to destabilise established knowledge systems. The stories also contribute to disrupt the notion of a 'single me', a fixed subjectivity. They demonstrate how people are embedded in complex webs of macrological and micrological power structures. The writers do not shy away from talking about the contradictions they inhabit. They also recreate identities that sometimes differ drastically from hegemonic identities, resisting gendered and other social norms. *Telling a Tale* is a political act in its effort to create new knowledge that resists stereotypes that box women into narrow and fixed subjectivities.

The collection as a whole can be read as a form of defiance and resistance to oppressive social norms and to the continued influence of gendered coloniality on subjectivity formation in Nepal. In this spirit, the tales are two-way strategies: women become knowers and producers of knowledge as they write personal stories from situated locations; and the collaborative effort to create non-androcentric knowledges becomes a political agenda of building solidarity and promoting ways of being other-wise. *Telling a Tale* is an endeavour of solidarity amongst women from various backgrounds writing collectively against dominant forms of knowledge that constrain women and relegate them to marginal positions. The tales are anchored in the idea of a heterogeneous feminine force in solidarity, yet they do not desire to conquer the centre. Instead, they want to draw attention to their voices and be heard. They undercut the stereotyped homogenous knowledge regarding 'women' and celebrate plurality with heterogeneous reality. In this sense, they contribute to constitute a 'plural ecology of knowledge' (Nandy 1989), enhancing alternative ideas in the corpus of non-androcentric knowledge and opening up the horizon of possibilities for epistemic equality in knowledge production.

Bibliography

Ali, Suki. 2007. 'Introduction: Feminist and Postcolonial: Challenging Knowledge.' *Ethnic and Racial Studies* 30 (2): 191–212. doi:10.1080/01419870601143877.

Allison, Katherine. 2015. 'Feminist Security Studies and Feminist International Political Economy: Considering Feminist Stories.' *Politics & Gender* 11 (02): 430–34. doi:10.1017/S1743923X1500015X.

Anzaldúa, Gloria. 2012. *Borderlands/La Frontera: The New Mestiza.* Fourth Edition. San Francisco: Aunt Lute Books.

Casas, Maribel. 2006. 'WAN & Activist Research: Toward Building Decolonial and Feminist Projects.' *World Anthropologies Network (WAN) Red de Antropologías Del Mundo (RAM)*, 75.

Castro-Gómez, Santiago. 2005. *La hybris del punto cero: ciencia, raza e ilustración en la Nueva Granada (1750–1816).* Bogota: Pontificia Universidad Javeriana.

Césaire, Aimé. 2000. *Discourse on Colonialism.* Monthly Review Press.

Chakrabarty, Dipesh. 2001. *Provincializing Europe: Postcolonial Thought and Historical Difference (New Edition).* Princeton University Press.

———. 2002. *Habitations of Modernity: Essays in the Wake of Subaltern Studies.* University of Chicago Press.

Dauphinee, Elizabeth. 2013. 'Writing as Hope: Reflections on the Politics of Exile.' *Security Dialogue* 44 (4): 347–61. doi:10.1177/0967010613492838.

Des Chene, Mary. 2007. 'Is Nepal in South Asia? The Condition of Non-Postcoloniality.' *Studies in Nepali History and Society* 12 (2): 207–23.

Doty, Roxanne Lynn. 2004. 'Maladies of Our Souls: Identity and Voice in the Writing of Academic International Relations.' *Cambridge Review of International Affairs* 17 (2): 377–92. doi:10.1080/0955757042000245951.

Enloe, Cynthia. 2015. 'Closing Reflection: Militiamen Get Paid; Women Borrowers Get Beaten.' *Politics & Gender* 11 (02): 435–8. doi:10.1017/S1743923X15000161.

Fanon, Frantz 1994. *Black Skin, White Masks.* Grove Press.

Fujikura, Tatsuro. 1996. 'Technologies of Improvement, Locations of Culture: American Discourses of Democracy and "Community Development" in Nepal.' *Studies in Nepali History and Society* 1 (2): 271–311.

Gaztambide-Fernández, Rubén. 2014. 'Decolonial Options and Artistic/AestheSic Entanglements: An Interview with Walter Mignolo.' *Decolonization: Indigeneity, Education & Society* 3 (1). https://decolonization.org/index.php/des/article/view/21310.

Gupta, Pallabi. 2010. 'Full Moon, Facts, and Faults'. In *Telling a Tale*, edited by Archana Thapa, 86–91. Kathmandu: Akshar Creations. http://www.pandulipibooks.com/telling.php.

Gurung, Amrita. 2010. 'Not Being a Fool Anymore!' In *Telling a Tale*, edited by Archana Thapa, 13–17. Kathmandu: Akshar Creations. http://www.pandulipibooks.com/telling.php.

Inayatullah, Naeem, and Elizabeth Dauphinee, eds. 2016. *Narrative Global Politics: Theory, History and the Personal in International Relations.* London; New York: Routledge.

International Crisis Group. 2005. 'Nepal's Maoists: Their Aims, Structure and Strategy.' 104. Asia Report. http://www.crisisgroup.org/~/media/Files/asia/south-asia/nepal/104_nepal_s_maoists_their_aims_structure_and_strategy.ashx.

Jauhola, Marjaana. 2015. 'Scraps of Home: Banda Acehnese Life Narratives Contesting the Reconstruction Discourse of a Post-Tsunami City That Is "Built Back Better".' *Asian Journal of Social Science* 43 (6): 738–59. doi:10.1163/15685314-04306005.

Khadka, Geeta. 2010. 'Window to My Heart.' In *Telling a Tale*, edited by Archana Thapa, 40–52. Kathmandu: Akshar Creations. http://www.pandulipibooks.com/telling.php.

Lohani-Chase, Rama S. 2008. 'Women and Gender in the Maoist People's War in Nepal: Militarism and Dislocation.' Dissertation, Rutgers State University of New Jersey,

Lugones, María. 2010. 'Toward a Decolonial Feminism.' *Hypatia* 25 (4): 742–59. doi:10.1111/j.1527-2001.2010.01137.x.

Maese-Cohen, Marcelle. 2010. 'Introduction: Toward Planetary Decolonial Feminisms.' *Qui Parle: Critical Humanities and Social Sciences* 18 (2): 3–27. doi:10.1353/qui.0.0015.
Malik, Shiera S. el-. 2016. 'Subjectivity.' In *Critical Imaginations in International Relations*, edited by Ni Mhurchu and Reiko Shindo, 212–27. Routledge. https://works.bepress.com/shiera_malik/10/download/.
Mansfield, Nicholas. 2000. *Subjectivity: Modern and Postmodern Theories of the Self.* St. Leonards, N.S.W.: Allen & Unwin.
Mignolo, Walter D. 2012. *Local Histories/Global Designs: Coloniality, Subaltern Knowledges, and Border Thinking (New in Paper).* Princeton University Press.
Mishra, Indira. 2010. 'Trapped in a Liminal Persona.' In *Telling a Tale*, edited by Archana Thapa, 53–60. Kathmandu: Akshar Creations. http://www.pandulipibooks.com/telling.php.
Mittra, Sangh, and Bachchan Kumar. 2004. *Encyclopaedia of Women in South Asia: Nepal.* Gyan Publishing House.
Mohanty, Chandra Talpade. 1984. 'Under Western Eyes: Feminist Scholarship and Colonial Discourses.' *Boundary 2* 12 (3): 333–58.
Nandy, Ashis. 1983. *The Intimate Enemy: Loss and Recovery of Self Under Colonialism.* Oxford University Press.
———. 1989. 'Shamans, Savages and the Wilderness: On the Audibility of Dissent and the Future of Civilizations.' *Alternatives: Global, Local, Political* 14 (3): 263–77. doi:10.1177/030437548901400301.
Naumes, Sarah. 2015. 'Is All "I"IR?' *Millennium-Journal of International Studies* 43 (3): 820–32.
Ojha, Nisha. 2010. 'Within My Heart Lies Mustache-Ache.' In *Telling a Tale*, edited by Archana Thapa, 81–5. Kathmandu: Akshar Creations. http://www.pandulipibooks.com/telling.php.
Pérez, Emma. 1999. *The Decolonial Imaginary: Writing Chicanas into History.* Indiana University Press.
Pigg, Stacy Leigh. 1992. 'Inventing Social Categories through Place: Social Representations and Development in Nepal.' *Comparative Studies in Society and History* 34 (3): 491–513.
Pokharel, Neeta. 2010. 'Keeping up Appearances.' In *Telling a Tale*, edited by Archana Thapa, 76–80. Kathmandu: Akshar Creations. http://www.pandulipibooks.com/telling.php.
Ranji, Ashmina. 2010. 'Yes, It's Spelled with 'Sh'. Ashmina.' In *Telling a Tale*, edited by Archana Thapa, 24–8. Kathmandu: Akshar Creations. http://www.pandulipibooks.com/telling.php.
Razack, Sherene H. 2004. *Dark Threats and White Knights: The Somalia Affair, Peacekeeping, and the New Imperialism.* University of Toronto Press.
Roma. 2010. 'Memories of a Girlhood in Kathmandu.' In *Telling a Tale*, edited by Archana Thapa, 110–15. Kathmandu: Akshar Creations. http://www.pandulipibooks.com/telling.php.
Said, Edward W. 1979. *Orientalism.* Knopf Doubleday Publishing Group.
Sharma, Prayag Raj. 2004. *The State and Society in Nepal: Historical Foundations and Contemporary Trends.* Kathmandu: Himal Books. http://himalbooks.com/shop/products/The-State-and-Society-in-Nepal%3A-Historical-foundations-and-contemporary-trends.html.
Sheila, Rashmi. 2010. 'Being Different'. In *Telling a Tale*, edited by Archana Thapa, 100–109. Kathmandu: Akshar Creations. http://www.pandulipibooks.com/telling.php.
Shrestha, Swastika. 2010. 'Spinning Dreams for a Life'. In *Telling a Tale*, edited by Archana Thapa, 194–202. Kathmandu: Akshar Creations. http://www.pandulipibooks.com/telling.php.
Spivak, Gayatri Chakravorty. 1985. 'Three Women's Texts and a Critique of Imperialism.' *Critical Inquiry* 12 (1): 243–61.
———. 1988. 'Can the Subaltern Speak?' In *Marxism and the Interpretation of Culture*, edited by Cary Nelson and Lawrence Grossberg. London: Macmillan. http://www.maldura.unipd.it/dllags/docentianglo/materiali_oboe_lm/2581_001.pdf.
Tamang, Seira. 2009. 'The Politics of Conflict and Difference or the Difference of Conflict in Politics: The Women's Movement in Nepal.' *Feminist Review* 91 (1): 61–80.
Thapa, Archana, ed. 2010. *Telling a Tale.* Kathmandu: Akshar Creations. http://www.pandulipibooks.com/telling.php.
Thapa, Manjushree. 2010. 'Rhymes with Fun Jew Free.' In *Telling a Tale*, edited by Archana Thapa, 67–75. Kathmandu: Akshar Creations. http://www.pandulipibooks.com/telling.php.
Tickner, J. Ann. 2006. 'On the Frontlines or Sidelines of Knowledge and Power? Feminist Practices of Responsible Scholarship.' *International Studies Review* 8 (3): 383–95.
Toulmin, Stephen. 1992. *Cosmopolis: The Hidden Agenda of Modernity.* University of Chicago Press.
Yadav, Punam. 2016. *Social Transformation in Post-Conflict Nepal: A Gender Perspective.* Routledge.

Notes

1 The Rana dynasty ruled the kingdom of Nepal from 1846–1951 (Des Chene 2007).
2 It is important to note that this is based on a particular understanding of Hinduism, although other interpretations also exist. Thus, for example, the Blue Diamond Society, one of the main LGBTI associations in Nepal, uses Hindu imagery as an inspiration to challenge and broaden dichotomous understandings of gender and sexuality (personal discussions with BDS representatives, Kathmandu, January 2015).
3 *Telling a Tale* includes only English-writing authors. As such, it does not claim to represent the whole diversity of Nepali women's experiences, nor do they claim the superiority that is often adopted by the standpoint of privileged women's position.
4 The choice of focusing on *Telling a Tale* has another personal dimension: the book kept coming up during conversations between Archana and Rahel since 2014. In 2015, Rahel invited Archana to come and present the book at the University of Lausanne in a seminar entitled 'Narrating the Self'. During her research visits in Kathmandu while working on gender politics in Nepal, Rahel also met with some of the authors to talk about their contributions to the book and their broader activities.
5 This comment was made at a book discussion group in Kathmandu in 2010.
6 The fact that the collection was subsequently transformed into a theatre play whereby some authors performed their own life stories further contributes to challenge disciplinary boundaries.

33

DU BOIS, GHANA AND CAIRO JAZZ

The geo-politics of Malcolm X

Hisham Aidi

I

In the mid-1950s, when W.E.B. Du Bois was barred from foreign travel – accused by the Justice Department of spreading the propaganda of foreign governments – Gamal Abdel Nasser of Egypt invited the eighty-two-year-old scholar and his wife Shirley Graham to settle in Cairo, offering them a beautiful home on the Nile. Nasser had proclaimed solidarity with the African-American struggle and even began offering scholarships to black students in the South (Nolte 1956). When Du Bois and Graham finally had their passports returned, following a Supreme Court ruling in 1958, they traveled extensively, and though Du Bois did visit Cairo in 1962, he and his wife chose to settle in Ghana, taking on Ghanaian citizenship and working closely with Ghanaian leader Kwame Nkrumah.

But David Graham Du Bois – Shirley's son (W. E. B. Du Bois's stepson) – would settle in Cairo, in 1960, living in the Egyptian capital continuously for a dozen years, and on and off until the mid-nineties. A leftist, journalist and professor of American literature at Cairo University, Du Bois was also a bon vivant and inveterate jazzman (an alumnus of the Oberlin Conservatory of Music). He knew the black activists who spent time in Cairo – Malcolm X, Maya Angelou, Stokely Carmichael – as well as the jazz artists who passed through (Louis Armstrong, Duke Ellington, Sun Ra.) Old-timers still smile about the lavish New Year parties that David threw deep into the 1980s – at 76 Nile Street in Giza, apt#24 – in that grand apartment, where every room had a view of the Nile. The apartment, a gift from Nasser to the Du Boises, was in the famed 'Farid El Atrache building,' named so after the Arab crooner who lived there as well. David Du Bois's end-of-year gatherings always recalled the early sixties, bringing together South African freedom fighters, Albanian Marxists, members of the Afro-Asian Solidarity Committee, white radicals from New York, with local jazzheads and Egyptian police sergeants.[1]

In 1975, Du Bois published a semi-autobiographical novel, ... *And Bid Him Sing*, chronicling life in Cairo from the early 1960s through the 1967 War. This was a hopeful moment, when Cairo was home to several African liberation movements, when Radio Cairo broadcast in Zulu, and when Maya Angelou lived in Egypt, writing for *The Arab Observer*. Told through the eyes of veteran journalist, Bob Jones – a stand-in for Du Bois himself – the novel revolves around the budding Egyptian jazz scene, chronicling the lives of African-Americans who have made Cairo their home: a sundry crew of Marxists, black nationalists, Nation of Islam and Sunni 'Muslims' who divide their time between local jazz bars, Al Azhar university, news bureaus and 'café-au-lait women.' Jones goes about his reporting, while trying to create a 'progressive' jazz culture in Cairo, helping newly-arrived expats like Suliman ibn Rashid, a poet who came to study at Al-Azhar, get gigs at local clubs. These exiles are trying to find a place in Nasser's pan-African project, while remaining connected to the struggles back home, keeping a distance from the 'Goddamned [American] embassy,' yet aware that, for all their misgivings, in moments of crisis, they are still viewed as American.

Malcolm X's 1964 sojourn in Cairo is rendered vividly. During the day, 'El Hag Shabbazz' – as Egyptians call him – meets with diplomats and dignitaries at the Organization of African Unity conference. In the evening, the 'brothers' gather in Malcolm's suite at the Shepheard Hotel – to help him type up his speech to the Organization of African Unity, and talk about how to build the Cairo branch of his recently-launched Organization of Afro-American Unity. At one point, finding himself alone with Malcolm X, Bob Jones – a nonbeliever surrounded by converts – asks the civil rights leader the question he's long wanted to ask: Is it necessary to believe in God, or any religion, to be part of the revolution? Malcolm X sips from his glass of lemonade and offers a layered response. 'For me…Islam…has been like a harness, a guide to how I should behave…I needed to be reined in. I needed guidelines…limits beyond which not to go. Islam provides these for me.' He looks up, 'Perhaps everybody doesn't need guidelines imposed from outside, a harness to keep him on the straight and narrow…on the right road.' Then seeing how relieved Jones looks, Malcolm smiles and adds, 'You'd make a good Muslim.'

The question of God's role in revolution, and who wants or needs God's guidelines, is of course a matter that is still playing out today, furiously, in Egypt and beyond. Yet for the first time since the heady sixties, we're seeing young people beyond America's borders turning towards Malcolm X for guidance – and governments are paying close attention.

II

In May 1999, I was a graduate student running around Cairo looking for a dissertation topic. Seeing I was interested in 'Third World labor movements,' a friend suggested I talk to Gamal al Banna – a liberation theologian, trade unionist and the youngest brother of Hasan al Banna, the founder of the Muslim Brotherhood. 'He met all the Third World revolutionaries – including Malcolm X,' my friend Patrick had said. And so I went to see Banna at his home office. I remember sitting across from a soft-spoken gentleman, then seventy-nine years old, in a gray Maoist jacket, as he talked about Islamic humanism, the pitfalls of the free market, and why he had never joined the Muslim Brotherhood. A gray cat hopped around the piles of book on and around his desk. After an hour or so, I asked him about Malcolm X. 'He sat in the seat you're sitting in now,' said Banna with a twinkle in his eye. He spoke of Malcolm X's courage, charm, curiosity; he kept referring to him as a youth (*shab*) and lamented that in Egypt only the aged, his cohort, seemed to have heard of this remarkable American.

When I returned to New York, I went to see Manning Marable, Malcolm X's would-be biographer, who was about to launch a multi-media project about the civil rights leader. I mentioned my meeting with Banna, and suggested that there were people – a dozen or so in Egypt alone – but elsewhere (in Sudan, Ghana, Senegal, Tanzania, Algeria, Lebanon, etc.) – who had met or accompanied Malcolm X during his travels, and whom we needed to interview. Professor Marable asked me to compile a list of these individuals, and told me to get in touch with his friend David Du Bois, who in turn directed me to his novel, and told me to look up a 1962 Arabic translation of Langston Hughes's *The First Book of Jazz*.

That was the nineties.

Earlier that decade, rap artists like Public Enemy and Ice Cube were sampling Malcolm X's speeches. The video for Public Enemy's 'Shut 'Em Down' showed Malcolm's face on the dollar bill. Hip-hop would go global in the middle of the 1990s, and with that, all the references to Islam and Malcolm X. America's main musical export would reach distant corners, introducing youth worldwide to African-American history and the black freedom struggle, and to the various types of Islam referenced therein. Today there are thriving hip-hop scenes in São Paulo, Havana, Marseilles, Istanbul and Dar es Salaam. A rich melding took place: marginalized youth now express their politics in distinctly African-American terms, some are embracing Islam, others are launching Black Panther-like movements. Malcolm X's visage today appears in assorted places – murals in Caracas, posters in Parisian banlieues, spray-painted silhouettes in Istanbul's streets – but especially in the Muslim world, and the Muslim enclaves of Europe. Indeed the most well-known European Muslim leader, Tariq Ramadan – a nephew of Gamal al-Banna's – explicitly models himself on Malcolm X.

A Life of Reinvention (2011), Manning Marable's Pulitzer-prize winning biography of Malcolm X, is a heroically-detailed account of Malcolm X's rise from street hustler to ambassador-at-large for the earth's wretched. Marable brightly evokes the sights and sounds of mid-century America – the zoot suits, trolley cars, bebop, Harlem terracotta facades and so on – that backdropped Malcolm's multiple self-inventions. Marable attributes Malcolm's posthumous odyssey from purported demagogue to cultural icon, to Alex Haley's biography, released in late 1965, stating that Malcolm X's 'latter-day metamorphosis from angry Black militant into a multicultural American icon was the product of the extraordinary success of Haley's *The Autobiography of Malcolm X*.' But *A Life of Reinvention* was also intended as a corrective to *The Autobiography*. Marable set out to highlight and explain Haley's role. Malcolm's amanuensis, notes Marable, was a liberal Republican who disliked the Nation of Islam, and who, unbeknownst to Malcolm, left out several statements and chapters, and to use today's parlance, tried to 'deradicalize' the Muslim leader – presenting him as an integrationist and liberal reformer.

In March 2002, a trove of Malcolm X's personal writings – hundreds of pages of letters, photographs, diaries, handwritten drafts of speeches – turned up for sale at an auction house in San Francisco. The Shabazz family would reclaim the material and lend it to the Schomburg public library in Harlem, where it has been on display since 2008. The collection, at least what's available for public viewing, shows Malcolm X as an avid reader and meticulous chronicler, and includes everything from letters to diplomats Richard Holbrooke and Ralph Bunche, to Paris metro ticket-stubs and a marked-up translation of Sartre's *Black Orpheus*. The diaries, in particular, are a delight to read, showing the activist's political evolution, but also a more quotidian side: there is Malcolm crossing Tahrir Square, to go have some lemonade at Groppi's – a still-standing pastry shop – then he's buying pajamas, picking up Vitamin C tablets, (because he's feeling kind of 'woozy,') going to the cinema, and so on.

Marable makes use of this new archive, as well as hundreds of declassified FBI files, to make several arguments. First: as is well-known, Malcolm X was initially opposed to integration and political participation but, in debating integrationists – Bayard Rustin in particular – he would abandon separatism, and come to believe in civic engagement and voting, as tools for a 'bloodless revolution.' Rustin – the liberal integrationist who wrote the famous essay 'From Protest to Politics' – forms a curious moral counterpoint, or shadow, to Malcolm X throughout the book, and his thinking, per Marable's telling, is ultimately vindicated. Towards the end of his life, the 'mature Malcolm' has moved close to Rustin's position, believing that African-Americans could use the electoral system to achieve meaningful change. Marable also met with Gregory Reed, the lawyer who purchased the 'missing chapters' from the Alex Haley estate. (In lieu of these chapters, Haley inserted an epilogue that he wrote.) The unpublished chapters, it turns out, discuss political organizing and show that in his final year, Malcolm envisioned a broad-based 'pluralistic united front' that would unite integrationists and civic organizations with black separatists, under the leadership of the Black Muslims. And it is this plan – Malcolm's political organizing – that got him killed. 'Malcolm X, the real Malcolm X, was infinitely more remarkable than the personality presented in *The Autobiography*,' writes Marable, and with his unique potential to unite black integrationists with black nationalists, with support from a range of post-colonial states, he 'had the potential to become much more dangerous to white America than any other single individual had ever been.' Hence, Haley's censorship.

A Life is crucial for understanding Malcolm's life. Marable reveals that Malcolm – during his Detroit Red phase – when he danced and playing drums at jazz bars, under the stage name Jack Carlton (the name a tribute to his late brother Earl Jr, who had performed as Jimmy Carlton). Marable revisits the assassination, noting that by 1964 there was a 'convergence of interests' among the Nation of Islam, the FBI and Bureau of Special Services, all of whom wanted Malcolm silenced. Parsing declassified police records, he shows that the FBI and NYPD – who had planted informants in the NOI, Muslim Mosque Inc. and OAAU – knew of the threats against the Muslim leader, but did not provide security when he spoke at the Audubon that night in February 1965. The assassins were linked to the Nation of Islam mosque in Newark – and the lead suspect, whom Marable names, is still alive and living in New Jersey. Yet given that thousands of FBI and CIA files remain declassified, we still don't know who gave the order, and if the murder was committed by a government informant. Marable also tries to make Malcolm more accessible, showing that the leader made tactical political errors, often felt vulnerable and was 'no saint.' The historian speculates – on admittedly thin evidence – that Malcolm X 'probably' had homosexual encounters during his time as a street hustler, and that he and Betty Shabazz were unfaithful to each other.

Professor Marable expected *A Life* to stir some controversy. Malcolm X's daughters had, after all, worked strenuously to prevent him from accessing their father's papers and diaries, once they got wind of his narrative – and decided to deposit the papers at the Schomburg Library instead of at Columbia. But still, Marable, who died three days before the book's publication, would have been surprised by the furor, and the political, racial and generational fissures that his work exposed. Two books have already been written in response (Herb Boyd's edited volume *By Any Means Necessary Malcolm X: Real, Not Reinvented* and Jared Ball's *The Lie of Reinvention*) and Malcolm's eldest daughter, Ilyasah Shabazz, recently co-published an annotated version of her father's travel diaries, also intended to counter Marable's account.

The responses to *A Life* have been revealing. The book was well-received by the mainstream media, praised by critics as a corrective not only to Haley's autobiography, but also to Spike Lee's film, which presented Malcolm 'sentimentally' (Remnick 2011). But the book was roundly criticized by the black press, for stating that Malcolm at the end of his life had abandoned revolution for the ballot box, and become an integrationist or social democrat. Marable's aim was to expose how Haley had tried to moderate and mainstream Malcolm, and yet he (Marable) had done the same, superimposing his politics onto his subject. Marable's claims that Malcolm X was a 'misogynist,' dissembled about his past, made insensitive remarks about whites and Jews also caused a flap, threatening to eclipse the larger questions raised by the book. And the fact that – of all the books published on Malcolm X – the 'white media' raved over *A Life* was proof that the mainstream wanted a Malcolm cut down to size (and that Marable had done the leader a disservice.) Amiri Baraka, a close friend of Marable, said the historian had 'slandered' Malcolm.

A *Life* was well-received by scholars and activists who knew Marable as a giant in the field of Black Studies, and understood what he was trying to do, devoting years of his life, as his health faltered, to reconstructing Malcolm's story. So what exactly was he trying to do?

Marable once observed that since the mid-nineteenth century, three visions have characterized African-American political thought: the school of racial separatism, the school of integrationism, and the school of radical democracy, the latter being grounded in anti-imperialism and internationalism. These currents surge and recede, depending on political-economic circumstances (Marable 2005, 209). Marable himself came of age when that third school, of progressive black internationalism, was ascendant, when African-American politics was enriched with an engagement with the world, when black expat communities emerged in Africa, Asia and Europe. This was also the era when peoples struggling for independence abroad, found inspiration in the black freedom movement, and saw African-Americans as America's conscience, a vanguard of sorts. Having lived in East Africa as a young man, part of the expat communities of Nairobi and Dar es Salaam, and having written a dissertation about Kenya, Marable situated himself solidly within this tradition of transnational solidarity and Third World socialism. And like others of that generation (think Harry Belafonte's recent spats with Jay Z), he was dismayed by the decline of the black left, of this internationalist spirit, and the lack of interest in black history among youth today.

'How can the authentic history of black people be brought to life?' Marable (2006, 21) asks in his penultimate book, *Living Black History*. One answer: Malcolm X. Marable knew that Malcolm still commands respect across Black America, and if anyone could awaken an interest in black history and reignite black internationalism – not so as to move to Kenya, but to have a progressive engagement with the world's languages and cultures – it would be Malcolm and his riveting story. *A Life* has not resurrected Malcolm – the way Lee's film did, but the Malcolm X narrative – and Marable's book – have had a jolting effect among youth beyond America's border. One important prediction that Marable made and, which is spot-on, is that Malcolm's legacy will increasingly be shaped by Islam.

III

'I have difficulty praying. My big toe is not used to it,' Malcolm told his diary on April 20, 1964 shortly after arriving in Mecca. Having recently left the Nation of Islam with their practices, he was still acclimating to sitting on his knees during prayer. Despite the pain, the following day he embarks on the journey to Mount Arafat, part of the hajj pilgrimage, joining 'hundreds of thousands of pilgrims, all colors, buses, car, camel, donkey & foot.' Mecca, he writes, is surrounded by the:

> cruelest looking mts [mountains] I've ever seen. They seem to be made of the waste material from a blast furnace. No vegetation on them at all. The houses are old & modern. Some sections of the city are no different than when the Prophet Abraham was here over 4000 [years ago] – other sections look like a Miami suburb.

Wandering among the pilgrims, he describes the rituals, the seven stones cast at the devil, the circumambulating of the *kaaba*, and observes, 'This would be an anthropologist's paradise.'

Malcolm X is a powerful optic through which to understand America's post-war ascendance and expansion into the Middle East. His is the perspective of a ghetto-dweller who has transcended the borders drawn around him. '[A]s though I had stepped out of prison,' he writes, when he travels abroad. The diaries – several notebooks of single-spaced handwriting – show an anthropologist's eye. Malcolm comments on the landscape, the politics, cultural and religious differences, with humorous asides. When a friend arrives late, he quips, 'Arab time!!' At one point, he observes, 'The worst most dangerous habit among Arab Muslims is cigarettes. They smoke constantly, even on the Hajj.' There are also personal reflections on his mood, health and intense solitude. The words 'lonesome' and 'alone' appear on almost every other page. His thoughts on Saudi Arabia support the standard narrative that the hajj was transformative.

Yet the diaries show something else: when not in Arabia, Malcolm seemed to enjoy being away from his role as a religious leader, and away from religious strictures as well. Whether in Ghana, Guinea, Kenya or Egypt, he immerses himself in the cultural life of these newly independent states, and the younger Malcolm, the music aficionado, resurfaces, as he frequents nightclubs and dance centers again. In Nairobi, he goes to see his friend Gee Gee sing at the Equator Club, and then accompanies Vice-president Oginga Odinga to a party at the Goan Institute of Dance. ('The PM is a good dancer, remarkably for his age,' he writes.) In Guinea, he attends a wedding party, then goes to a nightclub and, 'watche[s] some Americans from the Ship-hope try to dance.' He rejoices in seeing newly independent states shunt aside European colonial music and celebrate their own musical traditions. In Accra – accompanied by Maya Angelou – he attends a party at the Ghana Press Club and enjoys 'Highlife,' which would become the country's national music (Angelou 1986, 134). But it's mostly in Egypt, which he saw as the bridge between Africa and Asia, a key player in the Non-Aligned Movement, that he spent the most time and experienced the most cultural immersion.

The story of Egyptian jazz dates back to the Harlem Renaissance, when African-American musicians who had settled in Paris, ventured east. In December 1921, Eugene Bullard, the Georgia-born military pilot, drummer and prize fighter, traveled from Paris to Alexandria, Egypt. For six months, he played with the jazz ensemble at the Hotel Claridge, and fought two fights while in Egypt (Lloyd 2000, 79). A decade later, the blues singer Alberta Hunter followed suit, singing in Istanbul and Cairo (Shack 2001, 43). The trumpeter and vocalist Bill Coleman would live in Cairo from 1939 to 1940, leading the Harlem Rhythmakers/Swing Stars. As Islam began to take hold in American cities and within jazz circles, Muslim jazz musicians would journey to Egypt. In 1932, an African-American Muslim with a saxophone turned up in Cairo, saying that he was working his way to Mecca (Berger 1964). With America's post-war ascent, jazz would spread around the world carried by servicemen, Hollywood and Voice of America broadcasts. In 1958, the bassist Jamil Nasir, trumpeter Idrees Sulieman, and pianist Oscar Dennard traveled to Tangier, where a VOA relay station would broadcast Willis Conover's *Jazz Hour* to listeners behind the Iron Curtain, where they recorded an album. They then went on to Cairo. In the Egyptian capital, the thirty-two-year-old Dennard would fall ill and die from typhoid fever; he would be buried in the city, his grave a regular stop for visiting jazz musicians.

All to say, by the time David Du Bois arrived in Cairo in 1960, there was already a local jazz scene and the State Department had launched its jazz diplomacy tours aimed at countering Soviet propaganda. Du Bois and his friends – with the support of the Egyptian Ministry of Culture – would try to create a music culture different from that sponsored by the US government. The Egyptian government was also leery of the jazz tours, and turned back 'jambassador' Dizzy Gillespie at Cairo airport in 1956 following the Suez War.

This was the buoyant cultural moment that Malcolm X encounters when he arrives in July 1964. Egypt is flourishing culturally, a regional leader in music, cinema and literature. Malcolm's diary entries from Egypt confirm the events and personalities described in Du Bois' novel. David Du Bois is working as an announcer at Radio Cairo, and lobbying

Egyptian officials to have his father's books – especially *Black Flame Trilogy* – translated. (*Black Boy* by Richard Wright was the only work of African-American literature available in Arabic, he would write to his mother in November 1960; he wanted the government to translate Lorraine Hansberry's *Raisin in the Sun* and Langston Hughes' primer on jazz.) The local jazz scene was feeding off musical trends in the US, as American jazz artists wrote compositions in honor of Africa and Afro-Asian solidarity. Malcolm would soak up the scene in Cairo and Alexandria, attending weddings and concerts, socializing at Cairo's elite social clubs, sailing down the Nile to the Valley of Kings. It's in Cairo that he meets Fifi, a Swiss woman who works for the UN, and who is quite smitten by him. All along, of course, he is networking with regime officials and scholars hoping to build a branch of Al-Azhar in Harlem. When he travels from Cairo to Saudi Arabia for hajj, he is struck by how culturally barren the kingdom is compared to Egypt.

The diaries in effect show a man who has landed smack in the middle of the 'Arab Cold War' of the early 1960s, which pitted Nasser's Egypt and her socialist allies against Saudi Arabia and the conservative monarchies backed by the US. As part of the Non-Aligned Movement, Nasser had stepped up his rhetorical attacks on American-allied monarchies in the region, through Radio Cairo, denouncing the royals for their social conservatism and alliance with the West. Music was at the heart of this propaganda effort, as top musicians were enlisted to sing the praises of 'our destiny' and 'historical leader.' And the expat jazz artists were solidly on the Egyptian side. One of the musicians, saxophonist Othman Karim, would set up the Cairo Jazz Quartet and record a track called '*Yayeesh Nasser*' ('Long Live Nasser') (Du Bois 1964, 47). Karim would go on to collaborate with Salah Ragab, a young drummer and major in the Egyptian army, who would become Egypt's most famous jazz musician, working with Sun Ra and Randy Weston.[2] When Malcolm X arrives in Cairo, he negotiates this cultural tug of war, hanging with the 'bros' but also listening to jazz with Morroe Berger, a Princeton Arabist, expert on Black Muslims and organizer of State Department jazz tours. This contest is subtly rendered in Du Bois' novel. Both Ragab and Karim make appearances – as characters named Salah Janin and Muhammad X – performing at the Cairo Jazz Combo. The Saudis would soon respond to Nasser's cultural diplomacy, creating a radio station with religious broadcasts. In 1964, they launched their own ideological offensive, setting up the Muslim World League, to mobilize various Islamist groups to counter the spread of socialism and secular Arab nationalism.

American officials were wary of which side Malcolm was going to take in this regional Cold War. According to cables at the National Security Archive in Maryland, American diplomats were displeased by the 'sympathetic stories' that Malcolm X – and that '[Black] Islam' in general – were receiving in the Arab press. Officials were convinced that the Nation of Islam was infiltrated by Communists, and wanted to keep Malcolm away from leftist movements abroad as well. It was around this time that the Muslim World League began considering sending emissaries around the world to spread Salafi Islam, including to cities in the West. Diplomatic cables from the early to mid-1960s show Mohammed Surur, then Secretary-General of the Muslim World League, asking the American embassy in Jeddah for permission to set up a branch office in the US to 'propagate the faith' and 'help raise the level of Islamic education in the US and particularly in the Black Muslim Movement,' whose 'doctrines' were 'in flat contradiction to the teachings of Islam.'[3] American officials would soon come to view the Muslim World League as an antidote to Black Muslim militancy.

Most of the diplomatic cables detailing Malcolm X's visits to Egypt and Saudi Arabia were written by Richard Murphy, now a retired career diplomat and fellow at the Council of Foreign

Relations. I spoke to Murphy last year and he recalled that Saudi Arabia and the Muslim World League had sponsored Malcolm's visit to the kingdom in 1964, as a way to 'peel' him away from Nasser's influence – and the US supported that effort. 'Back then, we thought Islam was a potential friend in dealing with the radical black community,' recalled Murphy:

> We had a benevolent attitude toward what we called Wahhabi Islam. We saw the Saudis as devout, quaint, but not dangerous. Washington thought a better understanding of Islam could help deal with some of the violent tendencies in the black American community. The better Muslims they [Black Muslims] are, the less violent they'll be back home. Malcolm X was a prime example.[4]

Nowadays it is well-known that the US mobilized the Islamic right in South Asia and the Middle East to counter nationalist movements, but there is also the corollary idea – heard often in the Muslim American community – that in the 1960s the government used immigrant Muslims to counter or 'tame' Black Muslim organizations. COINTELPRO – the Counter-intelligence Program set up by the FBI – did see the Nation of Islam as a threat, and wanted to change the movement's philosophy 'to one of the strictly religious and self-improvement orientation, deleting the race hatred and separate nationhood aspects;' but there is no evidence to suggest that immigrant Muslims were used to neutralize Black Muslim organizations.[5] What seems to have occurred was that, as part of a broader Cold War strategy, American diplomats allowed the Muslim World League to set up a branch office in the US and to dispatch teachers of orthodox Islam to Muslim communities across the United States – in part to 'moderate' black militancy.

Malcolm X in turn was testing the waters, navigating the Cold War's shifting currents, assessing which nation-state or movement to align his new Muslim Mosque Inc. with, and even presenting himself as a bridge between rival camps. He was courted by the (Salafi) Muslim World League and the Muslim Brotherhood, who competed to pull him into their school of Sunni Islam. In September 1964, after undergoing training in Mecca and being appointed an official representative of the organization, Malcolm would consider establishing his Muslim Mosque Inc. in Harlem as a 'legal branch of the Muslim World League.' But his affection for Egypt ran deep. In a confidential letter to Muhammad Tawfik Oweida, Secretary-General for the Supreme Council for Islamic Affairs in Egypt, Malcolm explains to the Egyptian official why he is building relations with the Muslim World League and the Muslim Brotherhood, two movements anathema to the Nasserist regime. 'My heart is in Cairo,' writes the civil rights leader, noting that the most progressive social forces in the Muslim world are in the Egyptian capital, but 'I can be more helpful and of more value' to these progressive forces by having strong ties to the conservative forces 'that are headquartered in Mecca.' He adds, 'When I passed through Geneva I even took time to speak with [the exiled Muslim Brotherhood leader] Said Ramadan so that I could find out what he was thinking without ever letting him know what I was really thinking.'[6]

In his final years, Malcolm X had embraced Sunni Islam, but which ideology or state he would have aligned with is today the subject of intense debate, with observers projecting their own ideological predilections onto his future trajectory. In Egypt he found a cosmopolitan progressivism but was wary of Nasser's secularism; in Saudi he found the religious orthodoxy to counter NOI teachings, but was suspicious of the kingdom's reactionary politics. By early 1965, Malcolm was still searching for a theology that could speak to racism, inequality and imperialism, not unlike Muslim youth today.

IV

One warm Monday morning last May, hundreds of people lined up to board buses on 125th Street and Seventh Avenue. Signs on the buses read, 'Annual Malcolm X Day and Pilgrimage.' The excursion is organized by the Organization of Afro-American Unity (an outfit that Malcolm founded in 1964), and has taken place on his birthday every year since his death. The caravan of buses left Harlem and wound its way up to Ferncliff Cemetery in Hartsdale, some twenty minutes north of the Manhattan. Upon arrival, the visitors – including dozens of schoolchildren - lined up, waiting for the ceremony to begin. A low wooden throne-like chair was placed near the adjacent graves of Malcolm X and Betty Shabazz; an embroidered golden cloth and a framed portrait of the civil rights leader were placed on the 'throne.' The drumming began, and young men in white robes and skullcaps walked in file towards the grave, forming two lines in front of the wooden chair; other groups followed into the ceremony area and formed a semi-circle around the grave.

The event draws black groups from around the country and the Caribbean. The tone and attire recall an earlier era: young men and women in Black Panther and Garveyite military uniforms, older men in flowing white-sleeved African robes, women in resplendent gowns and head wraps. For two hours, Imam Talib 'Abdur-Rashid, a Harlem-based cleric, emcees a program which includes speeches, testimonies and prayers, and concludes with the folding of the red, black and green pan-African flag, which is then handed to someone who was close to Malcolm, a family member or one of his two bodyguards, now in their eighties.

I have been attending this 'pilgrimage' for over a decade and have watched it grow and change. It's still largely an African-American affair, but each year brings more visitors from other communities and from overseas – mostly young European Muslims. The pilgrims pay their respect differently. Once the flag is folded, devotees usually approach the grave, pour some water on the soil around it, and have their children place their hands on the bronze memorial plaque. But now people are also leaving offerings, like fruits or candles, and collecting a little soil to take back home with them. Visitors will leave their prayer stones or beads on the grave during the ceremony to absorb the martyr's *baraka*.

Malcolm X has become central to Muslim youth consciousness over the last decade. Young Muslim visitors now stop by Ferncliff cemetery throughout the year, wandering around trying to find 'Brother Malcolm's' grave, while tweeting to their friends. The Malcolm X story has circled the globe thanks to hip-hop, Lee's film and the internet. The interest on the part of Muslim youth, however, is part of a larger turn towards race and black internationalism, a response to recent political convulsions. With few exceptions, across North America and Western Europe, Muslim communities find themselves wedged between surveillance states, right-wing xenophobic movements and American state power. The situation in the wider Muslim world is equally dispiriting: civil wars in Iraq and Syria; drone strikes in Pakistan and Somalia; the wave of revolts that swept North Africa and the Middle East in 2011 has been suppressed by a massive counter-revolution launched by Saudi Arabia and her allies, as the Western-sponsored subjugation of Palestine enters its second century. The sense of besiegement has aggravated questions of belonging and identity among Muslim youth. There is a suspiciousness of the nation-state, which divides and demeans the *ummah*. And particularly in Europe's urban periphery, there is a need for a narrative of social justice that can make sense of the 'global Muslim predicament.'

This quest has often led the young European or American Muslim – often converts – toward Africa or the Middle East, in search of an authentic Islam. The student-traveler who heads East – traveling through space and time – in search of spiritual knowledge, and comes back bedecked in Middle Eastern or African robes, and with a bit of an accent, is now a familiar figure. But today it's also common to see young Muslims from Europe or elsewhere head westward across the Atlantic, to an American metropolis, in search of religious freedom or simply to immerse themselves in black history. The reason for this westward drift is partly the dismal state of progressive politics in the Muslim world. Cold War policies and local authoritarianism have created a Muslim political landscape dominated by the Right – by groups like the center-right Muslim Brotherhood, the ultra-conservative Salafi movement and the latter's more murderous offshoots – jihadist groups like Boko Haram, Al Qaeda and ISIS. The black freedom movement fills a political void.

W.E.B. Du Bois once observed that African-Americans have a 'great message' for humanity, and would offer the world a conception of freedom that would rival the French or Greek idea of liberty and that that would be conveyed through the 'gift of art,' more precisely, the Negro's 'magnificent art impulse.'[7] Since the end of the Cold War, the black freedom movement – with its message of social solidarity, and opposition to racism, militarism and imperialism – has emerged as the progressive alternative, appealing to marginalized groups worldwide, but especially to Muslim youth it seems. At a time when organized hostility and state persecution of Muslims transcends borders, when the US, UK and Australia are passing laws to strip their Muslim citizens of their passports, the experiences and internationalism of Du Bois and Paul Robeson resonate profoundly. In the mid-1950s, frustrated by the antics of Middle Eastern regimes, Elijah Muhammad briefly instructed followers of the Nation of Islam to face the direction of Chicago instead of Mecca for their prayers. Nowadays young Muslims searching for a narrative of social justice are figuratively turning towards Chicago, and towards black history more broadly.

Malcolm X is at the center of this process. If Islam is the unofficial religion of hip-hop culture, Malcolm X is the prophet or at the very least, the patron saint; his speeches are quoted, his dress and demeanor imitated. If hip-hop celebrates the rise of the outsider, the Nation of Islam activist's awesome trajectory from street hustler to the global arena, rising above any and all states, freed from the shackles of patriotism and national allegiance, fearing only Allah, is riveting to young Muslims (and non-Muslims) chafing under state domination in the favela, the *banlieue* or their appendage institution, the prison. For those who find black history liberating, here is an individual to whom history clung like metal shavings to a magnet.

Politically, varying Muslim interpretations of Malcolm are emerging. If younger Muslims are drawn to Malcolm X's radical internationalism and embrace of a political identity that transcended the nation-state, older integrationist Muslims argue that toward the end of his life – when he delivered his speech 'The Ballot or the Bullet,' Malcolm had come to terms with America and the nation-state. What is striking is that fifty years after his death, the Muslim conversation about the significance of Malcolm has taken a distinct theological turn and 'Imam Shabazz' is gradually becoming almost a saintly figure, a *wali*, whose life offers personal and spiritual guidance. Sheikhs now debate various aspects of Malcolm X's life, his views on music, marriage, parenting, political participation and so on. Prominent clerics like Imran Hosein of Trinidad issue opinions on whether Malcolm X's receiving an advance for his autobiography from Grove Press in 1964 constituted *riba* (interest). And it's not unusual to hear those with Sufi leanings describe the pilgrimage to Malcolm's grave as a *mausam* and his death anniversary as an *urs* (a saint's union with their beloved God.)

Thus not surprisingly Muslim readers have taken a rather dim view of Marable's book as well. Many were irritated by Marable's claim in the prologue that the civil rights leader adopted a pro-Palestinian position simply to gain Nasser's support. The more religious were incensed by how Marable had (allegedly) sullied the martyr's reputation. In *A Life*, Nation of Islam leader

Louis Farrakhan tells Marable that 'Malcolm was like a clock...I never saw Malcolm smoke. I never saw Malcolm curse. I never saw Malcolm wink at a woman. I never saw Malcolm eat in between meals. He ate one meal a day. He got up at 5 o'clock in the morning to say his prayers.' This is the image that Muslim community leaders have of Malcolm as well – a startlingly self-disciplined and self-abnegating individual, who stands as a testament to the power of Islam to inspire and rehabilitate. But Marable punctures this image describing a man who enjoyed a rum and coke, had a roving eye, and – at least when overseas – had more than one meal a day.

The recently-released *Diary of Malcolm X 1964* published by Ilyasah Al-Shabazz and Herb Boyd (2014), tries to restore Malcolm's image, presenting the leader in his own words. The volume hews closely to the original diary, but doesn't include Malcolm's random jottings in between daily entries. Thus on his trip to Gaza in September 1964, for instance, readers won't see his scribbled reference to the Khan Yunis refugee camp, his attempts to write in Arabic script or his hand-written rendition of a poem about Palestinian exile by poet Harun Hashim Rashid whom he meets in Gaza. The edits and commentary in the published diary don't seem to be trying to assuage the pique of religious conservatives or left-wing critics. For example, on November 15 1964, Malcolm arrives in Geneva and checks into the Hôtel du Rhône, and then Fifi, the UN secretary he had met in Cairo comes to see him. They talked for several hours until 5pm. 'She claims she is in love with me & seems willing to do <u>anything</u> to prove it.' The following morning Malcolm wrote, 'I slept late then went to buy an overcoat,' took a tour of the city and the UN headquarters, 'had a glass of wine' and then went to meet with Dr. Said Ramadan. At 9:15pm, he returns to his hotel room, 'Fifi was knocking on my door as I came up the stairs... We talked till 11pm and she left. I went for a walk in the rain, alone and feeling lonely....thinking of Betty.' This potentially controversial passage is reproduced in full but for some reason the phrase 'thinking of Betty' is redacted out.

The daughters, who commissioned the publication of the travel diary, seem mainly interested in protecting their father's reputation against Marable's allegations of infidelity. Marable claimed that Malcolm, by 1965, had 're-connected' with his old girlfriend Evelyn Williams from Boston, and had started an affair with an eighteen-year-old named Sharon Poole – and speculates that he spent the night of Feb 20 – his last night – with the latter at the New York Hilton. Marable's claims were based on interviews with Abdullah Abdur-Razzaq, Malcolm X's personal assistant, who insisted – until his passing last November –that he was grossly misquoted.[8] To be sure, in the published diary, there is one passing mention of Evelyn and none of Sharon; the notebook from early 1964, which does describe a conversation that Malcolm had with Evelyn about her relationship to Elijah Muhammad, has not been published.

V

European and American officials were initially unalarmed by the rise of Islam-inflected hip-hop or the growing interest in Malcolm X in the 1990s. Right-wing Islamist groups like the Muslim Brotherhood and the Salafi movement were given space in Western cities from the mid-1960s onwards, often seen as a force against urban disorder, and, in the US, a counter to black groups supported by Nasser and Castro. Yet with the 1967 War, the political geography of the region was redrawn, altering the direction of black and Muslim movements in the West. With Nasser's defeat, Elijah Muhammad would find himself deprived of a key ally. As states that were Soviet clients gradually entered America's orbit, they withdrew their support for leftist African-American movements. In 1973, Algeria renewed its ties with the US – broken since 1967 – and expelled the Black Panthers, who had established their headquarters in Algiers. Likewise, when Anwar Sadat left the Soviet camp and forged a strong alliance with the US and Saudi Arabia, he quickly abandoned his predecessor's language of pan-Africanism and Third World solidarity. David Du Bois would leave Cairo in 1972, repulsed by Sadat's crackdown on leftists, but also because an editor at Random House, a woman by the name of Toni Morrison, expressed interest in the manuscript of his novel; he would settle in Oakland, where he became the editor of the Black Panther Party's newspaper.

After the Camp David Accord and the cementing of the Egyptian-Saudi alliance – which would become the linchpin of American power in the Arab world – left-leaning Black Muslim groups would find themselves bereft of economic and political support. The Saudis withdrew their support for Muslim Mosque Inc. upon Malcolm X's death.[9] The Salafi movement and the Muslim Brotherhood would expand their presence in Western cities further following the first Gulf War. The Muslim Brotherhood is economically and socially conservative but believes in political participation and coexistence with non-Muslims. The Salafi movement, on the other hand, while also economically conservative, is with few exceptions largely opposed to political participation, seeing it as corrupting, preferring to separate from the larger society and focus on 'self-rectification.'

But the Salafis' libertarian political attitude – not asking the state for anything – fit well with the Reaganite and Thatcherite free-market thinking of the 1980s and 1990s: as the state stopped providing services and amenities, religious groups, including Islamists, stepped in to fill the vacuum. The Salafis' ultraconservatism and intolerant rhetoric, though recognized as a potential problem, was, proponents argued, mitigated by their political quietism. To be sure, similar arguments were made in the 1960s in defense of the Nation of Islam's economic and social conservatism. In their pioneering study *Beyond the Melting Pot*, Nathan Glazer and Daniel Patrick Moynihan lamented the NOI's 'nationalist and racist' tendencies while lauding the movement's 'traditional values' and 'Horatio Alger' entrepreneurial spirit. In the 1990s, Islamist groups' ability to patrol the streets, rehabilitate young men, restrain anti-state sentiment and mobilize capital through their economic networks was seen as an asset to cash-strapped city governments. (Interestingly, the Nation of Islam and the Salafis are also conspicuously absent from the annual pilgrimage to Malcolm's grave; in addition to a neo-liberal/libertarian outlook, both groups also share a disdain for graveside rituals.)

After 9/11 – and following the London and Madrid bombings – as it became evident that the quietest Salafis could not control the violent extremists in their midst, the Bush and Blair governments cracked down on Salafi organizations and began to look for an alternative Islam to back. It was around this time that state officials would gain a keen interest in Malcolm X, prompted by the case of John Walker Lindh, a young American who in October 2001 was found in Afghanistan fighting with the Taliban. Just how did this middle-class boy from Marin County end up joining the Taliban? His online postings, experts argued, offered a clue; in hip-hop chat rooms, Lindh often posed as black, adopting the name Professor J. 'Our blackness does not make white people hate us, it is THEIR racism that causes hate,' he once wrote. Experts would trace the young man's 'journey' to radicalism to the age of twelve, when his mother took him to see Spike Lee's film Malcolm X, after which he read Haley's *Autobiography* and began listening to hip-hop. American and European officials would thereafter note the centrality of Malcolm X to Muslim youth politics, and argue that a 'moderate' understanding of the 'Malcolm X narrative' can help 'rein in' Muslim youth.

In the early 2000s, a movement appeared in Antwerp, Belgium, that illustrates just how present and pervasive the influence of Malcolm X is. The Arab European League (AEL) started off as a local immigrant-advocacy organization, but grew more militant in response to Vlaams Blok, a far-right party that had gained power in Flanders. By the end of 2003, AEL was one of the most organized youth organizations in Western Europe. With followers in several countries, the AEL hoped to build a civil rights movement that mobilized Muslim youth across borders. What struck observers was how American this Antwerpian movement was, and how it drew heavily on the Black Power movement. The AEL organized Black Panther-style patrols to 'police the police,' with groups of unarmed youth dressed in black following the police around Antwerp and Brussels, carrying video cameras. The media soon began referring to these youths as the 'Arabian Panthers' and the movement's Lebanese-born leader, Dyab Abou Jahjah, as the 'Arab Malcolm X.' Abou Jahjah embraced the role. He appeared at media events surrounded by bodyguards, speaking in short sound bites, declaring that integration was 'degrading,' demanding '100 percent rights;' he warned that European Muslims would get their rights 'By Any Means Necessary!' The Belgian government cracked down hard on this movement.

In Europe and the Americas, the specter of Malcolm X tends to arise among urban-beleaguered minorities in peripheral areas where states, despite heavy policing, don't fully reach (i.e. ghettos, banlieues, favelas) and – these days mostly among Afro-Latinos in South America, and Muslims in Europe. In recent years, we have seen the emergence of the New Black Panthers in Paris, the *Pantrarna* in Gothenburg, and the Black Panthers of Athens, the latter formed by immigrants for self-defense against the far-right Golden Dawn party. In North Africa and the Middle East, interest in Malcolm X surges during democratic openings, when the political left stirs. It's not a coincidence that it is in Turkey, the region's oldest democracy, where Haley's *Autobiography* was first translated, and where there is a slew of books in Turkish on the leader's speeches and ideas, including an illustrated biography for high school students (*Malcolm X* by Alex Haley 1995; *Malcolm X* by Andrew Young 2007; Senturk 2008). The first Arabic translation appeared in Morocco in 1996, just as the ruling monarch began liberalizing, allowing more space for political parties and civil society (Abouzied 1996; Al Issa 2007).

The revolts of 2011 sparked a new wave of interest. In August 2011, a bookstore owner in Cairo told the newspaper *Al-Akhbar* that since Mubarak's downfall, Che Guevara's and Malcolm X's memoirs had become bestsellers (Shair 2011). The current interest is partly because of the parallels between the 'Arab Cold War' of the 1960s, and the current 'Middle Eastern Cold War' between Saudi Arabia and her allies (Egypt and the American-backed monarchies) and Iran and her allies (Syria, Iraq and Hizbullah). It's not surprising that interest in Malcolm X surged in Egypt during a moment when a transition seemed possible, and it seemed like the country could wiggle out of the Saudi-American chokehold. In chatrooms, students asked what would Malcolm think of the Muslim Brotherhood? Or of the Sunni–Shia conflict?

Iran had claimed Malcolm X's legacy in 1984, releasing a stamp in his honor to promote the Universal Day of Struggle Against Race Discrimination (fifteen years before the US issued its own stamp). After the invasion of Iraq in 2003, as Iran seemed ascendant, a number of young Muslim activists argued that Shi'ism, with its tradition of protest and minority consciousness, was better suited for Muslims in the West than Sunni Islam. This argument would be famously made by Malcolm Lateef Shabazz Jr., the civil rights leader's late grandson, who embraced Shia Islam and moved to Syria in 2007. The twenty-seven-year-old became quite popular among Muslim youth in Europe and the US, lecturing and starring in political hip-hop videos, but caused an uproar at an event in Detroit in 2011 when he spoke negatively about the *sahaba* (the Prophet's companions) and declared that had his grandfather lived, he would have become Shia. Marable's book quickly got caught up in the cultural politics of the revolts. The author's most incendiary claim, in this regard, was that Malcolm X may have been influenced by Shiism and inspired by Hussein's tragic murder in Karbala. 'Like Husayn [sic], Malcolm made the conscious decision not to avoid or escape death,' writes the historian. 'Perhaps, like Husayn, he wanted his death to be symbolic, a passion-play representing his beliefs.' Marable's book, published in April 2011 when sectarian tensions were running high, and as youth in Europe were organizing reading groups around this book, seemed to support the argument made by Malcolm Jr.

The states trying to contain Iran would in turn underline Malcolm X's Sunni credentials. The Saudi-based Salafi evangelists who appear on Saudi television regularly reference Malcolm X, as do the Muslim-American hip-hop ambassadors dispatched by the State Department. Ironically, Malcolm who despised American diplomacy and the United States Information Agency's efforts to use black culture for propaganda purposes is today seen as a useful diplomatic tool – and not just by the US.

VI

In one letter to his mother written in November 1960, David Du Bois confides that in Egypt he wants to work in 'the general area of propaganda in the interest of African freedom, possibly with the Afro-Asian Committee in Cairo, or some other Pan-African organization.' He asks her to send him books, because the little that is available on 'Negro life' and which comes from 'official sources' at the US embassy is 'incomplete' and 'erroneous.'[10] (Shirley Graham would join her son in Cairo shortly after Nkrumah is overthrown in February 1966.) But Du Bois lists the books he wants translated, clearly seeing black culture and history as an antidote to whatever American diplomats were spouting. His novel, ... *And Bid Him Sing*, broaches the dangers of trying to counter American propaganda. The Cairo Jazz Combo wants to play compositions about black suffering and Afro-Asian ascendance for Egyptians and members of liberation movements based in Cairo, but US officials (from the 'embassy of Babylon') keep showing up at their gigs. Suliman the poet is in a particularly tight spot: he works for USAID, studies at Al-Azhar, and wants to perform his poetry but is worried about 'whiteys from the embassy' sitting in the front row.

A year after Du Bois published his novel, the Chicago-born writer Sam Greenlee who is today better remembered for his novel *The Spook Who Sat by the Door*, published *Baghdad Blues*, which eerily parallels Du Bois's book. It's a semi-autobiographical novel depicting Greenlee's deep alienation as an officer working for the United States Information Agency in Baghdad on the eve of the 1958 revolution, which topples that country's American-backed monarchy. (The book cover, evoking the blaxploitation era, shows the protagonist Chicago-native Dave Burell in a white suit standing legs apart in front of two tanks, and behind him is a veiled woman, armed Bedouins and Iraqi soldiers.) Burell is angered by the way his 'liberal' white colleagues speak about the Iraqis, and how his superiors want to use him to 'dispel negative attitudes' about America's race problem. 'You have great representational potential.' his boss tells him at one point, 'The Arabs seem to like you.' Burell (Greenlee) is sent to Mosul and Kirkuk to screen American films to villagers. 'You must know by now how distorted and exaggerated the race question is in the European and Arab press. They either don't know about Ralph Bunche or people like that, or they find it convenient to ignore them,' explains his boss, 'So don't be hesitant to discuss our racial situation in the United States with Arabs ... Your own accomplishments are as good an example as any that it is possible for Negroes to progress if they want to in our country' (Greenlee 1976, 48). He distances himself from his colleagues, stays home drinking and listening to his jazz records or wanders the streets of belle époque Baghdad frequenting bars on the Euphrates, until he makes some Iraqi friends, some of whom are plotting to overthrow the country's pro-American king. Then the intrigue begins.

A recurring theme in these novels – ... *And Bid Him Sing*, *Baghdad Blues*, and one can include journalist William Gardner Smith's *The Stone Face* about the Paris Massacre of 1961 – is that black Americans exist in a liminal state; US citizenship is neither full nor secure, and acceptance by other states is not guaranteed either. As such, they are transnational actors, allies of Third World peoples, unbound by borders and politically obliged to counter the public message of the State Department. This certainly was uppermost on Malcolm X's mind as he traveled through Africa and the Middle East, excoriating the USIA (United States Information Agency) and its 'propaganda,' all along expecting to have his passport revoked. In Cairo, he notes the admiration people have for President Kennedy, 'Most people here idolize JFK because they thought he seriously tried: I shot holes in the JFK image so fast.' This was, in fact, part of his ongoing debate with Bayard Rustin – who said that that 'if you want to criticize the United States you do it at home' – and with diplomat Ralph Bunche, who thought African-Americans had a special role to play in American diplomacy, 'owing to their unique ability to gain more readily the confidence of the Native.' Malcolm X dismissed the government's 'information agents,' calling out Bunche himself.

This – Malcolm's contempt for American public diplomacy and for the idea of an inviolable state sovereignty, as seen in his efforts to use the UN to address racialism in America – is what sealed his fate. But the disputes between Bunche and Malcolm, Rustin and Malcolm – on state allegiance versus transnational solidarity, on whether to partake in public diplomacy or not – are just getting started in Muslim communities today; and each camp, it seems – the separatists, integrationists and radical internationalists, to borrow Marable's framing – is using the language and ideas of the civil rights movement to make its case. It's thus ironic, but not surprising, that over the last decade Malcolm X has emerged at the center of American diplomacy towards the Muslim world.

In May 2011, with the Arab revolts at full throttle, the US embassy in Tunis organized a public-speaking competition for youth who want to be like Malcolm X, 'Are you the next Martin Luther King? The next Gamal Abdel Nasser? The next Malcolm X? Can you inspire and move people with your words?' American officials are aware of the hunger for African-American history among Muslim youth, and the power of black music; and various soft-power projects have been launched to tap this awe. State Department planners now speak of hip-hop with its adulation of Malcolm X as a 'natural connector' to the Muslim world, which sounds rather ominous given recent revelations of USAID's attempts to use hip-hop to infiltrate youth movements in Cuba, Tunisia and Lebanon (Weaver 2014). In November 2008, Al Qaeda released a video following Obama's electoral victory in 2008, celebrating Malcolm X's militancy and describing the president-elect as a 'house slave.' (Islamists now regularly use the term 'house Muslim' to discredit their liberal adversaries.) American embassies soon began sponsoring events during Black History Month and on Malcolm X's birthday, celebrating Obama and post-hajj Malcolm X together, accenting their meteoric rise to international eminence and relationship to Islam, stressing that it was Malcolm X, a 'symbol of a vital, open America,' who made Obama possible.

The British government also began to support Muslim organizations that had a 'moderate' understanding of Malcolm X, again focusing on his post-hajj transformation. Peter Mandaville, a political scientist and former member of Hillary Clinton's Policy Planning staff, argues that the resurging interest in Malcolm X, as seen in the 'aggressive and confrontational' lyrics of British Muslim hip-hop acts, has implications for national security. Mandaville has praised the work of the British government in funding a 'counter-radicalization' project that combined 'traditional Islamic scholarship and social consciousness with hip-hop sensibilities' and sought to mobilize British Muslim youth around the 'more cosmopolitanism impulses of Malcolm X after his break with the Nation of Islam and subsequent global travels' (Mandaville 2010).

VII

It's hard to exaggerate all the geo-political maneuvering and counter-movements that Malcolm provoked. He inspired most obviously the Black Power movement, yet his critiques of Christianity as the 'white man's religion,' would also trigger a crisis of faith in Christian thinkers like James H. Cone (1969) and give rise to Black Liberation theology. Likewise, for all that has been written about neoconservatism in the last decade, little has been said about how this ideology emerged partly in response to black radicalism and the discourse of Afro-Arab solidarity put forth by Malcolm X and then Stokely Carmichael. For the neoconservatives – most of whom were leftists in their youth – the militancy of Black Power, the calls for racial quotas, the Soviet Union's oppression of Soviet Jews and the radical left's embrace of the Palestinian cause only bolstered their anticommunism and defense of a hyper-liberalism. That the black nationalists and African-American Muslims were claiming solidarity with the Arab world, describing Islam as color-blind and not talking about the trans-Saharan slave trade, was particularly galling to the neoconservatives.

'We can understand why many blacks would give up the name and language of the white men who bought them as slaves, but why on earth would they want to adopt the name and language of the Arabs who sold them into slavery?' asked Bernard Lewis. Lewis, a British scholar of Islam, had been warily watching Malcolm and the rise of Islam among African-Americans from his perch at the University of London. In 1970, he published *Race and Color in Islam*, which directly challenged Malcolm X's view of Islam and questioned the epiphany he experienced at hajj. Lewis wrote that although 'Malcolm X was an acute and sensitive observer ... the [Islamic] beliefs which he had acquired' prevented him from seeing the 'Alabama-like quality' and 'Southern impression' of Arab life.

Today tensions between black and Jewish nationalism in the US have largely abated, but this discourse has traveled to Europe. The 'Eurabia' literature that warns of a weak Europe being overrun by Muslims, is informed not only by an American Cold War outlook but also by the memory of Black Muslim agitation and the racial tumult of the 1960s. French and Dutch commentators cringe when Malcolm-style agitators start speaking of Black or Muslim power, finding the language so distastefully American. The 'Eurabia' genre tends to single out Tariq Ramadan, the Egyptian-Swiss theologian, for reproach. One reason is that Ramadan's grandfather was the founder of the Muslim Brotherhood. Another is that the dapper, globe-trotting scholar, popular among Muslim youth worldwide, not unintentionally evokes the specter of Malcolm, posing like the leader in photographs, telling rapt audiences how he sat on Malcolm's knee as a toddler, and how the last letter on Malcolm's desk was addressed to his father whom he claims brought the American into Sunni Islam. 'Ramadan is said to have been influenced by the example of Malcolm X in the United States, or at least by Spike Lee's Malcolm X,' writes Paul Berman, another American leftist-turned-Eurabia-alarmist, in a twenty-eight-thousand-word profile of the Swiss scholar published in *The New Republic*, though granting that 'Ramadan, who has something of Malcolm's air of touchy dignity, has nothing of Malcolm's demeanor of unstated threats.'

The irony is that Malcolm has become central to American soft power at a time when we are told that interest in Malcolm X has dipped at home, or differently put, that the country has moved on – beyond either hating or adulating 1960s' icons. That is, the nineties may have seen a public celebration of Malcolm and other sixties radicals (recall boxer Muhammad Ali lighting the Olympic flame in Atlanta in 1996), but the new century brought us the rise of Obama, an HBO documentary that exposed Muhammad Ali as a charlatan, and the Marable biography that, according to *The New Yorker*, showed that Malcolm's best decision was 'choosing to entrust his story to Alex Haley.' Obama's victory was thus presented as evidence that Rustin's and Martin Luther King Jr's integrationism had triumphed over the black separatists and the radical internationalists, with their fanciful visions. The image that best captured this mood, plastered on posters at the inauguration, was a photo-shopped version of the famous photo of Malcolm X shaking hands with King in Washington; the 2008 version showed King shaking hands with – in lieu of Malcolm – a smiling Barack Obama. 'The Dreamer and the Dream,' read the caption.

Yet policymakers in Europe and the US who see the parallels and connections between the racial militancy of 1960s' America and the Islamist militancy of today realize that Malcolm can't so easily be airbrushed out. Malcolm is 'the bridge' connecting these eras and communities; through him the history of black protest flows to Europe's urban periphery. That is why black protest is now part of American 'strategic communication' and public diplomacy efforts. Even the security policies once used to neutralize black militancy are now being used to contain or 'de-transnationalize' Muslim youth. The NYPD's surveillance program, for example, is modeled on the FBI's Ghetto Informant program introduced in the 1960s to monitor black neighborhoods (Apuzzo and Goldman 2013, 130). And American policies from 'broken windows' to 'race classification' to 'citizenship stripping' are now being exported to Europe, just as the SWAT teams and armored vehicles used in Afghanistan are being deployed on the streets of America. Even the public discourse about Muslim youth echoes the narrative about 'undersocialized' black youth: it's cultural pathology, bad behavior and unbridled sexuality – and not policy – that holds these young men back, and the solution is a belief system that teaches hard work, respectability and self-improvement. If in the 1960s, the FBI was trying to get the embassies of Pakistan and Egypt to denounce and isolate Black Muslim groups, today the US government is more likely to send someone from the Black Caucus or NAACP to help 'moderate' youth in Islamabad or Cairo.

This past year was a difficult one for champions of black internationalism. Amiri Baraka, Maya Angelou, Sam Greenlee and Ali Mazrui died within months of each other. One wonders what these elders would make of the current tumult; they left just when the troubles began. But their words are in the air. 'We can hear their whispers,' as Pastor Mike of Harlem recently said. When shocked or in crisis, this country has been known to circle back towards the 'great message.' And now with nationwide protests and new solidarities forming, with youth in Ferguson, Missouri, proclaiming their support for Mexico's missing students, and activists in Syria holding signs saying 'I Can't Breathe,' we may see young Americans rediscover Malcolm and American internationalism all over again.

Bibliography

Abouzeid, Laila, translator. *Alex Haley, Malkum Aks: Sira Thatia* (Bisan, Beirut 1996).

Al Issa, Hamad, translator. *Malcolm X: Al Nusus Al Muharamat* (Airpbooks, Cairo 2007).

Al-Shabazz, Ilyasah and Herb Boyd, eds. *The Diary of Malcolm X: El-Hajj Malik El-Shabazz, 1964* (Chicago: Third World Press 2014).

Angelou, Maya. *All God's Children Need Traveling Shoes* (Knopf 1986).

Apuzzo, Matt and Adam Goldman. *Enemies Within: Inside the NYPD's Secret Spying Unit and bin Laden's Final Plot Against America* (New York: Touchstone 2013).

Berger, Morroe. 'The Black Muslims,' *Horizon* (Winter 1964).

Cone, James H. *Black Theology and Black Power* (Seabury Press 1969).

Du Bois, David Graham. '1-Man US Progressive Jazz Wave Hits Cairo & Flips Those Arab Cats,' *Variety* (Dec. 16, 1964).

——— ... *And Bid Him Sing* (California: Ramparts Press 1975).

Evanzz, Karl. *The Messenger: The Rise and Fall of Elijah Muhammad* (Durham, NC: Duke University Press 1999).
Greenlee, Sam. *Baghdad Blues* (New York: Bantam Books 1976).
Haley, Alex. *Malcolm X*, translated by Yaşar Kaplan (İnsan Yayınları1995 Istanbul).
Lloyd, Craig. *Eugene Bullard: Black Expatriate in Jazz-Age Paris* (Athens: University of Georgia Press 2000).
Mandaville, Peter. 'The Rise of Islamic Rap,' *Yale Global Online* (August 2010).
Marable, Manning. *W. E. B. Du Bois: Black Radical Democrat* (Boston: Twayne 1986).
———'The Divided Mind of Black America,' in Manning Marable, *Beyond Black and White: Transforming African-American Politics* (Verso 2005).
———*Living Black History: How Reimagining the African-American Past Can Remake America's Racial Future* (Basic Civitas 2006).
———*Malcolm X: A Life of Reinvention* (Viking 2011).
Nolte, Richard. 'Pure White Democracy: Egyptian Reactions to the Affair of Autherine Lucy,' *American Universities Field Staff Reports, Northeast Africa Series* 1/1 (1956).
Remnick, David. 'This American Life,' *The New Yorker* (April 25, 2011).
Senturk, Recep. *Malcolm X İnsan Hakları* (Mücadelesi İlke Yayıncılık 2008).
Shack, William A. *Harlem in Montmartre: A Paris Jazz Story between the Great Wars* (Berkeley: University of California Press 2001).
Shair, Mohammed. 'Malcolm X wa Guifara wa … al-dustur al-masri' ('Malcolm X and Guevara and … the Egyptian Constitution'), *Al-Akhbar* (August 2011).
Weaver, Matthew. 'US Agency Infiltrated Cuban Hip-hop Scene to Spark Youth Unrest,' *The Guardian* (December 10, 2014).
Young, Andrew. *Malcolm X*, translated by Eylemin Öteki Yüzü (2007).

Notes

1 Interviews with Esther Cooper Jackson, friend and colleague of W.E.B Du Bois and editor of *Freedomways*, August 21 2014; and interview with Max Rodenbeck of *The Economist* (May 12, 2014 Cairo, Egypt).
2 Interview with Ahmed Aladdin, grandson of Salah Ragab. May 12, 2014, Cairo, Egypt.
3 Richard W. Murphy, 'Memorandum of Conversation,' aerogram, Department of State, Jeddah, Saudi Arabia, October 30, 1965; Nicholas G. Thacher, 'Muslim World League Representatives to Visit US to Investigate Black Muslims,' aerogram, Department of State, Jeddah, Saudi Arabia, May 26, 1964, A-397.
4 Richard W. Murphy, 'Malcolm X Visits Jidda,' aerogram, Department of State, Jeddah, Saudi Arabia, September 29, 1964. 240; Richard W. Murphy, 'Activities of Malcolm X,' aerogram, Department of State, Jeddah, Saudi Arabia, September 29, 1964.
5 Letter from Director's Office to Chicago Agent Marlin Johnson Counterintelligence Program, FBI File Date, January 7, 1969, cited in Evanzz (1999, 476–477).
6 Letter to H. S. Muhammad Tawfik Oweida, the Supreme Council for Islamic Affairs, Cairo, UAR, November 30, 1964, Reel #3, Box #3 (Correspondence), Folder #4, Malcolm X Collection, Schomburg Center.
7 Wrote Du Bois: 'We are that people whose subtle sense of song has given America its only American music, its only American fairy tales, its only touch of pathos and humor amid its mad money-getting plutocracy.' See Marable (1986, 36–8).
8 Interview with author May 19, 2013; Panel on Malcolm X, Schomburg Library, May 20, 2011.
9 Richard W. Murphy, 'Muslim World League No Longer Assisting Muslim Mosques, Inc.,' aerogram, Department of State, Jeddah, Saudi Arabia, June 26, 1965, A-378.
10 Letter from David Graham Du Bois to Shirley Graham Du Bois, November 20, 1960, Papers of Shirley Graham Du Bois, Radcliffe Institute for Advanced Study at Harvard University.

34

BLESI DOUB/HERIDAS DOBLES/ DUAL WOUNDS

Re-writing the island

Alanna Lockward

Introduction

To read a book – one book – we must divide it in two. Ancient traditions say that the creation of the world may have only been possible by the powerful force of polarization, differentiation: Man/Woman, Ying/Yang and Light/Darkness. The number two is then the same number one, the manifestation of the same reality, but in opposite directions.

To articulate the complicated historical scenery of the two nations that dwell in La Hispaniola, it is also necessary to separate them, polarize them. The emergence of Haiti and the Dominican Republic, and of their respective cultures, has been canonized by their chroniclers in such a way as to assume this natural splitting process – in their eagerness to define by opposition, they have obviated the absolute interdependency of Haiti and the Dominican Republic. Yet, they were twins; two creatures were born in the same island, gestated in the belly of plantation economy, the machine invented by Europe for the New World.

The following text is an exercise in the hidden sight of this unique reality in the Caribbean that challenges the beatific hypothesis of an anti-apocalyptic Caribbean, as argued by Antonio Benítez Rojo or as prophesized by Edouard Glissant, who both talk about a model of Caribbean creolization for the world. Over the mountains of this island – the only in the Caribbean with a territorial dividing line between two nation/states – lie presaging clouds that threaten to liberate them with their humid truths; the exceptional life of the serpent-island that eats its own tail: that must be two to be one.

Demetaphorization of the colonial wound

A recent account on the constant robberies at a cultural art center in Puerto Plata, a coastal town in the North of the Dominican Republic, brought tears of laughter to my disconcert. How was it possible that the thieves 'visited' the place so often that the director, after returning from filing a complaint for a burglary, found that he was hit again by yet another break-in? These anecdotes are everyday life in the Dominican Republic where the level of criminality is significantly higher than in Haiti.[1] Against all evidence, however, the common assumptions of these shared realities implies the opposite. And it is precisely in these epistemic limbos, in this tragic accumulation of misconceptions that both populations have experienced the coloniality of sensing, being and doing that Jacques Viau Renaud's epically characterizes in his poem 'Nada Permance Tanto como el Llanto'(Nothing Lingers so Long as the Weeping).

The following ideas on healing the coloniality of being-sensing and thinking through performance art in the island and its diasporas orbit around the seeds of a shared humanity depicted in Viau Renaud's meticulous lyrical account of a chain of historical circumstances that overshadow any aim of atonement. These seeds are as present as the shared wounds, 'Dual Wounds' as I call them here, resonating with the phenomenal political and literary legacy of this martyr and poet, articulated always from the notion of the inseparability of our co-existence:

> 'We took refuge under the distracted shadow of trees
> and from them
> ran to meet the mutilated life,
> we removed the earth
> and found the essence of love
> deeply rooted in the hearts of our dead.'[2]

At the moment of Viau's untimely death, visual artists, poets and intellectuals were self-organized in different collectives,[3] in circumstances still unparalleled in Saint-Domingue's[4] history. The legacy of the radical art of the 1960s in the Dominican Republic, a direct outcome of the struggle against dictatorial rule and later of the US invasion of 1965, was defined by the budding solidarity between the two populations of Saint Domingue. This unity found concrete expression in the more than 100 anti-Duvalier exiles who fought side by side with Dominicans against this second US Marine occupation.

Poetry as a healing tool has been consecrated by many, and the words of Audre Lorde's are particularly relevant for the ideas that follow:

> Over the last few years, writing a novel on tight finances, I came to appreciate the enormous differences in the material demands between poetry and prose. As we reclaim our literature, poetry has been the major voice of poor, working class, and Colored women. [...]. The actual requirements to produce the visual arts also help determine, along class lines, whose art is whose.[5]

Moreover, Lorde resumes in this powerful statement the distinctive intersectionality of the synergy between healing, poetry, political activism and the visual arts, which is clearly observable in the way that performance practices are embodied by Saint-Domingue's artists, and which is the focus of this examination. And in this assertion, those living in the Diaspora are equally included; my curatorial and theoretical work has consistently spiraled around this axis. Marked by economic and political exile, this quintessential Caribbean quality demands to be analyzed in the context of two brutal dictatorships and their immediate successors.[6] This particular demetaphorization[7] of the colonial and imperial wounds is what I intend to highlight with the use of 'Dual Wounds'. In their shared (diasporic) social persona, the inhabitants of this exceptional Antillean imaginary are constantly confronted with the freshness of the blood shed by two barbarous dictators. In Saint Domingue the heroes and heroines of anti-dictatorial activism and their descendants are sharing the same moment in history right now with their murderers and their offspring. Moreover, the grandsons of both Duvalier and Trujillo, born and raised outside of the island, are currently politically active in each country.

Beyond eloquent, and ultimately effective, were the recent protests organized by victims and descendants of the Duvalier regime who use political performance to sabotage President Michel

Martelly's plans to honor Jean-Claude Duvalier's burial with the protocol of a former head of state. Artist Barbara Prézeau-Stephenson, took part in the protest denouncing these plans. It is empowering to report that this collective performance, supported by those living in the island and the Diaspora, was successful and that many of the main instigators were women.

As opposed to Haiti, where Papa Doc and Baby Doc are indivisible, canonical historiography systematically avoids scrutiny of the continuities between Trujillo's dictatorship and Joaquín Balaguer's 'constitutional' rulings. In the elections of 1996, the presidential candidate, José Francisco Peña Gómez, a Dominican of Haitian descent who was orphaned by Trujillo's massacre of 1937[8] and had the support of half of the population, was defeated by a coalition between Balaguer and the Dominican Liberation Party (PLD) founded and ruled by Juan Bosch, his traditional 'enemy'. At the core of this infamous pact, 'El Frente Patriótico Nacional' (The National Patriotic Front), represented the alleged impossibility of allowing a politician of Haitian descent to rule the country. The PLD has capitalized since this first victory on the anti-Haitian sentiments institutionalized by the Trujillo-Balaguer tandem and it is currently in complete control of the executive, judiciary and legislative powers. In the same pendular dynamic of power 'mastered' by the Trujillo-Balaguer era,[9] the PLD only lost the authority of its almost two decades of political reign for a short period between 2000 and 2004. The winning candidate, Hipólito Mejía from Peña-Gómez' party, the Partido Revolucionario Dominicano (PRD), is currently one of the public figures openly supporting Trujillo's grandson's political ambitions, who have smoothly entered the local sphere without major public upheavals. In other words, the overall picture of anti-Haitian sentiments and policies, which has been consecrated in the shameful Constitutional Ruling 168/13 is taking place in an atmosphere of uncanny socio-political consensus (Canton and McMullen 2014).

Narratives of reconciliation: beyond the Parsley Massacre

The 1937 massacre of Haitian citizens ordered by Trujillo has been, until the Constitutional Rule 168/13, the most prominent subject of conversation on Haitian territory and its Diaspora with regards to its neighbors. In my experience spending long periods of time living in Haiti since 1994, this is a fact about our shared history that every single Haitian knows about. In contrast, the period of the 22 years of Jean-Pierre Boyer's ruling of the entire island is only referred to in school books with 12 lines and correspondingly, the same happens with the absence of Dominican characters in Haitian literature, as exposed by French literary critic Léon-François Hoffmann, which could explain how the same phenomena is applicable to the visual arts:

> Up to the American occupation, and despite the turbulent history and frequent contacts between the two countries, the Dominican Republic and its citizens are virtually absent in Haitian literature. There is, in my knowledge, no historical novel about the invasion of Dessalines, the occupation under Boyer, the invasions of Soulouque. Nor a novel or a story that is set in the Dominican Republic, or a protagonist is a Dominican or is about a Haitian-Dominican community. It is as if the writers had decided to treat their neighbors with contempt and silence.[10]

Eliú Almonte, as well as some intellectuals like Freddy Prestol Castillo, who in his novel *El Masacre se Pasa a Pie* (*The Massacre Is Crossed by Foot*) recreates his own account of what Dominicans call 'El Corte' (The Cutting), and Haitians refer to as 'Kout kouto a' (The Knife Blow), has dealt with this moment in history in a rigorous manner. In 2000, Almonte presented the commissioned installation 'La isla ofendida' at X-Teresa Arte Actual in Mexico City as part of a group show dedicated to Dominican artists on the island and the Diaspora. Two plexiglass maps of the island mirrored each other, one on the floor, the other hanging from the ceiling. On the floor, the different racializing categories used in Dominican territory to 'classify' people across class divides were printed in red, covered with bare bones sprinkled with sea salt. On top, the second map was completely covered with dozens of parsley bunches.[11] The challenging self-explanatory allegory to the 1937 Massacre represented by this herb, suspended from above, suggested a permanent state of alertness with regards to this indeed inescapable issue in our shared history. The inclusion of Almonte's provocative and redemptory piece in this exhibition responds to my insistence in including Haiti in what is considered to be a 'Dominican' exhibition or essay. This emphasis has also been extensive to the regional conundrum on the Spanish-colonized Caribbean, which until very recently has systematically excluded the irrefutable historical relevance of Haiti, especially of the Haitian Revolution.[12] In this sense, the iconoclastic work of Eliú Almonte is explicit in many dimensions. Almonte's commitment to political commentary in his installations and performances combined with the healing tools of historical re-enactments are an integral part of his practice.

As in the case of Eliú Almonte, historical and collective memory's re-enactments are also recurrent in the works of Teresa María Díaz Nerio, Sasha Huber and Jochi Muñoz. A series of recent performances by Jochi Muñoz, inspired by and dedicated to Jacques Viau Renaud, testify to the poet's enduring of the anti-imperialist legacy on Dominican soil.

Stapling, re-enactments and healing

Born and raised in Switzerland from a Haitian mother and a Swiss father, Sasha Huber has only been able to visit Haiti twice in her life. The epic narratives of her nation and her family history as grandchild of the prominent Haitian painter, Georges Ramponneau, and her mother being also a painter have permeated her own definition as an artist.

In the 'Shooting Back Series', Huber literally shoots back at the narrative of the brutal repression of Duvalierism, something she did not experience personally but that defines her sensing, being and thinking in the world, which is also the case with Teresa María Díaz Nerio's mimicry of Trujillo's persona discussed further on. The physicality of this action and the sound of the stapling machine also operate as a self-healing method assisting the artist in the process of facing the 'Dual Wounds' of the Saint Domingue condition. According to Huber, each staple represents the death of countless *indiviDuals* as part of the tragic legacies of Duvalierism.

From the dictatorial legacies of the Dual Wound, Teresa María Díaz Nerio echoes in '*Throne of Gold*' and '*Trujillo's Island*' (2007) the narratives of a history that she as well as Huber has mainly heard from historical and familiar accounts, and later on invested considerable time in researching. In these two performances, Díaz Nerio comments on the hyper-masculinity embedded in an autocratic persona. Avoiding oversimplifications by mimicry or caricaturization, these portrayals rely on a hieratic mode.

In a radically new direction, the staged paralysis of Díaz Nerio's previous works is transformed into dance and spoken word in the lecture-performance 'Ni "mamita", Ni "mulatita"' (2013). In her analysis of the hyper-sexualized 'mulata' and the 'faithful servant' or 'mamita', in the Cuban film *Yambaó* (1956), Díaz Nerio describes how these figures emerged in Cuba during colonialism, often becoming symbols of nationalist renderings after independence. Alternatively dancing a rumba, screening sequences of the film and reading her analysis, Díaz Nerio departs from the hypothesis that:

> These roles are so ingrained in the Caribbean women's view of themselves that it greatly affects their choice of social performance. In turn, these stereotypes are being

> taken for granted by *white* Europeans, which in the long run contributes to perpetuate the misrepresentation of Caribbean women and in this regard prevents their accessibility to other spheres of life in the West.
>
> (Díaz Nerio 2013)

By challenging these heteronormative parameters, Díaz Nerio provides a much-needed space for knowledge creation from a Black woman's perspective, honoring at the same time African ancestral devotions. In her performance at Nikolaj Kunsthal, Copenhagen, as part of BE.BOP 2014. SPIRITUAL REVOLUTIONS AND THE 'SCRAMBLE' FOR AFRICA', she was playing the claves, an instrument of Cuban Rumba that marks the rhythm, while the audience took their seats. Dressed in yellow, the color that identifies Ochún as the goddess of love, she rang bells at different moments to invoke the loas. Towards the end, as a final decolonizing gesture, Díaz Nerio removed from her neck an *iruke,* a horse tail used in Cuban Yoruba religion, in this case made from her own hair interlaced with gold leaves, and a *nazar boncuğu,* a Turkish evil eye pendant. By swinging both amulets on top of the audience heads whispering a protection blessing, a moment of intimate communion materialized in the name of some of the spiritualities that inform her daily life in Amsterdam.

Expansion and reverberations of hair politics

Hair as a signifier of racialization and particularly in relation to Blackness is a recurrent theme in iconic works by artists such as Ellen Gallagher and Ingrid Mwangi Robert Hutter. The level of involvement of Black women with their hair is epic and its implications could be considered encyclopedic. The multiplicity of codes brought up by the interplays within a constructed Otherness and the dialectic between an empowered self-affirmation and an ostracized self-deprecation with regards to a *white* hegemonic norm of 'beauty' and 'cleanliness' are already a subject of many scientific publications (Prince 2010) and art projects (Opiah 2013) in the US, the Caribbean and elsewhere.

In *Dynamo* (2013) Élodie Barthelémy's melodramatic dreadlocks are paired with classical music and action painting, two emblematic examples of Western discursive hegemonies. The dreads of the maroon, of the rebel, that Bob Marley popularized in an almost unmeasurable manner, are paired to a cello concerto as well as to the signature of Jackson Pollock's legacy: action painting. The juxtaposition of these elements is yet another lyrical provocation to the hegemony of Western canons.

Dominican diaspora emergent artist, Joiri Minaya, who has won several national awards with performances, videos and installations that rely frequently on hair as a medium, experimented during a residency at Skowhegan with her peers, creating a landscape of interlaced humanity invoking on her own terms the power of hair as a multi-dimensional signifier.

An equally puzzling and revealing space of shared trust in the island is manifested in the startling success of Dominican hair dressers in Haitian territory and elsewhere in the Caribbean and beyond. The ambition of approaching *whiteness* at all costs is at the core of the phenomenal skills cultivated in this trade by generations of Dominican women. Accompanied by their legendary entrepreneurial stamina, they have achieved a unique status that facilitates their social mobility conjuring common places associating them with the sex industry.[13]

Nicolás Dumit Estévez has also addressed these issues from a queer perspective. The artist traveled from his home in the South Bronx to his birthplace in Santiago de los Treinta Caballeros, Dominican Republic, in order to trace any genealogical roots that he may possibly have to the neighboring Republic of Haiti. Carefully 'staged' in the diaspora, in Estévez' adoptive home, the South Bronx, the braiding of his hair was part of the process of facing his own contradictory relationship to Blackness.

Marassás in the mirrors of decoloniality

The metaphor of inseparability of the Duality, of the twin principle of the *Marassá*, the *loa* that symbolizes the status of Saint Domingue as the only Caribbean space with two island-nations sharing the same territory, is dealt with in 'All Tied Up/Atados'. Charo Oquet tied herself back-to-back to a Haitian vendor outside the Museo de Arte Moderno in an action reminiscent of Tehching Hsieh and Linda Montano's legendary durational piece. The impossibility of moving in any direction without the consent of the other is dramatically accentuated by the choice of tying both counterparts back-to-back.

The rope is staged as a symbol of the multi-dimensional character of human relations in Élodie Barthelémy's 'Cordes à Cailloux' (2014), a collaborative work with the rope acrobat Nicolle Perrier and the musicians Chiara Simeone and Joran Le Nabat. Sometimes the rope is in the middle somehow elevated, and at other times it duplicates the physicality of the borders between the two women on stage. The dramaturgy is deliberately enigmatic and consists in the juxtaposition of the elements on stage and their manipulation by the performers.

There is a self-evident connection with the idiosyncratic Dual collective subconscious of the Saint Domingue condition. Barthélemy is tied-up and frees herself from her counterpart, revealing the tensions and frustrations of the inescapable *Marassá* status of Saint Domingue and in doing so she also introduced her inherent potential for achieving her own healing. As in any curative agenda, a diagnosis is already part of the remedy, which can only materialize upon exploring and naming our shared realities and calling its elements by their right names.

Furthermore, I will argue as in previous conversations with Dominican critic and curator Sara Hermann, that this association of entanglements and inescapable realities typifies the particular diasporic stamina of the Saint Domingue condition. According to Dominican and Haitian statistics,[14] the local economies are significantly supported by international wires, known as *'remesas'* in Spanish and as *'transfé'* in Haitian Creole. The proportion is remarkable and goes to show to which extent in each imaginary the absence of those that departed is truly illusory. How much of this economic input is generated by Dominican sexual workers is a pending assignment of government statistics that painfully illustrates the double standards at play.

The financial entanglements between Saint Domingue communities in the Diaspora and their local island counterparts is conclusive in the mirroring nature of their social and political interactions. Therefore, the Saint Domingue diasporic condition, as an experience, becomes part of the narrative of self-identification even for those who have lived in the island permanently. Obviously, each experience is informed differently across gender, class and racialization, but what is important here is to highlight how this communal diasporic-self beyond geographical boundaries is transformed into an identifiable territory.

In 2005, David Pérez Karmadavis asked a Haitian vendor to write on a piece of paper his own diagnosis of the traumatic, to say it lightly, relationship between both nations and then had this message tattooed on his arm in public during the first Festival de Arte Corporal, in Caracas. As is the case with a vast majority of Dominicans, although the artist has dedicated many of his performance pieces to the exploration of the relation between both populations, until now he has never himself visited Haiti. Since he does not speak Haitian Creole, Karmadavis had no idea of what the piece of paper said. He only found out later on when Haitians would talk to him in the street asking him why he had that sentence tattooed on his arm. This is in the most strict sense a conversational piece and as durational as it gets, for that matter. The text says that all the problems between the two nations have been created by its respective economic and political elites: 'Biznis gouvenman benefis gouvenman'.

Beyond the spectrum: documenting the intimate in/and the public space

A work outside of what Huey Copeland refers to as 'the storied history of performance'[15] is Miami-based Adler Guerrier's 'Is what Chomsky said about Prometheus (Nine to Five)' (2001), a three-channel video featuring a man in a suit carrying a briefcase. He waits at the bus stop; walks down the street; walks into a building; enters a cafeteria. However, his activities begin at 9 p.m., when it is dark and downtown is completely deserted. This is definitively the view of an immigrant that sees himself as part of the scene, not as an accessory; there is a strong sense of dignity and self-respect in this perspective. According to Guerrier (Zorach 2014, 80), this film was based on three jazz compositions: Charles Mingus's 'Haitian Fight Song' [1955], Duke Ellington's 'Fleurette Africaine' (African Flower) [1963], and the Modern Jazz Quartet's 'Valeria' [1972]. 'Haitian Fight Song' is the piece more strongly connected to the above-mentioned sequences of the film, where the idea of the Situationist's flâneur[16] is linked to the maroon[17] leaders who conceived and ultimately achieved the first successful enslaved people uprising, the Haitian Revolution, which created the first Black Republic.

This particular type of awareness implied by the presence of the Black body in the urban landscape represents both a transgression and an affirmation of being. In Guerrier's native Haiti, young people also transgress the unmarked boundaries of class and racialization by becoming contemporary *pa gen pwogram,* defying pervasive notions of belonging attached to public spaces such as those beaches that until very recently were only accessible to the elite, as well as the streets of Pétion-Ville, which today are as promiscuous socially as the traditionally crowded areas of downtown Port-au-Prince. This displacement of landscapes' 'legitimacy' dooms any attempt at social engineering to be an exercise in futility. The illegality of the Black body is a de facto impossibility in Haiti and the absurdity of its criminalization is what keeps the legacy of the Haitian Revolution a glorious reminder in the face of Ferguson et al. Here the Black body in the landscape has a decolonial history that is as real as it gets, a living memory that has been consistently and painfully erased by colonial archives on the African continent and elsewhere.

Underlining the conundrums of absence–presence in performance art, different healing actions for what I refer to as 'post-earthquake healing performance', have been poetically embraced by Sasha Huber and Barbara Prézeau-Stephenson, and Jean-Ulrick Désert. 'Bol du Ciel' is an elegiac action conceived by Désert to mourn the earthquake victims and their survivors. A poster reproducing the landscape of the sky at the official time when the earthquake of January 10, 2010 occurred portrays each of the 750 stars with a metal low relief miniature profile of Josephine Baker. Crushed to form a ball, the posters will be sold by a street vendor holding on her/his head a typical market basket. She/he will offer the artist's work for a nominal fee with a simple proclamation: 'Bol du Ciel'. When opened, the buyer will see in this crushed paper relevant information about the performance in Haitian Creole, French, English and German. The physical presence of the artist is redundant in this piece which is a dynamic that permeates some of his recent performances as explained above. This action is still awaiting its crystallization on Haitian soil but was presented as an installation at the major exhibition 'Haïti, Deux Siecles de Creation Artistique', 11.19.2014–02.15.2015 (Haiti, Two Hundred Years of Artistic Creation), presented at the Grand Palais, in Paris.

Accompanying these healing tools seen from the perspective of a mourning diaspora, Sasha Huber in 'Haïti Cherie', yet another private performance, is dressed symbolically with the colors of the Haitian flag while drawing angels on the snow. Her impotent grief, intensified by distance, has an individual and social undertone distinctively spiritual and formally executed with her characteristic visual precision.

In 'The Fréda Circle' (2013), the myth of the seductive Erzulie Fréda is invoked by the Vodoun chanting of seven women while they embroider petals of artificial flowers on a transparent veil circle measuring five meters in diameter. Originally conceived as spiritual and emotional support for women who lost their partners during the earthquake, the essential components of this piece celebrating womanhood and solidarity, spoken word and embroidering, are also exposed in 'The Fabrication of the Creole Woman' (2014), presented at Yale University.

Six women (including Prézeau-Stephenson) prepared blog posts in advance about the role of sewing in their families. After contemplating and sharing these stories, they came together, bringing assorted scraps of fabric brought from home. The result was a multimedia performance experience, documented through pictures and texts, and dedicated to Audre Lorde. Mirroring the legacy of this inspiring Caribbean diaspora Black feminist, the body politics and knowledge creation of Saint Domingue artists sharing their Dual Wounds have been changing the tone and subject of the conversation on aesthetics, aesthesis, gender, spirituality and healing, among other liberation agendas. By means of re-interpreting socio-political misconceptions across racialized class boundaries and filling historical vacuums using performance art as a medium, they are facilitating much-needed curative spaces in the island and beyond.

Bibliography

Cosentino, Donald J. (1998). *Vodou Things. The Art of Pierrot Barra and Marie Cassaise*. Jackson: University Press of Mississippi.

Hall, Stuart (1989). Cultural Identity and Diaspora. Framework (no. 36). http://www.rlwclarke.net/Theory/PrimarySources/HallCulturalIdentityandDiaspora.pdf (Downloaded 10.06.2014).

Hermann, Sara (2002). 'Eliú Almonte: Aspavientos'. In: *Arte Contemporáneo Dominicano*. Madrid: Turner/Casa de América.

——— (2001). Presentación. Dimensiones Heroicas. Santo Domingo: Museo de Arte Moderno.

Hoffmann, Léon-François (2008). 'La République Dominicaine et les Dominicains dans la fiction haïtienne'. In: *The Caribbean Writer as Warrior of the Imaginary – L'Ecrivain caribéen, guerrier de l'imaginaire*. Gyssels, Kathleen and Bénédicte Ledent (eds.). Amsterdam/New York: Rodopi. PP. 345–58.

Lao Montes, Agustín (2007). 'Hilos Descoloniales. Trans-localizando los espacios de la Diáspora Africana'. *Tabula Rasa*. Bogotá Colombia, No. 7: 47–79, July–December 2007.

——— (2006). 'Stages of a Panic Curator. My Catharsis with the Holy Infant of Prague (aka Nicolàs Dumit Estévez)'. New York: Franklin Furnace. http://www.franklinfurnace.org/research/related/Estévez.php (Downloaded 11.06.2014).

Lockward Artiles, Antonio (2009). *Haitianos y Cocolos en la Literatura Dominicana*. Santo Domingo: Editora Universitaria UASD.

——— (1965). 'Prólogo'. In: *Permanencia del Llanto*. Santo Domingo: Ediciones del Frente Cultural. http://www.marxists.org/espanol/tematica/literatura/viaurenaud/permanenciadlelllanto.pdf (Downloaded 10.07.2014).

Lorde, Audre (1984). 'Age, Race, Class and Sex: Women Redefining Difference'. In: *Sister Outsider*, Los Angeles: Freedom, 114–23.

Mignolo, Walter (2012a). 'Decolonial Aesthesis and Other Options Related to Aesthetics'. In: *BE.BOP 2012. Black Europe Body Politics*, Alanna Lockward, W Mignolo, eds. Berlin: Ballhaus Naunynstrasse. http://blackeuropebodypolitics.wordpress.com/catalogue/

Viau Renaud, Jacques. *Poesía Completa* (1985/2006/2010). Santo Domingo–Berlín 2006. First edition: CEDEE, Santo Domingo, 1985. Second edition: Ediciones del Cielonaranja, 2006. Third edition: Ediciones Cielonaranja, 2010.

Notes

1 At the moment of writing this text, the Haitian Ambassador Fritz Cinéas was robbed in his house by two policemen and four civilians. During his visit to the police national headquarters for a press conference on the matter, his cellular phone was apparently stolen. After prompt inquiries the phone was recovered. The incident has been explained as a result of the chaotic atmosphere of the press conference. The phone's disappearance, whether accidental or criminal, is a painfully illustrative episode that reveals the absolute insecurity that the population must endure on a daily basis with the systematic involvement of the police in their adversities. http://acento.com.do/2015/actualidad/8222650-aparece-celular-robado-embajador-de-haiti-durante-rueda-de-prensa-en-palacio-pn/

2 'Nos refugiamos bajo las sombras distraídas de los árboles
y desde ellas
corrimos al encuentro de la vida mutilada,
removimos la tierra
y encontramos las raíces del amor
profundamente arraigadas al corazón de nuestros muertos'.
Renaud (2010, 108), translation by the author.

3 A pioneering overview of these contributions is compiled in the catalogue of the exhibition *Dimensiones Heroicas*. Museo de Arte Moderno, July 2001, Santo Domingo.

4 The usage of the colonial term used by the French to name the island is meant to emphasize the conundrums of translation and coloniality. The name is taken from the 'original' Spanish colonial apellation which previously referred to the island as 'La Española'. The fact that the capital of the Dominican Republic is Santo Domingo reflects the ambivalences of canonical historiographies which very often uses the same term to refer to Haiti as well as the entire island as *Saint-Domingue*. An illustrative example of how confusing the naming politics of the island are, is materialized in C. L. R. James legendary 'The Black Jacobins: Toussaint L'Ouverture and the San Domingo Revolution' (1938). San Domingo never existed, instead, Ayïti and Quisqueya are the original people's designations for the island.

5 Lorde (1984, 116).

6 François Duvalier 1957–1971 + Jean-Claude Duvalier 1971–1986. Rafael Leónidas Trujillo Molina 1930–1961 + Joaquín Balaguer 1960–1962; 1966–1978 (For its ferocious prosecution of political opponents, this period is known as 'Los Doce Años', *The Twelve Years*) and 1986 to 1996.

7 I am very thankful to Silvio Torres-Saillant for the inspiring conversation on this particular matter.

8 The massacre of an indeterminate number of Haitians and Dominicans of Haitian descent, ordered in 1937 by the dictator Rafael Leonidas Trujillo Molina, despotically in place for 31 years, is an open wound in the relations between the two peoples. The only local public exposure of this tragedy was championed by foreign Protestant ministers. The agreement on the border of the only island in the Caribbean with these characteristics dates back to 1936, as a result of the negotiation between President Sténio Vincent and Trujillo, who added new clauses to the 'original' version of 1929 by the American occupation authorities (Haiti 1915–1934, Dominican Republic 1916–1924). The year following the ratification of this agreement, Trujillo ordered the massacre.

9 Balaguer was defeated for re-election in 1978 and was out of power for the next eight years.

10 Hoffmann (2008, 349) continues analyzing the specific role that Dominican identity plays in the Haitian literary imagination which until today is strictly circumscribed to representing Dominican women as seductresses and prostitutes. Male characters are symptomatically absent.

11 'Perejil' is parsley in Spanish. The 'r' sound was used as a mean to identify who would pronounce it as a Haitian or a Dominican.

12 I have done this consistently since my physical and mental decolonization processes started in 1988, after my participation as a dancer in the Afro-Dominican choreography *Vidas y Muertes de una Isla,* by Marilí Gallardo, dedicated to *Saint Domingue*, and in 1994 after my first visit to Port-au-Prince, in my curatorial and theoretical work as well as a writer and journalist. Furthermore, after the Constitutional Ruling 168/13, I have defined myself as an epistemic Haitian and a Dominican in transit.

13 Haitian men's preference for Dominican sex workers is documented by historian Georges Corvington in one of the volumes of his extensive work *Port-au-Prince au Cours des Ans (1743–1950.* According to the author, the exotic prostitution was installed in the city starting in 1923, much to the detriment of their Haitian peers. The first customers were the American soldiers that occupied then the entire island, followed by local ones motivated by curiosity. At that time, upper-class Haitians disapproved of the proliferation of Dominican brothels (then called 'dancings'). Nowdays, after more than seven decades of

uninterrupted exercise, the status of the Dominican sex worker in Haiti is recognized and forms part of the next meeting of the Bilateral Commission headed by the Foreign Secretaries of the two countries. According to a statement by the Haitian Embassy's chargé d'affaires, Guy Lammothe, this new point of negotiation is the latest addition to the agenda to be discussed in January 1998. See Lockward (2014, 35).

14 In an unpublished interview Gabriel Bidegain, chief technical advisor of the United Nations Population Fund (UNFPA) in Haiti states in this regard that: 'Remittances exceed 30% of the Gross Domestic Product (GDP) and at the household level, 52% reach the end of the month thanks to money transfers from their working relatives abroad. In those places, mainly in the United States, migrants have improved their educational level. 16.5% have licentiate level, masters or PhDs. The main negative impact is the brain drain (skilled personnel at different levels migrating) affecting the country's development.'

According to Dominican official data: 'Dominican Republic is the sixth recipient of remittances in Latin America and the Caribbean. From the macroeconomic standpoint, remittance income plays an important role, and in the period 2000–2007 accounted for 8% of GDP on average. According to figures from the Central Bank of the Dominican Republic, the remittance income in the balance of payments increased from USD 1.689 million in 2000 to USD 3.111 million in 2008. Moreover, remittances are the second largest source of income, second only to the tourism sector': 'Programa de mejora de la información y procedimientos de los Bancos Centrales en el área de remesas' (2010).

15 Taken together, Guerrier's flâneur-style pictures from the late 1990s to the present offer a peculiar articulation of imagistic practice that stands in contrast both to contemporary large-format color photography, which aims for the immersive effect of a tableau, and to the storied history of performance documentation, perhaps the series' closest analogue in terms of its structural underpinnings. [...] Even more importantly, in his practice there is no initial target that spurs either action or interaction, distinguishing his work not only from performance art more broadly, but also from influential models of African diasporic urban intervention predicated on the [B]lack subject's visual recognition by unnamed passersby. As opposed to Stanley Brouwn's requests for directions in early 1960s' Amsterdam, Adrian Piper's cross-dressing as a black man on the make in 1970s Cambridge, or William Pope. L's abject crawls through 1980s' Manhattan, the ambit and ambition of Guerrier's movements through space seem less testaments to the racialization of civil society and more functions of the unknowable terrain of his own subjective inclinations at a given moment in time. See Copeland (2014, 44).

16 Literally translatable as 'stroll; strolling; sauntering', flânerie is most often associated with a rich tradition of unencumbered, non-confrontational movement through physically and socially shifting Francophone geographies. In late 19th-century Parisian visual and poetic discourse, the aimless looking of the 'gentleman of leisure' was key to understandings of the city's spatial transformation into a center of modern capital. For Haitian writers in the 1920s living under American occupation, the wanderings of bourgeois *pa gen pwogram*, meaning those with no program or schedule, were seen as central to the gathering of native knowledges that might be amassed and mobilised in the making of a national culture. And amid the upheavals of mid-20th-century France, the related concept of the *dérive*, or drift – an uncharted, meandering journey through an urban landscape – would become central to the radical practice of the Situationist International, particularly group members' exploration of 'the effects of the geographical environment on the emotions and behaviors of individuals'. See Copeland (2014, 45).

17 Marronage – the lifestyle, ethics and socio-political organisation of runaway enslaved communities outside the plantation system during colonialism – has been an intrinsic component of the radical imagination of countless liberation struggles in the Americas.

35
AFRICAN VIOLET
Hybrid of circumstance

Denize LeDeatte

Introduction

'Painting,
brushstrokes
of humanity,
on to
the world canvas
of world history.
Monumental.
picture of inhumanity
winter blue, brutality
ice cold white, calamity
terrifying greyed, tragedy
buried black, deeply,
for purpled, prosperity.
Yet the roots remain
within reach
to be easily
watered,
by the fertility
of fear, of hate
and poverty.
So paint
the love
of brilliant blue black hues,
saluting the sun,
bending its rays,
one by one,
pouring through a prism,
pan fried cool caramel,

into the vibrant orange
mangoed fleshed gold,
pumpkin tones, gently warmed
burnished copper browns,
dark earthed chocolate,
through to the beauty of midnight,
where the colours alight!'

Britain, like much of Europe, has a hypocritical love affair with the memory of its colonial past, yet there are many whose memory is, and always will be, different from that 'narrowed narrative'. As an artist, I believe that transatlantic slavery and the brutal plantation as an agricultural cauldron which laid the foundations for the industrial revolution, is everybody's history. Without repairing that legacy, the damage to the fabric of society simply continues to deepen and the idea that 'privilege views equality as discrimination' and its monologue becomes the voice of society. The arts provide a mechanism to balance the dominant narrative of 'academic history', which has evolved into academic genocide and in that process, prohibited snapshots of the past from being more complete in their rendering of the human story.

The legacy of European Empire is one of wealth accumulation through dehumanisation. This continues to manifest chameleon-like, in a contemporary context, most notably through constant debate on immigration.

'African Violet' is a body of artwork, which is my contribution as an artist towards the development of an artistic language for *Debate on Africa and Its Diaspora by Africa and Its Diaspora*. As an artist, through my own reflective process of creative expression, I have made a philosophical and artistic journey which has been documented in a way which allows others to take that journey. Below is a snapshot of that timeline of evolution which began at a micro level, triggered by death then culminating in a more macro perspective, exploring a personal relationship to British history. It is my belief that the importance of knowing yourself identifies the nature of your contribution to the dialogue of who we are as human beings – it also allows you to know others…

If you wish to know who I am
If you wish me to teach you what I know,
Cease for the while to be what you are
And forget what you know

Tierno Bokar, Sage of Bandiagara (1875–1939)

African Violet … Hybrid of Circumstance – 'Painting in a Book', is a personified voice of the past and the present which continually unfolds. She has evolved from experience across generations, having responded to terminal illness as a catalyst, complete with those acute observations which inspire unusual levels of self-reflection. She lends her voice to the developing 'De-colonial pedagogy' through a growing body of artistic dialogue, which has evolved to democratise unchallenged knowledge traditions often accepted as the 'Norm'.

My peculiar context as an artist is rooted in the United Kingdom born of Caribbean parents with an upbringing grounded in the robust and disciplined style of the Caribbean; which sharply contrasted against the backdrop of life in the UK at the time. Thus manifests my 'Hybridism'! My perspective is shored up as a consequence of positioning both geographical and political: exposure to the struggles of peoples across Africa, including Steve Biko, Ken Sarawira and Mandela, just to name but a few, and the narrative of African leaders such as Kenyatta, Rawlings, Lumumba and Seghor, who expanded the narrative of 'Blackness'. In addition, intimate engagement with the civil rights movement in all of its manifestations drew us into the Martin Luther King Jr and Malcolm X African, Black Panther Civil Rights African-American narrative.

Our immediate ancestral Caribbean heritage provided us with a window into the Caribbean struggles for independence almost island by island via the regular pale blue 'Airmail' correspondence which was our lifeline, and thus we became familiar with Premier Bird, Williams, James, Manley, Seaga, Burnhan and Jagan, Bishop and Charles among others. We absorbed the history of Harlem and its renaissance alongside its Negritude cousin and other relatives such as the Black Jacobbins, all the while being surrounded by the sounds of Pan, Sparrow, Kitchener, The Wailers with Rita and Marcia, The Heptones, and learning the virtues of 'The Harder They Come' juxtaposed against 'Smile Orange' all against the timeline of a periodic open house carnage of Jamaican political elections, which historically left both casualty and corpses as a consequence of camps polarised in opposition to gain favour with politicians.

We listened to our parents listening to Mahalia and Sam Cooke, Ray Charles, Motown, sounds of Philly, Isaac and Curtis. We watched them dance to Treasure Isles latest, Trojans's trophy sounds and saw the nation respond to Millie, Desmond Dekker and the Israelite. We funked to Bootsy and Funkadelic, to Roy's Sunshine, to Miles and Grover. We absorbed Studio One, Prince Jammy's paid homage to the crown prince Brown, and marvelled at how cool the Cool Ruler was. Police and Thieves were in the street and we heard about Pablo's hard times and still went out in the rain with Webby Jay. Like smooth molasses, the remnants of this mixture pored themselves into the mould of our very own Brown Sugar Lovers Rock (documented by Menelik Shabazz). Then later British Soul of Hi-Tension and Light of the World, peaking with Soul II Soul as movements (and industries), recording and reflecting our very own evolving history, creating the toffee which still binds us together in the sticky mess of our peculiar lives – a world within a world.

We built new industries – mobile disco and boom boxes exploded after our creative response to lack of social venues when we built on our parents' blues and sound system innovation; car audio evolved after we extended these adaptations of sound into cars. Few escaped the apprenticeship of the sound system, the car mechanic circuit or alternately the church musician apprenticeship...where many learned their craft of instrument (including vocals). And yes the 'dreads' made sportswear cool and a new sector of leisurewear added margins to Adidas, Puma, etc. mirrored by our brothers and sisters in arms on the other side of the Atlantic through the DJ and hip-hop fraternity.

All of these external factors individually fashioned the 'blocks' that we were – they were dwarfed, however, by the context of our more immediate environment which yielded a much sharper tool which carved deep and lasting marks in our identity ... the legacy of enslavement and colonisation is a cutlass which cuts both sides at once by force. The context of this heritage cannot be divorced from its narrative because it affords a perspective which is critical ...

Our conscious encounters with the colonial commenced in school, the battlefields in the war on our psyches. Our battles were multiple battles fought daily with different enemies at various levels, everyday brought fresh assault particularly trying to avoid the 'Sin Bin' (now called 'PRU's) and required new tactics ... 2016 illustrates that the battle has escalated! We were assaulted by our teachers' attitudes to the new and exotic, by their colonial language and attitude, we were assaulted by the 'dinner ladies' who appointed themselves front line law enforcement who would reinforce the colour line and ensure our being at the school would remain a segregated and very separate experience. As children, of course, our largest battles were reserved for the playground ...

In my schools, I learned about different attitudes to the challenges of survival, particularly assimilation which simply meant that you would tolerate regular name calling, beatings and other forms of abuse without protest or retaliation. Being spat at in the street by adults and told to 'go home wog' was also a new and interesting experience, it challenged all of my Caribbean upbringing not to respond, because of the deep-rooted respect we were expected to hold for our elders, so I like many others, just got on with the life that was rolled out in front of us.

School battles ensued at every level and stage then into college, amongst my peer group there was little talk of university so our focus was work, only to encounter new skirmishes in employment. The first of which were 'already filled' but 'advertised' job vacancies, a strange phenomenon of being given an interview: on arrival you were told that the vacancy was already filled – however, if you called again with a very 'white'-sounding voice, the job suddenly reappeared and so it went on. Again, many of us just stepped over that particular merry-go-round and pushed further afield and made inroads into more and more diverse occupations.

There are so many stories which are a part of this story which remain untold … SUS, mental health sectioning, borstals, deaths in custody, skin head assaults and beating, etc., and hearing them would alter the widely-held view that the civil rights era was only relevant to the USA. It would help to illustrate why repair and reparations are necessary to the Diaspora here in the UK. Unfortunately, the majority will take their stories with them when they finally close the doors on life…

I needed to empty my soul
of the darkness
which has left it
in the shadow of life!
I had to be thrown
into the well,
of myself
and so I fell,
through times and spaces,
peoples and places,
through history and its many faces.
Past, now smiling
at the present,
and winking at the future
as I reach the depths …
of the night when it closeth,
of the morning when it breathes
in the afterglow of the sunset
of that journey.

'African Violet' explores the historic and contemporary landscape of Britain which gave birth to her very existence. She encompasses aspects of the universal, including how poverty and fear of the unknown impact upon compassion. Beyond dialogue, there is a need to delve into broader literary conversations; our refugee crisis presents a critical period in the timeline of humanity and an honest reflection on the past can impact our present. Understanding the emotional impact of historic persecution of the human spirit reconnects us and facilitates repair. Whilst this is valuable to the world, it is equally important to the 'British' sense of national identity.

I am going to tell you a little more about the story of the story – and 'a butterfly is pivotal'. Just as a butterfly emerging from a chrysalis and unfolding its shaky wings has to wait a while to get the strength to fly, African Violet, too, unwrapped her tiny petals as she burst through the darkness of the earth finally strong enough to face the majesty of the sun …

The journey

There is an interesting programme in the UK titled 'Who do you think you are?' which allows celebrities to trace their heritage. Almost without exception, the intimate emotional impact which they each experience following the revelations illustrates that there is something significant which connects people to their past.

*Carib…**Being***
*The Caribbean, pivotal piece of the **jigsaw***
*of the African **Diaspora**.*
*Widely acknowledged **unequivocally**,*
as a unique melting pot and blend
*of culture as a consequence of **History**.*
***Regionally** here,*
Africa blends
with China, India
Seamlessly
and the length and breadth of Europe.
***Visually** every race can see something of itself there;*
***Culturally** through music, food and language*
*all peoples find latent **Familiarity,***
strands of the haunting residues of History,
*Infused in the peoples, strands of the **Legacies**,*
diverse narrative in a chapter of African History
*conveyed **Genetically**,*
***Philosophically**, many find themselves*
uniquely positioned
*to comment on the narrative of their own **Humanity …***

Like many others from the island of Antigua, Mary Prince and Papa Sammy Smith believed in the power of story …

Good grief … a postman's legacy

Our family values are always questioned and yet! My father was a man of principle and values were extremely important to him, he balanced this with a profound and emotional love that he held for my mother, we his children were the reason for his living, nothing else mattered to him more in this world, nothing. He sacrificed his entire life for the benefit of his children and it was a selfless sacrifice as nothing was too good for us. He was known for his principled perspective, he was very proud and disciplined and yet he laughed heartily at Scooby Doo, would remember our favourite sweets, books and hobbies, and he encouraged us to excel. I remember that he would keep small treats in his pocket and produce them at opportune times to squeals of delight.

These may seem like ordinary things that fathers do, but the context here is important; to grasp it, you must return to the 60s and the optimistic warm winds of Caribbean migration which blew across the British Isles meeting the cool chilled reception which quickly froze, causing frostbite amongst the newcomers. The pessimism of reality quickly dimmed the gloss of potential for many people, but from the little that I understand it had a profound effect on the Caribbean men, many of whom experienced challenges in providing for their families as well as protecting their women and their children in a hostile environment. While the majority of them rose effectively to embrace those challenges, this left consequences which continue to impact on our community until the present day.

> Throughout his life he had always asked himself what we as a race had done to the world to incur so much hatred; he died still asking that question.
>
> My father for all of his strengths was nothing without my mother and he often said as much, he often called her his rock. Let me introduce you to her …
>
> My mother is kind to a fault, generous and the most forgiving person I have ever known. Her story like that of so many women of the Caribbean is all at once different and the same, like them she had to make her way and cultivate her family without the support of her mother, her grandmother or her aunts, something she would have had in the Caribbean.
>
> In her early 20s, she was the first in her family to migrate and so while she was able to give the benefit of her experience to her siblings, she did not benefit from the same support. She married like many others with little family support and settled in a land which made little effort to accommodate her, as a woman she suffered like the others, the double discrimination of being black and being a woman.
>
> My mother like my father moved from factory work into national industry, I often wonder what contributions both of them would have made to the world if things had been different. It is so ironic the 'no Irish, no dogs and no blacks' sign forced many to ultimately purchase houses and they all stayed to honour the debt; if they had rented, many who I have spoken to admit that they would have returned to the Caribbean within five years – my parents included.

African Violet as creative expression is a process of personal reconciliation … 'a coming to terms with', which is healing to the soul. It is a creative process of dealing with negativity surrounding British slavery, empire, race and death…a narrative communicating imperialism in the context of race; by one who has experienced it directly and which challenges narrated history. This chapter of history is British history; Britain must simply accept it as very present and an undeniable part of the fabric of the West, with its European Diaspora.

Contemporary manifestation

My 'Art Practice' is concerned with the tangible dimension of words; their physical manifestation and translation of impact, with their essence of emotion and the colour of their composition. I use words to paint, to sculpt absence of form and shape the sound of silence.

Words of beauty …
So time and time again,
after the downpour of the rain,
when the storm becomes the calm,
you pour words of beauty,
as a balm,
onto my heart.
and so slowly,
cover and coat,
the fine raw hurt,

and unhealed grief,
with the magic of belief.
Time and time and time
again,
after the downpour of the rain,
you send the medicine for my pain.'

First...
The First Wave...
Our parents – well they came

They came...
They know not,
for what
after the war
was as far,
as they had thought
to rebuild
restore.
Leaving the ships – again
they came ashore.'

As people ... They lived and they loved

Seasons of love

Summer, fierce heat of independence
battling, yet more new realities
belonging anew,
communities formed and grew,
new life,
planting seeds in different soil,
more reason to work and toil,
together but alone,
social gaggles
brides, babies and loss,
flights back home.
The blue spot, the blues dance
another chance
to jump and prance,
together, but alone!

Contemporary context

2007 – I watched Wilberforce celebrations of the bicentenary unfold across the UK with incredulity ... 2007 was cited as the celebration of the 200th year of abolition of British slavery, all of the substantive events across the country had been engineered to focus on the abolitionists, particularly

William Wilberforce. The Anglican Church used the celebration to focus on some aspects of its role and made various efforts to apologise for its historic role. Events culminated in a church service attended by Queen Elizabeth and heads of Commonwealth during which the then Prime Minister Tony Blair simply expressed regret for Britain's role in the slave trade. The celebration had provided an opportunity for critical dialogue but most of the resources allocated had been absorbed by government institutions that facilitated the abolishment narrative, reinforcing a mythical narrative about Britain's humanitarian stance. Professor Robert Beckford was one of a few exceptions and produced a documentary on the financial legacy of sugar, which I believe has been pivotal to the on-going dialogue on compensation and reparations, laying the foundation for the UCL 'Legacies of British Slave Ownership' database. Luckily my parents had taught us about the resistors…African Violet was my comment – she spoke through paper and canvas … at the time I didn't really know what to do with her.

Heritage and legacy given the context makes the question of macro heritage feel like this …

First there is your mother …

African violet
tropical,
exotic,
vibrant,
violet, pink, purple
bloom,
she stretches her neck
long elegant and slender
towards the morning sun
already in the sky, blazing a trail
and leaving playful footprints of new day hues,
tossing vivid reds and plum blues.
Fierce yellows,
dwarf the shrinking indigo of midnight
of majestic, gentle, orange, golden light
reigning itself in and
just peeping delicately, through the clouds
slowly, but carelessly, across the skies.
Unfurling her leaves, one by one, she collects herself and looks down.

Imagine yet your father a brutal rapist! You remind her of him, you are constantly reminded of him and what he has done but he is also a part of you.

Beyond the horizon,
equally unaware,
he sets sail.
Stalk tall, threadlike and frail
lord lavender,
cold,
pale,

empty and
wanting.
Wakes restless from his bitter, tormented sleep
already needing warmth.

You cannot escape your past nor change it so continue to live with the conundrum and unsure as a consequence.

Another world.
Transplanted,
all at once.
Different
but
same.
The soil, rich
Its warm brown earth
Flourishes,
but is
nourished,
by the flow of blood.
The sun still dances
in the sky,
but no longer
for her,
her gaze
is in the past
for her, no future.
he walks that soil.
Free, but bound
it holds him fast,
a captive too!
Also gazing in the past
as every lash,
tears a strip,
from his soul,
until he is no longer whole,
but lives for a time when,
he will be.

Your father and his family refuse to acknowledge your existence despite the irrefutable likeness of him in you. In full knowledge of the violation they leave you and your mother destitute in the hope that you will just die and be removed from memory from existence.

Hard as the stick he wields,
he lives to survey the fields
uneasy, he watches
the new blooms, from a distance

detached
yet, he sees the lavender
teasing gently through,
that violet hue,
taunting him,
with haunting familiarity.
Unmistakable legacies
for future worlds,
the new blooms
blossom, in new soil
and unwrap, buds and petals
to display an
impressive array,
of colour, tints and tones
each just, a little whiter shade of pale,
betraying, circumstantial tales …

Driven by insatiable greed well-financed planters leave *en masse* to seek even more profitable potential from the poverty of others…including India.

Leaving
the sinking ships,
in which they came,
scavenging for new terrain.
New worlds,
East India Company,
The floating jail,
Imprisoning, all who sail,
towards an Indian acquisition.
Leaving behind the chaos of legacy,
the future's concern,
stagnant,
stalemate,
slow deathbed,
ghost towns,
shadows,
of former selves.
Islands lie,
lame,
in the lazy heat
barren,
bare,
stripped,
of possibility,
finally too
they leave,
another exodus.

But we didn't all die.

The seed
literally, torn in two,
facing a reality,
ripped,
stripped,
of
history,
it
grows
with confusion,
harbours
illusion,
about
the origins
of the fusion,
carefully watered
over tended,
but lack of sunlight
makes it grow in the midnight,
the wrong side
of right,
blonde black
Korean keratin,
Indian complexions,
imitation pale,
in the shadow
of lavender.
Small souls
steeped
in
big history,
they know not
or
care not.

...So here we are!

After centuries of hopelessness,
dying they are still trying
to be accepted,
but even in death,
still rejected.
Their youth wasted, chasing shadows
of themselves,
illusive, intrusive

confusive!
They gather strength for a final push
legacy is all they have,
they are simply black not African.
They are Foreign seeds in western soil, spoiled.

And what of their parents, parents, parents?

Chapters of Shadow Empire

The world watched in silence for over 300 years ... As the scaffolding was being built for the framework of its greatest monument to inhumanity. Many accepted that it was necessary to die fighting ... Claude McKay Jamaica (1889–1948) wrote the poem which Winston Churchill appropriated for Britain during the war.

If we must die, let it not be like hogs
Hunted and penned in an inglorious spot,
While round us bark the mad and hungry dogs,
Making their mock at our accursed lot.
If we must die, O let us nobly die,
So that our precious blood may not be shed
In vain; then even the monsters we defy
Shall be constrained to honour us though dead!
O kinsmen! We must meet the common foe!
Though far outnumbered let us show us brave,
And for their thousand blows deal one deathblow!
What though before us lies the open grave?
Like men we'll face the murderous, cowardly pack,
Pressed to the wall, dying, but fighting back!

Chapters of Shadow Empire – COSE © reflects the ancestry of African Violet which is responsible for the hybridity of her contemporary circumstance; it looks at key countries, some in a representational capacity like Nigeria and Jamaica and the others specific as a consequence of their actual roles, i.e. Britain and Haiti.

2010 – Haiti was shaken by a devastating earthquake. The earthquake turned up the volume for me, on Haiti, tapping into an underlying frustration regarding its role in world history, which eventually poured itself into Mme Haiti within the same week of the earthquake. Haiti is yet to find a resolution ... and she is yet to be acknowledged for her unquestionable pivotal role in world history!

Mademoiselle Haiti

Extremely rare and wealthy beauty,
precious, priceless bijoux
coveted commodity,
a cruelly chained captive

of circumstance,
proud
and fierce,
determined
to prise apart every link
in the cast iron chains, that binds her,
a fervent wish to wrest and free her soul
from the desperate, salacious, slimy, grasp
of monsieur François,
too odious, too hideous.

In 2010, the world watched Haiti's earthquake reveal a bitter legacy of enslavement courtesy of the infamous loan repayment to France as punishment for freeing herself from enslavement, which has spilt over into the twenty-first century. That same year I experienced my own personal earthquake, my father died and then I realised that I had watched Death …

I have watched
Death
walking, slowly
very slowly
sometimes, almost standing
still.
he seems, yes he seems very heavy
yet, he walks lightly
almost sprightly
sometimes, he rests for a while
surveying the beauty of this world,
he takes the time
to look at the crisp, clear vacuous blue sky
or the grass, green beyond,
every blade sharpened
to perfection, reflecting
the bright silver hue
vibrating in the sunlight
or, instead, the cool, dark earth
musky and damp,
rich and fertile with possibility.
Having rested, he rises
and continues with his journey.

For the first time in my life – I heard my father say that he had lived to regret coming to Britain … then he died! His death left a void which can never be filled. The architecture of my entire landscape collapsed as its tallest building had fallen. My pain though, was nothing compared to that of my mother, she was the Butterfly. The significance of the colonial legacy is about its continued impact and how this impact translates into ordinary people's lives, past present and potentially futures.

My mother was the Butterfly!

A butterfly with a broken wing
can still fly,
albeit slowly,
and care fully,
still has a delicate charm.
Momentarily,
Disorientated and
unbalanced, whilst adjusting
all the while to her broken wing.

2011 was Nigeria's 50th year of independence; Oba Naija evolved. He is an ancestral representative for the West African dynamic of the story and a narrative in his own right.

His-story
of kings,
lavish kingdoms, Oba's,
significant empires,
civilized, cultured,
buried, deeply,
in the lush oil soaked soil,
rich, black gold, opulent
but smothering the shabby poverty,
of wretched souls and 17th century his-story,
crystallized with wanton bloodshed,
fierce, resistant sweat
futile and frustrated tears,
of the stolen ones.

2012 a year later during Jamaica's celebration of its 50th year of independence, Grandma Jamaica evolved in the midst of substantial triumph during the 2012 Olympics.

Backbone of the brutish, British, Caribbean
the treasured colony.
Orphaned and estranged,
de-terrained and desolate,
in the hands of the deranged.
Awaiting the fate
of those, in the new world.
New victims of the newly qualified,
oppressors, recent graduates
themselves, only one step removed
from the degradation of servitude.
Exiled Jews from Brazil, smooth the Portugal path to sugar
with money and Dutch sense.

2012 'In Tribute' evolved as many of my friends were also burying their parents and we were losing elders, across the community here and abroad. I honoured them … the generation of trees … who changed the face of the UK forever.

The Tree …
Nobody nourishes the tree,
solid, strong, slender, long.
The tree that gives everybody shelter from the storm,
and shade from the warm
rays of the sun on a hot summer's day.
Everybody comes, they pick the leaves, peel the bark, cut new shoots
of growth and dig up pieces of its roots.
constantly stripping it of its future possibility,
no-one cares to nourish the tree.
Nobody sees the fungus of its poverty,
deep set, damaging it to its core;
it is rich yet it is so very poor.
Maybe even beyond repair, maybe none care,
so the fungus dances just on agitating and dehydrating,

2013–2014 saw continuing immigration headlines, African Violet speaks to Great Aunt Britannia. Essence of Poverty manifested in response to a number of evolving headlines regarding growing debt, repossessions, food-banks and my continued exploration of the history of the working classes in the UK … eventually 'The Myth of White Supremacy' emerges.

End of a journey …
the challenge of white supremacy!
wearily
I clamber
over the debris,
of my history,
the longest journey
of my life.
Arduous but necessary
to dismiss the recollections
of hostility
and find new possibility;
and now it is so much easier
to see.

Stories, like many things, are not equal as a consequence of the dynamics of power, so many stories are more equal than others, but prominence does not denote significance or importance in the scheme of things.

Contemporary legacies

A Recent YouGov poll 2014 showed that 'By three to one, British people think the Empire is something to be proud of rather than ashamed of – they also tend to think it left the colonies better off, and a third would like it to still exist'. The European psyche has normalised over centuries, their referencing and behaviour in response to 'Blackness' in many ways; objectification has been a constant and facilitates the type of distance required to sustain the dehumanising modus operandi which is deeply embedded in western society.

The mechanics of European empire were built on fear and hate, both still exist today ensuring the legacy remains hard to dismantle – yet it is impossible to fear and hate others without damaging yourself. The poem 'The Age Demanded' by Ernest M. Hemingway nods in agreement.

And yet more conundrums …

Wealth supremacy masquerades as white supremacy, its agenda of global colonisation, mass poverty and control affect our total existence. Once race and then religion, thin out the lifeblood of humanity, class will present itself anew, as the enemy to be defeated; then the machinery of war, ever present, will simply and effortlessly realign itself! White supremacy is the Trojan horse of the wealth supremacists.

Yet, 'The Money' is the chief weapon
in the war,
against the poor!
Money, commanding vast armies, globally
conquering new territory, daily.
Its generals constantly discussing fresh military strategy,
its frontline troops enforce compliance, creating endless possibilities,
to oppress, to control, to deceive, to cajole,
to induce, to entice all to lure into the vice!
Until all are like spidered trapped flies,
surprised, when the delicate threads hold tight and fast.
Caught, enslaved new chains of promised progress.
the promised progress, a complete illusion
simply employed to cause confusion,
a five hundred yeared empirically clothed dissolution,
as usury unveils himself to be
the proud sponsor of poverty.
Usury, the terrorist in the war on humanity
universally accepted, uncontested in his supremacy.
The Journey continues with the Light of the New Dawn … I realised that I had been working on the same painting.

A new dawn, a new day,
gentle morning hours,
signal of hope on the horizon
shows us a new way to look at yesterday,
who has happily skipped away.
And truly, that which comes after,
will be better than the present.
So once again, we breathe
like that newborn breath, sharp intake,
finally alert, mercifully more awake

to the beauty of reality.
Awake, we see with eyes anew
those people, those places, those familiar faces.

From my perspective, Art feels like an ancient language. William Butler Yeats told us that: 'Supreme art is a traditional statement of certain heroic and religious truths, passed on from age to age, modified by individual genius, but never abandoned. The revolt of individualism came because the tradition had become degraded, or rather because a spurious copy has been accepted in its stead'. Rumi also shares his take on the matter when he says 'You think the shadow is the substance.'

In the context of my practice; I believe one of the most powerful words that will help contemporary society to cross that bridge of the past is the word 'Terrorism'. People across the world can engage with the emotions, thoughts and feelings associated with the contemporary global fear of terror... They can translate those emotions very personally, particularly those close to or directly affected by events and apply all of the associated emotion retrospectively, facilitating in the process access to an unfortunate unique window of opportunity and its legacy.

Let the Artists speak ...
We are the epitome of pain, let us heal.
In the misery of darkness, we beg for light of mercy to see,
let every man say that light is in me
that it shines through the truth of beauty,
and that the beauty of art of the heart,
is the very fabric of society.
Repair
that fabric tear,
means the very idea
of repair,
must challenge
the fear,
of the hopelessness,
which brings its own despair.

In the hands of the 'artist', this window, gateway or door to the past provides an opportunity to explore parallels in history... the terrorism of colonial Empire mirrors contemporary terrorism. *As an Artist, if I consider an exercise rebranding of meanings then I would ask* – how the words colonial terrorism (empire building) fits into the debate on terror; especially in the dialogue which attributes the nexus on human emotion and the urge to use violence ... I would ask – is a weapon of mass destruction responsible for genocide and oppression globally over the last 500 years and the symbol of Western civilisation and democracy – the gun? What if we were to rebrand all colonial activity retrospectively as terrorism, what does that now say about the state of the world, perception of civilisation – or the developed world and its acquisitions? The dialogue would have to explore the successive journeys of early refugees, migrants from the European Diaspora, (especially Britain) who have permanently reshaped the world irreversibly. It would also have to acknowledge that the consequences of that reshaping have spilled into the contemporary landscape for all modern war.

The words 'West Indian' evoke conflicting emotions and provide an interesting dynamic, as the word 'Caribbean' is more contemporary; historically they have been used interchangeably. From a perspective of impact, it makes for an interesting exploration. In the UK, the Docklands Light Railway enshrines the memory of the period which was the height of British colonisation and enslavement of the West Indies and their slave merchants, by naming a station West India Quay. The historic use of the word 'West Indian' exclusively refers to slavers, classified as either 'merchants' or the sanitised term of 'planter' instead of 'Slavemerchant' which speak more to the gravity of circumstance. The contemporary reference to this geographic region is the 'Caribbean' and its use has both positive and negative implications within British history. Consider the potential sparks of enquiry in making the association with the Docklands as a consequence of naming the DLR station Caribbean Quay; it would make an immediate contemporary connection.

Much of the highly studied classic British literature skirts around its enslavement with 'words' which are unhinged from their reality and rob society of the opportunity to make pertinent association. The classics form a substantive part of an academic battle for supremacy and attempts at every available opportunity to either re-write history or justify it. Because contemporary studies insist on preservation of the past and uses the same literature, the pattern has continued uninterrupted. This provides the oil which smoulders and burns the fire of reparations; which is slowly spreading.

The propaganda of colonialism was supported by many in the literary circles

Rudyard Kipling 1899 captured the essence …

Take up the White Man's burden –
Send forth the best ye breed –
Go bind your sons to exile
To serve your captives' need;
To wait in heavy harness
On fluttered folk and wild –
Your new-caught sullen peoples,
Half devil and half child.
Take up the White Man's burden –
In patience to abide
To veil the threat of terror
And check the show of pride;
By open speech and simple,
An hundred times made plain,
To seek another's profit,
And work another's gain.

Many others answered … amongst them:

Farrakhan – white man's heaven
When the white man came to America
He told the Indian, 'I am your white brother'
He said, 'Red man, I'll treat you the best'

Yet and still he pushed the Indian further west
With his white woman and firewater
Tricks and lies, he stole America
The original owner of this nation
Is cooped up on a reservation
So my friend, it's easy to tell
White man's heaven is black man hell
He needed someone to work the land
His back was too weak – he needed you, black man
So he commissioned Sir John Hawkins
To commit the worst, most grievous sin
To take a man who's born to be free
And bring him down slavery
Sell a man as merchandise
On his body, put a price
Oh my friend, it's easy to tell
White man heaven is a black man hell

Words used in context as part of a collective form part of a present and tangible body of evidence which can anchor Empire to its reality. The absence of this reality results in the type of opinion poll such as the recent YouGov 2014 survey which shows substantive misplaced support and pride for the British Empire. The working classes did not benefit from the Empire yet white supremacy masks this reality. The Legacy of Empire in the context of African Diaspora is unprecedented and has never been addressed adequately, the deliberate reshaping and modification of people for profit has cause profound and irreversible damage.

Great Aunt Britannia travels...

Unaware, of a future fate.
welcoming hosts,
effectively eliminated
after making a date...
With the ***white widow***
who only offers death as reward,
a curious trade
for honour and integrity,
but that's ***the only gift she brings***
on her travels,
from god's own country...
over centuries!

Contemporary slavery sits on a platform of unspoken acceptability because transatlantic enslavement has never been dealt with effectively in the context of world history, unlike the Jewish holocaust which holds a sacred place in human consciousness. Equally, world history needs to acknowledge the British Genocide of the American Indians as a benchmark crime against humanity.

Child of fallen empire...
I am but a footprint,

in the journey
of humanity.
A footprint
of the journey
of mankind,
towards itself,
walking towards
its ailing terminal health.
A footprint across
the landscape of history,
of conquest
made manifest.
Across time and space,
across the construct of race,
across the acquisitions of place.
A footprint in the global legacy
of stellar stars and galaxy,
of alphaic infinite creativity
of earth mothered, covered
synchronicity
a footprint which walks
from incomprehensible
mystery,
to,
the sterile poverty of misery,
through the vastness,
of that rich humanity,
reduced to a twisted story.

More recently; a UK television drama of the young Queen Victoria (2016), attempts to re-write history portraying both the queen and her husband as extremely sympathetic to the abolition of transatlantic enslavement. The world needs to acknowledge damage and pursue an agenda of repair…so that we can eventually cross the many bridges which span both time and generations of the colonial!

arts as pedagogy,
connecting the dots
of history.
A history of human misery
to reveal the picture
so that none can say they didn't see
before they leave …
Timelines of music
the soul's release,
from slow murder,
the poet's prose,
those
translating pain,

again and again
to keep them sane.
The artist who see
unfortunately,
hold vision
of hell,
farrakhan said it well...
Those who danced
to free their being
alive still, just
and then film and the plays,
expanding the many ways,
to simply say,
we are still here
and despite the genocides
will not go away.

Rigid structures of pure academic research find their limitations in capturing and conveying the magnitude of emotion; however, this 'emotional legacy' is equal to the analysis of material and evidence unearthed in research ...

Academic genocide,
warm
maturity
of
legacy,
left to brew
quietly,
stewing nicely,
served gently,
confidently,
masqueraded
as normality,
how dare we ...
say differently,
we – the expert unworthy,
must regress into the invisibility,
designed and allocated for us globally.

Historically this construct has been identified at many levels by those in the Diaspora, 'Intellectuals ought to study the past not for the pleasure they find in so doing, but to derive lessons from It.'

Cheikh Anta Diop

Contemporary global order

There are a number of Black Artists of the Diaspora including Lawson Oyekan, who have engaged themselves with the impact of the loss to humanity, as a consequence of the absence of African Art in the art history narrative. He has created a body of work which reflects the critical elements of the universality of humanity within this context. Throughout his work, Oyekan continually asks us, 'What do you see with your eyes?' It is a question which remains unanswered. Some simply cannot see and we must accept this with sincerity, others can see but they are afraid. This, we must understand without judgement since we are not here to judge. Like much that is ancient, art history has been deliberately distorted and destroyed to serve those who seek to contain and control. Oyekan states that:

> It was a combination of both white superiority, as well as the inability of those academics who were engaged in the process of exploration at the time, to recognise what were in fact pieces of an extremely sophisticated, rich tapestry of a superior intellectual language that allowed access to the world of African Art. This white superiority succeeded in convincing the world that Africans had no validity in the world at all, to date, few inroads have been made to redress this position especially within the art world, which unashamedly announced the 2012 sale of El Anat Sui's work in May 2012 at Bonham's in London for £541,250 ($850,000) as a world record for the highest sale for a Ghanaian. A figure dwarfed on a regular basis by very junior European contemporaries or recent European graduates especially on the UK art scene.

Einstein said, 'The world will not be destroyed by those who do evil, but by those who watch without doing anything.'

I believe that it is time to let artists speak … to the condition of the world! Artists have a language which transcends the political sound-bites that are thrown around like bolts of lightning across the political spectrum. In the midst of the contemporary chaos, with all of its associated confusion and noise of 'vested interest polarities', there is an urgent need for another sound. The Arts, however, need to be subject to a serious 'colonial gaze scrutiny', which cannot be achieved internally by those affected. Money in my opinion predominantly dictates the manner in which we respond to one another as individuals and talks in a language of inhumanity and one consequence is the devaluation of the 'artist' in society. Artistic social observation and narration provides a unique, critical, historical, recorded perspective of life which is an essential tool for humanity; imbalance and manipulation of the arts damage us all.

As an artist, my perspective on the British Empire takes its cue from the thoughts, feelings recollections, stories and discussions of empire … from those who have directly experienced its supremacist legacy over the generations! Statesman and poet Aimé Césaire says it well when he says, 'It is not the head of civilization that rots first, it is the heart.'

For me, Britain has an entire 'world within' as a consequence of British 'Immigration through Empire'. London, in particular, has a love affair with the memory of its colonial past. Yet, there are many whose memory of London is different from its 'narrowed narrative'.

Susan Okokon, author, is one of many contributors (2009) to an expansion of that narrative with *Black Londoners: A History*. The contemporary narrative of refugees in London, unsettling though it is, remains familiar, as it sits on a keg of gunpowder which has ingredients of the continual geographies of migration, trajectories of flight mixed with the romances of adventure, resulting in re-territorialisation of an unsettled city, forced to accommodate mobility and citizenship, over centuries from other parts of the country. The keg of gunpowder sits in the warehouse of its history of inequality fashioned by the carpenters of global trade networks, mercantile capitalism against metropolitan cultural hegemony and the imperial *mythos* built from the wood of its landscapes of slavery, transportation and service, as well as historic rebellions ignited by unbearable poverty.

The thread of this narrative weaves its way through the fabric of neo-colonial refashioning and memorialisation of London's colonial past, its poetic and rhetorical appropriation of its subjugated conquests, through its ownership of paradisal islands, steeped in the escapism of dreary reality by exoticism. The thread of the narrative is the voice of the literati. There seems to be much which was and continues to be accepted as normal; particularly the inevitable connection between the working classes, poverty and debt ... slavery forms the foundation of the working classes. The role of 'usury' is now accepted as the norm and yet that 'usury' is the seed of debt which then grows into a young plant of poverty and finally branches out into a tree of slavery for someone...somewhere.

Unchallenged in world history, this 'narrative apathy' has manifested in continued collaborative global 'terrorism abroad' for the British.

For the Americans, it manifests in uninterrupted genocide of the original Americans, centuries of state-sponsored terrorism for African-Americans, inhumane detention and deportation of Mexicans along the Mexican border and an engineered war across much of the Middle East. Guantanamo Bay and more recently the refugee crisis visibly assault our humanity and yet continue to evoke an apathy which demonstrates that we have not learned from our past. The 'narrative apathy' is built on the premise that we are insignificant in the systems which control our everyday lives and are therefore powerless to resist or make changes.

Understanding the emotional impact of historic persecution of the human soul reconnects us to our humanity, this is especially important for the contemporary refugee crisis. It is also a part of the challenge of refiguring 'Britishness' and the validity of re-aligning racial identity and reframing questions of statehood in the light of globalisation. Established economic systems over centuries have prohibited fair exchange of skills between individuals, interrupting a well-established system of barter over centuries and deskilling humanity as a consequence. Art success has become the aspiration to create for the elite few. The link between money, poverty and slavery cannot be overlooked because they exist as interrelated ingredients in modern society. London has been and still remains crowned global king of banking and finance, yet its silent parallel, poverty, speaks volumes!

Conclusion: white supremacy in the context of poverty

Middle and Working classes,
in your masses
we have travelled
some distance
together,
in the same carriage
an uneasy marriage,
for some time.
yet your superiority
strangely should
never have allowed this to be. i raise my hand and i often do feel the chain
what do you suppose is stopping you?

INDEX

Printed in Great Britain
by Amazon